SEALS AND SOCIETY

SEALS AND SOCIETY

MEDIEVAL WALES, THE WELSH MARCHES AND THEIR ENGLISH BORDER REGION

Edited by P. R. Schofield and E. A. New
with S. M. Johns and J. A. McEwan

UNIVERSITY OF WALES PRESS
2016

© The Contributors, 2016

All rights reserved. No part of this book may be reproduced in any material form (including photocopying or storing it in any medium by electronic means and whether or not transiently or incidentally to some other use of this publication) without the written permission of the copyright owner. Applications for the copyright owner's written permission to reproduce any part of this publication should be addressed to the University of Wales Press, 10 Columbus Walk, Brigantine Place, Cardiff CF10 4UP.

www.uwp.co.uk

British Library CIP Data

A catalogue record for this book is available from the British Library

ISBN   978-1-78316-871-2 (hardback)
            978-1-78316-875-0 (paperback)
eISBN 978-1-78316-872-9

The right of the Contributors to be identified as authors of this work has been asserted in accordance with sections 77 and 79 of the Copyright, Designs and Patents Act 1988.

Designed and typeset by Chris Bell, cbdesign
Printed by CPI Antony Rowe, Chippenham, Wiltshire

CONTENTS

Acknowledgements	vii
List of figures	ix
List of maps and tables	xii
List of abbreviations	xv
Introduction *Elizabeth A. New and Phillipp R. Schofield*	1
1. Seals in Medieval Wales and its Neighbouring Counties: Trends in Motifs *John A. McEwan*	13
2. Seals: Administration and Law *Phillipp R. Schofield*	35
3. Seals and Exchange *Phillipp R. Schofield*	49
4. Ecclesiastical Seals *Elizabeth A. New*	61
5. Seals and Lordship *Susan M. Johns*	79
6. Seals, Women, Gender and Identity *Susan M. Johns*	91
7. Seals as Expressions of Identity *Elizabeth A. New*	105
Conclusion *Elizabeth A. New and Phillipp R. Schofield*	121
Appendix *Elizabeth A. New, John A. McEwan and Phillipp R. Schofield*	127
Bibliography	327
Index	341

ACKNOWLEDGEMENTS

THIS VOLUME arises from a project funded by the Arts and Humanities Research Council (AH/G010994/1), *Seals in Medieval Wales*. The project team is extremely grateful for the support and advice of the advisory board to the project, Dr Susan Davies, Professor Paul Harvey, Professor Mark Ormrod and Mr Glyn Parry. The Revd Dr David Williams has also, from the outset, been most generous with his time, support and access to his own catalogues and materials. The team also acknowledges with gratitude the invaluable support provided by staff at the following archives and repositories: Bangor University Archives, The British Library, Cheshire Archives and Local Studies, Gwent Record Office, Gwynedd Archives, Hereford Cathedral Archive, Herefordshire Record Office, the National Archives, the National Library of Wales, the National Museum of Wales, and Shropshire Archives. Images presented in this volume are reproduced with the kind permission of Bangor University Archives (figures 1.10, 1.12, 1.15, 1.21, 2.3, 3.3, 4.3, 5.1, 5.2, 6.6, 7.9, 7.13), The British Library (figures 1.8, 3.9, 5.8, 6.9, 7.1, 7.2, 7.3, 7.14), Cheshire Archives and Local Studies (figures 3.11, 7.10, 7.11), Hereford Cathedral Archive (figures 1.18, 4.1, 4.2, 4.5, 7.5), Herefordshire Record Office (figures 1.6, 1.20), the National Library of Wales (figures 1.1, 1.3, 1.4, 1.7, 1.11, 1.13, 1.14, 1.16, 1.17, 1.19, 2.1, 2.2, 3.1, 3.2, 3.4, 3.5, 3.6, 3.7, 3.8, 3.12, 3.13, 3.14, 4.4, 4.6, 4.7, 4.8, 5.3, 5.4, 5.5, 5.6, 5.7, 6.1, 6.2, 6.5, 6.8, 6.10, 6.11, 7.4, 7.7, 7.8, 7.12, 7.16) and Shropshire Archives (figures 1.2, 1.5, 1.9, 3.10, 6.3, 6.4, 6.7, 7.6, 7.15). The team is also most grateful to Mr Thomas Lloyd for helping secure permission to publish seal images from National Library of Wales, Bronwydd Estate Records (figures 1.19 and 3.14). The publishing team at the University of Wales Press, including Siân Chapman, Production and Editorial Manager, Dr Dafydd Jones, Editor of the Press, and Sarah Lewis, Head of Commissioning, have been unfailingly helpful and supportive throughout the process. The publication of the volume was also supported by a grant from Aberystwyth University.

The editors
27 April 2016

FIGURES

Fig. 1.1: NLW PITORD/1248 (Seal 2055), armoured man on horseback

Fig. 1.2: SHA 972/1/1/428 (Seal 2436), bird

Fig. 1.3: NLW PITORD/466 (Seal 1887), bust

Fig. 1.4: NLW PITORD/413, s.1 (Seal 1850), Christogram

Fig. 1.5: SHA 20/6/122 (Seal 2271), crossed hands

Fig. 1.6: HAS F8/II/17 (Seal 706), hare on hound

Fig. 1.7: NLW PITORD/12 (Seal 1581), hawk hunting

Fig. 1.8: BL Harl. Ch. 75 B 6, s.2 rev. (Seal 41), lamb and staff

Fig. 1.9: SHA 972/1/1/427 (Seal 2435), lion

Fig. 1.10: BUAS PENR/311, s.1 (Seal 242), lion sleeping

Fig. 1.11: NLW PENRICE: GLAM/342, s.5 (Seal 1374), merchant mark

Fig. 1.12: BUAS PENR/220 (Seal 243), pelican in piety

Fig. 1.13: NLW PENRICE: GLAM/2056, s.3 (Seal 1237), radial device

Fig. 1.14: NLW PITORD/54 (Seal 1610), shield

Fig. 1.15: BUAS PENR/407 (Seal 294), squirrel

Fig. 1.16: NLW PENRICE: GLAM/119 (Seal, 1201), stag

Fig. 1.17: NLW PITORD/1144 (Seal 1630), stag head

Fig. 1.18: HCA Deed122 (Seal 764), stylised lily

Fig. 1.19: NLW BRONWYDD/1031 (966), text

Fig. 1.20: HAS D52/B/1/2, s.7 (Seal 697), two heads

Fig. 1.21: BUAS MOST/1629/vii (Seal 144), woman and child

Fig. 1.22: Motifs by period

Fig. 2.1: NLW PENRICE: GLAM/54 (Seal 56), grant to Margam under lord's seal

Fig. 2.2: NLW PITORD/519 (Seal 1919), seals of the burgesses of Bridgnorth(?)

Fig. 2.3: BUAS MOST/718 (Seal 106), tir prid deed

Fig. 3.1: NLW PENRICE: GLAM/2798 (Seal 1550), Amibilia daughter of Walter the Miller to John Pervath of Kenfig and Alice his wife

Fig. 3.2: NLW PENRICE: GLAM/183 (Seal 1266), Robert son of Robert Raul to Philip son of Robert Plamer

Fig. 3.3: BUAS PENR/219 (Seal 242), sale of neif and his 'brood'

Fig. 3.4: NLW WIGFAIR/627 (Seal 2205), seal of Gilbert Osemund, depicting peacocks with 'tree of life'

Fig. 3.5: NLW PENRICE: GLAM/348, s.2 (Seal 1378), used by Henry Bassett

Fig. 3.6: NLW PENRICE: GLAM/348, s.1 (Seal 1377), used by William Bassett

Fig. 3.7: NLW PENRICE: GLAM/1978 (Seal 96), seal of Geoffrey Sturmi

Fig. 3.8: NLW PENRICE: GLAM/1986 (Seal 1503), seal of Roger Sturmi, jnr

Fig. 3.9: BL Harl. Ch. 75 D 6 (Seal 99), seal of William Sturmi

Fig. 3.10: SHA 972/1/1/610, s.2 (Seal 2460), hare on hound

Fig. 3.11: CALS DLL/4/47, s.1 (Seal 427), seal used by John de Hesketh

Fig. 3.12: NLW PITORD/489 (Seal 1901), sleeping lion seal

Fig. 3.13: NLW PENRICE: GLAM/1993 (Seal 1504), seal of Margery daughter of Roger

Fig. 3.14: NLW BRONWYDD/1332 (Seal 1028), seal used by Gwalter ap Gourwared Vawr

Fig. 4.1: HCA Deed 1084, s.1 (Seal 845), subsidiary(?) seal of Peter of Aigueblanche, Bishop of Hereford (1240–68)

Fig. 4.2: HCA Deed 1084, s.2 (Seal 846), seal of Anselm, Preceptor General in England of the Hospital of St Anthony of Vienne

Fig. 4.3: BUAS PENR/12 (Seal 216), seal of Julian (Giuliano Della Rovere), Cardinal-Bishop of Sabina

Fig. 4.4: NLW PITORD/236 (Seal 1667), seal of the Official of the Dean of Bridgnorth

Fig. 4.5: HCA Deed 2003 (Seal 871), seal of the parson of Kinnersley

Fig. 4.6: NLW PITORD/1057, s.2 (Seal 1983), seal of the Worcester Franciscans

Fig. 4.7: NLW PITORD/605, s.1 (Seal 1950), convent of the Franciscan friars of Bridgenorth

Fig. 4.8: NLW PITORD/605, s.2 (Seal 1951), seal of the Guardian of the Bridgnorth Franciscans

Fig. 5.1: BUAS PENR/166 (Seal 215), front, seal of Henry V as Chamberlain of Wales

Fig. 5.2: BUAS PENR/166 (Seal 215), back, seal of Henry V as Chamberlain of Wales

Fig. 5.3: NLW PENRICE: GLAM/126, s.1 (Seal 1210), seal of Philip son of Kedic

FIGURES

Fig. 5.4: NLW PENRICE: GLAM/126, s.2 (Seal 1211), seal of Madog son of Kedig

Fig. 5.5: NLW PENRICE: GLAM/126, s.3 (Seal 1212), seal of Idenard son of Kedic

Fig. 5.6: NLW PENRICE: GLAM/126, s.4 (Seal 1213), seal of Madog son of Meurig

Fig. 5.7: NLW PENRICE: GLAM/72 (Seal 1174), seal of Ifor Fychan and his sons

Fig. 5.8: BL Harl. Ch. 75 B 12 (Seal 45), seal of John de Bonville

Fig. 6.1: NLW PENRICE: GLAM/2042, front (Seal 1195), seal of Isabella, Countess of Gloucester

Fig. 6.2: NLW PENRICE: GLAM/2042, back (Seal 1194), seal of Isabella, Countess of Gloucester

Fig. 6.3: SHA 972/1/1/432 (Seal 2438), seal of Isabella wife of Roger

Fig. 6.4: SHA 322/2/14 (Seal 2318), seal of Emma wife of William Banastre

Fig. 6.5: NLW PENRICE: GLAM/69 (Seal 1171), seal of Thatherech

Fig. 6.6: BUAS PENR/311, s.2 (Seal 242), seal used by Gwenllian daughter of Gwerfil

Fig. 6.7: SHA 322/2/117, s.2 (Seal 2353), seal of Ela la Botiliere

Fig. 6.8: NLW PITORD/537, s.2 (Seal 1603), seal of Alice, wife of Edmund Pitchford

Fig. 6.9: BL Add. Ch. 24275, s. 2 (Seal 16), seal of Gwenllian daughter of Philip

Fig. 6.10: NLW PITORD/1356 (Seal 2106), seal used by Sibilla widow of William Waters

Fig. 6.11: NLW PENRICE: GLAM/214 (Seal 1305), seal used by Iseuda la Welere

Fig. 7.1: BL Harl. Ch. 75 C 44 (Seal 87), seal of Adam the Porter

Fig. 7.2: BL Harl. Ch. 75 C 46 (Seal 88), seal of Grunu ap Philip

Fig. 7.3: BL Harl. Ch. 75 B 36 (Seal 61), seal of Sibyl de Bonville

Fig. 7.4: NLW PITORD/242, s.2 (Seal 1740), seal used by Maurice Gwyneth of Shrewsbury, chaplain

Fig. 7.5: HCA Deed 23 (Seal 739), seal of William the Chaplain

Fig. 7.6: SHA 972/1/1/442, s. 2 (Seal 2447), seal of Robert Scissor

Fig. 7.7: NLW PITORD/373 (Seal 1817), seal of Richard Brun

Fig. 7.8: NLW PITORD/333 (Seal 1795), seal of Edmund de Pitchford

Fig. 7.9: BUAS MOST/3008 (Seal 186), seal of Ieuan son of Ifor Gough

Fig. 7.10: CALS D3785/1/16 (Seal 321), high-quality 'hare and hound' seal

Fig. 7.11: CALS D3785/1/15 pt.1 (Seal 319), lower quality 'hare and hound' seal

Fig. 7.12: NLW PENRICE: GLAM/2013 (Seal 1513), seal of Richard Norries

Fig. 7.13: BUAS PENR/25 (Seal 221), seal used by Johanna, late wife of Gwilym ap Gruffudd

Fig. 7.14: BL Harl. Ch. 75 B 17 (Seal 46), seal of William de Boneville

Fig. 7.15: SHA 20/7/43, s.2 (Seal 2307), seal depicting the martyrdom of St Edmund

Fig. 7.16: NLW PITORD/10 (Seal 1579), seal used by John son of Robert the locksmith

MAPS AND TABLES

Map I.1: Location of seals by place of sealing and by extent of sealing recorded
Table I.1: Medieval seal matrix finds by Welsh county
Table 1.1: Total number of cases by period
Table 1.2: Distribution of motifs by class, 1175 to 1524
Table 1.3: Definition of motifs
Table 1.4: Percentage of cases in each temporal group

ABBREVIATIONS

Acts	H. Pryce, *The Acts of Welsh Rulers, 1120–1283* (Cardiff, 2005)
BBCS	*Bulletin of the Board of Celtic Studies*
Birch	W. de Gray Birch, *Catalogue of Seals in the Department of Manuscripts in the British Museum*, 6 vols (London, 1887–1900)
BUAS MOST	Bangor University Archives, Mostyn Manuscripts
BUAS PENR	Bangor University Archives, Penrhyn Castle
BL Harl. Ch.	British Library, Harley Charters
BL Add. Ch.	British Library, Additional Charters
CALS DWN	Cheshire Archives and Local Studies, Wilbraham of Nantwich Collection
CALS DLL	Cheshire Archives and Local Studies, Leigh of West Hall, High Legh
CALS D3785/1	Cheshire Archives and Local Studies, Professor G. Barraclough: Deeds and Research Papers (Bulkley and Bickerton Deeds)
CMCS	*Cambrian Medieval Celtic Studies*
GA D8/1	Gwent Record Office, John Capel Hanbury (D8/1)
GA D2, GA D583	Gwent Record Office, Llanarth Court MSS
GACRO XD2	Gwynedd Archives: Caernarfon Record Office, Newborough Archives
GACRO Vaynol/Glan	Gwynedd Archives: Caernarfon Record Office, Vaynol Papers
Good Impressions	N. Adams, J. Cherry and J. Robinson (eds), *Good Impressions: Image and Authority in Medieval Seals* (London, 2007)
Guide	P. D. A. Harvey and A. McGuiness, *A Guide to British Medieval Seals* (London, 1996)

HAS A95	Herefordshire Record Office, Pateshall Family of Allensmore
HAS D52	Herefordshire Record Office, Wellington Inheritance Brobury (Garnons)
HAS AA26/II	Herefordshire Record Office, Records of the Barton Colwall Estate
HAS CF54	Herefordshire Record Office, Pilley Collection: Manuscripts
HAS F8/II	Herefordshire Record Office, Hill Court
HCA	Hereford Cathedral Archives
Margam	W. de Grey Birch, *A History of Margam Abbey* (London, 1897)
NLW BACBYD	Llyfrgell Genedlaethol Cymru / National Library of Wales, Bachymbyd Estate Deeds and Documents
NLW BRONWYDD	Llyfrgell Genedlaethol Cymru / National Library of Wales, Bronwydd Estate Records
NLW CHIRK	Llyfrgell Genedlaethol Cymru / National Library of Wales, Chirk Castle Estate Records
NLW MYNDE	Llyfrgell Genedlaethol Cymru / National Library of Wales, Mynde Park Deeds and Documents
NLW PITORD	Llyfrgell Genedlaethol Cymru / National Library of Wales, Ottley (Pitchford Hall) Estate 1
NLW PENRICE: GLAM	Llyfrgell Genedlaethol Cymru / National Library of Wales, Penrice and Margam Estate Records
NLW WIGFAIR	Llyfrgell Genedlaethol Cymru / National Library of Wales, Wigfair Deeds and Documents
NLW Strata Marchella	Llyfrgell Genedlaethol Cymru / National Library of Wales, Wynnstay Estate Records 1945 Deposit (Ystrad Marchell)
NLWJ	*National Library of Wales Journal*
NMW	National Museum of Wales
PAS	Portable Antiquities Scheme
Scriptorium	R. B. Patterson, *The Scriptorium of Margam Abbey and the Scribes of Early Angevin Glamorgan: Secretarial Administration in a Welsh Marcher Barony* (Woodbridge, 2002)

ABBREVIATIONS

Seal 1–2497	Reference to seal as listed in the main appendix to this volume
Seals and Sealing Practices	E. A. New, *Seals and Sealing Practices*, British Records Association Archives and the User 11 (London, 2010)
Seliau	J. McEwan and E. A. New (eds), *Seliau yn eu Cyd-destun: Cymru o'r Mers yn yr Oesoedd Canol / Seals in Context: Medieval Wales and the Welsh Marches* (Aberystwyth, 2012)
SHA 322/2	Shropshire Archives, Acton Reynald (Corbet Family)
SHA 5981/B	Shropshire Archives, Powis Estate Records
SHA 20	Shropshire Archives, Oakley Park Collection
SHA 972	Shropshire Archives, Lilleshall Collection
SiMeW	*Seals in Medieval Wales, 1200–1500*, project funded by the Arts and Humanities Research Council (AH/G010994/1)
TNA	The National Archives
Welsh Heraldry	M. P. Siddons, *The Development of Welsh Heraldry*, 4 vols (Aberystwyth, 1991–2006)
WHR	*Welsh History Review*

INTRODUCTION

Elizabeth A. New and Phillipp R. Schofield

THIS VOLUME IS THE PRODUCT of an Arts and Humanities Research Council-funded project, *Seals in Medieval Wales*, a collaborative project between the universities of Aberystwyth and Bangor, the project based in the Department of History and Welsh History at Aberystwyth University.[1] *Seals in Medieval Wales* (hereafter *SiMeW*) was the largest and best-funded project of its kind ever undertaken in Britain. In the present volume the project team has set out a preliminary exploration of some of the resulting material as well as providing an appendix of all seals listed in the project's database. Supported also by a sample of images representative of the content of the dataset, it is hoped that the present volume will not only shed additional light on the developing study of seals as well as the medieval history of Wales, the March and neighbouring English counties, but also encourage future research with this corpus of material as well as the greater body of largely unexamined material still awaiting close investigation.

Seals have been used by societies across the world for more than seven thousand years, and are indeed some of the earliest historical records. In a British context, medieval seals are particularly important because they were usually the choice of their owner, and as such provide a unique insight into the personal concerns of women and men across the social spectrum, including those for whom little other evidence survives. While personal seals offer glimpses into the lives of individuals, official seals provide information about institutions and people in positions of power, and their images and words were frequently used as a vehicle of propaganda. In addition, seal impressions that are still attached to the documents that they validated are closely dateable, vital information frequently lacking from other material sources, and this offers potential for iconographical and stylistic chronology. The volume examines both the history of seal usage in the Middle Ages, and highlights the use of sigillographic evidence to provide important new insights into the history of medieval Wales and the English border counties, bringing novel analytical and thematic approaches to Wales in this period.

In this introductory section we reflect upon seals and their usage in the Middle Ages, as well as provide a general overview of sealing practices, the establishment of the parameters of the investigations (i.e. the project remit) and the dataset. It is also an opportunity to offer some reflections upon the ways in which sigillography has been employed in medieval Welsh history to date. Thereafter, individually authored chapters will address themes central to the study of seals and their use and allow sigillography to be set within the context of medieval history and, more particularly, the context of Wales, its March and its neighbouring counties.

As with the more general study of medieval Wales and the Marches, *SiMeW* has been able both to build upon, and contribute to, previous work on seals and sealing practices in the region. In common with much of the rest of Britain, there was considerable interest in seals from across Wales and the Marches in the late eighteenth and, especially, the nineteenth century.[2] *The Journal of the Chester Architectural, Archaeological and Historical Society* included several references to seals in its 1849 inaugural issue, *Archaeologia Cambrensis* published the first of many seal-focused articles in 1860, and seals (many illustrated) featured prominently in Robert Eyton's twelve-volume *Antiquities of Shropshire*, for example, while the Victoria County History volumes for the English border counties made note of official and institutional seals. Most of the nineteenth-century references to seals take the form of descriptive notes, but are very valuable nonetheless, especially for items that have either subsequently been damaged or destroyed, or cannot now be located.[3] In the later nineteenth century, Walter de Gray Birch, a noted sigillographer whose catalogues of British seals remain invaluable to researchers, included careful notes of seals and sealing practices associated with Margam Abbey, including some brief discursive notes and observations.[4]

The decline in interest in seals, especially by academic historians, in the inter-war period and into the later twentieth century, was as marked in Wales as elsewhere in Britain, and it was only really with the work of David H. Williams and Michael Powell Siddons that Welsh sigillographic studies started to see a revival in the later 1980s. Siddons's work has focused on seals with armorial and equestrian devices, and is particularly important for highlighting material held outside Wales, as well as for demonstrating the crucial role of sigillographic evidence for the study of heraldry in the country.[5] In addition to important work cataloguing matrices and casts in the National Museum of Wales, and the production of unpublished catalogues of seals within several collections held at the National Library of Wales, Williams's great contribution to Welsh sigillography has been his extensive work on ecclesiastical, and especially Cistercian, seals and sealing practice. The catalogue of Welsh ecclesiastical seals, published across several volumes of *Archaeologia Cambrensis*, provides a very full (if, by Williams's own admission, not exhaustive) record of known material, while his work contextualising Cistercian seals has added considerably to this field.[6] As well as academic studies, David H. Williams has also helped promote seals as valid and valuable source for the history of Wales to a general audience.[7] In addition to focused studies of seals, sigillographic material has also been incorporated into a number of different works about Welsh society, while some reference is made to seals in the editions of important collections of Welsh charters that have appeared since the 1980s.[8]

In contrast to the situation in Wales, the study of seals and their incorporation into investigations of the medieval period across the English border counties has suffered markedly from the decline in interest in matters sigillographic since the early-to-mid twentieth century. Apart from the Victoria County History's policy of recording official seals whenever possible, and a scattering of (sometimes unpublished) lists of seals in particular repositories, surprisingly little use has been made of the sigillographic material available in this region.[9] An example of this decline in interest in seals is exemplified by the *Transactions of the Woolhope Naturalist's Field Club*, the principal publication concerned with Herefordshire. Between 1900 and 1936, six articles in the *Transactions* were solely or principally devoted to seals; between 1937 and 2000, only one focused on, and one other mentioned, seals. Recent studies of the March and Marcher families have started to take some notice of sigillographic material, but at the time of writing seals and sealing practices in the border counties remain remarkably under-studied.[10]

The *SiMeW* project: the selection of material and the recording process

In order to offer a fuller context to this volume, it will be helpful, then, to begin with a discussion of the research and data-gathering processes, which also permits an early perspective on the period and geographical range of the material. The material recorded for the *SiMeW* project was drawn from across Wales and the English border counties, within the timeframe of *c*.1150–1550. The decision to include areas beyond the March, even in its broadest context, was made to provide the greatest potential for the identification of regional and local patterns in an area that saw both significant political and cultural divides, as well as a great deal of movement and exchange of people and commodities.[11] The scope of the project meant that it was impossible to record all extant material, but great care was taken to ensure that, as far as possible, all areas within the project's geographical boundaries were included. This was done through identifying repositories and collections known to have sealed documents that fell within the project's remit; in addition to online and analogue finding aids, the project team was fortunate to receive invaluable advice from archivists in a number of repositories, and benefit from Dr Susan

Davies's extensive knowledge of Welsh archival material.[12] Care was also taken to ensure that a range of different types of collection, from the muniments of monastic houses and cathedrals to the archives of Marcher lords, secular estates and small towns, were also included in the sample. The *SiMeW* research questions were predicated on obtaining as broad a picture as possible and so, unlike the majority of existing catalogues of seals in Britain, care was taken not to cherry-pick by type of sigillant, seal or seal-motif. Therefore, with three exceptions, all documents within a collection that fell within the geographic and chronological parameters of the project were examined, and all those with extant seal impressions were recorded.[13]

In practice, however, the recording process was, almost inevitably, not as straightforward as had been hoped, and highlighted the crucial importance to researchers of item-level description of collections (especially with reference to the presence or absence of a seal), and of the specialist knowledge of archival professionals. Collections occasionally contained far fewer medieval documents than the available description suggested, or it was found that the seal impressions had deliberately been removed from documents.[14] At the other extreme, some collections and repositories proved to be unexpectedly fruitful (usually the result of the inconsistent noting of the presence of seals, thus masking the true extent of the material to be recorded), while on one occasion a very recent acquisition with no publicly accessible information about the contents provided valuable additional items.[15] In addition, since all sealed items within a collection that met the project's temporal and geographical criteria were recorded (see below), more data were inevitably gathered for certain locations depending on the size of collections.[16] A further complicating factor was the loss or inaccessibility of material. For example, there are known to be a few sealed deeds relating to medieval Ceredigion and the borough of Aberystwyth within the Gogerddan Estate Records in the National Library of Wales, but this extensive collection is listed only at fonds level, and the time required to extract the small number of relevant items was deemed prohibitive for the very limited amount of data that would have been obtained.[17] There are also a scattering of medieval documents relating to land held by the Cistercian houses of Cwmhir and Cymer in a number of collections, while the loss of virtually all Strata Florida material is regrettable since this would, presumably, have provided material relating to the heart of *Pura Walia*.[18] Despite these caveats, the *SiMeW* dataset represents a robust sample of sealed documents, and thus evidence of sealing practices, from across Wales and the border counties, and adds further confirmation to the existing scholarly consensus regarding the adoption or rejection of the sealed instrument across Wales, as discussed below and in chapter 2.[19]

In addition to gathering material for the project itself, part of the remit of *SiMeW* was to establish a practical template for the recording of sigillographic data in an archival context that could be considered for future programmes of seal recording in the UK, and this flexibility and adaptability was kept in mind when designing the project template. Drawing upon previous experience and best practice,[20] and in conjunction with advice from the project's own oversight board, especially Dr Susan Davies and Professor P. D. A. Harvey, and taking into consideration the requirements of the International Standard for Archival Description (General) (ISAD(G)), John McEwan and Elizabeth New therefore designed a template that would enable many different features of the sealed instrument consistently to be recorded. McEwan proceeded to design a relational database that would capture this information, as well as enabling editing at the review stage of the project. The use of a relational database was essential, and enabled the researchers to record a large amount of data, as well as making data output extremely flexible. This model also treated the sealed instrument as a whole and recorded significant data from the parent document (such as type of document and date). Physical aspects of the seal were also recorded, such as form of attachment, colour, condition (completeness), using controlled vocabulary and check / drop boxes when possible. The recording of the seal motif and legend were undertaken using free-text fields according to a detailed form of description established by the project team. *SiMeW* also obtained permission to take reference photographs from all the repositories involved, and digitally imaged all the documents and seal impressions that were recorded. In order to facilitate research and enhance accessibility, a system of keywords for the principal motif on each seal was also devised.[21]

Seals in context

The following chapters in this volume represent first attempts to use the material gathered by *SiMeW* and, as importantly, to encourage others to do so. The subject range of the chapters move through a discussion of seal usage and its legal and administrative setting, as well as the place of seal usage in exchange in medieval economy and society, to discussion of the ways in which seals within a Welsh and Marcher context allow historians to approach issues of identity in this period, as well as such themes as piety, the representation of women and of power and lordship. In his analysis of the data extracted by the *SiMeW* project, John McEwan identifies some of the broad trends established by these data and discusses the main identifiable changes in the form of seals across the period from the twelfth century to the sixteenth. In general terms these are consistent with trends already identified in earlier work, but the range and depth of the material studied here allows a more concrete view of such developments as well as the opportunity for a more nuanced sense of shifts in design. McEwan necessarily sets out these developments in largely generalised terms and, as such, provides a broad schema against which future work can be set.

One important element of that future work is likely to be investigation of change over time, set within particular regional and local contexts. As we will see on more than one occasion in this volume, data gathered here suggest regional and local patterns in seal usage and in choice of seal motif, even within the context of general developments in seal usage; it is very much hoped that further work on this and associated material will test this suggestion. For the present, chapters in this volume employ these broad developments and set them within particular thematic contexts. Schofield's chapter on law and administration sets out the main ways in which seals were used in order to support administrative structures in Wales and its periphery. In reflecting upon change over time in this respect, and especially a more general development in seal usage, Schofield also notes two important features in seal usage. In the first instance, in Wales there is an important difference between the area of the March and *Pura Walia*. As was discussed above, in this introduction, the survival or lack of survival of relevant material may accentuate the distinction but there seems little doubt, and it is a feature already noted by other historians working in this area,[22] that *Pura Walia* is, relatively speaking, an area relatively free of seal usage in the high and late Middle Ages in comparison to northern, southern and eastern Wales and its border regions. This is a pattern that an initial quantification of medieval seal matrix finds also seems to corroborate. A simple county-level search of the Portable Antiquities Scheme (PAS) database, using the criteria 'medieval' for period and 'seal matrix' for object type, suggests interesting disparities in the number of finds to date by modern Welsh county and a pattern largely consistent with that described by surviving seal impressions.[23] Among the notable absentees from table I.1 are, of course, the modern counties of Ceredigion and Gwynedd, and for neither county have there been recorded finds of matrices to date.[24]

Table I.1: Medieval seal matrix finds by Welsh county

County	Number of matrix finds
Bridgend	2
Carmarthenshire	3
Conwy	3
Denbighshire	3
Flintshire	3
Monmouthshire	11
Newport	1
Pembrokeshire	4
Powys	6
Rhondda Cynon Taf	1
Swansea	1
Vale of Glamorgan	19
Wrexham	9

Source: Portable Antiquities Scheme database at *https://finds.org.uk/database/search/results/objecttype/SEAL+MATRIX/broadperiod/MEDIEVAL/regionID/41424/show/100* (last accessed 9 June 2015)

INTRODUCTION

In fact, this distinction between a Welshry and Englishry writ large sits at the heart of much relevant writing on medieval Wales as historians have grappled in different ways with the distinctions and shared features of medieval Wales and its neighbour. So, for instance, discussions of the relationship between Welsh and English law, or of the nature of urban and rural settlement in Wales make important distinctions between Wales within and beyond areas of close contact with England and Anglo-Norman society.[25]

The frequency of regional seal usage is identified in map I.1 below, which also illustrates the concentration of material within particular locations. This concentration of material must to some degree or other slightly 'skew' the more general picture, and we look forward to future work aimed at establishing and/or correcting the patterns and discussions set out in this volume. Further programmes of recording and research projects will almost certainly enable an even more nuanced picture to emerge as more material is investigated. For the present, the chapters in this volume have drawn upon material set within this particular regional context.

Map I.1: Location of seals by place of sealing and by extent of sealing recorded

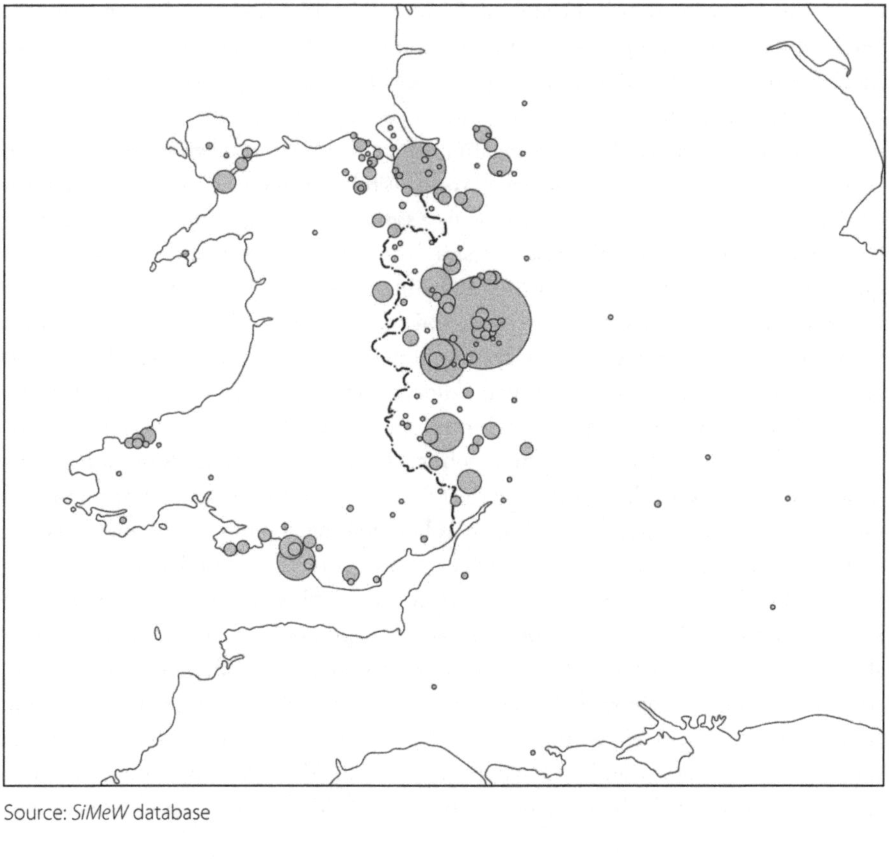

Source: *SiMeW* database

So, for instance, Elizabeth New's investigation of seals and religion illustrates how seals add to the message of an international church operating within Wales. New also suggests ways in which the historical understanding of the administration of the church might be extended through close analysis of seals, as for instance in the role of the Official of the Dean of Bridgnorth and the variety of contexts in which the Official came to use his seal. In addition, New shows how, within Wales and its neighbouring counties, ecclesiastics and religious worked within their own shared conventions and developed motifs in personalised ways, reflecting both corporate and individual identities. Identity, in particular, looms large as a theme in a number of the discussions here. In her chapter on expressions of identity, New moves beyond the more immediate consideration of clerical and religious devices to extend her discussion of the ways in which individuals sought to use seals in order to represent themselves. Here she begins to challenge Brigitte Bedos-Rezak's contention that the message of seals can be contained by semiotic devices as to negate the impact of personal expression.[26] This may work with a particular socioeconomic context in mind when considering the semiotic force of shared motifs, but New moves well beyond familiar, and often dominant seal types in terms of the historiography, such as equestrian seals and seals with heraldic devices. Even in such instances, seal owners can be identified adjusting 'conventional' motifs and intruding their own personal conventions into seal designs and motifs. Sometimes these can be light-hearted references to the person or their name while, for instance, in others they may be deeply spiritual and apparently representative of their personal piety. As New remarks, close investigation of such subtleties takes us beyond more familiar interpretations of the medieval world. While the question as to whether a seal used by a female sigillant actually represents a squirrel cracking a nut or a fox playing a flute may appear the most abstruse of research topics, in reality it and similar types of question point us to the ways in which individuals chose to represent themselves, the involved semiotic devices they employed, and the ways in which seal design intersects with and represents shared social and cultural mores. Similar themes are addressed in Sue Johns's chapters on lordship and on women. High-status seal usage has been at the core of sigillographic research since its inception, a focus that reflects a persistent historiographical focus upon elites and high politics. In her chapter on lordship, Johns aims to address the ways in which seals may shed more light on the perceived importance of lordship and its associated features, such as landholding. Taking a particular perspective upon seals, their use and their social construction, Johns emphasises the power associated with seal usage and suggests ways in which seals were part of an 'armoury' of seigneurial power. Power also features in Johns's chapter on women and seals in which she seeks to show that ideas about gender and women were reflected in seal design, while a changing chronology of female usage of seals may also illustrate a changing role for women, notably in seigneurial households. In addition, seals became opportunities for a variety of collective and personal features to coincide with shared cultural expression mediated through the expectations of the individual seal owner. Schofield also examines related themes in his chapter on seals and exchange. While, inevitably, part of Schofield's focus is upon the ways in which sealed documents facilitated exchange of different kinds and not those uniquely associated with the transfer of free land, Schofield also observes that the very nature and process of sealing were opportunities for other kinds of exchange. So, for instance, the sharing through seal designs of cultural norms such as customary or local conventions arising from popular imagery might be one such feature of exchange, as might shared legal knowledge relating to seal usage, its force and its applicability within particular jurisdictions and contexts.

Finally, in each instance, chapter authors have worked to distinguish the particular message of the seal from its associated document. There is the inevitable risk that the document is left to speak alone or, by extension, for the seal; here, unusually in historical analysis, the seal takes centre stage and it is the additional or contrary message of the seal that is sought throughout the discussion as set out in the following chapters.

Notes

1   *Seals in Medieval Wales, 1200–1500*, funded by the Arts and Humanities Research Council (AH/G010994/1): principal investigator, Phillipp Schofield; co-investigator, Sue Johns; senior research officer, Elizabeth New; and research officer, John McEwan.
2   For recent overviews of the study of seals in Britain and Europe, see B. M. Bedos-Rezak, 'Outcast. Seals of the medieval West and their epistemological frameworks (XIIth–XXIst centuries)', in *From Minor to Major: the Minor Arts in Medieval Art History*, ed. Colum Hourihane (Princeton, 2012), pp. 122–40; *Seals and Sealing Practices*, pp. 29–32.
3   An impression of the seal of the Hospital of St James, Bridgnorth, is discussed and illustrated by Eyton, but the document to which this was attached was in private hands at the time and cannot now be located. R. W. Eyton, *The Antiquities of Shropshire*, vol. 1 (London, 1854), p. 349, and vol. 2 (London, 1855), plate facing p. 16.
4   *Margam*. See for example p. 52, where Birch describes the seal of Grunu son of Phillip as an example of 'native art'.
5   See for example M. P. Siddons, 'Welsh seals in Paris', *Bulletin of the Board of Celtic Studies*, 29 (1981), 531–44; *Welsh Heraldry*, vol. 1, esp. pp. 13–18.
6   See, for example, D. H. Williams, 'Medieval Cistercian seals with special reference to "hand-and-staff" seals', *Archaeologia Cambrensis*, 154 (2007 for 2005), 153–78.
7   D. H. Williams, *Welsh History through Seals* (Cardiff, 1982); idem, *Images of Welsh History* (Aberystwyth, 2007).
8   C. Lloyd-Morgan, 'More written about than writing? Welsh women and the written word', in H. Pryce (ed.), *Literacy in Medieval Celtic Societies* (Cambridge, 1998), pp. 149–65, at p. 150, mentions the importance of seals as evidence for women's status and engagement with administration, for example, while the seals of the princes of Wales (including Glyndŵr) have elicited frequent comment in an Anglo-Welsh political context. Both G. C. G. Thomas (ed.), *The Charters of the Abbey of Ystrad Marchell* (Aberystwyth, 1997), pp. 99–100, and D. Crouch (ed.), *Llandaff Episcopal Acta 1140–1287* (Cardiff, 1989), p. xliv, provide useful, but brief and descriptive sections about the seals within their respective collections of charters. *Acts*, pp. 86–9, provides a more discursive overview of seals and sealing practices.

9   F. C. and P. E. Morgan, *A Concise List of Seals Belonging to the Dean and Chapter of Hereford Cathedral* (Hereford, 1966), is one of the few published lists.
10 M. Julian-Jones, 'Land of the raven and the wolf: a comparative study of family power and strategy in the Welsh March, *c.*1199–1300' (unpublished Cardiff University PhD, 2014), incorporates sigillographic material, for example.
11 The difficulty in defining the March and Marches of Wales has been noted by a number of scholars. See, for example, R. R. Davies, *Lordship and Society in the March of Wales 1282–1400* (Oxford, 1978), esp. pp. 2–3, 15–17.
12 Dr Susan Davies also acted as *SiMeW*'s archival advisor for the duration of the project. For a full list of the collections recorded by *SiMeW*, see appendix.
13 Samples were taken from Hereford Cathedral Archives, the British Library Additional Charters and the British Library Harley Charters, because the size and nature of these collections and timescale of the project precluded full recording. The Margam material in the BL Harley Charters was prioritised because it enabled *SiMeW* to include almost all of the important Abbey collection, the project team having already recorded the Penrice and Margam collection in the NLW. At Hereford Cathedral, runs of documents were sampled to provide an overview of this extensive collection, while material relating to Cardiff (surprisingly underrepresented in other collections) was identified and recorded from the BL Additional Charters.
14 The Newborough Archives in Caernarfon Record Office is one collection where the fonds-level description suggested a greater number of medieval sealed items than actually survive. The most extreme example of the removal of seals was the Whitney and Clifford collection in the Bangor University Archives, where all the seal impressions had been cut off (prior to deposit with the university archives) to make it easier to store the documents.
15 The Professor G. Barraclough Deeds and Research Papers in Cheshire Archives and Local Studies. We are grateful to Jonathan Pepler, past county archivist for Cheshire, for drawing our attention to this collection, and enabling us to record it prior to item-level cataloguing.
16 The Ottley (Pitchford Hall) Estate 1 collection in the National Library of Wales proved especially rich, for example.
17 See *http://www.archiveswales.org.uk/anw/get_collection.php?inst_id=1&coll_id=20144&expand* (last accessed 26 January 2016). At the time of writing, a National Library of Wales project to catalogue all 120 boxes of the Gogerddan Estate Records has recently started.
18 A few fifteenth-century Cymer documents survive in the Nannau Manuscripts collection in the Bangor University Archives, for example.
19 For discussions about the adoption of the sealed instrument across Wales, see, for example, Ll. B. Smith, 'Inkhorn and spectacles: the impact of literacy in late medieval Wales', in H. Pryce (ed.), *Literacy in Medieval Celtic Societies*, Cambridge Studies in Medieval Literature, 33 (Cambridge, 1998), pp. 202–22, and A. D. Carr, ' "This is my act and deed": the writing of private deeds in late medieval north Wales', in H. Pryce (ed.), *Literacy in Medieval Celtic Societies*. Cambridge Studies in Medieval Literature 33 (Cambridge, 1998), 223–237, esp. p. 223, and pp. 36–7 in the present volume.
20 Principally the V*ocabulaire international de la sigillographie* and the data-capture model on that established by Professor P. D. A. Harvey for the catalogue of seals in TNA DL25 and DL26, compiled in the 1990s.
21 This was devised by John McEwan and Elizabeth New, and subsequently has been developed by Dr McEwan as part of his ongoing research; see J. McEwan, 'The challenge of the visual: making medieval seals accessible in the digital age', *Journal of Documentation*, 71 (2015), 999–1028.
22 Smith, 'Inkhorn and spectacles', pp. 215–16.
23 Of course, this is a simple and inaccurate indicative test; error will be introduced here by other

factors, not least the density of modern populations and the likely consequence for relative activity of detectorists within different parts of Wales. For the available data, using the same broad search terms, see *https://finds.org.uk/database/search/results/objecttype/SEAL+MATRIX/broadperiod/MEDIEVAL/regionID/41424/show/100* (last accessed 9 June 2015).

24 This points stands only as regards finds recorded in Portable Antiquities Scheme; there is some evidence for finds within these counties, such as the papal bulla at Strata Florida, D. H. Williams, 'Seal finds in Wales', in P. R. Schofield (ed.), *Seals and their Context in the Middle Ages* (Oxford, 2015), pp. 196–7, although it is interesting to note that the bulla were associated with documents sent to the house from elsewhere.

25 For recent reflections on aspects of this distinction see essays in R. A. Griffiths and P. R. Schofield (eds), *Wales and the Welsh in the Middle Ages* (Cardiff, 2011).

26 B. M. Bedos-Rezak, 'Replica: images of identity and the identity of images', in J. F. Hamburger and A-M. Bouché (eds), *The Mind's Eye: Art and Theological Argument in the Middles Ages* (Princeton, 2006), pp. 46–64.

SEALS IN MEDIEVAL WALES AND ITS NEIGHBOURING COUNTIES
TRENDS IN MOTIFS

John A. McEwan

IN 1292 COUNT AMADEUS of Savoy was travelling in the south-east of England, where he bought luxury goods, including two silver matrices.[1] The official keeping his accounts noted their cost, but nothing about the text and images on the seals. This is typical of the written sources from this period, which occasionally identify the artisans who made seals and how much they were paid, but offer little information on what the seals expressed.[2] To determine what types of seals people wanted, therefore, scholars need to look at the seals themselves. Although medieval seals of the British Isles survive in exceptional numbers, they have not yet been systematically surveyed. Consequently, as Paul Harvey has commented, apart from seals of the English monarchy 'we have not even the most elementary typology, the simplest chronological outline of their development'.[3] Without this information, it is difficult to determine the extent to which the motifs people selected for their seals were dictated by function or by fashion. This chapter surveys the motifs of the approximately 2,500 seals in the *SiMeW* dataset to establish what motifs were popular and how quickly their popularity changed over time in medieval Wales and its neighbouring counties. In these regions, people used an extremely wide range of motifs, but the favoured motifs gradually shifted. Within this broad history of changes in the fashions in seal motifs in this region, three phases of development can be discerned, defined by the changing role of seals as tools of identification.[4]

The surviving seal impressions from medieval Britain present a variety of motifs. A random sample, such as those listed on the first page of one catalogue of 'personal' seals in the National Archives, includes a shield of arms, a griffin's head, a stylised flower, a man on horseback, a monogram, and a heart.[5] As seal catalogues usually present the seals surviving in a particular repository, they typically bring together examples from many different locations and times. Although a large number of motifs were used on seals over the course of the Middle Ages, the level of diversity among the seals circulating in a particular time and place may not always have been high. The well-known charter recording an agreement made between Ranulf, Earl of Chester and Lincoln, and a group of his rural tenants in Lincolnshire shows that those tenants favoured certain motifs.[6] The copy sealed by the men survives with forty-eight of their seal impressions and thus reveals the seal motifs typical of one particular area at a given moment. While one man used a seal with a 'lamb and staff' (Lamb of God) motif and another a 'bird', the remainder can be broadly characterised as presenting 'foliate' motifs.[7] Cases such as this suggest that in particular times and places, particular seal motifs predominated. The co-existence of such cases with the wide range of motifs on surviving seals of the larger period suggests that the popularity of motifs fluctuated, and fluctuated within a dynamic system.

Scholars have long recognised that people in different periods favoured different motifs. T. A. Heslop has suggested that in the second half of the twelfth century people outside the aristocracy commonly used 'animals and birds, stylised flowers or an elaborate cross' and in the fourteenth century representations of various animals, as well as religious and heraldic motifs.[8] However, such generalisations need to be tested and refined. French scholars have demonstrated the value of quantitative approaches, but attempts to apply them to seals from the British Isles have so far been limited.[9] Nonetheless, there is a wealth of evidence with which to work. The precise number of surviving seal impressions from medieval Britain is unknown because they have never been systematically counted, but it is significant. Harvey has estimated that the National Archives holds 50,000 examples and that in the nation there could be several hundreds of thousands.[10] Before they can be analysed, however, those seals need to be recorded. As detailed in the introduction, the seals in the *SiMeW* dataset are associated with locations across Wales and its neighbouring counties in England, including a significant proportion issuing from the English counties of Shropshire (35 per cent), Chester (13 per cent) and Hereford (9 per cent), together with a large group from Glamorgan (20 per cent). The seals are temporally well distributed, as they range from *c.*1150 to 1550. The approximately 2,500 seals described by the *SiMeW* project are a fraction of those that exist, but they provide an opportunity to conduct an initial survey to determine which motifs were popular and how quickly their popularity changed.

The first step in the analysis is to organise the seals into temporal groups. Each seal matrix was made at a particular date and then used for a period of time. The date of fabrication of a given seal is generally not recorded, but the period of its use is revealed by its surviving impressions, for these are attached to documents that can normally be dated precisely. These impressions therefore offer a *terminus ante quem* for the manufacture of the seal matrix. Yet since an individual could use a single seal matrix throughout his or her life, the date of the earliest surviving impression can be later than the date when the seal matrix was made; if a man acquired a seal matrix in December 1299, he might continue to use it well into the fourteenth century. As the date of each seal's fabrication is difficult to infer with precision, it is appropriate, for the purpose of analysis, to group together seals from the same period. For this discussion, the seals are organised into seven temporal groups, ranging from *c.*1200 to *c.*1500. Each temporal group is defined as the seals whose impressions are first recorded within twenty-five years of the group's titular date; thus the *c.*1300 group includes seals attached to documents dated 1275 to 1324 (see table 1.1). For this analysis seals from the *SiMeW* dataset whose dates set them outside these temporal groups have been discarded, leaving only those from 1175 to 1524.

The seals analysed here have also been selected according to social criteria. The seals of popes, bishops, kings, earls and corporate bodies, such as monastic houses and cathedrals, together with their officials and obedientiaries, reveal a distinctive set of purposes in the selection of their motifs.[11] Corporate institutions could retain the same seals for decades – if not centuries – as a sign of their continuity. Similarly, kings normally acquired seals with the same motifs as those of their predecessors in order to underline the legitimacy of their succession.[12] Furthermore, the seals of institutions and the elite are overrepresented in the historical record because they were appended to important documents that their recipients were especially likely to retain. By contrast, the seals of more humble people are comparatively underrepresented, for only a fraction of the millions that were probably once in circulation survive.[13] Nonetheless, there are still many examples and they have been largely overlooked by historians.[14] Excluding the seals of the corporate bodies and the most elite members of society enables us to focus on the seals associated with the remaining members of society. Thus the seven temporal groups include 1,955 seals, which constitute more than 78 per cent of the total number in the *SiMeW* dataset.

Table 1.1: Total number of cases by period

Group	Period	Cases
1	*c.*1200 (1175–1224)	136
2	*c.*1250 (1225–1274)	242
3	*c.*1300 (1275–1324)	309
4	*c.*1350 (1325–1374)	387
5	*c.*1400 (1375–1424)	308
6	*c.*1450 (1425–1474)	300
7	*c.*1500 (1475–1524)	273
		Total = 1955

Source: *SiMeW* dataset

Before the motifs on the seals can be analysed quantitatively, they need to be classified. Medieval seals are typically a few centimetres tall and include a band around the outer edge reserved for text. Consequently the area available at the centre of the seal for visual content is minimal. It was into this restricted space that medieval artisans inserted a motif that could serve as a distinctive and identifiable mark. These physical constraints encouraged artisans to design seals with a single clearly expressed motif, which makes them amenable to classification. The International Council on Archives sigillography committee's typology is perhaps the most authoritative.[15] Although it is not a formal classification system, it offers a set of categories. This typology reflects the traditional priorities and concerns of seal scholars, who have focused on the seals of the upper levels of society. Thus, for example, the typology includes three separate categories for representations of men on horseback – a motif often used by members of the social elite. However, the typology does not provide specific categories for most of the motifs favoured by people of lesser standing, yet these are the motifs that most commonly appear in British collections. Thus the typology is not appropriate for this study, which requires a system that can sort with some precision the typical seals in British collections.

Instead, this analysis employs *SiMeW*'s classification system, which is based on the general nature of motifs at the primary level of meaning.[16] Visual materials do not necessarily have precise linguistic equivalents, so there are often several ways in which a motif can be described. A description can be general (a lion), or it can include additional qualifiers that indicate the motif's particular features (a lion facing to the left with foliage behind). A further complication is that any visual content can be described on a number of levels. Panofsky has argued that any visual resource has a 'primary' (or natural) subject matter.[17] A description of a visual resource at the primary level is factual: this is a painting of thirteen men having dinner. Panofsky distinguished this primary level from what he called the 'secondary' (or conventional) subject matter. A description of a visual resource at the secondary level is iconographic and depends on cultural knowledge: this is a painting not just of thirteen men having dinner, but of the Last Supper. Scholars aim to grasp the secondary-level meaning of the motifs, but that understanding is founded on the primary-level meaning. For the purposes of an initial and provisional quantitative survey of motifs on seals from Wales and the Welsh Marches it is thus appropriate to employ a simplified version of *SiMeW*'s classification system, which focuses on the primary level of meaning (see table 1.3).[18] However, it must be emphasised that classification entails bringing together seals whose motifs express a common idea, rather than motifs that are precisely identical.[19] Thus a crude and badly engraved seal that depicts a man on horseback can be placed in the same class as a seal with the same motif carefully executed by a skilled artisan. The classification process groups together motifs irrespective of their quality and style. Once the seals are sorted into their classes, it is clear that some motifs are more popular than others for some classes hold only a handful of examples. When only those classes with ten or more cases are retained, the list of classes is reduced to a set of twenty-two, which accommodate 77 per cent of the seals. For this discussion, those twenty-two classes will be termed the 'standard' classes (see table 1.2).

When the seals in all seven temporal groups are considered together, it is clear that some motifs predominate. The 'text' class, which holds motifs where the key or principal element is one or more letters, contains 16.56 per cent of the total number of seals (see figure 1.19 and table 1.3). The portion of cases in the 'shield' class, motifs that consist of a shield or shield-like surface upon which is depicted a coat of arms (which may or may not conform precisely to heraldic conventions), is similar at 15.3 per cent (see figure 1.14 and table 1.3). The radial motifs, which are decorative designs symmetrical along a number of axes, with arms or radii extending from a central point, are 13.88 per cent of the total (see figure 1.13 and table 1.3). Together, the 'text', 'shield'

Table 1.2: Distribution of motifs by class, 1175 to 1524

Percentage	Class
23.42	unclassified (miscellaneous)
16.56	text
15.3	shield
13.88	radial
6.81	stylised lily
4.95	bird
2.22	bust
1.97	woman holding child
1.72	lion
1.62	armoured man on horseback
1.41	squirrel
1.26	merchant mark
1.36	pelican in piety
1.36	lamb and staff
1.06	lion sleeping
0.91	stag head
0.91	two heads
0.81	crossed hands
0.76	stag
0.61	hawk hunting
0.61	Christogram
0.5	hare on hound

Source: *SiMeW* dataset

and 'radial' classes have 45.74 per cent of the cases, which is significantly higher than the 30.82 per cent of the total shared by the eighteen other classes. (A further class consists of 'unclassified' or miscellaneous motifs, which make up the remaining 23.42 per cent.) The most important of those classes is the 'stylised lily' (see figure 1.18 and table 1.3). This is a decorative motif in the form of a stylised iris or lily, which is commonly called the 'fleur-de-lys', usually with three curled petals, but occasionally with five, one of which forms the central axis to the symmetrical design. Seals in this class form 6.81 per cent of the total, while the remaining classes all have less than 5 per cent. The 'bird' class has 4.95 per cent; the 'bust', 2.22 per cent (see figures 1.2, 1.3 and table 1.3). Eight other classes hold between 1 per cent to 2 per cent of the total and another seven less than 1 per cent. Thus, almost half the motifs are 'shield', 'radial' or 'text', a third fall into the eighteen other 'standard' classes, and the remaining quarter are miscellaneous. With this broad distribution of seal motifs across the entirety of the period *c.*1175–*c.*1524 established, we can now consider shifts in the relative popularity of motifs over shorter periods of time (see table 1.4). However, to understand the changes to be revealed, we need first to consider shifts in the functions of seals.

The first temporal group are the seals from 1175 to 1224. In the *SiMeW* dataset there are only a handful of examples of seals used by people who were not kings, earls or great men prior to this period. A man simply called Marescot who made a gift to a church in Shropshire, perhaps in the third quarter of the twelfth century, had a seal displaying a lion.[20] Roger Parvus, who in the period 1148–55, gave the monks of St Peter's Gloucester eight acres of land and used a seal displaying a lion with its tail curled between its legs.[21] However, the data become considerable richer in the final quarter of the twelfth century, and even more so in the early thirteenth. Thus an analysis of the motifs that people favoured must begin with those from the period 1175–1224. To explain why it is from this period that substantial numbers of seals associated with people outside the very top ranks of society survive, it is important to consider both the function of seals and their social significance.

In England, in the 1160s, Richard de Lucy, an English royal justice, while considering a dispute involving Battle Abbey and Gilbert de Bailleul, was inspired to consider the social significance of seal ownership. He observed that 'it was not the custom in the past … for every petty knight to have a seal, which is appropriate only to kings and great men'.[22] Despite the reservations of men such as Richard de Lucy, the social significance of seal ownership was shifting in the mid-twelfth century, because people in an expanding range of social categories were using them. Those people who were not 'kings and great men' who acquired seals in the second half of the twelfth century may have been partly motivated by social pretension, but changes in how the judicial system operated were also important. Richard de Lucy was inspired to reflect on the history of seals when Gilbert de Bailleul objected to documents that the Abbey's representatives presented to support their claims, on the grounds 'that he did not see the evidence of their seals appended to them'. James Holt has argued that records the monks presented as evidence of their claims were manufactured at the time of the dispute, as Gilbert may well have recognised.[23] By pointing out that the documents lacked seals, Gilbert perhaps hoped that the court would reject the documents. The presentation of written records of property exchanges in courts, and the acceptance of seals as a method of authenticating records, created the conditions that encouraged the parties to these agreements to use seals, regardless of their social standing. Gilbert de Bailleul and Battle Abbey were involved in a dispute over property, which suggests that property owners were among the earliest group to use seals, but formal records were also prepared in other circumstances, such as to record debts.[24] A late twelfth century treatise advises justices adjudicating debt cases on what to do when a litigant denied 'that the charter was made by, or with the consent of, himself or his ancestors' but still acknowledged the legitimacy of the seal, or when the litigant denied the validity of both the charter and the seal.[25] Thus, another group who might need seals in this period were those who borrowed money. In England, over the course of the twelfth century, seal ownership ceased to be associated with 'kings and great men' and instead became generally available to those participating in the production of formal documents. By the beginning of the thirteenth century, as Harvey and McGuinness have observed, the seal-using segment of society in England 'comprised everyone who had free land or property to convey or other business to be agreed in formal writing.'[26]

Nonetheless, those people who were not 'king and great men' but who did use seals to authenticate records in the late twelfth and early thirteenth centuries outside of the English counties may have been exceptional. McGuinness has suggested, based on evidence from England, that in this period 'it was probably the case that anyone who held land that could be freely sold also owned a seal'.[27] In reality, this is more difficult to determine for Wales than it is for medieval England. Those people who did adopt seals in this period could be encouraged to do so by religious institutions, which particularly appreciated the power of sealed documents. Margam Abbey's records offer good evidence for the process whereby the people of one particular area gradually became accustomed to using seals. The abbey was founded and endowed with land in Glamorgan by Richard, Earl of Gloucester, shortly before his death in 1147; subsequently other benefactors gave it additional gifts, and the monks also made purchases. The monks ensured that these exchanges were recorded in writing. The deeds were often prepared in advance of the ceremony of conveyance, and Robert Patterson has argued that the scribes were often connected with the abbey, so it was preparing the documents that recorded transactions of which it was the beneficiary.[28] To avoid accusations of forgery, the monks of Margam ensured deeds were authenticated or validated. The monks wanted records for large and significant exchanges as well as those involving just a few acres of land. In the period 1186–91, for example, Margam acquired one acre from Hugh, son of Robert de Lantcarvan,[29] and two acres from Milisant daughter of William Mitdehorguill,[30] and in both cases the monks ensured that the exchanges were recorded in a charter sealed by the grantor. The monks' desire for sealed records thus affected members of all social categories that owned land, rather than only those of exceptional social standing. Nonetheless, in the early years, when the monks of Margam asked donors to authenticate the deeds with their seals, the monks could encounter a problem. Property owners in Glamorgan were not accustomed to recording property conveyances in writing, and thus many people did not have their own seals. In July 1188, for example, William the Clerk granted land to Margam, but as he did not have a seal, one of the witnesses, Hugh of Hereford, lent William his ring to use as a seal.[31] A more common expedient was for the grantor to have the deed validated by a man of authority. Circa 1170, a group of men quitclaimed their rights in a parcel of land to Margam. They made the declaration before the Bishop of Llandaff, and then he sealed the deed that recorded this event.[32] In 1172 x 79, Roger Sturmi and his wife made a grant to the monastery. While he had a seal that he could use to validate a deed, his wife did not, so her deed was validated by officials of Llandaff Cathedral.[33] However, by the end of the twelfth century, people in social categories that had previously not had seals, such as women, were now appearing at exchanges equipped with them.[34] Thanks in part to the efforts of institutions such as Margam Abbey that promoted the use of written records, by the end of the twelfth century, the segment of society in Glamorgan using seals encompassed those who owned property. However, those property owners who owned a seal in the late twelfth century and early thirteenth century in Wales may have been exceptional.

By c.1200, in England, and to a lesser extent in Wales, there were particular places where many people had adopted seals, but there were also areas where seals were just gaining acceptance. In 1191, Gwenwynwyn son of Owain, prince of southern Powys, gave land to the monastery of Strata Marchella, and the charter prepared as a record of this event explains its purpose: 'as nothing is more effective than writing against oblivion and challenge, and nothing should hinder the intention of holy work, he [Gwenwynwyn] has ordered the terms of his gift and alms to be written down to perpetuate the memory of them'.[35] The document concludes with the injunction that 'lest any claim should arise in the future on this his gift and alms, it is sealed and subscribed by witnesses'. In 1197–1202, when he made another grant to the monastery, the deed concludes with the statement: 'so that this gift might be held firm and ratified, he has strengthened and confirmed it by the attestation of good men and with the impression of his seal'.[36] Gwenwynwyn son of Owain was a member of a ruling dynasty, but his views on the significance and utility of seals were probably in keeping with the opinions of many of his contemporaries in Wales, even if only a fraction of them probably had their own seals at this time. By the beginning of the thirteenth century, certainly in the English counties bordering Wales, and to a lesser extent in Wales itself, people were becoming familiar with the practice of using seals and some examples survive, so this is where a survey of the history of the motifs can begin.

In Wales, religious institutions helped establish among people outside the nobility the practice of recording property conveyances in writing. In England, members of the ecclesiastical leadership were precocious in adopting seals of office, and religious houses also used corporate seals from an early date.[37] However, the Church did more than set a pattern that the rest of society could follow, for some of the earliest surviving deeds were written by scribes connected to religious houses, and leading ecclesiastical officials validated documents for people who did not have their own seals. Why the Church was a proponent of the sealed deed is not difficult to explain, for written records offered the Church an opportunity to reinforce its claims to land. Ecclesiastical leadership, therefore, was crucial in establishing the practice of recording property conveyances in documents authenticated by seals. Whether the Church also influenced the motifs people selected for their seals is more difficult to determine.

Most of the seals from the period *c*.1200 (1174–1224) have standard motifs (see figure 1.22 and table 1.4). Seals with the 'stylised lily' are an important group, constituting 17 per cent of the total, which is much higher than the 6.81 per cent they represent for the full period of this study. The percentage of seals with 'radial' motifs is even higher, at around 20 per cent. The portion of 'stylised lily' and 'radial' seals is so large that it calls for explanation. Harvey has suggested that in the period before seal ownership was common, landowners who wanted their tenants to seal a document might supply them with seals.[38] If this were the case, then the 'stylised lily' and 'radial' motifs may initially have proliferated because landowners regarded these designs as appropriate for people of humble standing and thus encouraged their tenants to use them, and perhaps even distributed them to their tenants. Regardless of the precise mechanism whereby the 'stylised lily' and the 'radial' motif came to be established as favoured motifs, by the turn of the thirteenth century, when most people possessed their own seals and other seal motifs were in circulation, these motifs remained the most popular choices. Although some of the early thirteenth century examples were crudely executed and were perhaps intended to be used only once, others were engraved with considerable care and used repeatedly by their owners over many years. These latter examples suggest that their owners selected their seals, and their 'stylised lily' or 'radial' motifs, themselves, over and against alternatives.

For those people who wanted a seal with a standard motif, but one more distinctive than the 'stylised lily' or the 'radial', the alternatives included motifs that appear to have carried strong connotations of elevated social status or aspirations and those that do not. Almost 17 per cent of the seals in the *c*.1200 temporal group display an 'armoured man on horseback' (see figure 1.1 and table 1.3). Since these were the seals frequently used by members of the male aristocracy, this motif was attractive to men with social aspirations.[39] Another small group of seals, 2 per cent of the total, display a 'bust' (see figure 1.3 and table 1.3). Some impressions of these seals show signs that they were made using a seal matrix that incorporated an antique gem.[40] These were costly objects, so this motif too may have been favoured by those with social aspirations. The portion of seals with a 'bird' motif is slightly higher, at 5 per cent,

SEALS AND SOCIETY

Figure 1.22: Motifs by period

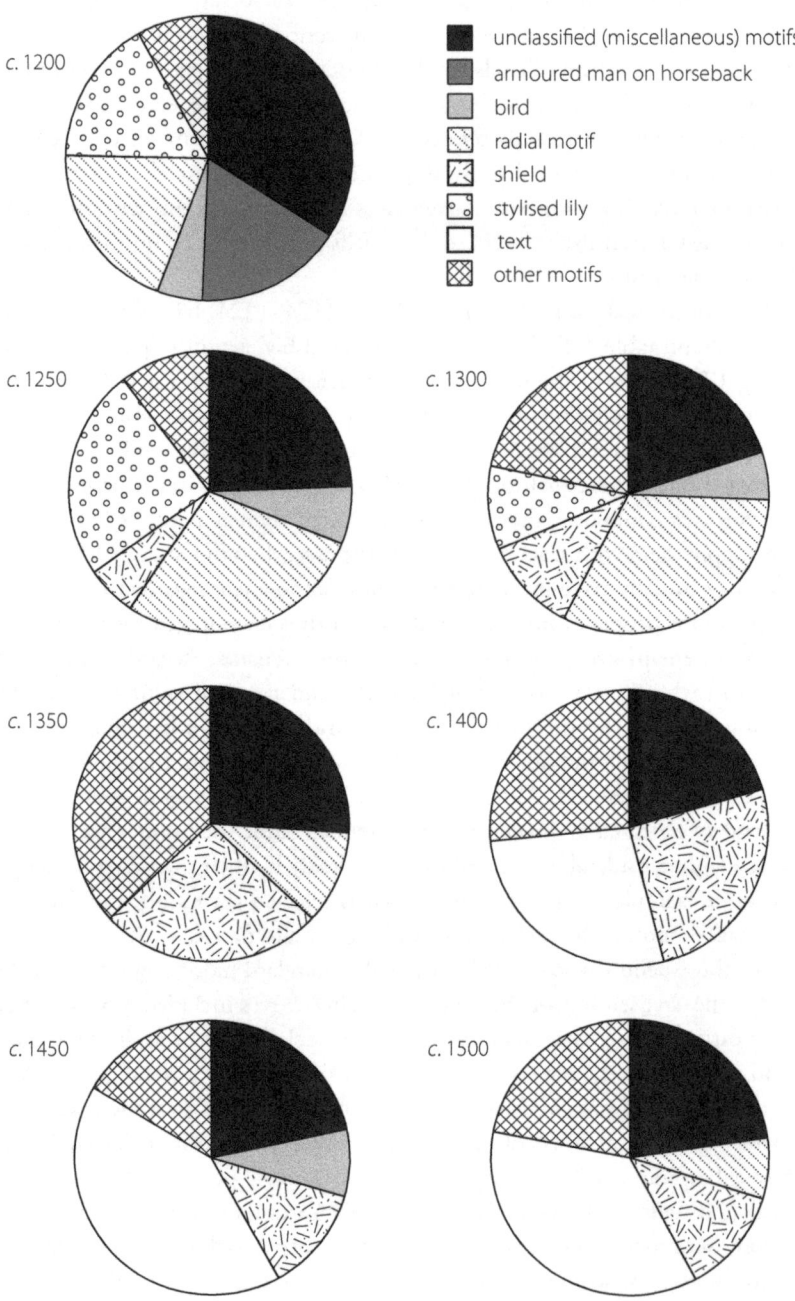

followed closely by those with a 'lion' motif at 4 per cent (see figures 1.2, 1.9 and table 1.3). These two motifs were the most important alternatives to the 'stylised lily' and 'radial' motifs for people who do not appear to have intended to communicate social aspirations through their seals. However, although most people were using seals with these six standard motifs, 34 per cent of the seals in use fall outside these categories. The number of exceptional cases is remarkably high by comparison with later periods. As in later periods, people commonly used seals with decorative motifs or depictions of objects, animals and human figures, but the particular subjects they selected could be distinctive. For instance, Hugh de Hereford's seal depicts a sword pointed down, a motif that does not appear elsewhere amongst the seals in the *SiMeW* sample.[41] Some of the human figures, too, are peculiar. Gilbert Burdini's seal presents a full-length bearded man, emerging from the left into the image field and wearing a short tunic, while holding by its base a short staff with an emblem at its top in his raised left hand, pinched between his thumb and forefinger.[42] Although such unusual motifs appear among the seals of all periods, they form a particularly high proportion of those c.1200. Their preponderance suggests that the burgeoning use of seals in this period brought with it innovation and experimentation in the motifs adopted for seals. But there is also evidence that many people were not looking to innovate.

In the mid-thirteenth century, the portion of seals without a standard motif remains significant but declines from 34 per cent to 28 per cent. At the same time, the popularity of both the 'stylised lily' and the 'radial' motifs appears to have increased. Together, these motifs account for more than half of the entire group, with 'stylised lily' seals climbing to 24 per cent and 'radial' seals to 29 per cent. Their combined growth from 37 per cent to 53 per cent of the total shows, on the one hand, that the mid-thirteenth century was a period in which many people selected motifs that conformed to the established patterns, but it may also reflect a change in the social composition of the group of people whose seals survive. The 242 seals from c.1250 are almost double the number available from c.1200, and this increase probably reflects a greater rate of survival among the seals of people of relatively humble standing. The decline in the portion of seals with an 'armoured man on horseback', from 17 per cent to 3 per cent of the total, might be thought to provide further evidence of a dramatic shift in the social origins of surviving seals. As this motif was associated with men with social aspirations, the decline implies that the seals of members of this group formed a much smaller portion of the total. However, this period also sees the rise of the 'shield' motif, which could likewise be used to assert social standing. At 6 per cent of the total, the growth in popularity of this motif compensated to an extent for the decline of the 'armoured man on horseback' and suggests that men with social aspirations may have adopted the 'shield' in place of the 'armoured man on horseback' as that earlier motif's use became restricted. By contrast, people of lesser standing appear to have been largely content with the existing motifs. The portion of seals with 'bird' motifs rises slightly to 7 per cent, while the 'lion' declines to 2 per cent. In the mid-thirteenth century, it was the leading members of society who introduced the most important new motif.

By contrast, it was people outside the nobility whose preferences had the strongest impact on the fashions of the period c.1300. It has been suggested that in this period both the range of subjects and language that ordinary people could use on seals expanded, such that, in contrast to earlier periods, seals offered them 'a serious possibility for the expression of status, piety, taste and even humour'.[43] Certainly the range of types of textual statements on seals expands. In the twelfth and thirteenth centuries, people routinely used seal matrices inscribed with their names.[44] In the c.1200 temporal group 98 per cent include a name and 96 per cent c.1250. However, in c.1300 it slips to 82 per cent. One alternative to a legend with a name was to use a seal with no legend but only a motif, and 3 per cent of seals have this form in the c.1300 group. The remainder of the seals have a legend with a so-called 'anonymous' legend.[46] These texts can take a variety of forms, ranging from hunting cries to religious invocations.[47] The rise of the 'anonymous' legends and the gradual decline in seals with a name is significant because it reveals a change in the function of seals.

In thirteenth-century England, people considered it possible to seal a document with a borrowed seal. Indeed, the mid-thirteenth century justice Henry of Bracton argued that the act of sealing was more important than who owned the seal itself: 'it is not of great importance whether it [the document] is sealed with his own seal or another's'.[48] Nonetheless, the borrowing of seals was discouraged, for when parties authenticated documents with seals other than their own, this could make authenticating the document more difficult in the event of a dispute.[49] For example, a set of procedures governing the lending of money by Jews to Christians details how the Christians were to use their seals to record agreements. The loan was to be recorded in a bipartite chirograph, and the Christian borrowing the money had to seal one part with a seal inscribed with his 'proper name'.[50] In the fourteenth century, because of the limitations of seals as tools of authentication, people adopted some new methods of securing information that often complemented the sealed record. Places to enrol loan agreements, for instance, were established in urban centres, such as London, so that an incontestable record of the agreement would be available in the event of a dispute.[51] Perhaps as a consequence of such changes, people gradually become more comfortable using seals that did not identify them. Harvey has observed that in the fourteenth century 'many lesser people would sign with a seal that the clerk, or perhaps a friend, supplied'.[52] Indeed, such cases are also common in this period in the *SiMeW* dataset. From c.1300 onwards, the portion of people using borrowed seals increased, as did the portion of people using seals with an 'anonymous' legend or no legend at all. Consequently, as McGuinness has commented, in this period 'seals were, on the whole, less personal'.[53] In the fourteenth century those people who did use a seal that genuinely identified them probably did so as a matter choice, rather than of necessity.

The change in the content of the legends is associated with a change in the motifs displayed on the seals. People continued to use most of the motifs popular from the period *c.*1250, although their fortunes varied. The portion of seals with 'radial' motifs continues to climb, reaching 32 per cent of the total, but the 'stylised lily' drops sharply from 24 per cent to 10 per cent and is surpassed by the 'shield' motif, which at 11 per cent of the total nearly doubles in popularity. The portion of seals with 'bird' or 'lion' motifs remains relatively stable, at 6 per cent and 4 per cent of the total respectively; the 'armoured man on horseback' motif all but disappears. However, a host of new motifs now appear in significant numbers. The 'sleeping lion' features on 3 per cent of the surviving seals (see figure 1.10 and table 1.3), while the 'hare riding a hound' appears on 2 per cent (see figure 1.6 and table 1.3). While the origins of many of these motifs – including the 'Christogram', the 'hawk hunting', the 'pelican in piety', the 'squirrel', the 'stag', and the 'woman holding child' – can be traced to *c.*1250, examples of these motifs only become numerous in *c.*1300 (see figures 1.4, 1.7, 1.12, 1.15, 1.16, 1.21 and table 1.3).[54] Many of these motifs were strongly associated with the use of an anonymous legend. These legends can comment on the motifs. For example, seals with the 'pelican in piety' motif can have a legend that reads 'SVM PELICANUS DEI'.[55] Some motifs, which were perhaps intended to be humorous, often have a legend in the vernacular. The seals with a 'squirrel' motif often have a legend that reads 'I CRAKE NOTIS'.[56] Those with the 'lion sleeping' motif, the legend 'WAKE ME NO MAN'. Such seals are revealing of popular humour and piety and they show that seals could be used to address topics that had hitherto not been usual subjects of seals. However, it would be wrong to presume that the advent of 'anonymous' seals precipitated an explosion of creativity. People in this period used all of the twenty-two standard motifs (see table 1.2 and table 1.3).[57] Although people were using a greater number of standard motifs, the motifs on seals were not necessarily more diverse. Indeed, it could be argued that they are less diverse than in previous periods, since standard motifs form a greater portion of the total. As the portion of seals with a standard motif increased, those with a non-standard motif decline from 34 per cent in *c.*1200, to 24 per cent in *c.*1250, to 20 per cent in *c.*1300. The desire of people outside the aristocracy for 'anonymous' seals allowed for the expansion in the number of 'standard' motifs, and this was accompanied by a change in the types of messages that seals conveyed, but most people remained content to use 'standard' motifs.

In the mid-fourteenth century, those people who wanted a seal that would unequivocally identify them shifted to favouring the 'shield' motif. The portion of seals with legends that include a name continues to decline from 81 per cent to 50 per cent. In this period, the 'anonymous' legends reach the apex of their popularity, rising to 38 per cent of the cases, with the remaining cases possessing no legends, but only a motif. The 'radial' and the 'stylised lily' motifs, which were normally used with name legends in the preceding periods, lost much of their previous popularity. In *c.*1350, the portion of seals with the 'radial' motif contracts from 32 per cent to 11 per cent, and the 'stylised lily' from 9.7 per cent to 1.8 per cent. Much of the growth was well distributed across the other classes. Nineteen classes are represented among the motifs with less than 5 per cent of the total. The most important of these are 'squirrel', at 4 per cent. The motifs with less than 5 per cent of the total now collectively represent 37 per cent of the cases. This figure is similar to the portion of seals with an 'anonymous' legend, which is perhaps not surprising since many of the motifs in this group, such as 'squirrel', 'sleeping lion' and 'pelican in piety', were associated with the use of anonymous legends c.1300 and this remains true in c.1350. The number of 'unclassified' or exceptional cases rebounds somewhat to 26 per cent. However, there was a large increase in seals with the 'shield' motif, which more than doubles from 11 per cent to 26 per cent to become the single most widespread motif in this period. If the use of the 'shield' motif were restricted to the portion of society with elevated social standing, then this increase could be taken to indicate a fundamental change in seal ownership or survival. However, this increase coincides with the rise of heraldry, which became more pervasive in this period and led both people with an elevated place in society and those with only moderate social aspirations to adopt coats of arms.[58] People could use heraldry to claim social standing but also potentially to locate themselves in a particular family. Thus, the surge in seals with the 'shield' motif, together with the decline of the 'radial' and the 'stylised lily', suggests a reaction to the increasing anonymisation of seals in this period. A 'shield' motif could identify a person with a particular family through a visual symbol, but seals with heraldic motifs were also routinely reinforced with a name legend to clarify and underline the particular person that the seal represented. Indeed, while 50 per cent of seals from the c.1350 period have a legend that includes a name, among those with a 'shield' class motif the portion is much higher, at 92 per cent.[59] In the thirteenth century, people encountering any seal could assume that it identified its owner, but in the fourteenth century it was seals with the 'shield' motif that most commonly made an explicit reference, both through their texts and images, to their owners.

In the period c.1400, seals with humorous or, in some instances but not all, pious images with 'anonymous' legends began to pass out of fashion. The portion of seals with the 'shield' motif remains steady at 25 per cent, but there is a strong surge in demand for the 'text' motif, which rises to 27 per cent of the total. Many examples of the 'text' motif are strikingly simple designs engraved into relatively small matrices that have no legend but feature a single letter or a monogram as their main visual element (see figure 1.19 and table 1.3).[60] In c.1400, the seals with the 'shield' and 'text' motif form an exceptionally large share of the seals in circulation. In the first three periods surveyed, there were always at least two exceptionally popular motifs, which each reached 16 per cent to 30 per cent of the total, and one to three with 5 per cent to 10 per cent. In c.1350, there was a contraction to a single exceptionally popular motif (26 per cent), and a second at 11 per cent. In c.1400 the 'shield' and 'text' shared the leading role, but the rise of the 'text' motif in *c*.1400 was at the expense of other motifs (with the exception of 'shield'). The once-popular 'radial' motif is reduced to 3 per cent, while the 'stylised lily' falls to less than 1 per cent, along such motifs as the 'merchant mark', 'Christogram' and 'pelican in piety'. Indeed, people used a smaller portion of the standard motifs in *c*.1400 than in *c*.1350. However, in *c*.1400, aside from the dominant 'shield' and 'text' motifs, no other standard motif has more than 3.2 per cent of the total, and when added together, these motifs with only a small portion of the total had collectively fallen from 37 per cent to 27 per cent. In *c*.1400, although people continued to favour seals with the 'shield' motif, they were turning away from seals that made statements of piety, taste and humour, in preference for the 'text' motif, and thus the seals in circulation became more homogenous.

In the second half of the fifteenth century, the range of standard motifs in circulation further contracts. The most striking development *c*.1450 is the continuing rise in the portion of seals with a 'text' motif: from 27 per cent in *c*.1400 they climb to 42 per cent. Whereas in *c*.1400, the rise of the 'text' motif was at the expense of the motifs associated with 'anonymous' legends, in *c*.1450 it also affected the 'shield' motif. There is a nearly equivalent drop in the portion of seals with the 'shield' motif, which declines from 25 per cent to 12 per cent. At the other end of the scale, those motifs with less than 5 per cent of the total collectively decline from 25 per cent to 17 per cent of the total. However, the renewed popularity of the 'bird' motif is partly responsible for the decrease, for it climbs to 8 per cent, and thus is no longer included in this sub-category. When the standard motifs with less than 5 per cent of the total are examined closely, it is clear that once again the number in use has diminished. 'Radial', 'merchant mark', 'pelican in piety' and 'bust' all hold between 2 per cent to 3 per cent of the total, and eight other motifs have lesser portions. In *c*.1350 there were nineteen motifs represented with less than 5 per cent of the total, and in *c*.1450 there are seventeen. This process of retrenchment and declining diversity continues into the final period, *c*.1500. The portion of seals with the 'shield' motif remains constant at 12 per cent and the portion of seals with a 'text' motif declines from 41 per cent to 36 per cent. Nonetheless, in broad terms the pattern of distribution among the motifs in circulation is similar. There is renewed enthusiasm for the 'radial' motif, which captures 7 per cent of the total, while 'bird' slips to 4.5 per cent. The number of motifs represented among the seals in the less than 5 per cent category continues to constrict, falling to thirteen, and they hold a smaller portion of the cases, falling slightly from 25 per cent to 22 per cent of the total. The strong continuity across the period *c*.1450–*c*.1500 demonstrates that there had been a further decline in the diversity of the motifs.

The story of the development of the motifs presented on the seals of people active in medieval Wales and its neighbouring counties can be traced from the late twelfth century. From the earliest years, it is clear than most people wanted seals with standard and familiar motifs. By surveying the seals it is possible to discern what motifs people used and to chart shifts in their preferences. In the late twelfth and early thirteenth centuries, it was probably those with the greatest social aspirations who set the fashions, perhaps by supplying seals to their tenants, as Paul Harvey has suggested.[61] By *c.*1300, the population in general, which had until that period been largely content to use either the 'stylised lily' or 'radial', adopted a number of new motifs that could be used to make statements about an expanded range of topics, including taste, piety or humour. In the fifteenth century, many of the motifs favoured in the fourteenth century fell out of fashion, as people turned to seals with a 'text' motif. Throughout this period, the people of the region covered by this study did commission artisans to fabricate seals with unusual and distinctive images and legends. Nonetheless, people favoured a small set of motifs, even in the late twelfth century, when they were first becoming accustomed to using seals. The relative popularity of these motifs was always changing, and so the key question is what factors impelled change.

Judicial factors directed the development of seals in the broadest sense, for in the earliest years people were encouraged to acquire seals to authenticate documents for use in courts. Seals soon became established as a customary tool for authenticating important documents, and since this continued in subsequent centuries, people continued to need seals. However, there is little evidence that judicial requirements dictated what people depicted on their seals. The favoured motifs changed over time, and a motif could rise and fall in popularity within a few generations. This rate of change points to the importance of fashion, and helps to explain why motifs, such as the armoured man on horseback, could rapidly decline, while the popularity of others, such as the hare riding the hound, could be brief. Although individual motifs did rise and fall in popularity, there were three distinct phases of development. Until the end of the thirteenth century, people normally used a seal with a legend that named them and a motif that in broad terms located them in society. In the fourteenth century, the conventions shifted. People now had more freedom to choose whether they wanted a seal with their name, or a seal with an 'anonymous' legend, and they had a large range of standard motif from which to choose. In the fifteenth century, it was the seals that specifically identified their owners that were exceptional, as people increasingly used seals with no legends and 'text' motifs. Thus fashion probably did contribute to the rise and fall of particular motifs, but so too did the changing role of seals in the expression of identity.

Table 1.3: Definition of motifs

Motif	Definition	Example
armoured man on horseback	Motif consisting of a riding full-length humanoid in armour	Figure 1.1: NLW PITORD/1248 (Seal 2055)
bird	Motif consisting of a bird (any member of the Aves class of vertebrates), but excluding 'pelican in piety' and 'hawk hunting'	Figure 1.2: SHA 972/1/1/428 (Seal 2436)
bust	Motif consisting of the head or head and shoulders of a humanoid	Figure 1.3: NLW PITORD/466 (Seal 1887)
Christogram	Motif consisting of an abbreviation of the name of Jesus	Figure 1.4: NLW PITORD/413, s.1 (Seal 1850)
crossed hands	Motif consisting of a pair of clasped hands	Figure 1.5: SHA 20/6/122 (Seal 2271)
hare on hound	Motif consisting of a hare (a rodent of the genus Lepus) astride a dog (a domesticated carnivorous mammal, Canis familiaris)	Figure 1.6: HAS F8/II/17 (Seal 706)
hawk hunting	Motif consisting of a bird of prey taking another animal	Figure 1.7: NLW PITORD/12 (Seal 1581)
lamb and staff	Motif consisting of a sheep (an animal of the genus Ovis) with a cross tipped staff bearing a pennon	Figure 1.8: BL Harl. Ch. 75 B 6, s.2 rev. (Seal 41)
lion	Motif consisting of a lion (a carnivorous quadrupedal animal of the genus Felis leo)	Figure 1.9: SHA 972/1/1/427 (Seal 2435)
lion sleeping	Motif consisting of a sleeping lion (a carnivorous quadrupedal animal of the genus Felis leo)	Figure 1.10: BUAS PENR/311, s.1 (Seal 242)
merchant mark	Motif consisting of a type of mark conventionally known as a 'merchant mark': see Edward Mars Elmhirst and Leslie Dow, *Merchants' Marks* (London, 1959)	Figure 1.11: NLW PENRICE/ 342, s.5 (Seal 1374)
pelican in piety	Motif consisting of a bird perched on a nest feeding its young with its own blood	Figure 1.12: BUAS PENR/220 (Seal 243)
radial device	Motif consisting of two or more intersecting branches, leaves or lobes	Figure 1.13: NLW PENRICE/ 2056, s.3 (Seal 1237)
shield	Motif consisting of a shield (an implement of defensive armour carried in the hand or attached by a strap to the arm) or a shield-like surface upon which a coat of arms is depicted	Figure 1.14: NLW PITORD/54 (Seal 1610)

(continued)

Table 1.3: Definition of motifs *(continued)*

Motif	Definition	Example
squirrel	Motif consisting of a squirrel (a rodent of the genus Sciurus), having a long bushy tail and furry coat	Figure 1.15: BUAS PENR/407, s.2 (Seal 294)
stag	Motif consisting of a male deer (member of the family Cervidæ)	Figure 1.16: NLW PENRICE/119 (Seal, 1201)
stag head	Motif consisting of the head of a male deer (member of the family Cervidæ)	Figure 1.17: NLW PITORD/1144 (Seal 1630)
stylised lily	Motif consisting of a decorative motif in the form of a stylised iris or lily, usually with three curled petals, but occasionally with five, one of which forms the central axis to the symmetrical design	Figure 1.18: HCA Deed122 (Seal 764)
text	Motif consisting of one or more letters (excluding Christogram)	Figure 1.19: NLW BRONWYDD/1031 (966)
two heads	Motif consisting of a pair of heads	Figure 1.20: HAS D52/B/1/2, s.7 (Seal 697)
woman and child	Motif consisting of a woman holding a child	Figure 1.21: BUAS MOST/1629/vii (Seal 144)

Table 1.4: Percentage of cases in each temporal group*

	c.1200	c.1250	c.1300	c.1350	c.1400	c.1450	c.1500
unclassified	34.06	24.38	20.06	26.02	20.45	21.64	22.7
armoured man on horseback	16.67	3.31		0.26			
bird	5.07	6.61	5.5	3.32	2.56	7.87	4.61
bust	2.17	0.41	2.91	2.3	3.19	2.3	1.77
Christogram		0.41	0.32	0.77	1.92		0.35
crossed hands				1.62	2.81		
hare on hound			2.27	0.26	0.32	0.33	
hawk hunting		0.41	0.32	1.53	0.96	0.33	
lamb and staff	0.72	0.83	0.65	3.06	2.56		0.71
lion	4.35	2.07	3.56	1.28	0.64	0.98	0.71
lion sleeping			3.24	2.04	0.96		
merchant mark			0.32	1.02	1.28	2.62	2.84
pelican in piety		0.41	0.32	1.53	1.6	2.95	1.77
radial device	19.57	28.51	32.04	10.97	3.19	2.3	7.09

Table 1.4: Percentage of cases in each temporal group* *(continued)*

	c.1200	c.1250	c.1300	c.1350	c.1400	c.1450	c.1500
shield		5.79	11	26.02	25.56	12.46	12.41
squirrel		0.41	1.94	4.08	1.28		0.35
stag		0.41	0.65	0.77	1.28	0.66	1.06
stag head			1.29	2.04	0.64	0.66	0.71
stylised lily	16.67	24.38	9.71	1.79	0.64	1.31	3.55
text	0.72	0.41	0.32	2.81	27.48	41.64	35.82
two heads			1.29	2.04	0.64	0.66	0.71
woman and child		1.24	0.65	3.32	2.88	1.31	2.84

See table 1.1 for total number by temporal group.

Notes

1. A. J. Taylor, 'Count Amadeus of Savoy's visit to England in 1292', *Archaeologia*, 106 (1979), 125–6.
2. J. A. McEwan, 'Making a mark in medieval London: the social and economic standing of seal-makers', in P. R. Schofield (ed.), *Seals and their Context in the Middle Ages* (Oxford, 2015), pp. 77–88.
3. P. D. A. Harvey, 'Personal seals in thirteenth-century England', in G. A. Loud and I. N. Wood (eds), *Church and Chronicle in the Middle Ages: Essays Presented to John Taylor* (London, 1991), p. 117.
4. On the term 'identity', see D. Postles, 'Identity and identification: some recent research into the English medieval "forename" ', in D. Postles and J. T. Rosenthal (eds), *Studies on the Personal Name in Later Medieval England and Wales* (Kalamazoo, MI, 2006), pp. 29–31.
5. R. H. Ellis, *Catalogue of Seals in the Public Record Office: Personal Seals*, vol. 1 (London, 1978), p. 1.
6. TNA DL27/270.
7. T. A. Heslop, 'Peasant seals', in E. King (ed.), *Medieval England, 1066–1485* (Oxford, 1988), p. 214.
8. Heslop, 'Peasant seals', pp. 214–15.
9. A. F. McGuinness, 'Non-armigerous seals and seal-usage in thirteenth-century England', in P. R. Coss and S. D. Lloyd (eds), *Thirteenth Century England*, vol. 5 (Woodbridge, 1995), p. 167; for a notable exception, see Harvey, 'Personal seals', p. 120.
10. P. D. A. Harvey, 'Computer catalogue of seals in the Public Record Office, London', *Janus*, part 2 (1996), 29; idem, 'Seals and the dating of documents', in M. Gervers (ed.), *Dating Undated Medieval Charters* (Woodbridge, 2000), p. 207. It has been recently suggested that this estimate may be conservative: E. A. New, 'Text and image: the language of seals in medieval England and Wales', in M. Carruthers (ed.), *Multilingual Networks in Medieval Britain*, Harlaxton Medieval Studies, XXV. (Donnington, 2015), p. 60.
11. See also chapters on administration (chapter 2), lordship (chapter 5) and religion (chapter 4).
12. P. Chaplais, *English Royal Documents: King John–Henry VI 1199–1461* (Oxford, 1971), p. 2.
13. M. T. Clanchy, *From Memory to Written Record, England 1066–1307*, 2nd edn (Oxford, 1993), p. 50.

14 McGuinness, 'Non-armigerous seals', pp. 167–8; Harvey, 'Personal seals', p. 119; C. H. Jenkinson, *A Guide to Seals in the Public Record Office* (London, 1968), p. 6.
15 The International Council on Archives's sigillographic committee made considerable progress towards establishing a controlled vocabulary for sigillography in the late twentieth century. As part of this project, it set out a typology with twenty-six types: R. H. (ed.) Bautier, *Vocabulaire international de la sigillographie* (Rome, 1990), pp. 151–63; M. Fabre, *Sceau medieval: analyse d'une pratique culturelle* (Paris, 2001), pp. 134–54. See also T. Diederich, 'Reflexions sur la typologie des sceaux', *Janus: revue archivistique*, 1 (1993), 48–68.
16 For a description of the system and how it was created by the project team, see J. A. McEwan, 'The challenge of the visual: making medieval seals accessible in the digital age', *Journal of Documentation*, 71 (2015), 999–1028.
17 E. Panofsky, *Studies in Iconology: Humanistic Themes in the Art of the Renaissance* (New York, 1939), pp. 5–6.
18 The classes in the *SiMeW* system are based on the manner of describing sigillographic images established by Elizabeth New for *SiMeW*, which in turn is founded on the method developed by Paul Harvey for the National Archives's Duchy of Lancaster seal catalogue. Thus the most distinctive aspect of the *SiMeW* classification system is not the classes it contains, but rather their hierarchical arrangement and their mutual exclusivity: McEwan, 'The challenge of the visual', 1008. In the *SiMeW* system, each motif can only be assigned to one branch of the tree and fall into one class at each level. For the purposes of this analysis, the upper level 'parent' classes, such as 'animal', have been set aside leaving only the bottom level 'child' categories, such as 'hare on hound'. In the *SiMeW* classification system, the 'lion', 'bird' and 'text' classes have 'child' classes, such as 'Christogram', 'lion sleeping' and 'pelican in piety'. Rather than discard 'text', 'lion' and 'bird' they have been retained for cases that are not otherwise accommodated in their child categories, such as the various heraldic and pseudo-heraldic lions. Representations of people are divided into different classes based on their poses, so 'seated woman holding child', 'standing woman holding child' and 'half-length woman holding child' are distinguished, despite their similar general meaning. These three classes have been replaced with a single 'woman holding child' category.
19 McGuinness, 'Non-armigerous seals', p. 170.
20 Seal 2051.
21 Seal 868.
22 E. Searle (ed.), *The Chronicle of Battle Abbey* (Oxford, 1980), p. 215.
23 Forgery was a problem in this period. For the Battle Abbey case, see *The Chronicle of Battle Abbey*, p. 2; N. Vincent, 'King Henry II and the monks of Battle: the Battle Chronicle unmasked', in R. Gameson and H. Leyser (eds), *Belief and Culture in the Middle Ages: Studies Presented to Henry Mayr-Harting* (Oxford, 2001), p. 285; J. C. Holt, 'More Battle forgeries', *Reading Medieval Studies*, 11 (1985), 76–9. For forgery in the thirteenth century, see P. Brand, 'Seals and the law in thirteenth century England', in P. Schofield (ed.), *Seals and their Context in the Middle Ages* (Oxford, 2015), pp. 117–18.
24 H. Jenkinson, 'A money-lender's bonds of the twelfth century', in H. W. C. Davis (ed.), *Essays in History Presented to Reginald Lane Poole* (Oxford, 1927), pp. 193–94.
25 G. D. G. Hall (ed. and trans.), *The Treatise on the Laws and Customs of England Commonly Called Glanville* (Oxford, 1993), p. 127.
26 *Guide*, p. 77.
27 McGuinness, 'Non-armigerous seals', p. 167.
28 *Scriptorium*, p. 44.
29 NLW PENRICE: GLAM/38.

30 NLW PENRICE: GLAM/39; NLW PENRICE: GLAM/40.
31 NLW PENRICE: GLAM/36.
32 NLW PENRICE: GLAM/9.
33 NLW PENRICE: GLAM/11.
34 NLW PENRICE: GLAM /2061.
35 G. C. G. Thomas (ed.), *The Charters of the Abbey of Ystrad Marchell* (Aberystwyth, 1997), no. 14.
36 Thomas (ed.), *The Charters of the Abbey of Ystrad Marchell*, no. 51. See also B. M. Bedos-Rezak, 'In search of a semiotic paradigm: the matter of sealing in medieval thought and praxis (1050–1400)', in *Good Impressions*, p. 1.
37 For some examples of seals from the twelfth century, see T. A. Heslop, 'Seals', in G. Zarnecki, J. Allen and T. Holland (eds), *English Romanesque Art 1066–1200* (London, 1984), pp. 298–319.
38 Harvey, 'Personal seals', p. 127.
39 David Crouch, *The Image of Aristocracy in Britain, 1000–1300* (London, 1992), pp. 242–6.
40 M. Henig, 'The re-use and copying of ancient intaglios set in medieval personal seals, mainly found in England: an aspect of the Renaissance of the twelfth century', in *Good Impressions*, pp. 25–34.
41 Seal 1148
42 Seal 53. E. A. New, 'Lleision ap Morgan makes an impression: seals and the study of medieval Wales', *Welsh History Review*, 27:1 (2013), 327–50, pp. 340–1.
43 Heslop, 'Peasant seals', p. 215.
44 McGuinness, 'Non-armigerous seals', p. 168.
45 The content of the legends of some seals are difficult to determine because the surviving seal impressions are broken or otherwise illegible. For the purposes of this discussion, it is assumed that seals with 'name' and 'anonymous' legends are equally likely to become illegible and thus that the portions of seals in the legible categories is indicative of the overall distribution.
46 McGuinness, 'Non-armigerous seals', p. 174.
47 Harvey, 'Personal seals', p. 122.
48 Henry de Bracton, *On the Laws and Customs of England*, ed. G. E. Woodbine and S. E. Thorne, vol. 2 (Cambridge, 1968), p. 120. See also Bedos-Rezak, 'In search of a semiotic paradigm', p. 2.
49 J. M. Kaye, *Medieval English Conveyances* (Cambridge, 2009), p. 16.
50 Henry Thomas Riley (ed.), *Chronicles of the Mayors and Sheriffs of London*, (London, 1863), p. 200.
51 M. M. Postan, 'Private financial instruments in medieval England', *Vierteljahrschrift für Sozial und Wirtschaftsgeschichte*, 22 (1930), reprinted in M. M. Postan, *Medieval Trade and Finance* (Cambridge, 1973), pp. 28–64, at p. 35.
52 Harvey, 'Personal seals', p. 124.
53 McGuinness, 'Non-armigerous seals', p. 176.
54 For christograms, see New, 'Text and image', pp. 60–1.
55 Seal 1530.
56 Seal 2279.
57 Who made the seals is obscure, for the medieval artisans who made seals have been little studied: McEwan, 'Making a mark in medieval London', p. 84; H. S. Kingsford, 'Some medieval seal-engravers', *Archaeological Journal*, 97 (1940), 155–80; R. K. Lancaster, 'Artists, suppliers and clerks: the human factors in the art patronage of King Henry III', *Journal of the Warburg and Courtauld Institutes*, 35 (1972), 95.
58 Heslop, 'Peasant seals', p. 215.

59 In this period, artisans may have sometimes produced these types of seals as blanks, with empty shields and legends, and then engraved them on demand to suit the requirements of their clients: J. Cherry, 'Seal matrices', in P. Saunders and E. Saunders (eds), *Salisbury Museum Medieval Catalogue*, part 1 (Salisbury, 1991), p. 29.
60 Although these symbols are often very clearly engraved and the letters can correspond to the names of the parties using the seals, they often do not. Assuming that the letters did stand for names, then they are a deliberately ambiguous method of representing a name, which contrasts with the seals with name legends.
61 Harvey, 'Personal seals', p. 127.

SEALS: ADMINISTRATION AND LAW

Phillipp R. Schofield

THE IMPORTANCE OF SEALED instruments as foundations to interpersonal action, as evidence of things done, of past and future performance, is an established but evolving feature of the English medieval common law from the twelfth century. How far does that concept apply in medieval Wales and the March, and to what extent does it alter, in terms of social and political status, by region and over time (from the beginning of the thirteenth century to the middle years of the sixteenth century)? This chapter will discuss the legal significance of the seal, its adoption and use throughout medieval Welsh and Marcher society, as well as its importance within the administration of government, estates, towns and personal dealings. In a departure from the general discussion, the chapter will also include consideration of the alternatives to seal usage, the apparent resistance to the sealed instrument at all levels in the west of Wales, and the ways in which individuals might either choose not to employ seals or find themselves unable to use seals, issues also of relevance to such matters as identity and expression already discussed in this volume.

In many respects the defining features of seal usage in Wales and the Marches, in terms of administrative development, are broadly consistent with patterns exhibited in neighbouring medieval England; while some of the main developments, including the adoption of great seals by the nobility and a subsequent increase in the use of smaller ancillary seals, privy and secret seals, postdate similar changes in England, the general trends are the same, as is the adoption of seal usage by a wider population in the thirteenth century, including free tenants in the countryside as well as townspeople.[1] With this growth in seal usage came both the development of administrative process founded upon the use of seals and a growing reliance upon them as primary devices of validation; inevitably, hand-in-hand with such developments came case law intended to settle matters pertaining to the correct and incorrect/illegal usages associated with seals and sealing. The investigation of seals and their associated documents in the *SiMeW* project has necessarily directed the focus of research towards the process of using seals, including features of the administration of seal usage, as, for instance, in the commentary on usage contained within the sealing clauses of charters; it has less to say regarding dispute over seals and contemporary reflection upon seal usage, and for that, as we shall see in what follows, we need to look elsewhere in our sources.

An important feature of the use of seals within medieval Wales and the March is the suggestion, from the material sampled for this project, that seal usage did not extend significantly into western Wales and the principality during the high and late Middle Ages. This observation is also consistent with earlier investigation of the spread of literacy and the use of charters in medieval Wales. Llinos Smith has noted that 'remarkably few charters and deeds of late medieval data have survived from the counties of Carmarthen and Cardigan', a feature explicable in terms of the persistence of forms of conveyancing, notably surrender and admittance through local, seigneurial courts, which did not involve the use of charters.[2] One important reason for this is undoubtedly the vigour of medieval Welsh law that, itself a reflection of the age and society in which it was honed, was in no respect dependent upon the use of sealed instruments. 'Oaths and witness are the instruments of proof', as Dafydd Jenkins succinctly describes proof in the medieval Welsh law books.[3] Proof in Welsh law was founded upon compurgation, witnesses or oath helpers supporting the party to the dispute by attesting to the integrity of his or her oath, and that remained an important feature of Welsh law and practice throughout the Middle Ages. As Huw Pryce notes in his discussion of literacy in medieval Wales, it is quite possible to conceive of Welsh lawyers and other practitioners, who moved between worlds of Anglo-Norman and Welsh law, reserving practice to one or other sphere, as appropriate, and never seeking to unite the two.[4]

A. D. Carr observes that a significant proportion of pre-1282 grants by charter in Gwynedd and Powys tend to relate to grants by local lay lords to religious houses, the use of the charter, he contends, reflecting the expectations of the precociously literate religious institution in their dealings with a secular society that had yet fully to engage with literacy and written instruments.[5] Evidence of seal usage in central and west Wales in the earliest decades of this period mostly relates to high-status seal usage by Welsh princes and by monastic houses, the former adopting Anglo-Norman usage and the latter typically bringing with them common usage from England and the continent. To date, we have found far less, if indeed any, indication that lords and monastic houses in west Wales, at least during the high Middle Ages, were engaging, in their seal usage, with a wider local community similarly familiar with seal usage. Unless we posit the possibility that, even in everyday society, the inhabitants of west Wales were using both English and Welsh law as a matter of course, it is far from surprising that seal usage appears to have been so relatively slight. If we look further afield, for instance, to south Wales and the southern reaches of the March, we also, in fact, find similar features, with a slower take-up of seals among the wider populace, including relatively minor nobles and those of middling status in the later twelfth and early thirteenth century. Within a matter of decades however, and especially in the Marcher counties of Wales and its English borders, seal usage was widespread both among Welsh and English, a point reflected in other chapters in this volume. Beyond the principality of Wales, in the Marches, Anglo-Norman law, as regards conveyancing for instance, was key, and the same kinds of distinctions were not so strongly evident as might be found in those parts of Wales in which Welsh law operated. Thus, and as will be discussed in the next chapter, the permanent alienation of land was recorded by charter and validated by seal from the later twelfth century, while the use of sealed documents and seals more generally extended in the following centuries. This extension was accompanied by, and also of course reflected developments in both administration and law.

Administrative developments

Seals held by officers and institutions feature prominently in medieval Wales and the March just as they do elsewhere in medieval western Europe. Most obviously, seals of kings, princes and nobles feature significantly and are, as a proportion of all surviving seals, especially prevalent in the later twelfth and thirteenth centuries. Welsh princes from the later twelfth century possessed seals that reflected a wider Anglo-Norman tradition of high-status seal usage, though a number of Welsh rulers from this period used a single-sided equestrian seal rather than the two-sided seal of contemporary English kings and nobles with the individual enthroned on the obverse and mounted on horseback on the reverse.[6] These aspects are discussed more fully elsewhere in this volume, especially insofar as the employment of such motifs speaks to status and the physical representation of power.[7]

Here we need to consider more fully the use to which such seals were put and their particular significance in administrative terms. There is, in fact and hardly surprisingly, little to suggest that high-status seals were used in ways that were significantly different from other kinds of seal. The scale and public nature of transactions involving major secular figures of medieval Wales and the March encouraged the use of seals which in size and in the form of motif reflected the social status of the personage, as has been discussed in the previous chapter, but the kinds of transactions were, in strict legal and administrative terms, hardly distinctive and chiefly involved conveyance of land. So, for instance, gifts to religious houses are especially evident in early grants. In the early to mid-twelfth century it is likely that higher status lords possessed seals but even quite significant landowners of lesser status did not;

in such instances, and where the individual of lesser status wished to carry out an act, such as alienation, validated by seal, he or she might borrow his lord's seal. This happened, for instance, in the early to mid-twelfth century when Caradoc Uerbeis granted a considerable tract of land to the Cistercian house of Pendar, the precursor of Margam Abbey; not possessing a seal of his own he made use of that of his lord, Morgan ap Caradoc. The seal was a single-sided equestrian seal with a name legend: SIGILLUM (MAR)GANI FILII CRATOCI (see figure 2.1).[8] As seal usage, which was already known to extend to peasant sigillants by the later-twelfth and early-thirteenth century in parts of England, increased in medieval Wales and the March, the likelihood that grantors of the stature of Caradoc would have borrowed a seal for permanent lack of their own must have become increasingly remote.

As has also been discussed elsewhere in this volume, high-status sigillants came to employ both great seals and smaller, privy, seals in the thirteenth-century, the latter sometimes used as a counterseal and, in its design, often, but certainly not always, reflecting particular features of family and lineage.[9] The earls of Gloucester, for instance, used smaller privy seals, sometimes in the form of gems or intaglios, from the twelfth century, as for example, in the confirmation by William, Earl of Gloucester, of a grant by Gruffudd ab Ivor of land to Margam Abbey for the establishment of a hermitage or monastery beside the Taff.[10] In such instances, counterseals, using a different and smaller matrix, seem to have served only to reinforce the sealing with the earl's great seal (in this instance, a lion facing right with lily plant behind).[11]

We know that privy seals might be used, especially by those in positions of considerable authority, as an important and sometimes contentious alternative to great seals and other major seals of office, validating acts in a way that was potentially ad hoc and in a manner that might sidestep formal process. So, for instance, in England in the early fourteenth century, one of the many complaints aimed at Edward II and his supporters by the Ordainers was misuse of the privy seal.[12] As Pierre Chaplais makes clear, it is not always easy to distinguish policy in the separate use of privy and great seals, even in the case of a medieval king such as Edward I at the end of the thirteenth century;[13] this is even more the case when we turn to his tenants-in-chief and those immediately below them, as well as to the Welsh princes. As much as facilitating the kinds of administrative arrangements that privy seals certainly permitted, allowing the sigillant to act without the presence of his or her writing office and the great seal, the use of a privy seal also indicated status and a household that was complex and sophisticated in its administrative structures to an extent reflective of the size and power of the seal owner.[14] In this case, privy seals tended to be interchangeable with great seals and were used in conjunction with them, often, at least in terms of surviving instances, as counterseals. So, for instance, Llywelyn ap Iorwerth possessed a privy seal, an antique gem, with the legend SIGILLVM . SECRETVM . LEWLINI, which he used as a counterseal.[15] Gilbert de Clare, seventh earl of Gloucester and sixth of Hertford, had what appears to have a privy or secret seal in the later thirteenth century and we see it used to validate agreements carried out between the main parties, as in the sealing of a chirograph between the abbeys of Tewkesbury and Margam in 1265 regarding the tenure of tithes at St Leonard, Newcastle.[16]

There is also indication that privy seals were used to seal letters closed, especially those relating to correspondence that was more obviously private, and reflected a distance between official and less official correspondence, itself a consequence of a growing literate culture in the high Middle Ages.[17] By the second quarter of the fourteenth century in England and from the latter years of the reign of Edward II, kings had also introduced a third seal, a secret seal which was used by the king in sealing correspondence not requiring the great seal. In this case, the secret seal met a particular administrative function, allowing the king access to a personal seal at a time when the privy seal was absorbed into the developing bureaucracy of chancery with its own office and keeper; in time all three seals, great, privy and seal, came to represent royal and governmental authority.[18] Such developments, which reflected the unique complexities of English royal government, were echoed to a lesser degree among the greater magnates and their households in Wales and in England, and not least as the bureaucracy of the Marcher lordship and government in the Marches grew in its sophistication and complexity in the thirteenth and fourteenth centuries.[19] The complexity of large secular households and their estates also required that the officers responsible for the running of household and estate had their own seals of office or were responsible for the administration of the great seal and the other most important seals. So, for instance, the great seals of lords mirrored royal government in that they were, by the fourteenth century at least, in the custody of household officers; in 1338 the Lord of Glamorgan and Morgannwg, Hugh Despenser, in confirming grants by his predecessors to Margam, used his great seal, the sealing clause, making it clear that he instructed his chancery at Cardiff castle to place his seal on the inspeximus and confirmation.[20]

Earlier usage of so-called 'privy' and 'secret' seals, especially by magnates in medieval Wales and England, sometimes reflects not the same levels of complexity but rather the interchange and imprecision of terminology. As we have seen, by the mid-thirteenth century magnates also employed 'secret seals' in their dealings, and it is clear that the term was often interchangeable with 'privy seal'. As well as the example of Llywelyn ap Iorwerth mentioned above, there is the oft-cited instance of the private seal of Llywelyn ap Gruffudd, found upon his body in December 1282 and subsequently melted down, with the seals of Dafydd ap Gruffudd and Eleanor, to make a chalice in 1284.[21] Lords must have found secret or privy seals highly valuable in allowing them to deal with everyday business and matters of administration. In a dispute with tenants in the Dyffryn Clwyd commote of Colion in 1350, the Marcher lords, Reginald and John de Grey of Dyffryn Clwyd, appointed two of their officers by letters sealed under secret seal in order to oversee and bring to a conclusion the dispute on their behalf 'because we cannot terminate the said plea before our journey to England, because of the shortness of our stay at our castle in Wales'.[22]

Estate administration, insofar as we can observe it in Wales by the later thirteenth century, was increasingly dependent upon the use of seals and sealed instruments. Seals featured prominently in court records as well as in charters as instruments of the lord and his officers. For instance, in the regulation of the buying and selling of bread and ale under the assize of bread and ale, there are pronouncements from the court relating to the need for ale and grain to be sold according to prescribed and sealed measures, and amercements for those who fail to comply. So, at Dyffryn Clwyd, amercement of individual brewers and, more particularly, regraters for the illegal sale of ale by false measure typically makes reference to the failure of the seller to sell in measures 'not sealed by the lord's seal', a process overseen by ale tasters and other borough officials.[23] Orders of attachment of goods were also subject to the use of seals, the defendants' goods seized and then held under the lord's seal, the bailiff ordered to seal all of the goods so they were not dealt with otherwise (*sigillare omnia bona sua ut non ministrentur*). At the Great Court at Ruthin in 1353, in a case that most probably relates to seigneurial rights over the property of a deceased tenant, Margaret, the wife (possibly widow) of Gruffydd ap Bleddyn, was amerced 40d. for breaking the seal of the escheator 'placed on the door of the chamber'.[24]

The lord also communicated particular pieces of information to the court by means of sealed letter.[25] Estate officials also produced their own seals in handling the day-to-day administration of courts; in vouching the court rolls in a dispute over land, the relevant copies of rolls were produced under the seal of the steward, for instance, while transcripts of charters were also, on rare occasion, enrolled in the court rolls again by the authority of the steward's charter, a feature very familiar in English borough records.[26] Seals were also used to authenticate past acts and to secure rights over property where seisin may have been in dispute or at least subject to challenge, as in Margam Abbey's early thirteenth-century notice to the earl of Gloucester and Hertford insisting that a grantor to the abbey, David Scurlage, had been of sufficient age to deal with the abbey in granting land at an earlier date.[27] Inquests by local jurors were also validated by seal, as in the example from Swansea relating to a coroner's inquest from the early sixteenth century and discussed in the following chapter.[28] A similar collection of jurors' seals is attached to an inquest into the restoration of rights sought by Margam Abbey in 1329 in relation to seizures carried out in the thirteenth century by Gilbert de Clare, the grandfather of Alianora le Despenser, consort of the present lord of Glamorgan and Morgan, William de la Zouche.[29] The function of courts was also supported by sealed documents in other ways, as for instance, in sealed letters from litigants appointing attorneys to act in their stead, as for instance is recorded at Colion, a commotal court of Dyffryn Clwyd in 1344, whereby the plaintiff, William de Hampton, appointed his brother, John, as his attorney by means of a sealed letter produced in court.[30]

Unsurprisingly, also, the seals of ecclesiastics are familiar in this period and have been described in considerable detail by David Williams in particular. These vary in status and office much as do secular seals of magnates, with bishops using great seals as well as privy seals, the latter sometimes used as counter seals to great seals in the same way as we have seen in the case of lay magnates. In addition, bishops, especially by the fifteenth century, employed seals *ad causas*, intended for use in validating relatively minor deeds.[31] As well as the seals of bishops, other diocesan officers, including archdeacons and rural deans came to have their own seals of office in the thirteenth century, a development which reflects an expectation that such officials needed their own seals in order to meet the demands of their office.[32] This proliferation of ecclesiastical seals in the thirteenth and fourteenth centuries also encouraged interchangeability of seals by officials as, for instance, in 1397 when John Burghill, the bishop of Llandaff, used an official seal of the diocese rather than his own episcopal seal, which he did not have in his possession, in sealing an adjudication regarding the repair of church property.[33] In a case of disputed matrimony at Dyffryn Clwyd, discussed more fully later in this chapter, the variety of ecclesiastical seals and their lack of absolute specificity in certain instances are recognised, with an expectation that the husband in the dispute produced a proof validated by the relevant seal of a priest or ordinary or other holder of ecclesiastical office.[34]

Cistercian abbey seals in Wales, as discussed by Williams for instance, tended also to conform to type, as prescribed by the General Chapter of the Order; in the thirteenth century this meant that the abbot alone possessed a seal and this should not bear the abbot's name. The statute of Carlisle (1307) required the use of a common seal in religious houses, under the custody not of the abbot but the prior and a small body of monks; this development was also encouraged by the Cistercian General Chapter in the early fourteenth century. Given the general context in which such developments took place, it is unsurprising to find that Welsh houses did not deviate significantly or at all from seal usage elsewhere.[35]

Seals of towns and of burgesses are also common in medieval England and interesting examples also survive from medieval Wales, including some quite early and fairly basic seals from south Wales.[36] The early thirteenth-century common seal of the burgesses of Kenfig is a good example of an early corporate seal of this kind; though it obviously lacks the detail and involved representation of certain other British urban seals from the same period, especially those issuing from the larger towns and cities, its authority was not, as we have seen, diminished in this respect. Later seals from towns in medieval Wales and its border region do suggest attempts at civic representation, as in the burghal seal of Bridgnorth from the early fourteenth century.[37] Seals such as these facilitated shared action on the part of corporate bodies, the seal, *sigillum nostrum communi*, offering assurance of the shared commitment to an act. In an unusual but striking instance of such shared activity on the part of two corporate bodies, the seals of both the friars minor at Bridgnorth and the Bridgnorth burgesses were appended to an agreement from 1306 detailing obligations in relation to the maintenance and use of water courses in the town (see figure 2.2).[38]

Seals and law

It is clear that over time the defining features of Welsh and English law in terms of seal usage tended to undergo a degree of elision, no doubt a reflection of common practice and the sharing of forms of dealing; at the same time we can see persistence of features of Welsh law within legal practice that was, in essence, Anglo-Norman. Thus, for instance, deeds founded upon Welsh law and the form of leasing arrangement known as *tir prid* were, by the end of the thirteenth century, not only recorded in writing but also sealed, a mode of proof consistent with English but not Welsh law.[39] An agreement in 1340 in *tir prid* for a recurrent lease of four years in the first instance was also supported by sealed written indentures and recorded in the commotal court at Colion (Dyffryn Clwyd) in March 1341.[40]

This partial coming together of legal traditions, informed also by a rich vein of Welsh legal consciousness, is illustrated in litigation in commotal and Marcher courts, as at Ruthin in 1314 where the plaintiff sought to deny the oath of the defendant by insisting that the oral proof of his own contract counted as much in Wales as did written proof in England. In this he seems to have been consciously applying the legal maxim that 'specialty [i.e. a sealed written instrument] bars compurgation', and treating oral proof in Wales as such.[41] The same is also the case in terms of postmortem transfer of moveable goods where the evidence of local courts, such as those for the lordship of Dyffryn Clwyd, suggests that testators did not seek to secure their bequests through written wills but were quite attuned to the use of oral wills and deathbed transfers.[42]

A general regard for witness proof and oral evidence may also be hinted at in early sealing clauses from south Wales that appear to question the inherent legal force of particular seals, especially where the seal or the sigillant was unfamiliar. Most especially, personal seals were not always considered to be of sufficient authority to be used in support or validation of a particular act. While it seems evident that the parties had their own seals, seals of institutions or those greater collective or individual standing were often preferred. As we have seen earlier, in discussion of the seals of magnates, the relative force of a seal in securing or validating was in part conditioned by the prestige of the individual, the seals of the greatest magnates adding apparent force to agreements.[43] We can also detect this in the use of borough seals, the collective worth of the borough standing in the stead of the individual sigillant. So, for instance, by the early thirteenth century in Wales small and middling towns had their own common seals, as we have seen, and used them both in their own business and also as appropriate and respected alternates to those presented by one or other of the main parties to the contract. So, at Kenfig in south Wales we find the repeated formula that the party has used the common seal of the burgesses in addition to his or her own as the seal of the party to the agreement is not well known.[44]

In certain respects, this early formulation must reflect an uncertainty regarding the potency of seals, and especially personal seals, as effective devices in permitting recovery in case of a failed agreement and may illustrate a commitment to witness proof and public fame (*fama*) as the essential ingredients in securing a contract. In this, Welsh law was not so very far from high medieval conveyancing in medieval England; as more than one commentator has noted, early charters are 'evidential' rather than 'dispositive' and provided evidence of a public deed of granting itself typically supported by some physical act, such as the handing over of a sod of earth.[45] If this transition between oral and written forms of proof was clearly not unique to Wales and the March in this period, it is at least conceivable that it may have been accentuated by Welsh law's ingrained commitment to witness proof, as discussed earlier in this chapter.

A more general recognition of the importance of seals as proof in law is illustrated in cases of misuse of seals in this period. Paul Brand has recently discussed some of the ways in which the issue of seals and their misuse might feature prominently in contract litigation of various kinds in thirteenth and fourteenth century England.[46] An act seemingly carried out in error by an estate official at Dyffryn Clwyd illustrates, in terms of the remedies undertaken to resolve the problem, the perceived importance and force of sealed instruments. In 1344 at Aberchwiler, a commote of the Marcher lordship of Dyffryn Clwyd, the steward, allegedly in his ignorance (*per ignoranciam*) and presumably before anyone could point out his supposed error, cut the seal from a deed that had been introduced into the court by parties as evidence of the limit of rights owed to the lord; the sealed document which, before the steward's intervention had been good and whole, neither torn nor faulty (*bona et integra, non rasa nec vitiata*), was restored to its previous condition in the view of the full court, with the seal sown back on and the steward's own seal in red wax impressed upon the stitches so that the charter was then in no place faulty (*in nullo loco vitiabatur*); all of this was identified as a temporary expedient as the steward also undertook on his own security that the lord would renew the charter on his arrival at Ruthin.[47]

Seals were used to support rulings and to provide evidence of matters of law, and often a shared recognition of the potency and efficacy of seals is evident not least in anxiety over the validity of relevant sealed documents produced in such instances. When Gwerful daughter of Adda impleaded Einion ap Bleddyn in trespass, claiming he took livestock and grain from her, Einion acknowledged the seizure but sought to dismiss the claim of trespass on the basis that Gwerful was his wife, and so, as her husband, he had committed no wrong. The court requested that, in order to prove his case, he produce at the next court evidence 'under the seal of an ordinary where and when the marriage between them was solemnised'.[48] In the next court Einion produced 'a certain letter from the official of Bromfield sealed with his privy seal, as is asserted [by the defendant]'; the court was sceptical – 'full faith is not accorded to it' (*cui non adhibetur plena fides*) – and Einion was ordered to produce authentic testimony at the next court at his peril; his attorney's attempt to produce 'certain letters under the seal of Einion official of St Asaph' at the next court was also queried by the court, the officers of which demanding that the attorney 'produce in the next court at his peril letters of the bishop, dean or archdeacon testifying at what time the marriage was solemnised and if up to now they have cohabited as man and wife'. At the next court, with still no evidence of trustworthy documentation or other proof of his marital status, Einion's case collapsed.[49] The potency of seals as proof in matters of dispute is also revealed at Dyffryn Clwyd in 1317; a dispute over the ownership of a horse previously sold at Shrewsbury was eventually settled out of court when it was shown, by evidence of the 'common seal of the citizens of Shrewsbury' that the defendant had indeed bought the horse and paid toll at Shrewsbury for his purchase there.[50]

A likely growing regard for the force of sealed instruments and the potential for legal challenge helps explain both their use but also the development of a careful diplomatic in the high and later Middle Ages. The avoidance of future litigation undoubtedly informs the construction of carefully worded sealing clauses though the legal necessity for a sealing clause was never clearly essential; convention and the pursuit of a secure contract, correctly established, no doubt informed such choices, which tended to encourage 'more' (in terms of sigillants and appropriate sealing clauses) rather than 'less', as did, for instance, the ways in which seals were appended to documents, by tongue, tag or cord.[51] A document sealed with a magnate's great seal would not fail at law because it was appended by tongue rather than the far more typical cord used to append great seals, but no doubt it would offend diplomatic practice.[52] Carr's suggestion that grants in *tir prid* were often poorly and cheaply executed documents seems also to be supported by the preferred method of attachment of seal, which, in some instances at least, appears often to have been by tongue (see figure 2.3).[53] In addition, a developing law pronounced upon which of the parties were expected to seal certain kinds of agreement. Typically, it was the grantor whose seal was most necessary – evidence, if future evidence were needed, that the grant had taken place with the assent of the party whose property or goods were being alienated, as for example in the early thirteenth-century quitclaim made by Isabella the widow of John Callow 'in her urgent necessity' to Hugh le Vilein of a messuage and appurtenances next to the cemetery of St Juliana the Virgin at Shrewsbury. The quitclaim is sealed with Isabella's seal only.[54] In these respects, of course, the surviving instances from Wales and the March offer little that is novel or a departure from practice elsewhere.

Notes

1 For summaries of such developments, see, for instance, *Guide*; *Seals and Sealing Practices*.
2 Ll. B. Smith, 'Inkhorn and spectacles: the impact of literacy in late medieval Wales', in H. Pryce (ed.), *Literacy in Medieval Celtic Societies* (Cambridge, 1998), pp. 215–16.
3 D. Jenkins, 'The medieval Welsh idea of law', *Tijdschrift voor Rechtsgeschiedenis/Legal History Review*, 49 (1981), 332.

4   Jenkins, 'Medieval Welsh idea of law', 333; H. Pryce, 'Lawbooks and literacy in medieval Wales', *Speculum*, 75 (2000), 36, 66–7, and in particular the assertion that 'a striking feature of the Welsh lawbooks is the widening chasm between their assumptions about the legal uses of literacy and the practices of the increasingly document-minded society in which they were written. This suggests that the literate mentality represented, for example, by the use of deeds or the keeping and consultation of court rolls did not penetrate all spheres of Welsh life, even in the later Middle Ages' (66). On Welsh proof, see also H. Pryce, *Native Law and the Church in Medieval Wales* (Oxford, 1993), pp. 37–65.

5   A. D. Carr, '"This is my act and deed": the writing of private deeds in late medieval north Wales', in Pryce (ed.), *Literacy in Medieval Celtic Societies*, pp. 224–5.

6   *Acts*, pp. 86–7; for obverse and reverse of English great seals, see, for example, A. Ailes, 'Governmental seals of Richard I', in P. R. Schofield (ed.), *Seals and their Context in the Middle Ages* (Oxford, 2015), p. 102; *Guide*, pp. 27–34. See also M. P. Siddons, 'Welsh equestrian seals', *National Library of Wales Journal*, 23 (1983–4), 292–318.

7   See especially chapters 5 and 7.

8   Seal 56; *Margam*, pp. 9–10.

9   See below, chapter 5.

10 Seal 1145; *Margam*, p. 16.

11 Seal 1144; see appendix for various impressions.

12 J. H. Trueman, 'The privy seal and the English ordinances of 1311', *Speculum*, xxxi (1956).

13 Chaplais, *English Diplomatic Practice in the Middle Ages* (Hambledon and London, 2003), pp. 96–7.

14 See, for instance, the comments of *Acts*, pp. 87–8.

15 *Acts*, p. 87; Siddons, 'Welsh equestrian seals', 294.

16 NLW PENRICE: GLAM/177; *Margam*, pp. 282–3. I am grateful to Dr Elizabeth New for drawing my attention to this example. The seal is discussed and an image given in E. A. New, '(Un)conventional images. A case-study of radial motifs on personal seals', in Schofield (ed.), *Seals and their Context in the Middle Ages* (Oxford, 2015), p. 153.

17 Note, though, the ways in which privy seal and great seal interacted by the later thirteenth and early fourteenth centuries in England, D. Carpenter, 'The English royal chancery in the thirteenth century', in A. Jobson (ed.), *English Government in the Thirteenth Century* (Woodbridge, 2004), pp. 63–4.

18 Chaplais, *English Diplomatic Practice*, p. 98.

19 On this last point, see W. Rees, *South Wales and the March, 1284–1415. A Social and Agrarian Study* (Oxford, 1924), pp. 88–107. For a general discussion of the development of English government in the early part of this period, see Jobson (ed.), *English Government in the Thirteenth Century*.

20 See, for instance, NLW PENRICE: GLAM/2065; *Margam*, pp. 236–7. For an example of the seal, see *Seliau*, pp. 72–3; also *Margam*, p. 309.

21 *Acts*, p. 89.

22 TNA SC 218/2, m.18. The Dyffryn Clwyd examples use here are recorded in the project database arising from Economic and Social Research Council project, 'Dyffryn Clwyd Court Roll Database, 1294–1422', award numbers: R000232548; R000234070. The database arising from these projects is available for download through the UK data archive at *http://www.data-archive.ac.uk/* (last accessed 26 January 2016). For description of the project, see A. D. M. Barrell, R. R. Davies, O. J. Padel and Ll. B. Smith, 'The Dyffryn Clwyd Court Roll project, 1340–1352 and 1389–1399: a methodology and some preliminary findings', in Z. Razi and R. M. Smith (eds), *Medieval Society and the Manor Court* (Oxford, 1996), pp. 260–97.

23 Among numerous instances in the Great Court of Dyffryn Clwyd, see, for example, TNA SC 216/10, m.24d (Tudur le Trauenter, amerced 6d.); 216/12, m.14d (Tangwystl wife of William Saer, amerced 6d.). For a discussion of brewing and its regulation at Ruthin in the fourteenth century, see M. F. Stevens, *Urban Assimilation in Post-Conquest Wales. Ethnicity, Gender and Economy in Ruthin, 1282–1348* (Cardiff, 2010), pp. 138–53.
24 TNA SC 218/4, m.30.
25 As, for instance, the appointment of an attorney to represent parties in a claim to tenements at Ruthin, the attorney appointed 'before the lord at le Releghe…as is clear from the lord's letter under his seal', court of 10 March 1349, Ruthin, TNA, SC 217/14, m.32d.
26 Ruthin, court of 22 April 1343, TNA SC 217/8, m.6d; Llanerch, court of 6 November 1343, TNA SC 217/9, m.5. In medieval England, the use of the mayoral seal or that of officers of the borough was often applied to enrolments of deeds in borough courts, J. M. Kaye, *Medieval English Conveyances* (Cambridge, 2009), p. 15.
27 NLW PENRICE: GLAM/2049.
28 NLW PENRICE: GLAM/342, and below in chapter 7.
29 NLW PENRICE: GLAM/203; *Margam*, pp. 299–300.
30 Colion, court of 15 April 1344, TNA SC 217/9, m.22.
31 D. H. Williams, 'Catalogue of Welsh ecclesiastical seals as known down to 1600 AD. Part I. Episcopal seals', *Archaeologia Cambrensis*, cxxxiii (1984), 105.
32 D. H. Williams, 'Catalogue of Welsh ecclesiastical seals as known down to 1600 AD. Part II. Seals of ecclesiastical jurisdiction', *Archaeologia Cambrensis*, cxxxiv (1985), 162–3.
33 NLW PENRICE: GLAM/242.
34 See below, pp. 43–4.
35 D. H. Williams, 'Catalogue of Welsh ecclesiastical seals as known down to 1600 AD. Part IV. Seals of Cistercian Monasteries', *Archaeologia Cambrensis*, cxxxvi (1987), 138–9; see also idem, 'The seals of Strata Florida Abbey', *Ceredigion*, 14 (2003), 2. See also below, pp. 67–8, for some indication of local employment of these conventions.
36 See, for instance, E. New, 'Seals and status in medieval English towns: a case study of London, Newcastle and Durham', in N. Adams, J. Cherry and J. Robinson (eds), *Good Impressions: Image and Authority in Medieval Seals* (London, 2007), pp. 35–8.
37 Seal 1844.
38 NLW PITORD/519; while the sealing clauses suggests both parties appended their seals, only one seal is appended to the surviving portion of the indenture, possibly the communal seal of the burgesses, though the motif is entirely different from an earlier Bridgnorth common seal of the burgesses. It is possible therefore that the two parties each sealed one part of the chirograph or indenture, the original or the counterpart, each party retaining the part-sealed by the other party, as in the examples from later-twelfth- and early-thirteenth-century Pontefract discussed in Kaye, *Medieval English Conveyances*, p. 9. On occasion, sealing clauses made this arrangement evident, as in NLW PITORD/402, where it is clearly stated to be the case that each party received that part of the indenture that was secured by the other party's seal.
39 See, for example, the instances of sealed *tir prid* deeds in Ll. B. Smith, '*Tir prid*: deeds of gage of land in late medieval Wales', *Bulletin of the Board of Celtic Sstudies*, 27 (1977), 270–7.
40 TNA, 217/6, m.5d.
41 P. R. Schofield, 'English law and Welsh Marcher courts in the late-thirteenth and early-fourteenth centuries', in R. A. Griffiths and P. R. Schofield (eds), *Wales and the Welsh in the Middle Ages* (Cardiff, 2011), p. 117.

42 P. R. Schofield, 'Intestat et testaments paysans en Angleterre et Pays de Galles au XIIIe siècle et au début du XIVe siècle', in N. Vivier (ed.), *Ruralité française et britannique, xiiie–xxe siècles. Approches comparées* (Rennes, 2005), pp. 207–18.
43 On this point, see also Williams, 'Episcopal seals', 103.
44 NLW PENRICE: GLAM/198; 199; 200; 2059; see also *Margam*, pp. 297, 299. The communal seal of Kenfig is also discussed in New, '(Un)conventional images', p. 153.
45 See, for instance, Carr, ' "This is my act and deed" ', p. 224; for an early instance of a grant to a religious institution in which the initial grant, subsequently supported by a sealed testimony, was carried out in a public setting in the presence of a 'multitude' of witnesses, see NLW PITORD/2456, Testimony and confirmation of John Extraneus [Ext'neus] of a grant of the Church of Wroccestre [Wroxeter, co. Salop] by William son of Alan to the church of St John the Evangelist of Hagaman [Haughmond, co. Salop].
46 P. Brand, 'Seals and the law in thirteenth century England', in Schofield (ed.), *Seals and their Context*, pp. 111–19; see also Kaye, *Medieval English Conveyances*, pp. 16–17.
47 TNA 217/10, m.17, court of 12 October 1344.
48 TNA, SC 217/8, m.20d, Llanerch, court of 1 March 1343, filia Adda v. ap Bleddyn. For further discussion of sealed documents and the role of ecclesiastics in solemnising marriage, see also below, chapter 4.
49 TNA, SC 217/8, mm.20d, 21, 21d., Llanerch, courts of 20 March 1343, 24 April 1343, 8 May 1343, filia Adda v. ap Bleddyn.
50 TNA 215/76, m.14.
51 On sealing clauses, see, for instance, Kaye, *Medieval English Conveyances*, pp. 14–15.
52 See, for example, *Seals and Sealing Practice*, pp. 19–21; Sir H. Jenkinson, 'The study of English seals: illustrated chiefly from examples in the Public Record Office', *Journal of the British Archaeological Association*, 3rd ser., i (1937), 93–125, reprinted in *Selected writings of Sir Hilary Jenkinson* (Gloucester, 1980), pp. 147–85, and in particular pp. 159–60.
53 Carr, ' "This is my act and deed" ', p. 234; for example, BUAS MOST/718; 731.
54 SHA 972/1/1/ 432.

SEALS AND EXCHANGE

Phillipp R. Schofield

THE SEALED INSTRUMENT was, from the high Middle Ages, an important device for facilitating trade, and typically at a relatively elevated level. The ubiquity or otherwise of sealed instruments, their prevalence within certain economic and social groups, and their importance for particular kinds of economic and social exchange remain topics of importance in the wider social and economic literature for the Middle Ages. Only partially considered for medieval England, the material gathered here, for medieval Wales, the March and its bordering counties, presents an excellent opportunity to examine the ways in which seals and sealing practice facilitated economic exchange. Importantly, also, the reach of sealed instruments into wider society and economy, and the tendency, as evident from study of local courts of medieval England, for a high proportion of low-level exchange to operate without sealed instrument, needs also to be considered. This further encourages some reflection upon a wider exchange, including the exchange of motifs and seal forms and the underlying associations that may have encouraged such kinds of activity.

We can detect two main and developing strands in examining seal usage in terms of exchange. In the first instance, as has already been discussed on more than one occasion in this volume and is already familiar from other sigillographic studies, the social base of seal usage expanded from the end of the twelfth century so that, through the thirteenth century, it included greater numbers of low-status sigillants, including peasants and lowlier townsmen and townswomen. Secondly, and especially important here, while exchange of free land remained throughout the Middle Ages the single greatest factor in promoting seal usage, it is also clear that the kinds of issues involving the use of a seal grew in number, reflecting in some part the changing economic and social developments in high and later medieval England and Wales.

One of the most significant categories in the material examined in terms of seal usage relates to land and its transfer. Land was transferred in a variety of forms; whether in terms of transfer of seisin (the freehold transfer of land with all associated rights) or possession (typically, the grant of a limited term from one party to the other), transfers often, but not always, involved the use of a sealed instrument in order to secure the transfer and provide evidence for the incoming landholder. The earliest sealed documents from Wales, the March and neighbouring English counties reflect this inevitable focus upon landholding, and those from the later twelfth and early thirteenth centuries tend to involve higher status parties, both individuals, such as secular lords and princes and institutions, most obviously religious houses. Grants of land to the abbey of Ystrad Marchell show the significance of princely families as grantors in the decades either side of 1200, for instance.[1] The same is also reasonably evident in other early gatherings of charters relating to grants to religious houses. Grants to Margam Abbey in the later twelfth and early thirteenth century illustrate the important role of the high status secular grantor, speaking also to the considerable involvement of wealthy knightly families. Families such as the Sturmis, Scurlages, Luvels, Londres, de Bonevilles were all important donor families, and, engaged as they often were in serial transactions under seal with Margam, sometimes extending over generations, their sealing practice reflected their piety, self-regard and lineage.[2] Thus, for instance, as Elizabeth New has discussed, the sharing of radial motifs among a number of highly placed members of society in south Wales in the thirteenth century perhaps illustrates the sharing of motifs within extended family groups, as well as among members of the same socio-economic groups.[3] We will return to some examples of these grants later in this chapter when we consider exchange of motifs within families and over generations as well as indications of shared motifs within particular locales and socio-economic contexts.

There is also good indication that parties of lower social status were already using sealed instruments in support of transfers of relatively small plots by the later twelfth century in Wales. Thus, sealed contracts for transfers of messuages and burgage plots in towns by sealed instrument are already evident from late twelfth-century Wales, as in the transfer of property at Cardiff and Kenfig involving William son of Osmund and his son Tedbald.[4] Grouped together by repository and landholder, deeds relating to transfer of land often concentrate upon a particular location, such as a manor, small town or an area of a town in which the holder of the relevant deeds, such as a religious house, held properties and/or the head rent. At Shrewsbury, for instance, in the thirteenth century, Lilleshall Abbey collected rents on properties that were transferred between townspeople, as in the example of Hugh le Vilein who purchased from Isabel daughter of John Callow a messuage and appurtenances next to the cemetery of Juliana the Virgin within the town.[5] Other examples from later twelfth- and thirteenth-century Kenfig also illustrate the frequent transfer of land by charter supported by seal, as for instance in the alienation of one acre by Amibilia daughter of Walter the Miller of Kenfig to John Pervath of Kenfig and his wife Alice, or that, again of a single acre at Kenfig, from Robert, son of Robert Raul, to Philip, son of Robert Palmer (see figures 3.1 and 3.2).[6] This potentially lower status, relatively speaking, transfer of free land is consistent with that found at the same period in neighbouring England, where final concordances in the form of feets of fine illustrate a significant engagement in the transfer of small plots by poorer freemen, undoubtedly including peasants and smaller townsmen.[7] In terms of the actual exchange of land, seals were used in a variety of forms of conveyancing, and not just in simple transfer of seisin, including leases of land and gages.

Leases of land and mortgages were supported by seal, as in the lease and gage of land for four years granted by Gruffydd ap Dafydd Dey in September 1348.[8] Where Welsh law applied, strict alienation was not permitted but land continued to be transferred by the device of *tir prid*. *Tir prid* agreements, also often for four years in the first instance, were also supported by seal, as discussed in the previous chapter. Some of the earliest of these date from the early fourteenth century and reflect a coming together of Welsh and English law, a Welsh device intended to sidestep restrictions on free alienation by an individual of hereditary rights vested in the kindred located within an essentially Anglo-Norman framework of a Latin charter validated by seal. So, for instance, an early surviving example from Anglessey, while it does not refer to *tir prid*, makes it clear that the grant has been made for four years with the possibility of additional four year terms, the traditional structure of such arrangements.[9]

The distinction between Welsh and English conventions in terms of exchange is also illustrated by the provenance of grants of land issuing from religious houses situated in England or functioning according to English law. A small series of charters from the later thirteenth and early fourteenth centuries relating to grants and leases by Lilleshall Abbey (Shropshire), an Augustinian house, of their properties in Welshpool (*de la Pole*) is conducted according to the precepts of English law. As well as offering a fair amount of information on plots of land in the borough just a few decades after its foundation, the charters also illustrate the quite extensive seal usage, in terms of variety of design, to be found in a small urban centre such as Welshpool by the end of the thirteenth century. Striking also in this respect is the clear evidence for mid-Welsh seal usage; at Welshpool, in a new burghal foundation with a significant proportion of English residents and dealing in property owned by an English religious house, we have a combination of influences that allows us to see quite extensive seal usage at the close of the thirteenth century. The further west we head from Welshpool, the less evidence we find of similar usage in this period, a point discussed more fully in the previous chapter.

Given the very high proportion of sealed documents relating to the transfer of immoveable goods (most obviously, land and housing), we might reasonably suppose that seal usage, in terms of exchange and everyday dealing, was typically to be associated with the transfer of immoveables. While there are plenty of indications that this was not always the case, as we have seen earlier in this chapter, it is also evident that much economic dealing in moveables, such as grain, wool, or finished goods, and certainly at the level of wealthy peasantry and middling townspeople, was conducted without recourse to sealed documents. Where relatively rare instances do survive of moveable goods exchanged by means of a sealed instrument, we might explain this in terms of the random survival of a more common type that was typically not preserved subsequent to the transaction; however, given the plentiful evidence for non-use of seals, as outlined above,[10] it may be as reasonable to suppose that the relative rarity of lower status sealed documents involving the transfer of moveables reflects a 'real' distinction with the proportion of sealed documents relating to immoveables. That this distinction shows some slight sign of changing over time, again as suggested in the earlier discussion, is consistent with developments elsewhere in medieval Britain and may reveal a greater recourse to sealing in the later Middle Ages.

One form of 'moveable' to which we can associate seal usage from a relatively early period is people. On occasion, sealed documents were used to secure the sale of people, and more particularly neifs or villeins. The sale of villeins is quite commonly recorded in English charters, from the thirteenth century onwards;[11] fairly late instances from Wales also survive from the mid-fourteenth century and from the early fifteenth century. For instance, at Uchaf, Caernarfonshire in May 1416, William ap Ievan ap Gruffith ap Iorwerth ap Llewelyn, a free tenant of the commote sold under sealed instrument Hwlkin Bach, his neif or bondman [*nativus*] as well as his 'brood' [*sequela*], goods and chattels, reliefs, heriots (*amobwr*) and whatsoever other services and bondages applied to William ap Gruffith ap Gwilym (see figure 3.3).[12] As has been noted by more than one commentator, the focus of such transactions is likely to have been the tenanted land and the associated obligations, rather than the buying and selling of individuals.[13] However, it is striking, in a Welsh context, that the language of obligation persists so resolutely into the later Middle Ages, and no doubt reflects the strong and persistent distinctions between free and bonded commotes in parts of Wales. Sigillography adds only a little to our understanding here; we can reflect upon the changing seal design of those involved in the purchase and selling of villeins that are, unsurprisingly, consistent with general trends in seal design and reflect the fashions of individual seal ownership in the later Middle Ages. Of course, the seal ownership of the vendors and purchasers, often local freemen of no great social standing whose adopted seal designs were often geometric and quite ordinary, distinguished them at law from the bondsmen who were being bought and sold, their status generally, though certainly not wholly, deemed to be inconsistent with the employment of sealed instruments.[14]

If sealed instruments were used to record and secure the transfer of the unfree, sealed instruments were also used to evidence manumission. The grant of free status and the release from bondage was, again in England, a fairly common act in the twelfth and thirteenth centuries; a fine example of the same survives from the later thirteenth century by which Gilbert Osemund of Foxherd, Ida, his wife, Peter, his son, and Elen, his daughter, bondmen of Walter, son of Richard of Stokes, were granted their liberty by the said Walter.[15] As discussed elsewhere in this volume, the fine seal attached to the charter of manumission, detailing a lily-like plant flanked by peacocks, may reflect the personal piety of the grantor, and is also perhaps redolent of his status (see figure 3.4).[16] Sealed documents in relation to individuals and their labour also come to feature later in the period, a consequence not of serfdom and its constraints but instead of labour in a market economy. Thus, for instance, by the fifteenth century apprenticeship agreements could involve sealed documents, as in the example from Shrewsbury in 1410 by which John Ynge of Acton Burnell joined the household of John Harley for seven years; the sealed agreement set out not only the economic conditions of their contract but also issues of conduct, including the sexual conduct of the young apprentice within his new master's household.[17]

The survival of sealed bonds, and especially mercantile bonds, relating to moveable goods relative to the survival of sealed charters recording transfer of land is also quite limited. The database compiled for the *SiMeW* project includes very few instances of bonds and this is a pattern also reflected elsewhere.[18] Seals with merchant marks feature to some degree in the body of material gathered to date and, unsurprisingly given the prevalence of deeds, were most often used to validate charters transferring land rather than to support other kinds of mercantile activity. By the later fifteenth and early sixteenth century there is some slight indication that sealed bonds for loans of money were more common, at least within the surviving corpus of material, as in a small number of bonds for sizeable money loans recorded by sealed bonds from north Wales and quite probably Caernarfonshire in 1541; of the few surviving instances, the bonds were typically validated by seal carrying a merchant's mark. In two separate instances, the seal was the same, bearing the initials 'R' and 'S', and hints at least at sizeable loans issued from within the merchant community.[19] In this respect, scale was also certainly important, with very large money loans validated by seal as in the loan of £3,000 by the armiger, later knight and first lay owner of Margam Abbey at the Dissolution, Resio Mauncell or Rees Mansell, to three members of the Bassett family in November 1514. One of the seals was that of one of the recipients of the loan, possibly Henry Bassett judging by the location of his name on the tongue, and displayed a merchant mark; that of his relative, again possibly William, instead carried a simple five-petalled flower motif (see figures 3.5 and 3.6).[20]

While our focus has been to date upon the ways in which sealing of documents facilitated exchange at all levels of society, including the relatively lowly, it would not be correct to suggest that use of seals pervaded all kinds of transactions or indeed that the seal came to dominate as a mode of security and proof of contract at all levels of society and in all kinds of transaction. In the first instance, and as discussed earlier in this volume, securing of agreements under Welsh law was not dependent upon sealed documents and, instead, oral proof was the foundation to contract under Welsh law. That Welsh sigillants came to employ sealed instruments reflected the intrusion of

Anglo-Norman convention rather than an absorption of non-Welsh laws into Welsh law, points again that have been discussed earlier this volume.[21] Secondly, as was the case for much of the population of neighbouring England in the later Middle Ages, the availability of seals and sealing practice did not mean that seals were used or indeed required in all contexts. In an English context, it is striking in fact to what degree, even by the fourteenth century, contracts of some scale and complexity could be secured by something rather less secure than a sealed instrument, and typically by witness proof.[22] The same appears also to be the case insofar as we can observe it in local court records from Wales and the Marches. Thus, for instance, the later thirteenth- and fourteenth-century court rolls from Dyffryn Clwyd illustrate the ways in which transfers in small items of property might be conducted and the kinds of security typically employed. Thus, for instance, at Dogfeiling in June 1342, the defendant was able to prove by witnesses (*per videntes et audientes*: those who saw and heard the original contract) that he had repaid the small debt of 6½d.[23] In fact, a survey of entries in the Dyffryn Clwyd court rolls suggests that reference to written and sealed proof is rare and tends to be confined to rather particular agreements concerning land, as in the instances given above as well as in the previous chapter relating to tir prid, for instance,[24] or to matters originating within and beyond the estate but relating to matters issuing from other, and often higher, forms of dealing and, as often, administration.[25]

If we move from the sealed documents and the kinds of transactions with which they were or were not involved, and turn our attention instead to sealing practice within types of transaction, we can observe certain patterns and indications that suggest different kinds of exchange. These 'other' exchanges include the transfer of seals themselves as well as the exchange and sharing of form and motif also in terms of the seals. The shared use of standard motifs in seal usage is familiar and has been examined especially closely in the case of high-status seal usage. So, for instance, we are familiar with, to give some obvious examples, the widespread use of equestrian seals among the higher nobility or particular clerical designs as regards ecclesiastical institutions and offices.[26] We are also increasingly aware of the subtle distinctions that individuals might employ in order to establish relative positions and hierarchies even within rather closely defined cohorts.[27] Such shared reference to motifs has been studied far less for groups of a lower social status, though certain inroads have been made and the disproportionate attention paid to higher status sigillants acknowledged. Over half a century ago Rodney Hilton, discussing Gloucestershire Abbey leases from the thirteenth century, commented albeit briefly, on the seals used by peasant lessees and noted some consistencies of theme and design in the motifs used by the lessees.[28] Much more recently Elizabeth New has shown how family groups in south Wales, operating above the level of the peasantry, might share devices and forms across generations.[29] New also describes how apparently simple radial designs contained a variety of rather more complex messages and were capable of subtle interpretations by their users.[30]

It is clear that, on a fairly straightforward level, elements of designs were shared within particular socio-economic groupings so that, again to use the obvious instance, secular lords employed martial devices such as armed figures on horseback. Institutional association, office-holding and high-status lineage all, of course, encouraged a sharing of sealing motifs and the transmission of consistent and suitable forms from one individual to their successor. Discussion of such issues will also surface in other relevant chapters in this volume, especially those relating to lineage and nobility, as well as the church and religious institutions, and will not be considered further here.[31] There are, however, elements of this discussion that can be explored here, particularly those relating to exchange within family groups and the development of shared sealing practices within localities.

We can begin with sealing within family groups. Thus, for instance, a late fifteenth-century grant of a lease in Denbighshire, includes the seals of the five grantors, three of whom are from the same family, Eyton, a Denbighshire knightly family. Of the four surviving and easily discerned impressions, two are of stags, each identifiably different from the other but also sufficiently close in execution as to suggest a shared provenance.[32] This sharing of devices and motifs is evident in other family groups and often across generations. The Sturmi family's grants to Margam Abbey in the twelfth and thirteenth centuries illustrate the continuity of themes, including hunting spears and their associated imagery.[33] Details of these motifs appear to have carried over from one generation to the next and sometimes with significant modification but also retention of features. Thus, it appears possible, for instance, that the stylised device topping the spear of Roger Sturmi junior at the end of the twelfth century, itself in general form an echo of the seal of Roger's grandfather, Geoffrey Sturmi, was used by one of his successors, also Roger, as the central motif to his seal in the 1230s (see figures 3.7, 3.8 and 3.9).[34] It is also far from fanciful to suggest that echoes of the same stylised device are represented in later thirteenth-century radial motifs on seals of later members of the Sturmi family.[35] The examples offered here relate to relatively high-status knightly families engaged in quite high-level exchange of land, often involving grants to religious houses. It is less easy to follow similar instances of shared motifs across generations in lowlier families, though it is possible to identify some seemingly regionally distinctive patterns of shared motifs.

In the first instance, locality was important in the exchange and sharing of seal design. The later thirteenth- and early fourteenth-century devices employed at Welshpool in dealings with Lilleshall Abbey, also discussed earlier in this chapter, are not especially remarkable but they do suggest variety and also speak to a shared culture of representation, a number of the themes arising often in seals issuing from elsewhere in England and Wales. The small Welshpool corpus in fact falls into three main themes. There is a strong religious element that, as we have seen, is entirely consistent with themes identified elsewhere. So, for instance, late fourteenth seals from Welshpool depicted saints with suppliant figures, as in the seal appended to a grant of a tenement at Welshpool to William Flesshewer and his wife, Agnes.[36] There is also a common secular theme to a number of the devices, including such familiar themes as a hare riding a hound with the legend '*sohou [Robin]...*', a typical medieval hunting-call (see fig. 3.10).[37] There are good examples of this device from throughout England and Wales, including a similar and almost certainly closely contemporaneous seal matrix discovered at Chester.[38] Thirdly, there is also evidence of personal seals, including initialled or monogrammed seals of a kind consistent with personalised sealing. There is indication, in terms of relative types, that by the later Middle Ages Welsh-named sigillants at Welshpool opted for monogrammed designs, and that these were inscribed on signet rings rather than matrices. That said, while all sigillants who were identifiably Welsh (i.e. by name) sealed their charters with monogrammed signet rings, *c*.1400, such practice was consistent with broader practices across England and Wales in the later fourteenth and fifteenth centuries.[39] So, for instance, in Cheshire, by the end of the fourteenth century, monogrammed seals were in common usage, as a grant in 1394 by John de Hesketh, Thomas Frere and William Grenehilles of Preston to John de Midelton of Lancaster illustrates (see figure 3.11).[40] Elsewhere monogrammed seals were quite typical motifs of a kind used by burgesses within Wales, as for instance at Beaumaris, Newborough and Caernarfon in the fourteenth and early fifteenth centuries.[41]

In some instances the persistence of a seal motif within a particular local context is especially striking. Thus, for instance, with the *SiMeW* dataset almost 50 per cent of surviving seals (11 of 23) carrying the motif of the sleeping lion are from Bridgnorth (Shropshire) and its environs, while 25 per cent were from the area of Llanwys and a smaller number from Welshpool. The local concentration in and about Bridgnorth is especially interesting as the use of the sleeping lion motif covers a long time span, the first instance gathered here dating from 1279 and the last from 1344,[42] (see figure 3.12) and is used by more than one person or family within the locale. The device of the lion asleep beneath a tree is well known elsewhere from medieval England and Wales[43] but the concentration of impressions in and around Bridgnorth carrying this motif may suggest that the device found particular favour there; the same may also be true of hunting motifs, especially those with hares, as a high proportion of those from with the sample originate from Bridgnorth and associate with more than one family.[44] As already noted, radial motifs of quite a specific and nuanced kind have been identified as a persistent 'theme' in parts of south Wales in the high Middle Ages and may reflect similar shared traits to those described here for Bridgnorth and its later thirteenth- and early fourteenth-century sigillants.[45] These included seals of both men and women, including for instance one Margery the daughter of Roger, described in the charter by which she granted land to Margam Abbey as 'once the concubine of Richard Clerk of Kenfig' (see figure 3.13).[46]

Merchants also used distinctive designs and adopted devices that both distinguished them as a group through the use of 'merchant marks' but also allowed them to identify themselves uniquely. The use of seals in the style of merchant marks appears to have been quite frequent in and around Bayville in the barony of Kemes in Carmarthenshire, for instance, as also in the fifteenth-century grant by Gwallter ap Gourwared Vawr of Bayville, the sealing clause in this instance suggesting, if not absolutely confirming, that the seal was his own (see figure 3.14).[47] Elsewhere, as at Swansea at the beginning of the sixteenth century, a number of impressions with merchant marks appear in validation of the finding of an inquest regarding inheritance, suggestive of the shared role of respected local merchants.[48] Mercantile dealing throughout medieval Europe required both speed and certainty;[49] these principles, increasingly supported in the Middle Ages through the development of a distinct law merchant (*lex mercatoria*), both encouraged and on occasion worked against the use of seals. A fair amount of mercantile dealing, as we have seen and discussed for other sections of medieval society in terms of exchange, was as, and sometimes more, reliant upon word of mouth; seals in support of complex deals conducted often over long distance were common but merchants also relied upon 'lesser' forms of proof including a combination of witnesses and tallies (though the latter were also sometimes sealed).[50] That said, it is of course clear that merchants did use sealed bonds and the widespread survival of seals and impressions carrying merchant marks attests to this, as does the evidence of contemporary records, both in terms of bonds but also litigation over sealed contracts.

Of course, one further feature of the exchange of sealed motifs and an explanation of their apparent concentration within a local context is the localised or regionalised production and circulation of particular seals, perhaps produced by local seal makers.[51] Rodney Hilton noted, in an initial and brief examination of seals attached to Gloucester Abbey leases, that there was a fairly consistent resort to radial designs and pondered but did not closely explore the potential influence of Bristol merchants, their seals and the availability of their matrices on the choices made by later thirteenth-century Gloucestershire peasants in choosing their own seal designs.[52] As well as shared motifs, other intrinsic features are sometimes evident, not least quality. While the kinds of motifs within a locale or family grouping might be quite distinctive and without consistent pattern in terms of design, there is sometimes evidence of a consistency of high-quality seal making within a particular location suggestive of the shared commitment to possess seals of high-quality design and which were capable of displaying the individual choices made by seal owners in commissioning seals. Finally, and in ways that cannot easily be gleaned from the material available to us given that the source base is dominated by sealed documents of various kinds, but which refer us back to issues discussed in the previous chapter on law administration and seal usage, it is also the case that legal advice regarding the use of seals was also exchanged and traded. Advice on when to employ seals and when not, the particular contexts in which they should be used, as well as the correct approach to seal usage, must have informed all such dealing in the Middle Ages and would have been information capable of being exchanged, whether in a market context or an institutional one. Such informed choices are central to the discussion in the following chapters.

Notes

1. G. C. G. Thomas (ed.), *The charters of the Abbey of Ystrad Marchell* (Aberystwyth, 1997), pp. 40–6.
2. *Margam*, pp. 131–47; on the subtle development of devices reflecting both continuity and change in lineage, see, for instance, B. Kemp, 'Family identity: the seals of the Longespées', in P. R. Schofield (ed.), *Seals and their Context in the Middle Ages* (Oxford, 2015), pp. 137–50.
3. E. A. New, '(Un)conventional images. A case-study of radial motifs on personal seals', in P. R. Schofield (ed.), *Seals and their Context in the Middle Ages* (Oxford, 2015), pp. 151–60.
4. NLW PENRICE: GLAM/379.
5. SHA 972/1/1/432.
6. NLW PENRICE: GLAM/2798; 183.
7. For further discussion of this point and relevant references, see P. R. Schofield, 'The market in free land on the estates of Bury St Edmunds: sources and issues', in L. Feller and C. Wickham (eds), *Le marché de la terre au Moyen Âge* (Rome, 2005), pp. 273–95. See also M. Yates, 'The market in freehold land, 1300–1509: the evidence of feet of fines', *Economic History Review*, 66 (2013), 579–600.
8. BUAS MOST/715.
9. BUAS MOST/731; for discussion of the same see A. D. Carr, *Medieval Anglesey* (Llangefni, 1982), pp. 177–8; also Ll. B. Smith, 'The gage and the land market in late medieval Wales', *Economic History Review*, 29 (1976), 537–50. For further instances, see for example BUAS MOST/718 where a term of four years is also given and the grantor 'gives, concedes and gages [*impignoravi*]'. On gages of similar kind and more generally, see J. M. Kaye, *Medieval English Conveyances* (Cambridge, 2009), pp. 274–5.
10. On this point, see also P. R. Schofield, 'Peasant debt in English manorial courts: form and nature', in J-M. Claustre (ed.), *Endettement privé et justice au Moyen Age* (Paris, 2007), pp. 55–67; P. R. Schofield, 'Seals and the peasant economy in England and Marcher Wales, c.1300', in S. Solway (ed.), *Medieval Coins and Seals: Constructing Identity, Signifying Power* (Turnhout, 2015), pp. 347–58.
11. E. Miller and J. Hatcher, *Medieval England: Rural Economy and Society, 1086–1348* (Abingdon, 1978), pp. 114–15; P. R. Hyams, *Kings, Lords and Peasants in Medieval England* (Oxford, 1980), pp. 3–5. There are also instances from the fifteenth century for England, as discussed in M. Bailey, *The Decline of Serfdom in Late Medieval England. From Bondage to Freedom* (Woodbridge, 2014), pp. 62–5. On the evidence for later sales in Wales, see in particular, Carr, *Medieval Anglesey*, pp. 129–31.
12. BUAS PENR/219; see also BUAS PENR 407 for a similar instance from December 1330.
13. Carr, *Medieval Anglesey*, pp. 130–1.
14. For recent discussion of which, see Schofield, 'Seals and the peasant economy'.
15. NLW WIGFAIR/627. See also the enrolled charter of manumission in the court at Ruthin, 3 November 1394, TNA SC 220/9, m.34.
16. Peacocks and lilies are also discussed in chapter 7 below. The image of peacocks flanking a tree or plant is a well-used motif in Islamic, Asian and eastern Mediterranean art from the Middle Ages and is consistent with depictions of the 'tree of life'; see, for instance, G. Lechler, 'The tree of life in Indo-European and Islamic cultures', *Ars Islamica*, 4 (1937), 369–419.
17. NLW PITORD/126.
18. A search of 'bond' for seals catalogued in TNA Duchy of Lancaster DL 25 and DL 26 at *http://www.nationalarchives.gov.uk/records/research-guides/seals.htm* (last accessed 23 June 2015) indicates that 3.8 per cent (179 of 4,605) entries were identified as bonds.

19 GACRO Vaynol/Glan/1391 and 1394. Some bonds from this period include a Latin description of the bond followed by a condition or endorsement written in English, as for instance GACRO Vaynol/Glan/ 1398, and 1402; also NLW BRONWYDD/1155; on this see also A. D. Carr,' "This is my act and deed": the writing of private deeds in late medieval north Wales', in H. Pryce (ed.), *Literacy in Medieval Celtic Societies*, Cambridge Studies in Medieval Literature, 33 (Cambridge, 1998), p. 232.
20 NLW PENRICE: GLAM/348. There may though have been some inaccurate ordering of the seals relative to the written identification on the tongue as the merchant mark includes the initials 'T' and 'B', possibly standing for Thomas Bassett, the third recipient of the loan. Further, the other seal carries the motif of a pelican in its piety and is a seal used by William Bassett in a separate agreement with Resio Maunsell, NLW PENRICE: GLAM/, 20 January 1515.
21 See introduction and chapter 2 above.
22 See chapter 2; see also C. Briggs and P. Schofield, *Select Pleas in Manorial Courts* (Selden Society, forthcoming).
23 Dogfeiling, court of 6 June 1342, ap Madog v. Goh, TNA, SC 217/7, m.27.
24 See above in this chapter. See also above in chapter 2.
25 For which see chapter 2.
26 M. P. Siddons, 'Welsh equestrian seals', *National Library of Wales Journal*, 23 (1983–4); see also chapters 1, 2, 4 and 5.
27 See, for example, N. Vincent, 'The seals of King Henry II and his court', in Schofield (ed.), *Seals and their Context*, pp. 7–33; see also, for instance, chapter 7.
28 R. H. Hilton, 'Gloucester Abbey leases of the thirteen century', *University of Birmingham Historical Journal*, iv (1953–4).
29 E. A. New, 'Lleision ap Morgan makes an impression: seals and the study of medieval Wales', *Welsh History Review*, 27:1 (2013), pp. 338–9.
30 E. A. New, '(Un)conventional images'.
31 See also chapters 4 and 5, for instance.
32 Seal 125.
33 New, 'Lleision ap Morgan', 338–41; *Seliau*, pp. 78–80.
34 Roger Sturmi junior, 1193 x 1218, NLW PENRICE: GLAM/1986 (Seal 1503); Roger Sturmi, 1234: BL Harl. Ch75 D 5 (Seal 98). On early Sturmi grants to Margam, see also *Margam*, pp. 77–81. For discussion of BL Harl. Ch75 D 5, see *Margam*, p. 245. Birch (*Margam*) describes the Roger Sturmi of this charter as 'a late member of the family'.
35 William Sturmi, son of William Sturmi, BL Harl. Ch75 D 6 (Seal 99); also, *Margam*, p. 288, describes the motif as a 'rose of twelve points' but the variety of forms including apparent rods or crossings intersecting the foliage looks to reflect features of the earlier Sturmi seals. See Seals 1503 (detail) and 99.
36 Seal 2470.
37 Seal 2461; *Guide*, p. 118.
38 PAS LVPL-A17C66.
39 Seals 2471, 2472, 2474. See chapter 1.
40 Seal 427 and 428. See the numerous other instances of monogrammed seals also in CALS DLL/4: seals 431, 432, 434, 437, 438.
41 See, for instance, Seals 262, 278, 281.
42 Seals 1577 (1279), 1638 (1301), 1901 (1302/3), 2004 (1304/5), 1826 (1306/7), 1904 (1314), 1746 (1323), 1816 (1339), 1683 (1343), 1591 (1344). Date of associated document in brackets.

43 See for evidence of matrices with the same device, PAS Unique ID: IHS-E338C1 *https://finds. org.uk/database/artefacts/record/id/105546* (last accessed 19 March 2015). This motif compares very closely with Seal 1577.
44 See, for instance, Seals 1791, 1838, 1876.
45 See above, p. 54.
46 NLW PENRICE: GLAM/1993.
47 NLW BRONWYDD/1332.
48 Seals 1372, 1373 and 1374.
49 On lex mercatoria, see, for instance, J. Davis, *Medieval Market Morality. Life, Law and Ethics in the English Marketplace, 1200–1500* (Cambridge, 2012), pp. 207–11; see also the introduction to C. Gross (ed.), *Select Cases Concerning the Law Merchant. Vol. 1. Local Courts*, 23 (Selden Society, 1908).
50 On bonds in medieval trade, see M. M. Postan, 'Private financial instruments in medieval England', *Vierteljahrschrift für Sozial und Wirtschaftsgeschichte*, 22 (1930), reprinted in M. M. Postan, *Medieval Trade and Finance* (Cambridge, 1973), pp. 28–64, at pp. 33–4. Postan ponders the possibility that the use of sealed bonds in Britain, and more particularly England as the subject of his discussion, distinguished it from continental Europe where documents authenticated by notary were more common; on this same comparative point but set within a different context, see also C. Briggs, *Credit and Village Society in Fourteenth-Century England* (Oxford, 2009), pp. 95–9.
51 As also discussed in more detail in chapter 7.
52 Hilton, 'Gloucester Abbey leases'.

ECCLESIASTICAL SEALS

Elizabeth A. New

THE SEALS DISCUSSED in this chapter are the impressions of matrices that represented Church institutions, offices and personnel. Such seals, whether in the form of matrices, impressions or casts, are among the most widely recorded and best known seals from medieval Britain, with those from Wales particularly well documented.[1] The seals of ecclesiastics and religious institutions are however usually studied by 'type', according to owner or principal motif (the two frequently coinciding), or as part of an investigation of Church bureaucracy.[2] Here, instead, the emphasis will be upon what the seals and their use can reveal about the Church and faith in contemporary society.

(i) The international Church

Impressions of the seals of popes and papal officials, cardinals, archbishops and bishops, archdeacons, rural deans and their deputies, cathedral chapters and royal free chapels, along with hospitals, monastic and mendicant houses of varying sizes and orders, are all found attached to documents from Wales and the English border counties, providing an important reminder of the role of the medieval Church as a landholder, legal adjudicator and fulcrum of economic and social exchange. Many of the ecclesiastical officials and institutions were from different parts of Britain, and indeed from across Europe, while the Cistercians and some other religious orders looked overseas for ultimate authority, emphasising not only the Church's international nature but also that areas often seen as the 'periphery' were not in fact isolated from wider affairs or long-distance exchange.³ This can perhaps be seen most clearly though papal bulla, where the head of the Catholic Church intervened in or adjudicated upon sometimes very local affairs. Innocent III (1198–1216) twice confirmed grants and gifts made to Margam Abbey (Glamorgan), while Clement IV (1265–68) literally gave the seal of approval to an agreement made between Margam and Tewkesbury abbeys regarding the church of St Leonard in Newcastle (Glamorgan).⁴ The bulla that sanctioned the transfer of the patronage of the church of Afan (Glamorgan) to Margam Abbey provides a poignant insight into a society reeling from the plague that ravaged Britain during the fourteenth century, with the authorisation of Urban VI (1378–1389) stating that this was the result of effects of pestilence 'and other calamities'.⁵ However, two more papal bulla give a somewhat different view of southern Wales in the late fourteenth and early fifteenth centuries. A 1394 bull of Boniface IX (1389–1404) ordered the abbot of Neath to excommunicate all those who had 'concealed or detained' property, land or tithes from Margam Abbey, while the head of that abbey was in return instructed by Martin V (1417–31) to excommunicate the people who had 'injured or despoiled' Neath Abbey by cutting down groves, withholding tithes or other nefarious activities.⁶ The inference of these papal interventions clearly is that these neighbouring Cistercian houses were ignoring misdemeanours committed against each other, and that it required a firm hand from Rome to correct a problem in distant south Wales.

It is not only Cistercian seals that provide evidence of the Church in Wales and the English border counties as part of a national and international network. In common with many religious houses, Margam Abbey controlled property beyond its immediate environs, including lands held of Bath Abbey in the Somerset parish of Keynsham.⁷ The document confirming this arrangement took the form of a cyrograph, with Margam's extant copy validated with the impressions of the seals of both Bath Abbey (rare evidence of an eleventh-century matrix) and Robert of Lewes, Bishop of Bath (1136–66).⁸ Strictly speaking, only the abbey's conventual seal was required as corroboration, but it has been noted that this was a period of jurisdictional uncertainty and that Margam was therefore 'well advised' to ensure that it secured a seal of validation from any individual or institution that might lay claim to the property in question.⁹

Also relevant to a discussion of how seals can add to our appreciation of the Church as an international organisation are two documents that bear impressions of previously unrecorded seals relating to the Order of St Anthony of Vienne. The Order comprised a network of hospitals under the leadership of the priory of Vienne in south-eastern France, with a cell established in London in the 1240s.¹⁰ In 1243 Henry III gave the London hospital the advowson of All Saints, Hereford, although it was not until 1261 that the rector, Richard le Brun, resigned the living.¹¹ The document in which Brother Anselm, Preceptor General in England of the Hospital of St Anthony,¹² confirmed receipt of the advowson, was sealed by both Brother Anselm and Peter of Aigueblanche, Bishop of Hereford (1240–68), at the bishop's palace of Whitbourne, demonstrating that the royal gift was important enough for the preceptor to travel some distance to ensure its secure receipt (see figure 4.1).[13] The international nature of the Church is also reflected in the iconography of Brother Anselm's seal (see figure 4.2). The principal image shows Anthony's visit to Paul the Hermit with a raven descending with food for the holy men, an image found in Coptic art, on the eighth-century Northumbrian Ruthwell Cross and Pictish Nigg and St Vigeans Stones, and in the early thirteenth century windows of Chartres Cathedral, among other places.[14] Despite this wide geographical distribution, the image appears to have been quite unusual in medieval England and Wales, where the figure of Anthony with a Tau cross, often accompanied by a pig, was far more common.[15] It was however appropriate for a hospital dedicated to providing care and sustenance for the needy, and may have provided Brother Anselm with the opportunity for recounting the legend to those asked about the seal imagery.

Almost 200 years later, in 1442, John, son of Richard de Leigh, and his wife Johanna, received letters of confraternity issued by John Carpenter, Master of the House of St Anthony of Vienne in London.[16] The letters were sealed in Chester, so this may be evidence of a fundraising mission by Carpenter himself, rather than the more usual practice of farming the right to collect offerings to local agents.[17] The seal impression is fragmentary, but the figure of St Anthony with his Tau cross and a pig, can still clearly be discerned, images that may well have acted as a devotional aide-mémoire for John and Johanna, especially if they or someone to whom they showed the document could not read the text.[18] The sealed indulgence was preserved among the family papers, a rare survival of what would have been quite a common type of document. It also provides evidence of the international nature of the late medieval spiritual economy, with a gentry family from the Marches gaining remission of their sins from the pope in Rome, via the London house of what was originally a French religious order.[19]

Two more sealed instruments provide a reminder that the secular clergy, and not only the religious orders, brought an international dimension to local affairs. Among the Penrhyn Castle Papers in Bangor University Archives is a dispensation issued in 1480 by Julius (Giuliano Della Rovere, later Pope Julius II, d.1513), cardinal-bishop of Sabina and papal penitentiary, to William Gruffith and Joan, widow of William Butler, legitimising a marriage contract made by them in the diocese of Coventry and Lichfield.[20] The impression of the cardinal-bishop's seal was made into a cake of red wax that had been set in a frame of uncoloured wax, and was placed in a metal skippet (see figure 4.3). The overall effect, when the document was unfolded and the skippet opened, would have added to the sense of occasion and, perhaps, carried a note of the exotic (the shield and crest are clearly Italian in style), amid the legal implications of the instrument.[21]

(ii) The Church and the laity

While the ecclesiastical seals from across western Europe found their way into Wales and the English border counties, seals and sealing practices more often reveal insights about the Church on a local basis, especially in relation to interactions between churchmen and religious institutions and the laity.

Only five years before Della Rovere approved the union of William and Joan, a cleric far lower down the rungs of ecclesiastical administration and much closer to home sealed another marriage-related document. This time, however, it was Robert Pennarth, commissary of the bishop of St Asaph, who was validating the annulment, on grounds of sexual misconduct and consanguinity, of the marriage of Thomas ap Dafydd Says and Margaret verch Dafydd ap Iollyn.[22] The document would probably have made uncomfortable reading or listening for Thomas and Margaret, but the fragmentary seal impression provides us with valuable information about aspirations to status and the development of heraldry in north Wales at this time, for a shield with a griffin *statant* is clearly visible.[23]

Seals and sealing practices reveal insights into the legal processes related to probate as well as marriage. Four documents in the project dataset bear the (now fragmentary) impressions of the seal of the 'dean of Chester'. Probate for the will of Richard le Bruyn senior was granted under this official seal in 1337, and the same matrix was used forty years later to grant probate for the will of Alice, widow of Richard le Bruyn (possibly the kinsman named in the will of Richard senior), and then to release Alice's executors from further business in connection with the administration of her will.[24] Over a century later, in 1496, the impression of a different matrix, albeit of almost identical design, authorised a William Meylys to administer the goods and chattels of Elisabeth Meylys.[25] The dean in question was head of the collegiate church of St John, Chester, but although the importance of this ancient church is widely recognised by scholars, its exemption from the jurisdiction of the archdeacon of Chester, claimed as early as 1318 but not officially confirmed until 1542, is rarely discussed.[26] The sealed instruments provide important evidence about the active exercise of the independence claimed by the dean of St John's. It is also interesting to note that the sigillographic motif was secular; a garb (wheatsheaf, heraldic symbol of Chester) within a crenellated architectural surround. Was this perhaps a deliberate attempt to establish a legal identity in the face of opposition, or perhaps a reminder to those within the deaconal jurisdiction that in this context the relationship was first and foremost an administrative one?

Another minor ecclesiastic administrating an area of peculiar jurisdiction was the Official of the Dean of Bridgnorth, and here, too, surviving seal impressions and the use of the seal provide significant evidence for low-level interaction between the Church and the laity.[27] The collegiate church of St Mary Magdalene, Bridgnorth, was a royal free chapel with jurisdiction over several parishes in Shropshire, with a regular court held to deal with legal and administrative matters.[28] Records from the court are extant only for the period 1472–1523, but by studying surviving sealed documents it is possible to gain an insight into its activities, and the important role the Official played in local life.[29] The matrix of the seal of the Official would appear to have been engraved by an accomplished craftsman, perhaps, on stylistic grounds, in the later thirteenth century (see figure 4.4).[30] The seal of the Official was used for a range of administrative activities, such as grants of probate, including for the wills of Robert at Gate (*ad Portam*), clerk, in 1326, Walter Bagod in 1341, and Thomas '*dictus cognomina Robard*' of Bridgnorth in 1349,[31] and to validate a copy of the will of Robert de Pitchford, originally made in 1349, when it was brought before the court in order to confirm its legal validity.[32] In 1316 it was attached to the will of Christina, widow of William Canne of Bridgnorth, an item that may be a probate copy of the will.[33] It is however possible that Christina borrowed the matrix because she had no seal of her own and, if so, it suggests that the Official may on occasion have taken on a role usually filled by a parish priest by assisting the laity when making their wills.[34] The dean and prebendaries of Bridgnorth were supposed to provide curates to serve the community, but there is evidence that pastoral provision was often neglected, perhaps explaining why an ecclesiastical administrator might have felt compelled to fulfil a more pastoral role.[35]

Although a fairly minor cog in the bureaucratic wheels of the Church, the Official was, in the absence of senior clerics, also required to administer more complex cases, such as adjudicating on the wishes of Edmund de Pitchford with regard to his estate.[36] Edmund died intestate when he was 'feloniously killed' by John Pulley (Pohley), a painter,[37] but his widow, Alice, came before the court along with Brother Robert of Facham, a Franciscan who had been her husband's confessor, who swore that Edmund had intended to leave his goods and property to Alice once his debts had been paid and his illegitimate daughter Agnes provided for. The Official clearly accepted this, since he appended his seal as validation to the record of the case, although in this instance probate was granted by the commissary of the bishop of Hereford, presumably because Edmund held lands or property outside the area of peculiar jurisdiction.[38]

Above and beyond the validation of wills and granting of probate, the Official could be called upon to append his seal to documents as a means of additional authentication in cases where the principal parties wanted to ensure that a transaction could not easily be challenged. This was often connected with the honouring of the wishes of testators, such as the 1338 grant of a barn in Bridgnorth by William of Rudge and Simon Dod, executors of the will of Adam of Scheynton.[39] In this instance, William and Simon may have been especially keen to obtain an impression of the Official's seal, since they both used 'anonymous' matrices that could more easily have been challenged than those with name legends.[40]

This validation by the Official of what was in effect a property transfer is a reminder that seals and sealing practices provide important evidence for interactions between ecclesiastics and laity in economic terms. The Church was a major landholder, and impressions of seals representing religious institutions and officials survive appended to property deeds of various kinds. A number of the extant impressions of the common seal of Margam Abbey are, for example, appended to grants and leases, such as the 1484 lease of the revision of the grange of Hafodheulog to John ap Thomas ap Richard and Richard his brother, after the death of their father.[41] In a similar manner, the seal of John of Chetwynd (1308x30), Abbot of Lilleshall Abbey (Shropshire), validated a cyrograph made between the abbey and Roger Appeleye and Alice his wife relating to property in Welshpool, Powys, the fragmentary impression on the cyrograph being the only known impression of Chetywnd's seal.[42] While the lands and property in the previous examples were reasonably close to the grantor's house, seal impressions attached to some property deeds speak of ecclesiastical landholding on a national and even international scale. Thus, the lease of a fourth part of the township of Twemlowe (Cheshire), with one section assart, made to Reginald Brun in the second quarter of the thirteenth century was validated with impressions of the seal matrices of the Hospital of St John of Jerusalem in England and its then master, Prior Terricus de Nussa, since the Hospitallers held the land in question.[43]

As demonstrated by the seal of the Official of the Dean of Bridgnorth, seals of Church institutions and personnel were sometimes used to provide additional corroboration for transactions in which they were not directly involved. This might be because the principal sigillant was from a distant location, was using an unfamiliar matrix, or did not have a matrix of their own.[44] When Nicholas of 'Bremesberg' (?Bramburgh) granted a piece of land in Hereford to William Roc, chaplain, he impressed his own finely engraved seal matrix in validation, but he also asked the dean and chapter to corroborate by impressing their seal matrices.[45] The land in question was part of the dowry of his wife Helisend, daughter of William Albus of Hereford, so Nicholas may have wanted the additional security in case of a dispute over land acquired through marriage, or perhaps because he was from outside the city and marrying into an established Hereford family.

A most unusual type of ecclesiastical seal was used to validate what would otherwise have been a fairly standard grant in frankalmoin by Phillip, parson of Kinnersley (Herefordshire), to the newly founded hospital of St Ethelbert in Hereford.[46] As was usual for a grant in free alms, Phillip requested prayers for himself and his ancestors and successors in return for an annual gift of grain, and confirmed the documentary record with 'my seal' (*sigillo meo confirmatio*). The attached impression suggests a very finely engraved matrix, quite large at 25 millimetres in diameter, with a beautifully rendered scallop shell as the central motif (see figure 4.5). This image and the accompanying legend, *SECRET' P'SON [. . . . .]ARDES[.]'*, identify the seal as representing not Phillip as an individual, however, but the role he filled as parson of Kinnersley (the church was dedicated to St James the Great, one of whose symbols was a scallop shell). The seal matrix may well have been commissioned by, or considered the personal possession of, Phillip, but it functioned as a seal of office and could have been used by other parish priests. Furthermore, the term 'secret (seal)' was commonly used on matrices that were usually employed as subsidiary to another, larger or more formal, matrix, suggesting the possibility of another seal that represented the parish or its incumbent. Seals from medieval England and Wales that represented either a parish as a unit, or its incumbent in a generic manner, are exceptionally unusual, with only fourteen others having so far been identified.[47] Moreover, apart from an ambivalent cartulary reference, the secret seal of the parson of Kinnersley predates all other known parochial seals by approximately a century.[48] In the early thirteenth century the settlement of Kinnersley was within the parish of Leominster, itself a possession of Reading Abbey, but was later to emerge as a parish in its own right.[49] It is therefore tempting to speculate whether the acquisition of a seal to represent the parson was part of a move to establish a greater degree of independence for the church and its community.

The parson of Kinnersley's grant of free alms is a reminder that many ecclesiastical seals were employed to authenticate documents related to pious acts and spiritual matters as well as legal and economic exchange. A concentration of mid-thirteenth-century episcopal seals from across England and Wales found in the archives of the Dean and Chapter of Hereford are for example the result of the foundation of St Ethelbert's Hospital. Presumably part of a fundraising drive, no fewer than eight bishops issued indulgences to those contributing to the building of the hospital, all validated with their episcopal seal of dignity and, in most cases, a subsidiary seal.[50] The result is a valuable collection of episcopal seals from the 1220s and 1230s, including examples of the introduction of new features, such as the small sunken panels flanking the figure of the ecclesiastic on the seal of Edmund of Abingdon, Archbishop of Canterbury (1223–40),[51] details that may have influenced or been influenced by other seals,[52] and an image that may provide evidence of a lost building (the spire on the west tower of Ely Cathedral, represented on the subsidiary seal of Bishop Hugh of Northwold (1229–54)).[53]

(iii) Devotion and identity

The iconographic details of the episcopal seals attached to the St Ethelbert's Hospital indulgences are a reminder that ecclesiastical seals provide important evidence of both spiritual exchange and seals as vehicles for the expression of identity and devotion.

While most religious houses appear to have been reasonably free to decide what imagery and wording to employ on their seals, the Cistercian order was concerned about how its houses should be represented, and in 1200 the General Chapter ruled that all seals should depict either an abbot with a pastoral staff (the 'effigy' type) or a hand holding the staff.[54] David H. Williams has carefully documented the use of both motifs on the seals of Welsh Cistercian houses, while the strict conformity to the pattern can further be seen through impressions of seals from Cistercian houses from England and France that are preserved in archives across Wales and the borders.[55] An arbitration in 1208 of a dispute between Neath and Margam abbeys was, for example, sealed by the abbots of Fountains (Yorkshire), Warden (Bedfordshire) and Boxley (Kent), with all the seals being of the 'effigy' type.[56] The Warden seal is of particular note, since it does not appear previously to have been recorded in the public domain, and demonstrates that the abbey possessed two different matrices between its foundation in 1136 and 1208.[57] The 'hand and staff' image is also represented among the Margam Abbey documents, including a 1249 impression of the seal of the mother house of Clairvaux (Champagne, France).[58] Margam Abbey itself reflects changes to Cistercian sealing practices enforced by the 1307 Statute of Carlisle, which required religious houses to have a common seal, and the Constitution of the Reform of the Cistercian Order issued by Pope Benedict XII in 1335, which also included an injunction ordering the acquisition of a common seal (earlier Cistercian seals technically represented the abbot rather than the community).[59] The 'hand and staff' abbatical seal of Margam was, as a result, supplemented by a communal seal with the same motif, although this was quickly abandoned in favour of one with the image of the Virgin and Child, conforming to the 1335 General Chapter ruling that the new common seals should all depict the Virgin Mary.[60]

While the Cistercian seals present corporate identity in a highly regulated manner, two sets of seal impressions attached to documents in the Pitchford Hall collection show ecclesiastical institutions and officials creating highly individualised visual expressions of identity, and ones that, moreover, provide insights into local or personal devotion and theological interpretation. The first set of seals was used to validate the 1333 licence for a daily mass to be said by the Franciscans of Bridgnorth on behalf of Nicholas de Pitchford (Pitchford, Shropshire), Joan his wife, and their parents.[61] Nicholas was provost of Bridgnorth in 1302 and owned land and property in the town, clearly a well-to-do burgess seeking spiritual support to complement his worldly success.[62] One half of the indented licence, complete with a decorated initial, was carefully preserved among the family archive, and retains one fragmentary and one almost complete impression of the three that were originally attached.[63] The fragment is from the matrix of the Minister of the Franciscans in England, at that time Roger of Denemede,[64] and depicts the head of Christ in a small niche, a kneeling figure in the main part of the image, and the head and shoulders of a suppliant tonsured figure in the base. The main image almost certainly depicted the martyrdom of St Thomas of Canterbury, since this scene, with the head of God above, appears on three other seals of provincial ministers.[65] In iconographic terms it is very similar to the seal of Roger Marston, provincial minister 1292–8, supporting a suggestion that English provincial ministers employed personalised seals of office.[66]

The other surviving impression on the 1333 Pitchford licence is that of the seal of the Worcester Franciscans, in whose Custody the Bridgnorth house lay.[67] The matrix was obviously engraved by an accomplished craftsman, probably in the late thirteenth century, but it is the iconography that makes this seal so remarkable (see figure 4.6).

It depicts Christ carrying the cross, but instead of the usual plain wood it is quite clearly ragged, and closely resembles the 'flourishing' cross employed in a number of thirteenth- and fourteenth-century Crucifixions.[68] The 'flourishing' cross was a symbol of the new life offered through Christ's death and Resurrection, which makes sense in the context of the Crucifixion, but it is much more difficult to explain earlier in the Passion sequence.[69] St Bonaventure, the great Franciscan theologian, wrote a meditation on the *Lignum vitae*, but the imagery is again restricted to Christ's death on the cross.[70] It is possible that the seal-engraver simply decided on a whim to depict the cross as undressed timber, or had seen a 'flourishing' cross Crucifixion and transferred this to the earlier Passion scene, but such an unusual detail is far more likely to be a deliberate choice on the part of the patron. The Worcester Franciscans, perhaps inspired by Bonaventure's writing, may have decided that the redemptive power of Christ's blood, first spilled at the scourging, made the cross flourish even before Calvary, or could have been influenced by the typological roundels in Worcester Cathedral Chapter House, where the images of Aaron's rod flourishing in the Temple and the Crucifixion are explicitly connected through accompanying verses.[71] The imagery on the seal of the Worcester Franciscans is exceptionally rare and may even be unique, and its meaning remains ambiguous.[72] It is also tempting to speculate whether the friars took the opportunity afforded by witnesses to the act of sealing to expound upon the iconography, thus explaining to Nicholas and Joan and other contemporaries a nuanced meaning now lost.

Four years after this licence was granted, the scale of what was in effect the Pitchford's chantry was expanded, the indenture granting this again preserved among the family archives. This document, which simply increased liturgical provision rather than establishing a new commitment, did not require the seal of the provincial minister, but was instead authenticated with the common seal of the Bridgnorth Franciscans and their Guardian.[73] The central image of the common seal is the Virgin and Child flanked by Mary Magdalene to the left and an archiepiscopal saint to the right, with a shield of arms (England) below (see figure 4.7). The royal arms and presence of the Magdalene probably reflect the Royal Free Chapel of St Mary Magdalene in Bridgnorth, which dominated the town. The dedication of this chapel may also have influenced the choice of iconography for the seal of the Guardian, the Risen Christ appearing to Mary Magdalene (John 20:14–18), a scene closely associated with devotion to that saint (see figure 4.8).[74] Once again, the imagery may also have provided an opportunity for teaching or a devotional discussion, and, at the very least, the impressions in bright red wax of finely engraved matrices would have made the indenture a visually striking, as well as spiritually significant, document.

Impressions of the seals that represented Church institutions, offices and personnel were attached to a wide range of documents from medieval Wales and the English border counties. They provide insights into, among other things, the Church as an international organisation, its role in a plethora of legal and administrative affairs, ecclesiastical interaction with the laity on a secular and spiritual basis, representation and identity, and theological and devotional matters. They contribute to our understanding of ecclesiastical institutions and churchmen as an integral part of the society and economy in medieval Wales and England, and act as a reminder that religious sensibilities and devotional practices made an impression on contemporary culture in many different ways.

Notes

1   See, for example, W. de Gray Birch, *Catalogue of Seals in the Department of Manuscripts in the British Museum*, 6 vols (London, 1887–1900), nos 1169–4578; W. St John Hope, 'The seals of English bishops', *Proceedings of the Society of Antiquaries*, 2nd ser., 11 (1885–1887), 271–306; R. H. Ellis, *Catalogue of Seals in the Public Record Office: Monastic Seals* (London, 1986); D. H. Williams, 'Catalogue of Welsh ecclesiastical seals as known down to 1600 AD. Part IV. Seals of Cistercian monestaries', *Archaeologia Cambrensis*, cxxxvi (1987), 133–8; J. P. Dalton, *The Archiepiscopal and Deputed Seals of York, 1114–1500*, Borthwick Texts and Calendars 17 (York, 1992); D. H. Williams, *Catalogue of Seals in the National Museum of Wales. Vol 2: Ecclesiastical, Monastic and Collegiate Seals with a Supplement Concerning Wales* (Cardiff, 1998); D. H. Williams, 'Medieval Cistercian seals with special reference to "hand-and-staff" seals', *Archaeologia Cambrensis*, 154 (2007 for 2005), 153–78.
2   The *English Episcopal Acta* volumes all include a note of the episcopal seals as part of the form and diplomatic of the acta, for example.
3   Discussions of the idea of 'centre' and 'periphery', especially in relation to Wales, include, among others, A. D. Carr, 'Inside the tent looking out: the medieval Welsh world-view', in R. R. Davies and G. H. Jenkins (eds), *From Medieval to Modern Wales: Historical Essays in Honour of Kenneth O. Morgan and Ralph A. Griffiths* (Cardiff, 2004), pp. 30–44; R. Bartlett, 'Heartland and border: the mental and physical geography of medieval Europe', in H. Pryce and J. Watts (eds), *Power and Identity in the Middle Ages. Essays in Memory of Rees Davies* (Oxford, 2007), pp. 23–36.
4   NLW PENRICE: GLAM/83 and NLW PENRICE: GLAM/84 (Seal 1183), *Scriptorium*, no. 78 (Innocent III's confirmations); NLW PENRICE: GLAM/185 (Seal 1268), Patterson, *Scriptorium*, no. 79 (Clement IV).
5   NLW PENRICE: GLAM/236 (Seal 1318); D. H. Williams, *Images of Welsh History* (Aberystwyth, 2007), p. 41, fig. 126.
6   NLW PENRICE: GLAM/238 (Boniface IX's bull; Seal 1320); NLW PENRICE: GLAM/245 (Martin V's bull; Seal 1325).
7   BL Harl. Ch 75 A 30 (Seal 25); Patterson, *Scriptorium*, no. 306, dates the document to c.1157x66; M. F. Ramsey (ed.), *English Episcopal Acta X. Bath and Wells, 1061–1205* (Oxford, 1995), p. xcii, dates it to *c*.1151.
8   Bath Abbey: Seal 26; Birch 1437; G. Zarnecki, J. Holt and T. Holland (eds), *English Romanesque Art 1066–1200* (London, 1984), no. 348 (entry by T. A. Heslop); Bishop Roger: Seal 25; Birch 1409 (referencing a cast), Zarnecki, Holt and Holland (eds), *English Romanesque Art*, no. 343 (entry by T. A. Heslop), Ramsey (ed.), *EEA. X Bath and Wells*, p. xcii, plate I.

9   Zarnecki, Holt and Holland (eds), *English Romanesque Art*, no. 343 (entry by T. A. Heslop).
10 D. K. Maxfield, 'St Anthony's Hospital, London: a pardoner-supported alien priory, 1219–1461', in J. L. Gillespie (ed.), *The Age of Richard II* (Stroud, 1997), pp. 225–47; D. Lewis, 'The Hospital of St Anthony [of Vienne]', in C. M. Barron and M. Davies (eds), *The Religious Houses of London and Middlesex* (London, 2007), pp. 228–31.
11 R. Graham, 'The Order of St Antoine de Viennois and its English commandery in Threadneedle Street', *Archaeological Journal*, 84:1 (1927), 341–406, at 349, 351.
12 Anselm does not appear in the list of 'Masters or Wardens' of the hospital provided in Lewis, 'Hospital of St Anthony', p. 231, and is not mentioned by name in Graham, 'Order of St Antoine'.
13 HCA Deed 1084, Seal 1 (Bishop Peter; Seal 845) and 2 (Seal 846). This impression of Aigueblanche's subsidiary seal does not appear previously to have been noted, since it is not in Birch, the Morgans's list, or the list of known impressions provided in Julia Barrow (ed.), *English Episcopal Acta 35. Hereford, 1234–1275* (Oxford, 2009), pp. xcviii–xcix.
14 W. Dalrymple, *From The Holy Mountain: A Journey in the Shadow of Byzantium*, rev. edn (London, 2011), pp. 418–22; A. F. Saxl, 'The Ruthwell Cross', *Journal of the Warburg and Courtauld Institutes*, 6 (1943), 1–19, at 3, plate 1c; M. Carver, 'Sculpture in action: contexts for stone carving on the Tarbat peninsula, Easter Ross', in S. M. Foster and M. Cross (eds), *Able Minds and Practiced Hands: Scotland's Early Medieval Sculpture in the 21st Century* (Leeds, 2005), pp. 13–36, 24, 28 (Anthony and Paul appear on St Vigeans 7); the window at Chartres is illustrated and discussed at *www.medievalart.org.uk/chartres/030b_pages/Chartres_Bay030b_Panel15.htm* (last accessed 15 December 2014); image © Dr Stuart Whatling.
15 Depictions of St Anthony with a Tau cross and pig are found in glass in the church of St Nicholas, Stanford on Avon (Northamptonshire), and on painted screens at Smallburgh and Tacolneston, Norfolk, and Westhall, Suffolk. See, for example, K. Ayre, *Medieval English Figurative Roundels*, CVMA (GB) Summary Catalogue 6 (Oxford, 2002), no. 381; A. Baker, *English Panel Paintings 1400–1558*, ed. and updated A. Ballantyne and P. Plummer (London, 2011), p. 231.
16 CALS DLL/3/76; R. N. Swanson, *Indulgences in Medieval England: Passports to Paradise?* (Cambridge, 2007), p. 78, n.3. John was probably John son of Richard of the Leighs of High Hall, Cheshire; see J. Burke, *A Genealogical and Heraldic History of the Landed Gentry of Great Britain and Ireland*, 4 vols (London, 1838), vol. 4, p. 531.
17 Swanson, *Indulgences*, pp. 128–9, 137–9. Pope Eugenius IV authorised a five-year fundraising campaign for the hospital in 1441, and Swanson suggests that the three known letters of confraternity (DLL3/76 is the only original; the other two are enrolled copies) were directly related to this process, rather than being a more widespread practice; see Swanson, *Indulgences*, p. 78.
18 No impression of this seal has previously been recorded in print, although the matrix was in private hands in the eighteenth century; see A London Antiquary, 'Curious notices of antiquities of London', *The Gentleman's Magazine and Historical Chronicle*, 54, 2 (1784), 733, and fig. 4, plate facing p. 811. According to the note on p. 733, the anonymous antiquary had 'sight of an impression in *insinglas* [sic] of the seal of St Anthony's Hospital, London', while a Mr S. Ayscough claims on p. 811 to have been in possession of several impressions of this matrix. The current whereabouts of the matrix is unknown.
19 The hospital became a royal free chapel under the 1414 Alien Priories Act, Lewis, 'Hospital of St Anthony', p. 230.
20 BUAS PENR/12 (Seal 216). According to a family tree supplied by George Ormerod, Joan was the daughter of Sir William Troutbeck of Dunham, Cheshire, and her first husband was Sir William Butler of Bewsey; see G. Ormerod, *The History of the County Palatine and City of Chester. Vol. II: Containing the Hundreds of Edisbury, Wirral and Broxton* (London, 1819), p. 28.

21 Della Rovere possessed several matrices during his time as cardinal, but this particular seal does not appear previously to have been recorded; see M. J. Sillence, 'The cardinal's seal of dignity and the representation of identities, 1378–1533' (unpublished PhD thesis, University of East Anglia, 2009), esp. pp. 112–13. I am grateful to Dr Matthew Sillence for his helpful comments on Della Rovere's seals.
22 NLW WIGFAIR/268 (Seal 2201).
23 Williams, 'Catalogue of Welsh ecclesiastical seals as known down to 1600 AD. Part IV', incorrectly describes the charge as 'a lion *statant*'. No Robert Pennarth appears in M. P. Siddons, *Development of Welsh Heraldry*, 4 vols (Aberystwyth, 1991–2006). The arms may relate to the diocese or to Richard Redman, Bishop of St Asaph (1471–95), but this is unlikely, since the known fifteenth-century arms of St Asaph are two keys in saltire, while the Redman family arms are three cushions ermine, Siddons, *Development of Welsh Heraldry*, vol. 2, p. 514; Birch 12,947.
24 NLW PITORD/1281 (will of Richard le Bruyn senior), 322 (will of Alice, relict of Richard le Bruyn), 1394 (release of executors). Seal 1786.
25 CALS DWN/1/25 (Seal 459).
26 D. Jones, *The Church in Chester 1300–1540*, Chetham Society 3rd ser., vol. 8 (1957), p. 48 and note. The 1542 exemption from the jurisdiction of the archdeacon of Chester is for example mentioned only in passing in A. T. Thacker, 'Churches and religious bodies: the collegiate church of St John', in ed. C. P. Lewis and A. T. Thacker, *A History of the County of Chester*, vol. 5, part 2, (Woodbridge, 2005), pp. 125–33, p. 129; R. N. Swanson, 'Peculiar practices: the jurisdictional jigsaw of the pre-Reformation Church', *Midland History*, 26 (2001), 69–95, although observing that the archdeaconry of Chester, itself a peculiar, had 'relative autonomy' (70), does not mention the exempt collegiate church of St John.
27 Swanson, 'Peculiar practices', 71, observes that mention of an official is sometimes the only indication of the existence of a peculiar.
28 W. G. Clark-Maxwell, 'The College of St Mary Magdalene, Bridgnorth, with some account of its deans and prebends. Part 1. The college', *Archaeological Journal*, 84 (1927), 1–23, esp. 14; A. Hamilton Thompson, 'The College of St Mary Magdalene, Bridgnorth, with some account of its deans and prebends. Part 1. The deans and canons of Bridgnorth', *Archaeological Journal*, 84 (1927), 24–87, dismisses the activities of the peculiar court as being of secondary historical interest to the deans and canons (p. 25).
29 Shropshire Archives, SRR 6001/112; Clark-Maxwell, 'College of St Mary Magdalene', 14; Swanson, 'Peculiar practices', 75, notes that, most unusually, the dean and prebends held independent jurisdictions.
30 *Seliau*, no. 19, seal 3. The existence of the seal is mentioned in passing in Clark-Maxwell, 'College of St Mary Magdalene', 15, n.1, referencing a note in Oxford, Bodleian Library, Blakeway MS 18, but it does not otherwise appear to have been published. Seal 1667.
31 NLW PITORD/137, 587, 537.
32 NLW PITORD/1420. The dean is named as Nicholas 'Selak', probably Nicholas Slake, Dean 1387–91, Hamilton Thompson, 'College of St Mary Magdalene', 51. The hand of the main text and the corroboration clause are almost certainly the same, and could be as late as 1387. I am grateful to Dr Susan Davies for her helpful comments on this document.
33 NLW PITORD/1233. Probate copies usually had the relevant official's seal attached, although in this instance there is no note to confirm that it is a copy; see M. M. Sheehan, *The Will in Medieval England* (Toronto, 1963), p. 205.
34 Testators were advised to borrow a matrix to validate their wills if they had no seal of their own; see Sheehan, *Will in Medieval England*, p. 191. The borrowing of matrices without a

documentary note to this effect became increasingly common during the thirteenth century; see *Guide*, p. 90. A number of episcopal statutes and constitutions required priests to be present when testators were drawing up their will, Sheehan, *Will in Medieval England*, pp. 180–1.

35 In 1369 a royal inquisition was informed that, among other abuses perpetrated by, or allowed to continue through, the neglect of the dean and prebends of Bridgnorth, no parochial chaplain had been provided for the chapel of St Mary Magdalene for the previous twenty-one years, or for the church of St Leonard for the past fourteen years, *Calendar of Inquisitions Miscellaneous (Chancery) Preserved in the Public Record Office*, vol. 3 (London, 1937), no. 735.

36 NLW PITORD/236. The document is dated the feast of SS Fabian and Sebastian (20 January) 1355 (calendar year given), but, since Edmund witnessed a document dated the Sunday before Michaelmas 29 Edward III (27 September 1355), (Shropshire Archives, Mrs Dyas's Collection, 796/12), this must be a scribal error.

37 *Calendar of Inquisitions Miscellaneous (Chancery)*, vol. 3, no. 270.

38 A diocesan commissary court usually grated probate when a testator held property in different archdeaconries, see K. French, *The People of the Parish. Community Life in a Late Medieval English Diocese* (Philadelphia, 2001), p. 37.

39 NLW PITORD/227; *Seliau*, no. 19.

40 *Seliau*, no. 19.

41 NLW PENRICE: GLAM/268. Seal 1337; Williams, 'Catalogue of Welsh ecclesiastical seals as known down to 1600 AD. Part IV', 246a. Hafodheulog Grange is a couple of miles southeast of Margam, see D. H. Williams, *Atlas of Cistercian Lands in Wales* (Cardiff, 1990), p. 50 and map 12.

42 SHA 972/1/1/603; Seal 2457. For Lilleshall's property in Welshpool, and Abbot Chetwynd, see M. M. Chibnall, 'Houses of Augustinian canons: Abbey of Lilleshall', in ed. A. T. Gaydon, *A History of the County of Shropshire*, vol. 2 (Oxford, 1973), pp. 70–80, esp. p. 73.

43 DLL/2/2, undated, *c*.1237 x 1242. Birch 4533, Seal 330 (common seal); Birch 4534R, Seal 2270 (de Nussa's seal). See also L. J. Whatley, 'Visual self-fashioning and the seals of the Knights Hospitaller in England', in N. Paul and S. Yeager (eds), *Remembering the Crusades. Myth, Image and Identity* (Baltimore, 2012), pp. 252–69, at pp. 262–3 and fig. 11.5.

44 *Guide*, pp. 84, 86; *Seals and Sealing Practices*, pp. 100–1. The seals of secular magnates or corporations were also used in this manner. For an example of this from the *SiMeW* dataset, see, for example, E. A. New, 'Lleision ap Morgan makes an impression: seals and the study of medieval Wales', *Welsh History Review*, 27:1 (2013), 331.

45 HCA Deed159, undated (1201x1205 from internal evidence). Seal of Nicholas of Bremburgh: Seal 780. Seal of Hereford Cathedral Dean and Chapter (main): Seal 781, Birch 1613, F. C. Morgan, and P. E. Morgan, *A Concise List of Seals Belonging to the Dean and Chapter of Hereford Cathedral* (Hereford, 1966), p. 5.

46 HCA Deed 2003, Seal 871. The document is undated, but on palaeographical grounds appears to be from the mid-thirteenth century. The hospital was founded by Elias of Bristol, a canon of Hereford Cathedral, in *c*.1225, and was soon placed under the authority of the dean and chapter, see D. Whitehead, 'St Ethelbert's Hospital, Hereford', in G. Aylmer and J. Tiller (eds), *Hereford Cathedral: A History* (London and Rio Grande, 2000), pp. 599–609, at pp. 599–600.

47 E. A. New, 'Signs of community or marks of the exclusive? Parish and guild seals in later medieval England', in C. Burgess and E. Duffy (eds), *The Parish in Late Medieval England*, Harlaxton Medieval Studies, XIV (Stamford, 2006), pp. 113–28, at pp. 122–8. In addition

to those listed in this essay, casts of four other 'parochial' seals (two representing collegiate churches) and two seals of churchwardens are preserved among the seal casts of the Society of Antiquaries of London.

48 A 1154 reference to a church seal in the Blythburgh Cartulary is discussed in New, 'Signs of community', p. 123.

49 *English Episcopal Acta 7. Hereford, 1079–1234*, ed. Julia Barrow (Oxford, 1993), nos 11, 352. The fourteenth-century matrix of the vicar of Reculver (Kent) may be associated with Reculver's change in status to an area of peculiar deaconal jurisdiction in 1325; see G. Clinch, 'Seal of the vicar of Reculver', *Archaeologia Cantiana*, 23 (1918), 169–70, and New, 'Signs of community', pp. 126–7.

50 The grantors of the indulgences are: Edmund of Abingdon, Archbishop of Canterbury (1223–40), HCA Deed 2037; Seal 882 (seal of dignity), 881 (subsidiary seal); Birch 1202, 1202R; Morgan and Morgan, *A Concise List of Seals Belonging to the Dean and Chapter of Hereford Cathedral*, p. 7. Cadwgan, Bishop of Bangor (1215–36), HCA Deed 1514 (Seal 865); Williams, 'Catalogue of Welsh ecclesiastical seals as known down to 1600 AD. Part IV, no. 4. Alexander Stainsby, Bishop of Coventry (1224–38), HCA Deed 2038; Seal 884; Birch 1631, Morgan and Morgan, *A Concise List of Seals Belonging to the Dean and Chapter of Hereford Cathedral*, p. 7. Hugh of Northwold, Bishop of Ely (1229–54), HCA Deed 2041; Seal 886 (seal of dignity), 887 (subsidiary seal); Birch 1496; Morgan and Morgan, *A Concise List of Seals Belonging to the Dean and Chapter of Hereford Cathedral*, p. 7. Eustace of Fauconberg, Bishop of London (1221–8), HCA 2043; Seal 890 (seal of dignity), 891 (subsidiary seal); Birch 1907, 1907R. Anselm le Gros, Bishop of St Davids (1230–47), HCA Deed 1509; Seal 864; Williams, 'Catalogue of Welsh ecclesiastical seals as known down to 1600 AD. Part IV, no. 81. Robert Bingham, Bishop of Salisbury (1228–46), HCA 2037; Seal 882 (seal of dignity), 883 (subsidiary seal); Birch 2192, 2192R; Morgan and Morgan, *A Concise List of Seals Belonging to the Dean and Chapter of Hereford Cathedral*, p. 9. Jocelin of Wells, Bishop of Wells (1206–42), HCA Deed 2042; Seal 888 (seal of dignity), 889 (subsidiary seal); Birch 1412, 1412R; Morgan and Morgan, *A Concise List of Seals Belonging to the Dean and Chapter of Hereford Cathedral*, p. 7.

51 HCA Deed 2036, Seal 880. The seal of Richard Wethershed, Archbishop of Canterbury (1229–31) is usually cited as the earliest example of small panels with high-relief images, see Hope, 'Seals of English bishops', 275.

52 The figure of St Paul on Eustace of Fauconberg's subsidiary seals has close affinities with the image of the saint on the common seal of the city, see J. Alexander and P. Binski (eds), *Age of Chivalry: Art in Plantagenet England, 1200–1400* (London, 1985), no. 193 (entry by T. A. Heslop); E. A. New, 'The common seal and civic identity in medieval London', in S. Solway (ed.), *Medieval Coins and Seals: Constructing Identity, Signifying Power* (Turnhout, 2015), pp. 297–31.

53 For a discussion of the image as a possible likeness of the lost tower, see J. Maddison, *Ely Cathedral: Design and Meaning* (Ely, 2000), p. 44.

54 T. A. Heslop, 'Cistercian seals in England and Wales', in C. Norton and D Park (eds), *Cistercian Art and Architecture in the British Isles* (Cambridge, 1986), pp. 266–83, at p. 266.

55 Williams, 'Catalogue of Welsh ecclesiastical seals as known down to 1600 AD. Part IV', nos 218–62; Williams, 'Medieval Cistercian seals'.

56 NLW PENRICE: GLAM/101; Patterson, *Scriptorium*, no. 96. Fountains, Seal 1188, Birch 3170, Williams, NMW M311; Warden (Sartis), Seal 1189; Boxley, Seal 1190, Birch 2693; Neath (first seal), Seal 1191, Williams, 'Catalogue of Welsh ecclesiastical seals as known down to 1600 AD. Part IV', 222.

57 NLW PENRICE: GLAM/101 Seal 2 (Seal 1189). Heslop's reasonable assumption that the same matrix produced both the 1208 impression and the Society of Antiquaries' cast is however incorrect (Heslop, 'Cistercian seals', p. 269 and n.17, plate 139). The impression suggests a matrix engraved by an accomplished craftsman, stylistically of the early thirteenth century.
58 NLW PENRICE: GLAM/151 (Seal 1242). The seal of the abbot of Clairvaux is not the same as that impressed on the 1247 document reproduced in J-L. Chassel (ed.), *Sceaux et usages de sceaux. Images de la Champagne médiévale* (Paris, 2003), no. 4.
59 Williams, 'Catalogue of Welsh ecclesiastical seals as known down to 1600 AD. Part IV', 138–55, at 139.
60 First seal of abbot Seal 1136, Williams, 'Catalogue of Welsh ecclesiastical seals as known down to 1600 AD. Part IV', 220a, 220b; second seal of abbot Seal 31, Williams, 'Catalogue of Welsh ecclesiastical seals as known down to 1600 AD. Part IV', 221; Margam first common seal, Seal 1303, Williams, 'Catalogue of Welsh ecclesiastical seals as known down to 1600 AD. Part IV', 245; Margam second common seal, Seal 1337, Williams, 'Catalogue of Welsh ecclesiastical seals as known down to 1600 AD. Part IV', 246a. Idem, 'Catalogue of Welsh ecclesiastical seals as known down to 1600 AD. Part IV', 139, notes that the General Chapter further ruled that the matrices should be made of copper and round in shape; Margam's second common seal was in fact a pointed oval.
61 NLW PITORD/1057.
62 Nicholas of Pitchford was named as provost in the witness list of a 1302 deed, and is a party to several other deeds, NLW PITORD/371 (as provost), 10, 248, 387, 586, 605.
63 The lost impression was probably that of the communal seal of the Bridgnorth Franciscans or their Guardian.
64 NLW PITORD/1057, Seal 1, Seal 1982. The only record of Denemede comes from this document, A. G. Little, *Franciscan Papers, Lists and Documents* (Manchester, 1943), p. 196.
65 Birch 4438, 4439, 4440; H. S. Kingsford, 'The seals of the Franciscans', in A. G. Little (ed.), *Franciscan History and Legend in English Mediaeval Art* (Manchester, 1937), pp. 84–5, plate I.1–I.3.
66 Kingsford, 'Seals of the Franciscans', p. 85.
67 Little, *Franciscan Papers*, p. 220.
68 P. Binski, *Becket's Crown. Art and Imagination in Gothic England 1170–1300* (New Haven and London, 2004), pp. 212–18.
69 For a discussion of flourishing cross iconography in English art and theology, see Binski, *Becket's Crown*, pp. 87–101, 212–18.
70 One copy of Bonaventure's meditations on the Cross, produced in England (possibly Bury St Edmunds) in the third quarter of the thirteenth century, contains an illustration of the dead Christ on a flourishing cross, Binski, *Becket's Crown*, p. 217 and fig. 173.
71 T. A. Heslop, 'Art, nature and St Hugh's choir at Lincoln', in J. Mitchell (ed.), *England and the Continent in the Middle Ages*, Harlaxton Medieval Studies, VIII (Stamford, 2000), pp. 60–74, p. 73.
72 I am grateful to Professor Paul Binski for his helpful comments on this seal, and for his confirmation of the probable date and extremely unusual nature of the iconography.
73 NLW PITORD/605, Seal 1 (common seal), Seal 1950, Seal 2 (Guardian), Seal 1951. Kingsford, 'Seals of the Franciscans', p. 87, mistakenly dismisses these seals as being from Bruges, probably based upon an unreliable antiquarian source. The Victoria County History entry notes this error, but fails to cite the original document, see M. J. Angold, G. C. Baugh, M. M. Chibnall, D. C. Cox, D. T. W. Price, M. Tomlinson and B. S. Trinder, 'Friaries:

Franciscan friars', in ed. A. T. Gaydon and R. B. Pugh, *A History of the County of Shropshire*, vol. 2 (1973), pp. 89–91, *http://www.british-history.ac.uk/report.aspx?compid=39934* (last accessed 11 July 2014). Footnote 15 mentions the seal, f.n.28 notes the antiquarian error.

74 E. A. New, 'Biblical imagery on seals in medieval England and Wales', in M. Gill and J-L. Chassel (eds), *Pourquoi les sceaux? La sigillographie nouvel enjeu de l'histoire de l'art* (Lille, 2011), pp. 451–68, p. 459 and fig. 4.

SEALS AND LORDSHIP

Susan M. Johns

THIS CHAPTER EXPLORES the way that seals may be interpreted to reveal ideas about the importance of lordship, land tenure, political and economic and social realities, as well as the symbolic importance of the act of sealing. This analysis of seals explores some aspects of the political importance of seals in a context that takes account of political change, the growth in the use of seals, the spread of literacy and changes in social structures. It sees seals and their documents as one tool in the armoury of bureaucratic seigniorial lordship that was used to confirm and, in part, create and perpetuate ideas about social difference and social hierarchy. The spread in the use of seals was not only tied to the concerns of lordship; people of all social ranks acquired seals as the Middle Ages progressed. For the nobility in medieval Wales the work of, in particular, David H. Williams and Michael Siddons has done much to chart the way that seals and sealing developed.[1] The process of cultural diffusion that saw the use of seals spread through all social ranks through the late twelfth and thirteenth centuries occurred in a period of social transformation.[2] Social change and social differentiation, then, are the contexts in which the emergence of seals and sealing practice occurred and during the thirteenth century sealing had become widespread and routine and part of the proper procedural mechanisms for authenticating documents.[3]

The Norman conquests of Wales, which began in the late eleventh century, contributed to processes of change that fundamentally affected the Welsh polities. After Edward I's conquest of Wales in 1282–3 the subordination of Welsh political authority in the thirteenth century saw the creation of a Wales that was still a politically disunited kingdom predicated on the polities of Gwynedd and Deheubarth and Marcher lordships, and where political power was fragmented.[4] It was not until 1536 and 1543 that administrative unity was imposed. Yet the 1282 conquest had profound impacts on bureaucratic and literate practice in Wales and was a spur to change in the way that business and juridical matters were conducted. A. D. Carr has found that in north Wales following 1282, private deeds emulated English practice, although Welsh forms of pledges, originating in Welsh law, came to be used. For Carr, cultivated literacy had a 'cultural dimension'.[5] This occurred in a context whereby individuals and communities, both secular and ecclesiastical, became more literate as the volume of written records increased, and as written records proliferated they gradually replaced oral, traditional and non-literate ways of conducting business.[6] In Wales contact with English administrative practice, in part, had an impact on the ways that individuals conducted transactions. Llinos Beverley Smith has suggested that, following the conquest of Wales by Edward I, there was an increase in trust in written records and a growth in literacy that suited the concerns of the bureaucratic lordship. Written cultures served as a mechanism for social dominance, but also for spreading the use of seals, since in the king's courts in England actions of covenant were not acceptable unless they were sealed, whereas in Wales, as Smith points out, oral agreements were acceptable.[7] This was in part exclusionary since written culture was inaccessible to those who could neither create nor read such documents. Written records were thus a facet of the cultural domination of landholders. In high politics, political agreements were mediators of freighted symbolic meanings, for example, as Huw Pryce has found in his analysis of the 1272 Treaty of Montgomery, the ritual and symbolic aspects of medieval politics and diplomatic relations can also be evidence of the process of cultural integration. Pryce also notes that the power could be imposed through documentary culture since England had a more developed bureaucracy than Gwynedd and different ethnic and cultural contexts were important.[8] In 1282 the coronet of Llywelyn ap Gruffudd, his seal matrix and those of his wife and son were melted down and recast into a chalice that was given to Vale Royal Abbey after his defeat by Edward I: their destruction demonstrated the extinction of princely power in Wales.[9] That seals had deeply symbolic and cultural functions in the architecture of medieval lordship is without doubt. Seals were symbolically important as mediators of real political power. That seals could retain such symbolic functions in the thirteenth century despite the ubiquitous use of them throughout all levels of society is suggestive of the power of tradition and memory in medieval society. Seals in these contexts imaged the power of lordship and served as semiotic devices of personal, political, economic and cultural power. The intersection of the personal with these wider cultural contexts was imaged through a variety of devices on seals, and the equestrian seals of the military elite have long been seen as indicative of the function and role of such men in society.

By the later fourteenth century, the spread of literacy and the circulation of a range of contracts strained the judicial system and also social relations. The processes whereby the written record became an instrument for securing transactions had also become coercive since records were used to force individuals to fulfil their legal obligations. In the context of the tensions of the late fourteenth century, as Steiner has pointed out, contemporaries such as John Gower criticised abuses of documentary culture: the actions of peasants during 1381 in England when they destroyed written records have been seen as evidence of hostility to a literate culture.[10] Documents were seen as instruments of repression or as evidence of participation in insurrection suggesting the importance of the political and juridical contexts, but the emergence of legal practice as literary practice is key to the formation of documentary culture.[11] Nevertheless, the dominance of territory was key to the concerns of the landed elite, and securing access to power through administrative control of offices and through mechanisms such as the control of justice and courts, was critical. Although, therefore, documentary culture underwent profound changes in the period 1100–1500, seals mediated and represented similar ideas about authentication and identity throughout the period, and central to this the concerns about social status remained potent. On occasion, the spread in the use of seals could be the site of acknowledged contested boundaries. For example, the concerns with social status and the use of seals and their importance in defining status in the twelfth century can be seen in the famous statement of Richard de Lucy, the Justiciar of Henry II, who is recorded in the *Chronicle of Battle Abbey* (written in the 1180s) as saying that '[i]t was not formerly the custom in the past for every petty knight to have a seal, they are appropriate for kings and great men only.'[12] De Lucy here was merely stating a conception of past sealing practice in England as he perceived it: developments within society in terms of social stratification and economic change allied to political and urban developments meant that, in reality, de Lucy was archly defending an idea of sealing practice as an exclusionary aspect of the dominance of the elite even as sealing practice developed with rapidity in contemporary society. The spread in the use of seals is related to the management of economic resources and the need to authenticate that management. In *Glanville*, a book written to explain the developing English common law completed between 1187 and 1189, seals are only mentioned in the specific context of the developing law of debt.[13] In particular, the use of a sealed charter is envisaged by the user as one of two ways that an enforceable debt obligation could be created and proved at court. Sealed charters were given the same legal validity as transactions of debt contracted orally and which could be proved by trial by battle.[14] Within twenty years of de Lucy's derisory comment a charter of 22 February 1191, granted by Gwenwynwyn ab Owain Cyfeiliog of Powys (d.1216) to Strata Marcella Abbey, stated that 'nothing is more effective than writing against oblivion and challenge and nothing should hinder the intention behind holy work'. Gwenwynwyn had ordered the charter to be drawn up to perpetuate the memory of his grant, and his seal, featuring an equestrian device, appended to the document.[15] The Welsh male military elite used seals from the late twelfth century in common with their western European counterparts. Yet, even though the Welsh princes sealed documents and the same process of cultural diffusion saw the emergence of sealing across all social groups, some lacked seals and, for example, might have to perform suretyship in person. On 16 December 1275 in a letters patent of Owain ab Llywelyn ab Owain Fychan, his brother and other male lords acted as surety for Gruffudd ap *Bud rei hosan*. The seals of the lords were attached to the document: 'The seals of the aforesaid lords have been attached with those of other nobles who have seals: those who lack seals are bound to perform their suretyship with their own hands before the prince's attorney'.[16] This is significant because although it secures the document and the political agreement, the seal also takes the place of *performance* of surety. Huw Pryce has studied the 1272 Treaty of Montgomery in the context of its textual production. He focused on the phraseology and form of the document but noted the ritual and symbolic aspects of medieval politics and diplomatic relations and saw that the latter were part of a process of cultural integration. Pryce also notes that power could be imposed through documentary culture since England had a more developed bureaucracy than Gwynedd and different ethnic and cultural contexts were important. For Pryce, cultural differences were not as stark as between eastern and western Europe, but 'the prince of Gwynedd and the king of England were differentiated not only by a disparity in power but also by the distinctive ethnic and cultural complexion of their respective polities'.[17] Nevertheless their diplomatic practice were framed in similar ways, and perhaps the influence of the beneficiary here is key; for example, the *acta* produced at Haughmond were framed in similar ways to current Anglo-Norman or Angevin diplomatic practice.[18]

Secular rulers of lands in Wales created documents and sealed in much the same way as their English counterparts, as part of a noble and aristocratic material culture that constructed aristocracy.[19] The early seals of medieval Wales were not fundamentally different from English seals, but in the twelfth and thirteenth centuries the absence of heraldry and the names on legends is indicative of some differences in sealing practice. As Crouch suggests, the Welsh lay sealers authenticated their deeds in much the same way as English seal users, but the legends had different names and there were no heraldic devices on the seals of Welsh magnates in the twelfth and thirteenth centuries.[20] In the later Middle Ages the equestrian seal was used by high-status individuals and was associated with office. There are more than 172 impressions of equestrian seals in the *SiMeW* database, the majority from the twelfth and early thirteenth centuries, with fewer from the mid-thirteenth century and later. The earliest charter validated with the seal of an elite Welsh ruler is an equestrian seal of Cadell ap Gruffudd who had succeeded to the kingship of Deheubarth in 1143 and the seal dates from 1146 x 51.[21] Cadell was ruler of Deheubarth until 1151 and the land concerned was granted to Totnes priory and confirmed a previous gift of land that may have been given by Stephen, Constable of Cardigan castle during the reign of Henry I. His seal is no different from the use of equestrian imagery of other European male secular landholders who were adopting seal usage. There is a clear development in the trappings depicted on the equestrian seals, from the basic depictions of knights, such as the seal of Morgan ap Caradoc on horseback in use possibly as early as 1158[22] (see figure 5.1) to the more elaborate devices, such as that of Gilbert de Clare which depicts a knight on horseback in use 1217 x 1230,[23] the deputed great seal of Henry V as Chamberlain of Wales in use in 1413,[24] the Chamberlain of North Wales for Edward IV,[25] or that of Jasper Tudor's finely worked seal in use in 1486 and 1493. The latter seal (see figure 5.2) is double-sided and the front depicts a man in armour with an armorial shield with a horse with caparisons leaping over a dragon, the reverse is heraldic and incorporates a range of devices including dragons.[26] These later impressions of equestrian seals are finely developed and have been associated with high social status and office as in the seals of William de la Zouche, Lord of Glamorgan in use in 1329.[27] The former's seal is unusual since on the reverse it depicts a standing female holding the arms of her father.[28] Overall the dataset from the *SiMeW* project confirms the established contours for the developments in equestrian seals more generally.[29]

A further development in sealing practice occurred when the greater magnates in western Europe began to use great seals and privy seals in the late twelfth and early thirteenth centuries. Llywelyn ap Iorwerth, Prince of Gwynedd, had a great seal and a privy seal in use by 1220; his privy seal authenticated deeds in place of his great seal, although the reasons for this were clarified in the text of his letters.[30] Yet, Adrian Ailes has suggested that the use of two-faced seals may have had mediated different ideas about the role of the seal user. The equestrian seal may have reflected on the role of a male leader as 'feudal lord' and the image on the reverse 'all that the family stood for'.[31] The emergence of heraldic seals and the relationship of seal imagery with different social classes has been well charted by Ailes, who has shown how seals that displayed heraldic arms could also associate individuals increasingly with civilian functions. Civilian function is key to the depiction of the seal of Gilbert Burdin in 1200 x 1225.[32] Gilbert Burdin, his wife Agnes and their sons gave land to Margam near the wood of Sturmi, and in return the abbot of Margam gave Gilbert 20s., Agnes one bezant and a sum of beans, and his two sons were given red shoes. The agreement is sealed with Gilbert's seal, but the seal stood for the family agreement where Gilbert's superior status is indicated by the differing value of the countergifts given.[33] His sons confirmed his charter and used their father's seal since he had died before he had completed the transaction.[34] Birch noted the congruence between Gilbert Burdin's seal, which depicts a man holding a staff of office, and the depiction of the *penteulu* in law codes, and New has recently confirmed this association.[35] The image of a hand holding a staff of office is common on ecclesiastical seals where the standing figure might hold a staff, as in the seal of the Abbot of Neath which depicts a hand and arm wearing a maniple emerging from the lower right holding a pastoral staff.[36] The Abbot of Caerleon had a similar motif on his seal that was in use in 1203.[37] Both seals mediate images that refer to the user with pastoral office and function. There is a small group of seals from the end of the twelfth and early thirteenth centuries that depict a hand grasping a spear from which flies a pennon.[38] Adrian Ailes has discussed how the adoption of banners or pennons in the twelfth century emerged and in particular he noted that a number of twelfth century seals show men bearing pennons and gonfanons on lances. He comments on the description by Wace, writing episodically from the 1160s through to 1173/4, that the barons at Hastings bore gonfanons and knights pennons, to suggest that the distinction may not be as clearly defined since the terminology for banners was interchangeable.[39] That such imagery appears on seals is congruent with the emergence of the banneret as a status group, which has been discussed by David Crouch. The appearance of banners as a sign of high status in the late twelfth century was associated with the emergence of the banneret.[40] An early equestrian seal of William de London depicts a man on a horse holding a pennon.[41] In some later seals the pennon may have armorial designs, such as the seals of William, Madog, Espus and Iorwerth Fychan, sons of Iorwerth, which have as a device a lance with a pennon with four chevrons and pellets in the field, which a number of scholars have suggested are early examples of native Welsh heraldic devices.[42] Other objects held include a hand holding three lilies,[43] while two others depict the hand holding key(s), one of which may be an allusion to the user's office as a doorman (see chapter 7).[44] Other objects include bells, or possibly a cleaver,[45] while later examples include a hand holding a dagger.[46]

Seals as a consequence mediated ideas about function and could also symbolise the place of the individual in the family hierarchy and in wider social hierarchies of power. The place of the seal on a document may have indicated this, and individuals changed their seal when their circumstances changed, for example on becoming an heir, as in the case of the younger son of Morgan ap Caradog whose second seal in use 1208 x 1217 deployed an equestrian device and may have indicated his position as heir. His brother Lleision changed his seal as his place in the family hierarchy changed.[47] Family hierarchy could also be mediated on documents where family members conjointly sealed deeds with their own seals. For example, in *c*.1200 x 1225 Wrunu, Meurig and Rhys sons of Bleddyn sealed a deed in favour of Margam; the seal of Meurig depicts a flower, that of Wronu a nine-armed sun within a six-pointed star with a pellet in each angle, whilst the seal of Rhys has a stylised lily motif. Each seal has a legend with the forename of each sealer and the designation 'fil Bleddyn'.[48] In 1250 Philip, Madoc, and Idenard sons of Kedic and Madog son of Meurig gave lands to Margam Abbey. The seals of Philip and Madog son of Meurig are conventional and depict an ornate stylised lily, that of Idenard an ornamental floral device, while the seal of Madog ap Kedic depicts a bow and arrow, and it is just possible that he is therefore the elder son of Meurig. The use of the arrow motif may conceivably be related to Madog's military function (see figures 5.3–5.6).[49]

Both male and female Welsh landholders utilised seals in the twelfth and thirteenth centuries, for example Ivor Vaghan (Ifor Fychan) sealed a deed that authenticated a quitclaim that he made with his sons to Margam Abbey. The deed concerns a claim to twelve acres of land in the fee of Kenfig and dates from the period *c*.1225–50.

The seal is a stylised lily (upside down) and the legend reads: YVOR FYCHAN ET FILIOR'EY (see figure 5.7).[50] The reference to sons is unusual and is evidence of the possible routine sealing by Welsh male landholders as a family group in the context of a quitclaim of lands in the early thirteenth century. In 1225 x 1250 *Griffin Voil, Resus ab Yewan* and *Yeruard Du*, the sons of a Welsh landholder, Yewan ab Yustin, co-sealed a deed in favour of Margam. Gruffudd's seal depicts an inverted stylised lily, while his brother's seal depicts an arrow.[51] The other seal has not survived. Welsh free families were organised around patrilineal descent patterns and kin-group members could claim descent from a common ancestor in the male line from a great-grandfather. Land could thus be claimed by agnatic lineage connections and it is possible that land could not be alienated without the consent or involvement of kin.[52] In the Ivor Fychan example, family group authority was signalled as key on the legend. It is more usual that family members would attest a document as individuals and seal with their own seals, so this seal is important evidence of a seal serving as a family object of authentication. John de Boneville had two seals; while one [1193 x 1218] depicted a lion,[53] his other seal had an intaglio with Arabic lettering.[54] Another John de Bonville also had an unusual seal that decorated a cross with a foliate motif with a trio of pellets in each angle with a 'jewelled' border, a motif that Birch thought was 'early Welsh art' (see figure 5.8).[55]

The semiotic importance of the language of domination and control of territory and economic power is imaged in equestrian seals that encapsulate ideas about function and male military masculinity and social status. Military power and lordship but also crucially family power emerged on seals at a point of social change: as Crouch has pointed out, aristocratic affinities were significant in the late twelfth century as a key way that elites dominated localities.[56] The incorporation of heraldry that physically represented the significance of genealogy has been explored by Michael Siddons's magisterial four-volume work on the emergence of Welsh heraldry. Siddons found that there are no surviving examples of Welshmen who show the use of heraldic devices before 1300, and only a few examples from the fourteenth century, although he noted the early exception to this pattern in the seals of William, Madog, Epsus and Iowerth Fychan discussed above.[57] The use of personal seals and equestrian seals in Wales followed similar patterns to other parts of western Europe in the Middle Ages. Heraldry and the deployment of arms confirm the importance of family, function and inheritance in framing the identity of an individual.[58] Seals have little to tell us about ethnicity: symbols had universal associations of status, even though we know from other sources that attention to ethnicity became evident in twelfth-century discourses.[59] Thus, although it is possible to distinguish Welsh landholders and the Welsh military elite, the sociocultural changes of the twelfth century were fundamentally transformative – and the seals of landholders in Wales or anywhere else are elegant testimony to the universal nature of the semiotic discourse. The language of power in medieval Europe transcended ethnic boundaries, and seals reflect this in the twelfth century since emblems were universal in a written language informed by Christian theology.[60] Seals are important evidence of documentary culture that can also be read with sociocultural symbolisms, since they represent a collective body of evidence that intermeshes personal identity with authorisation, what Bedos-Rezak has termed a paradoxical connection whereby an 'inward-oriented symbolic object of personal identity' was a dialectical structure that constructed symbologies of power.[61]

Documents and their seals were at the nexus of a commemorative process and had legal functions. Yet, it is surprising that they are hardly mentioned in the key exposition of developing common law in England in the twelfth century, *Glanville*, and only in specific cases of the acknowledgement of debt. Seals also served to embed the memory of an action in the collective memory of those who read, or heard read, the documents that they ratified. Thus, seals were objects that constructed the present understanding of the past. As Markus Späth has discussed in his analysis of the seals of English cathedral priories, for example, seals memorialised the past of the religious institution.[62] They provided a focus for a collective understanding of authority and action. Seals were integral components of the process by which the written word became memorialised because they deployed words and symbols that relied upon the interpretation of the viewer to create an understanding and memory. Seals were thus objects that had a role in creating an active memory through the shape, colour and insignia deployed; as Michael Clanchy has pointed out, for example, the seal was the 'harbinger of literacy' and Exchequer demands for taxation brought 'the hated green wax' even into remote communities.[63] A variety of colours were used and this may well have had symbolic resonances; green, for example, on aristocratic seals, may have represented life, and green was the dominant colour on Welsh episcopal seals until the fourteenth century, with red used thereafter. Royal seals were also green, while privy seals and signets were red.[64] Such devices have drawn the attention of scholars since seals became objects of interest to antiquarians and early academics, and yet the interpretation of them tends to assume the cultural ascription of meaning that has an historical constant. Seals are not simple guides to gentry culture, knightly culture or social aspiration since they are culturally contingent and were also legal devices and the context of use changed as society developed. For example, in Glanville, in the mid-twelfth century, sealed instruments were only discussed in the specific actions to recognise debt. Yet, by the early fourteenth century, if a plaintiff denied a debt that was recorded in a sealed tally or charter, the plaintiff had recourse to jury trial rather than by wager of law. Later, debtors who wished to make a bond with a Jewish creditor had to own or have access to a seal.[65] Thus the sealed instrument had particular function in the specific context of debt recognition and thus the acquisition and widespread use of seals in some circumstances was directly related to developing legal practice as well as economic imperatives. Certainly, as Clanchy has pointed out, the Statute of Exeter of 1285 stated that bondsmen who wished to serve on inquests should have a seal.[66]

Economic and legal imperatives had cultural force but so did cultural interactions across political divides, as Huw Pryce's discussion of the form of the *acta* produced at Haughmond, framed in similar ways to current Anglo-Norman or Angevin diplomatic practice, has shown.[67] In Gwynedd, there was a conscious attempt to align the form of charters with English royal practice and that of the greater magnates.[68] Yet, intra-Welsh rivalry could shape the diplomatic. Crouch argues that Gwenwynwyn ab Owain Cyfeiliog, as ruler in Powys and the enemy of the ruler of Gwynedd, Llywelyn ap Iorwerth, styled himself as *Powisie princeps et dominus Arwistili*, 'either in rivalry or mockery' of Llywelyn.[69] His equestrian seal, however, deployed motifs congruent with the military aristocracy. A more detailed exploration of such themes is beyond the scope of this chapter, but, nevertheless, the intense rivalry between different dynasties within Wales is certainly an important context that can be explored through the diplomatics of charters. The key point is that it is debatable how far the language deployed on charters is reflective of diplomatic convention, or whether the diplomatic serves as the voice of donor pretension to status and wider claims. Huw Pryce has argued that the production of charters that conformed to contemporary European and English diplomatic norms could nevertheless produce documents that portrayed pretension to territorial hegemony, although there was variety in the forms used.[70] Without doubt, the specific words used within documents suggest the sensitivities of scribes to languages of power, and as Crouch reminds us, those who drew up charters were acutely aware of the aspirations of their patrons.[71] The titles used to describe rulers in Wales changed through the twelfth century with a noted change in the language of power in the emergence of the use *princeps* by Welsh rulers in the late twelfth century which replaced *rex*.[72] This documentary context is fundamental to the interpretation of the seals that authenticate the *acta*. The language of princely power emerges just as Welsh rulers begin to seal and their seals depict equestrian imagery. Thus, irrespective of the changing language of power with the decline in the appellation *rex* to the increasing use of *princeps*, the seals were what may be termed conventional sigillographic devices deploying images common to the elite of western Europe. There is thus a disconnect between the imagery and language of power deployed on seals and that within the charter. Thus, the seal, together with the text of the charters, mediated ideas about lordship that suggest the interrelationship between family connections and lordship, but fundamentally social function and status in a multifaceted legitimating discourse. Seal usage was ubiquitous by the end of the Middle Ages and their use and interpretation of such use is contingent on a wide array of interlocking symbolic, practical, cultural and legal and chronological contexts. Seals imaged motifs that referred to personal identity and ideas about function, since seals were, in certain respects and contexts and notably those pertaining to lordship, an emblem of class function and territorial domination – not just military dominance but part of a legitimating discourse within a context of changing social, political and economic realities.

Notes

1. D. H. Williams: 'The judicial seals of the Welsh Courts of Great Sessions', in *Good Impressions*, pp. 60–5; D. H. Williams, *Images of Welsh History: Seals of the National Library of Wales* (Aberystwyth, 2007); 'The seals of Strata Florida Abbey', *Ceredigion*, 14, no. 3 (2003), 1–6; 'Welsh seals at Canterbury', *Archaeologia Cambrensis*, 148 (2001 for 1999), 146–53; and the four parts of his 'Catalogue of Welsh ecclesiastical seals', published in four volumes of *Archaeologia Cambrensis*, cxxxiii through cxxxvi (1985–8). Equally significant are the following works by M. P. Siddons: 'Welsh equestrian seals', *National Library of Wales Journal*, 23 (1983–4), 292–318; 'Welsh equestrian seals: additions', *National Library of Wales Journal*, 33 (2003), 217–18; *The Development of Welsh Heraldry*, 4 vols (Aberystwyth, 1991–2006); 'Welsh seals in Paris', *Bulletin of the Board of Celtic Studies*, 29 (1981), 531–44. See also *Acts*, pp. 86–9; E. A. New, 'Christological personal seals and Christocentric devotion in later medieval England and Wales', *Antiquaries Journal*, 82 (2002), 47–68; eadem, 'Lleision ap Morgan makes an impression: seals and the study of medieval Wales', *Welsh History Review*, 27:1 (2013), 331. See also S. M. Johns, 'Seals, gender, identity, and social status in the late twelfth and early thirteenth centuries in Wales', in S. Solway (ed.), *Medieval Coins and Seals: Constructing Identity, Signifying Power* (Turnhout, 2015). My thanks to Phillipp Schofield and Elizabeth New for their helpful comments.
2. For discussion of this scholarship see D. Crouch, *The Birth of Nobility: Constructing Aristocracy in England and France, 900–1300* (Harlow, 2005), pp. 191–8; see also his *The English Aristocracy, 1070–1272: A Social Transformation* (New Haven and London, 2011) and *The Image of Aristocracy in Britain, 1000–1300* (London, 1992).
3. See chapter 2.
4. For the development of Wales in the Middle Ages generally see R. R. Davies, *Domination and Conquest: The Experience of Ireland, Scotland and Wales, 1100–1300* (Cambridge, 1990); idem, *The Matter of Britain and the Matter of England* (Oxford, 1996); idem, *The Age of Conquest: Wales 1063–1415*, new edn of his *Conquest, Coexistence and Change* (Oxford, 2000); for a discussion of the rulers of Wales in the period 1120–1283 see *Acts*, pp. 1–47.
5. A. D. Carr, '"This is my act and deed": the writing of private deeds in late medieval north Wales', in H. Pryce (ed.), *Literacy in Medieval Celtic Societies*, Cambridge Studies in Medieval Literature, 33 (Cambridge, 1998), pp. 223–35.
6. M. T. Clanchy, *From Memory to Written Record, England 1066–1307*, 2nd edn (Oxford, 1993); see also Richard Britnell (ed.), *Pragmatic Literacy, East and West* (Oxford, 1997); J. Goody, *The Logic of Writing and the Organization of Society* (Cambridge, 1986).
7. Ll. B. Smith, 'Inkhorn and spectacles: the impact of literacy in late medieval Wales', in H. Pryce (ed.), *Literacy in Medieval Celtic Societies* (Cambridge, 1998), pp. 202–22, at p. 214. For further discussion of these points, see chapter 2.
8. H. Pryce, 'Anglo-Welsh agreements, 1201–77', in R. A. Griffiths and P. R. Schofield (eds), *Wales and the Welsh in the Middle Ages* (Cardiff, 2011), pp. 1–19, at p. 2. Pryce notes disparity in power, ethnic and cultural differences, but also recognises some cultural similarities.
9. For a treatment of these themes, see S. M. Johns, *Gender, Nation and Conquest in the High Middle Ages: Nest of Deheubarth* (Manchester, 2013), pp. 105–7.
10. S. Justice, *Writing and Rebellion: England in 1381* (Berkeley, 1994).
11. E. Steiner, *Documentary Culture and the Making of Medieval English Literature* (Cambridge, 2003), pp. 4–5, 81–5.
12. As cited in Crouch, *English Aristocracy*, p. 53 and n.75 at p. 265; see also his comments in his *Image of Aristocracy*, pp. 138–9, 243; Clanchy, *Memory to Written Record*, p. 53, and n.23;

E. Searle (ed.), *The Chronicle of Battle Abbey* (Oxford, 1980), p. 214; P. Coss, *The Origins of the English Gentry* (Cambridge, 2003), p. 88.

13   *The Treatise on the Laws and Customs of England Commonly Called Glanville*, ed. and trans. G. D. G. Hall (Oxford, 1993), pp. 126–9.

14   P. Brand, 'Aspects of the law of debt, 1189–1307', in P. R. Schofield and N. J. Mayhew (eds), *Credit and Debt in Medieval England c.1180–c.1350* (Oxford, 2002), pp. 19–41, esp. pp. 21, 27 for comments on charters as sealed bonds.

15   Most of his charters are in favour of Strata Marcella Abbey, NLW, Wynnstay Estate Records, Ystrad Marchell Charters, no. 14 (*Acts*, no. 544). Other charters with his seal NLW, Wynnstay Estate Records, Ystrad Marchell Charters, nos 35, and no. 62 relate to periods when Gwenwynwyn was active as 'prince of Powys'. For his career and comment: *Acts*, pp. 41–4; G. C. G. Thomas (ed.), *Charters of the Abbey of Ystrad Marchell* (Aberystwyth, 1997), pp. 12–17; D. Stephenson, 'The politics of Powys Wenwynwyn in the thirteenth century', *Cambrian Medieval Celtic Studies*, 7 (1984), 39–61.

16   *Acts*, no. 612, pp. 809–10; Stephenson, 'Politics of Powys Wenwynwyn', 39–61.

17   Pryce, 'Anglo-Welsh agreements', p. 2.

18   H. Pryce, 'Culture, power and the charters of Welsh rulers', in M. T. Flanagan and J. Green (eds), *Charters and Charter Scholarship in Britain and Ireland* (Basingstoke and New York, 2005), pp. 184–202, esp. p. 188; D. Crouch, 'The earliest original charter of a Welsh king', *Bulletin of the Board of Celtic Studies*, 26 (1989), 128.

19   Crouch, *Birth of Nobility*, p. 211; also his *Image of Aristocracy*, pp. 242–7, 205–6.

20   Siddons, 'Welsh equestrian seals', 292–317; Crouch, *Image of Aristocracy*, p. 246.

21   Williams, *Images of Welsh History*, pp. 8 ff; Crouch, 'Earliest original charter of a Welsh king', 125–31; *Acts*, no. 22; New, 'Lleision ap Morgan', 331.

22   BL Harl. Ch. 75 B 29 [1158 x October 1191], Seal 55/56; NLW PENRICE: GLAM/202 [1186 x *c.*1208], *Acts*, no. 144; other impressions, BL, Harl. Ch. 75 B 30; NLW PENRICE: GLAM/88 [1189x1203], Seal 57; and for discussion of other examples *Acts*, pp. 258–80.

23   NLW PENRICE: GLAM/131; other impressions NLW PENRICE: GLAM/nos 2044, 2056, 2046, 2047, 2048.

24   BUAS PENR/166.

25   BUAS PENR/34.

26   Gwent Record Office, Hanbury D8/1/1814 (1486), /1794 (1493).

27   NLW PENRICE: GLAM/212 (Hugh le Despenser had a similar seal, see *Seliau*, p. 72); NLW PENRICE: GLAM/204 and 205. The seal depicts a lady standing on a corbel with her hands placed on two shields; the dexter shows three lions passant and the shield on the right depicts a carved panel of either traceried cusps. *Margam*, pp. 299–303; *Seliau*, p. 98.

28   His wife Eleanor was co-heiress of her father Earl Gilbert de Clare (d. 1295).

29   For further discussion of which see chapter 1.

30   Letter to Henry II (*c.* September 1220), *Acts*, no. 248, pp. 408–9 (he also swore on relics as well as sealing a document that confirmed a dependant's inheritance that suggests the connection between the practical and spiritual connections in the symbology of authentication that seals provided and the security that they represented); letter to William Marshal, Earl of Pembroke [1230], *Acts*, no. 262, pp. 429–31; swearing on relics and seal letter patent [1218], *Acts*, no. 240, pp. 396–7.

31   A. Ailes, 'Heraldry in twelfth-century England: the evidence', in D. Williams (ed.), *England in the Twelfth Century: Proceedings of the 1988 Harlaxton Symposium* (Woodbridge, 1990), pp. 1–16, at p. 7.

32 A. Ailes, 'The knight's alter ego: from equestrian to armorial', in N. Adams, J. Cherry and J. Robinson (eds), *Good Impressions: Image and Authority in Medieval Seals* (London, 2007), pp. 8–11, at p. 9; New, 'Lleision ap Morgan', pp. 340–1.
33 BL, Harl. Ch. 75 B. 26.
34 BL, Harl. Ch. 75 B. 27.
35 *Margam*, p. 33; New, 'Lleision ap Morgan', pp. 340–1.
36 BL Harl Ch 75 B 32. For a discussion of the emergence of the imagery of the staff of office, its early meanings and links to Christian theology see T. A. Heslop, 'Towards an iconology of Croziers', in ed. D. Buckton and T. A. Heslop (eds), *Studies in Medieval Art and Architecture Presented to Peter Laslo* (Stroud, 1994), pp. 36–45.
37 BL Harl Ch. 75 A 3; other examples of a pastoral staff NLW PENRICE: GLAM/133 [1228]
38 Espsus son of Caradoc hand holding a spear with a pennon NLW PENRICE: GLAM/2037 [1203 x 1208] other examples of this seal: NLW PENRICE: GLAM/nos 2038 [1175 x 1225] 2039 [1200 x 1225] and 15 [1175 x 1207]; hand and lance with pennon; NLW PENRICE: GLAM/95 [1208]; BL Harl Ch. 75 C 36 and BL Harl Ch. 75 C 37 [both 1208]; Gronw son of Phillip BL Harl Ch. 75 C 46 [1175 x 1225]; Filipp son of Wurkin, BL Harl Ch. 75 D 22 [1175 x 1200]; BL Harl Ch. 75 D 20 [1175 x 1225]; Kenwric son of Robert, BL Harl Ch. 75 C 47 [1175 x 1225]. See chapter 8 for detailed discussion.
39 A. Ailes, 'The knight, heraldry and recognition and the origins of heraldry', in C. Harper Bill and R. Harvey (eds), *Medieval Knighthood IV: Papers from the Fifth Strawberry Hill Conference 1990* (Woodbridge, 1992), pp. 14–15 and n.58. *The Roman de Rou*, trans. G. S. Burgess, with the text of A. J. Holden and notes by G. S. Burgess and E. van Houts (St Helier, 2002), ii, part 3, lines 6504–6, for a translation and comment see M. Bennett, 'Wace and warfare', in M. J. Strickland (ed.), *Anglo-Norman Warfare: Studies in Late Anglo-Saxon and Anglo-Norman Military Organization and Warfare* (Woodbridge, 1992); M. Bennett, 'Poetry as history? The "Roman de Rou" of Wace as a source for the Norman Conquest', *Anglo-Norman Studies*, 5 (1982), 21–39.
40 Crouch, *English Aristocracy*, pp. 53–4.
41 NLW PENRICE: GLAM/156 [1205 x 1214] other impressions NLW PENRICE: GLAM/158 [1205 x 1214] and BL Harl Ch. 75 C 31 [1175 x 1225].
42 NLW PENRICE: GLAM/128 [1225 x 1274], for which see also *Seliau*, pp. 80–1, no. 35; Williams, *Images of Welsh History*, p. 12 and fig. 24; *Welsh Heraldry*, vol. 1, pp. 3–4, vol. 2, p. 272; *Margam*, pp. 243–4.
43 Nicholas Ponti [1202]: NLW PENRICE: GLAM/50 and NLW PENRICE: GLAM/2049 [1200 x 1225].
44 BL Harl Ch. 75 C 44 [1175 x 1225]; another example of hand emerging holding a key(s) Hereford Cathedral Archives 1082 [1233]; NLW PENRICE: GLAM/179 [1265]; NLW PITORD/76 [1329 x 1330].
45 Richard de Warwick *c*.1200 x 1222, NLW PITORD/431 and 433.
46 NLW PENRICE: GLAM/350 [1516], and see below, chapter 7.
47 Owain's seal: BL, Harl. Ch. 75 C 37 (*Acts*, pp. 113, 298–9). Lleision's seal: NLW PENRICE: GLAM/109; BL, Harl. Ch. 75 C 34; BL, Harl. Ch. 75 C 35. For women and seals and their place in family hierarchy, see S. M. Johns, *Noblewomen, Aristocracy and Power in the Twelfth-Century Anglo-Norman Realm* (Manchester, 2003), p. 137. New, 'Lleision ap Morgan', pp. 345–8, suggests that the seals of Lleision ap Morgan may demonstrate the place of an individual in a kinship group; for the importance of family hierarchy and inheritance see Johns, *Noblewomen*; for discussion of an example of female co-heir group sealing where the seals of the younger sisters are smaller than their elders, *op. cit.*
48 BL Harl Ch. 75 B. 11. Seals 42–4.

49 NLW PENRICE: GLAM/126; *Margam*, pp. 145–6. Madog son of Meuric was the nephew of the other three principal grantors. Their father had associated them with a grant to Margam in 1225 x 1250; his seal was an eight-lobed flower with dots between the petals: NLW PENRICE: GLAM/1974 (dating: R. B. Patterson, T*he Scriptorium of Margam Abbey and the Scribes of Early Angevin Glamorgan: Secretarial Administration in a Welsh Marcher Barony* (Woodbridge, 2002), p. 117). Seal 1499. See also E. A. New, '(Un)conventional images. A case-study of radial motifs on personal seals', in P. R. Schofield (ed.), *Seals and their Context in the Middle Ages* (Oxford, 2015), pp. 151–60.
50 *Seliau*, no. 15
51 NLW PENRICE: GLAM/146. Seals 1239 and 1240.
52 Thomas (ed.), *Charters of the Abbey of Ystrad Marchell*, p. 13, n.1, which notes the view of H. Pryce, *Native Law and the Church in Medieval Wales* (Oxford, 1993), chapter 8; see also J. B. Smith, 'Dynastic succession in medieval Wales', *Bulletin of the Board of Celtic Studies*, 33 (1986), 199–232, and also idem, 'The succession to Welsh princely inheritance: the evidence reconsidered', in R. R Davies (ed.), T*he British Isles, 1100–1500: Comparisons, Contrasts and Connections* (Edinburgh, 1988), pp. 64–81.
53 BL Harl Ch. 75. B. 15 Seal 48.
54 See also *Seliau*, no. 26
55 BL Harl. Ch. 75 B. 12, Seal 45; the grant was to William the harper of twelve acres of land with meadow he subsequently granted this to Margam, *Margam*, p. 132.
56 Crouch, *English Aristocracy*, pp. 150–9, esp. p. 152.
57 *Welsh Heraldry*, I, p. 3.
58 Ailes, 'Knight's alter ego', p. 8.
59 Crouch, *English Aristocracy*, p. 248; J. Gillingham, *The English in the Twelfth Century: Imperialism, National Identity and Political Values* (Rochester, NY, 1999), p. xviii; J. Gillingham, 'Civilizing the English: the English histories of William of Malmesbury and David Hume', *Historical Research*, 74 (2001), 17–43, at 19; see also his 'The travels of Roger of Howden and his views of the Irish, Scots and Welsh', *Anglo-Norman Studies*, 20 (1998 for 1997), 151–69; Johns, *Gender, Nation and Conquest*, pp. 67–8.
60 For Christian theology and seals, see chapter 4 above.
61 B. Bedos-Rezak, 'Towns and seals: representation and signification in medieval France', *Bulletin of the John Rylands Library*, 72/3 (1990), 35–49, at 35–6.
62 M. Späth, 'Memorialising the glorious past: thirteenth-century seals from English cathedral priories and their artistic contexts', in P. R. Schofield (ed.), *Seals in their Context in the Middle Ages* (Oxford, 2015), pp. 161–2.
63 Clanchy, *From Memory to Written Record*, p. 317.
64 D. H. Williams, *Catalogue of Seals in the National Museum of Wales*. Vol I: *Seal Dies, Welsh Seals, Papal Bullae* (Cardiff, 1993), pp. i, 12, which notes that the appropriate colour was important when authenticity of a seal was in question.
65 Brand, 'Aspects of the law of debt', p. 27; R. R. Mundill, 'Jewish and Christian lending patterns and financial dealings during the twelfth and thirteenth centuries', in P. R. Schofield and N. J. Mayhew (eds), *Credit and Debt in Medieval England* (Oxford, 2002), p. 61.
66 Clanchy, *From Memory to Written Record*, p. 51.
67 H. Pryce, 'Culture, power and the charters of Welsh rulers', pp. 184–202, esp. p. 188; Crouch, 'Earliest original charter', 128.
68 C. Insley, 'From *rex Wallia* to *princeps Wallie*: charters and state formation in thirteenth-century Wales', in J. R. Maddicott and D. M. Palliser (eds), *The Medieval State: Essays Presented to James Campbell* (London, 2000), pp. 194–5.

69 Crouch, *Image of Aristocracy*, p. 93.
70 *Acts*, pp. 133, 141; for a comprehensive discussion of the diplomatic of the *acta* of the princes 1120–1283, see pp. 47–143.
71 Crouch, *Image of Aristocracy*, p. 89.
72 *Acts*, pp. 74–5.

SEALS, WOMEN, GENDER AND IDENTITY

Susan M. Johns

IN 1216 x 1217 ISABELLA, Countess of Gloucester and Essex, in her free widowhood, sealed a deed that gave lands in the fee of Kenfig to the monks of Margam Abbey in Glamorgan.[1] Isabella also augmented her grant to Margam later with a grant of lands in Newcastle (Glamorgan) and thus continued a family tradition of support for the foundation originated by her grandfather, Earl Robert of Gloucester and continued by his son, Isabella's father, Earl William of Gloucester. As a result of the patronage of Isabella's family, Margam Abbey became one of the wealthiest religious houses in medieval Wales by the end of the thirteenth century.[2] The vessica-shaped seal depicts a female figure in a long robe with long flowing maunches standing full face, holding a stylised lily up in her right hand and a bird on her left hand [the principal matrix] (see figure 6.1). Her subsidiary, an antique intaglio gem, depicts an eagle facing left with 'Roman' standards either side, a helmeted head facing right above with a small female to the top right, facing left. The legend on the seal impression identifies her as 'Isabelle, Countess of Gloucester and Mortain', while the legend on the counterseal reads 'EGOSVAQILACVSTOSDNEMEE' [I am the eagle and custodian of my lady] (see figure 6.2). The 1216 x 17 impression is made of green wax, attached to the charter by pink, blue and yellow cords. Patterson noted that Isabel's seal and counterseal were the same as, respectively, her mother and father's seal and counterseal, although there were some minor changes. The antique gem that was used as Isabella's counterseal had been used by her father and he had possibly inherited it from his father before him, and it had been reset or the mount recut to make the legend more suitable for a female seal user.[3] Isabella, a great heiress, had been married three times and was a widow of her third husband when she sealed her document. From 1189 to 1199 she had been married to King John, and it was from him that she acquired the title of Countess of Mortain.[4]

High-status female patronage of a monastic house associated with their family is not unusual in the early thirteenth century, but the seal appended to Isabella's charter gives us an insight into the basis of her status and power. Isabella's seals illustrate many of the significant areas of study identified by historians writing on seals and their meanings. Prominent among these are the importance of the iconography as it relates to the individual seal user, and the significance of the legend and counterseal if present. The context of Isabella's actions, too, illustrates core themes present in the study of medieval noblewomen: Isabella sealed in the context of religious patronage and family connections; she did so as a widow, and one of high status; and the motifs on the seal were standard devices utilised by women of the elite in the late twelfth and early thirteenth centuries. Motifs deployed on seals were important markers of identity and that they mediated ideas about gender is now accepted by scholars.[5] The legend refers to her temporal power, office gained through marriage, the iconography to her lineage and procreative roles through the deployment of the lily flower, an image associated with purity, virginity and genealogy. Isabella's status as a widow and as an heiress is accepted as providing key contexts that constructed women's power in the Middle Ages, and politics and family connections then interacted with each other and individual circumstance to both facilitate and constrict women's agency. The seal imaged these contexts directly. Although historians have discussed high-status women, there is much less known about non-elite females and women of lower social status than Isabella, whose family connections place her at the apex of the landed elite in late twelfth-century England and who was even married to a prince, later king. Thus, in its broader symbolisms relating to Isabella's individual status as heiress and widow, the seal underlines the importance of a careful reading of the motifs, legend and counterseal to understand the nature of the complex messages mediated through the seal impression. Seals also, however, raise questions about the nature of women's sealing as it relates to broader issues concerning women's family connections, social status and access to economic resources, and to current ideologies of power as they relate to gender, as well as the purpose of seals in a broader dialectic about legitimate power and authority involving women.

The following discussion will focus on women's seals through an analytical framework that takes account of the way that seals mediated ideas about women and gender. Set into a comparative analysis, the discussion will consider iconography in a framework which takes account of the documentary context to clarify similarities and differences in sealing practice between men and women. The following discussion will focus on the seals of women, while taking account of gender, since the seals of women have received less scholarly attention than men's, and also because the study of seals has been dominated by discussions of the male military elite, ecclesiastical hierarchy and institutions, kings and queens. The following exploration of women and seal usage will thus cast some light on questions concerning interactions between gender, power, identity and social status that were imaged on seals. It will further explore questions concerning ideologies of function and the imagined realities of power that were imaged by reference to gender identity. This methodology will allow for reflections on whether seals articulated a legitimating discourse for the exercise of power that was gendered, complex and multivocal in specific contexts. Women's seals were as legally authoritative as those of men, yet paradoxically women were of inferior legal status to men. Seals were symbols of the legitimate use of power and as such articulated an individualised image of the social, political, economic and cultural role of the seal user/owner.

Seal usage among the elite accompanied a European social transformation in the period of the high Middle Ages that saw the emergence of distinctive hierarchical groups within the landholding elite forming distinctive social categories or 'classes'.[6] This process saw the elite defined by modes of behaviour, by recourse to heraldry and by social practices that saw the creation of conscious, yet evolving, social classes. By the end of the Middle Ages different hierarchical groups had emerged in a medieval society that had become more complex, so there were recognisable social groups in the noble elite that included gendered categories of social status, as evident in the emergence of the peerage, knights, gentlemen and bannerets, distinctions reflected in seal ownership and usage. As Philip Morgan has pointed out, lordship was constructed through the dominance of territory, land ownership, elite mentality and a military ethos that gave it force.[7] Recent writings on the nobility reflect the more general interest in chivalry and kingship, and as a result it is possible to argue that a discourse on power emerged on seals that had at its heart a language of social definition. Women as a category apart conforms to medieval gendered classification systems that saw women as the other; the evidence from seals, however, tells us about complex social classifications that were enmeshed with broader sociocultural concerns. Social status interacted with ideas about the place of women in society, and the female lifecycle was key in determining women's roles in society. This cut across social status and was one way in which all women, irrespective of rank, were classified.[8] In English and Welsh law, wives were subject to the authority of their husbands or male kin, and daughters, like sons, were subject to the authority of their fathers or male kin until they married. In the case of female heiresses or wards of court they were under the control of their guardian who might, or might not, be a blood relative.[9] Much scholarship has explored the ways in which family contexts defined women's identity and roles in the gendered constructed categories of wives, widows, daughters and sisters.

The dominant historical paradigms inherent in the works of late nineteenth- and twentieth-century scholars such as John Horace Round or Sir Frank Stenton and, following him, his wife Lady Doris, gendered lordship as a male function. Lordship has been central to the way scholars have discussed Anglo-Norman polities and society. They thus articulated a paradigm that privileged male power and action and overlooked the participation of women in contemporary power structures and this became the dominant historiographical construct for historians of the Anglo-Norman realm. For example, Sir Frank Stenton overlooked the participation of Milicent de Gournay, the wife of Hugh de Gournay, in the twelfth century where he saw Hugh acting for his wife, when in fact the charter in question records joint action and therefore joint responsibility.[10] Joint sealing by husband and wife in charters where husband and wife acted conjointly was an important statement of such joint responsibility, power and authority.

There are about 300 seal impressions that identify women as the sole seal user in the *SiMeW* database; this represents just under 10 per cent of impressions of the 'personal' seals.[11] This can be compared with John Cherry's estimate that, considering seals used by women that were identifiable through personal names among the relatively well-catalogued medieval seals of Norfolk and Suffolk, about 20 per cent of all seals in use were employed by women.[12] The figures, both of course contingent upon the survival of artefacts, suggest that seal usage by an identifiably named female seal user is markedly lower than seal usage by named male seal users, and historians have noted this established pattern for the seals of high-status women.[13] Women's participation in business was affected by the impact of the female lifecycle, both wives and widows sealed medieval documents and seals identify women by marital and family ties. About 25 per cent of the women are identified as the wife of a named individual (*uxor*), either within the document or through the legend. Some wives had their own seal, which suggests an identity distinct from that of their husband.[14] About a fifth of the sample were probably widows and a variety of terms were used within documents, such as the deployment of *quondam uxor* (sometime wife) or *qui fuit uxor*. In one case dating from the 1340s, Margery, the wife of a clerk, was described as a concubine in the text of the deed, since under canon law those under holy orders could not marry.[15] The deed may clarify that the woman was involved through reference to *maritagium* or dower. About a third of the sample may be identified as 'the daughter' of [named father], which may suggest, in some circumstances, that the woman was an heiress.[16]

Although it is predominantly the case that a seal matrix was associated with a single individual, identities could be blended within a single matrix. As John Cherry has shown in an example from Lincolnshire, husband and wives could have a single seal matrix.[17] This is significant because it illustrates that the family unit, husband and wife, was a key unit of authorisation encapsulated in the very essence of the seal matrix since it served as the means by which the power of the family was authorised in family actions jointly applicable to both husband and wife. Brigitte Bedos-Rezak argued that seals had, among other uses, Christological functions that symbolised presence and were tools of social control and identity. Seals were stereotypic, that is they assigned sociocultural functions.[18] Seals assigned sociocultural functions, yet gender-neutral imagery and non-specific legends suggest that seals in effect functioned in a multivocal non-specific way in some contexts: they mediated different ideas about individuals, yet the motifs deployed could be interpreted in different ways. Some seal matrices were impersonal with no legend and some bore legends that served more personal functions, such as mottos.[19]

Linguistic change is a feature of medieval society; Latin replaced the vernacular as the language of royal and governmental records from the late eleventh century. With the Norman advances into Wales through the late eleventh and twelfth centuries, Wales became plurilingual. Seals, and their associated documents, constructed personal identity, and the choice of language used to identify individuals could potentially be analysed within a sociolinguistic framework to evaluate whether linguistic choice also interacted with gender to define an individual's identity. Language in twelfth-century England was an important aspect of social definition and part of the competing and multiple identities of the elite and may well express ideas about social status.[20]

Although in many cases legends are not legible, where the legend does survive it allows us to understand how the identity of women is represented in various categories and provides a complicated guide to personal identity. Some women are identified by use of an *uxor* formula, as in the examples of Isabella, the wife of Pain, whose seal depicted a bird with wings outstretched (see figure 6.3),[21] or Emma the wife of William Banastre (see figure 6.4).[22] The document that the latter example seals is a quitclaim given by Emma as a widow in her free widowhood and, even more significantly, after her marriage had ended: *post divortium celebratum inter me et Adam maritum meum*. Thus, although the seal legend identifies Emma as a wife, the text of the deed clarifies her marital state. Emma had been married three times, firstly to Simon of *Jagdon* (Yagdon), secondly to William Banastre, and thirdly to Adam. Emma thus sealed her document as a widow after the divorce from Adam. The lands that were the subject of the transaction were held by right of dower acquired through her first marriage. Thus Emma's identity as constructed on her seal was fixed as the widow of her second husband when she disposed of lands that she had acquired through marriage to her first husband. Women retained the name of previous husbands through subsequent marriages, yet Emma was known as the wife of William Banastre, not as the wife of Simon of *Jagdon*, her first husband by whom she had a son, Roger, who also in *c.*1220–30 quitclaimed lands to the same beneficiary, Haughmond Abbey, which had also received the quitclaim of Emma his mother. The quitclaim clarifies that one of the virgates that the donor granted was held in dower by his mother but that the land would revert to him on her death.[23] The lands relate to property in Edgebolton (Shropshire), and it is these lands that Emma Banastre confirmed to Haughmond as a widow in the period 1235–40.[24] Thus, the remarried widow/divorced Emma Banastre confirmed her gift of lands to Haughmond that were hers by right of dower from her first marriage. The foliate design on the field is a complicated motif that in some contexts was associated with freeholders in the thirteenth century, which is perhaps suggestive of Emma's social status, but which also was used in a variety of contexts and social groups and different statuses.[25] The *uxor* formula on Emma's personal seal is not a guide to the marital status of the female sealer at the moment of sealing. It represents instead one element of Emma's identity that, in effect, was her personal yet public identity, which was also indicated by the motif deployed at that specific moment when the document was agreed. Together with the documentary context, this provides an insight into the sealing practice of a woman of relatively modest social status, yet marriage is key to the public identity of Emma, as indicated by the *uxor* formula.

Marital status as wife (*uxor*) is a gendered category of identity since marriage changed the status of women in a way that did not apply to men. Usage of this formula declined concomitant with the emergence of bynames usually related to place which became stable and hereditary. This was a slow process that reflected, in the words of David Postles, 'daily, lived experiences'.[26] Bynames account for the majority of names on women's seals from the thirteenth and fourteenth centuries, and this could appear to reflect gender parity: it is more difficult to detect from seal legends whether the bynames indicate the adoption by women of the byname associated with their husband. A key question with the emergence of names and naming patterns in the context of bynames is therefore the importance of 'placeness'. The classification of toponymic names or locative names is fraught with methodological problems, and thus any assessment of the importance of gender complicates an already complex area. There are a number of seal legends that identify women with bynames and surnames; fluidity is key since the perception of an individual's identity must be seen within a social, communal and creative context within ongoing social processes.[27] Even more significant is the documentary provenance of names.

It is apparent that just as some women's seals that contain an *uxor* formula may not reflect their current marital status, so too the legends of seals that function to associate them with bynames, or patrilineal 'locative' names, may also not be connected to their current marital status or marital identity. Thus, legends may be one guide to a seal user's identity in the context of that moment when the deed was made or agreed, yet the seal should be read together with the narrative within the associated document. There are a small number of seals whose legends utilise the 'daughter of' [named father] or *filia* formula.[28] Two male seal users were identified as son of their mother and one similarly identifies the woman as the daughter of her mother.[29] The *filia* designation is not apparent on the seals of women later than the early thirteenth century. Bynames associated with placenames are represented on the seals of women in the *SiMeW* dataset, and out of the sample of seals that are legible, approximately one third have legends linked to placenames, accounting for approximately 0.05 per cent of the overall sample of seals in the dataset. Of the legends that are legible, only three contain Welsh female personal names; one belongs to Thaterech, another seal is appended to a document that was jointly given by Gwenhwyfar and Gwenllian, daughters of Gwerfil ferch Griffith ap Cynwrig ap Howel in 1415.[30] (See figures 6.5 and 6.6. and figure 1.10.) The legends on women's seals also feature bynames, and it is apparent that just as some women's seals that utilise the *uxor* formula thereby depict identities that may not have been connected with their husbands' identities, so the legends of seals that function as bynames, or 'locative' names, may also not be connected to women's marital status. There are very few seals that identify the female user by title: only three countesses are represented in this sample. The legend of the seal of Lady Wem of Shropshire – 'Ela la Botiliere' had a seal in 1337 that possible references her as 'lady' (see figure 6.7).[31] There are examples of women co-sealing with their sons, for example Alice de *Frombruge*.[32] There are also examples of women co-sealing as sisters.[33]

Medieval women's seals have been studied by scholars who have shown the importance of the iconography for the way that it represented women's power and authority.[34] It is important to set the study of seals into a context that takes account of lordship and power and the interactions between these constructs and individuals. Seals symbolise the power of the individual in many different ways, in some specific contexts their power to control land or other aspects of its value such as food renders or military service, which are manifestations of economic power rooted in the value of land. For the seals of the elite, ideas about power inherent in conceptions of lordship seals were an increasingly important manifestation of aspects of lordship and individual identity in the twelfth century, the appearance of elite women's seals suggests the importance of women within lordship and their roles in cultural, symbolic power as well as in the economic exploitation of resources, and participation in documentary culture for all ranks of society.

Seals of noblewomen deployed the motif of a standing female figure holding symbolic objects from the inception of sealing by the aristocracy and the nobility in the twelfth century into the fourteenth. The incorporation of heraldic arms onto the seals of the landholding elite occurred with the beginnings of secular noble sealing practice in the twelfth century. That the seals of women also depicted heraldic arms is significant; scholars such as Maurice Keen have argued that heraldic arms depicted on seals initially related to military function, that is heraldry emerged on the battlefield as a means of identifying individuals. Heraldic arms also referred to lineage on twelfth-century seals.[35] Heraldic images had different symbolic functions on men and women's seals. David Crouch and Keen have both noted that connections to lineage, which was the crucial function of heraldic imagery, necessarily involved the depiction of the genealogical connections brought to families by marriage. The use of heraldic images on women's seals therefore constructs women's sigillographic identity in terms of kinship and lineage. Seals then serve as a part of a legitimating discourse of noble power that is founded on differences rooted in gender. Seals of elite women confirm the importance of ideas about gender identity as performance of social function.

As the use of seals spread, so women of non-noble status began to seal documents. Rather less is known of the interactions of women and sealing in the context of urban settings than is of those interactions in the world beyond the town. In the later Middle Ages women's ability to dispose of property was circumscribed, and women were defined by their relationship to male kin, usually their husbands, fathers or sons in legal contexts. Seals in part reflect this, but also suggest that women's identities could be more complex. In the fourteenth century, Alice, the widow of Edmund Pitchford, was involved in a range of actions recorded on deeds that concern lands in Bridgnorth, Shropshire, in the period 1360–1. Her conventional seal deploys imagery typical of noblewomen: a standing female figure holding a shield in her right hand. The shield would have depicted the arms of her husband given that it was usual for the armorial seals of women to deploy the husband's arms on the left hand of the shield and indicates her noble status and the right of her husband's family to bear arms (see figure 6.8). The document is a final concord and the linguistic formula is typical of deeds of this nature, informing the reader of her marital status, family connections and her stage in the female lifecycle: Alice is identified by her personal name, marital status and her widowed state. Thus she is 'Alicia who was the wife of Edmund Pitchford' who sealed *in viduatate mea* and made an agreement concerning her orchard for 40s. The agreement was made with a husband and wife, Phillip Orreby and Felicia, and was witnessed by John de la Hulle then bailiff of Bridgnorth, among others.[36] Other deeds that conveyed property rights in the same period were also sealed with the same seal, and, further, her seal was appended to the will of Robert of Bridgnorth.[37] Alice was widowed by 1358, by which time she was involved in a suit to recover lands in Bridgnorth that were being denied to her by John, son of Thomas, son of Robert of Bridgnorth. The agreement was settled at Westminster and suggests that the complex process of litigation involved relatively small amounts of land.[38] In 1341 Alice's father, John Rondulph, made an agreement with Alice and her husband, Edmund de Pitchford, concerning various lands in Bridgnorth, and the copy that survives has a seal that depicts two busts facing each other with a stylised lily above. The seal owner is not identified: the legend reads in the vernacular 'LOVEMEANDEWE'. The *conventio* indicates that John Rondulph sealed his copy of the agreement and Alice and her husband retained that copy, while he retained the copy sealed by Alice and Edmund de Pitchford.[39] The two heads may signify the two families joined in marriage, the stylised lily that represents a developed form of a stylised lily as the central motif symbolised family lineage, and the two individuals face each other across the symbol. There is another example of a seal of a similar design and period that authenticates a joint deed of Hugh de Trotinale and Agnes his wife.[40] The legend of the Pitchford seal is a pun, both a command to 'love' the agreement as well as a reminder of the joint nature of any agreement. Here the seal is gender-neutral and authenticates a family agreement: Alice as a wife and daughter, Edmund as a husband and son-in-law, and John as the patrilineal grantor. The seal is a witty allusion to its function and is distinctive as a multivocal symbolic object of family, authority and memory, and also the busts of the human head indicate the human nature of the connections forged.

The documentary evidence, and associated seals, facilitates a complex picture of sales and settlements based on land values among the landholders of Bridgnorth, and there are evidently connections between parties over time established through male office-holding and female kinship. For example, the widowed mother of the above named John son of Thomas, in 1350–1 in *viduatate mea* sealed a quitclaim in favour of Peter de Colington of all her rights in the lands as given by her son John. The seal she used depicts St Katherine holding her wheel,[41] perhaps a personal choice given the popularity of the cult of St Katherine in late medieval England.[42] It is suggestive of the noble status of the female sealer given the use of the standing female form. Joanna, the widow of Nicholas de Pitchford, had, for a certain payment, granted a tenement to John Canne, who was her clerk.[43] Joanna de Pitchford may well be connected to the above Alice de Pitchford, and certainly her husband Nicholas de Pitchford witnessed documents that were also witnessed by the town's officers. The above examples reveal women involved in different types of transactions: we can see them involved in business (sales) and on a local basis we can begin to build up a chronology of use that indicates the potential of this body of evidence. For our purposes the use of seals by women reveals their public identity.

Variety in the seal motifs is a noted development in the Middle Ages and women's seals reflect this development with women using animals on their seals; for example Margery and Cecilia, daughters of Hugh son of Hugh de Haurthyrn, in 1364 x 1365 used a seal that depicted a rabbit with an arrow-shaft protruding from its back.[44] Rabbits or hares appear on seals from *c.*1315 and they peak mid-century; they are a gender-neutral motif appearing on both men and women's seals, with one example showing a hare blowing a horn.[45] Lower status women's seals usually identify them by a forename and a simple device, such as that of Thatherech daughter of Katherech datable to *c.*1225, which depicts an unusual fish motif (see figure 6.5). There are only two other examples of seals that deploy fish motifs in the *SiMeW* dataset; one dates from 1248 x 1285 and was used by a Matilda daughter of William, and another dates from 1438 x 1439, used by John Pykemere, and is an obvious pun.[46] Another example of a simple seal design dates from the early thirteenth century and was used by Gwenllian daughter of Phillip. Her seal depicts a radial motif in the form of a cross with rays emerging from a central pellet (see figure 6.9).[47] A later example is that of Gwenhyfar Holbache (1429 x 1430) whose seal depicts two letters interlaced.[48] Other seals feature animals or birds with pious religious symbolisms, not linked to gender, such as the pelican in its piety, a motif that develops from the late thirteenth century on the seals of men and women, such as on the seal of Lleucu, daughter of Ieuan ap Llywelyn, wife of David ap Dyc Bonnwyn, of 1476.[49] Other non-gender-specific motifs on the seals of women include the Lamb of God,[50] or zoomorphic devices featuring animals such as a fox[51] or a squirrel.[52]

The standing female figure motif was used on higher status women's seals from the twelfth century. Despite the variety in the different motifs used on women's seals, the standing female figure that may hold objects signifying family connections (heraldic devices) or lineage and procreation (fleur-de-lys or stylised lily flowers). There are later examples of seals that depict a standing figure associated with other emblems and especially from the fourteenth century motifs associated with specific saints. We have already observed the example of St Katherine,[53] and the seal used by Sibilla widow of William Waters of Burton [1368 x 1369] depicts a standing female figure who can be identified as St Margaret; other examples that reference St Margaret all date from the latter part of the fourteenth century (see figure 6.10).[54] The fourteenth century thus saw a development whereby female saints, especially St Katherine, and other female saints such as SS Helen, Milburga or Winefrid were referenced on seals.[55] Iseuda la Welere as a widow used a seal that depicted the Virgin and Child, another popular motif, in 1339 (see figure 6.11).[56] That such allusions may reflect personal piety is probable (see chapter 7 below). Scriptural allusions to the language of sealing gave force to the sacred and 'magical' qualities of sealing.[57] The connection with the sacred is evident in the life of St Margaret of Antioch, a popular saint for women as the patron saint of childbirth. The language of contract was deployed in the text popular in the fourteenth century.[58] The text relates that Margaret states, at the peak of her sufferings, that her promise to God was marked on her body: 'My lord has put a seal on each of my limbs, and in return for the jewel that I gave him has prepared and granted me a victor's crown.'[59] Here the language of contract shaped the text, but for our purposes it is striking that the language of sealing was associated with marking Margaret's body: and the language deployed used sigillographic imagery and suggests the marks on her were indelible. Her body had been tortured by candles and changed and moulded, the allusion to her body as a soft object that was malleable is then alluded to in the sealing imagery, and was a symbolic medium, and metaphorically alluded to the cultural dichotomies inherent in medieval symbolisms. Walker Bynum has suggested that women's sense of self was formed by reference to theological traditions and dominant symbologies.[60] Taking this idea forward, sealing for women as a process, and by reference to the motifs deployed on seals, may perhaps have assumed, in some respects, different meanings even when they used the same symbols on their seals.

Seals and the deeds that they validate are thus important sources that have much to tell us about the cultural norms and ideological constructs of contemporary societies. Ideas about women and gender influenced the deployment of motifs on the seals of men and women and this is apparent particularly on the seals of elite women's seals of the high Middle Ages, but so, too, other influences shaped the iconography of the seal, such as the emergence of armorials and heraldry. Social status and the economic context had an influence too and seals reveal the ongoing dialogue between text, seal and audience that was multivocal and variable, fluid and developing. If charters can be seen as moments in an ongoing narrative of cultural exchange, then seals serve as an iconographic statement of function and identity of the individual in a complex cultural context. For women, this language of power was based on ideas about their position in the family and kin as well as the female lifecycle, and the ongoing imperatives of other factors, such as lordship and economic exchange affected the presentation of individual identity in a communal context. The process of cultural diffusion and the widespread use of seals created a form of functional literacy where the interplay of gender, function, charter production, legal functions and sigillographic contexts interacted to create individualised identities, yet also confirmed group cohesion and family boundaries: all these, as well as social status, thus underpinned the iconography of seals, which has much to reveal about contemporary norms. Seals and their associated documents demonstrate the importance of the lifecycle, gender, patterns of seal usage and the variety in motifs deployed on seals, as well as the importance of interacting contexts of family, place and social status on creating individualised identities in a fluid sociocultural context.

Notes

1. NLW PENRICE: GLAM/113; other impressions all NLW PENRICE: GLAM/104 [1217]; NLW PENRICE: GLAM/2042 [1216 x 1217]; NLW PENRICE: GLAM/2043 [1214 x 1216] NLW PENRICE: GLAM/2043 [1214 x 1216]; *Margam*, pp. 212, 213; *Cartae*, no. 350; R. B. Patterson (ed.), *Earldom of Gloucester Charters: The Charters and Scribes of the Earls and Countesses of Gloucester to AD 1217* (Oxford, 1973), no. 146; Susan M. Johns, *Noblewomen, Aristocracy and Power in the Twelfth-Century Anglo-Norman Realm* (Manchester, 2003), p. 214 (no. 55); *Scriptorium*, p. 120; David H. Williams, *Images of Welsh History* (Aberystwyth, 2007), p. 14, fig. 30. For discussion of the importance of seals and the significance of colour, see D. H. Williams, *Catalogue of Seals in the National Museum of Wales. Vol. I: Seal Dies, Welsh Seals and Papal Bullae* (Cardiff, 1993), p. 12. See also chapter 5. My thanks to Phillipp Schofield and Elizabeth New for their helpful comments.
2. D. Robinson (ed.), *The Cistercian Abbeys of Britain: Far from the Concourse of Men* (London, 1998), p. 138: the abbey's income by 1291 was £256.
3. Patterson, *Earldom of Gloucester Charters*, pp. 24–5; M. M. Archibald, 'The lion coinage of Robert earl of Gloucester and William earl of Gloucester', *British Numismatic Journal*, 71 (2001), 71–86, at 74; for the heritability of counterseals, see *Guide*, pp. 58–9, n.9; T. A. Heslop, 'Seals', in G. Zarnecki, J. Allen and T. Holland (eds), *English Romanesque Art 1066–1200*, Hayward Gallery exhibition catalogue (London, 1984), p. 308, no. 345.
4. For her titles see Patterson, *Earldom of Gloucester Charters*, pp. 23–5.
5. B. Bedos-Rezak, 'Women, seals and power in medieval France, 1150–1350', in M. Erler and M. Kowaleski (eds), *Women and Power in the Middle Ages* (Athens, GA, and London, 1988), pp. 61–82; Johns, *Noblewomen, Aristocracy and Power*, pp. 122–51; E. Danbury, 'Queens and powerful women: image and authority', in *Good Impressions*, pp. 17–24. Work on identity includes J. Cherry, 'Personal and impersonal impressions: identity revealed through seals,' in S. Worrell, G. Egan, J. Naylor, K. Leahy and M. Lewis (eds), *A Decade of Discovery: Proceedings of the Portable Antiquities Scheme Conference 2007*, BAR British Series, 520 (Oxford, 2010), pp. 225–34.
6. D. Crouch, *The English Aristocracy, 1070–1272: A Social Transformation* (New Haven and London, 2011), pp. xiv–xv, 53, 166. For the later Middle Ages see S. H. Rigby, *English Society in the Later Middle Ages: Class, Status and Gender* (Basingstoke, 1995).
7. P. Morgan, 'Making the English gentry', in P. R. Coss and S. D. Lloyd (eds), *Thirteenth-Century England V* (Woodbridge, 1995), pp. 21–35. See also Crouch, *English Aristocracy*, p. xvi.
8. M. E. Mate, *Women in Medieval English Society* (Cambridge, 1999), p. 2.

9   For discussion of medieval women and the law generally see S. S. Walker, 'Introduction', in S. S. Walker (ed.), *Wife and Widow in Medieval England* (Ann Arbor, MI, 1993), pp. 1–16; more recently the collection of essays in N. J. Menuge (ed.), *Medieval Women and the Law* (Woodbridge, 2003); for Welsh laws see D. Jenkins and M. E. Owen (eds), *The Welsh Law of Women: Studies Presented to Professor Daniel A. Binchy on his Eightieth Birthday, 3 June 1980* (Cardiff, 1980); G. Richards, *Welsh Noblewomen in the Thirteenth Century: An Historical Study of Medieval Welsh Law and Gender Roles* (Lewiston, NY; Queenston, Ontario; and Lampeter, 2009). For a discussion of aspects of the Welsh laws and women of the elite see S. M. Johns, *Gender, Nation and Conquest in the High Middle Ages: Nest of Deheubarth* (Manchester, 2013), pp. 30–4, 99–101.

10   F. M. Stenton, *First Century of English Feudalism* (Oxford, 1932), pp. 107–8; D. M. Stenton, *The Englishwoman in History* (London, 1957); J. H. Round, 'The introduction of Knight Service into England', in J. H. Round, *Feudal England: Historical Studies on the Eleventh and Twelfth Centuries* (London, 1895; repr. London, 1964), pp. 182–245; for comment see Johns, *Noblewomen, Aristocracy and Power*, pp. 2–4.

11   There are 309 impressions.

12   Cherry, 'Personal and impersonal impressions', pp. 225–34, at p. 228.

13   Danbury, 'Queens and powerful women', p. 17.

14   See the discussion at pp. 96–8.

15   NLW PENRICE: GLAM/289; for comment, *Margam*, p. 152.

16   There are ninety-seven in total. For a detailed discussion of this principle see Johns, *Noblewomen, Aristocracy and Power*, pp. 135–6 and B. Bedos-Rezak, 'Medieval women in French sigillographic sources', in J. T. Rosenthal (ed.), *Medieval Women and the Sources of Medieval History* (Athens, GA, and London, 1990), pp. 1–36.

17   Cherry, 'Personal and impersonal impressions', p. 225.

18   B. Bedos-Rezak, 'In search of a semiotic paradigm: the matter of sealing in medieval thought and praxis (1050–1400)', in N. Adams, J. Cherry and J. Robinson (eds), *Good Impressions: Image and Authority in Medieval Seals* (London, 2007), pp. 1–7.

19   Cherry, 'Personal and impersonal impressions', p. 225.

20   See I. Short, '*Tam Angli quam Franci*: self-definition in Anglo-Norman England', *Anglo-Norman Studies*, 18 (1996 for 1995), 153–75, which suggests ways that language was a part of social definition, and that the subject of names and identity has diverse range of scholarship. The potential for the *SiMeW* dataset to shed light on naming choices, identity, cultural interactions and gender will be explored in a paper to be published in P. Skinner (ed.), *Beyond Arthur: the Welsh and the World in the Middle Ages* (Cardiff, forthcoming).

21   Seal 2438.

22   SIGILL'AMMEVXORISWILL'IBANAST', Seal 2318.

23   Una Rees (ed.), *The Cartulary of Haughmond Abbey* (Cardiff, 1985), p. 76, no. 305.

24   *Cartulary of Haughmond Abbey*, p. 76, no. 307.

25   E. A. New, '(Un)conventional images. A case-study of radial motifs on personal seals', in P. R. Schofield (ed.), *Seals and their Context in the Middle Ages* (Oxford, 2015), pp. 151–60.

26   D. Postles, *The North through its Names: A Phenomenology of Medieval and Early Modern Northern England*, English Surnames Survey, 8 (Oxford, 2007), p. 8.

27   Postles, *North through its Names*, p. 8.

28   Seal 1271; Seal 1645; Seal 759; Seal 764.

29   William son of Susanne: Seal 1166; Stephen son of Mary: Seal 870; Alice daughter of Christine de BiþWelle: Seal 800.

30   NLW PENRICE: GLAM/69 [1225]; BUAS PENR/311.

31   Seal 2353: *S'ELE LA BOT[........]M[.]E for ?domine, it features armorial devices.

32 BL Add. Ch. 24269 [1225 x 1274] Alice, mother of Adam son and heir of Philip Alexander; other impressions: BL Add. Ch. 24270, BL Add. Ch. 24272 [both 1225 x 1274]; seal depicts a stylised lily.
33 Agnes, Christine and Alice daughters of William co-sealed a document in 1262, each had their own seal: HCA Deed 269.
34 Danbury, 'Queens and powerful women', pp. 17–24; Johns, *Noblewomen, Aristocracy and Power*. Work on identity includes Cherry, 'Personal and impersonal impressions'.
35 M. Keen, 'Heraldry and the medieval gentlewoman', *History Today*, 53 (2003), 24. See also his *Origins of the English Gentleman: Heraldry, Chivalry and Gentility in Medieval England, c.1300–c.1500* (Stroud, 2002); P. Coss, *The Lady in Medieval England, 1000–1500* (Stroud, 1998); D. Crouch, *The Image of Aristocracy in Britain 1000–1300* (London, 1992); P. Coss and M. Keen (eds), *Heraldry, Pageantry and Social Display in Medieval England* (Woodbridge, 2002), chapters 1 and 2 (by P. Coss and D. Crouch).
36 NLW PITORD/38, 46, 437, 1293.
37 Agreements with male recipients: NLW PITORD/1293; NLW PITORD/46; Will of Robert of Bridgnorth NLW PITORD/537.
38 TNA, CP 25/1/195/16, no. 20.
39 NLW PITORD/57; for another agreement with similar sealing clause NLW PITORD/404.
40 NLW PITORD/1162. For discussion of 'love and loyalty' seals see *Guide*, pp. 89–90; T. A. Heslop, 'Peasant seals', in E. King (ed.), *Medieval England 1066–1485* (London, 1988), pp. 214–15, notes that love and loyalty seals were probably used for personal correspondence and had anonymous legends, usually in French.
41 Seal 1605.
42 K. Lewis, *The Cult of St Katherine of Alexandria in Late Medieval England* (Woodbridge, 2002), and see also C. Pearce, 'The cult of St Margaret of Antioch', *Feminist Theology: The Journal of the Britain and Ireland School of Feminist Theology*, 16 (1997), 70–85.
43 SA Mrs Dyas Deeds, 796/6, 14 Edward III [3 October 1340].
44 Seal 1769.
45 Seal 1616; Seal 1579 (for further discussion of which, see also below, pp. 114–15); Seal 1838; Seal 1847; Seal 1946; Seal 2281; Seal 2231; Seal 201; Seal 631; Seal 2154; Seal 674.
46 Thatherech daughter of Katherech: Seal 1171, in favour of Margam Abbey. Matilda daughter of Robert: Seal 2450. John Pykemere: Seal 260.
47 Seal 17.
48 Seal 1966.
49 Seal 108, Lleucu was jointly involved in a suit of court with her husband in 1444, NLW Bronwydd Ch. 826. There are 33 impressions that feature the pelican in its piety. Early examples: Seal 2443; BUAS PENR/408 [1334 x 1335]. See chapter 5, on seals and religion.
50 Gwenllian, daughter of David Vychan [1385]; Seal 177.
51 Seal 221: Johanna the wife of John of Pykemere. Her husband used a punning fish motif, see above, p. 99. For examples of fox motif: Seal 272; Seal 645.
52 Thirty-three seals feature squirrels. For an early example [1250]: Seal 359; most date from the mid-fourteenth century onwards; Amy White, a spinster, had a seal with this motif in 1530: Seal 1005.
53 Above, n. 24; saints are usually depicted as a standing figure, in common with the seals of women and ecclesiastics; for other examples from the *SiMeW* data set see also Seal 1628; Seal 1659; Seal 1971; Seal 2053; Seal 2216; Seal 2213; Seal 2289; Seal 753; Seals 794–6. The spiked wheel of St Katherine appears on a deed of Richard de la Hulle, rector of Pichford church: Seal 1894.

54 Seal 2106; Seal 2153.
55 St Miliburga and St Winefrid: Seal 2165. St Helen: Seal 2462. There is much scholarship on female saints and their cults; see, for example, D. Weinstein and R. M. Bell, *Saints and Society: The Two Worlds of Western Christendom 1000–1700* (Chicago and London, 1982); K. A Winstead, *Virgin Martyrs: Legends of Sainthood in Late Medieval England* (Ithaca, NY, and London, 1997); Lewis, *Cult of St Katherine*. See T. A. Heslop, 'The Virgin Mary's regalia and 12th century English seals', in A. Borg and A. Martindale (eds), *Studies Presented to Christopher Hohler* (Oxford, 1981), pp. 53–62, which demonstrates the fusion of Christian theology with depictions of the Virgin.
56 Seal 1305. Fifty-one seals in the *SiMeW* dataset include identified motifs that reference the Virgin and Child, for example Seal 831; Seal 699, one of eleven surviving impressions on the deed; Seal 463; Seal 2365; Seal 1662; Seal 1519; Seal 1632; Seal 1636; Seal 850; Seal 2288; Seal 235; Seal 149; Seal 2191. The examples given date from the early thirteenth to the late fifteenth century consecutively. The 'Virgin and Child' motif was a popular devotional motif on ecclesiastical seals through the Middle Ages and until the dissolution, for example for the abbot of Margam, 1530: Seal 1337. For further discussion see chapter 5.
57 M. T. Clanchy, *From Memory to Written Record, England 1066–1307*, 2nd edn (Oxford, 1993), pp. 311–17; Williams, *Catalogue of Seals*, pp. 1, 7, 17.
58 Pearce, 'Cult of St Margaret', 79.
59 B. Millett and J. W. Brown (eds), *Medieval English Prose for Women: Selections from the Katherine Group and Ancrene Wisse* (Oxford, 1990), pp. 74–5.
60 More could be done on the different meanings of seal motifs taking account of perspectives offered by cultural anthropologists. See C. W. Bynum, 'Men's use of female symbols', in L. K. Little and B. K. Rosenwein (eds), *Debating the Middle Ages: Issues and Readings* (Oxford, 1998), pp. 277–89, esp. nn.4 and 5 for useful reading and perspectives; S. Ortner, 'Is female to male as nature is to culture?', in M. Rosaldo and L. Lamphere (eds), *Women, Culture and Society* (Stanford, 1974), pp. 67–87.

SEALS AS EXPRESSIONS OF IDENTITY

Elizabeth A. New

THIS CHAPTER WILL EXPLORE in different ways some of the themes and issues discussed in earlier chapters, especially those on power-politics and gender; it will also highlight the importance of investigating representation and identity as expressed by seals across the whole of society rather than just elites or very specific groups. Brigitte Bedos-Rezak has proposed that 'the semiotic principal at work in seal imagery tended to thwart individualised references'.[1] While this may be true in some contexts, seals can in fact offer examples of highly individualised images, some – notably canting or rebus designs (essentially a visual pun on or allusion to a name) – which are inexplicable unless associated with a particular man or woman. Taking Bedos-Rezak's hypothesis as a starting point, this chapter will explore the ways in which the designs of seals owned by people, especially those from below the elites, could be used to project identity.[2] It will also offer opportunities to reflect upon constructed identities and their significance in informing historical views of social mobility and aspiration in this period.

One complication when discussing 'personal' seals is a definition of this term.[3] There are, for example, a number of seals in the project sample that were used by magnates or leading ecclesiastics acting in an official capacity, but which do not name the office held by that individual. The subsidiary seals of twelfth and early thirteenth century bishops are a case in point, with the matrices employed to counterseal the episcopal seal of dignity being used in an official capacity but frequently being 'personal' in that they had non-standardised imagery and often failed to give the seal owner's formal title.[4] Therefore, for the purposes of the following discussion, seals are considered to be 'personal' unless either they make specific reference to an office, institution or corporation, or diplomatic evidence demonstrates that they were used exclusively in an official capacity.

(i) Identity through family and hierarchical status

One of the best-known and most thoroughly investigated sigillographic images that place the seal owner within a social category is that of an armed warrior on horseback, a transnational motif of secular power used by the Anglo-Norman elite in Wales and the Marches and rapidly adopted by the native nobility.[5] Even so, a tendency towards individualisation can be seen, both with the development of heraldry (discussed below and in chapter 5 in relation to social hierarchy),[6] and in adjustments that were sometimes made to the conventional image, such as the foliage held in place of the usual sword by the equestrian figure on the seals of Payne (III) de Turberville (d.c.1208), and which probably relates to the name and nature of his lordship of Coity in Glamorgan.[7] Another well-known stereotypic image is that of a standing female figure, principally used on the seals of very high-status women.[8] What is notable about this motif, especially when one considers how much scholarly attention it has received, is how few examples there are within the project's dataset (see appendix of index references in the present volume), suggesting that its usage was even more restricted than previously recognised.

A number of seals used in the late twelfth and early thirteenth centuries suggest a degree of experimentation, while still working within the boundaries of sigillographic motifs that provided a socially constructed representation of the equestrian image type. One such group are 'hand and object' seals, and within the project's dataset a particular subset may be identified, all used by laymen between 1175 and 1225 (their use chiefly clustered around 1200) and validating documents from south Wales. Five of these depict a hand grasping a spear from which flies a pennon, one shows a hand holding three lilies, while on another the hand is holding a large key (see figure 7.1).[9] While in a secular context they may seem somewhat experimental, moving from a complete figure to a part of the body, in another respect they fit comfortably within the framework of sigillographic imagery that was coalescing at this time.[10] The model for these seals may well have been Cistercian seals that depicted a hand holding a staff, signifying the pastoral role of the abbot.[11] The hand and object seals of the laity sometimes seem to have acted in the same way, signifying a particular role, such as that of Adam the porter (*portarius*) of Cardiff, which depicts a hand holding a large key.[12] The lance-pennon seals are a rather more complex group, however, not least because they seem to challenge some ideas about the representation of noble status. As David Crouch notes in his discussion of the emergence of the 'banneret' as a 'magnate-knight', a banner is usually thought to have been the prerogative of a leader.[13] One might therefore expect the lance-pennon seals to belong to men in this category, but this does not seem to be the case. Three of the lance-pennon seal owners were Welshmen,[14] one a younger son of a cadet branch of one of the Welsh ruling families, but the other two cannot be identified beyond their participation in fairly small-scale exchanges suggesting that they were not the dominant figure in their kinship group (see figure 7.2). The other two lance-pennon seal owners have names that suggest Anglo-Norman or Anglo-Welsh origins, but likewise remain difficult to trace in the historical record beyond their involvement in small-scale exchanges with Margam Abbey. It is therefore unlikely that any of these men fitted Crouch's definition of a 'banneret', but while in most parts of England this would be a puzzle, it may be suggested that this motif was adopted because it represented military power and leadership, but did not compete directly with those men of even more elevated status within the kinship group or district who used the equestrian warrior image – something to be avoided in a hierarchical society where an accidental slight could lead to feuds.[15]

Familial relationships and one's place within the kinship group of course played a very important part in the construction of medieval identity, with heraldry widely used as a means of displaying this on seals.[16] Welsh society is considered to have been comparatively late, in western European terms, in adopting hereditary armorial bearings,[17] although caution must be exercised here since it is clear that motifs associated with kinship – such as the hand and lance-pennon discussed above – were current and used on seals in Wales from the mid-twelfth century onwards.[18] One of the earliest examples of possibly heraldic devices on seals from Wales are the impressions of the seals of four brothers, attached to a thirteenth-century grant to Margam Abbey, where in each case the principal motif is a banner charged with three chevrons.[19] The device on the banners is usually associated with the chevrons of the powerful Clare family, whose Welsh lands included the lordship of Glamorgan, and is presumed also to have influenced the adoption of similar arms by the d'Avene family in Glamorgan.[20] This is a particularly interesting case, since the first 'd'Avene' known to have used an armorial seal was Lleision ap Morgan ap Morgan Fychan.[21] As his name suggests, he was a member of one of the native Welsh ruling dynasties in the areas, the later family name being a Francophone version of their lordship of Afan, indicating a reorientation of familial identity in order more fully to integrate with the Anglo-Norman elite, of which the acquisition of a heraldic seal would surely have played a part.

While the d'Avene family used seals as a means of better identifying with English society, other heraldic seals suggest that native Welsh culture was an important part of the identity of some families. Thomas Vaughan, son of Sir Roger Vaughan of Tretower (Powys), is a case in point. His first seal has the motif of the head of a boy with a snake wrapped around his neck, a device that later became the family's heraldic badge, while his second seal placed the image as a charge on a shield.[22] This international form of expressing elite status was however given a specifically Welsh dimension, since the snake in the motif adopted by Thomas Vaughan is referenced in a number of fifteenth and sixteenth-century praise-poems written in honour of the extended family.[23]

Family identity could be expressed in ways other than heraldry, however, such as when Roger Sturmi, junior, used on his seal a very similar image (a man dressed and equipped as a hunter) as that employed by his grandfather Geoffrey, possibly as a means of associating himself with a pioneer of Anglo-Norman settlement in south Wales (see figures 3.7 and 3.8).[24] In one instance, a combination of image and text appear to be representing both an individual's natal and marriage family through a motif that also has connotations of social status and cultural identity. The legend, clear on the impression attached to a document dated 1217, declares that it is the seal of Sibyl de Bonville, a member of the Anglo-Norman family who settled in the lordship of Glamorgan in the later twelfth century and founded the settlement of Bonvilston.[25] The seal has as its central motif the beautifully rendered image of a harp, and at first glance this could be interpreted as an indication of musical ability or patronage (possibly bardic) (see figure 7.3).[26] The document validated by the impression of the seal reveals that Sibyl was in fact widow of William *Citharedi*, the harper, however, and through a combination of image and text her seal thus neatly identified her through her paternal and uxorial relationships.

(ii) Occupational identity

No impressions of the seal of William the harper have been identified, and it is interesting to speculate whether he used his seal to identify himself by occupation, as some seal owners chose to do. One hand-and-object motif seal, much later in date than the group discussed above, also relates to a specific status, that of priest, an occupation and a way of life that set ordained men apart from the rest of society. The seal used in 1438 by Maurice Gwyneth of Shrewsbury, a chaplain, depicts a hand, emerging from a large sleeve, holding an object that appears to be either a monstrance or a candle (see figure 7.4).[27] This image could be interpreted as devotional, but would also have identified the seal owner as a priest, the only type of person allowed to carry the consecrated Host in this manner. Other priests identified themselves as such on their seals in a rather more straightforward manner, through the use of an image of a tonsured head. This motif was found on seals across Britain (indeed those with the anonymous legend *caput servi dei*, 'head of the servant of God', could be bought off the shelf), but among those in the project dataset are two of exceptional quality, one which may possibly have been a representation from life of the seal owner, suggesting that this rather conventional means of identifying status could also be very personal (see figure 7.5).[28]

In the secular sphere, seals associated with occupational identity would appear, unsurprisingly, to be more prevalent in urban areas where craft specialisation was at its greatest.[29] There are for example a range of different occupation-related motifs (that is a tool or item associated with a specific craft or occupation, or the representation of someone engaged in a trade-related activity) among a sample of seals of London men from the twelfth and thirteenth centuries.[30] Only a handful of such motifs can be identified from the *SiMeW* dataset, where the material is drawn from a region with few towns of any size, however. Chester and Shrewsbury were the largest urban centres in the region and provide most of the seals with occupation-related motifs in the project dataset, including that of Thurstan 'the armourer', whose seal has a closed helm as its central motif.[31] An apparently clear example of a secular occupations identifier on a seal in the project sample, the seal of Robert *Sissor* (Tailor), with an image of a pair of open shears, used in Shrewsbury in the later thirteenth century, is however complicated by the fact that the document to which the impression is attached names the seal owner as son of William the Tailor, suggesting that this could also have been a canting device for an inherited or family byname (see figure 7.6).[32] This did not mean that trade-related devices were unknown in Wales, as evidenced by a matrix, naming the owner as John the carpenter and with a pair of dividers as the motif, found in Pembrokeshire,[33] but that such devices formed a much smaller part of the sigillographic lexicon in some parts of the country than in others.

From the later thirteenth century, so-called 'merchant marks' start to appear on seals across England and Wales, although it should be noted that such marks were also used by craftsmen and were closely related to masons' and carpenters' marks.[34] These 'trade marks' were used for marking goods and products, and also appear on tombs and in relation to patronage in glass and other items, and it has been suggested that their extensive use in later medieval urban centres was related to a developing sense of communal identity among merchants, wealthier craftsmen, and perhaps even citizens more generally.[35] As with occupation-related motifs, the modest number of merchant mark seals in the project dataset (fifty-three separate seals) is therefore unsurprising for a region with no major cities, and indeed in this context it is interesting to note that five of the examples were used by merchants from London, Bristol and Oxford.[36] What is perhaps significant is the number of seals (twenty-one of the fifty-three examples) where the merchant mark has been placed on a shield in a manner that at first glance makes them appear heraldic, such as on the seal of Richard Brun of Bridgnorth (see figure 7.7).[37] This could be seen as means of the seal owner insinuating that they were of a more elevated status, a member of the amigerous elite rather than a merchant or craftsman. An instance where this may have been a motive for the adoption of such a motif is the seal of another Bridgnorth man, Edmund de Pitchford. From the evidence of surviving impressions, he seems to have acquired a matrix with a pseudo-armorial merchant mark at about the same time as his marriage into a family of apparently higher status than his own (see figure 7.8).[38] Furthermore, his new in-laws appear to have been armigerous, with his father-in-law, John Rondulph, using a seal with two shields of arms held aloft by St Katherine, while Edmund's wife, Alice, had a seal with the image of a woman standing holding a large shield.[39] The origins of both families are obscure, but the use of what appear to be 'correct' armorial bearing by the Rondulph father and daughter may well explain why Edmund felt it necessary to acquire a seal with a motif on a shield, even if, in his case, the change was in fact a form of 'merchant mark'.[40]

We must however be cautious about making such assumptions with regard to the adoption of pseudo-armorial devices. It has, for example, been noted that many wealthy and powerful London citizens had seals with a merchant mark on a shield or adopted devices that were only later recognised as heraldic, while still clearly identifying themselves first and foremost as citizens and merchants.[41] More generally, it is important not to take an anachronistic view of armorial devices; we know that some were adopted as hereditary and at some point sanctioned by heralds, but during the thirteenth and fourteenth centuries the heraldic lexicon was developing and experimentation was part of this process.[42] Thus the occupational, and perhaps name-related, shears displayed on a shield on the fourteenth-century seal of Walter Sherman of Hereford would, to contemporaries, have seemed entirely suitable.[43] Finally, we should perhaps also recognise that, even when the heralds started trying to enforce rules, not everyone knew or cared about what was deemed correct, especially in more remote locations and among those of lower status. It is, for example, hard to imagine that the crudely rendered shield with a geometric pattern on the seal of Ieuan 'le Tayllour' son of Ifor Gough, used to validate a document relating to property in Whitford (Flint) in 1346, was going to make anyone assume that Ieuan was of high social rank, but it does perhaps suggest an awareness on the sigillant's part that such a device was a useful way of identifying himself (see figure 7.9).[44]

(iii) Humour and subversion

A number of examples of rebus and allusive seals, those where the motif or part of an image alludes to or stands in for a name, have already been mentioned, and are a means of expressing identity that is perhaps particularly attractive for historians trying to understand men and women in the Middle Ages. The Welsh use of patronymics, which continued in many places into the early modern period, means that such devices are far less common in Wales and the Marches than across England, but people with Anglo-Norman and English name forms did use them on seals in this region. Examples include the seal of George Haukeston, impressed in validation of a document in Shrewsbury in 1427, which bears the image of a hawk, pecking the letter 'g' followed by the letters 'stun', and that of Ralph Springhose, a minor Shropshire landholder, whose seal bears the image of a leg dressed in hose that has 'sprung' undone.[45]

Some seal designs are, essentially, fun, but although it is usually very difficult to associate them with a specific individual – those with any wording usually have anonymous legends – they do reveal a willingness to engage with sometimes quite subversive humour. The image of a hare riding to hunt on the back of a hound, which appears on twelve seals from the Marches of Wales is, for example, part of the 'world turned upside down' genre also found in manuscripts and carvings (see also chapter 3 on exchange in the present volume).[46] Three impressions of seals with this device occur in one very small collection of deeds relating to one Cheshire family. One, attached to an indenture of 1318, suggests a matrix made by a reasonably skilled craftsman, while a second, while very similar in design and size, would appear to be from a matrix of rather lower quality; the third impression, attached to a deed of 1332 (in favour of the son of one of the parties in the previous two documents), indicates a matrix of very low quality, both in terms of artistic ability and workmanship (see figures 7.10 and 7.11).[47] It seems from this evidence quite possible that one member of the family acquired a matrix with this design that was then copied, and that a few years later this image had become associated with the original seal user and was copied again, although this time by a low-skilled and possibly local craftsman; perhaps an instance where the whimsy of one generation became a mark of family identity for the next.

On occasion, some non-rebus humorous / subversive seal motifs can directly be associated with particular individuals, and offer insights into how such imagery could be incorporated into an expression of personal representation and identity. Hybrid creatures and grotesques, similar to those found in manuscripts and stone and wood carvings, had, it has been suggested, a mnemonic function in a sigillographic context, the use of a seal with such an image helping the witnesses remember the sigillant and act of sealing.[48] The great majority of such seals were anonymous, but one late twelfth or early thirteenth century example has a legend that clearly identifies it as having been made for Richard Norries, a member of an Anglo-Norman family who held a fee within the lordship of Glamorgan.[49] As with so many sigillographic images, the reason for Richard choosing a bird with a man's head and a foliate tail as the motif for his seal is now lost, but it would have been reasonable for him to expect others to remember this striking image (see figure 7.12).

Such personalisation of generic types of humorous or subversive seal motif is also interesting because it suggests that the seal owner wanted others to appreciate a particular aspect of their persona, although one is sometimes left wondering exactly why. Impressions of one matrix survive on five documents from the Bangor area of north Wales dating 1442–77, and in each case one of the principal parties is Johanna, late wife of Gwilym ap Gruffudd ap Gwilym.[50] The seal has no legend, but the letters 'i' and 'g' are engraved in the main field, respectively to the left and slightly above the image of an animal (see figure 7.13). All of the impressions are slightly worn or damaged, so it is impossible to be certain whether this is intended to be a squirrel eating a nut or, more probably, a fox seated playing a flute.[51] What is really puzzling is why Johanna or her husband would have personalised either image in this manner, since in contemporary culture the squirrel had connotations of sexual licentiousness, while the fox was seen as a trickster.[52]

(iv) Devotional expression and religious identity

While some people may have wished to be identified through their sense of humour, or represent their family and socially constructed identity in their choice of motif, others used their seal to express something more spiritual about themselves. Within the project dataset, 235 separate seals may be identified as bearing a devotional image or text, representing approximately 10 per cent of the total, in line with findings from other samples.[53] While this may seem a rather small proportion in an era when religious observance formed part of everyday life, it should be remembered that, by choosing a seal with devotional content, owners were effectively rejecting the opportunity to represent the secular aspects of a socially constructed identity.

One problem with identifying 'religious' seals is, however, that some images may have had a devotional meaning now lost to us, while the pious significance of other motifs is an area where caution must be exercised. In particular, while the lily has clear Trinitarian and Marian connotations in the culture of medieval Christendom, the question of whether the owners of matrices that display a lily-type motif actively associated these sigillographic images with devotion to the Holy Trinity or Blessed Virgin Mary is moot. On the one hand, the period when this motif is most prevalent on seals – the later twelfth and thirteenth centuries – quite neatly mirrors that of an increased focus on Mary and promotion of Marian devotion.[54] The problem with suggesting a more direct connection is, however, complicated by the fact that none of the seals with the lily motif have devotional texts, or indicate a specific devotion to the Blessed Virgin. Therefore, while the lily motif on a seal may well have stirred pious thoughts about the Virgin Mary or the Holy Trinity in some individuals, a direct correlation cannot be drawn between image and devotional expression in this instance.

Within the general category of 'religious' personal seals, a few devotional motifs dominate.[55] Most prevalent are seals with representations of the Virgin and Child, a trend reflected in identified material from Wales and the border counties. Within the project dataset, a broad chronological distribution may also be discerned, with impressions attached to documents dating from the early thirteenth century to the late fifteenth century.[56] In a number of cases the Virgin and Child are accompanied by a suppliant figure, while the imagery is often complemented by a devotional text, reflecting the popularity of Marian devotion in late medieval society. While most of the imagery is conventional, with the Virgin standing or sitting holding the Christ Child, the earliest of the Marian seal examples in the project dataset is in fact an ancient gem depicting what appears to be a half-naked figure with a billowing cloak and holding up an object. That this has been reinterpreted as a Christian image is evidenced by the legend, AVE MA[. . .]AMEN, a phenomenon, known from other ancient gems reset with devotional texts, that provides a useful reminder of the world-view of medieval seal owners.[57]

Another popular devotion motif on seals was the Lamb of God, an image with Christocentric connotations, but also connected with John the Baptist.[58] One example from early thirteenth century south Wales belonged to William de Bonneville, the matrix taking the form of a stone, possibly engraved in Italy (on stylistic grounds), set into a metal mount (see figure 7.14).[59] The evidence of surviving matrices suggests that many of the stones employed in matrices were perceived in the Middle Ages to have atrophic qualities, and this may further have enhanced the significance of this item.[60] In one instance the image of the Lamb of God is used in an ambivalent manner, apparently expressing both personal devotion (possibly associated with the owner's name-saint) and, by being placed above a shield of arms, co-opting the religious iconography into an armorial – and therefore secular – context.[61]

Other popular devotional images found on seals across Wales mainly follow patterns identified in England and mirror more general trends in pious expression. Thus, there are thirty-three seals in the project dataset that employ the image of 'pelican in piety' (a Christocentric and Eucharistic motif),[62] and seventeen with the image of St Katherine, a very popular saint.[63] St John the Baptist, popular across Britain, is similarly well represented, with sixteen seals depicting either the standing saint or the rather grizzly image of a head on a dish.[64] Indeed, one very interesting feature of 'religious' seals from across Wales and the English border counties is the use of internationally recognised motifs and absence of any identifiable Welsh iconography, with none of the numerous Welsh saints represented. This is even more surprising when one considers that St Edmund, an East-Anglian saint, features on two seals from western Shropshire (see figure 7.15).[65] This could possibly be because Welsh saints generally had very minor or non-standardised attributes, making them difficult to identify even in larger media such as glass and sculpture, although invocatory legends would have solved this problem.[66] It could well be that it is a result of supply and demand, with seal makers almost certainly restricted to a few of the larger towns in the region and their products beyond the financial as well as physical reach of middle and lower status seal owners with a devotion to a very localised saint.

The question of agency is important for how we can use 'religious' personal seals to draw conclusions about personal piety. When a devotional image on a seal is accompanied by an anonymous legend, we have the immediate problem of not being able to associate it with any degree of confidence to the person who used it, unless perhaps all the known impressions were made by the same or related sigillants. In a couple of instances, however, there does seem to be evidence not only of ownership of a 'religious' seal without a name-legend, but for the matrix having become a family heirloom, perhaps because such matrices were also in effect devotional images. A matrix featuring the Lamb of God but no legend was, for example, used in 1488 by Hywel ap Jankyn, and by his son William ab Hywel ap Jenkyn on two occasions in 1508.[67]

In addition to fairly generic devotional motifs, there were also a number of seal matrices featuring highly individualised religious imagery or which incorporate name-legends, and provide tantalising insights into personal piety. For example, the seal of John Mygnoth, used to validate a grant to Margam in the early thirteenth century, is a carefully rendered 'passion flower', with chalices on the petals and nails as the stamens; a sophisticated expression of Eucharistic piety at a time when devotion to Corpus Christi was developing in Britain.[68] While this example indicates a specific devotion, some 'religious' seals suggest a generally pious outlook, such as that of Alexander Russell, a chaplain who validated an exchange of land in Conwy in 1393 with his seal depicting the head of John the Baptist accompanied by an invocation beseeching God's help.[69] One instance where seals, combined with the purpose for which they were used, is suggestive of a religiously conscientious individual is the case of Walter, son of Richard of Stokes. As discussed by Phillipp Schofield in chapter 3 on seals and exchange, Walter confirmed a later thirteenth-century grant of manumission with what appears to have been a finely engraved matrix with the image of peacocks between a plant, possibly a lily, a symbol of the tree of life and immortality.[70] In addition, Walter countersealed with another matrix, this time with the image of a stag with a cross between its antlers and the legend TIMETE DEVM (Fear God).[71] This combination of motif and wording is not in itself uncommon, with sixteen other examples in the project dataset and further examples known from across England, but the use of two matrices with devotional content to validate an act that could be seen as pious (although which of course usually had an economic function), does suggest that Walter may have had a particularly pious turn of mind.

In conclusion, it is perhaps appropriate to focus on one seal from the project dataset that combines many of the themes already discussed, since it brings together ideas of family and occupational identity, expressions of piety, and a possible glimpse into the mindset of a seal owner. The seal used in 1330 by John son of Robert the Locksmith to validate a grant of property in the small town of Bridgnorth, Shropshire, has on it the image of three hares or rabbits running in a counter-clockwise direction (see figure 7.16).[72] On careful inspection, one realises that each hare has two ears when viewed as a single entity, but that there are in total only three ears. This symbol has been used by a number of different cultures around the world, from central Asia to western Europe, and many interpretations have been suggested.[73] It is often said that, in medieval western Europe, the image of the three separate hares made whole by the shared ears had devotional connotations, and it can be seen as a neat visual means of expressing the theological complexity of the Holy Trinity, but, as Susan Andrew has noted, its positioning in manuscripts and the location of bosses in churches may also suggest more negative connotations, perhaps with reference to the three spiritual enemies of man.[74] Its use on a seal could therefore indicate either devotion to the Holy Trinity or serve as a warning for the viewer not to give in to temptation (in the context of the object, perhaps not to bear false witness or defraud), or perhaps act in both capacities. The motif of the three hares each with two ears is also a visual puzzle, and as such could reflect the owner's sense of humour.⁷⁵ Finally, it may reference the owner's familial and occupational identity, since the puzzle is revealed, as an early sixteenth-century French rhyme suggests, by the viewer being required to 'turn and turn again', just as one turns a key to open a lock.⁷⁶ In a similar way, it is crucially important for us to be prepared to consider all the information packaged within seals and their use in order to unlock their potential for understanding the creation and expression of identity in the Middle Ages.

Notes

1   B. M. Bedos-Rezak, 'Replica: Images of Identity and the identity of images', in J. F. Hamburger and A-M. Bouché (eds), *The Mind's Eye: Art and Theological Argument in the Middle Ages* (Princeton, 2006), pp. 46–64, p. 55.
2   The question of the individual and 'identity' in the Middle Ages remains a topic for much discussion, but most scholars agree that medieval men and women had a sense of 'self', and that the projection of that 'self' accommodated unique features as well as socially constructed identity. For discussions of identity and the individual in relation to seals see,for example, Bedos-Rezak, 'Replica: Images of Identity and the Identity of Images', pp. 46–64; B. M. Bedos-Rezak, 'Signe d'identité et principes d'altérité au XIIe siècle', in B. M. Bedos-Rezak and D. Iogna-Prat (eds), *L'Individu au Moyen Âge. Individuation et individualisation avant la modernité* (Paris, 2005), pp. 43–57. For more general discussions of the medieval concepts of the individual, the 'self', and identity see, for example, D. Postles, 'Identity and identification: some recent research into the English medieval "forename" ', in D. Postles and J. T. Rosenthal (eds), *Studies on the Personal Name in Later Medieval England and Wales* (Kalamazoo, MI, 2006), pp. 29–62, esp. 30–1, nn.5, 6; C. W. Bynum, *Jesus as Mother* (Berkeley and Los Angeles, 1982), pp. 82–109.
3   With regard to the challenges of defining exactly what constitutes a 'personal' seal, Roger Ellis commented that to 'aim for absolute consistency could delay indefinitely the publication' of his catalogue. See R. Ellis, *Catalogue of Seals in the Public Record Office: Personal Seals*, vol. 1 (London, 1978), p. vii, n.1.
4   An example of how complex this issue can be is the subsidiary seals of the early thirteenth century archbishops of Canterbury. Hubert Walter chose to depict the martyrdom of Thomas Becket, accompanied by a personalised devotional legend, on the matrix he used as a subsidiary seal, this imagery later becoming the standard for archiepiscopal subsidiary seals and eventually transferring to the seal of dignity. See Birch, nos 1187R–1238.
5   M. P. Siddons, 'Welsh equestrian seals', *National Library of Wales Journal*, 23 (1983–4), 292–318; E. A. New, 'Lleision ap Morgan makes an impression: seals and the study of medieval Wales', *Welsh History Review*, 27:1 (2013), 327–50, at 333–8. See also chapter 5 in the present volume.
6   This point is also made in a wider European context by Brigitte Bedos-Rezak, 'In search of a semiotic paradigm: the matter of sealing in medieval thought and praxis (1050–1400)', in *Good Impressions*, p. 2.
7   New, 'Lleision ap Morgan', pp. 336–7; Seal 1151.
8   See also chapter 6.
9   Seals 1142, 1186, 83, 88, 104, lance-pennon seals; Seal 1155, lilies; Seal 87, key.

10 This is not unique to England and Wales, heads being used to represent a group on a number of communal seals in France and the Empire at about this time, M. Späth, 'The body and its parts: iconographical metaphors of corporate identity in 13th century common seals', in J-L. Chassel and M. Gil (eds), *Pourquoi les sceaux? La sigillographie nouvel enjeu de l'histoire de l'art* (Lille, 2011), pp. 383–99.
11 T. A. Heslop, 'Cistercian Seals in England and Wales', in C. Norton and D. Park (eds), *Cistercian Art and Architecture in the British Isles* (Cambridge, 1986), pp. 266–83, p. 267
12 Seal 87; BL Harl. Ch. 75 C 44; D. H. Williams, *Welsh History through Seals* (Cardiff, 1982), p. 25, fig. 54.
13 D. Crouch, *The English Aristocracy, 1070–1272: A Social Transformation* (New Haven and London, 2011), pp. 53–5.
14 Owein ap Morgan ap Caradog, BL Harl. Ch. 75 C 36, 75 C 37 (Seal 83); Grunu ap Philip, BL Harl. Ch. 75 C 46 Seal 88); Espus ap Caradog Du, Seal 1142; NLW PENRICE: GLAM 2037, 2038, 2039.
15 The spear features extensively in Welsh poetry, and the bardic imagery of the spear and pennon in relation to the use of this motif on seals is an area that I am currently exploring in more detail.
16 M. P. Siddons, *The Development of Welsh Heraldry*, vol. 1 (Aberystwyth, 1991), p. 18.
17 *Welsh Heraldry*, vol. 1, esp. pp. 1–4.
18 A particular form of radial motif may have expressed nuances of status, including those associated with the place in a kinship group, in early thirteenth-century Glamorgan, for example. See E. A. New, '(Un)conventional images. A case-study of radial motifs on personal seals', in P. R. Schofield (ed.), *Seals and their Context in the Middle Ages* (Oxford, 2015), pp. 154–7.
19 *Seliau*, pp. 82–3, no. 35; *Welsh Heraldry*, vol. 1, pp. 3–4.
20 *Welsh Heraldry*, vol. 1, pp. 8, 263–4; For John d'Avene's heraldic seal, in use by 1330, see Seal 1301.
21 *Welsh Heraldry*, vol. 1, p. 8. Lleision ap Morgan was using an armorial seal by 1313.
22 Seal 518, 504; *Welsh Heraldry*, vol. 1, pp. 14–15, figs. 15, 16; M. P. Siddons, *Heraldic Badges of England and Wales. II.2: Non-Royal Badges* (Woodbridge, 2009), p. 298.
23 *Welsh Heraldry*, vol. 1, pp. 120, 127–9.
24 New, 'Lleision ap Morgan', 338–9; *Seliau*, pp. 78–9.
25 L. D. Nicholl, *The Normans in Glamorgan, Gower and Kidweli* (Cardiff, 1936), p. 129.
26 Seal 61 (BL, Harley Ch. 75 B 36). This appears to be one of the earliest representations of a harp known from Wales.
27 Seal 1740. Very few medieval monstrances survive, but the section that held the Host could be quite small, such as the mid-fifteenth-century Italian example now in the Victoria and Albert Museum, *http://collections.vam.ac.uk/item/O39534/monstrance-unknown/* (last accessed 26 January 2016).
28 Seal 1398, seal of William the Chaplain (*Seliau*, no. 45 and p. 110); Seal 739, seal of William de Fostone, chaplain. The rather jolly-looking, heavy-set and big-nosed man on de Fostone's seal could be the result of the whim of the manufacturer, but what appears to have been lifelike representations of Henry of Blois, Bishop of Winchester, and Nigel, Bishop of Ely, have been noted (N. Karn (ed.), *English Episcopal Acta 31. Ely, 1109–1197* (Oxford, 2005), p. cxlvi), and so this could be an image based on the chaplain's actual appearance.
29 See, for example, E. A. New, 'Representation and identity in medieval London: the evidence of personal seals', in M. Davies and A. Prescott (eds), *London and the Kingdom*, Harlaxton Medieval Studies, XVI (Stamford, 2008), pp. 246–58, table 3.
30 J. McEwan, 'Occupation and identity in medieval London', in C. M. Barron and A. F. Sutton (eds), *The Medieval Merchant*, Harlaxton Medieval Studies, XXIV (Donington, 2014), pp. 357–9.

31 Seal 1788 (NLW PITORD/324). The release from Thurstan 'le Armurer' to Richard le Bruyn, citizen of Chester, relates to Chester property and was sealed in Chester, so it is assumed that Thurstan lived and worked there.
32 Seal 2446. Andrew McGuinness also makes this point about some late thirteenth-century seals from Newcastle: A. F. McGuinness, 'Non-armigerous seals and seal-usage in thirteenth-century England', in P. R. Coss and S. D. Lloyd (eds), *Thirteenth Century England*, vol. 5 (Woodbridge, 1995), pp. 170–1.
33 D. H. Williams, 'Seal finds in Wales', in P. R. Schofield (ed.), *Seals and their Context in the Middle Ages* (Oxford, 2015), p. 203 and fig. 14.22.
34 McGuinness, 'Non-armigerous seals', p. 172; E. Elmhurst, *Merchant Marks*, Harleian Society (London, 1959), pp. vii–viii.
35 McGuinness, 'Non-armigerous seals', pp. 171–2.
36 Seals 1653, 1759, 1451, 719, 2139.
37 Seals 1817. Impressions of Richard Brun's seals survive on six documents dated between 1363 and 1374.
38 Seal 1795, impressions attached to NLW PITORD/332, 333, 375. The same seal was used by an Alice, wife of Richard le Bruyn (who may possibly have been Edmund de Pitchford's widow) in 1371 (NLW PITORD/1310, 1311), and by a John Peole in 1426 (NLW PITORD/1322), this last instance suggesting that the matrix had become an heirloom, or possibly the possession of a scribe who loaned it to those who did not have a matrix themselves.
39 Seal 1749, NLW PITORD/251, 566, 1126 (John Rondulph's seal); Seal 1603, NLW PITORD/38, 46, 537 s.2, 1293 Seal 1603 (Alice's seal). The shield on Alice's seal appears to be a fess, possibly with a bordure. On John Rondulph's dexter shield the charge appears to be barry, but impressions of the sinister shield are indistinct. Although the shield held to dexter by the figure of a woman is traditionally that of her husband, there is no evidence that the Pitchfords were armigerous (nor can Edmund de Pitchford securely be associated with the Anglo-Norman knightly family of de Pitchford, who held the manor of Pitchford in the twelfth and thirteenth centuries), and the use of a pseudo-armorial device by both Edmund and his brother William (see Seal 1613, NLW PITORD/61) further supports the premise that they were not. A third Pitchford bother, Robert, also used a seal with a shield charged with a device, but the only identified impression is worn and the charge indistinct; Seal 1584, NLW PITORD/15. At the time of writing, Laura Evans, a PhD student at Aberystwyth University, is investigating the community of Bridgnorth in the fourteenth century, and it is to be hoped that origins of, and relationship between, both families will become clearer. For an alternative interpretation of these seals, see chapter 6.
40 Edmund de Pitchford used a number of other matrices to validate documents, but none that identify him as an individual and which are therefore assumed either to be borrowed or secondary, less personalised, items. For an alternative interpretation of these seals and sigillants, see chapter 6.
41 C. Barron, 'Chivalry, pageantry and merchant culture in medieval London', in P. Coss and M. Keen (eds), *Heraldry, Pageantry and Social Display in Medieval England* (Woodbridge, 2002), pp. 219–41, 232–5.
42 See, for example, P. Coss, 'Knighthood, heraldry and social exclusion in Edwardian England', in P. Coss and M. Keen (eds), *Heraldry, Pageantry and Social Display in Medieval England* (Woodbridge, 2002), pp. 39–68.
43 Seal 744 (HCA Deed 32, s.2)
44 Seal 186 (BUAS MOST/3008).

45 Haukeston's seal, Seal 2167, NLW PITORD/2482, s.4; Springhose's seal, NLW PITORD/341, Seal 1802 (seal used to validate a document of 1321); E. A. New, 'Text and image: the language of seals in medieval England and Wales', in M. Carruthers (ed.), *Multilingual Networks in Medieval Britain*, Harlaxton Medieval Studies, XXV (Donnington, 2015), pp. 59–73, p. 65, figs. 6 and 7.
46 McGuinness, 'Non-armigerous seals', pp. 174–5; New, 'Text and Image', p. 64. John Cherry notes that impressions of seals with this image in the Durham collections have only been found on documents datable to 1312–29, J. Cherry, 'Ie su sel nul tel: no seal like it?', in M. Gill and J-L. Chassel (eds), *Pourquoi Les Sceaux. La sigillographie nouvel enjeu de l'histoire de l'art* (Lille, 2011), p. 198. The *SiMeW* examples cover a considerably wider date range, from 1292 (Seal 706) to 1473 (Seal 2068).
47 CALS D3785/1/16 (1318 document, highest-quality seal), 15, part 2 (second 1318 document), 17, part 1 (1332, lowest-quality seal). I am grateful to Jonathon Pelper, County Archivist at Cheshire Archives and Local Studies, for drawing my attention to this uncatalogued collection of Bulkeligh deeds.
48 Cherry, 'Ie su Sel nul tel', p. 200.
49 *Seliau*, p. 39, no. 16; Seal 1513 (NLW PENRICE: GLAM/2013). The document has been dated to 1175 x 1231, R. B. Patterson, *The Scriptorium of Margam Abbey and the Scribes of Early Angevin Glamorgan: Secretarial Administration in a Welsh Marcher Barony* (Woodbridge, 2002), p. 119. The Norries family of Penllyn held a fee from 1166, but Richard himself has not otherwise been identified, J. Beverley Smith, 'The kingdom of Morgannwg and the Norman conquest of Glamorgan, in T. B Pugh (ed.), *Glamorgan County History, Volume 3: The Middle Ages* (Cardiff, 1971), p. 17.
50 BUAS PENR/24 (1443), 25 (1442), 26 (1443), 28 (1447) and 170 (1477) Seal 221. In the first four documents Johanna is also named as late wife of John Pykemere.
51 The image of a squirrel eating a nut is not an uncommon sigillographic motif in the fourteenth and fifteenth centuries, but the image of a fox playing a musical instrument is very rare outside manuscripts and no published reference to another such image on a seal has been identified. For images of a fox playing a musical instrument, see K. Varty, *Reynard the Fox. A Study of the Fox in Medieval English Art* (Leicester, 1967), figs 117–19.
52 M. Camille, *Mirror in Parchment. The Luttrell Psalter and the Making of Medieval England* (London, 1998), p. 299 and n.68; Varty, *Reynard the Fox*, esp. pp. 22–3.
53 New, 'Representation and identity', pp. 246–58, p. 251.
54 See chapter 1.
55 This is of course based only on the small proportion of impressions and matrices that have been catalogued, but this material represents most areas and the whole medieval period, and the popular images generally reflect what else is known about devotional trends.
56 HCA Deed 234 (back), Seal 810, undated document of *c*.1225 x 1250; SHA 322/2/280, s.1 and s.3, Seal 2430, 2432, document dated 1484.
57 Seal 810. For the reinterpretation of ancient gems, see M. Henig, 'The re-use and copying of ancient intaglios set in medieval personal seals, mainly found in England: an aspect of the Renaissance of the twelfth century', in *Good Impressions*, pp. 30–1.
58 E. A. New, 'Christological seals and Christocentric devotion in later medieval England and Wales', *Antiquaries Journal*, 82 (2002), 47–68, esp. 49.
59 BL Harl. Ch. 75 B 13, 17, 16, Seal 46. Patterson dates Harley Ch. 75 B 16 and 17 to *c*.1200 x 1231, and Harley Ch. 75 B 13 to *c*.1250 x 1275. The user in each case was William de Bonneville.
60 J. Cherry, 'Medieval and post-medieval seals', in D. Collon (ed.), *7000 Years of Seals* (London, 1997), pp. 124–42, pp. 133–4.

61   Seal of John d'Avene; NLW PENRICE: GLAM/207, 217, 218, 219 (Seal 1301), documents dated 1330–41. See above for a discussion of the armorial seals of this family.
62   Examples date from 1260 x 70 (Seal 2443, SHA 972/1/1/439, s.1) until the 1540s (Seal 560, GA D583/99, s.2).
63   The date range of the St Katherine seals is rather more limited than for the 'pelican in piety', with the earliest impression from 1319 and the latest from 1428, Seal 2101, 2218.
64   The St John the Baptist seals are most prevalent in the second half of the fourteenth century, with ten examples attached to documents dated 1351–1400.
65   Seal 2377 (SHA 322/2/174) and 2309 (SHA 20/7/43).
66   M. Gray, Images of Piety: *The Iconography of Traditional Religion in Late Medieval Wales*, BAR British Series, 316 (Oxford, 2000), p. 34.
67   Seal 950 (NLW BRONWYDD/965, 991, 993).
68   New, '(Un)conventional images', p. 153, fig. 11.1; D. H. Williams, *Images of Welsh History* (Aberystwyth, 2007), p. 20; M. Rubin, *Corpus Christi: The Eucharist in Late Medieval Culture* (Cambridge, 1991), esp. pp. 164–210.
69   Seal 1100, NLW CHIRK/11594.
70   Seal 2205. F. Klingender, *Animals in Art and Thought to the End of the Middle Ages* (London, 1971), p. 272; P. Murray and L. Murray, *The Oxford Companion to Christian Art and Architecture* (Oxford, 1996), p. 58.
71   Seal 2206.
72   Seal 1579, NLW PITORD/10.
73   S. Andrew, 'Late medieval bosses in the churches of Devon' (unpublished PhD, University of Plymouth, 2011), p. 210, n.107; J. Baltrušaitis, *Le Moyen-Âge Fantastique*, new edn (Paris, 1981), pp. 144–6; http://trois-lievres.skyrock.com; http://www.chrischapmanphotography.co.uk/hares/index.html (last accessed 26 January 2016). At the time of writing, Andrew and a colleague are preparing a book on the subject.
74   Andrew, 'Late medieval bosses', p. 214.
75   Klingender, *Animals in Art and Thought to the End of the Middle Ages*, p. 434, is uncharacteristically dismissive of the potential meanings of the image, saying it 'appealed primarily as an amusing trick'.
76   Baltrušaitis, *Le Moyen-Âge Fantastique*, p. 144.

CONCLUSION

Elizabeth A. New and Phillipp R. Schofield

THE *SEALS IN MEDIEVAL WALES* project represents both continuity with and new developments in, the study of medieval Wales and the English border counties and in sigillographic research. Foregrounding seals in terms of recording and analysis has also enabled the project team to build upon existing scholarship, while at the same time offer fresh interpretations, and indeed a fresh corpus of material for future investigation. In this volume the authors have sought to highlight the findings of the project, but also to make others aware of the research potential of this material and to illustrate the ways in which seals and sealing practices can enrich our understanding of medieval society. The following concluding comments allow some further reflection on the processes central to the research that underpins this volume and above all a consideration of future research approaches and the questions that may be applied to further work in this area.

One important facet of the *SiMeW* project has been the gathering of a wealth of seals data and, through a recording template developed for the project, to allow its careful scrutiny and analysis. In the first instance, the recording template, intended as a model for further research in this area, has enabled a robust and wide-ranging interrogation of the data for the current volume as well as other publications associated with the project.[1] As part of the recording process, digital photographs were taken of all the seal impressions and sealed instruments, a sample of which, from the more than 5,000 images gathered by the team, illustrate this volume. Since seals are visual items, the importance of images cannot be underestimated, and advances in digital photography have made the photography of large numbers of them increasingly easy and financially viable. While from a technological perspective digital images are revolutionising the ways in which we can study seals (there are, for example, a number of instances where impressions from the same matrix are impossible to identify without photographs for comparison, especially when the items are held in different repositories), it is worth noting here that a number of challenges are posed by this additional resource. Chief among these are concerns raised by custodians of the original sealed instruments, mindful of issues of the security and control of digital images. This is understandable from one perspective, especially in straightened times where the reproduction of images can be a valuable source of income, but restrictions on the use, accessibility and ease of sharing of visual material is detrimental to research, and it is to be hoped that future sigillographic projects will benefit from new methods of protecting images, especially online, such as watermarking and limited resolution, and thus further realise and more effectively preserve the potential of this academically highly valuable material.[2]

While the technical side of *SiMeW* will, it is hoped, provide a valuable and tangible legacy, the project has been one founded upon academic research, utilising seals to investigate different aspects of medieval society and culture in fresh ways. This volume demonstrates some of the approaches that can be taken, but has already provided new evidence and insights, many of which in turn force us to re-evaluate assumptions and to ask still more questions. In particular, by recording all seal impressions within a collection, those owned and used by men and women from below the very highest levels of society, and those displaying what are often dismissed as 'conventional' motifs, have been investigated with the same rigour as the seals of institutions and elites that have for so long dominated sigillographically based research. This is of course not to the exclusion of such high-status and institutional seals and their owners, and this volume has been careful to include a wide range of approaches and discussions.

A close exploration of the use of seals in an administrative and legal context has provided further support for the conclusion of a number of scholars that native law, which rejected the sealed instrument as a means of proof, remained dominant across *pura Walia* for most of the Middle Ages, and that, as a result, very few seals are found in these areas. While reconfirming this general pattern, and previous investigations of the importance of religious orders (most notably the Cistercians) in promoting the use of seals among the Welsh, the work of the project team has uncovered significant nuances in the adoption of the practice of sealing in Wales, and in the variety of exchanges for which seals were an integral part, both in Wales and across the English border counties. When considering exchange in a broader context, the work of *SiMeW* is important for highlighting local, national and international connections, from bonds exchanged to confirm small-scale trade, through to Papal intervention in a dispute between neighbouring religious houses. That much exchange took place without recourse to, and sometimes with the explicit exclusion of, seals has also been highlighted, and important questions have been raised about who exactly formed the 'sealing' sector of society, especially when individuals and institutions frequently engaged in different types of transaction, inviting further investigation.

The use of seals by different elements in society, for different purposes and with different results, has also been explored in some detail. Women from Welsh, Anglo-Welsh and English backgrounds could all employ seals, and although a number of questions with regard to agency and choice remain, it is clear that at least some women utilised motifs that emphasised their roles as landholders, or provided insights into family connections or cross-cultural exchange. It is, further to this, quite likely that women were, for instance through marriage, especially at elite levels, potentially important agents in effecting change and served an important role in encouraging cultural and administrative change.[3] The majority of seal owners and users were men, however, but here the *SiMeW* approach has added to the existing scholarship, and potential new areas of further research have been identified. That powerful men used certain types of nationally and internationally recognised motifs has long been established, but details of these motifs, and how they might be adapted and adopted, has been further investigated here. Far less work has previously been undertaken on sigillants lower down the social scale, and initial work on the *SiMeW* corpus of material is starting to reveal significant information, as well as posing fresh challenges for the medievalist.

General patterns in the principal motifs used on seals appear, from the work of the project, to be very similar to what was previously known, but this in itself is of interest, especially within the context of semiotic studies. Furthermore, the temporal breakdown of seal motifs within the *SiMeW* dataset is especially important, and enables us to track with some certainty trends that have until now been assumed and have been based largely upon the personal experience and detailed knowledge of individual scholars. When one starts to explore details within general categories, significant subtleties are revealed, and it is hoped that the examples and case studies highlighted in this volume will encourage far more work of this kind. While it seems most likely that seal owners often introduced such subtleties into their seal designs, the wider context of seal ownership, commissioning of designs, seal production, and so on, themes not considered here and indeed seldom dealt with at all by historians, merit further work and will direct historians and sigillographers into other bodies of material, including investigation of matrices and, as in the instance used by John McEwan at the beginning of his chapter on motifs, to financial accounts.[4]

This survey has also raised other potential future research questions. A number of these relate to issues of transmission. There is, as this discussion has shown in numerous instances, plentiful indication that Welsh men and women were using seals, some of them carrying their name as legends, from the first instances of seal usage in Wales in the twelfth century. Importantly, this was not confined, again from the outset, to elites, though it is also evident that the socio-economic range in terms of seal usage expanded in the following century and more. Cross-border transfer, again not only including elites and their alliances, but also mercantile and trading, must have helped encourage transmission of seal usage into Wales.

In addition, some results presented in this volume, such as the apparent absence of Welsh saints on seals other than those used by the institutional Church, appear to answer questions posed by the *SiMeW* project team at the inception of the project. However, even here, further questions are raised: why are saints from Wales not represented, or are there in fact seals with such saints still awaiting discovery? It may be that the seal within Wales remained above all essentially an Anglo-Norman device. While Welsh men and women used seals, and with some considerable regularity throughout the period, the close cultural association of seal usage with Wales and the Welsh, sufficient to encourage motifs that truly reflected local cultural expression, was limited. This again, as more than once throughout this volume, returns us to the reflection that seals and seal usage were not predominant in *Pura Walia*; this key observation, which supports comment made by Smith and others, needs to be tested and challenged by future research, especially on collections not represented in the present sample utilised here.[5] Furthermore, the discussion in the preceding chapters has touched from time to time upon the particularly local features and typicality of seal usage; local fashion and trends in usage will undoubtedly merit further work in this area. There is an evident sense of local form and motif that will reward further research; allied to the kinds of close prosopographical research that was not possible for a survey of the kind undertaken here, and set in the context of the sorts of multilayered reading of all seal types, including lower status seals, it may be possible to show subtle continuities and interconnections of form at the regional and local level.[6] These, in turn, as has been suggested in parts of the preceding discussion, speak to such themes as shared cultural norms, local conventions and issues of lineage. And further to this point, and to return to observations with which we began, inevitably much of the discussion throughout this volume has been founded upon the seals and their associated documents; only occasionally have the authors moved beyond the immediate source. Again, future research perhaps focused upon individual, familial, local or regional case studies, will be well placed to set a study of seals and seal usage within such a context, and one informed by a range of ancillary documentation. Such documentation is likely to involve use of estate and manorial material, as well as the burgeoning body of material associated with small finds as recorded through the Portable Antiquities Scheme. This may be especially fruitful for local studies or studies that choose to focus upon particular family, social or administrative groups. There is much that can be done in this respect to deepen the kind of analysis suggested in this survey. By bringing such material together, and by foregrounding the seal and its associated document, new questions will be posed in otherwise familiar contexts and new insights offered. The present project and its publications are intended to encourage such approaches and to generate further reflections.

Notes

1. For example E. A. New, '(Un)conventional images. A case-study of radial motifs on personal seals', in P. R. Schofield (ed.), *Seals and their Context in the Middle Ages* (Oxford, 2015), pp. 151–60. The recording template has also been tested through its use, in a slightly adapted form, for the British Academy *Seals in a Local Context* project, and the template and keyword index for motifs disseminated though demonstrations at conferences and workshops, and through technical articles. At the time of writing, the results of the *Seals in a Local Context* project are being prepared for publication. See also J. McEwan, 'The challenge of the visual: making medieval seals accessible in the digital age', *Journal of Documentation*, 71 (2015), 999–1028.
2. A further indicative sample of images arising from the *SiMeW* project has been published online and is hosted by the National Library of Wales at *http://seliau.llgc.org.uk/project/* (last accessed 26 January 2016).
3. Note, for instance, evidence for Welsh-English marriage among the high nobility in the twelfth and thirteenth centuries, *Acts*, pp. 412, 643, 658, 773.
4. For a recent discussion of relevant themes, see E. A. New, 'Text and image: the language of seals in medieval England and Wales', in M. Carruthers (ed.), *Multilingual Networks in Medieval Britain*, Harlaxton Medieval Studies, XXV (Donnington, 2015), pp. 66–71.
5. Ll. B. Smith, 'Inkhorn and spectacles: the impact of literacy in late medieval Wales', in H. Pryce (ed.), *Literacy in Medieval Celtic Societies* (Cambridge, 1998), pp. 215–16, and in the introduction and chapter 2 of the present volume.
6. As proposed in New, '(Un)conventional images', for example.

APPENDIX

SEALS IN MEDIEVAL WALES (SiMeW): SEALS RECORDED

Elizabeth A. New, John A. McEwan and Phillipp R. Schofield

THE SEALS RECORDED BY *SiMeW* are presented in a format similar to that of a number of existing catalogues, notably Roger Ellis's *Catalogue of Seals in the Public Record Office*, but with adaptations that reflect the nature of the recording process and the general approach of the project to the material under investigation. Each 'Seal' entry represents an individual seal matrix, as expressed through one or more impressions attached to a document or documents. When only a single impression has been recorded the description is of this item, even if damaged. When a seal survives in more than one impression the description is drawn from all those impressions to recreate as completely and accurately as possible the original image, text and dimensions. The image and text of royal and governmental seals is, however, not usually described, since this information is readily available in various publications, chiefly Birch's Catalogue of Seals in the Department of Manuscripts in the British Museum. The archival reference(s) for all impressions recorded by *SiMeW* is provided, but this does not necessarily mean that other impressions do not survive elsewhere. This is especially true for royal and episcopal seals, where the project team may only have recorded one or two impressions, but multiple other impressions might be scattered across numerous repositories.

The descriptions for all the seals recorded take a standard format:

- The unique identification number for each individual 'seal' (an individual matrix expressed through one or more extant impression(1))

- The shape, when this can be determined, and size of the seal. All measurements are in millimetres, with vertical and horizontal measurements listed in that order except for round seals. When a seal is fragmentary or damaged, this is indicated by an approximate measurement that is taken from the surviving impressions(s), and does not necessarily reflect the original full size of the matrix. In some cases, where a measurement was not recorded, the entry is 'nm' (no measurement).
- The image(s) on the seal. The description of the image is intended to be as clear as possible, but except in the case of armorial devices or iconographic attributes the description is kept at quite a high level; 'armoured man' rather than 'man in chain-mail with an enclosed helm', for example. Saints, where they can be identified, are named, but a description of their iconographic attribute(s) is also provided for clarity. In a complex or compartmentalised scheme, the principal motif is given first. Uncertain elements are indicated by a question mark.
- The legend (text), if any. Legends are transcribed as seen, with missing letters indicated by '…' (each period representing a lost or illegible letter) and missing sections clearly identified. Illegible and lost legends are indicated; 'none' indicates that no legend ever accompanied the central motif.
- The date of and reference number for the item to which each impression is attached. Only impressions actually recorded by the *SiMeW* project team are listed here.

There are a number of ways in which a catalogue of seals can be organised in printed form, with those grouping seals by type or alphabetically by name of the presumed owner being the most familiar. The *SiMeW* project deliberately recorded material without prioritising types of seal or seal owner, however, and so it seemed most appropriate to present the results in as neutral a manner as possible. Furthermore, since the great majority of presumed seal owners (those instances where the legend names whose seal it was) in the *SiMeW* sample are from below the highest levels in society and distributed widely across time and location, it was decided that an order based on name would not be particularly helpful in any case. The catalogue is therefore ordered by repository, and collections generally listed together. It is also anticipated that the *SiMeW* data will in due course become available online, thus facilitating searches by motif, name and so on linked to the seal number given in each instance here.

Abbreviations

BL Add. Ch.	British Library, Additional Charters
BL Harl. Ch.	British Library, Harley Charters
BUAS MOST	Bangor University Archives, Mostyn Manuscripts
BUAS PENR	Bangor University Archives, Penrhyn Castle
CALS D3785/1	Cheshire Archives and Local Studies, Professor G. Barraclough: Deeds and Research Papers (Bulkley and Bickerton Deeds)

APPENDIX

CALS DLL	Cheshire Archives and Local Studies, Leigh of West Hall, High Legh
CALS DWN	Cheshire Archives and Local Studies, Wilbraham of Nantwich Collection
GA D2, GA D583	Gwent Record Office, Llanarth Court MSS
GA D8/1	Gwent Record Office, John Capel Hanbury (D8/1)
GACRO Vaynol/Glan	Gwynedd Archives: Caernarfon Record Office, Vaynol Papers
GACRO XD2	Gwynedd Archives: Caernarfon Record Office, Newborough Archives
HAS A95	Herefordshire Record Office, Pateshall Family of Allensmore
HAS AA26/II	Herefordshire Record Office, Records of the Barton Colwall Estate
HAS CF54	Herefordshire Record Office, Pilley Collection: Manuscripts
HAS D52	Herefordshire Record Office, Wellington Inheritance Brobury (Garnons)
HAS F8/II	Herefordshire Record Office, Hill Court
HCA	Hereford Cathedral Archives
NLW BACBYD	Llyfrgell Genedlaethol Cymru / National Library of Wales, Bachymbyd Estate Deeds and Documents
NLW BRONWYDD	Llyfrgell Genedlaethol Cymru / National Library of Wales, Bronwydd Estate Records
NLW CHIRK	Llyfrgell Genedlaethol Cymru / National Library of Wales, Chirk Castle Estate Records
NLW MYNDE	Llyfrgell Genedlaethol Cymru / National Library of Wales, Mynde Park Deeds and Documents
NLW PENRICE: GLAM	Llyfrgell Genedlaethol Cymru / National Library of Wales, Penrice and Margam Estate Records
NLW PITORD	Llyfrgell Genedlaethol Cymru / National Library of Wales, Ottley (Pitchford Hall) Estate 1
NLW Strata Marchella	Llyfrgell Genedlaethol Cymru / National Library of Wales, Wynnstay Estate Records 1945 Deposit (Ystrad Marchell)
NLW WIGFAIR	Llyfrgell Genedlaethol Cymru / National Library of Wales, Wigfair Deeds and Documents
SHA 20	Shropshire Archives, Oakley Park Collection
SHA 322/2	Shropshire Archives, Acton Reynald (Corbet Family)
SHA 972	Shropshire Archives, Lilleshall Collection
SHA 5981/B	Shropshire Archives, Powis Estate Records

Seals

SEAL 1
Round, nm
Armoured man on a horse galloping to the right
Legend: +SIGILL [section lost] G [section lost] I
GACRO XD2/1113, dated 1207 x 1207
BL Add. Ch. 10637, dated 1228

SEAL 2
Rounded oval, nm
Uncertain (?Gem: ?bust)
Legend: [. . . . .]CI FIL[. . . . .]
BL Add. Ch. 10637, dated 1228

SEAL 3
Round, 25
Sixteen-petalled stylised flower
Legend: + S' IOhI'S ¶ POR[. .] ¶
BL Harl. Ch. 75 C 43, dated 1225 x 1274
BL Add. Ch. 24248, dated 1225 x 1274

SEAL 4
Round, 27
Stylised lily
Legend: + S[. . .]BERTI T'VRGOD
BL Add. Ch. 24250, dated 1243

SEAL 5
Round, 26
Stylised lily
Legend: + S'. WILL' [. . .][section lost]
BL Add. Ch. 24251, dated 1225 x 1274

SEAL 6
Round, 23
Four stylised leaves
Legend: + S' WALTERI [. . . . .]
BL Add. Ch. 24252, dated 1225 x 1274

SEAL 7
Round, 28
Stylised lily with two small cross bourdonny in place of 'seed heads'
Legend: + S' ADE . PANChOLF
BL Add. Ch. 24253, dated 1225 x 1274

SEAL 8
Round, 25
Eight-petalled stylised flower
Legend: + S' ADE : YSAAC
BL Add. Ch. 24255, dated 1225 x 1274

SEAL 9
Round, 22
Stylised lily
Legend: + S' ADE : KENE
BL Add. Ch. 24256, dated 1225 x 1274

SEAL 10
Pointed oval, $c.22$x $c.19$
Stylised lily (upside down in relation to legend)
Legend: + SIG[. . . . .]AC
BL Add. Ch. 24257, dated 1200 x 1299

SEAL 11
Round, 28
Four-petalled stylised flower in form of double loops
Legend: [. . .] PhI' . S[. .]ONIS
BL Add. Ch. 24259, dated 1125 x 1174

SEAL 12
Round, 25
Eight-petalled stylised flower
Legend: + S' WAL[. . . .]CARPVT'I
BL Add. Ch. 24260, dated 1225 x 1274

SEAL 13
Round, 25
Stylised flower in form of a cross saltire formed by four rays emerging from a central pellet, four larger pellets in the angles
Legend: + S'. ADE . FIL'.Ph'I
BL Add. Ch. 24269, dated 1225 x 1274
BL Add. Ch. 24272, dated 1225 x 1274
BL Add. Ch. 24270, dated 1225 x 1274

SEAL 14
Pointed oval, $c.30$x19
Stylised lily
Legend: + S' ALIS.DE FROMBRVGE

APPENDIX

BL Add. Ch. 24270, seal 2, dated 1225 x 1274
BL Add. Ch. 24269, seal 2, dated 1225 x 1274
BL Add. Ch. 24272, seal 2, dated 1225 x 1274

SEAL 15
Round, 22
Eight-petalled stylised flower
Legend: + S' ADE.FIL'L.ThOME
BL Add. Ch. 24275, dated 1225 x 1274

SEAL 16
Round, 26
Stylised flower in form of a cross saltire formed by four rays emerging from a central pellet, four larger pellets in the angles
Legend: + S'WENLIAN.FIL'.PhILIPPI
BL Add. Ch. 24275, seal 2, dated 1225 x 1274

SEAL 17
Round, 25
Stylised flower in form of cross saltire formed by four rays emerging from a central pellet, four larger pellets in the angles
Legend: + S'hENRICI . DE . ANGLIA
BL Add. Ch. 24281, dated 1275 x 1324

SEAL 18
Round, 25
Stylised lily
Legend: + S' IOhIS.DE.ANGLIA
BL Add. Ch. 24282, dated 1225 x 1274

SEAL 19
Round, 30
Bird (?hawk / ?fighting cock) facing right with wings and talons raised
Legend: + S,:WIL[. .]MI.FIL'.WALTERI
BL Add. Ch. 24290, dated 1225 x 1274

SEAL 20
Pointed oval, c.23x19
Stylised lily-like plant with a trefoil leaf at the top
Legend: [.]S':AVICIE : DE : KERDIF
BL Add. Ch. 24299, dated 1200 x 1299

SEAL 21
Round, 29
Stylised lily
Legend: + S' +ROBI'.:FILL':ROB':[.]V[.]
BL Add. Ch. 24301, dated 1225 x 1274

SEAL 22
Round, 22
Shield of arms (three covered cups) with a lion's head caboshed above, two small wyverns in the field at the base of the shield
Legend: * . [. . . . . .]IOhANNIS B[. . . .]ER
BL Harl. Ch. 46 I 37, dated 1438 x 1439

SEAL 23
Pointed oval, 63x40
Mitred man vested for Mass standing full-face blessing with right hand, holding a pastoral staff in the left hand
Legend: [. .]GILL' : HENRICI [. . . . .] VENSIS EPISCOPI
BL Harl. Ch. 75 A 21, front, dated 1193 x 1218
BL Harl. Ch. 75 A 23, front, dated 1193 x 1218

SEAL 24
Pointed oval, 37x23
Winged and robed figure standing full-face holding a Latin cross up in their right hand, a book held to their chest in their left hand (Archangel)
Legend: +SECRET'hENR':LANDAV'EPISCOP'
NLW PENRICE: GLAM/102, back, dated 1203 x 1213
NLW PENRICE: GLAM/48, back, dated 1200 x 1218
BL Harl. Ch. 75 A 21, back, dated 1193 x 1218
BL Harl. Ch. 75 A 23, back, dated 1193 x 1218

SEAL 25
Pointed oval, nm
Mitred man vested for Mass standing full-face blessing with right hand, holding a crozier in his left hand
Legend: +SI[section lost]D?E[section lost]?BA[section lost]PI
BL Harl. Ch. 75 A 30, dated 1157 x 1166

SEAL 26
Round, 56
Building composed of a central tower with a conical roof, to the left and right shorter towers with conical roofs; structure decorated with vertical lines
Legend: +SIGILLVM. SC+PETRI:BADONISECLLESIEA
BL Harl. Ch. 75 A 30, seal 2, dated 1157 x 1166
SBH Deed 1325, dated *c*.1220

SEAL 27
Round, 29
Hand and arm emerging from right wearing a maniple and holding a pastoral staff, small ?suns (?stars) in upper left and right, lower left
Legend: [. . . . . .] ABB'IS DE [. . .]RLIO[.]
BL Harl. Ch. 75 A 32, seal 2, dated 1203

SEAL 28
Pointed oval, nm
Within an ornate canopied niche, Virgin and Child holding in the right hand a flower on stem seated full-face with below, beneath a rounded arch, a half-length suppliant man full-face with foliage to left and right
Legend: Sig [section lost] nis. [section lost] A [.]nda [section lost]
BL Harl. Ch. 75 A 33, dated 1385

SEAL 29
Round, nm
Shield of arms (three bars)
Legend: [.]IGILL' REIMVNDI : DE S[. . . .]
BL Harl. Ch. 75 A 35, dated 1230
NLW PENRICE: GLAM/2054, dated 1200 x 1250

SEAL 30
Round, *c*.15
Shield of arms (cross fleuretty between four billets)
Legend: [. .'NI.IOhANNIS [. . . . . .]
BL Harl. Ch. 75 A 36, dated 1270 x 1295
BL Harl. Ch. 75 C 38, dated 1270 x 1295

SEAL 31
Pointed oval, nm
Tonsured man standing full-face holding a pastoral staff in the right hand, left hand holding a ?book, crescent and ?star in lower left, crescent and ?sun to right
Legend: lost
BL Harl. Ch. 75 A 38, dated 1225 x 1274

SEAL 32
Round, 32
Eight-petalled stylised flower
Legend: +SIG[.]L'MIC[.]AE [.]: TVSAR[section lost]
BL Harl. Ch. 75 A 41, dated 1260

SEAL 33
Pointed oval, 35x23
Double-headed axe
Legend: +S'T [. . . .]E.SPODVR
BL Harl. Ch. 75 A 42, dated 1291

SEAL 34
Round, 24
Sixteen-petalled stylised flower
Legend: [section lost]WILLI.WRO [section lost]
BL Harl. Ch. 75 A 43, dated 1308

SEAL 35
Round, 21
Stylised flower (?twelve-petalled)
Legend: [. .]C[.][section lost][. . . . . .]
BL Harl. Ch. 75 A 44, dated 1349

SEAL 36
Pointed oval, *c*.29x24
Stylised lily

APPENDIX

Legend: INS [section lost] SSERO[. .]R'M
BL Harl. Ch. 75 B 2, seal 1, dated 1220 x 1230

SEAL 37
Round, c.22
Lamb of God facing right
Legend: [section lost] VIR [section lost]
BL Harl. Ch. 75 B 2, seal 3, dated 1220 x 1230

SEAL 38
Pointed oval, 71x44
Mitred man vested for Mass standing full-face on a corbel blessing with right hand, holding a pastoral staff in the left hand
Legend: ELIAS:DEI:GRACIA:LAN-DAVENSIS:EPISCOPVS
BL Harl. Ch. 75 B 8, seal 1, front, dated 1234
BL Harl. Ch. 75 B 6, seal 1, front, dated 1230 x 1240
BL Harl. Ch. 75 B 9, seal 1, front, dated 1234
HCA Deed 1515, front, dated 1230 x 1240
NLW PENRICE: GLAM/139, front, dated 1238 x 1240
NLW PENRICE: GLAM/136, front, dated 1239
NLW PENRICE: GLAM/137, front, dated 1230 x 1240
BL Harl. Ch. 75 B 40, seal 2, front, dated 1234

SEAL 39
Pointed oval, 67x43
Building with a rounded arched doorway with a row of three windows above, a tower with a conical spire above, smaller towers surmounted by crosses to the left and right
Legend: [.]SIG[.]CAPITVLI.LANDAVENSISECLESIE[.]
BL Harl. Ch. 75 B 6, seal 2, front, dated 1230 x 1240
BL Harl. Ch. 75 B 9, seal 2, front, dated 1234
BL Harl. Ch. 75 B 8, seal 2, front, dated 1234
NLW PENRICE: GLAM/241, dated 1397

SEAL 40
Pointed oval, 36x24
Arm emerging from base with hand blessing
Legend: +SECRETV' ELIE:LANDAVENSISEPISCOPI
HCA Deed 1515, back, dated 1230 x 1240
BL Harl. Ch. 75 B 8, seal 1, back, dated 1234
BL Harl. Ch. 75 B 9, seal 1, back, dated 1234
BL Harl. Ch. 75 B 40, seal 2, back, dated 1234
BL Harl. Ch. 75 B 6, seal 1, back, dated 1230 x 1240
NLW PENRICE: GLAM/139, back, dated 1238 x 1240
NLW PENRICE: GLAM/136, back, dated 1239
NLW PENRICE: GLAM/137, back, dated 1230 x 1240

SEAL 41
Pointed oval, 41x26
Lamb of God facing right
Legend: SECRETVMLANDAVENSISECCLESIE
BL Harl. Ch. 75 B 9, seal 2, back, dated 1234
BL Harl. Ch. 75 B 8, seal 2, back, dated 1234
BL Harl. Ch. 75 B 6, seal 2, back, dated 1230 x 1240
NLW PENRICE: GLAM/145, seal 2, dated 1246

SEAL 42
Round, 38
Six-petalled stylised flower
Legend: +SIGILL'MEVRICFILIIBLEThIN
BL Harl. Ch. 75 B 11, dated 1200 x 1225

SEAL 43
Round, 38
Nine-armed sun within a six pointed star with a pellet in each angle
Legend: +SIGILL'WR?ONVFILIIBLE[. . .]
BL Harl. Ch. 75 B 11, seal 2, dated 1200 x 1225

SEAL 44
Round, 38
Stylised lily
Legend: +SIGILL'.RESI.FIL[section lost]N
BL Harl. Ch. 75 B 11, seal 3, dated 1200 x 1225

SEAL 45
Round, 38,
Cross potent with a foliate motif extending from each arm and a trio of pellets in each angle
Legend: + ¶ SIGILLVMIOHANNI [.] E BONAVILLA
BL Harl. Ch. 75 B 12, dated 1250 x 1299

SEAL 46
Pointed oval, 22x28
Gem: Lamb of God facing left
Legend: + SIGILLVM WILLI': DE BONEVILLA:
BL Harl. Ch. 75 B 13, dated 1225 x 1275
BL Harl. Ch. 75 B 16, dated 1200 x 1231
BL Harl. Ch. 75 B 17, dated 1200 x 1231

SEAL 47
Rounded oval, 28x23
Three lines of Arabic script
Legend: +S'MABILLE:DEBONAVILLA
BL Harl. Ch. 75 B 14, dated 1200 x 1250

SEAL 48
Round, 38
Lion walking left with head facing back, tail passing between its legs and raised above its back
Legend: +S[section lost]IO ¶ hANNISDEBOHEVILE
BL Harl. Ch. 75 B 15, dated 1193 x 1218

SEAL 49
Pointed oval, 35x28
Stylised lily, inverted, on the upper right and left, a cross pomey
Legend: +SIGILLVMROBERTIDEBONEVILE
BL Harl. Ch. 75 B 19, dated 1200 x 1231
BL Harl. Ch. 75 B 20, dated 1200 x 1231

SEAL 50
Round, 21
Within a sexfoil, a shield of arms (three bars) with three flowers on tendrils in the field
Legend: *SIGILL'REMVNDESVLIE
BL Harl. Ch. 75 B 22, dated 1302
NLW PENRICE: GLAM/194, dated 1312

SEAL 51
Round, 21
Stylised six-petalled flower
Legend: +S':IOh'IS.BONEVIL':
BL Harl. Ch. 75 B 22, seal 2, dated 1302
NLW PENRICE: GLAM/194, seal 2, dated 1312

SEAL 52
Pointed oval, 80x56
Building with rounded doorway, circular windows, tall central tower surmounted by a cross, a large cross at the right end of the roof, a tall ?round tower and apse to the left, ?stylised foliage in the field to the left
Legend: [. .]IGILLVM LA[.]DA[. .]ENSIS ECCLESI¶E.
BL Harl. Ch. 75 B 25, dated 1175 x 1200
NLW PENRICE: GLAM/10, dated 1150 x 1199
NLW PENRICE: GLAM/11, seal 1, dated 1172 x 1179

SEAL 53
Pointed oval, 59x37
Bearded man wearing a short tunic and hat emerging from left walking right holding up in his left hand an object with a long handle
Legend: +SIGILLVMGILL[.]ERTIBURDINI
BL Harl. Ch. 75 B 27, dated 1200
BL Harl. Ch. 75 B 26, dated 1150 x 1199

SEAL 54
Round, 45
Long tendril with stylised leaves curled around itself terminating in trefoil leaf
Legend: + SIGILLVM MOREDVCFILII CARADOCI .
BL Harl. Ch. 75 B 28, dated 1186 x 1199

SEAL 55
Round, nm
Armoured man on a horse galloping to the right
Legend: +SIGILL' [.] CA [section lost] IF [section lost]RATOCI⸱
BL Harl. Ch. 75 B 29, dated 1158 x 1191

SEAL 56
Round, 50
Armoured man on a horse galloping to the right
Legend: + ⸱ SIGILLVM [. . .]G ⸱ ANI : FI[. . .] ⸱ CRATOCI
NLW PENRICE: GLAM/54, dated 1175 x 1200
BL Harl. Ch. 75 B 29, seal 2, dated 1158 x 1191

SEAL 57
Round, 54
Armoured man on a horse walking to right
Legend: + SIGILLVM MARGAN FILII CARADOCI
BL Harl. Ch. 75 B 31, dated 1205 x 1208
NLW PENRICE: GLAM/2019, dated 1189 x 1208
NLW PENRICE: GLAM/51, dated 1199
NLW PENRICE: GLAM/59, dated 1200
NLW PENRICE: GLAM/2026, dated 1200
NLW PENRICE: GLAM/2003, dated 1193 x 1203
NLW PENRICE: GLAM/2025, dated 1200 x 1208
NLW PENRICE: GLAM/2023, dated 1189 x 1208
NLW PENRICE: GLAM/2022, dated 1189 x 1208
NLW PENRICE: GLAM/2020, dated 1186 x 1208
BL Harl. Ch. 75 B 30, dated 1205
NLW PENRICE: GLAM/2018, dated 1197
NLW PENRICE: GLAM/2017, dated 1199
NLW PENRICE: GLAM/92, dated 1208
NLW PENRICE: GLAM/100, dated 1208
NLW PENRICE: GLAM/95, seal 2, dated 1208
NLW PENRICE: GLAM/2021, dated 1189 x 1208
NLW PENRICE: GLAM/93, dated 1197
NLW PENRICE: GLAM/85, dated 1205
NLW PENRICE: GLAM/91, dated 1205 x 1208
NLW PENRICE: GLAM/89, dated 1193 x 1199
NLW PENRICE: GLAM/88, dated 1189 x 1203
NLW PENRICE: GLAM/87, dated 1205 x 1208
NLW PENRICE: GLAM/90, dated 1208
NLW PENRICE: GLAM/86, dated 1205

SEAL 58
Pointed oval, nm
Hand and arm wearing maniple emerging from lower right holding a pastoral staff
Legend: +SIGILLAB[. .]DENETH
BL Harl. Ch. 75 B 32, seal 1, dated 1175 x 1224

SEAL 59
Pointed oval, 55x36
Eagle displayed
Legend: +SIGILLVVRBANI:ARChiDIA-CLANDAVIE
BL Harl. Ch. 75 B 32, seal 2, dated 1175 x 1224

SEAL 60
Round, 32
Sixteen-petalled stylised flower
Legend: +SIGILL'GRIFINI
BL Harl. Ch. 75 B 33, dated 1205
NLW PENRICE: GLAM/18, dated 1175 x 1225

SEAL 61
Round, 30x31
Harp with small sprig of stylised foliage to left and right
Legend: +SIGILLVM:SIBILLE:DEBOHVIL'
BL Harl. Ch. 75 B 36, dated 1217

SEAL 62
Unknown, nm
Armoured man on a horse with armorial caparisons (chevrony) galloping to the right
Legend: lost
BL Harl. Ch. 75 B 37, front, dated 1217 x 1218

SEAL 63
Round, 25
Shield of arms (three chevrons)
Legend: +SIGILL':GILEBERTI DE CLARA
NLW PENRICE: GLAM/2048, back, dated 1218 x 1230
BL Harl. Ch. 75 B 37, back, dated 1217 x 1218
BL Harl. Ch. 75 B 38, back, dated 1218 x 1230
NLW PENRICE: GLAM/131, back, dated 1218 x 1230

SEAL 64
Round, nm
Armoured man on a horse ?walking to right
Legend: [section lost] SIGILL G[section lost]
BL Harl. Ch. 75 B 38, front, dated 1218 x 1230

SEAL 65
Round, 29
Radial design of twelve spokes with a roundel at the tip (stylised teasels?) emerging from central boss
Legend: +SIGILLVM: [G]RIFIT:ABRES
BL Harl. Ch. 75 B 39, dated 1225 x 1250

SEAL 66
Round, 36
Nineteen-petalled stylised flower
Legend: +SIGILL':MAVRICII:FILII:RESI:COH
BL Harl. Ch. 75 B 39, seal 2, dated 1225 x 1250

SEAL 67
Round, 27
Stylised lily
Legend: +SIGILL':RESI:FIL':RESI:COH
BL Harl. Ch. 75 B 39, seal 3, dated 1225 x 1250

SEAL 68
Round, 33
Sixteen-petalled stylised flower
Legend: +SIGILL'RESI:COH:IVNIORIS
BL Harl. Ch. 75 B 40, seal 1, dated 1234

SEAL 69
Pointed oval, 39x27
Man on horse walking to left
Legend: +SIGILL'VN ? NODGANICAM
NLW PENRICE: GLAM/1973, seal 2, dated 1225 x 1250
BL Harl. Ch. 75 B 40, seal 3, dated 1234

SEAL 70
Round, 38
Bow and arrow pointing down, ready for shooting
Legend: +SIGILL':ROGERI:GRA[.]MVS
NLW PENRICE: GLAM/1988, dated 1175 x 1200
BL Harl. Ch. 75 C 3, dated 1202
NLW PENRICE: GLAM/1987, dated 1203

SEAL 71
Rectangular, 31
Stylised lily
Legend: + S' : ROGERI : GRAMVS
BL Harl. Ch. 75 C 5, dated 1200 x 1225

SEAL 72
Round, 29
Stylised lily with pellets in the field
Legend: +SIGILL : THOME GRAMMVS
NLW PENRICE: GLAM/1989, dated 1225 x 1274
NLW PENRICE: GLAM/1992, dated 1225 x 1250
BL Harl. Ch. 75 C 5, seal 2, dated 1200 x 1225

APPENDIX

SEAL 73
Round, 26
Eight-petalled stylised flower formed by small stylised lilies joined at base
Legend: + S' MAVRICI ' GRAMMVS
BL Harl. Ch. 75 C 16, dated 1250 x 1299

SEAL 74
Round, 32
Lion walking to right
Legend: + SIGILL' : MOGANI : FILII : KAD[. .]
BL Harl. Ch. 75 C 19, dated 1217 x 1228

SEAL 75
Round, 37
Stylised lily
Legend: +SIGIL'MILONISCAIRVS
BL Harl. Ch. 75 C 20, dated 1175 x 1225

SEAL 76
Round, 38
Armoured man on a horse galloping to the right
Legend: +[.]IGILLVM MORGANIIGAM*
NLW PENRICE: GLAM/73, dated 1217 x 1241
BL Harl. Ch. 75 C 21, dated 1217 x 1241

SEAL 77
Round, 36
Radial design of central boss from which emerge eight spokes with stylised teasels at the tips
Legend: + SIGILL' RIERED FILL'.KENOH'
BL Harl. Ch. 75 C 24, dated 1175 x 1225

SEAL 78
Round, 28
Standing cup with foliate fronds emerging from top, two ?hand (?palm-type fronds) flanking the stem, two ?leaves pointing up from base of cup bowl
Legend: + SIGILL' : GRIFID : L'TIMER
BL Harl. Ch. 75 C 29, dated 1225 x 1250

SEAL 79
Rounded oval, 32x39
Gem: figure holding a lance with a ?pennant on a horse galloping to the left
Legend: + SIILLVM WILL'IDELONDONIIS
NLW PENRICE: GLAM/158, dated 1205 x 1214
BL Harl. Ch. 75 C 31, dated 1175 x 1225
NLW PENRICE: GLAM/156, dated 1205 x 1214

SEAL 80
Round, 22
Eight-petalled stylised flower
Legend: + SIGILL' : EGELINE
BL Harl. Ch. 75 C 32, dated 1200 x 1249

SEAL 81
Round, 54
Figure wearing archaic mitre (?wimple) and long flowing gown seated full-face on ornate stool blessing with right hand, left hand holding oblong object with tassels (?book with straps undone / ?sealed charter), to the left a kneeling suppliant man in a short tunic and cloak facing right
Legend: + SIGILLVM ¶ LEISAN . FI ¶ LII MORGANI
BL Harl. Ch. 75 C 34, dated 1175 x 1208
NLW PENRICE: GLAM/110/b, dated 1208 x 1217
NLW PENRICE: GLAM/111, dated 1208 x 1217
NLW PENRICE: GLAM/112, dated 1203 x 1205

SEAL 82
Round, 54
Armoured man on a horse galloping right
Legend: + SIGILLW¶M LEISAV ¶ N FILII MORGAN
NLW PENRICE: GLAM/108, dated 1213
NLW PENRICE: GLAM/2032, seal 2, dated 1208 x 1217
NLW PENRICE: GLAM/2031, dated 1208 x 1214

NLW PENRICE: GLAM/2030, dated 1208 x 1217
NLW PENRICE: GLAM/149, dated 1247
NLW PENRICE: GLAM/2027, dated 1208 x 1217
NLW PENRICE: GLAM/106, dated 1205 x 1207
NLW PENRICE: GLAM/107, dated 1213
BL Harl. Ch. 75 C 35, dated 1215 x 1217

SEAL 83
Round, 38
Hand emerging from right holding up a spear with a striped pennon flying to the right
Legend: + SIGILL : HOWENI [section lost] NI .:.
BL Harl. Ch. 75 C 36, dated 1186 x 1208
BL Harl. Ch. 75 C 37, dated 1203 x 1208

SEAL 84
Unknown, 21x15
Indistinct
Legend: + [section lost] R [.]TI
BL Harl. Ch. 75 C 39, dated 1175 x 1225

SEAL 85
Round, 26
Eight-petalled stylised flower
Legend: + SI' : PhI' :FILII : WILL'
BL Harl. Ch. 75 C 40, dated 1261

SEAL 86
Round, 27
Scallop shell
Legend: +SIGILL' MILON:DEP[. .]EI
BL Harl. Ch. 75 C 41, dated 1225 x 1250

SEAL 87
Round, 34
Hand emerging from the right holding a key
Legend: +SIGILLVM ADE PORTARI
BL Harl. Ch. 75 C 44, dated 1175 x 1225

SEAL 88
Pointed oval, 50x30
Arm emerging from the right hand holding up a spear with striped pennant flying to the right, small suns to right and left of spear-tip, small trefoil flowers on stems emerging from the base
Legend: + SIGILL' GRVNV ҁ FILII PHILIPPI
BL Harl. Ch. 75 C 46, dated 1175 x 1225

SEAL 89
Round, 34
Radial design of eight spokes with a roundel at the tip (stylised teasels?)
Legend: +SIGIL'TVDER [section lost]
BL Harl. Ch. 75 C 47, dated 1175 x 1225

SEAL 90
Round, 43
Lance with pennant to right
Legend: +SIGIL'KENWRECFIL'ROb'TI
BL Harl. Ch. 75 C 47, seal 2, dated 1175 x 1225

SEAL 91
Round, 41
Stylised eight-petalled flower
Legend: +SIGIL'GRVNVFIL'ROb'TI
BL Harl. Ch. 75 C 47, seal 3, dated 1175 x 1225

SEAL 92
Round, 39
Five-petalled stylised flower
Legend: +SIGLL'V. [.]ERBERTIFILII. RODBERTI
BL Harl. Ch. 75 C 48, dated 1175 x 1225

SEAL 93
Unknown, c.40xc.33
Stylised lily (upside-down in relation to legend)
Legend: S' R[. . . . .]I. RV[. . . . . .]AIONIS
BL Harl. Ch. 75 C 50, dated 1200 x 1299
BL Harl. Ch. 75 C 49, dated 1261

SEAL 94
Round, 25
Eight-petalled stylised flower

APPENDIX

Legend: + S': ROBERTI : FILII : MILOTI
BL Harl. Ch. 75 C 51, dated 1261

SEAL 95
Round, nm
Within a cusped quatrafoil, a shield of arms (a chevron) hanging from a bush that extends into the legend band, foliate tendrils in the field
Legend: ¶ Sig[. . . . .] Rad[. . . . .] St[section lost]
BL Harl. Ch. 75 C 55, dated 1359 x 1360

SEAL 96
Pointed oval, 68x44
Man ?wearing crested helm and short belted tunic facing right holding a spear point up in his right hand and blowing a horn held up in his left hand
Legend: + SIGILLVM GALFRIDISTVRMI
BL Harl. Ch. 75 D 1, dated 1150 x 1174
NLW PENRICE: GLAM/1978, dated 1150 x 1175
NLW PENRICE: GLAM/1979, dated 1183

SEAL 97
Round, 59
Lion walking to right
Legend: +SIGILLVM:ROGERI:STVRMI
NLW PENRICE: GLAM/1980, dated 1166 x 1193
BL Harl. Ch. 75 D 3, dated 1175 x 1200
NLW PENRICE: GLAM/1983, dated 1150 x 1199
NLW PENRICE: GLAM/1982, dated 1150 x 1199
BL Harl. Ch. 75 D 2, dated 1150 x 1174
NLW PENRICE: GLAM/1981, dated 1150 x 1199
NLW PENRICE: GLAM/1984, dated 1150 x 1199

SEAL 98
Round, 35
Stylised lily
Legend: + SIGILL' : ROGERI : STRMI
BL Harl. Ch. 75 D 5, dated 1234

SEAL 99
Round, 23
Twelve-petalled stylised flower
Legend: +S'WILLELMISTVRMI
BL Harl. Ch. 75 D 6, dated 1250 x 1299

SEAL 100
Round, 55
Armoured man on a horse walking to the right
Legend: ¶ +SIG[. .]LVM ADAM DE VM [.]E [.]¶ I
BL Harl. Ch. 75 D 8, dated 1175 x 1200
BL Harl. Ch. 75 D 7, dated 1175 x 1200

SEAL 101
Round, 23
Seven-petalled flower
Legend: +SECRETVMhENRICI
BL Harl. Ch. 75 D 14, dated 1217
NLW PENRICE: GLAM/118, dated 1217

SEAL 102
Pointed oval, c.38x29
Spear point up with pennant flying to left (?held by hand emerging from lower right)
Legend: [. . . .]LL' ENIAVN FIL' WRVN [. . . .]
BL Harl. Ch. 75 D 20, dated 1175 x 1225

SEAL 103
Round, 33
Eight-petalled stylised flower
Legend: + SIGILL'.MEVRICII.GOVH ¶
BL Harl. Ch. 75 D 21, dated 1200 x 1249

SEAL 104
Pointed oval, 55x31
Arm emerging from right with hand holding a spear with tasselled pennant flying to the right
Legend: + SIGILL' FILIPPI : F : WVRKENI
BL Harl. Ch. 75 D 22, dated 1175 x 1200

SEAL 105
Round, nm
Uncertain
Legend: none
BUAS MOST/717, dated 1378 x 1379

SEAL 106
Round, 17
Within an ornate border, a shield of arms (three objects between a chevron, an object in chief)
Legend: illegible
BUAS MOST/718, dated 1392 x 1393

SEAL 107
Round, 14
Merchant mark
Legend: none
BUAS MOST/752, dated 1496 x 1497

SEAL 108
Rounded oval, nm
Pelican in its piety facing left
Legend: none
BUAS MOST/787, seal 2, dated 1476

SEAL 109
Unknown, nm
Letter T
Legend: none
BUAS MOST/788, dated 1476 x 1477

SEAL 110
Rounded oval, 13x16
Lamb of God facing left
Legend: none
BUAS MOST/791, dated 1492 x 1493

SEAL 111
Rectangular, 12x9
Letter E
Legend: none
BUAS MOST/794, dated 1498 x 1499

SEAL 112
Rounded oval, 11x14
Bird with three stalks of wheat in its beak facing left
Legend: none
BUAS MOST/891, dated 1485 x 1486

SEAL 113
Seal of the ?Exchequer of Henry VII
BUAS MOST/954, dated 1487 x 1488

SEAL 114
Unknown, nm
Uncertain (?head of unicorn facing right, foliage in the field)
Legend: none
BUAS MOST/1028, dated 1486 x 1487

SEAL 115
Round, 17
Crowned letter R, stylised branch on either side
Legend: none
BUAS MOST/1094, dated 1438 x 1439

SEAL 116
Hexagonal, 10x12
Heart with foliate tendrils emerging from top and drooping down sides
Legend: none
BUAS MOST/1187, dated 1457 x 1458

SEAL 117
Round, nm
?Letter ?H (two parallel lines)
Legend: none
BUAS MOST/1189, dated 1496 x 1497

SEAL 118
Round, 14
Bird (?stork) facing right
Legend: none
BUAS MOST/1379, dated 1445 x 1446

SEAL 119
Round, 11
Eight-pointed star
Legend: none
BUAS MOST/1380, dated 1446 x 1447

APPENDIX

SEAL 120
Undetermined, 18x13
Shield (crescent with cross in chief)
Legend: none
BUAS MOST/1535, dated 1423

SEAL 121
Round, 15
Letter T
Legend: none
BUAS MOST/1535, seal 2, dated 1423

SEAL 122
Round, 11
Letters dd (?w)
Legend: none
BUAS MOST/1536, dated 1450 x 1451

SEAL 123
Round, 13x12
Eagle displayed
Legend: none
BUAS MOST/1537, dated 1469 x 1470

SEAL 124
Unknown, nm
Uncertain (fragment)
Legend: none
BUAS MOST/1539, dated 1473 x 1474

SEAL 125
Round, 13
Animal running to left, letter ?g to left, letters ?cs to right
Legend: [. .]p[.]
BUAS MOST/1540, dated 1480 x 1481

SEAL 126
Round, nm
Animal (?lion / ?squirrel) on haunches facing right
Legend: none
BUAS MOST/1540, seal 3, dated 1480 x 1481

SEAL 127
Unknown, nm
Letter W
Legend: none
BUAS MOST/1540, seal 4, dated 1480 x 1481

SEAL 128
Round, 14
Stag seated facing left
Legend: none
BUAS MOST/1540, seal 5, dated 1480 x 1481

SEAL 129
Round, nm
Four-petalled flower
Legend: [. . . . .]WRIO[. .]IOR[. . . .]
BUAS MOST/1627/iv, dated 1332 x 1333

SEAL 130
Rounded oval, nm
?Three lines of script:
Legend: [. . . . . R . .]
BUAS MOST/1627/v, seal 2, dated 1343 x 1344
BUAS MOST/1627/v, dated 1343 x 1344

SEAL 131
Round, 25
Stylised eight-petalled flower
Legend: + ADDAF : AP : KYN
BUAS MOST/1627/xii, dated 1381

SEAL 132
Round, 12
Stylised eight-petalled flower
Legend: none
BUAS MOST/1627/xiv, dated 1480
BUAS MOST/1627/xv, dated 1482

SEAL 133
Round, 12
Saltire cross with extra line forming a border on exterior of arms
Legend: none
BUAS MOST/1627/xv, seal 2, dated 1482

SEAL 134
Round, 12
?Letter ?N (?R)
Legend: none
BUAS MOST/1627/xvi, dated 1491

SEAL 135
Round, 12
Pelican in its piety facing left
Legend: none
BUAS MOST/1627/xvi, seal 2, dated 1491

SEAL 136
Round, 23
Four branches
Legend: S'IOR[. . . . .]WRIC
BUAS MOST/1628/i, dated 1344 x 1345
BUAS MOST/1628/vi, dated 1344

SEAL 137
Round, nm
Four conifer branches
Legend: [. . . . .]ER[. . .]D[. . . .]
BUAS MOST/1627/vii, dated 1347

SEAL 138
Round, nm
?Bird displayed (?stylised lily)
Legend: +[. . . . .]
BUAS MOST/1627/viii, dated 1347

SEAL 139
Round, 11
Within a quatrefoil, letter 'I' with pellet on either side
Legend: none
BUAS MOST/1628/ii, dated 1499 x 1500

SEAL 140
Unknown, nm
?branches
Legend: none
BUAS MOST/1628/iv, dated 1393 x 1394

SEAL 141
Round, 25
Stylised eight-petalled flower
Legend: S'MADOCIAPIEVAN¶
BUAS MOST/1629/iii, dated 1330 x 1330

SEAL 142
Round, 29
Shield of arms (bendy)
Legend: lost
BUAS MOST/1629/iv, dated 1393 x 1394

SEAL 143
Rounded oval, 23x19
Indistinct
Legend: none or lost
BUAS MOST/1629/vi, dated 1300 x 1399

SEAL 144
Round, 20
Within an ornate border, Virgin and Child standing full-face
Legend: *:\SIGILLV + EINION + ILWYD
BUAS MOST/1629/vii, dated 1389 x 1390

SEAL 145
Round, nm
Four conifer branches
Legend: SI[?O][. . . .]R [remainder lost]
BUAS MOST/1630, dated 1300 x 1399

SEAL 146
Round, nm
Four conifer branches with four small pellets in the angles
Legend: [section lost] VAN [section lost]
BUAS MOST/1636, dated 1376 x 1377

SEAL 147
Unknown, nm
Illegible (fragment)
Legend: lost, if any
BUAS MOST/1639, dated 1300 x 1399

SEAL 148
Rounded oval, nm
Letter h, stylised branch to the left, foliate sprig emerging from right of ascender

Figure 1.1 NLW PITORD/1248 (Seal 2055)

Figure 1.2 SHA 972/1/1/428 (Seal 2436)

Figure 1.3 NLW PITORD/466 (Seal 1887)

Figure 1.5 SHA 20/6/122 (Seal 2271)

Figure 1.6 HAS F8/II/17 (Seal 706)

Figure 1.7 NLW PITORD/12 (Seal 1581)

Figure 1.8 BL Harl. Ch. 75 B 6, s.2 rev. (Seal 41)

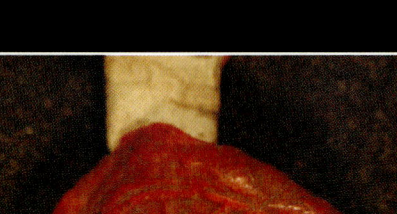

Figure 1.9 SHA 972/1/1/427 (Seal 2435)

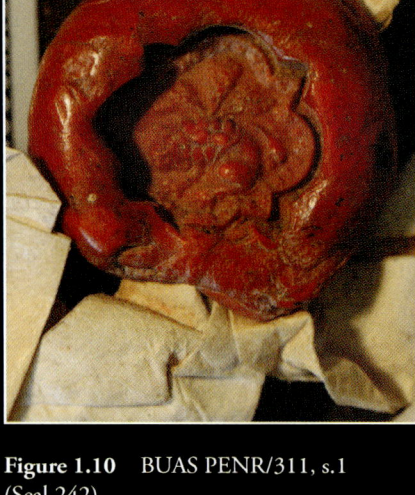

Figure 1.10 BUAS PENR/311, s.1 (Seal 242)

Figure 1.11 NLW PENRICE: GLAM/342, s.5 (Seal 1374)

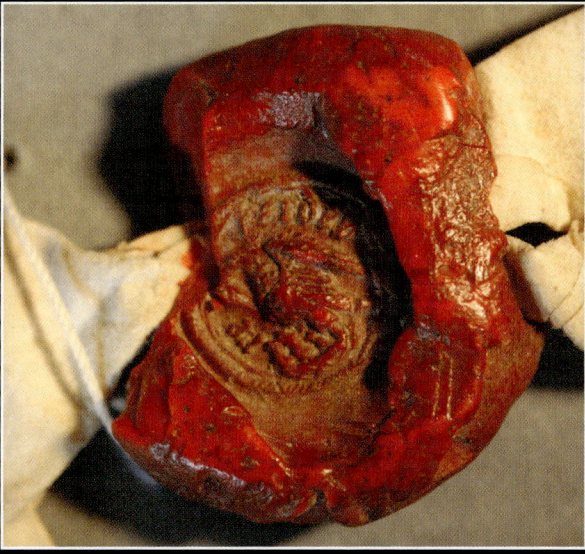

Figure 1.12 BUAS PENR/220 (Seal 243)

Figure 1.13 NLW PENRICE: GLAM/2056, s.3 (Seal 1237)

Figure 1.14 NLW PITORD/54 (Seal 1610)

Figure 1.15 BUAS PENR/407, s.2 (Seal 294)

Figure 1.16 NLW PENRICE: GLAM/119 (Seal 1201)

Figure 1.17 NLW PITORD/1144 (Seal 1630)

Figure 1.18 HCA Deed122 (Seal 764)

Figure 1.19 NLW BRONWYDD/1031 (Seal 966)

Figure 1.20 HAS D52/B/1/2, s.7

Figure 1.21 BUAS MOST/1629/vii

Figure 2.1 *(above)* NLW, PENRICE: GLAM/54 (Seal 56)

Figure 2.2 *(left)* NLW PITORD/519 (Seal 1919)

Figure 2.3 BUAS MOST/718 (Seal 106)

Figure 3.1 NLW PENRICE: GLAM/2798 (Seal 1550)

Figure 3.2 NLW PENRICE: GLAM/183 (Seal 1266)

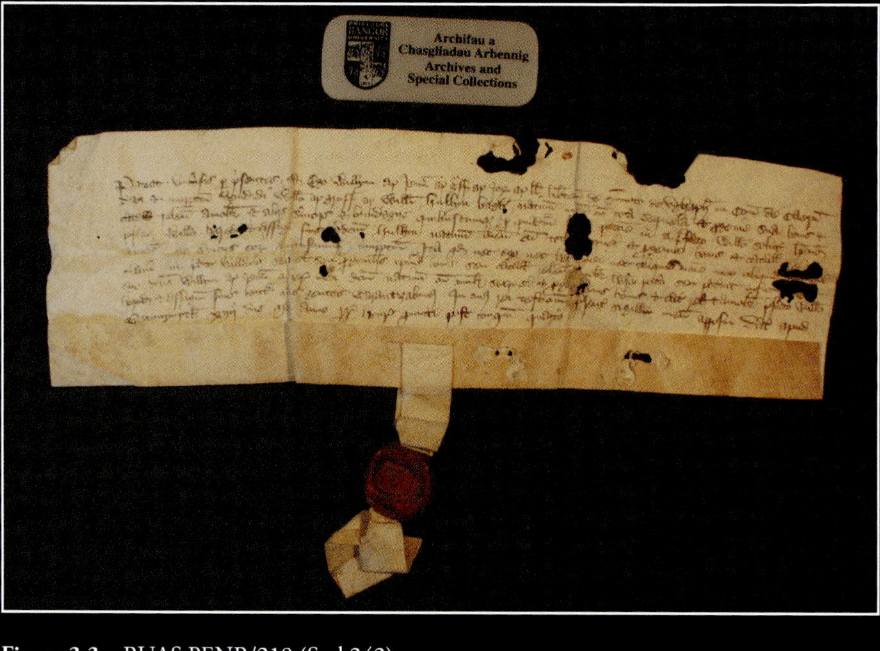

Figure 3.3 BUAS PENR/219 (Seal 242)

Figure 3.4 NLW WIGFAIR/627 (Seal 2205)

Figure 3.5 NLW PENRICE: GLAM/348, s.2 (Seal 1378)

Figure 3.6 NLW PENRICE: GLAM/348, s.1 (Seal 1377)

Figure 3.7 NLW PENRICE: GLAM/1978 (Seal 96)

Figure 3.8 *(left)*   NLW PENRICE: GLAM/1986 (Seal 1503)

Figure 3.9   BL Harl. Ch. 75 D 6 (Seal 99)

Figure 3.10 *(left)* SHA 972/1/1/610, s.2 (Seal 2460)

Figure 3.11 CALS DLL/4/47, s.1 (Seal 427)

Figure 3.12 NLW PITORD/489 (Seal 1901)

Figure 3.13 NLW PENRICE: GLAM/1993 (Seal 1504)

Figure 3.14 NLW BRONWYDD/1332 (Seal 1028)

APPENDIX

Legend: none
BUAS MOST/1935, dated 1428 x 1429

SEAL 149
Rounded oval, nm
Virgin and Child standing to left facing half right, to right a kneeling suppliant figure facing left, two flowers on long stems above suppliant's hands
Legend: illegible
BUAS MOST/2007, dated 1389 x 1390

SEAL 150
Round, nm
Stylised lily
Legend: [. . . . .]On
BUAS MOST/2008, dated 1275 x 1325

SEAL 151
Round, nm
Illegible
Legend: [. . .]NI[. . . .]E[. . . .]
BUAS MOST/2153, dated 1328 x 1329

SEAL 152
Round, nm
Four ?branches
Legend: lost
BUAS MOST/2155, dated 1344

SEAL 153
Round, 26
Four conifer branches
Legend: +S':KINWRIC.F.hYLIN
BUAS MOST/2167, dated 1304

SEAL 154
Round, 28
Four conifer branches
Legend: + S' . K[?E]NVRIC [. .] MADOC
BUAS MOST/2170, dated 1334

SEAL 155
Unknown, nm
Indistinct (?foliate motif)
Legend: lost
BUAS MOST/2171, dated 1336

SEAL 156
Round, 22
Within a wavy border, a man walking to right within a crescent holding a staff with a bundle over his shoulder (man in the moon)
Legend: illegible
BUAS MOST/2172, dated 1337

SEAL 157
Round, 28
Four conifer branches
Legend: DEV[. . . . .] (start-point uncertain)
BUAS MOST/2173, dated 1349

SEAL 158
Round, 26
Four conifer branches
Legend: +S'.IOh'IS:FIL'MADOCI
BUAS MOST/2195, seal 1, dated 1315

SEAL 159
Round, nm
Stylised lily
Legend: lost
BUAS MOST/2195, seal 2, dated 1315

SEAL 160
Round, nm
Includes?three branches arranged in radial pattern
Legend: V[?A]F[. .]R [ost] (start point uncertain)
BUAS MOST/2198, dated 1330

SEAL 161
Round, 31
Three branches arranged in radial pattern
Legend: +SIORWERTh[. . . . .]WERTh
BUAS MOST/2198, seal 2, dated 1330

SEAL 162
Round, 27
Four branches
Legend: Includes DE, otherwise illegible (start-point uncertain)
BUAS MOST/2199, dated 1333

SEAL 163
Round, 18
Within an ornate border, a shield of arms (three objects between a chevron, three objects in chief)
Legend: *SVG[. . . . .]M[section illegible].
BUAS MOST/2317, dated 1410 x 1411

SEAL 164
Round, nm
Stylised lily
Legend: + S'. GRVFVd : FI [section lost]
BUAS MOST/2462, dated 1303

SEAL 165
Round, 28
Stylised eight-petalled flower
Legend: + S' dd VOYL . FI[. . . .]VEN
BUAS MOST/2463, dated 1306

SEAL 166
Round, nm
Uncertain; fragment only
Legend: * S' GREO [section lost] LEKICI
BUAS MOST/2466, dated 1308

SEAL 167
Rounded oval, nm
Woman with ?long hair (?head covering) ?standing full-face, ?stylised foliage to left and right
Legend: I [. . . .]
BUAS MOST/2477, dated 1388

SEAL 168
Rectangular, nm
Letter ?R
Legend: none
BUAS MOST/2478, dated 1444

SEAL 169
Round, 28
Three confier branches
Legend: S' G[.]YFVD F' IORVERTh
BUAS MOST/2487, dated 1327

SEAL 170
Round, nm
Four conifer branches
Legend: + S [. . . . .] IOR'
BUAS MOST/2496, dated 1352 x 1353

SEAL 171
Pointed oval, nm
?Standing figure beneath a canopy, below, beneath a ?pointed arch, a ?kneeling ?figure
Legend: [section lost] A[.]E [section lost]
BUAS MOST/2516, dated 1338

SEAL 172
Round, nm
Crowned letters IM
Legend: none
BUAS MOST/2517, dated 1459

SEAL 173
Round, 12
Indistinct
Legend: none
BUAS MOST/2527, dated 1497 x 1498

SEAL 174
Round, 11
Eagle displayed
Legend: none
BUAS MOST/2527, seal 2, dated 1497 x 1498

SEAL 175
Round, 27
Stylised lily
Legend: [.]GORO[?NV][section lost]
BUAS MOST/2700, seal 1, dated 1324

SEAL 176
Round, 25
Stylised eight-petalled flower
Legend: [section lost] GOR[.]NV
BUAS MOST/2700, seal 2, dated 1324

SEAL 177
Round, 17

APPENDIX

Lamb of God facing left
Legend: *E[. . . . .]NVS[. .]E
BUAS MOST/2788, dated 1385

SEAL 178
Round, 28
Shield of arms (three chevrons)
Legend: N/A
BUAS MOST/2810, dated 1332 x 1333

SEAL 179
Pointed oval, 27
Stylised eight-petalled flower
Legend: +[?S][. .]IO[?D][. . . . . .][EN]
BUAS MOST/2943, dated 1277 x 1308

SEAL 180
Round, 21
Stylised eight-petalled flower
Legend: none
BUAS MOST/2970, dated 1331 x 1332

SEAL 181
Round, 27
Indistinct
Legend: none
BUAS MOST/2987, dated 1341

SEAL 182
Round, 26
Stylised four-petalled flower
Legend: S'GRVFVO[. . . . . .]
BUAS MOST/2990, dated 1341

SEAL 183
Round, 27
Stylised eight-petalled flower
Legend: [section lost]V[section lost]V[?M]:
BUAS MOST/2996, dated 1342

SEAL 184
Round, 24
Stylised eight-pointed star
Legend: +[.]DAVIDF'K[. . .]
BUAS MOST/2998, dated 1343

SEAL 185
Round, nm
Letter M
Legend: S IEVAN F' M[. . .]C
BUAS MOST/3005, dated 1345 x 1346
BUAS MOST/3323, dated 1345

SEAL 186
Rounded oval, 28x25
Shield of arms (per pale, dexter ?barry, sinister void)
Legend: + S' IEVAN F' IORT'
BUAS MOST/3008, dated 1346 x 1347

SEAL 187
Round, 29
Four conifer branches
Legend: + S': DAVID : F' : GWERYL
BUAS MOST/3010, dated 1346

SEAL 188
Round, 24
Within an ornately cusped border, a shield of arms (charge uncertain)
Legend: * S[. . . . . . .][. . . .] ap [. . . .]in
BUAS MOST/3022, dated 1381

SEAL 189
Round, 28
Three conifer branches, with three ?conifer branches (?ears of wheat) arranged lengthways between the tips of the radial branches
Legend: + S IORVE[. . . . . . .]E[.]
BUAS MOST/3097, dated 1312

SEAL 190
Round, nm
Stylised eight-petalled flower
Legend: S' DA[. . . . .]
BUAS MOST/3103, dated 1345

SEAL 191
Rounded oval, 14x12
Crowned letter R, stylised branch to left
Legend: none
BUAS MOST/3108, dated 1407 x 1408

SEAL 192
Round, 15
Four lines intersecting to form an open cross saltire
Legend: none
BUAS MOST/3220, dated 1495 x 1496

SEAL 193
Round, 20
Within an ornate border, a shield of arms (lozengy)
Legend: [. .]LLEW[. . . .]IhEL[section illegible]
BUAS MOST/3227, dated 1338

SEAL 194
Round, 28
Stylised eight-petalled flower
Legend: [section lost][.]I[.][section lost]
BUAS MOST/3236, dated 1331

SEAL 195
Round, 27
Stylised four-petalled flower
Legend: [. . .]ME[. . . . . .] (start-point uncertain)
BUAS MOST/3237, dated 1332

SEAL 196
Round, 29
Four conifer branches
Legend: [section lost][.]B[. . .]IN[. .]
BUAS MOST/3241, dated 1338 x 1339

SEAL 197
Round, 23
Within an ornate border, a shield of arms (a chevron between three ?roundels)
Legend: [. .]IGILLVM.M[. . . . .].GLODEI [section lost]
BUAS MOST/3264, dated 1340

SEAL 198
Round, 20
Indistinct (?four-petalled flower)
Legend: Includes ih [rest lost, start-point uncertain]
BUAS MOST/3325, dated 1346 x 1347

SEAL 199
Round, nm
Stylised ?eight-petalled flwoer
Legend: none
BUAS MOST/3519, dated 1437 x 1438

SEAL 200
Rounded oval, 12x9
Indistinct (?animal)
Legend: none
BUAS MOST/3518, dated 1341 x 1342

SEAL 201
Rounded oval, 17x16
Hare facing right
Legend: [.]AERE[.]WhPEMVRA[section lost]
BUAS MOST/3320, dated 1315 x 1316

SEAL 202
Rectangular, 13x14
Letter B
Legend: none
BUAS MOST/3706, dated 1492 x 1493

SEAL 203
Round, 27
Stylised eight-petalled flower
Legend: SRN[?E]FIL.[.]G[. . . . .] (start-point uncertain)
BUAS MOST/4132, dated 1329 x 1330

SEAL 204
Round, 14
Letter W, stylised foliage above, six small pellets arranged around sides in semicircles
Legend: none
BUAS MOST/4198, dated 1396 x 1397

SEAL 205
Round, 22
Within an ornate cusped border, a shield of arms (bend)
Legend: *S'IOhANISDSChAYIG[. .]N
BUAS MOST/4285, dated 1357

APPENDIX

SEAL 206
Round, nm
Within a cusped border a shield of arms (?fretty)
Legend: [. . . . . .] DE [. . .]ES [section lost]
BUAS MOST/4287, dated 1392 x 1393

SEAL 207
Round, 27
Stylised lily
Legend: +S'WILL'I:PVNT[. . . .]ING
BUAS MOST/4337, dated 1300 x 1399

SEAL 208
Round, 21
Within a pear-shaped cusped border, a merchant mark on a shield (includes letter T), cross-tipped staff emerging from the top
Legend: SIG ThOME [.]E [. .]SALE
BUAS MOST/4338, dated 1389 x 1390

SEAL 209
Rounded oval, 14x11
Letter W, eight-pointed star above, stylised branch to left
Legend: none
BUAS MOST/4497, dated 1425

SEAL 210
Rectangular, 13x9
Letter T, descender ending in stylised leaf, crown above and stylised branch to the left
Legend: none
BUAS MOST/4498, dated 1446

SEAL 211
Rounded oval, 18
?Gem (?bust)
Legend: none
BUAS MOST/5249, dated 1314

SEAL 212
Octagonal, nm
Letter R, ?crown above
Legend: none
BUAS MOST/5284, seal 2, dated 1471 x 1472

SEAL 213
Pointed oval, nm
Within an ornate canopied niche a mitred man vested for Mass seated full-face blessing within his right hand and holding a long cross-tipped staff in his left hand with below, beneath a pointed arch, a half-length suppliant man full-face
Legend: ¶ Sigillum [. .]om[.] ¶ arc[. . . . .] [section lost]
BUAS PENR/5, dated 1376

SEAL 214
Round, 10
Letters ?X 1 ?X
Legend: none
BUAS PENR/10, dated 1409 x 1410

SEAL 215
Round, 69
Deputed great seal of Henry V: seal of the Chamberlain of North Wales
BUAS PENR/166, dated 1415 x 1416
BUAS PENR/11, 1413 x 1414

SEAL 216
Pointed oval, 65x42
Within an ornate architectural niche, Virgin and Child seated full-face, a shield of arms (crossed keys) and crest (?papal mitre) below
Legend: SIGILL[section lost][. .]IISA-CRE§P[section lost]
BUAS PENR/12, dated 1479 x 1480

SEAL 217
Round, 29
Shield of arms (a chevron between three closed helms) hanging form a bush
Legend: ¶ Sigill' : Willelmi [. . . . .]ythe
BUAS PENR/14, dated 1430

SEAL 218
Round, nm
Obverse: shield; Reverse: ?equestrian
Legend: lost
BUAS PENR/17, dated 1431 x 1432

SEAL 219
Deputed Great Seal for Wales
BL PENR ADDMS 0, dated 1414
BUAS PENR/20, dated 1437 x 1438

SEAL 220
Seal of Chamberlain of North Wales
(Henry VI)
BUAS PENR/23, dated 1442 x 1443
BUAS PENR/167, dated 1429 x 1430
BUAS PENR/224, dated 1448 x 1449

SEAL 221
Round, 13
?Fox seated on hind-legs facing left
playing flute (?squirrel eating nut), letter ?g
(?I / ?s) below animal's front paws, letter S
in upper left
Legend: none
BUAS PENR/170, seal 2, dated 1447 x 1448
BUAS PENR/28, dated 1447 x 1448
BUAS PENR/24, dated 1442 x 1443
BUAS PENR/25, dated 1442 x 1443
BUAS PENR/26, dated 1442 x 1443

SEAL 222
Rectangular, 12x10
Pelican in piety facing left
Legend: none
BUAS PENR/27, seal 1, dated 1442 x 1443

SEAL 223
Square, 9x9
Five-lobed leaf
Legend: none
BUAS PENR/27, seal 2, dated 1442 x 1443

SEAL 224
Round, nm
Uncertain
Legend: lost, if any
BUAS PENR/29, dated 1448 x 1449

SEAL 225
Unknown, nm
Crowned letter ?P
Legend: none
BUAS PENR/29, seal 2, dated 1448 x 1449
BUAS PENR/30, dated 1448 x 1449

SEAL 226
Octagonal, 12x10
?Monogram: crowned letters ?h and ?b
Legend: none
BUAS PENR/30, seal 3, dated 1448 x 1449
BUAS PENR/29, seal 3, dated 1448 x 1449

SEAL 227
Rounded oval, 9x8
Stag's head full-face, letter ?i to left, letter
(illegible) to right
Legend: none
BUAS PENR/393, seal 3, dated 1446 x 1447
BUAS PENR/29, seal 4, dated 1448 x 1449
BUAS PENR/30, seal 4, dated 1448 x 1449

SEAL 228
Rounded oval, nm
Bird facing left
Legend: none
BUAS PENR/30, dated 1448 x 1449
BUAS PENR/393, seal 2, dated 1446 x 1447

SEAL 229
Rounded oval, nm
Crowned letter h
Legend: none
BUAS PENR/31, seal 2, dated 1448 x 1449

SEAL 230
Rounded oval, 12x10
Crowned letter I, ?clover leaf either side
Legend: none
BUAS PENR/31, seal 3, dated 1448 x 1449

SEAL 231
Round, 10
Crowned letter T
Legend: none
BUAS PENR/31, seal 4, dated 1448 x 1449

APPENDIX

SEAL 232
Rectangular, nm
Crowned letter I
Legend: none
BUAS PENR/31, seal 5, dated 1448 x 1449

SEAL 233
Seal of ?Chamberlain North Wales for Edward IV
BUAS PENR/34, dated 1466 x 1467

SEAL 234
Pointed oval, nm
Within an architectural niche, a man standing full-face, ?vested for Mass
Legend: lost
BUAS PENR/39, dated 1483
BUAS PENR/38, dated 1483

SEAL 235
Unknown, nm
Virgin and Child ?seated beneath a canopy, the moon, sun and star above
Legend: lost, if any
BUAS PENR/162, dated 1380 x 1381

SEAL 236
Undetermined, 16
Lion sleeping facing left beneath a tree
Legend: illegible
BUAS PENR/163, dated 1417 x 1418

SEAL 237
Octagonal, 13x10
?Head of animal (?horse)
Legend: none
BUAS PENR/165, dated 1416 x 1417

SEAL 238
Round, 19
Shield of arms (three chevrons)
Legend: +S'IO[.] IS [. . . . . .]IS
BUAS PENR/381, seal 2, dated 1341 x 1342
BUAS PENR/170, dated 1447 x 1448

SEAL 239
Round, 15
Stylised eight-petalled flower
Legend: none
BUAS PENR/216, seal 2, dated 1315 x 1315

SEAL 240
Undetermined, 16
Lion sleeping facing left beneath a tree
Legend: illegible
BUAS PENR/217, seal 2, dated 1347

SEAL 241
Round, 11
Monogram: letter 'W'
Legend: none
BUAS PENR/217, seal 3, dated 1347

SEAL 242
Octagonal, 8x10
Diamond at the centre of a saltire cross
Legend: none
BUAS PENR/311, seal 2, dated 1415 x 1416
BUAS PENR/219, dated 1416 x 1417

SEAL 243
Round, 11
Pelican in its piety facing left
Legend: re [. . .]de[.]
BUAS PENR/220, dated 1416 x 1417

SEAL 244
Octagonal, nm
Uncertain: star in top left corner
Legend: none
BUAS PENR/221, dated 1417 x 1418

SEAL 245
Octagonal, 10x12
Head of woman full-face to left, to right a cockerel (?with human head) walking to right with head turned back
Legend: none
BUAS PENR/226, dated 1458 x 1459

SEAL 246
Round, 10
Uncertain (?letter ?I)
Legend: none
BUAS PENR/227, dated 1476 x 1477

SEAL 247
Rounded oval, 9x8
Head of ?woman facing left ?wearing a wreath
Legend: none
BUAS PENR/229, dated 1486 x 1487

SEAL 248
Rounded oval, 15
Letter I, crown above
Legend: none
BUAS PENR/254, dated 1474 x 1475

SEAL 249
Round, 15
Head of man with beard facing left
Legend: g[?o]u [.] g[. . . . . . .]
BUAS PENR/255, dated 1474 x 1475

SEAL 250
Round, 16
Double-headed eagle displayed
Legend: none
BUAS PENR/256, seal 2, dated 1480 x 1481

SEAL 251
Square
Letter H
Legend: none
BUAS PENR/258, seal 1, dated 1498 x 1499

SEAL 252
Square, 13
Legend: none
BUAS PENR/258, seal 2, dated 1498 x 1499

SEAL 253
Octagonal, 13x10
Head of unicorn facing left, stylised branch to the right, letters ?r m above
Legend: none
BUAS PENR/261, dated 1420 x 1421
BUAS PENR/385, dated 1413 x 1414

SEAL 254
Round, 20
Within a cusped border, ?two heads both facing in, an object between them
Legend: illegible, partially lost
BUAS PENR/282, dated 1318 x 1319

SEAL 255
Round, 19
Indistinct
Legend: S'IOhAnnIS.[. . . .] AUnTO[. . .]S
BUAS PENR/283, dated 1336 x 1337

SEAL 256
Round, nm
?Stylised flower
Legend: illegible, partially lost
BUAS PENR/284, dated 1340 x 1341

SEAL 257
Round, 23
Within a cusped border, a shield of arms (a chevron between three lion's heads) handing from a bush
Legend: ¶ S' . Willelm[.]s de h[.]ntone
BUAS PENR/286, dated 1371 x 1372

SEAL 258
Round, nm
Within a cusped border, a shield of arms (a bird (?goose)) handing from a bush
Legend: ¶[. .] icard [rest lost]
BUAS PENR/286, seal 2, dated 1371 x 1372

SEAL 259
Round, 20
Within a six-pointed star (formed by two intersecting cusped triangles), Vernicle Head of Christ
Legend: * S' . Ih's . [. . . . .]ENVS[?R][. . .] DEOR'
BUAS PENR/286, seal 3, dated 1371 x 1372

APPENDIX

SEAL 260
Octagonal, 8x11
Fish (?pike) swimming to left with waves below, letters m[.][?r]e above
Legend: none
BUAS PENR/287, dated 1438 x 1439

SEAL 261
Round, 11
Four-petalled flower with letters in the petals, a heart at the centre (M-AR-?-?)
Legend: none
BUAS PENR/288, dated 1438 x 1439

SEAL 262
Round, 19
Crowned letter R, foliage on either side
Legend: none
BUAS PENR/288, seal 2, dated 1438 x 1439

SEAL 263
Hexagonal, nm
?Serpent (long body, no evidence of legs or wings) facing left
Legend: none
BUAS PENR/289, seal 1, dated 1445 x 1446

SEAL 264
Rounded oval, nm
Crowned letter T
Legend: none
BUAS PENR/289, seal 2, dated 1445 x 1446

SEAL 265
Round, nm
Shield of arms (three leopards passant guardant with a label of three points), a branch with three leafy stems to the right
Legend: [. . .] OMVNITA [rest lost]
BUAS PENR/290, dated 1450

SEAL 266
Unknown, 14x10
Indistinct
Legend: none
BUAS PENR/291, dated 1454 x 1455

SEAL 267
Round, 13
Pelican in its piety facing left
Legend: none
BUAS PENR/292, dated 1457 x 1458

SEAL 268
Square, 11
Griffin walking left
Legend: none
BUAS PENR/293, dated 1457 x 1458

SEAL 269
Rounded oval, 13
Crowned letter ?W,
Legend: none
BUAS PENR/294, dated 1482 x 1483

SEAL 270
Round, 10
Stylised eight-petalled flower
Legend: none
BUAS PENR/295, dated 1482 x 1483

SEAL 271
Round, 12
Letters r ?t (?c)
Legend: none
BUAS PENR/296, dated 1495 x 1496

SEAL 272
Round, 19
?Fox running left (?squirrel facing left)
Legend: [. .]IVE[. . . . . . .] (start-point uncertain)
BUAS PENR/309, dated 1375 x 1376

SEAL 273
Undetermined, 16
Lion sleeping facing left beneath a tree
Legend: none
BUAS PENR/311, seal 1, dated 1415 x 1416

SEAL 274
Round, 20
Head in dish
Legend: PRI[. . . . . .]
BUAS PENR/314, dated 1430 x 1431

SEAL 275
Round, 12
Eagle facing left clasping a ?flaming brand (?teasel) in its right claw
Legend: none
BUAS PENR/316, dated 1463 x 1464

SEAL 276
Round, 20
Indistinct
Legend: none
BUAS PENR/317, dated 1496 x 1497

SEAL 277
Round, 14
Indistinct
Legend: none
BUAS PENR/319, dated 1498 x 1499

SEAL 278
Octagonal, 10x8
Letter R
Legend: none
BUAS PENR/320, dated 1498 x 1499

SEAL 279
Round, 14x9
Crowned letter I
Legend: none
BUAS PENR/381, dated 1341 x 1342

SEAL 280
Rounded oval, 10x6
Four vertical lines and two horizontal lines (very rough)
Legend: none
BUAS PENR/382, dated 1361

SEAL 281
Round, 16
Letter W (left ascender is a stylised branch), stylised leaf above
Legend: none
BUAS PENR/383, dated 1396 x 1397

SEAL 282
Rounded oval, 14x9
Includes ?cross
Legend: none
BUAS PENR/384, dated 1408 x 1409

SEAL 283
Rounded oval, 13x10
Crowned letter I, foliage on either side
Legend: none
BUAS PENR/388, dated 1443 x 1444

SEAL 284
Rounded oval, 12x10
Crowned letter I, foliage on either side
Legend: none
BUAS PENR/391, dated 1442 x 1443

SEAL 285
Round, 12
Foliage ?growing in a large pot on legs, small rosette either side of the pot, legend around edge of upper part of design field
Legend: [. .]m[. .]l[.] [. . . . . .]a
BUAS PENR/392, dated 1446 x 1447

SEAL 286
Round, 12
Clover-leaf with a letter (illegible) on each of the constituent sub-leaves
Legend: none
BUAS PENR/392, seal 2, dated 1446 x 1447

SEAL 287
Octagonal, nm
Mermaid full-face (right side lost)
Legend: none
BUAS PENR/393, seal 1, dated 1446 x 1447

SEAL 288
Rounded oval,12x13
Letter 'I' with foliage on either side

Legend: none
BUAS PENR/394, dated 1455 x 1456

SEAL 289
Round, 14
Stylised lily
Legend: none
BUAS PENR/395, dated 1456 x 1457

SEAL 290
Rounded oval, 14x10
Letters I O with arched suspension bar above
Legend: none
BUAS PENR/399, dated 1497 x 1498

SEAL 291
Round, nm
Shield of arms (lion rampant)
Legend: [. . .]v[. . . . . .] [section lost]
BUAS PENR/405, dated 1311

SEAL 292
Round, 19
Lion sleeping facing right
Legend: * [. . . . .]RVS
BUAS PENR/405, seal 2, dated 1311

SEAL 293
Round, nm
Head of ?boar facing right
Legend: none
BUAS PENR/405, seal 3, dated 1311

SEAL 294
Round, 20
Squirrel facing right eating a nut
Legend: ThOME[.]AR[. . . . . . .]E[. . . . .]
BUAS PENR/407, seal 2, dated 1330 x 1331
BUAS PENR/406, dated 1316

SEAL 295
Round, 23
Eight conifer branches
Legend: hOWELAPE[. . . .]AD[.]
BUAS PENR/406, seal 2, dated 1316

SEAL 296
Round, 23
Uncertain (?bird)
Legend: [section lost]IAP[section lost]
BUAS PENR/406, seal 3, dated 1316

SEAL 297
Round, 22
With a cusped quatrefoil, lion facing left sleeping beneath a tree
Legend: lost
BUAS PENR/407, seal 1, dated 1330 x 1331

SEAL 298
Rounded oval, 19x15
Gem: head and shoulders facing right wearing a wreath
Legend: +S[. . .]SE[. . .]E[. . . . .]E
BUAS PENR/407, seal 3, dated 1330 x 1331

SEAL 299
Round, nm
Within a cusped quatrefoil, lion facing left sleeping beneath a tree
Legend: none
BUAS PENR/407, seal 4, dated 1330 x 1331

SEAL 300
Round, 24
Four conifer branches
Legend: [. . . . .]NERIS:[. . . . . . .]
BUAS PENR/407, seal 5, dated 1330 x 1331

SEAL 301
Round, 23
Pelican in its piety facing left
Legend: * S' ROBTI DE BETEWS
BUAS PENR/408, dated 1334 x 1335

SEAL 302
Round, 17
Eagle displayed
Legend: *DEIVCDV
BUAS PENR/411, dated 1400 x 1499

SEAL 303
Round, nm
Shield of arms (a ?boar / ?elephant) with foliage in the field in lower left
Legend: S': ddio ap [. . . .]
BUAS PENR/412, dated 1449 x 1450

SEAL 304
Round, 14
Stylised lily
Legend: none
BUAS PENR/413, dated 1462 x 1463

SEAL 305
Seal of Edward, Prince of Wales (b.1454, s. of Henry VI)
BUAS PENR/2195, front, dated 1459 x 1460

SEAL 306
Round, 20
Helm with ?plumed crest (?stylised lily crest)
Legend: [. . . .]VALE[. . . . . . .]
CALS D3785/1/3, dated 1275 x 1299

SEAL 307
Hexagonal, 18x18
Within a 'star of David' a lion sleeping facing right
Legend: none
CALS D3785/1/4, dated 1300 x 1349

SEAL 308
Round, 24
Stylised eight-petalled flower
Legend: *S'hVG[. .] DEB [. .] kIRT'
CALS D3785/1/5, dated 1300 x 1349

SEAL 309
Round, c.24
Sun with six rays
Legend: + S' WILLI [. . . . .]
CALS D3785/1/6, dated 1302

SEAL 310
Round, 23
Sun with five rays
Legend: *S' [. . . . . . .IL' RIC[.]DIS
CALS D3785/1/10, dated 1306 x 1306
CALS D3785/1/8, dated 1305 x 1305

SEAL 311
Rounded oval, 22x18
?Cockerel facing left (?seated figure facing right)
Legend: illegible
CALS D3785/1/8, seal 2, dated 1305 x 1305

SEAL 312
Round, 17
Squirrel facing right
Legend: illegible
CALS D3785/1/8, seal 3 and 5, dated 1305 x 1305

SEAL 313
Pointed oval, 32x22
Stylised lily
Legend: * S' ThOMA hORSAL'
CALS D3785/1/8, seal 4, dated 1305 x 1305

SEAL 314
Round, 24
?Star (very worn)
Legend: + S' WILL'I FIL' IOh'IS
CALS D3785/1/8, seal 6, dated 1305 x 1305

SEAL 315
Round, 15
Within an ornate eight-pointed border, a lion sleeping facing right
Legend: illegible
CALS D3785/1/9, dated 1306 x 1306

SEAL 316
Round, 14
Uncertain – ?bird (?squirrel)
Legend: illegible
CALS D3785/1/10, seal 2, dated 1306 x 1306

APPENDIX

SEAL 317
Rectangular, 14
?Bird (animal) walking to the left with ?foliage in its beak
Legend: lost
CALS D3785/1/11, dated 1312 x 1312

SEAL 318
Round, 15
Lion's head full-face
Legend: illegible
CALS D3785/1/13, dated 1314

SEAL 319
Round, 17
Hare blowing a horn riding a hound walking to the left
Legend: illegible
CALS D3785/1/15/2, dated 1318

SEAL 320
Round, 17
Lion rampant facing left
Legend: illegible
CALS D3785/1/14, dated 1315

SEAL 321
Round, 20
Hare ?blowing a horn riding a hound walking to the right
Legend: illegible
CALS D3785/1/16, dated 1318

SEAL 322
Hexagonal, 14x14
Illegible
Legend: lost, if any
CALS D3785/1/17/2, dated 1332

SEAL 323
Rounded oval, 16x12
Crowned letter W
Legend: none
CALS D3785/1/19, dated 1407 x 1408

SEAL 324
Pointed oval, $c.30$ x $c.24$
Figure (?man) standing full-face within a niche holding a ?sword (?palm) in their left hand within below, beneath a rounded arch, a half-length ?tonsured man full-face
Legend: lost
CALS D3785/1/20, dated 1439

SEAL 325
Round, $c.37$
Within a cusped octofoila shield of arms (three leopards passant guardant)
Legend: lost
CALS DLL/1/2, dated 1369 x 1370

SEAL 326
Round, 12
Stylised tree with five-pointed star to left and right
Legend: [. . . .]god
CALS DLL/1/3, dated 1399 x 1400

SEAL 327
Round, $c.18$
Hawk taking a bird, facing left
Legend: lost
CALS DLL/1/4, seal 3, dated 1396 x 1397

SEAL 328
Round, 44
Statue merchant seal (for Chester?).
CALS DLL/1/5, dated 1393 x 1394
NLW PITORD/135, back, dated 1377 x 1378

SEAL 329
Round, 21
Within an ornate trefoil, a shield of arms (indistinct)
Legend: ?WA[.] [section lost] D?A [section illegible]
CALS DLL/2/1, dated 1200 x 1299

SEAL 330
Round, 40
Head of bearded man with long hair full-face, ?pellets in the field
Legend: +S':PRIORIS:hOSPI...IER...ANGL':
CALS DLL/2/2, front, dated 1235 x 1247

SEAL 331
Round, 30
Boar's head with crown facing left
Legend: [...]TOE: NVS[.......]SAM [...]
CALS DLL/2/2, back, dated 1235 x 1247

SEAL 332
Round, 32
Four branches with stems in the angles
Legend: +S'REINALDI:DE. ?T[?H]VMMEL
CALS DLL/2/3, dated 1225 x 1274

SEAL 333
Pointed oval, 27x23
Stylised lily
Legend: [..]RIC[......]
CALS DLL/2/6, dated 1200 x 1299

SEAL 334
Pointed oval, 19x25
?Horse running right
Legend: SALI[....]M
CALS DLL/2/6, seal 2, dated 1200 x 1299

SEAL 335
Pointed oval, c.30x25
Stylised lily
Legend: [.....] . FIL' . [...]IN[...]
CALS DLL/2/7, dated 1250 x 1299

SEAL 336
Round, 29
Sun with twelve rays
Legend: +S [.....]CROXTO [.]
CALS DLL/2/8, dated 1250 x 1299

SEAL 337
Pointed oval, 36x27
Stylised lily
Legend: +S'WARIN[..] [?D]E [.....]
CALS DLL/2/9, dated 1250 x 1299

SEAL 338
Round, 17
Sacred monogram (IHC) with a cross crosslet above
Legend: +[.] S [.........]
CALS DLL/2/11, dated 1329 x 1330

SEAL 339
Round, 20
Within an ornate cusped border, a lozenge (two bars)
Legend: *SIGAINORE [........] DE [........]
CALS DLL/2/12, dated 1336 x 1337

SEAL 340
Round, 19
Within an ornate cusped border, a bird with foliage in its beak facing left
Legend: illegible
CALS DLL/2/14, dated 1372 x 1373

SEAL 341
Octagonal, 16x13
Crowned letter I
Legend: DDMOVR
CALS DLL/2/16, seal 1 and 2, dated 1422 x 1423
CALS DLL/2/15, dated 1422 x 1423

SEAL 342
Round, 12x10
Crowned letter T
Legend: none
CALS DLL/2/26, dated 1459 x 1460
CALS DLL/2/22, seal 2, dated 1433 x 1434
CALS DLL/2/21, seal 1 and 2, dated 1433 x 1434
CALS DLL/2/18, dated 1433 x 1434
CALS DLL/2/20, seal 2 and 3, dated 1433 x 1434

APPENDIX

SEAL 343
Round, 13
Star with a pellet at the centre
Legend: none
CALS DLL/2/22, seal 5, dated 1433 x 1434
CALS DLL/2/21, seal 5, dated 1433 x 1434
CALS DLL/2/18, seal 2, dated 1433 x 1434

SEAL 344
Octagonal, 9x8
Merchant mark (includes letter r)
Legend: none
CALS DLL/2/19, dated 1433 x 1434
CALS DLL/2/22, seal 3, dated 1433 x 1434
CALS DLL/2/21, seal 4, dated 1433 x 1434

SEAL 345
Rounded oval, 19x15
Letter W
Legend: none
CALS DLL/2/20, dated 1433 x 1434
CALS DLL/2/22, seal 1, dated 1433 x 1434

SEAL 346
Round, 13
Star with four pellets in the centre, a pellet in two of the points, and a pellet in each angle
Legend: none
CALS DLL/2/21, seal 3, dated 1433 x 1434

SEAL 347
Round, 11
Crowned letter I, foliage to left and right
Legend: none
CALS DLL/2/22, seal 4, dated 1433 x 1434

SEAL 348
Octagonal, 11x11
?Bear's (?dog's) head erased facing left
Legend: none
CALS DLL/2/23, dated 1452 x 1453

SEAL 349
Rounded oval, 15x12
Bird's head erased
Legend: none
CALS DLL/2/24, dated 1456 x 1457

SEAL 350
Round, 22
?Flower within wreath of foliage
Legend: none
CALS DLL/2/26, seal 2, dated 1459 x 1460

SEAL 351
Rounded oval, 12x9
Crowned letter G
Legend: none
CALS DLL/2/28, dated 1467 x 1468

SEAL 352
Round, 13
letter 'I' within a border of rays
Legend: none
CALS DLL/2/30, dated 1476 x 1477

SEAL 353
Round, 12
Letter R
Legend: none
CALS DLL/2/31, dated 1476 x 1477

SEAL 354
Round, 17
Animal facing right
Legend: lost, if any
CALS DLL/2/32, dated 1382 x 1383

SEAL 355
Round, 22
Within a quatrefoil, a headless man standing full-face holding a crowned head in their hands (St Oswald) flanked by two shields of arms (dexter, a chevron; sinister, a lion rampant)
Legend: *[?S][. .]TRIS [?G]ILBERTI DE GASTENO[.]
CALS DLL/2/33, dated 1389 x 1390

SEAL 356
Round, 19
Head (of John the Baptist) face-up in shallow dish, ?sword facing left above
Legend: [. . . .]O[?I] B[. . . . .]
CALS DLL/2/34, dated 1395

SEAL 357
Round, 20
Cross patonce between four circles, a bird facing left above
Legend: * S' WALTERI . AT[?E][?D][?V]RG
CALS DLL/2/35, dated 1395
CALS DLL/2/36, dated 1395

SEAL 358
Round, c.30
Uncertain (?stylised lily)
Legend: + [. . .][?E] [. . . . . . .]
CALS DLL/3/1, dated 1200 x 1299

SEAL 359
Round, 20
?Squirrel facing left with ?nut
Legend: illegible
CALS DLL/3/5, dated 1250 x 1299

SEAL 360
Round, 18
Shield of arms: (indistinct)
Legend: [. . . .] MASC [section lost]
CALS DLL/3/7, dated 1250 x 1299

SEAL 361
Pointed oval, 28x19
Stylised lily
Legend: +S:IOH.FILHVG:D'[. .]
CALS DLL/3/9, dated 1275 x 1324
CALS DLL/3/10, dated 1275 x 1324

SEAL 362
Round, 18
Squirrel facing right on top of a stylised bush, ?eating a nut
Legend: * S' RADVLFID hAWIRDIn
CALS DLL/3/11, dated 1305 x 1306

SEAL 363
Round, 14
Shield of arms (bendy of six)
Legend: * [. . . . . . .]SETCET[?E]R[?N]
CALS DLL/3/12, dated 1305

SEAL 364
Round, 20
Animal facing ?right
Legend: illegible
CALS DLL/3/17, dated 1300 x 1349

SEAL 365
Round, 17
Bird (?cockerel) walking to the right, foliage above and below
Legend: SIGIL[?L?V?M] [. .] DE[. . . .]
CALS DLL/3/20, dated 1316 x 1317

SEAL 366
Rounded oval, 16x14
?Stylised lily
Legend: illegible
CALS DLL/3/23, dated 1325

SEAL 367
Round, 17
Shield of arms (illegible)
Legend: illegible, partially lost
CALS DLL/3/24, dated 1326

SEAL 368
Round, 20
Two figures facing in with?hands raised towards each other, ?stylised leaf (?bird) above [?Annunciation]
Legend: [.]IES[.]¶S¶[?E?L][. .]
CALS DLL/3/25, dated 1336
CALS DLL/3/49, dated 1416 x 1417

SEAL 369
Round, 19
Within an ornate border, a shield of arms (?lozengy)
Legend: ?*STh [section lost] ?D [.] ERS §
CALS DLL/3/30, dated 1338 x 1339

SEAL 370
Round, 11
Lamb of God facing right
Legend: none
CALS DLL/3/45, dated 1407 x 1408

APPENDIX

SEAL 371
Round, 12
Letter I, stylised foliage to right and left
Legend: none
CALS DLL/3/53, dated 1419 x 1420

SEAL 372
Octagonal, 14x10
Head of a man with long hair and a beard facing left
Legend: none
CALS DLL/4/62, dated 1410 x 1411
CALS DLL/3/58, dated 1428 x 1429
CALS DLL/3/59, dated 1428 x 1429

SEAL 373
Unknown (?rounded oval), 14x9
Letter ?R, foliage either side
Legend: none
CALS DLL/3/64, seal 1, dated 1423 x 1424

SEAL 374
Round, 18
Letter W
Legend: none
CALS DLL/3/64, seal 2, dated 1423 x 1424

SEAL 375
Hexagonal, 14x17
?Bird's (?lion's) head erased facing right, to right letter in field
Legend: l[?e]g[?v]
CALS DLL/3/68, dated 1426 x 1427

SEAL 376
Round, 18
Four (?clover) leaves
Legend: illegible
CALS DLL/3/70, dated 1439 x 1440

SEAL 377
Round, 9
Armorial badge: ermine
Legend: deu aid
CALS DLL/3/73, seal 1, dated 1440

SEAL 378
Round, 33
Tower with central gateway with portcullis, two levels of battlements above, to left a stylised lily and letter 'd', to right a ?lion passant guardant, one either side a tower surmounted by a star
Legend: +S:ObL [section lost] ?US [section lost] : §
CALS DLL/3/73, seal 2, dated 1440

SEAL 379
Rounded oval, 11x9
Stylised lily
Legend: none
CALS DLL/3/74, seal 1, dated 1441 x 1442

SEAL 380
Round, 15
Crowned letter I, stylised foliage to left and right
Legend: none
CALS DLL/3/74, seal 2, dated 1441 x 1442

SEAL 381
Rounded oval, 11x9
Crowned letter R
Legend: none
CALS DLL/3/74, seal 3, dated 1441 x 1442

SEAL 382
Round, 36
Nimbed man in long robe standing full-face holding a Tao-cross staff in his left hand (St Anthony), to left and right seven figures standing full-face, below, beneath an arch, a pig wearing a bell around its neck facing left
Legend: +[section lost] ntatis § [section lost] london :
CALS DLL/3/76, dated 1442

SEAL 383
Unknown, nm
Letter ?I
Legend: none
CALS DLL/3/78, dated 1442 x 1443

SEAL 384
Round, 11
Bird facing left
Legend: none
CALS DLL/3/79, dated 1445 x 1446

SEAL 385
Octagonal, nm
Letters ?pp (?dd)
Legend: none
CALS DLL/3/80, dated 1412 x 1413

SEAL 386
Rectangular, 13x10
?Griffin's head erased, foliage in the field
Legend: none
CALS DLL/3/81, dated 1427 x 1427

SEAL 387
Round, 12
?Calf (?lamb) standing facing left, letters t d in upper right, foliage in lower left
Legend: none
CALS DLL/3/82, dated 1448 x 1449

SEAL 388
Rectangular, 9x8
Letter ?R (?K)
Legend: none
CALS DLL/3/82, seal 2, dated 1448 x 1449

SEAL 389
Round, 11
Letter R, small sprigs of stylised foliage to left and right
Legend: none
CALS DLL/3/82, seal 3, dated 1448 x 1449

SEAL 390
Unknown (?rounded oval; fragment), c.10x8
Letter ?I
Legend: none
CALS DLL/3/83, dated 1450 x 1451

SEAL 391
Round, 14
Crowned letter I, stylised foliage to left and right
Legend: none
CALS DLL/3/83, seal 2, dated 1450 x 1451

SEAL 392
Square, 14xc.11
Within a cusped quatrefoil, a shield of arms (bendy, a frett dancetty)
Legend: none
CALS DLL/3/83, seal 3, dated 1450 x 1451

SEAL 393
Round, c.17
Within a six-pointed star, a ?head facing left, to the right an object
Legend: none
CALS DLL/3/85, dated 1456 x 1457

SEAL 394
Round, 14
Hawk taking a bird, facing left
Legend: none
CALS DLL/3/88, seal 1, dated 1460 x 1461

SEAL 395
Round, 20
Letter I, stylised foliage to left and right
Legend: none
CALS DLL/3/88, seal 2, dated 1460 x 1461

SEAL 396
Round, 14
Crowned letter n
Legend: none
CALS DLL/3/88, seal 3, dated 1460 x 1461

SEAL 397
Rounded oval, 18x16
Six-pointed star with a device (indistinct) at centre
Legend: none
CALS DLL/3/91, seal 1, dated 1463 x 1464

SEAL 398
Round, 12
Boar's head facing left with foliage above

APPENDIX

Legend: none
CALS DLL/3/91, seal 2, dated 1463 x 1464
CALS DLL/3/99, dated 1475 x 1476

SEAL 399
Round, nm
Letter M
Legend: none
CALS DLL/3/92, dated 1463 x 1464

SEAL 400
Round, nm
Head of unicorn facing left (fragment only)
Legend: none
CALS DLL/3/94, dated 1461 x 1462

SEAL 401
Octagonal, *c.*12x*c.*9
Uncertain (?foliate motif)
Legend: none
CALS DLL/3/101, dated 1478 x 1479

SEAL 402
Round, 13
Radial design with eight arms
Legend: none
CALS DLL/3/105, seal 1, dated 1478 x 1479

SEAL 403
Round, 17
Shield of arms (?cross fimbrated)
Legend: none
CALS DLL/3/105, seal 2, dated 1478 x 1479

SEAL 404
Unknown, *c.*14x13
Shield of arms: (?label of three points)
Legend: none
CALS DLL/3/106, dated 1479 x 1480

SEAL 405
Round, 23
Within an ornate border, a shield of arms (indistinct)
Legend: [.]SIGILLUM [. . .] OME : DE : LE [. .]
CALS DLL/3/110, dated 1391 x 1392

SEAL 406
Round, 23
Within a cusped quatrefoil, a shield of arms (a fess dancetty between ?two ermines)
Legend: [.] Sigillum * Petri * de * Legh
CALS DLL/3/112, seal 2, dated 1392 x 1393

SEAL 407
Round, *c.*20
Within an ornate border, a shield of arms (a chevron between three letters T) hanging from a staple
Legend: none
CALS DLL/3/113, dated 1393 x 1394

SEAL 408
Hexagonal, 15x14
Cross saltire formed by on wide and one thin line, objects in the field
Legend: none
CALS DLL/3/114, seal 1, dated 1397 x 1398

SEAL 409
Round, 15
Head (of ?woman) full-face
Legend: illegible
CALS DLL/3/114, seal 2, dated 1397 x 1398

SEAL 410
Round, 15
Letter ?G (?b), foliate tendrils in the field
Legend: none
CALS DLL/3/117, seal 1, dated 1481 x 1482

SEAL 411
Round, 12
Letter W, foliage in the field
Legend: none
CALS DLL/3/117, seal 2, dated 1481 x 1482

SEAL 412
Round, *c.*12
Ewer (spout to left)
Legend: [section lost] [.]ames
CALS DLL/3/117, seal 3, dated 1481 x 1482

SEAL 413
Pointed oval, 48x30
Within an ornate architectural niche, a figure ?full-face
Legend: illegible, partially lost
CALS DLL/3/122, dated 1486

SEAL 414
Round, 12
Wolf's head facing left
Legend: none
CALS DLL/3/134, dated 1498

SEAL 415
Rounded oval, 12x9
Crowned letter ?G (?S)
Legend: none
CALS DLL/3/135, dated 1424

SEAL 416
Pointed oval, 30x20
Stylised stemmed plant
Legend: [. . . . . .] S [. . . . .]
CALS DLL/3/207, dated 1275 x 1324

SEAL 417
Round, 28
Indistinct
Legend: none
CALS DLL/4/1, dated 1200 x 1299

SEAL 418
Pointed oval, 43x27
Stylised lily
Legend: illegible
CALS DLL/4/4, dated 1200 x 1299

SEAL 419
Round, 32
Stylised lily
Legend: [. . . . .]RINIFIL'RICDECRO[. .]
CALS DLL/4/15, dated 1300 x 1349

SEAL 420
Unknown, nm
Shield of arms (charge illegible)
Legend: lost
CALS DLL/4/17, seal 3, dated 1266 x 1267

SEAL 421
Unknown, 20x11
Shield of arms (indistinct)
Legend: [section lost] ?MCT [section lost]
CALS DLL/4/17, seal 4, dated 1266 x 1267

SEAL 422
Pointed oval, nm
Stylised foliate motif (?lily)
Legend: [section lost] DEVALE[section lost]
CALS DLL/4/21, dated 1300

SEAL 423
Pointed oval, 32x20
Stylised lily
Legend: illegible
CALS DLL/4/22, dated 1307

SEAL 424
Hexagonal, 17x17
Heart with stars to left and right
Legend: none
CALS DLL/4/29, seal 1, dated 1329

SEAL 425
Scutiform, 17x13
Lion to left facing right fighting a beast to right facing left
Legend: none
CALS DLL/4/29, seal 2, dated 1329

SEAL 426
Round, 18
Six-petalled flower with voided centre
Legend: * S [. . .]O[.]IS
CALS DLL/4/38, dated 1363 x 1364

SEAL 427
Rounded oval, 12x10
Letter I, stylised foliage to left and right
Legend: none
CALS DLL/4/47, seal 1, dated 1393 x 1394

APPENDIX

SEAL 428
Round, 19
Uncertain (?Tree, to the left a ?man, to the right a ?quadruped facing left)
Legend: * [. . . . .]A[. . . .]
CALS DLL/4/47, seal 2, dated 1393 x 1394

SEAL 429
Rounded oval, 10x8
Letter ?T
Legend: none
CALS DLL/4/47, seal 3, dated 1393 x 1394

SEAL 430
Round, 26
Shield of arms (a chevron between three lozenges)
Legend: * S' GALFRIDI * MASSY
CALS DLL/4/48, dated 1395 x 1396

SEAL 431
Round, 17
Letter S reversed
Legend: none
CALS DLL/4/49, dated 1380

SEAL 432
Round, 17
Letters AL in 'frame' of rays in place of legend band
Legend: none
CALS DLL/4/49/A, dated 1398

SEAL 433
Rounded oval, 10x8
Dragon serjeant, facing left
Legend: none
CALS DLL/4/50, dated 1400 x 1401

SEAL 434
Rectangular, 17x17
Crowned letter W
Legend: none
CALS DLL/4/52, dated 1406 x 1407

SEAL 435
Round, 11
Five-petalled flower (Tudor-style rose)
Legend: none
CALS DLL/4/58, dated 1407 x 1408
CALS DLL/4/53, dated 1407 x 1408

SEAL 436
Round, 24
Within an ornate border, a shield of arms (dexter hand, couped at wrist apaume, a bordure indented) couche, a helm with crest (wings) above
Legend: [section lost] manley:
CALS DLL/4/56, dated 1408 x 1409

SEAL 437
Round, 15
Within a six-pointed star with pellets in the angles, ?letter I (?eagle displayed)
Legend: none
CALS DLL/4/57, dated 1407 x 1408

SEAL 438
Round, 18
Letter G
Legend: none
CALS DLL/4/60, dated 1409 x 1410

SEAL 439
Octagonal, 12x10
Heart with three flowers springing from the top
Legend: [. . . . .]s
CALS DLL/4/63, dated 1411 x 1412

SEAL 440
Round, 28
Eight-petalled stylised flower
Legend: S' hVGONIS : NASE
CALS DWN/1/1, dated 1260

SEAL 441
Round, 24
Eight-petalled stylised flower
Legend: +S'ROBERTILEBRET
CALS DWN/1/2, dated 1263

SEAL 442
Pointed oval, c.30x19
Foliate motif of 'S' shaped stem with leaves either end
Legend: + S' Th'E [. . .]LESCI
CALS DWN/1/3, dated 1300 x 1320

SEAL 443
Round, 24
Four leaves with three pointed branches in the angles
Legend: +S'AYDROPDEMVLNITON
CALS DWN/1/4, dated 1300 x 1320

SEAL 444
Rounded oval, 20x18
Gem: ?stag facing left
Legend: * S' RICADI : DE : F[. . . . . . .]
CALS DWN/1/5, dated 1316 x 1317

SEAL 445
Round, c.21
Within a niche a winged figure facing right with hand raised in salutation, to the right a tall plant (?Annunciation) [Fragment only]
Legend: [section lost] [.]ENA : DOMI [. . . . . . .]
CALS DWN/1/6, dated 1346 x 1346

SEAL 446
Round, 23
?Stag facing left
Legend: [section lost]S[?I]D [. .]M [.] [E?] R
CALS DWN/1/9, dated 1362 x 1363

SEAL 447
Rectangular, c.15x16
Letters R B with star between and sprig of stylised foliage above and below
Legend: none
CALS DWN/1/10, dated 1406

SEAL 448
Round, c.20
Lamb of God facing left
Legend: [. .] D [. . . . . .]
CALS DWN/1/11, dated 1406

SEAL 449
Round, 20
Within an ornate cusped border, a shield of arms (indistinct) hanging from a hook, to right a bird
Legend: * [.] ES [.] SE [.] ?D [. .] M [. . . .]E [.]
CALS DWN/1/12, dated 1409

SEAL 450
Round, 26
Shield of arms (?quarterly; charge illegible) couche, a helm with crest (indistinct) above, foliate tendrils in the field
Legend: ¶ S : iohis : + ¶ + : kyn[. . . . .]
CALS DWN/1/13, dated 1413 x 1414
CALS DWN/1/19, seal 2, dated 1445 x 1446

SEAL 451
Rectangular, 9x7
Wheatsheaf
Legend: lost
CALS DWN/1/15, dated 1425

SEAL 452
Round, 27
Within a scutiform beaded border, a shield of arms (ermine, a chevron between three garbs)
Legend: * Sigill . ¶ um : thome . ¶ mai[. . . .]son
CALS DWN/1/14, dated 1425

SEAL 453
Octagonal, 11x9
?Wolf's (?lion's) head erased
Legend: [. . .]mas wyn [.] a [.]
CALS DWN/1/17, dated 1440 x 1441
CALS DWN/1/16, dated 1440 x 1441

SEAL 454
Rounded oval, c.20x17
Virgin and Child standing to left facing half right, to right a kneeling suppliant figure facing left, a ?rose on a long stem between them
Legend: [. . . . . . .]E[. . . . .]
CALS DWN/1/18, dated 1444 x 1445

APPENDIX

SEAL 455
Octagonal, 11x10
Stag facing left, above right letter ?P
Legend: N/A
CALS DWN/1/20, dated 1457 x 1458

SEAL 456
Octagonal, 12x9
Bird walking to the left, ?leaves in the field
Legend: none
CALS DWN/1/19, seal 1, dated 1445 x 1446

SEAL 457
Round, 11
Six-petalled stylised flower
Legend: none
CALS DWN/1/23, seal 2, dated 1474 x 1475

SEAL 458
Round, 11
Shield of arms (a pheon)
Legend: none
CALS DWN/1/24, dated 1495 x 1496

SEAL 459
Pointed oval, c.34x23
A wheatsheaf (garb) beneath an arch within a crenellated niche
Legend: [.] [D]ECANA[. . .] CES[. . . .]
CALS DWN/1/25, dated 1496

SEAL 460
Round, 28
Stylised lily
Legend: +S'ROBERTI:F [section lost]
CALS DWN/2/2, dated 1260 x 1290

SEAL 461
Round, 19
A ?head full-face
Legend: * CRE[. .] MIChI
CALS DWN/2/8, dated 1281 x 1299

SEAL 462
Round, 20
?Bird with ?wings raised walking left
(?wyvern walking left)
Legend: illegible
CALS DWN/2/20, dated 1330 x 1331

SEAL 463
Round, 23
Virgin and Child stranding full-face, foliage to left and right, above right a ?shooting star (crescent with star above)
Legend: *S'ANC[.]E § MA [section lost]
CALS DWN/2/21, dated 1340 x 1341

SEAL 464
Round, 24
Centaur walking to the right
Legend: [. . VA[. . . .]EYR[?G][. . . . . . .]R[.]
CALS DWN/2/24, dated 1393

SEAL 465
Round, 20
Within a cusped border, a hare blowing a horn on a dog walking to the right
Legend: * [. . . . .][?b][. .]I[. . . . . .]
CALS DWN/2/25, dated 1397

SEAL 466
Round, 25
Lamb of God facing left
Legend: illegible, partially lost
CALS DWN/2/26, dated 1398 x 1399

SEAL 467
Octagonal, c.15x11
Merchant mark in form of a shield (includes letters ?C, O) cross-tipped staff with banner emerging from top
Legend: none
CALS DWN/2/27, dated 1406 x 1407

SEAL 468
Round, 14
Indistinct
Legend: lost, if any
CALS DWN/2/28, dated 1413 x 1414

SEAL 469
Rounded oval, 14x17
Sacred Monogram (ihc) small six-pointed star to right and left, small sprig of stylised foliage below
Legend: none
CALS DWN/2/35, dated 1436 x 1437
CALS DWN/2/33, dated 1435 x 1436
CALS DWN/2/29, dated 1413 x 1414

SEAL 470
Rounded oval, 15x11
Bird's head erased
Legend: none
CALS DWN/2/30, dated 1416 x 1417

SEAL 471
Square, 11
Letter h
Legend: none
CALS DWN/2/36, dated 1436 x 1437

SEAL 472
Unknown, nm
Indistinct
Legend: none
CALS DWN/2/37, dated 1445 x 1446

SEAL 473
Round, 12
Heart with crown above, flanked by ?rays (?wings)
Legend: none
CALS DWN/2/38, dated 1452 x 1453

SEAL 474
Round, 14
?Horse's head erased
Legend: none
CALS DWN/2/40, dated 1452 x 1453
CALS DWN/2/39, dated 1452 x 1553

SEAL 475
Unknown, c.10
?Winged bull facing left holding ?scroll
Legend: none
CALS DWN/2/42, dated 1453 x 1454
CALS DWN/2/43, dated 1453 x 1454

SEAL 476
Round, 12
?Head full-face (?heart) with small star above
Legend: none
CALS DWN/2/44, dated 1456 x 1457

SEAL 477
Rectangular, 12x10
Letter ?B
Legend: none
CALS DWN/2/45, dated 1458 x 1459

SEAL 478
Round, 13
Letter A
Legend: none
CALS DWN/2/47, dated 1460

SEAL 479
Unknown, nm
Letter W
Legend: none
CALS DWN/2/49, dated 1465 x 1466

SEAL 480
Rectangular, 11x10
Crowned letter I, stylised foliage to right and left
Legend: none
CALS DWN/2/51, dated 1468 x 1469

SEAL 481
Round, 10
?Merchant mark: horizontal ?key with open-topped loop
Legend: none
CALS DWN/2/51, seal 2, dated 1468 x 1469

SEAL 482
Octagonal, 10x12
Letter I flanked by small three-petalled flowers on stems
Legend: none
CALS DWN/2/53, dated 1468 x 1469

APPENDIX

SEAL 483
Rounded oval, 12x13
Monogram: 'DI' (or ID)
Legend: none
CALS DWN/2/55, dated 1498 x 1499

SEAL 484
Rounded oval, 22x19
Illegible (?gem)
Legend: +SIGILLV[section lost] BELLET
GA D2/2, dated 1302 x 1303
GA D2/17, dated 1302 x 1303

SEAL 485
Round, 41
Stylised lily
Legend: +SIGILL'RA[.]SFILIEVLNOL
GA D2/3, dated 1175 x 1224

SEAL 486
Round, 21
Uncertain (?bird)
Legend: illegible
GA D2/8, dated 1300 x 1349

SEAL 487
Round, 21
Stylised eight-petalled flower
Legend: [.]S'I [. .]ANL [.] V [.]
GA D2/10, dated 1275 x 1324

SEAL 488
Round, 22
Woman standing full-face holding a large object up to the right (?Virgin and Child), foliate stems on either side
Legend: *A[. . . . .]A[. . . . . .]NA
GA D2/25, dated 1347 x 1348

SEAL 489
Round, 24
Saltire cross with a?petals in each angle
Legend: +S'PhILIPFIL[. . . . . . .]oT
GA D2/26, dated 1333 x 1334

SEAL 490
Round, 19
Lion rampant facing left
Legend: [. . .] ?M [.] E [.] [section lost]
GA D2/28, dated 1393 x 1394

SEAL 491
Rectangular, 18x15
Letter ?T (?G)
Legend: none
GA D2/29, dated 1424 x 1425

SEAL 492
Unknown, nm
Within an architectural niche, Annunciation (top lost)
Legend: lost
GA D2/30, dated 1441

SEAL 493
Round, 10
Stag's head facing half left, a stylised lily between the antlers
Legend: none
GA D2/31, seal 1, dated 1452 x 1453

SEAL 494
Octagonal, 15x14
Pelican in its piety facing left
Legend: none
GA D2/31, seal 2, dated 1452 x 1453

SEAL 495
Round, 12
Illegible
Legend: none
GA D2/32, dated 1453 x 1454

SEAL 496
Round, 10
Bird facing left
Legend: none
GA D2/45, dated 1545 x 1546

SEAL 497
Rounded oval, 10x14
Illegible
Legend: none
GA D8/1/133, dated 1467 x 1468

SEAL 498
Round, 12
Shield of arms (a chevron between three objects)
Legend: none
GA D8/1/133, seal 2, dated 1467 x 1468

SEAL 499
Round
Obverse: Armoured man wearing cap / crest on helm, with armorial shield (quarterly England and France modern with a borure) on a horse with armorial caparisons galloping to left
Legend: Obverse: [section lost] [. . . .] Pem[. .]ockie [section lost]
GA D8/1/156, dated 1491 x 1492
GA D8/1/156, back, dated 1491 x 1492

SEAL 500
Hexagonal, 11x10
Letter T
Legend: none
GA D8/1/627, dated 1433 x 1434

SEAL 501
Round, 18
Illegible
Legend: none
GA D8/1/630, dated 1523 x 1524

SEAL 502
Unknown, 10x13
Squirrel sitting facing right
Legend: none
GA D8/1/632, seal 1, 2 and3, dated 1524 x 1525

SEAL 503
Round, 13
Pattern (?letters)
Legend: none
GA D8/1/634, dated 1534 x 1535

SEAL 504
Round, nm
Shield of arms (bust full-face with ribbon wound around neck) with letters tv above, all on a diaper ground
Legend: none
GA D8/1/1717, dated 1492 x 1493
GA D8/1/1857, dated 1492 x 1493

SEAL 505
Round, nm
Illegible
Legend: none
GA D8/1/1719, dated 1544 x 1545

SEAL 506
Round, nm
Large letter I, small letter d to left, letter ?d to right, all within border of rays
Legend: none
GA D8/1/1729, dated 1513 x 1514

SEAL 507
Square, nm
Three horizontal and three vertical lines forming grid pattern
Legend: none
GA D8/1/1733, dated 1535 x 1536
GA D8/1/1734, dated 1535 x 1536

SEAL 508
Round, nm
Pattern: cross with diagonal lines to the right
Legend: none
GA D8/1/1735, dated 1538 x 1539

SEAL 509
Round, 11
Letter R with small crown above
Legend: none
GA D8/1/1822, seal 2, dated 1507 x 1508
GA D8/1/1736, dated, seal 1 and 2, 1507 x 1508

APPENDIX

GA D8/1/1790, seal 2, dated 1507 x 1508
GA D8/1/1822, dated 1507 x 1508
GA D8/1/1763, seal 1 and 2, dated 1507 x 1508

SEAL 510
Rectangular, 15x13
Letter H
Legend: none
GA D8/1/1739, dated 1500 x 1550

SEAL 511
Round, 10
Sixteen-petalled flower formed by intersecting cross and saltire with short rays in the angles
Legend: N/A
GA D8/1/1741, seal 1, dated 1534 x 1535
GA D8/1/1915, seal 2, dated 1534 x 1535

SEAL 512
Square, nm
Letter W
Legend: none
GA D8/1/1915, seal 3, dated 1534 x 1535
GA D8/1/1741, seal 2, dated 1534 x 1535

SEAL 513
Round, 13
Stylised eight-petalled flower
Legend: none
GA D8/1/1741, seal 3, dated 1534 x 1535
GA D8/1/1915, dated 1534 x 1535

SEAL 514
Rectangular, 12x9
Letter E
Legend: none
GA D8/1/1862, dated 1526 x 1527
GA D8/1/1825, dated 1524 x 1525
GA D8/1/1925, dated 1544 x 1545
GA D8/1/1746, dated 1526 x 1527

SEAL 515
Octagonal, 14x12
Letter I with foliate branches above and below, foliate motif either side
Legend: N/A
GA D8/1/1746, seal 2, dated 1526 x 1527
GA D8/1/1862, seal 2, dated 1526 x 1527

SEAL 516
Round, 12
Letter M
Legend: none
GA D8/1/1757, dated 1524 x 1525

SEAL 517
Round, 13
Shield of arms (?dragon / ?wyvern facing up)
Legend: none
GA D8/1/1758, dated 1479 x 1480

SEAL 518
Round, 15
Head and shoulders full-face with a serpent around the neck
Legend: Thomas Vaughan
GA D8/1/1759, dated 1475 x 1476

SEAL 519
Octagonal, 13x9
Merchant mark on a shield (includes inverted Y, letter I, M), long cross-tipped staff with banner emerging from top
Legend: none
GA D8/1/1799, dated 1480 x 1481
GA D8/1/1762, dated 1480 x 1481

SEAL 520
Round, nm
Nine diagonal lines intersecting to form diaper pattern
Legend: none
GA D8/1/1768, seal 1 and 2, dated 1533 x 1534
GA D8/1/1791, dated 1534 x 1535

SEAL 521
Round, nm
Letter I
Legend: none
GA D8/1/1769, dated 1535 x 1536

SEAL 522
Rectangular, nm
Letter W
Legend: none
GA D8/1/1770, dated 1537 x 1538

SEAL 523
Undetermined, nm
Stylised four-petalled flower
Legend: none
GA D8/1/1771, dated 1524 x 1525

SEAL 524
Round, 18
Shield of arms (griffin rampant)
Legend: [. . .]n e[. .]
GA D8/1/1772, seal 1 and 2, dated 1505 x 1506

SEAL 525
Round, 11
Wheel with six spokes
Legend: none
GA D8/1/1788, dated 1484 x 1485

SEAL 526
Round, 84
Obverse: Armoured man with crested and mantled helm and armorial shield (quarterly England and France modern with a boudre) on a horse with caparisons galloping to the right trampling on a dragon
Reverse: shield of arms (quarterly France modern and England, a boudre with seven ?martlets), with a coronet and supporters (two dragons)
Legend: Obverse: [. . .]illu' : iaspar' : fratriSsunuch' : [.]e[. .] dux : bed[. . . . .]e dne' : glam[. . . .]em'
Reverse: illegible
GA D8/1/1794, dated 1493 x 1494
GA D8/1/1814, dated 1486 x 1487

SEAL 527
Rounded oval, 12x10
Letter I
Legend: none
GA D8/1/1798, seal 1 and 2, dated 1484 x 1485

SEAL 528
Round, nm
Letter h, stylised branch to left
Legend: none
GA D8/1/1801, dated 1431 x 1432

SEAL 529
Round, 9
Letter T
Legend: none
GA D8/1/1802, dated 1485 x 1486

SEAL 530
Round, 12
Letter ?ic (?v) flanked by stylised branches, ?stylised lily above
Legend: none
GA D8/1/1806, dated 1431 x 1432

SEAL 531
Rounded oval, nm
Shield of arms (?bird facing left)
Legend: none
GA D8/1/1808, dated 1492 x 1493

SEAL 532
Round, nm
?Griffin (?lion) facing left
Legend: none
GA D8/1/1817, dated 1450 x 1499

SEAL 533
Round, nm
Stylised six-petalled flower
Legend: lost
GA D8/1/1827, dated 1400 x 1401

SEAL 534
Rounded oval, nm
Letter T
Legend: none
GA D8/1/1828, dated 1479 x 1480

APPENDIX

SEAL 535
Square, nm
Three vertical bars
Legend: none
GA D8/1/1847, dated 1535 x 1536
GA D8/1/1915, seal 4, dated 1534 x 1535

SEAL 536
Round, nm
?Two ?hands clasped
Legend: illegible
GA D8/1/1858, dated 1370 x 1371

SEAL 537
Round, 12
?Stylised lily
Legend: none
GA D8/1/1859, dated 1498 x 1499

SEAL 538
Undetermined, nm
Tudor-style rose
Legend: none
GA D8/1/1860, dated 1514 x 1515

SEAL 539
Undetermined, nm
Four-petalled flower with five trefoil leaves around the edge
Legend: none
GA D8/1/1860, seal 2, dated 1514 x 1515

SEAL 540
Round, nm
Eagle displayed
Legend: none
GA D8/1/1880, dated 1519 x 1520

SEAL 541
Rectangular, nm
Letter W
Legend: none
GA D8/1/1882, dated 1533 x 1534

SEAL 542
Round, nm
Six diagonal lines forming diaper pattern
Legend: none
GA D8/1/1894, dated 1544 x 1545

SEAL 543
Round, nm
Letter I with foliage ?either side
Legend: none
GA D8/1/1895, seal 1 and 2, dated 1492 x 1492

SEAL 544
Round, nm
Letter R
Legend: none
GA D8/1/1910, dated 1417 x 1418

SEAL 545
Rounded oval, nm
Crowned letter ?W
Legend: none
GA D8/1/1916, seal 1, dated 1519 x 1520

SEAL 546
Round, nm
Letter M
Legend: none
GA D8/1/1916, seal 2, dated 1519 x 1520

SEAL 547
Round, nm
Eight diagonal lines (3, 5) forming diaper pattern
Legend: none
GA D8/1/1917, dated 1534 x 1535

SEAL 548
Round, 11x12
Bird walking left, on the left a single minim (?'L'), on the right a 'W'
Legend: none
GA D583/1, seal 1, dated 1464 x 1465

SEAL 549
Rounded oval, 14x10
Illegible (?lost)
Legend: none
GA D583/1, seal 2, dated 1464 x 1465

SEAL 550
Round, 12
Stylised lily
Legend: none
GA D583/9, dated 1472 x 1473

SEAL 551
Round, 14
Lamb of God facing left
Legend: illegible
GA D583/14, dated 1362 x 1363

SEAL 552
Round, 39
?Shield of arms
Legend: illegible, partially lost
GA D583/15, dated 1450 x 1451

SEAL 553
Round, 11
?deer facing left
Legend: none
GA D583/16, dated 1483 x 1484

SEAL 554
Round, 14
Letter M
Legend: none
GA D583/17, dated 1400 x 1401

SEAL 555
Round, 11
Bird walking to right
Legend: none
GA D583/18, dated 1473 x 1474

SEAL 556
Round, 9
Scallop shell
Legend: none
GA D583/45, dated 1496 x 1497

SEAL 557
Round, 14
Letter W
Legend: none
GA D583/61, dated 1548 x 1549

SEAL 558
Round, 14
Letters GW, stylised branch below
Legend: none
GA D583/90, dated 1542 x 1543

SEAL 559
Rounded oval, 16x12
Shield of arms (quadruped facing left), mantling behind
Legend: none
GA D583/99, seal 1, dated 1548 x 1549

SEAL 560
Round, 13
Pelican in its piety facing left
Legend: none
GA D583/99, seal 2, dated 1548 x 1549

SEAL 561
Rounded oval, 15x12
Stylised lily
Legend: none
GA D583/101, dated 1515 x 1516

SEAL 562
Round, 10
Cross
Legend: none
GA D583/104, dated 1534 x 1535

SEAL 563
Round, 10
Stylised eight-petalled flower (?eight-pointed star)
Legend: none
GA D583/104, seal 2, dated 1534 x 1535

SEAL 564
Round, 11
Letter I with two quatrefoils on either side
Legend: none
GA D583/104, seal 3, dated 1534 x 1535

SEAL 565
Round, 14
Lion rampant facing right, five-pointed star

in lower right
Legend: none
GA D583/265, dated 1517 x 1518

SEAL 566
Round, nm
Illegible
Legend: none
GACRO Vaynol/Ches/1434, dated 1200

SEAL 567
Round, 47
Lion walking to right
Legend: +SIG [rest lost0
GACRO Vaynol/Ches/1437, dated 1200 x 1299

SEAL 568
Rectangular, 11x7
Letter R with foliage above and to left
Legend: none
GACRO Vaynol/Ches/1442, seal 1, dated 1433

SEAL 569
Rectangular, 13x8
Crowned letter I, foliage to right and left
Legend: none
GACRO Vaynol/Ches/1442, seal 2, dated 1433

SEAL 570
Rounded oval, 12x11
Bird with wings displayed and foliage in its beak facing left
Legend: h longley
GACRO Vaynol/Ches/1442, seal 3, dated 1433
GACRO Vaynol/Ches/1444, seal 3, dated 1433

SEAL 571
Octagonal, 11x9
Scallop shell
Legend: I Straengwis
GACRO Vaynol/Ches/1442, seal 4, dated 1433

SEAL 572
Octagonal, 10x10
Bird (?hawk) facing left
Legend: I io[?h][. . . . . . .]
GACRO Vaynol/Ches/1444, dated 1433
GACRO Vaynol/Ches/1442, seal 6, dated 1433

SEAL 573
Round, nm
Lion rampant facing left (probably supporter; fragment only)
Legend: [. .]icardi Lestra [rest lost]
GACRO Vaynol/Ches/1443, dated 1433

SEAL 574
Round, 10
Six-pointed star with leaves in each angel
Legend: none
GACRO Vaynol/Ches/1444, seal 4, dated 1433

SEAL 575
Unknown, 16
Uncertain
Legend: none
GACRO Vaynol/Glan/1349/a, dated 1427 x 1428

SEAL 576
Round, 14
Trefoil overlaying a triangle
Legend: none
GACRO Vaynol/Glan/1353, dated 1479

SEAL 577
Round, 13
Letter R
Legend: none
GACRO Vaynol/Glan/1357, dated 1505

SEAL 578
Round, 18
Letters EG
Legend: none
GACRO Vaynol/Glan/1358, dated 1507

SEAL 579
Round, 12
Pentagram
Legend: none
GACRO Vaynol/Glan/1360, dated 1509

SEAL 580
Round, 10
Abstract pattern: triangle with radiating lines
Legend: none
GACRO Vaynol/Glan/1363, dated 1512

SEAL 581
Square, 11
Letter A
Legend: none
GACRO Vaynol/Glan/1365, dated 1513

SEAL 582
Square, 11
Letter E
Legend: none
GACRO Vaynol/Glan/1366, dated 1514

SEAL 583
Round, 14
Letter W
Legend: none
GACRO Vaynol/Glan/1368/b, dated 1518

SEAL 584
Rounded oval, 12x9
?Cross patty
Legend: none
GACRO Vaynol/Glan/1369, dated 1516

SEAL 585
Square, 13
Letter B (?R)
Legend: none
GACRO Vaynol/Glan/1371, dated 1519

SEAL 586
Round, 9
Stylised eight-petalled flower
Legend: none
GACRO Vaynol/Glan/1372, dated 1519

SEAL 587
Round, 12
Stylised eight-petalled flower
Legend: none
GACRO Vaynol/Glan/1373, dated 1519 x 1520

SEAL 588
Rounded oval, nm
Bird facing right
Legend: none
GACRO Vaynol/Glan/1374, dated 1521 x 1522

SEAL 589
Round, 11
Two vertical lines with, on either side, three lines at 45 degrees
Legend: none
GACRO Vaynol/Glan/1375/a, dated 1522

SEAL 590
Rounded oval, 12x10
Pattern of 'arrow head' with line to left (?letter W)
Legend: none
GACRO Vaynol/Glan/1375/b, seal 2, dated 1522

SEAL 591
Round, 13
Pattern of intersecting lines forming 'star of David' with pellet in centre
Legend: none
GACRO Vaynol/Glan/1376, dated 1522

SEAL 592
Round, 10
Pattern (?letter W)
Legend: none
GACRO Vaynol/Glan/1377, dated 1523

APPENDIX

SEAL 593
Unknown, nm
Letters RW
Legend: none
GACRO Vaynol/Glan/1378, dated 1526

SEAL 594
Unknown, nm
Indistinct (?animal)
Legend: none
GACRO Vaynol/Glan/1379, dated 1528

SEAL 595
Rounded oval, 12x13
Clover leaf
Legend: none
GACRO Vaynol/Glan/1380, dated 1529

SEAL 596
Round, 15
Lamb of God facing left
Legend: none
GACRO Vaynol/Glan/1381, dated 1529

SEAL 597
Pointed oval, nm
Figure standing full-face within a niche, a shield of arms (quarterly: 1 and 3 France modern; 2 and 4 England) below
Legend: illegible, partially lost
GACRO Vaynol/Glan/1382, dated 1531

SEAL 598
Round, 9
Illegible
Legend: none
GACRO Vaynol/Glan/1383, dated 1534

SEAL 599
Round, 10
Illegible
Legend: none
GACRO Vaynol/Glan/1384, dated 1535

SEAL 600
Round, 10
Interlaced pattern
Legend: none
GACRO Vaynol/Glan/1384, seal 3, dated 1535

SEAL 601
Unknown, nm
Small cross with objects below (fragment only)
Legend: none
GACRO Vaynol/Glan/1385, dated 1536

SEAL 602
Rectangular, 14x13
Stag's head full-face, object between antlers
Legend: none
GACRO Vaynol/Glan/1387, seal 1, dated 1539

SEAL 603
Square, 11x12
Interlaced pattern
Legend: none
GACRO Vaynol/Glan/1387, seal 2 and 3, dated 1539

SEAL 604
Unknown, nm
Indistinct
Legend: none
GACRO Vaynol/Glan/1388, dated 1539

SEAL 605
Scutiform, 18x15
Letters WB, a ?bid (?lion seated) facing left below
Legend: none
GACRO Vaynol/Glan/1390, dated 1540

SEAL 606
Round, 13
Merchant mark (heart-shaped, includes letters RS)
Legend: none
GACRO Vaynol/Glan/1391, seal 1, dated 1541
GACRO Vaynol/Glan/1394, seal 1, dated 1541

SEAL 607
Round, 11
Monogram A v
Legend: none
GACRO Vaynol/Glan/1391, seal 2, dated 1541
GACRO Vaynol/Glan/1394, seal 2, dated 1541

SEAL 608
Round, 19
Heart with small cross above
Legend: none
GACRO Vaynol/Glan/1395, dated 1541

SEAL 609
Unknown, 10
?Cross patonce
Legend: none
GACRO Vaynol/Glan/1396, dated 1541

SEAL 610
Round, 10
Illegible
Legend: none
GACRO Vaynol/Glan/1397, dated 1541

SEAL 611
Round, 10
Merchant mark (includes letters TW)
Legend: none
GACRO Vaynol/Glan/1399, dated 1542

SEAL 612
Round, 11
Letter S reversed between stylised branches
Legend: none
GACRO Vaynol/Glan/1400, dated 1542

SEAL 613
Round, 10
Abstract pattern: three vertical strokes and two horizontal
Legend: none
GACRO Vaynol/Glan/1401, dated 1544

SEAL 614
Round, 12
Stylised eight-petalled flower
Legend: none
GACRO Vaynol/Glan/1404, seal 1, dated 1547

SEAL 615
Round, nm
Letter ?M
Legend: none
GACRO Vaynol/Glan/1404, seal 2, dated 1547

SEAL 616
Round, nm
Letter n (?H)
Legend: none
GACRO XD2/549, dated 1515

SEAL 617
Round, nm
Letter T
Legend: none
GACRO XD2/554, dated 1455

SEAL 618
Round, nm
Pelican in its piety facing left
Legend: none
GACRO XD2/558, seal 3, dated 1546

SEAL 619
Undetermined, nm
Illegible
Legend: none
GACRO XD2/570, dated 1501

SEAL 620
Round, nm
Diamond with rays emerging from voided centre
Legend: none
GACRO XD2/571, dated 1513

APPENDIX

SEAL 621
Unknown, nm
Wing of ?dragon to left, above scroll with ?fleur-de-lys
Legend: none
GACRO XD2/575, dated 1497

SEAL 622
Round, nm
Letters ?D ?, a ?five-pointed star between, a ?branch above
Legend: none
GACRO XD2/582, dated 1542

SEAL 623
Hexagonal, 10x12
Letter ?A
Legend: none
GACRO XD2/595, dated 1519

SEAL 624
Round, nm
Monogram H B
Legend: none
GACRO XD2/597, dated 1538

SEAL 625
Rounded oval, nm
Stylised plant with three flowers and two leaves flanked by stylised branches
Legend: none
GACRO XD2/606, dated 1444

SEAL 626
Octagonal, nm
Bird with wings raised walking to left
Legend: none
GACRO XD2/606, seal 2, dated 1444

SEAL 627
Round, nm
Head of ?horse facing right
Legend: none
GACRO XD2/611, dated 1481

SEAL 628
Hexagonal, nm
Letter ?R
Legend: none
GACRO XD2/612, seal 2, dated 1481

SEAL 629
Round, nm
Letters ?I ?n (?h i)
Legend: none
GACRO XD2/622, dated 1490

SEAL 630
Unknown, nm
Shield of arms (?per pale, three fusils)
Legend: none
GACRO XD2/638, dated 1528

SEAL 631
Round, nm
Hare seated facing left
Legend: none
GACRO XD2/639, dated 1529

SEAL 632
Rectangular, nm
Letter R
Legend: none
GACRO XD2/640, dated 1530

SEAL 633
Round, nm
Letter T
Legend: none
GACRO XD2/643, seal 2, dated 1536
GACRO XD2/642, seal 1, dated 1532

SEAL 634
Round, nm
Pattern (?stylised five-petalled flower)
Legend: none
GACRO XD2/642, seal 2, dated 1532

SEAL 635
Round, nm
Within an eight-pointed star, a merchant mark (includes inverted Y)
Legend: none
GACRO XD2/643, dated 1536

SEAL 636
Pointed oval, nm
Illegible
Legend: none
GACRO XD2/648, dated 1548

SEAL 637
Round, nm
Letter B
Legend: none
GACRO XD2/687, seal 4, dated 1511

SEAL 638
Round, nm
Shield (any charge now lost)
Legend: none
GACRO XD2/735, dated 1512
GACRO XD2/687, seal 5, dated 1511

SEAL 639
Round, nm
Illegible
Legend: none
GACRO XD2/690, dated 1515

SEAL 640
Round, nm
Letter B (?R)
Legend: none
GACRO XD2/772, seal 2, dated 1523

SEAL 641
Rounded oval, nm
Foliage and ?animals
Legend: none
GACRO XD2/932, seal 1, dated 1548

SEAL 642
Round, nm
Shield of arms (a bar with three roundels between three hounds ?courant)
Legend: none
GACRO XD2/932, seal 2, dated 1548

SEAL 643
Rounded oval, nm
Shield of arms (Quarterly: 1 per pale, dexter a cross engrailed, sinister a cross moile; 2 sub-quarterly, i and iv a lion rampant, ii and iii a fret; 3 per pale, dexter a lion rampant, sinister six crosses between a fess dancetty 4 indistinct)
Legend: none
GACRO XD2/933, seal 2, dated 1549

SEAL 644
Round, nm
Armoured man on horse galloping to right
Legend: + SIGIL [section lost] L
GACRO XD2/1111, dated 1176

SEAL 645
Rounded oval, nm
Shield of arms (a fox's head couped)
Legend: none
GACRO XD2/1241, dated 1549

SEAL 646
Undetermined, 8x10
Letter ?R (?B)
Legend: none
HAS A95/2/35, dated 1455 x 1456

SEAL 647
Hexagonal, 14x10
Letter I, stylised branches to left and right
Legend: none
HAS A95/2/36, dated 1479 x 1480

SEAL 648
Round, 31
Shield of arms (barry of ?12)
Legend: +SIG[. . . . . . .]RICI.D.PINBRVG
HAS A95/2/46, dated 1225 x 1274

SEAL 649
Pointed oval, 34x19
Indistinct
Legend: lost, if any
HAS A95/5/2, dated 1275 x 1324

SEAL 650
Rounded oval, 29x18

APPENDIX

Vertical zigzag line with pellets in the angles
Legend: S'WIIL'I LEWITE.
HAS A95/5/3, dated 1293 x 1294

SEAL 651
Round, 23
Four conifer branches with leaves in the angles
Legend: +S'IOhANNESDEhERSE[. . .]
HAS A95/5/4, dated 1250 x 1299

SEAL 652
Pointed oval, 32x19
Indistinct
Legend: [section lost] ISDE [section illegible]
HAS A95/5/5, dated 1300 x 1349

SEAL 653
Rounded oval, 28x25
Stylised lily
Legend: S'MILONISLEhERT
HAS A95/5/7, dated 1250 x 1299

SEAL 654
Round, 18
Two birds addorsed
Legend: illegible
HAS A95/5/8, dated 1250 x 1299

SEAL 655
Pointed oval, 31x21
Stylised double-lily plant
Legend: +S'WILLELMIEDRIh[.]
HAS A95/5/9, dated 1250 x 1299

SEAL 656
Round, 19
Lamb of God facing left
Legend: [. .]D [?IVEI . . . . .]
HAS A95/5/12, dated 1365 x 1366

SEAL 657
Round, 15
Crowned letter h, to left a crescent facing down, to right a star
Legend: none

HAS A95/5/14, dated 1430 x 1431
HAS A95/5/15, dated 1430 x 1431

SEAL 658
Round, c.14
Crowned letter P
Legend: none
HAS A95/5/17, seal 1, dated 1477 x 1478

SEAL 659
Round, 13
Crowned letter N, stylised foliage to right
Legend: none
HAS A95/5/17, seal 2, dated 1477 x 1478

SEAL 660
Round, 14
Letter W with small stylised lily above
Legend: none
HAS A95/5/18, dated 1492 x 1493

SEAL 661
Round, 13
Letter I
Legend: none
HAS A95/5/18, seal 2, dated 1492 x 1493

SEAL 662
Unknown, c.19xc.14
Uncertain – ?figure
Legend: lost, if any
HAS A95/5/24, dated 1381 x 1382

SEAL 663
Round, 21
Shield of arms (?paly)
Legend: * S [. . . . .]E
HAS A95/5/25, dated 1401 x 1402

SEAL 664
Rounded oval, 25x23
Shield of arms (a ?manunch, with ?roundels in chief)
Legend: none
HAS A95/5/26, seal 1, dated 1405 x 1406

SEAL 665
Round, 21
Shield of arms (a ?quadruped (?dog))
Legend: illegible
HAS A95/5/26, seal 2, dated 1405 x 1406

SEAL 666
Round, c.18
Letter ?I
Legend: none
HAS A95/5/28, dated 1437

SEAL 667
Round, c.14
Letter E (E with ?S interlaced)
Legend: none
HAS A95/5/29, dated 1448 x 1449

SEAL 668
Round, 13
Uncertain: ?bust
Legend: [. . .][?h] [remainder lost]
HAS A95/5/30, dated 1493 x 1494

SEAL 669
Round, 16
Merchant mark
Legend: lost, if any
HAS A95/5/43, dated 1361 x 1362

SEAL 670
Round, 19
Squirrel facing left
Legend: [.] C[.]A[. . . . . .]
HAS AA26/II/2, dated 1300 x 1300

SEAL 671
Round, 19
?Abstract design (?heart surrounded by six (visible) pellets)
Legend: none
HAS AA26/II/3, dated 1300 x 1300

SEAL 672
Round, c.20
Six petalled stylised flower with small pellets between the petals
Legend: [. . . . . . .]RNG[.]
HAS AA26/II/7, dated 1300 x 1300

SEAL 673
Round, 19
Lion rampant facing left
Legend: * SV[?M]LEOFRTIS
HAS AA26/II/10, dated 1320 x 1321

SEAL 674
Round, 26
Hare facing left
Legend: illegible
HAS AA26/II/11, dated 1322 x 1323

SEAL 675
Round, 18
Lamb of God facing left
Legend: [.]CCE [. . . . .]
HAS AA26/II/20, dated 1336 x 1337

SEAL 676
Round, 21
Bird facing left with object below (?hawk taking prey / ? Pelican in its piety)
Legend: illegible, partially lost
HAS AA26/II/26, dated 1352 x 1353

SEAL 677
Round, 19
Three small flowers on stems, ?two ?hands joined below
Legend: lost
HAS AA26/II/26, seal 4, dated 1352 x 1353

SEAL 678
Round, 17
Stag's head full-face with a cross between the antlers
Legend: + S[. . .]D[. . . . .]
HAS AA26/II/30, dated 1355 x 1356

SEAL 679
Rounded oval, 19x17
Head and shoulders of man facing right

APPENDIX

Legend: * CAPVD [. .]RVI DEI
HAS AA26/II/30, seal 2, dated 1355 x 1356

SEAL 680
Scutiform, 18x14
Head of man (?wearing a ?coif) facing right
Legend: [. .]AREIN[?O?C][. . . . .]
HAS AA26/II/33, dated 1367 x 1368

SEAL 681
Round, nm
Lamb of God facing left
Legend: lost
HAS AA26/II/35, dated 1414 x 1415

SEAL 682
Round, 13
Bird with wings outstretched walking to right
Legend: none
HAS AA26/II/37, dated 1457
HAS AA26/II/36, dated 1457

SEAL 683
Round,
Indistinct
Legend: [section lost] ERIDE [section lost]
HAS CF54/2/1, dated 1300 x 1349

SEAL 684
Round, 20
Lamb of God facing right
Legend: S' [. . . . .]ENE [. . . . .]
HAS CF54/1, dated 1375 x 1376

SEAL 685
Round, 20
Squirrel facing left
Legend: N/Aillegible
HAS CF54/1, dated 1393 x 1394

SEAL 686
Round, nm
Squirrel facing left
Legend: [section lost] ICRA [section lost]
HAS CF54/1, dated 1403 x 1404

SEAL 687
Unknown, 14
letter ?W
Legend: none
HAS CF54/1, dated 1430 x 1431

SEAL 688
Unknown, 22
Within a cusped quatrefoil, a figure holding a ?hawk (?cross) on their left hand mounted on a horse walking to left
Legend: N/A
HAS CF54/1, dated 1457 x 1458

SEAL 689
Round, 11
Letter T
Legend: N/A
HAS CF54/1, dated 1466 x 1467

SEAL 690
Octagonal, 11x11
Letter W
Legend: ?
HAS CF54/1, seal 2, dated 1457 x 1458

SEAL 691
Round, 20
Shield of arms (eagle displayed)
Legend: * SIGIL' IOHANIS / KYDE
HAS CF54/2, dated 1360 x 1361

SEAL 692
Round, 20
Stag's head full-face with a cross between its antlers, stylised foliage (?branches) to left and right
Legend: [. .]R[. . . .]V[. . .]
HAS CF54/2/4, dated 1351 x 1352

SEAL 693
Round, c.23
Four conifer branches
Legend: * S' [. . . . . .]ETLAN
HAS CF54/2/3, dated 1324 x 1325

SEALS AND SOCIETY

SEAL 694
Round, 29
Boar walking to the left
Legend: + S'RICARDI . [. . . . .]RTIL'
HAS D52/B/1/2, dated 1250 x 1299

SEAL 695
Pointed oval, c.27x18
Stylised lily
Legend: [.] S' IOIS [. . . . . .]
HAS D52/B/1/2, seal 10, dated 1250 x 1299

SEAL 696
Round, 20
Closed helm facing right with small stylised lily above (?crest), star (many-armed) to left, crescent to right
Legend: * [. . . . .] LE HA[. . . .]R
HAS D52/B/1/2, seal 11, dated 1250 x 1299

SEAL 697
Round, 19
Two heads facing in, a plant (?stylised lily) above
Legend: + S' IOHE DE HER[. . .]E
HAS D52/B/1/2, seal 4, 7 and 12, dated 1250 x 1299

SEAL 698
Pointed oval, c.30x22
Eight-petalled stylised flower
Legend: + S' MA[?R][. .]RE[. . .]AD' LciT[?E]
HAS D52/B/1/2, seal 2 and 13, dated 1250 x 1299

SEAL 699
Pointed oval, 28x19
Virgin and Child seated full-face
Legend: illegible
HAS D52/B/1/2, seal 6 and 9, dated 1250 x 1299

SEAL 700
Pointed oval, c.28x18
Eight-petalled stylised flower
Legend: + S' RICAR[. .] : ALB[.]
HAS D52/B/1/2, seal 8, dated 1250 x 1299

SEAL 701
Round, 25
Four-petalled stylised flower with small leaves between petals
Legend: [.] PhI LE ꝗSSChI[. . . .]
HAS D52/B/1/5, dated 1329 x 1330

SEAL 702
Rounded oval, 11x8
Tonsured and bearded head full-face
Legend: none
HAS D52/B/1/11, dated 1530 x 1531

SEAL 703
Rectangular, 11x14
Letter ?h
Legend: none
HAS D52/B/1/12, dated 1534 x 1535

SEAL 704
Round, 26
Four petals in a radial pattern, a branch and a pellet in each angle
Legend: +S'WA[. . .]RIISTERRE
HAS F8/II/7, dated 1250 x 1299

SEAL 705
Round, 22
Five-armed radial device
Legend: S'WILL'FIL'WILL
HAS F8/II/15, dated 1275 x 1324

SEAL 706
Round, 17
Hare ?blowing a ?horn seated on a hound walking to right, and arrow in the upper left
Legend: +[. . . .]RE [. . . . .] INOSVA [. .]
HAS F8/II/17, dated 1292 x 1293

SEAL 707
Round, 19
Four ?leaves

Legend: illegible
HAS F8/II/18, dated 1352 x 1353

SEAL 708
Round, 14
Letter S
Legend: none
HAS F8/II/23, dated 1373 x 1374

SEAL 709
Round, 12
Within an ornate border, a shield of arms (charge illegible) couche, a helm ?with chapeau above
Legend: S'ALEXAND [section lost]
HAS F8/II/24, dated 1375 x 1376

SEAL 710
Unknown, nm
Curved line and small pellets (fragment)
Legend: none
HAS F8/II/25, dated 1379 x 1380

SEAL 711
Round, 19
Indistinct
Legend: lost, if any
HAS F8/II/28, dated 1407 x 1408

SEAL 712
Round, 23
Shield of arms (a chevron between three objects)
Legend: lost
HAS F8/II/29, dated 1418 x 1419

SEAL 713
Round, nm
Shield of arms (charge illegible) couche, a helm with crest (dog's head) above, supporters (lions serjant)
Legend: illegible
HAS F8/II/30, seal 1, dated 1408 x 1409

SEAL 714
Round, 11
Merchant mark (includes letter ?d), stylised foliage to left and right
Legend: none
HAS F8/II/31, dated 1432 x 1433

SEAL 715
Octagonal, 13x12
Indistinct
Legend: lost, if any
HAS F8/II/32, dated 1438 x 1439

SEAL 716
Round, 12
Crowned letter B, stylised foliage to left and right
Legend: none
HAS F8/II/33, dated 1433 x 1434

SEAL 717
Rounded oval, 11x13l
Letter T
Legend: none
HAS F8/II/34, dated 1436 x 1437

SEAL 718
Octagonal, 13x10
Monogram: dp with crown above
Legend: none
HAS F8/II/35, dated 1442 x 1443

SEAL 719
Round, 11
Merchant mark (includes 4 shape, letter W reversed S)
Legend: none
HAS F8/II/37, dated 1445 x 1446

SEAL 720
Octagonal, 12
Letter B
Legend: none
HAS F8/II/39, dated 1449 x 1450

SEAL 721
Rounded oval, 14x8
Crowned letter ?T (?M)
Legend: none
HAS F8/II/40, dated 1453 x 1454

SEAL 722
Rounded oval, 12x10
Letter E
Legend: N/A
HAS F8/II/41, dated 1454 x 1455

SEAL 723
Round, 18
Pelican in its piety facing left
Legend: none
HAS F8/II/43, dated 1405 x 1406

SEAL 724
Unknown, 11
Pelican in its piety facing left, ?letter in upper right
Legend: none
HAS F8/II/46, seal 1, dated 1467 x 1468

SEAL 725
Round, 10
Letter W
Legend: none
HAS F8/II/46, seal 2, dated 1467 x 1468

SEAL 726
Rounded oval, 11x8
Crowned letter R
Legend: none
HAS F8/II/54, dated 1473 x 1474
HAS F8/II/47, seal 1 and 2, dated 1468 x 1469
HAS F8/II/53, dated 1473 x 1474
HAS F8/II/51, dated 1471 x 1472

SEAL 727
Rectangular, c.12x10
Pelican in its piety facing left, illegible letters in upper right
Legend: none
HAS F8/II/49, seal 1, dated 1405 x 1406
HAS F8/II/48, seal 1, dated 1467 x 1468

SEAL 728
Round, 10
Letter W
Legend: none
HAS F8/II/49, seal 2, dated 1405 x 1406
HAS F8/II/48, seal 2, dated 1467 x 1468

SEAL 729
Rounded oval, 14x11
Crowned letter I, stylised foliage to left and right
Legend: none
HAS F8/II/53, seal 2, dated 1473 x 1474
HAS F8/II/54, seal 2, dated 1473 x 1474

SEAL 730
Round, 13
Letter ?I
Legend: none
HAS F8/II/55, dated 1478 x 1479

SEAL 731
Round, 11
Monogram: letter P with small letter T inside
Legend: none
HAS F8/II/56, dated 1482

SEAL 732
Round, 41
Bird with wings raised walking to right looking back to left
Legend: +SIGIL [section lost] N:
HCA Deed 1, dated 1194

SEAL 733
Round, 28
Eight-petalled stylised flower
Legend: [. . . .]COLA [.] D[. .] CA [. . . . . .]
HCA Deed 5, dated 1290
HCA Deed 9, dated 1290

SEAL 734
Round, 30
Eight-petalled stylised flower
Legend: S'NIChOLAID'LACALEWE
HCA Deed10, dated 1290
HCA Deed7, dated 1275 x 1324
HCA Deed8, dated 1275 x 1324

APPENDIX

SEAL 735
Round, 29
Eight-petalled stylised flower
Legend: [.] IOH'IS . BRVN .D' BR[. . . . .]
HCA Deed 16, dated 1300
HCA Deed 17, dated 1313
HCA Deed 15, dated 1300

SEAL 736
Round, 29
Sun with five arms
Legend: +S'PhILIPI:hOW[.]L
HCA Deed 18, dated 1290

SEAL 737
Pointed oval, 41x27
Eight-petalled stylised flower
Legend: * S' EVE : DE LA HAIORRI
HCA Deed 19, dated 1300

SEAL 738
Round, 29
Four conifer branches with pine cones in the angles
Legend: + S' WILL' : BERCHER :
HCA Deed 21, dated 1300

SEAL 739
Round, 19
Tonsured head facing left, a crescent with a pellet in upper left, to the right a star
Legend: *S'WILL'I. [.]E [. .] ?A [.] D[?C] A[?P] E [?LLI]
HCA Deed 23, dated 1300

SEAL 740
Round, 22
Eight-petalled stylised flower
Legend: + S' : ROG' : D' : ASWILLE
HCA Deed 25, dated 1319 x 1320

SEAL 741
Round, 31
Eight-petalled stylised flower
Legend: *S'IOh':DELABERNE [?T]O
HCA Deed 26, dated 1315
HCA Deed 27, dated 1315

SEAL 742
Pointed oval, 39x25
Eight-petalled stylised flower
Legend: +S'ISABEL'D'.LABERNE
HCA Deed 27, seal 2, dated 1315
HCA Deed 26, seal 2, dated 1315

SEAL 743
Round, 19
Man standing to left facing half right with right hand pointing to disk with Lamb of God held in left hand (St John the Baptist), flanked on left by ?heron and right by ?wheatsheaf, to right a kneeling suppliant figure facing left
Legend: * SIGILL' [. . . . . . .] HOV[.]G[. .]E
HCA Deed 32, seal 1, dated 1362

SEAL 744
Round, c.25
Shield with device (shears point up), a cross-tipped staff with banner emerging from top
Legend: + S' . W[. . .]GE[. . . . .]
HCA Deed 32, seal 2, dated 1362

SEAL 745
Pointed oval, 38x24
Eight-petalled stylised flower
Legend: * S' ALDIÞELENORRAIS
HCA Deed 36, dated 1290

SEAL 746
Round, 23
Eight-pointed star
Legend: S'ROB[. .]E [.] A [. . . .] RI
HCA Deed 39, dated 1317 x 1318

SEAL 747
Pointed oval, 38x24
Four conifer branches with pinecones in the angles
Legend: + S' IOVANE : BROMVED
HCA Deed 41, seal 2, dated 1317

SEAL 748
Round, 27
Eight-pointed star with a pellet in each angle
Legend: +S'WILL'DE.MVLDENhAL
HCA Deed 58, dated 1300
HCA Deed 111, dated 1275 x 1299

SEAL 749
Round, 30
Wolf's head facing right
Legend: + SIGILL' . HVGONIS DOVVEL :
HCA Deed 72, dated 1256

SEAL 750
Round, 30
Six-petalled flower with large central motif
Legend: *S'ADE:FREWIN
HCA Deed 73, dated 1290

SEAL 751
Pointed oval, 28x17
Lion rampant facing left
Legend: +S'IOhISDEBRVNEShOPE
HCA Deed 77, dated 1289

SEAL 752
Pointed oval, 36x23
Virgin and Child full-face half-length with below, beneath pointed arch, kneeling suppliant man facing right
Legend: [. . . . . .]ARDI : DE ¶ BRAVMPFOD
HCA Deed 81, dated 1290

SEAL 753
Round, 24
Crowned woman standing full-face holding up a spiked wheel (St Katherine), to the left three flowers on a long stem
Legend: [. .]NCTA : K¶ ATERINA
HCA Deed 82, dated 1349

SEAL 754
Rounded oval, 8x11
Lion walking to left
Legend: none
HCA Deed 95, dated 1425

SEAL 755
Round, 20
Ape holding an owl riding an ?ass (?goat) walking to left, stylised foliage in upper right
Legend: * MORNELASAPOV[. . . . . . .]
HCA Deed 98, dated 1337

SEAL 756
Round, 27
Eagle displayed
Legend: * S' : IOHANNIS : FIL' : RICARD'
HCA Deed 102, dated 1260 x 1230

SEAL 757
Round, 37
Stylised lily (ornate)
Legend: + SIGILLVM ROGER[.] DE HEREFORDIA :
HCA Deed 114, dated 1200 x 1230

SEAL 758
Round, c.29
Eagle displayed
Legend: + SIG[. . . . .] WALE
HCA Deed 115, dated 1230

SEAL 759
Pointed oval, 29x19
Stylised lily
Legend: +S'.CRISTINE:FIL:WILL' [.]
HCA Deed 269, seal 2, dated 1262
HCA Deed 118, dated 1262
HCA Deed 124, seal 2, dated 1261
HCA Deed 261, seal 2, dated 1262

SEAL 760
Round, 30
Four conifer branches with pinecones in the angles
Legend: + S' OSBAR' . GALANT
HCA Deed 119, dated 1308

SEAL 761
Rounded oval, 14x13
Letter R
Legend: none
HCA Deed 121, dated 1476

APPENDIX

SEAL 762
Unknown, 13
Three-lobed leaf
Legend: none
HCA Deed 121, seal 2, dated 1476

SEAL 763
Round, 19
Stag's head full-face with a cross between the antlers
Legend: illegible
HCA Deed 121, seal 3, dated 1476

SEAL 764
Round, 34
Stylised lily
Legend: +SIGILL':MATILLISFIL'EhVGONIS:
HCA Deed 122, dated 1200 x 1230

SEAL 765
Pointed oval, 30x19
Crescent with sun above
Legend: +S'ALISCIDLAMOR
HCA Deed 268, dated 1262
HCA Deed 261, dated 1262
HCA Deed 124, dated 1261

SEAL 766
Round, 27
Stylised plant with three fronds
Legend: +S'RADVL[.]ILE BARVNDMOR'
HCA Deed 126, dated 1300

SEAL 767
Pointed oval, 32x22
Stylised lily
Legend: +S'MARGERIE [.] DELAMORE
HCA Deed 127, dated 1262

SEAL 768
Pointed oval, 41x25
Stylised lily
Legend: +S'MARGERIDEMORE:
HCA Deed 127, dated 1262

SEAL 769
Rounded oval, 21x17
Head (?of man) facing right
Legend: [.] S' IOHE DE [. . . .]
HCA Deed 133, dated 1404

SEAL 770
Round, 23
Shield of arms (on a chevron engrailed between three leopard's heads, a charge), stylised foliage above
Legend: +S'DNI.[section lost]VERNOVN
HCA Deed 137, dated 1425

SEAL 771
Round, 21
Within a hexagon, a lion's head full-face
Legend: illegible
HCA Deed 138, dated 1362

SEAL 772
Round, 27
Stylised lily
Legend: [. . .]GIL' STEFFANIFIL' [. . .]O[. . .]
HCA Deed 141, dated 1230

SEAL 773
Round, 23
Within a cusped border, a shield of arms (a chevron between three animal (?bull) heads caboshed)
Legend: *SIG[. . . . .]
HCA Deed 144, dated 1398

SEAL 774
Round, 16
Crowned letter W, three small pellets to left and right
Legend: none
HCA Deed 145, dated 1403

SEAL 775
Round, 26
Eight-petalled stylised flower
Legend: S'.STEFANI.FINT
HCA Deed 148, dated 1270

SEAL 776
Pointed oval, 32x21
Foliate stem in inverted 'S' shape with two trefoil leaves
Legend: + S' ROB'TI : BOKE CAPLL'I
HCA Deed 149, dated 1225 x 1275

SEAL 777
Round, 22
Squirrel facing left
Legend: *[. . . . .]
HCA Deed 154, dated 1342

SEAL 778
Round, 34
Within a cusped octofoil, a shield of arms (three lions passant guardant)
Legend: + S'BALLI[.]O[. . . .] IVITATIS [. . . .]FORDIE
HCA Deed 2022, dated 1494
HCA Deed 154, seal 2, dated 1342

SEAL 779
Rounded oval, 22x20
Gem: head of ?woman facing right
Legend: + SIGILLVM ROGERI
HCA Deed 156, dated 1200 x 1215

SEAL 780
Round, 18
Stylised lily
Legend: +SIGILL' NICOLAI DE BREMMESBERGE
HCA Deed 159, dated 1201

SEAL 781
Pointed oval, 76x61
Building with a rounded-arched doorway flanked by round windows and a conical tower above, to the left a conical tower with five windows and rounded apsefoliate motifs in field in upper left and right
Legend: [. . . . . .]E.MARIA.ET S [section lost]RDENS'EC [section lost]
HCA Deed 1092, dated 1173 x 1182
HCA Deed 159, seal 2, front, dated 1201
HCA Deed 233, dated 1190
HCA Deed 786, dated 1234 x 1247
HCA Deed 274, dated 1186 x 1200
HCA Deed 793, front, dated 1248

SEAL 782
Pointed oval, 40x25
Crowned man seated full-face holding an orb out in his right hand, a sceptre in his left hand
Legend: +SIGILLVMCA[section lost] hEREFORDIE
HCA Deed 159, seal 2, back, dated 1201
HCA Deed 793, back, dated 1248

SEAL 783
Round, 28
Eight-petalled stylised flower with rays in the angles
Legend: + S' NICHOLAI DEVENES
HCA Deed 172, dated 1262

SEAL 784
Hexagonal, 12x10
Crowned letter W
Legend: none
HCA Deed 184, dated 1423

SEAL 785
Rounded oval, 13x9
Crowned letter W, stylised branches to left and right
Legend: none
HCA Deed 185, dated 1441

SEAL 786
Octagonal, 13x14
Merchant mark on a shield (includes letters r,?e), long cross-tipped staff with banner emerging from the top
Legend: none
HCA Deed 188, dated 1477

SEAL 787
Round, 30
Eight-petalled stylised flower
Legend: *.S'WILL'I CLEMENT.
HCA Deed 190, dated 1272

APPENDIX

SEAL 788
Round, 28
Eight-petalled stylised flower
Legend: *S'hVGONISCLEMENT
HCA Deed 190, seal 2, dated 1272

SEAL 789
Round, 25
Twelve-petalled stylised flower (six large and six small petals)
Legend: * S' ROGERI DELVDEDE
HCA Deed 196, dated 1316

SEAL 790
Pointed oval, 33x23
Eight-petalled stylised flower
Legend: * S' CRISTA' DE PIPA
HCA Deed 204, dated 1275 x 1299

SEAL 791
Drop-shaped, 31x30
Stylised lily
Legend: +S [.] G[. . . .] AL[.]ERIPAPPE
HCA Deed 205, dated 1199

SEAL 792
Round, 18
Two hands clasped, stars to left and right, trefoil foliate motif above
Legend: * T[. .]ET[. . . .]V
HCA Deed 208, seal 1, dated 1368

SEAL 793
Round, c.22
Head of ?cow full-face with long foliate stems emerging from its mouth and enclosing the head
Legend: none
HCA Deed 208, seal 2, dated 1368

SEAL 794
Rounded oval, 22x16
To the left, crowned woman standing facing half right holding a spiked wheel up in her left hand (St Katherine), to the right a kneeling suppliant man in clerical dress facing left with letter R?I in centre, foliate stems in the field
Legend: AR[. . .][?K]INEPRIERE[. . . . .] OYSEYTANYE
HCA Deed 211, seal 1, dated 1371

SEAL 795
Round, c.19
Crowned woman standing full-face holding a spiked wheel up in her left hand
(St Katherine)
Legend: * S. WA[?L]T[. . .] [Section lost][.]
HCA Deed 211, seal 2, dated 1371

SEAL 796
Round, c.24
Within a cusped border, nimbed man in short robe standing full-face with right hand pointing to Lamb of God in roundel in his left hand (St John the Baptist), four stars around his head, to the left letter W, to the right letter ?K
Legend: [section lost] [.]e me:
HCA Deed 211, seal 3, dated 1371

SEAL 797
Round, 19
Monogram tb
Legend: none
HCA Deed 211, seal 4, dated 1371

SEAL 798
Round, c.17
Within a cusped quatrefoil, bird walking to the right with foliage in its beak
Legend: [. .]RAVE[.]LE[.]A[.] [section lost]
HCA Deed 211, seal 6, dated 1371

SEAL 799
Round, 32
Four conifer branches with a leaf in each angle
Legend: +S':RICARDI [.] OCVLE
HCA Deed 213, dated 1260

SEAL 800
Round, 35
Stylised lily
Legend:
+SIGILL'ALIZFIL':CRISTINEBIþEWALLE
HCA Deed 214, dated 1200 x 1250

SEAL 801
Round, 34
Stylised lily-type plant
Legend: +SIGILL'.SI [.]ONIS DE hIDA
HCA Deed 216, dated 1200 x 1299

SEAL 802
Round, 32
Stylised tree with three foliate branches
Legend: S'IOh'IS.FIL'.ROG.DE.BRVN-SO[?H]P
HCA Deed 218, dated 1311

SEAL 803
Pointed oval, 30x20
Eight-petalled stylised flower
Legend: +S'IOhISLE [. . . . .]
HCA Deed 219, dated 1317

SEAL 804
Pointed oval, 33x23
Head facing left, 'Manus Dei' above
Legend: +S'WILLELMI.
DEEVEShAMCAPELLANI
HCA Deed 220, dated 1290 x 1300

SEAL 805
Round, 25
Eight-petalled stylised flower
Legend: * S' WILLELMI.CLEMENT
HCA Deed 221, dated 1271

SEAL 806
Round, 45
Armoured man on a horse galloping to the right
Legend: ¶ SIGILL' ALES[. . . .] ?FI[. .] WINESTV[.]
HCA Deed 227, dated 1175 x 1199

SEAL 807
Pointed oval, 36x22
Eight-petalled stylised flower
Legend: + S' HAWISIE . ChAVMPONEIS
HCA Deed 231, dated 1225 x 1275
HCA Deed 228, dated 1225 x 1275

SEAL 808
Round, 29
Cross fleury with four elongated pellets in the angles
Legend: * S' NICH'I : FIL[. .]OG'I : SVTORIS
HCA Deed 232, dated 1271

SEAL 809
Rounded oval, 39x33
Gem: To the left a lion leaping right, to right a figure standing facing left with right arm outstretched (?holding a spear), two plants below, an object above
Legend: +SIGILL'IOh[. . . . .]R
HCA Deed 234, front, dated 1225 x 1275

SEAL 810
Rounded oval, 24x20
Gem: Figure standing facing right with arms outstretched, to the right a ?kneeling figure ?facing left
Legend: AVEMA[. . . .]AMEN
HCA Deed 234, back, dated 1225 x 1275

SEAL 811
Round, 32
Stylised flower formed by small pierced cinquefoil with pellet in centre surrounded by nine rays with nine small pellets between them
Legend: + S' WALTERI FIL' WALTERI SIVAR
HCA Deed 239, dated 1200 x 1299
HCA Deed 235, dated 1225 x 1275

SEAL 812
Round, 22
Within an ornate border, a shield of arms (a ?cross with An object in dexter chief)
Legend: *SIG[. . . .]M:RICARDI:PERRERS
HCA Deed 236, dated 1342

APPENDIX

SEAL 813
Round, 31
Eagle with wings outstretched facing half left, head turned back to right
Legend: + SIGILL' : RICARDI : FIL'. PE[. .] I : D' WIZ
HCA Deed 240, dated 1200

SEAL 814
Pointed oval, c.28x19
Woman standing full-face (very stylised)
Legend: [. . .] MATILDE.DE: [. . .]ENhVLL'
HCA Deed 245, dated 1200 x 1299

SEAL 815
Rounded oval, c.24x20
Noli me Tangere (Risen Christ to right)
Legend: * [. . . . . . .]E[.]S [section lost] * P[. . . . . . .]SE[. . .]
HCA Deed 250, dated 1342

SEAL 816
Pointed oval, 29x20
Uncertain; ?human head full-face (very stylised)
Legend: + S' CRISTINI [. . . .]O[. . .]
HCA Deed 268, seal 2, dated 1262

SEAL 817
Pointed oval, 30x20
Crescent
Legend: [.]S':ALIS:FIL'.WILLAM
HCA Deed 269, dated 1262

SEAL 818
Pointed oval, 30x19
Eight-petalled stylised flower
Legend: +S'ANGNETIS:FIL'WILELMI
HCA Deed 269, seal 3, dated 1262

SEAL 819
Pointed oval, 34x22
Bird walking to left with foliage in its beak
Legend: * S' WALTERIWALES
HCA Deed 280, dated 1300

SEAL 820
Round, 68
Man standing facing left holding large armorial shield (paly) before him and a sword up in his right hand, to right a lion facing left springing up to attack man
Legend: [. .]GILLV [section lost] ER [section lost] C?HEL [section lost]
HCA Deed 775, dated 1148 x 1161

SEAL 821
Rounded oval, 31x27
Gem: figure mounted on a hippocampus galloping to right
Legend: [. . . . . .]V' NIChOLAIDE SCA' BRIGIDA
HCA Deed 778, dated 1175 x 1205

SEAL 822
Round, 30
Stylised lily
Legend: + SIGILL' GERALDI MARSCALLI
HCA Deed 780, dated 1200 x 1250

SEAL 823
Pointed oval, 44x27
Indistinct
Legend: [section lost] LL' hE [section lost] E T?E?L
HCA Deed 781, dated 1225 x 1230

SEAL 824
Pointed oval, 47x27
?Tonsured man vested as a deacon standing full-face on a corbel holding an object (?book) before him
Legend: +SIGILL':hELIEDECANIDPEN-CRA:[.]:D':TETEhal'
HCA Deed 783, dated 1225

SEAL 825
Pointed oval, 45x29
?Tonsured man in a long robe standing full-face, in his right hand a ?document, in his left hand an object
Legend: +SIGILLVM RIC[.]RDI AR [. . . . .]DIACON[section lost]ENSIS
HCA Deed 784, dated 1164 x 1179

SEAL 826
Round, 50
Bird with wings raised walking right
Legend: +SIG[ill]l'
HVGONISDEBAREVILLA
HCA Deed 785, dated 1150 x 1199

SEAL 827
Pointed oval, 36x23
Virgin and Child seated facing left, to left a kneeling suppliant tonsured man facing right, letters MARIA in upper left
Legend: + SIGILLVM IOhAN⸹ NIS FOLIOT
HCA Deed 787, dated 1234 x 1247

SEAL 828
Round, 64
Man holding a hawk up on his left hand on a horse walking to the left
Legend: [. . . .]ILLVM : RICARDI : DE ALCRINTVN
HCA Deed 791, dated 1150 x 1199

SEAL 829
Round, 48
Armoured man on a horse galloping to the right
Legend: +SIGILLV[.]⸹ RICARDI ⸹ ESCOTOT⸹
HCA Deed 792, dated 1198

SEAL 830
Pointed oval, 73x46
Mitred man vested for Mass standing full-face on a corbel blessing with his right hand, holding a pastoral staff in his left hand, to left and right small niches each with a head full-face, all on a diapered field
Legend: ⸹ RADULPVS[. . . .]RACIA[. . . . . .] RDENSIS[. .]ISCOPVS
HCA Deed 795, front, dated 1236

SEAL 831
Pointed oval, 42x25
Within a pointed arch, Virgin and Child half-length facing half right, with below, beneath a cusped arch, a half-length mitred suppliant man facing left
Legend: AVE [. . .] IAGRAPLENADOMINVSTEC
HCA Deed 795, back, dated 1236

SEAL 832
Round, 35
Bird with wings raised walking to left
Legend: +SIGILL'ROBERTIFIL'ROWELAN
HCA Deed 796, dated 1212

SEAL 833
Round, 68
Armoured man with an armorial shield (a chevron) on a horse galloping to the right
Legend: ⸹ + SIGILL[. . . .]BERTI DE ⸹ BERCKELAY ⸹
HCA Deed 797, front, dated 1216 x 1250

SEAL 834
Rounded oval, 34x37
Gem: man holding ?sword in his left hand, blade resting on his shoulder, on a horse galloping to the left
Legend: + SIGILLVM ROBERTI DE BERKELAI
HCA Deed 797, back, dated 1216 x 1250

SEAL 835
Unknown, nm
Indistinct
Legend: [section lost] SR [section lost]
HCA Deed 798, dated 1123 x 1199

SEAL 836
Unknown, 37x35
Hind legs of a horse (fragment)
Legend: [section lost] DEL [section lost]
HCA Deed 798, dated 1123 x 1199

SEAL 837
Pointed oval, nm
Tonsured man wearing cloak fastened at front seated full-face holding a book up in his left hand (object in right hand lost)
Legend: N/A

APPENDIX

NLW PENRICE: GLAM/129, front, dated 1205 x 1224
HCA Deed 799, dated 1205 x 1216
NLW PENRICE: GLAM/132, front, dated 1205 x 1224

SEAL 838
Round, 71
Armoured man on a horse walking to the right
Legend: [. . . . . .] hE?NR[.]CIDEPOME [section lost]
HCA Deed 1604, dated 1165 x 1180
HCA Deed 800, dated 1165 x 1180

SEAL 839
Pointed oval, 42x32
Three-quarter length man standing full-face vested for Mass holding a crozier in his right hand, a ?book in his left hand held before him, to left a crescent, to right a six-pointed star
Legend: [. . . . . . .]M ABB[. . . . .] SA[. . . .]
HCA Deed 801, front, dated 1236

SEAL 840
Pointed oval, 27x19
Lamb of God facing right
Legend: + SIGILLV[.] SECRETI
HCA Deed 801, back, dated 1236

SEAL 841
Pointed oval, 28x19
Stylised lily
Legend: [. .] AVISSE:RUDDVC
HCA Deed 1079, dated 1270

SEAL 842
Round, 34
Eagle displayed
Legend: +SIG[. . . . .]BERTIDEChANDOS
HCA Deed 1080, dated 1262 x 1271

SEAL 843
Round, 32
Small central quatrefoil with five long curved stems emerging, each terminating in a trefoil

Legend: + S' WATERI [. . .] DENEWEY
HCA Deed 1081, dated 1253

SEAL 844
Round, 46
Hand and arm emerging from the right holding a key
Legend: +S [section lost] IS
HCA Deed 1082, dated 1233

SEAL 845
Pointed oval, c.43x32
Virgin and Child seated full-face on a bench beneath an ornate architectural canopy with below, beneath a trefoil arch, a half-length mitred suppliant man facing left
Legend: ¶ VIRGO [.]ET [section lost] [. . . . .]RGO
HCA Deed 1084, seal 1, dated 1261

SEAL 846
Pointed oval, c.31x24
To the left a bearded man seated facing right with right hand raised, to the right a man seated facing left with left hand raised, right hand leaning on a Tau-cross staff, a bird descending from above with a large object in its beak (St Paul the Hermit and St Anthony), with below, beneath trefoil arch, the tonsured head and shoulders of a suppliant man
Legend: ¶ S' PRIS [. . . . .]ER[.]
HCA Deed 1084, seal 2, dated 1261

SEAL 847
Round, 20
Hawk facing right perched on a gloved hand emerging from upper right
Legend: *S'NICOLE.LESE[?C]UI[.]ER [.]
HCA Deed 1470, dated 1273

SEAL 848
Round, 22
Three-quarter length tonsured man standing full-face holding two large keys up in his left hand (St Peter), three ears of wheat on stems to left
Legend: [.]ANCTVS ¶ [. .]TRV[.]
HCA Deed 1474, dated 1350

SEAL 849
Rounded oval, c.30xc.24
Within a cusped octofoil, a shield of arms (on a chevron bordeau three mullets, a bourdeau engrailed) placed on an eagle displayed
Legend: * SIGILL[. .] TH[. . . . .]YT
HCA Deed 1475, seal 1, dated 1366

SEAL 850
Round, 25
Within a cusped octofoil, Virgin and Child seated full-face
Legend: * SIGILLVM § WILLELMI § WROTHE §
HCA Deed 1475, seal 2, dated 1366

SEAL 851
Round, 33
Plant with three branches tipped with lobbed leaves
Legend: +S'RICARDID'MEDIMOR
HCA Deed 1490, dated 1225 x 1275
HCA Deed 1484, dated 1275 x 1324

SEAL 852
Round, 18
Crossed hands, three leaves above
Legend: +IESVS[. . .]EAM
HCA Deed 1486, dated 1323

SEAL 853
Round, 26
Within a cusped quatrefoil, a shield of arms (on a chevron, three ?roses) hanging from a tree
Legend: ¶ Sigillum . Iohannis . Haro[. .]
HCA Deed 1491, dated 1388

SEAL 854
Round, c.20
Shield of arms (a ?Lion rampant)
Legend: [. . . . .]ome : mo[. . . .]
HCA Deed 1491, seal 2, dated 1388

SEAL 855
Round, 21
Within a cusped quatrefoil, a nimbed and winged figure standing full-face holding a spear in left hand with the point in the mouth of a dragon lying beneath figure's feet (St Michael), to the right a kneeling suppliant figure facing left
Legend: [. . . .]le [. . . . . . .]I[. . . . .] EL
HCA Deed 1491, seal 3, dated 1388

SEAL 856
Round, c.21
Within a cusped quatrefoil, monogram IG
Legend: * S' I[. . . . .]ston
HCA Deed 1491, seal 4, dated 1388

SEAL 857
Round, 10
Letter A
Legend: none
HCA Deed 1491, seal 5, dated 1388

SEAL 858
Round, 11
Crowned letter W
Legend:
HCA Deed 1493, dated 1404

SEAL 859
Round, 14
Stylised lily
Legend: N/A
HCA Deed 1493, seal 2, dated 1404

SEAL 860
Pointed oval, 45x29l
Within an ornate architectural niche, Virgin and Child standing full-face
Legend: SIGILL': COE':VICARIOR [. .] ECCLESIE : HEREFORD'IS'
HCA Deed 1495, dated 1413

SEAL 861
Seventh Great Seal of Edward III
HCA Deed 1498, dated 1368

SEAL 862
Pointed oval, c.46x32
Nimbed man in long tunic crucified on

saltire cross (St Andrew) flanked by two six-pointed stars, with below a shield of arms (a fess, on chief a ?label of five points)
Legend: § DAVI[. . . . .]A ME[. . . . .] EPISCOP[.] AD : CA[. . .]S
HCA Deed 1504, dated 1309

SEAL 863
Pointed oval, 37x24
Within an architectural canopy, a man standing full-length facing half left holding a ?cup with snake in his right hand and a ?book up in his left hand (?St John), a bird walking left below
Legend: [. . . . . . .] PRIOR [section lost] DE KEN [. . .] RT [. .]
HCA Deed 1505, dated 1309

SEAL 864
Pointed oval, c.51xc.24
Mitred man vested for Mass standing full-face blessing with his right hand, holding a crozier in his left hand
Legend: [fragment only] SC
HCA Deed 1509, dated 1231 x 1247

SEAL 865
Pointed oval, 67x42
Mitred man vested for Mass standing on a corbel blessing with his right hand, holding a pastoral staff in his left hand
Legend: [. . . . .]:CADVCAN [.] PISCOPI:BANGORENS
HCA Deed 1514, dated 1225 x 1235

SEAL 866
Round, 25
Four-petalled stylised flower with four six-pointed stars in the angles
Legend: +S'LEWELINAPOWEIN
HCA Deed 1523, dated 1314

SEAL 867
Round, 23
Cross potent with six-pointed stars in angles
Legend: +S'CRADO [. . . . .]GAN
HCA Deed 1523, seal 2, dated 1314

SEAL 868
Round, nm
Lion standing facing right with its tail curled between its legs, ornate foliate motifs in the field
Legend: [section lost] R ⁊ [. . .] [section lost]
HCA Deed 1602, dated 1148 x 1155

SEAL 869
Round, 27
Plant with three conifer-type branches
Legend: + SIGILL' WILL' [. .]IEMEN
HCA Deed 2002, dated 1225

SEAL 870
Round, 38
Lion walking to right
Legend: +SIGILLSTEFANIFIL[. .] MARIE
HCA Deed 2005, dated 1200 x 1299

SEAL 871
Round, 25
Scallop shell
Legend: + SECRET' P'SON [. . . . .] ARDES[.]'
HCA Deed 2003, dated 1225

SEAL 872
Round, 35
Bird with wings raised facing left
Legend: +SIGI [. .] L'SAMSONIS
HCA Deed 2006, dated 1225

SEAL 873
Round, 19
Shield of arms: (fess, in chief three objects)
Legend: +SIGILLVM [.] SABELE
HCA Deed 2007, dated 1225

SEAL 874
Round, 30
Plant with three stems, central conifer-type flanked by two ivy-type leaves
Legend: + SIG' XPINE : FIL'E : RADULFI
HCA Deed 2014, dated 1225 x 1275

SEAL 875
Round, 32
Plant with four pairs of stems each tipped with lobbed leaves, three small ?leaves at top
Legend: +SIGILL' WILL'MIFIL'WARNERI
HCA Deed 2017, dated 1225 x 1250

SEAL 876
Round, 28
Bird with wings raised and ?foliage in its beak walking to right
Legend: +S' IOhAMMISDEGL[. .]ERN[.]
HCA Deed 2019, dated 1275 x 1299

SEAL 877
Pointed oval, 63x44
Cross formée within a circular legend band containing the text: +SIT NOMEN DOMINI BENEDICT, below, a crescent enclosing a seven pointed star with, to left and right, a seven pointed star
Legend: +SIGILL' DO?M' ELEMO[. . .] ARIE:SCI:A[.]ELBERTI
HCA Deed 2026, dated 1558
HCA Deed 2025, dated 1542

SEAL 878
Round, 21
Shield of arms (three ?martlets on a bend engrailed between two mullets)
Legend: * S[. .] WILLELMI SEN[.]LER
HCA Deed 2028, dated 1406

SEAL 879
Round, 16
Letter I between two stylised branches
Legend: none
HCA Deed 2028, seal 2, dated 1406

SEAL 880
Pointed oval, 73x49
Mitred man vested for Mass and wearing a pallium standing full-face on a corbel blessing with his right hand, holding a pastoral staff in the left hand, three foiled recesses on either side of man, the central two containing heads full-face, all on a diapered field
Legend: [section lost]AN [. . . .]ENSIS AR [. . .]EPISCOP [section lost]
HCA Deed 2036, front, dated 1234

SEAL 881
Pointed oval, 54x32
Martyrdom of Thomas Becket, with below, beneath an arch, a suppliant mitred man facing right
Legend: ¶ EADMUND [. .] DOCEAT:MORS:MEA:DE:TIMEAT:
HCA Deed 2036, back, dated 1234

SEAL 882
Pointed oval, c.65x45
Mitred man vested for Mass standing full-face on a corbel blessing with right hand, holding a crozier in left hand, to the left a sun, with a trefoil arch below
Legend: ROBERT[. . .]A GRA : SAL¶ [. .] BIRIENS : EPISCOP[. .]
HCA Deed 2037, front, dated 1229 x 1246

SEAL 883
Pointed oval, 47x28
Beneath a trefoil canopy, Virgin and Child three-quarter length facing half left with foliate stems to left and right, with below, beneath a rounded arch, half-length suppliant mitred man with crozier facing right
Legend: § SALVE SCA' PARENS : ENIXA PVER PEREGVM
HCA Deed 2037, back, dated 1229 x 1246

SEAL 884
Pointed oval, c.59x44
Mitred man vested for Mass standing full-face on a corbel blessing with right hand, holding a crozier in left hand, to either side a cusped oval with a building with a central tower, all on a diapered field
Legend: [. . . . . . .]DER DEI GRA [.]OVE [section lost] EN[. . . .]E[. . . .]PIS[. . . . .]
HCA Deed 2038, front, dated 1225 x 1238

SEAL 885
Pointed oval, 33x22

APPENDIX

Gem: naked ?man standing facing half left leaning on staff held in left hand, playing a ?pipe held up in right hand, to left a small quadruped (?goat) facing right leaping up towards figure
Legend: [. . . . . . .] MVNDOSIS MVDVS INISTO
HCA Deed 2038, back, dated 1225 x 1238

SEAL 886
Pointed oval, 73x46
Mitred man vested for Mass standing full-face on a corbel blessing with right hand, holding a pastoral staff in the left hand
Legend: HVGO DEI GRAC[section lost] NSIS EPISCOPI
HCA Deed 2041, front, dated 1229 x 1254

SEAL 887
Pointed oval, 51x31
To the right a nimbed female standing full-face blessing with her right hand and holding a ?pastoral staff in her left hand (St Etheldreda), to the left a nimbed man standing full-face holding a sceptre in his right hand and ?two arrows up in his left hand (St Edmund), between them an ornate spire, a nimbed head in a compartment above, with below, beneath a trefoil arch, a suppliant mitred man facing right
Legend: + ME IVVET EADM[. . .] E [. . . .] DE SIM PRECE MVNDVS
HCA Deed 2041, back, dated 1229 x 1254

SEAL 888
Pointed oval, 69x43
Mitred man vested for Mass standing full-face on a corbel, blessing with right hand, holding pastoral staff in left hand
Legend: + IOSCELINVS DEI GRATIA ⁋ BATHO[. .]ENSIS [. .]ISCOPVS
HCA Deed 2042, front, dated 1226

SEAL 889
Pointed oval, 50x30
Virgin and Child seated full-face on platform supported by two robed men, both facing in, with below, beneath trefoil arch, a half-length mitred suppliant man facing left
Legend: § [. . .]: TIBI : PATRONI S[. . . .] OCELINE : BONI
HCA Deed 2042, back, dated 1226

SEAL 890
Pointed oval, 78x46
Mitred man vested for Mass standing full-face on a corbel blessing with right hand, holding crozier in the left hand
Legend: § EVSTACHIVS : DEI : G[. . . .]A ⁋ LONDONIENSIS : EPISCOPVS
HCA Deed 2043, dated 1226

SEAL 891
Pointed oval, 49x29
Nimbed and ?bearded man standing full-face on a corbel holding a sword up in his right hand and a book in his left hand (St Paul)
Legend: + EVSTACIAM : PAVLI DOCET ⁋ L[.]BER AD[. . . .] ⁋ [. .]IS
HCA Deed 2043, dated 1226

SEAL 892
Round, 17
Lion rampant facing left
Legend: *S'YORWARThAP[. . .]
NLW BACBYD/1, dated 1275 x 1324

SEAL 893
Round, 25
Plant with seven branches
Legend: +S'LEWELMI:F':YORVARTh
NLW BACBYD/1, seal 2, dated 1275 x 1324

SEAL 894
Round, 25
Plant with seven branches
Legend: +S'YORVARTh.F'.YORVARTh
NLW BACBYD/1, seal 3, dated 1275 x 1324

SEAL 895
Round, 26
Four conifer branches
Legend: S' [section lost] I :F' YORVA [section lost]
NLW BACBYD/1, seal 4, dated 1275 x 1324

SEAL 896
Round, c.65
Armoured man on a horse with armorial caparisons (lozengy) galloping to the right
Legend: lost
NLW BACBYD/2, front, dated 1346 x 1356

SEAL 897
Round, 37
Within an ornate octofoil a shield of arms (three lozenges with a bourdure)
Legend: *S'. Willi' . d' . monteacuto co'itis . Sar' . dni' man'ie d' dy'begh'
NLW BACBYD/2, back, dated 1346 x 1356

SEAL 898
Round, 9
Eagle's head erased
Legend: none
NLW BACBYD/5, dated 1486

SEAL 899
Round, 41
Shield of arms (quarterly: 1, 4, barry, in chief three torteaux; 2, 3, quarterly, 1, 4 a maunch, 2, 3, barry of eight, an orle of ten martlets), a helm with chapeaux and crest (wings) above, supporters (wodehouses), trees in outer field.
Legend: illegible, partially lost
NLW BACBYD/519, dated 1433
NLW BACBYD/219, dated 1417 x 1418
NLW BACBYD/51, dated 1431

SEAL 900
Round, nm
Deputed Great Seal for North Wales (judicial seal); reverse lost
NLW BACBYD/94, dated 1428

SEAL 901
Round, 16
Scallop shell
Legend: none
NLW BACBYD/111, dated 1486

SEAL 902
Rounded oval, 13x9
Dragon facing left
Legend: none
NLW BACBYD/112, dated 1487

SEAL 903
Rounded oval, 14x12
Four diagonal lines (three top to base)
Legend: none
NLW BACBYD/168, dated 1476

SEAL 904
Round, nm
?Shield of arms (charge lost)
Legend: none
NLW BACBYD/220, seal 1, dated 1418

SEAL 905
Rounded oval, c.23xc.21
Heart with crown above and cross below, ?letter ?I to left, ?letter t to right, small quatrefoils in lower left and right
Legend: none
NLW BACBYD/220, seal 2, dated 1418

SEAL 906
Round, 82
Shield of arms: (Quarterly, 1, 4: barry with escutcheon (blazon lost); 2, 3: cross) with supporters (greyhounds), coronet above.
Legend: +Sigillu' hen [. . . . . .] [section lost] dei gra [section lost] [. . .] comitat': [. .] : wa [. . .]
NLW BACBYD/351, dated 1487

SEAL 907
Round, 14
?Griffin (?dog) seated facing left, ?animal (?object) in lower left
Legend: none
NLW BACBYD/362, dated 1476

SEAL 908
Octagonal, 12x10
Letter h
Legend: none

APPENDIX

NLW BRONWYDD/780, dated 1483
NLW BRONWYDD/1347, dated 1493

SEAL 909
Round, 10
Letters ?F P
Legend: none
NLW BRONWYDD/781, dated 1520

SEAL 910
Round, 11
Letter ?B (?A)
Legend: none
NLW BRONWYDD/781, seal 3, dated 1520

SEAL 911
Round, 12
Letter P
Legend: none
NLW BRONWYDD/793, dated 1467 x 1468

SEAL 912
Rounded oval, 11x10
Virgin and Child seated full-face (very odd style)
Legend: none
NLW BRONWYDD/798, dated 1484

SEAL 913
Round, 12
Two interlaced elongated links forming a cross (Monogram ?d ?d)
Legend: none
NLW BRONWYDD/1054, dated 1473 x 1474
NLW BRONWYDD/1337, dated 1463
NLW BRONWYDD/799, dated 1475

SEAL 914
Rounded oval, 14x13
Shield of arms (two bars)
Legend: none
NLW BRONWYDD/802, seal 1, dated 1406

SEAL 915
Square, 10x10
Pelican in its piety facing left
Legend: none
NLW BRONWYDD/802, seal 2, dated 1406

SEAL 916
Rounded oval, 12x8
Gem: figure with wings in long robe standing facing left
Legend: none
NLW BRONWYDD/802, seal 3, dated 1406

SEAL 917
Round, 14
Indistinct
Legend: none
NLW BRONWYDD/804, seal 1 and 2, dated 1476

SEAL 918
Round, 11
?Letters ?IH
Legend: none
NLW BRONWYDD/806, dated 1465

SEAL 919
Round, 13
?Letter A (?abstract pattern similar to Arabic 4)
Legend: none
NLW BRONWYDD/808, dated 1472 x 1473

SEAL 920
Undetermined, c.17x16
Crowned h
Legend: none
NLW BRONWYDD/813, dated 1483

SEAL 921
Round, 9x10
Letter W
Legend: none
NLW BRONWYDD/818, dated 1535

SEAL 922
Rounded oval, 14x11
Letter R, stylised branch to left
Legend: none
NLW BRONWYDD/819, dated 1456

SEAL 923
Round, 20
Shield of arms (lion rampant)
Legend: [. . .] [section lost] W[?R] [. . .]
NLW BRONWYDD/820, dated 1449

SEAL 924
Scutiform, 16x14
On a shield, ?saddle-tree with stirrup below
Legend: none
NLW BRONWYDD/821, dated 1427

SEAL 925
Round, 12
Letter R
Legend: none
NLW BRONWYDD/822, dated 1480

SEAL 926
Unknown (?round), c.13
Letter ?W, stylised branch above
Legend: none
NLW BRONWYDD/823, dated 1406

SEAL 927
Rounded oval, 14x10
Gem: man in short cloak standing facing right holding a long pole over his right shoulder, to right a small figure in a short ?tunic (?short cloak) standing facing left, a small ?altar between them
Legend: [. . . .]G[. .]T[. . . .]S[. . .]
NLW BRONWYDD/824, seal 1, dated 1428

SEAL 928
Round, 11
Letter ?W (?M)
Legend: none
NLW BRONWYDD/824, seal 2, dated 1428

SEAL 929
Round nm
Seal of the Chancery of Pembroke
NLW BRONWYDD/826, dated 1444

SEAL 930
Rounded oval, 14x11
Pelican in piety, facing left
Legend: none
NLW BRONWYDD/827, dated 1455

SEAL 931
Round, 22
Lamb of God facing right, stylised foliage to left and stylised tendril to the right
Legend: none
NLW BRONWYDD/828, dated 1370
NLW PITORD/467, dated 1366 x 1367

SEAL 932
Round? (fragment) nm
Seal of Chancery of Pembroke
NLW BRONWYDD/891, dated 1523 x 1524
NLW BRONWYDD/1415, dated 1510

SEAL 933
Round, 22
Shield of arms (three lions passant on a bend cotised) hanging from a branch with two ?wyverns as supporters
Legend: ❡ WILL[. . . . .] R[. . .]
NLW BRONWYDD/943, dated 1508
NLW BRONWYDD/942, dated 1508

SEAL 934
Octagonal, 15x13
Merchant mark (includes inverted Y letters I, M)
Legend: none
NLW BRONWYDD/946, seal 2, dated 1499 x 1500
NLW BRONWYDD/974, dated 1497 x 1498
NLW BRONWYDD/944, dated 1498

APPENDIX

SEAL 935
Rounded oval, 10x12
Stag walking to left
Legend: none
NLW BRONWYDD/946, seal 1, dated
1499 x 1500

SEAL 936
Unknown (?round), *c*.11
Illegible
Legend: none
NLW BRONWYDD/947, dated 1504

SEAL 937
Round, 13x11
Shield of arms (?stag's head) on a two-headed eagle
Legend: none
NLW BRONWYDD/948, dated 1508

SEAL 938
Rounded oval, 14x12
Eagle displayed
Legend: none
NLW BRONWYDD/951, dated 1508 x 1509

SEAL 939
Round, 16
Quadruped facing left
Legend: none
NLW BRONWYDD/953, seal 3, dated 1508
NLW BRONWYDD/953, dated 1508

SEAL 940
Round, 17
Shield of arms (lion rampant)
Legend: none
NLW BRONWYDD/953, seal 2, dated 1508
NLW BRONWYDD/992, dated 1508

SEAL 941
Unknown, nm
Stylised lily
Legend: none
NLW BRONWYDD/953, seal 3, dated 1508

SEAL 942
Unknown
NLW BRONWYDD/953, seal 5, dated 1508

SEAL 943
Rounded oval, 11x9
Stylised lily
Legend: none
NLW BRONWYDD/954, dated 1506

SEAL 944
Round, 13
Geometric pattern: diamond with, extending from each point, an additional diamond
Legend: none
NLW BRONWYDD/955, dated 1506

SEAL 945
Round, 17
Within an ornate border a ?shield of arms (charge illegible)
Legend: none
NLW BRONWYDD/957, dated 1506

SEAL 946
Rounded oval, 11x14
Letter ?B
Legend: none
NLW BRONWYDD/958, dated 1503

SEAL 947
Round, 15
Letters hC
Legend: none
NLW BRONWYDD/961, dated 1486

SEAL 948
Unknown, nm
Indistinct
Legend: none
NLW BRONWYDD/962, dated 1487

SEAL 949
Round, 17
Shield of arms (lion rampant sinister)
Legend: none
NLW BRONWYDD/963, dated 1487 x 1488

SEAL 950
Round, 12
Lamb of God (stylised lily in place of cross-tipped banner)
Legend: none
NLW BRONWYDD/991, dated 1508
NLW BRONWYDD/993, dated 1508
NLW BRONWYDD/965, dated 1488

SEAL 951
Rounded oval, c.21x16
Stylised lily
Legend: none
NLW BRONWYDD/965, seal 2, dated 1488

SEAL 952
Round, c.17
Uncertain; ?letters
Legend: none
NLW BRONWYDD/968, dated 1492

SEAL 953
Rounded oval, 12x8
?Shield of arms (charge indistinct)
Legend: none
NLW BRONWYDD/969, dated 1493
NLW BRONWYDD/1041, dated 1520

SEAL 954
Round, 14
Uncertain; ?shield
Legend: none
NLW BRONWYDD/970, dated 1494

SEAL 955
Round, 9
Indistinct (?two pellets)
Legend: none
NLW BRONWYDD/971, dated 1498

SEAL 956
Round, 11
Within a cusped border, a human hand
Legend: none
NLW BRONWYDD/972, dated 1497

SEAL 957
Unknown, c.9x8
Illegible
Legend: none
NLW BRONWYDD/974, seal 2, dated 1497 x 1498

SEAL 958
Rounded oval, 13x11
Stylised lily
Legend: none
NLW BRONWYDD/978, dated 1499
NLW BRONWYDD/979, dated 1499

SEAL 959
Rectangular, 14x12
Letter B
Legend: none
NLW BRONWYDD/981, dated 1499

SEAL 960
Rectangular, 13x11
Letter I flanked by elongated pellets
Legend: none
NLW BRONWYDD/982, dated 1520

SEAL 961
Round, 11
Letter ?W
Legend: none
NLW BRONWYDD/983, dated 1501

SEAL 962
Rounded oval, 13x10
Head wearing a laurel wreath facing left
Legend: none
NLW BRONWYDD/984, dated 1503

SEAL 963
Round, nm
Stylised foliage

APPENDIX

Legend: none
NLW BRONWYDD/985, dated 1502

SEAL 964
Round, 14
A barrel on its side with ?flames (?hop flowers) emerging from the top, letter S to left
Legend: none
NLW BRONWYDD/986, dated 1503

SEAL 965
Round, 29
Shield of arms (?lozengy)
Legend: [section lost]:de:ne[section lost]
NLW BRONWYDD/1013, dated 1374

SEAL 966
Rectangular, 14x12
Letter R
Legend: none
NLW BRONWYDD/1036, dated 1510
NLW BRONWYDD/1049, seal 5 and 8, dated 1520
NLW BRONWYDD/1044, dated 1518
NLW BRONWYDD/1031, dated 1517

SEAL 967
Round, 15
Seven-petalled stylised flower
Legend: none
NLW BRONWYDD/1032, seal 2, dated 1494

SEAL 968
Round, 13
A butterfly with wings displayed
Legend: none
NLW BRONWYDD/1414, dated 1535
NLW BRONWYDD/1198, dated 1526
NLW BRONWYDD/7012, dated 1522
NLW BRONWYDD/1146, dated 1542
NLW BRONWYDD/1182, back, dated 1542
NLW BRONWYDD/1047, dated 1523
NLW BRONWYDD/1411, back, dated 1542
NLW BRONWYDD/1033, dated 1516

SEAL 969
Rounded oval, c.14x12
Animal (?pig)
Legend: none
NLW BRONWYDD/1035, dated 1524

SEAL 970
Rounded oval, 13x10
Stylised lily
Legend: none
NLW BRONWYDD/1039, dated 1520

SEAL 971
Unknown (?round), c.18
Pattern (?monogram)
Legend: none
NLW BRONWYDD/1040, dated 1521

SEAL 972
Rectangular, 14x11
Letter W
Legend: none
NLW BRONWYDD/1043, dated 1511 x 1512

SEAL 973
Round, 11
Triangle
Legend: none
NLW BRONWYDD/1045, dated 1515

SEAL 974
Round, nm
Heart with saltire cross within (?merchant mark)
Legend: none
NLW BRONWYDD/1046, dated 1515

SEAL 975
Unknown (?round) nm
Lost
Legend: OR[.] [rest lost; start-point uncertain]
NLW BRONWYDD/1047, seal 2, dated 1523

SEAL 976
Round, 48
Shield of arms (quarterly: 1, 4 a fret; 2 ermine, a chevron; 3 two bars) with a helm and crest (out of a coronet, a crowned swan) and mantling, a butterfly in the field dexter and sinister
Legend: ¶ SIGILLVM : IOHAN[. . .] ¶ [. .] A[. . . . . . .]
NLW BRONWYDD/1414, dated 1535
NLW BRONWYDD/1048, dated 1523 x 1524
NLW BRONWYDD/1411, front, dated 1542
NLW BRONWYDD/1182, front, dated 1542

SEAL 977
Round, 18
Wavy pattern in two lines
Legend: none
NLW BRONWYDD/1049, seal 10, dated 1520

SEAL 978
Rectangular, 12x18
Letter W
Legend: none
NLW BRONWYDD/1049, seal 12, dated 1520

SEAL 979
Round, 14
Geometric pattern: a 'V' crossed by a horizontal line
Legend: none
NLW BRONWYDD/1049, seal 2, dated 1520

SEAL 980
Unknown, nm
Indistinct
Legend: none
NLW BRONWYDD/1049, seal 3, dated 1520

SEAL 981
Round, 18
Three vertical lines crossed by a horizontal line
Legend: none
NLW BRONWYDD/1049, seal 4, dated 1520

SEAL 982
Scutiform, 12x14
Inverted pyramid bisected by vertical line
Legend: none
NLW BRONWYDD/1049, seal 6, dated 1520

SEAL 983
Square, 10x10
Letter W
Legend: none
NLW BRONWYDD/1049, seal 7, dated 1520

SEAL 984
Rectangular, 5x8
Letter B
Legend: none
NLW BRONWYDD/1049, seal 8, dated 1520

SEAL 985
Round, 11
Letter W
Legend: none
NLW BRONWYDD/1050, dated 1490

SEAL 986
Round, 16
Sacred Monogram (ihc)
Legend: none
NLW BRONWYDD/1053, dated 1475

SEAL 987
Rounded oval, 10x8
Crowned letter h
Legend: none
NLW BRONWYDD/1058, dated 1408
NLW BRONWYDD/1059, dated 1489

APPENDIX

SEAL 988
Round, 20
Illegible
Legend: none
NLW BRONWYDD/1067, dated 1409 x 1410

SEAL 989
Round, 10
Stylised lily
Legend: none
NLW BRONWYDD/1117, dated 1523 x 1524

SEAL 990
Round, 12
Cockerel facing left, letter ?T above
Legend: none
NLW BRONWYDD/1119, dated 1466

SEAL 991
Round, 12
Letters I ?N
Legend: none
NLW BRONWYDD/1123, dated 1432

SEAL 992
Unknown, nm
Pattern of two lines intersecting third line at right-angles
Legend: none
NLW BRONWYDD/1124, dated 1547

SEAL 993
Round, 14
Letters RM, stylised foliage above and below
Legend: none
NLW BRONWYDD/1127, dated 1549

SEAL 994
Round, 13
Letter W ?P, stylised foliage above and below
Legend: none
NLW BRONWYDD/1127, seal 2, dated 1549

SEAL 995
Round, 13
Letter R
Legend: none
NLW BRONWYDD/1131, dated 1549

SEAL 996
Round, 14
Letters W ?P, ?wheatsheaf above
Legend: none
NLW BRONWYDD/1132, dated 1549

SEAL 997
Round, $c.15$
Saltire cross formed by 10 diagonal lines
Legend: none
NLW BRONWYDD/1139, dated 1543
NLW BRONWYDD/1148, dated 1543

SEAL 998
Round, $c.16$
Indistinct
Legend: none
NLW BRONWYDD/1141, dated 1526

SEAL 999
Rounded oval, 13x10
Letter I
Legend: none
NLW BRONWYDD/1143, dated 1531

SEAL 1000
Unknown, $c.9 x c.7$
Letter ?h (?n)
Legend: none
NLW BRONWYDD/1144, dated 1545

SEAL 1001
Round, 11
Letters W. O with arched bar above
Legend: none
NLW BRONWYDD/1145, dated 1542

SEAL 1002
Hexagonal, $18 x c.16$
Letter M
Legend: none
NLW BRONWYDD/1147, dated 1546

SEAL 1003
Round, 10
Stylised lily
Legend: none
NLW BRONWYDD/1150, dated 1541

SEAL 1004
Round, c.15
Sacred Monogram ihc
Legend: none
NLW BRONWYDD/1151, dated 1541

SEAL 1005
Round, c.14
Squirrel facing left eating a nut, to the left a ?Latin cross (?letter t), to the right letter I
Legend: none
NLW BRONWYDD/1153, dated 1530

SEAL 1006
Round, 14
Letters I T, stylised grass stem above and below
Legend: none
NLW BRONWYDD/1154, dated 1545

SEAL 1007
Rounded oval, c.18xc.15
Merchant mark (includes inverted Y), cross-tipped staff emerging from top with letter B impaled
Legend: none
NLW BRONWYDD/1155, dated 1542

SEAL 1008
Rounded oval, 13x10
Crowned letter T
Legend: none
NLW BRONWYDD/1158, dated 1491

SEAL 1009
Unknown nm
Letter W
Legend: none
NLW BRONWYDD/1159, dated 1517

SEAL 1010
Round, 17
Two vertical lines joined by two short horizontal lines ('ladder' effect)
Legend: none
NLW BRONWYDD/1160, dated 1473

SEAL 1011
Round, c.19
Monogram: letter T within large letter C
Legend: none
NLW BRONWYDD/1173, dated 1519
NLW BRONWYDD/1175, dated 1519

SEAL 1012
Rounded oval, 12x10
Stylised lily
Legend: none
NLW BRONWYDD/1195, seal 1, dated 1515 x 1516

SEAL 1013
Square, 8x8
Letters ct
Legend: none
NLW BRONWYDD/1195, seal 2, dated 1515 x 1516

SEAL 1014
Round, 12
Bird with wings raised facing half left
Legend: none
NLW BRONWYDD/1200, seal 1, dated 1523

SEAL 1015
Round, 11
Three-petalled flower (?clover leaf with central disk)
Legend: none
NLW BRONWYDD/1200, seal 2, dated 1523

SEAL 1016
Round, c.15
Two horizontal lines bisected by one vertical line to the left

Figure 4.1 HCA Deed 1084, s.1 (Seal 845)

Figure 4.2 HCA Deed 1084, s.2 (Seal 846)

Figure 4.3 BUAS PENR/12 (Seal 216)

Figure 4.4 NLW PITORD/236 (Seal 1667)

Figure 4.5 HCA Deed 2003 (Seal 871)

Figure 4.6 NLW PITORD/1057, s.2 (Seal 1983)

Figure 4.7 NLW PITORD/605, s.1 (Seal 1950)

Figure 4.8 NLW PITORD/605, s.2 (Seal 1951)

Figure 5.1 BUAS PENR/166 (Seal 215)

Figure 5.2 BUAS PENR/166 (Seal 215)

Figure 5.3 NLW PENRICE: GLAM/126, s.1 (Seal 1210)

Figure 5.4 NLW PENRICE: GLAM/126, s.2 (Seal 1211)

Figure 5.5 NLW PENRICE: GLAM/126, s.3 (Seal 1212)

Figure 5.6 NLW PENRICE: GLAM/126, s.4 (Seal 1213)

Figure 5.7 *(left)*   NLW PENRICE: GLAM/72 (Seal 1174)

Figure 5.8   BL Harl. Ch. 75 B 12 (Seal 45)

Figure 6.1 NLW PENRICE: GLAM/2042, front (Seal 1195)

Figure 6.2 NLW PENRICE: GLAM/2042, back (Seal 1194)

Figure 6.3 SHA 972/1/1/432 (Seal 2438)

Figure 6.4 SHA 322/2/14 (Seal 2318)

Figure 6.5 NLW PENRICE: GLAM/69 (Seal 1171)

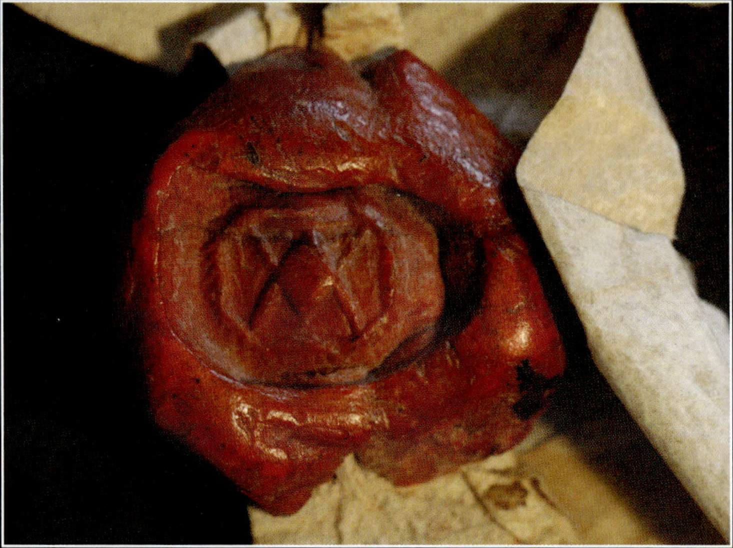

Figure 6.6 BUAS PENR/311, s.2 (Seal 242)

Figure 6.7 SHA 322/2/117, s.2 (Seal 2353)

Figure 6.8 NLW PITORD/537, s.2 (Seal 1603)

Figure 6.9 BL Add. Ch. 24275, s. 2 (Seal 16)

Figure 6.10 NLW PITORD/1356 (Seal 2106)

Figure 6.11 NLW PENRICE: GLAM/214 (Seal 1305)

Figure 7.1 BL Harl. Ch. 75 C 44 (Seal 87)

Figure 7.2 BL Harl. Ch. 75 C 46 (Seal 88)

Figure 7.3 BL Harl. Ch. 75 B 36 (Seal 61)

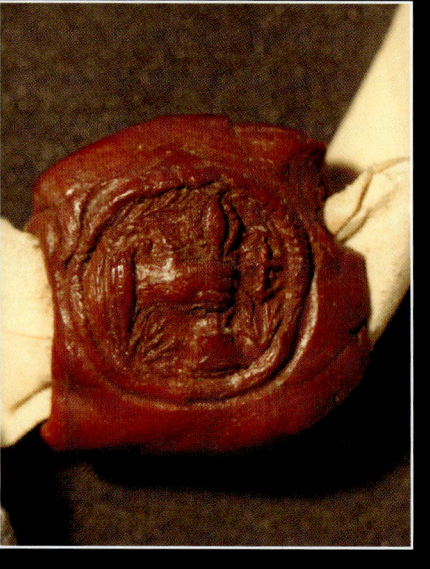

Figure 7.4 NLW PITORD/242, s.2 (Seal 1740)

Figure 7.5 HCA Deed 23 (Seal 739)

Figure 7.6 SHA 972/1/1/442, s. 2 (Seal 2447)

Figure 7.7 NLW PITORD/373 (Seal 1817)

Figure 7.8 NLW PITORD/333

Figure 7.9 BUAS MOST/3008 (Seal 186)

Figure 7.10   CALS D3785/1/16 (Seal 321)

Figure 7.11   CALS D3785/1/15 pt.1 (Seal 319)

Figure 7.12 NLW PENRICE: GLAM/2013 (Seal 1513)

Figure 7.13 BUAS PENR/25 (Seal 221)

Figure 7.14 BL Harl. Ch. 75 B 17 (Seal 46)

Figure 7.15 SHA 20/7/43, s.2 (Seal 2307)

Figure 7.16 NLW PITORD/10 (Seal 1579)

APPENDIX

Legend: none
NLW BRONWYDD/1200, seal 3, dated 1523

SEAL 1017
Round, 12
Letter W
Legend: none
NLW BRONWYDD/1270, dated 1493 x 1494

SEAL 1018
Unknown nm
Letter h
Legend: none
NLW BRONWYDD/1289, dated 1481

SEAL 1019
Round, 20
Shield of arms (lion rampant)
Legend: *S[..]WELYN.[.].WILIM
NLW BRONWYDD/1283, dated 1412

SEAL 1020
Unknown, c.13xc.14
Monogram ?HP
Legend: none
NLW BRONWYDD/1316, dated 1502

SEAL 1021
Round, 15
Six-petalled stylised flower
Legend: none
NLW BRONWYDD/1318, dated 1503

SEAL 1022
Round, 16
Square with small squares at each corner, ?foliage within, ?stylised lily above
Legend: none
NLW BRONWYDD/1320, seal 2, dated 1497

SEAL 1023
Round, 12
Within a cusped border, a hand
Legend: none
NLW BRONWYDD/1320, seal 1, dated 1497

SEAL 1024
Round, c.23
Lamb of God facing left (fragmentary)
Legend: illegible, partially lost
NLW BRONWYDD/1321, dated 1358

SEAL 1025
Round, 8
Letter W
Legend: none
NLW BRONWYDD/1322, dated 1539 x 1540

SEAL 1026
Round, 19
Hawk taking a bird, both facing left
Legend: none
NLW BRONWYDD/1323, dated 1300 x 1399

SEAL 1027
Round, c.13
Letter H, stylised branch in centre above crossbar
Legend: none
NLW BRONWYDD/1331, dated 1547

SEAL 1028
Round, 12
Merchant mark (includes letter W, cross-tipped staff with banner)
Legend: none
NLW BRONWYDD/1332, dated 1445

SEAL 1029
Round, 19
Animal (?squirrel / ?lion)
Legend: illegible, partially lost
NLW BRONWYDD/1333, dated 1362

SEAL 1030
Round, 11
Letter M
Legend: none
NLW BRONWYDD/1336, dated 1463 x 1464

SEAL 1031
Round, c.13
?Interlaced links
Legend: none
NLW BRONWYDD/1338, dated 1491

SEAL 1032
Round, 14
Shield (charge illegible)
Legend: none
NLW BRONWYDD/1342, dated 1397 x 1398

SEAL 1033
Round, c.16
Eagle displayed
Legend: none
NLW BRONWYDD/1344, dated 1471

SEAL 1034
Round, 14
Quadruped walking to left, object above (?hare on hound)
Legend: none
NLW BRONWYDD/1345, dated 1418

SEAL 1035
Round, 19
Stag's head full-face with patriarchal cross between antlers (top of cross intrudes into legend-band to form start-point for legend)
Legend: + IESV[?S] MERCI
NLW BRONWYDD/1348, dated 1370

SEAL 1036
Round, 14
Letters WG
Legend: none
NLW BRONWYDD/1358, dated 1548

SEAL 1037
Rounded oval, c.12xc.10
?Letter (fragment)
Legend: lost, if any
NLW BRONWYDD/1359, dated 1484

SEAL 1038
Round, c.14
Letters ?IO, arched bar above, three ?flower on short stem below
Legend: none
NLW BRONWYDD/1365, dated 1550

SEAL 1039
Round, 49x47
Shield of arms (quarterly: 1, 4 a fret; 2, 3 ermine, a chevron), a helm and crest (out of a coronet, a ?swan) and mantling, a butterfly in the field dexter and sinister
Legend: [. . . .]LLVM :.: IOHANNES ⁋ DOMINE :.: de [. . . . . .]
NLW BRONWYDD/1408, dated 1514
NLW BRONWYDD/7012, dated 1522

SEAL 1040
Round, 12
Ostrich walking to the left
Legend: none
NLW BRONWYDD/1414, seal 2, dated 1535

SEAL 1041
Round nm
Seal of the Principality of the south (Carmarthen)
NLW BRONWYDD/2392, dated 1519

SEAL 1042
Hexagonal, 10x12
Letters GW
Legend: none
NLW BRONWYDD/2394, seal 1, dated 1519

SEAL 1043
Rectangular, 11x15
Griffin walking to left
Legend: none
NLW BRONWYDD/2394, seal 2, dated 1519

SEAL 1044
Octagonal, 14x10
Letter I

APPENDIX

Legend: none
NLW BRONWYDD/2495, dated 1430

SEAL 1045
Unknown, c.11xc.11
Indistinct
Legend: none
NLW BRONWYDD/2499, dated 1389

SEAL 1046
Round, 14
Indistinct
Legend: none
NLW BRONWYDD/2500, seal 1, dated 1545

SEAL 1047
Round, 15
?Monogram (horizontal line with circle to right and centre, to right a vertical line, triangle below)
Legend: none
NLW BRONWYDD/2500, seal 2, dated 1545

SEAL 1048
Round, nm
Illegible
Legend: none
NLW BRONWYDD/2501, seal 1, dated 1547

SEAL 1049
Round, c.18
Merchant mark
Legend: none
NLW BRONWYDD/2501, seal 2, dated 1547

SEAL 1050
Seal of the Chancellery of Gower
NLW BRONWYDD/3042, dated 1417

SEAL 1051
Rounded oval, 14x11
Shield of arms (two bars, in chief a lion passant guardant)
Legend: none

NLW BRONWYDD/7009, dated 1349
NLW BRONWYDD/7010, dated 1349

SEAL 1052
Round, 29
Stylised lily
Legend: [S]ThO[.....]EWERN
NLW BRONWYDD/7015, dated 1241

SEAL 1053
Round, nm
Second Great Seal of Richard II
NLW BRONWYDD/7016, dated 1378

SEAL 1054
Round, c.26
Shield of arms (fretty, a lable of ?three points)
Legend: illegible, partially lost
NLW BRONWYDD/7230, dated 1373

SEAL 1055
Round, 29
Shield arms (two bars, a label of five points)
Legend: +S'[......]IIM[..] TI [..]
NLW BRONWYDD/7274, dated 1273 x 1281

SEAL 1056
Unknown, nm
Undetermined (includes cross-shape and roundel)
Legend: none
NLW CHIRK/1, dated 1550

SEAL 1057
Rounded oval, 18
Undetermined (?ornate shield)
Legend: none
NLW CHIRK/161, dated 1541

SEAL 1058
Rounded oval, 14x12
Gem: man wearing helm crouching facing left holding a ?sword up in his right hand, a shield held behind him on his left arm
Legend: none
NLW CHIRK/442/B, dated 1545

SEAL 1059
Round, 49
A yale passant ducally gorged and chained, a coronet above
Legend: +SIGIL[section lost] ONORI SO[. .] [section lost] EIRKLo
NLW CHIRK/475, dated 1536

SEAL 1060
Rectangular, 11x9
Scallop shell with a sword, point down, behind
Legend: none
NLW CHIRK/491, seal 1, dated 1505 x 1506

SEAL 1061
Scutiform, nm
Shield of arms (barry of three)
Legend: none
NLW CHIRK/491, seal 2, dated 1505 x 1506

SEAL 1062
Round, 12
Owl walking to left, stylised foliage to right
Legend: none
NLW CHIRK/493, dated 1518
NLW CHIRK/494, dated 1527 x 1528

SEAL 1063
Rounded oval, 13x11
Tree (?stem with branches)
Legend: none
NLW CHIRK/665, dated 1455

SEAL 1064
Round, 15
Cockerel walking to the left
Legend: none
NLW CHIRK/867, seal 1 and 2, dated 1543

SEAL 1065
Round, 16
Letters R E with interlaced cord above, between and below
Legend: none
NLW CHIRK/870, dated 1549
NLW CHIRK/868, dated 1546 x 1547

SEAL 1066
Round, 57
Shield of arms (lion rampant) hanging from a tassel in the legend, with supporters (two wodehouses seated on lions), trefoils semy in the field
Legend: S:Edwar[.]I:Cha[. . . . .] § domini : powi[.]e :
NLW Strata Marchella/89, dated 1420
NLW CHIRK/908, dated 1420

SEAL 1067
Rectangular, 16x12
Letter H
Legend: none
NLW CHIRK/933, dated 1511

SEAL 1068
Rounded oval, nm
Shield of arms (charge illegible) hanging from a ?bush, letter E to the right
Legend: none
NLW CHIRK/1079, dated 1516

SEAL 1069
Round, 11
Uncertain (fragment only)
Legend: none
NLW CHIRK/1081, dated 1538

SEAL 1070
Rounded oval, 14x12
Gem: head and shoulders of ?man facing right
Legend: none
NLW CHIRK/1803, seal 1, dated 1545

SEAL 1071
Rounded oval, 10x8
Gem: figure walking right, right hand holding up a ?club, left hand extended and holding short staff with point on ground
Legend: none
NLW CHIRK/1803, seal 2, dated 1545
NLW CHIRK/1804, dated 1545

APPENDIX

SEAL 1072
Rounded oval, 10x13
Letter W surrounded by dots
Legend: none
NLW CHIRK/2094, dated 1536
NLW CHIRK/2095, dated 1536

SEAL 1073
Round, 8
Letters W S, stylised foliage above and below
Legend: none
NLW CHIRK/2096, seal 2, dated 1546

SEAL 1074
Unknown, nm
Letter ?A
Legend: none
NLW CHIRK/2096, seal 4, dated 1546

SEAL 1075
Undetermined, 13x8
Irregular crescent with broad wavy base, two small disks inside (?not true seal matrix)
Legend: none
NLW CHIRK/2390, dated 1366

SEAL 1076
Rounded oval, 19x17
Vertical line with inverted 's' shaped curve on either side (?letter K or h designed to be viewed from both above and below?)
Legend: none
NLW CHIRK/2391, dated 1418

SEAL 1077
Hexagonal, 16x14
Letters HR conjoined, ?foliage to left
Legend: none
NLW CHIRK/2398, dated 1517 x 1518

SEAL 1078
Round, 16
Cross over cross saltire (akin to Union Jack)
Legend: none
NLW CHIRK/2403, dated 1534

SEAL 1079
Round, 13
Letter M
Legend: none
NLW CHIRK/2404, dated 1544

SEAL 1080
Round, 13
?Letter W (?blades of ?grass)
Legend: none
NLW CHIRK/2451, dated 1545

SEAL 1081
Round, 14
Shield of arms (a chevron between three mullets)
Legend: none
NLW CHIRK/2452, dated 1550 x 1551

SEAL 1082
Round, nm
Pelican in its piety facing left
Legend: none
NLW CHIRK/9866, dated 1445 x 1446

SEAL 1083
Round, nm
Uncertain (fragment)
Legend: lost, if any
NLW CHIRK/9877, dated 1406 x 1407

SEAL 1084
Round, 16
Letter ?R with ?crown above
Legend: none
NLW CHIRK/9878, dated 1468 x 1469

SEAL 1085
Round, 13
Letters W B, stylised lily at angle below
Legend: none
NLW CHIRK/9881, dated 1548 x 1549

SEAL 1086
Round, 23
Shield (charge illegible) with cross-tipped staff with banner emerging from top
Legend: * Sigillum I[. .] [section lost]
NLW CHIRK/9883, dated 1406 x 1407

SEAL 1087
Round, 12
Pelican in its piety facing left
Legend: none
NLW CHIRK/9885, seal 2, dated 1488 x 1489

SEAL 1088
Octagonal, 13x10
Crowned letter R
Legend: none
NLW CHIRK/9886, dated 1450

SEAL 1089
Round, 112
First Great Seal of Henry VIII
NLW CHIRK/9893, dated 1528
NLW PITORD/1274, dated 1514 x 1515
NLW PITORD/1608, dated 1513 x 1514
NLW PITORD/2458, dated 1517 x 1518

SEAL 1090
Round, 12
An eagle's head erased, illegible ?letters (?rays) to either side
Legend: none
NLW CHIRK/9894, dated 1477 x 1478

SEAL 1091
Round, 12
Lion's head erased facing left, letter I to left, illegible letters to right
Legend: none
NLW CHIRK/9894, seal 2, dated 1477 x 1478

SEAL 1092
Round, 12
Three-quarter length bearded man standing full-face holding a sword point up in his right hand and a ?book up in his left hand (?St Paul), letters to either side
Legend: [. . . .] [.]p[. . .]
NLW CHIRK/9894, seal 3, dated 1477 x 1478

SEAL 1093
Round, 13
Dog running to right, a tree behind
Legend: none
NLW CHIRK/9894, seal 4, dated 1477 x 1478

SEAL 1094
Round, 27
Uncertain
Legend: none
NLW CHIRK/10757, dated 1363

SEAL 1095
Round, 27
Uncertain; ?letter / ?foliate motif
Legend: +S' GV[.]N[. . .]ER . I' : LEV[. .]
NLW CHIRK/10757, seal 2, dated 1363

SEAL 1096
Unknown, nm
Uncertain (fragment)
Legend: none
NLW CHIRK/10760, dated 1368 x 1369

SEAL 1097
Rounded oval, 24x17
?Seated figure
Legend: none
NLW CHIRK/10760, seal 2, dated 1368 x 1369

SEAL 1098
Round, 15
Stylised seven-petalled flower (?seven-pointed star)
Legend: none
NLW CHIRK/11487, dated 1522

SEAL 1099
Rectangular, 14x12
Cross paty

APPENDIX

Legend: none
NLW CHIRK/11487, seal 2, dated 1522

SEAL 1100
Round, 19
Head face up in shallow bowl with low base (head of St John the Baptist)
Legend: * GOD HELP A[. . .]ED[.]
NLW CHIRK/11594, dated 1393 x 1394

SEAL 1101
Rounded oval, 15x12
Letter T
Legend: none
NLW CHIRK/11711, dated 1458 x 1459

SEAL 1102
Rounded oval, 18x16
Gem: figure ?with wings standing facing right, to right a ?bird
Legend: [section illegible]SE?C[section lost]?I:IOh'IS§
NLW CHIRK/12646, dated 1395 x 1396

SEAL 1103
Unknown, nm
Crenellated wall with large pointed-oval gateway, two towers behind, ?waves below
Legend: lost, if any
NLW CHIRK/12685, dated 1383 x 1384

SEAL 1104
Round, nm
Portcullis
Legend: [section lost] e castell[. .] [section lost]
NLW CHIRK/12708, dated 1506 x 1507

SEAL 1105
Round, 54
Portcullis with crown above
Legend: [section lost] DEI . GRA . REGI : A [section lost] [. . . . .]HIRK'
NLW CHIRK/13276, dated 1545

SEAL 1106
Round, c.28
Letter T with ?leaves in the field
Legend: * [. . . . . .] RE[.]V
NLW MYNDE/20, dated 1370

SEAL 1107
Hexagonal, c.17xc.11
Letter T, ?foliage above
Legend: none
NLW MYNDE/22, dated 1458

SEAL 1108
Round, c.9
Letter ?M (left side lost)
Legend: none
NLW MYNDE/33, dated 1497 x 1498

SEAL 1109
Round, 11
Seven-petalled stylised flower
Legend: none
NLW MYNDE/34, seal 1 and 2, dated 1498

SEAL 1110
Round, 14
Eagle displayed
Legend: none
NLW MYNDE/37, dated 1444

SEAL 1111
Round, c.17
Letter W flanked by small roundels
Legend: none
NLW MYNDE/44, dated 1541

SEAL 1112
Rectangular, 12xc.8
Letter I
Legend: none
NLW MYNDE/67, seal 1, dated 1511

SEAL 1113
Rounded oval, 13x15
Letters ?t P
Legend: none
NLW MYNDE/67, seal 2, dated 1511

SEAL 1114
Round, c.19
A ?griffin walking to left
Legend: none
NLW MYNDE/73, dated 1531

SEAL 1115
Unknown, c.20
?letter ?B
Legend: none
NLW MYNDE/83, dated 1451

SEAL 1116
Round, 28
Crescent with eight-pointed star above
Legend: * S' RADVL[. . . . .]E MADELE
NLW MYNDE/85, dated 1331

SEAL 1117
Round, c.19
Beast (?winged) standing on crescent facing right (?man carrying sack over his back walking right on a crescent (?man in the moon))
Legend: none
NLW MYNDE/87, dated 1364

SEAL 1118
Round, 24
Letter L, stylised branch to left, two small pellets to right
Legend: * [. . . . . . .]
NLW MYNDE/90, dated 1403

SEAL 1119
Unknown (?round), c.20xc.16
Shield of arms (quarterly; 1 lost; 2, 3 a fess between ?three roundels; 4, a chevron between three roundels)
Legend: none
NLW MYNDE/96, dated 1514

SEAL 1120
Round, 21
Four leaves (?four-leafed clover)
Legend: * [.]E[. . . . . .]V[.][?T]
NLW MYNDE/107, seal 1, 2 and 3, dated 1385

SEAL 1121
Round, 15
Monogram tA (or At)
Legend: none
NLW MYNDE/110, seal 1, dated 1425

SEAL 1122
Octagonal, 8xc.11
?Shield of arms (charge illegible)
Legend: none
NLW MYNDE/110, seal 2, dated 1425

SEAL 1123
Rounded oval, 15x19
?Gem: ?stag (?antelope) seated facing right
Legend: none
NLW MYNDE/113, dated 1438

SEAL 1124
Rounded oval, 18x15
Crowned letter R, branches to left and right
Legend: none
NLW MYNDE/140, seal 1, dated 1439

SEAL 1125
Hexagonal, 13xc.8
Crowned letter R
Legend: none
NLW MYNDE/140, seal 2, dated 1439

SEAL 1126
Unknown (?round), c.22xc.14
Crowned letter T
Legend: none
NLW MYNDE/160, seal 2, dated 1465

SEAL 1127
Round, c.27
Lost, within cusped border
Legend: * S' IOh [rest lost]
NLW MYNDE/173, dated 1371

SEAL 1128
Octagonal, c.8xc.13
Letter ?G within a beaded border

APPENDIX

Legend: none
NLW MYNDE/180, dated 1437

SEAL 1129
Octagonal, 18x13
Letter I
Legend: *§ E[?M]O§Vn §
NLW MYNDE/188, seal 1, dated 1431

SEAL 1130
Round, 13
Crowned letters IM
Legend: none
NLW MYNDE/188, seal 2, dated 1431

SEAL 1131
Scutiform, c.22x 17
Shield of arms (quarterly; 1, 4, a fret; 2, ?3, a chevron between eight pellets)
Legend: none
NLW MYNDE/288, seal 1 and 3, dated 1448

SEAL 1132
Round, nm
Illegible
Legend: none
NLW MYNDE/288, seal 2, dated 1448

SEAL 1133
Pointed oval, 76x52
Mitred man vested for Mass standing full-face blessing with right hand, left hand holding a crozier
Legend: [. . . . .]¶ [. . . . .] N[. . .]O [. . . . .]A LANDAVENSIS EPISCOP[.]
NLW PENRICE: GLAM/2, dated 1150 x 1166
NLW PENRICE: GLAM/1, dated 1148 x 1183

SEAL 1134
Round, 47
Armoured man on a horse galloping to the right
Legend: +SIGILLVMWIL[section lost]

GRE[. . .]II
NLW PENRICE: GLAM/4, dated 1166 x 1183

SEAL 1135
Unknown, nm
Building with tall central crenellated tower flanked to left and right by shorter crenellated towers
Legend: lost
NLW PENRICE: GLAM/5, dated 1154 x 1170

SEAL 1136
Pointed oval, 40x27
Half-length tonsured man full-face holding a pastoral staff in his right hand and a book in his left hand (both hands folded into chest), five dots in cruciform pattern in the upper right of the design field.
Legend: +SIGILLVM:ABBATISDEMARGAN
NLW PENRICE: GLAM/27, dated 1225 x 1250
NLW PENRICE: GLAM/6, dated 1166 x 1193
NLW PENRICE: GLAM/151, seal 6, dated 1249
NLW PENRICE: GLAM/26, dated 1213 x 1225

SEAL 1137
Pointed oval, 80x53
Man vested for Mass and wearing an archaic mitre standing full-face blessing with right hand, holding a crozier in left hand
Legend: [.section lost]GIL¶VM NICOLAI. DEIGRACIA[section lost]AVENSISEPISC[-section lost]
NLW PENRICE: GLAM/7, dated 1148 x 1183

SEAL 1138
Round, 29
Stylised lily with long stem
Legend: +[. . . .]LLV[.]RO[. . . .]IFILII[. . . .]O[. .]II
NLW PENRICE: GLAM/7, seal 2, dated 1148 x 1183

SEAL 1139
Round, 46
Figure with left hand raised on a horse galloping to the right
Legend: [. . . .]LV[.] PA[. .]NI DE T⸱ BE[. . . .]
NLW PENRICE: GLAM/8, dated 1186 x 1191

SEAL 1140
Pointed oval, 33x21
Eagle displayed, foliage in its beak
Legend: + SI[. .]LL'I : LAND' : ARCHIDIA
NLW PENRICE: GLAM/11, seal 2, dated 1172 x 1179

SEAL 1141
Round, 90
Second Great Seal of Henry II, obv and rev
NLW PENRICE: GLAM/12, dated 1154 x 1163
NLW PENRICE: GLAM/13, dated 1174 x 1179
NLW PENRICE: GLAM/14, dated 1174 x 1179

SEAL 1142
Pointed oval, 46x28
Hand emerging from lower right holding a spear point up with a pennon to right
Legend: +SIGILL' ESPVS:⸱ FILII CRADOCI
NLW PENRICE: GLAM/2039, dated 1200 x 1225
NLW PENRICE: GLAM/2038, dated 1175 x 1225
NLW PENRICE: GLAM/2037, dated 1203 x 1208
NLW PENRICE: GLAM/15, dated 1175 x 1207

SEAL 1143
Pointed oval, 69x42
Tonsured man in long robe (?monastic habit) standing facing half left holding a scroll up in his right hand and a book in his left hand
Legend: +SIGILLVM:PRIORIS:SCI':MICHAEL':DE:VGGOMOR'
NLW PENRICE: GLAM/17, dated 1166 x 1193
NLW PENRICE: GLAM/19, dated 1166 x 1193
NLW PENRICE: GLAM/16, dated 1166 x 1188

SEAL 1144
Round, 72
Lion walking to right, a tall lily plant behind
Legend: +SIGILLV[.] VVIL[. . .]MI [.] LOENCESTR[. . .]ONSVLIS
NLW PENRICE: GLAM/22, front, dated 1147 x 1166
NLW PENRICE: GLAM/23, dated 1158 x 1183
NLW PENRICE: GLAM/20, front, dated 1147 x 1183
NLW PENRICE: GLAM/1943, front, dated 1183
NLW PENRICE: GLAM/1944, dated 1150 x 1176
NLW PENRICE: GLAM/1945, front, dated 1147 x 1176
NLW PENRICE: GLAM/1946, front, dated 1150 x 1166

SEAL 1145
Rounded oval, 29x24
Gem: a bird walking left, with a thin vertical object on either side, head of a bearded man in profile facing right above, on either side of the head winged figures holding wreaths
Legend: +AQVILASV' ET C[section lost]
NLW PENRICE: GLAM/23, dated 1158 x 1183
NLW PENRICE: GLAM/22, back, dated 1147 x 1166
NLW PENRICE: GLAM/20, back, dated 1147 x 1183
NLW PENRICE: GLAM/1944, dated 1150 x 1176
NLW PENRICE: GLAM/1945, back, dated 1147 x 1176
NLW PENRICE: GLAM/1946, back, dated 1150 x 1166
NLW PENRICE: GLAM/1943, back, dated 1183

APPENDIX

SEAL 1146
Pointed oval, 26x19
Stylised lily
Legend: + SIGILLVM § DAVID
NLW PENRICE: GLAM/29, dated 1200 x 1250
NLW PENRICE: GLAM/28, dated 1213 x 1237
NLW PENRICE: GLAM/154, dated 1225 x 1274

SEAL 1147
Rounded oval, 21x19
Gem: ?female head facing right
Legend: +SIGILLVM HVGONIS HERE8o
NLW PENRICE: GLAM/32, back, dated 1183
NLW PENRICE: GLAM/33, back, dated 1183
NLW PENRICE: GLAM/34, back, dated 1168 x 1183
NLW PENRICE: GLAM/31, dated 1199

SEAL 1148
Round, 46
A sword point down
Legend: § SIGILL' : HVGONIS : DE : HEREFORD
NLW PENRICE: GLAM/33, front, dated 1183
NLW PENRICE: GLAM/32, front, dated 1183
NLW PENRICE: GLAM/34, front, dated 1168 x 1183

SEAL 1149
Round, 42
Stylised lily
Legend: +SIGILL'HVGONISFILLIROBERTI
NLW PENRICE: GLAM/2010, dated 1186 x 1191
NLW PENRICE: GLAM/37, dated 1186 x 1191
NLW PENRICE: GLAM/38, dated 1186 x 1191

SEAL 1150
Pointed oval, 43x30
Woman facing half left, holding a stylised lily (in outline) up in her right hand, her left hand at her hip ?holding an object (?distaff)
Legend: +SIGILLVMMILISENT
NLW PENRICE: GLAM/39, dated 1186 x 1191
NLW PENRICE: GLAM/40, dated 1186 x 1191

SEAL 1151
Round, 57
Man holding foliage up in his right hand and blowing a horn held in his left hand, on a horse galloping to the right
Legend: ¶+SI¶GILLV¶M. PAGANIDET¶VRBERVILLA
NLW PENRICE: GLAM/42, dated 1186 x 1191
NLW PENRICE: GLAM/41, dated 1186 x 1191

SEAL 1152
Pointed oval, 43x27
Stylised lily plant
Legend: + SIGILLVM WALTERI LUVELLI
NLW PENRICE: GLAM/43, dated 1186 x 1191
NLW PENRICE: GLAM/44, dated 1186 x 1191

SEAL 1153
Unknown, nm
Figure on horse facing right
Legend: [section lost]M[section lost]
NLW PENRICE: GLAM/47, dated 1197 x 1219

SEAL 1154
Pointed oval, 72x44
Mitred man vested for Mass standing full-face on a corbel blessing with his right hand and holding a pastoral staff in his left hand
Legend: + SIGILL' hENRICI DEI GRACIA ¶ LANDAVENSIS EPISCOPI

NLW PENRICE: GLAM/102, front, dated 1203 x 1213
NLW PENRICE: GLAM/48, front, dated 1200 x 1218

SEAL 1155
Round, 41
Hand and arm emerging from right holding up a bunch of lilies
Legend: +SIGILLVMNIChOLAIPONTII.
NLW PENRICE: GLAM/50, dated 1193 x 1202
NLW PENRICE: GLAM/2049, dated 1200 x 1225

SEAL 1156
Pointed oval, 30x19
Stylised lily
Legend: +SIGILL'WALTVLHI
NLW PENRICE: GLAM/52, dated 1193 x 1218

SEAL 1157
Round, nm
?Armoured man on horse galloping to right
Legend: lost
NLW PENRICE: GLAM/53, dated 1175 x 1191

SEAL 1158
Rounded oval, 26x37
Gem: lion to left racing right, quadruped (?bull) to right facing left, between them a tree
Legend: +SIGILLVM [. .]HANNIS' MON[.]MVA[. .]
NLW PENRICE: GLAM/55/a, dated 1200 x 1248

SEAL 1159
Rounded oval, nm
?Gem: Hindquarters of an animal facing right
Legend: SIG [rest lost]
NLW PENRICE: GLAM/55/b, dated 1200 x 1225

SEAL 1160
Round, 37
Ornate six-petalled stylised flower
Legend: +SIGILLVMGISTE[. . .]D[.]
NLW PENRICE: GLAM/56, dated 1175 x 1225

SEAL 1161
Round, 40
Bow with arrow (point down) ready for shooting with two ?teasels above and two foliate stems below the bow
Legend: +SIGILL'WALAVETG[. .]LE
NLW PENRICE: GLAM/57, dated 1199 x 1214
NLW PENRICE: GLAM/1953, dated 1175 x 1225

SEAL 1162
Round, 27
Stylised four-petalled flower with trefoil petals ('snowflake' pattern), two leaves in the angles between petals
Legend: +S' K[. . . .] FILII : GILEMIhEL
NLW PENRICE: GLAM/58, dated 1225 x 1250

SEAL 1163
Round, 28
Foliate motif formed by five rows of nine small cinquefoils and four small trefoils (rows of 1, 3, 5, 3, 1; trefoils flank central cinquefoil forming central block)
Legend: + S' YVOR : FILII . GILLEMIhEL
NLW PENRICE: GLAM/58, seal 2, dated 1225 x 1250

SEAL 1164
Rounded oval, 24x19
Gem: ?winged figure facing right on back of creature facing right
Legend: +SIGILL' DD' : SCVRLAG
NLW PENRICE: GLAM/60, dated 1217 x 1230

SEAL 1165
Round, 31

APPENDIX

Stylised eight-petalled flower (long 'stems' with main petal at end)
Legend: +SIGILL' DAVID SCURLAG
NLW PENRICE: GLAM/2016, dated 1200 x 1225
NLW PENRICE: GLAM/61, dated 1202

SEAL 1166
Round, 25
Stylised fourteen-petalled flower
Legend: +SIGILL'WILL'FILIISVSANNE
NLW PENRICE: GLAM/64, dated 1200 x 1225

SEAL 1167
Rounded oval, 29x25
Gem: three lines of Arabic script
Legend: + SIGILLI' : IOHANN' DE BONEVILE
NLW PENRICE: GLAM/65, dated 1200 x 1225

SEAL 1168
Round, 30
Stylised ?five-petalled flower (small petals on ends of long 'stems')
Legend: + [......]UERICI
NLW PENRICE: GLAM/66, dated 1200

SEAL 1169
Rounded oval, 24
Gem: head (?wearing helmet) facing right
Legend: +SIGILL'IVRDANFIL'ACERE
NLW PENRICE: GLAM/67, dated 1231

SEAL 1170
Round, 39
Six ?cones with long stems between alternate ones
Legend: +SIGILL'.IEREVORDI.FILII.GISTELARDI
NLW PENRICE: GLAM/68, dated 1200 x 1225

SEAL 1171
Pointed oval, 29x18
Fish facing up
Legend: +SIGILLVMTADERECI
NLW PENRICE: GLAM/69, dated 1225

SEAL 1172
Pointed oval, 37x24
Stylised lily facing down, five small pellets in lower left of design field
Legend: +SIGILLV'FILIORVIOR-VERTGI[?...]R
NLW PENRICE: GLAM/70, dated 1225 x 1250

SEAL 1173
Round, 25
Stylised sixteen-petalled flower (very thin petals)
Legend: + S' ROBERTI : CVRTEIS
NLW PENRICE: GLAM/71, dated 1200 x 1250

SEAL 1174
Round, 32
Stylised lily (upside down in relation to legend) flanked at the top by two pellets
Legend: + S'IGILL' YVOR VAChAN ET[?H]ILI[?C?A]'EY
NLW PENRICE: GLAM/72, dated 1225 x 1250

SEAL 1175
Round, 25
Stylised eight-petalled flower
Legend: +SIGILL':WORVA[.]D:COH
NLW PENRICE: GLAM/74, dated 1225 x 1241

SEAL 1176
Round, 20
Foliate-style motif formed by five petals with chalices upon them, a nail point inwards, between each petal, a ?many-petalled flower (lion's head) in the centre
Legend: * S' IOhIS : MINOT §
NLW PENRICE: GLAM/75, dated 1193 x 1203

SEAL 1177
Pointed oval, 34x24
Stylised lily facing down, five small pellets to left and right in design field
Legend: +SIGI[. . . . . . .]EYLINP[.]EN
NLW PENRICE: GLAM/76, seal 2, dated 1225 x 1250

SEAL 1178
Round, 38
Stylised six-petalled flower
Legend: + SIGILL' [. . . .]ERTh . FILII TV[.]VR
NLW PENRICE: GLAM/77, dated 1205

SEAL 1179
Pointed oval, 33x20
Flower (?lily) on stem with two leaves
Legend: + SIGILL' : GILLE : SE[.]S
NLW PENRICE: GLAM/78, dated 1200 x 1225

SEAL 1180
Undetermined, 24x24
Stylised lily between two multi-armed ?stars (?suns)
Legend: none
NLW PENRICE: GLAM/2005, dated 1175 x 1225
NLW PENRICE: GLAM/79, dated 1216

SEAL 1181
Round, 35
Wolf walking to right
Legend: +SIGILLVM : WALTERILWEL :
NLW PENRICE: GLAM/2058, dated 1200 x 1225
NLW PENRICE: GLAM/1975, seal 2, dated 1200 x 1225
NLW PENRICE: GLAM/80, dated 1202

SEAL 1182
Pointed oval, 34x25
Stylised lily
Legend: +SIGILL'WALTERILOVEL
NLW PENRICE: GLAM/81, dated 1225 x 1250

SEAL 1183
Round, 35
Bulla of Innocent III
NLW PENRICE: GLAM/84, dated 1203
NLW PENRICE: GLAM/83, dated 1203
NLW PENRICE: GLAM/82, dated 1203

SEAL 1184
Pointed oval, nm
Spear pointing up
Legend: +SIGI[section lost]HOWELI
NLW PENRICE: GLAM/90, seal 2, dated 1208

SEAL 1185
Pointed oval, 31x24
Stylised lily
Legend: + SIGILL' . ROGERI . WIAN
NLW PENRICE: GLAM/94, dated 1208
NLW PENRICE: GLAM/95, dated 1208

SEAL 1186
Round, 41
Gloved hand emerging from lower right holding a lance, point up, with a pennon to the right
Legend: + S[. . . .]L' : KENE[.]ERC : [. . . . . .]AN
NLW PENRICE: GLAM/95, seal 3, dated 1208

SEAL 1187
Round, nm
Great Seal of King John
NLW PENRICE: GLAM/96, dated 1205
NLW PENRICE: GLAM/98, dated 1207
NLW PENRICE: GLAM/99, dated 1207

SEAL 1188
Pointed oval, nm
Tonsured man vested for Mass standing full-face holding a pastoral staff in his right hand and a book up in his left hand
Legend: SIGILLV[.] ABBAT[. . . . . . .]TAINS
NLW PENRICE: GLAM/101, dated 1208

APPENDIX

SEAL 1189
Pointed oval, 45x26
Tonsured man vested for Mass standing full-face holding a pastoral staff in his right hand and a book in his left hand
Legend: + SIGILLVM ABBATIS DE SARTIS
NLW PENRICE: GLAM/101, seal 2, dated 1208

SEAL 1190
Pointed oval, nm
Man vested for Mass standing full-face holding a pastoral staff in his right hand, left hand ?held up in salutation
Legend: [. . . . .]BBATIS DE . BOXE[. . .]
NLW PENRICE: GLAM/101, seal 3, dated 1208

SEAL 1191
Pointed oval, nm
Man vested for Mass standing full-face holding a pastoral staff with both hands obliquely across his body
Legend: [. .]GILL : ABBATIS [. . . . . . .]
NLW PENRICE: GLAM/101, seal 4, dated 1208

SEAL 1192
Pointed oval, 66x42
Tonsured man vested for Mass standing full-face holding a ?pastoral staff in his right hand and a book up in his left hand
Legend: + WALTE[. . . . .]ABIE : ThE[. . . . .]E
NLW PENRICE: GLAM/103, dated 1203 x 1214

SEAL 1193
Round, 44
Building with four round-arched windows, central tower, lower extension to left ending in short rounded tower, curving finials at edge of roof and central tower
Legend: + SI [. . . . .] ATIE . [. . . . . . .] SIS
NLW PENRICE: GLAM/103, seal 2, dated 1203 x 1214
NLW PENRICE: GLAM/177, seal 3, dated 1265

SEAL 1194
Rounded oval, 29x24
Gem: a bird walking left, with a thin vertical object on either side, above head of a bearded man in profile facing right, on either side winged figures holding wreaths
Legend:
+EGOSVAQILACVSTOSDNEMEE
NLW PENRICE: GLAM/2041, front, dated 1217
NLW PENRICE: GLAM/104, front, dated 1217
NLW PENRICE: GLAM/113, dated 1214 x 1216
NLW PENRICE: GLAM/113/c, back, dated 1216 x 1217
NLW PENRICE: GLAM/2042, back, dated 1216 x 1217
NLW PENRICE: GLAM/2043, back, dated 1216 x 1214

SEAL 1195
Pointed oval, 84x54
Woman standing full-face in long gown with long flowing cuffs holding a stylised lily up in her right hand and a bird on her left hand
Legend: +SIGILLVMISAB[.]LCOMI [. . . . . .] LOECESTRIEETMORETVN
NLW PENRICE: GLAM/113/c, front, dated 1216 x 1217
NLW PENRICE: GLAM/2041, front, dated 1217
NLW PENRICE: GLAM/2043, front, dated 1216 x 1214
NLW PENRICE: GLAM/104, front, dated 1217
NLW PENRICE: GLAM/2042, front, dated 1216 x 1217
NLW PENRICE: GLAM/113, dated 1214 x 1216

SEAL 1196
Round, 37
Foliate motif formed by central swirl of nine tightly packed petals surrounded by five lozenges and two (?more) disks
Legend: + S[. . . . .] GIL[.]ERT[.] GRAMVS
NLW PENRICE: GLAM/105, dated 1203 x 1213

SEAL 1197
Round, 38
Armoured man on a horse walking to the right
Legend: + SIGILL' LEISAN FIL' MOR¶¶GANI :
NLW PENRICE: GLAM/110/a, dated 1208 x 1217
NLW PENRICE: GLAM/109, dated 1203 x 1205

SEAL 1198
Round, 32
Shield of arms (quarterly, 1 and 4 blank, 2 and 3 vair (archaic))
Legend: +SIGILL' : GALF[. . . . .] EMAVNDEVIL'
NLW PENRICE: GLAM/113/b, dated 1214 x 1216

SEAL 1199
Pointed oval, nm
?scallop shell (?ermine spot)
Legend: + S . ROB . D [. . . . .]
NLW PENRICE: GLAM/114, dated 1225 x 1250

SEAL 1200
Round, 39
Small central pellet surrounded by five thin concentric circles (the outer one forming the edge of the legend band)
Legend: ZIGILL' . ENER . VAChAN
NLW PENRICE: GLAM/116, dated 1225

SEAL 1201
Round, 29
stag running to right
Legend: +S'hE[.]R¶ICID¶ESVTTONE
NLW PENRICE: GLAM/119, dated 1225 x 1250

SEAL 1202
Pointed oval, nm
Man ?vested for Mass standing full-face, right hand raised in blessing
Legend: [section lost] NSIS EPISCOPVS
NLW PENRICE: GLAM/120, seal 1, front, dated 1215 x 1222

SEAL 1203
Pointed oval, nm
Mitred man vested for Mass standing full-face on a corbel holding a pastoral staff in his left hand
Legend: [. .]GILLVM GERVASII [rest lost]
NLW PENRICE: GLAM/120, seal 1, front, dated 1215 x 1222

SEAL 1204
Pointed oval, 35x23
Stylised lily (ornate)
Legend: + S' MORGANIABOEIN
NLW PENRICE: GLAM/140, seal 3, dated 1246
NLW PENRICE: GLAM/120, seal 2, dated 1215 x 1222
NLW PENRICE: GLAM/523, dated 1215 x 1222

SEAL 1205
Rounded oval, 31x28
Inverted stylised lily flanked by two pellets
Legend: +SIG[. . . .]M:GRI[.] INIAbWRVNI
NLW PENRICE: GLAM/121, dated 1225 x 1250

SEAL 1206
Unknown, nm
Motif lost
Legend: [section lost]AN[section lost]
NLW PENRICE: GLAM/122, dated 1215

APPENDIX

SEAL 1207
Round, 19
Lost (if motif existed)
Legend: none
NLW PENRICE: GLAM/123, dated 1208 x 1217

SEAL 1208
Round, 27
Cross formy with three pellets on each arm
Legend: + SIGILL. WI[.]O[. . . .]LI'
NLW PENRICE: GLAM/162, dated 1253
NLW PENRICE: GLAM/124, dated 1219

SEAL 1209
Pointed oval, 41x26
Stylised lily
Legend: +SIGIL':WALTERI:DE:REIN'
NLW PENRICE: GLAM/125, dated 1225 x 1250

SEAL 1210
Pointed oval, 30x20
Stylised lily
Legend: + S' . PhILIPPI . AB : KhEDIhK
NLW PENRICE: GLAM/126, dated 1250 x 1299

SEAL 1211
Pointed oval, 29x19
Bow with arrow ready to shoot facing left
Legend: + SIGILL' . MADOC : AB KEDIC
NLW PENRICE: GLAM/126, seal 2, dated 1250 x 1299

SEAL 1212
Pointed oval, 28x19
Stylised plant with a five-pointed star at top of central frond
Legend: +S' [. . . . . . .]D AB.KEDIC
NLW PENRICE: GLAM/126, seal 3, dated 1250 x 1299

SEAL 1213
Pointed oval, 27x20
Stylised lily (elaborate)
Legend: + S' . MADOC AB MEVRI
NLW PENRICE: GLAM/126, seal 4, dated 1250 x 1299

SEAL 1214
Round, 22
Lance with pennon (four chevrons) to the right, in the field three pellets on the right and six pellets on the left
Legend: S'.WILL'I.FI[.]L'I.YORVER'AB.ESP'
NLW PENRICE: GLAM/128, dated 1225 x 1274

SEAL 1215
Round, 21
Lance with pennon (four chevrons) to the right, in the field three pellets on the right and six pellets on the left
Legend: +S'MAD[. . .]FIL'I.YORIE[?T].AB.ESP'
NLW PENRICE: GLAM/128, seal 2, dated 1225 x 1274

SEAL 1216
Round, 22
Lance with pennon (four chevrons) to the left, in the field six pellets on the right and three pellets on the left
Legend: +S'YSPOIS.FIL'.YERVRET.AB.ESP[.]
NLW PENRICE: GLAM/128, seal 3, dated 1225 x 1274

SEAL 1217
Round, 21
Lance with pennon (four chevrons) to the right, in the field three pellets on the right and six pellets on the left
Legend: +S'.Y[. . . . . .]AhAN.FIL'.YORV'.AB.EP'
NLW PENRICE: GLAM/128, seal 4, dated 1225 x 1274

SEAL 1218
Pointed oval, 45x25
Tonsured man standing full-face vested for Mass holding a pastoral staff in his right hand, a book up in his left hand

223

Legend: +
SECRETVM:ABBATISGLOVECESTRIE
NLW PENRICE: GLAM/132, back, dated 1205 x 1224
NLW PENRICE: GLAM/129, back, dated 1205 x 1224

SEAL 1219
Round, 72
Armoured man with an armorial shield (?3 chevrons) on a horse in armorial caparisons (chevrony) galloping to the right
Legend: ¶ SIGILL' GILBE¶ ERTI : DE : CLARE : CO¶MITIS : DE : hERTFORDI ¶E
NLW PENRICE: GLAM/2046, front, dated 1218 x 1230
NLW PENRICE: GLAM/2045, front, dated 1217 x 1218
NLW PENRICE: GLAM/2044, front, dated 1217 x 1218
NLW PENRICE: GLAM/2048, front, dated 1218 x 1230
NLW PENRICE: GLAM/131, front, dated 1218 x 1230
NLW PENRICE: GLAM/2047, front, dated 1200 x 1225

SEAL 1220
Pointed oval, c.24xc.11
?Hand emerging from right holding a pastoral staff
Legend: SIGILL' [rest lost]
NLW PENRICE: GLAM/133, seal 15, dated 1228

SEAL 1221
Pointed oval, c.32xc.20
Hand emerging from right holding a pastoral staff
Legend: lost
NLW PENRICE: GLAM/133, seal 17, dated 1228

SEAL 1222
Pointed oval, c.32xc.15
Tonsured man vested for Mass standing full-face holding a pastoral staff in his right hand
Legend: lost
NLW PENRICE: GLAM/133, seal 9, dated 1228

SEAL 1223
Round, 96
First Great Seal: Henry III
NLW PENRICE: GLAM/134, dated 1236

SEAL 1224
Pointed oval, c.40xc.27
Tonsured man standing full-face holding a pastoral staff in his right hand and a book up in his left hand
Legend: [. .]GI [. . . . .] S DE RIEVAL[. .]
NLW PENRICE: GLAM/135, dated 1237

SEAL 1225
Pointed oval, c.38xc.26
Man vested for Mass standing full-face
Legend: [. . . . .] ABBA[. . .] DE [section lost]
NLW PENRICE: GLAM/135, seal 2, dated 1237

SEAL 1226
Pointed oval, c.44xc.28
Man vested for Mass standing full-face holding ?pastoral staff in right hand
Legend: [section lost] A[. . . .] KINGESW [. . .]
NLW PENRICE: GLAM/135, seal 3, dated 1237

SEAL 1227
Pointed oval, c.40xc.27
Man vested for Mass standing full-face holding pastoral staff in right hand and book in left hand
Legend: [. . . . .] : ABBABIS : DE [. . . . .]
NLW PENRICE: GLAM/135, seal 4, dated 1237

SEAL 1228
Round, 20
Lion's head facing left

APPENDIX

Legend: [. . . .] NI.WILL'MI.DE.BREUS
[. .]
NLW PENRICE: GLAM/139/B, dated 1275 x 1324

SEAL 1229
Pointed oval, *c*.58x*c*.40
Man vested for Mass standing full-face on corbel blessing with right hand and left hand holding pastoral staff, on diaper ground with crescents in the voids
Legend: [. .]LLELMVS⁊ DEI § GR [section lost] VENSIS ⁊ [. . . . .]
NLW PENRICE: GLAM/140, seal 1, front, dated 1246
NLW PENRICE: GLAM/148, front, dated 1245 x 1253
NLW PENRICE: GLAM/145, seal 1, front, dated 1246
NLW PENRICE: GLAM/147, front, dated 1247

SEAL 1230
Round, *c*.70
Obverse: Armoured man in armorial surcoat (chevrony) and shield (chevrony) on horse in armorial caparisons (chevrons) galloping to right.
Legend: Obverse:[section lost] ⁊ DI . DE . C [section lost]
NLW PENRICE: GLAM/140, seal 2, front, dated 1246
Round
Reverse: Shield of arms (three chevrons) suspended by strap from stylised foliage, a supporter (lion rampant) to the left
Legend: Rev: [section lost] RE COMI [section lost]
NLW PENRICE: GLAM/140, seal 2, back, dated 1246

SEAL 1231
Pointed oval, *c*.40x*c*.26
Annunciation with below, beneath rounded arch, head and shoulders of suppliant figure facing right
Legend: +VE DELENS P AVE:PIA⁊P TE. LIBERER: [.]VE

NLW PENRICE: GLAM/147, back, dated 1247
NLW PENRICE: GLAM/140, seal 1, back, dated 1246
NLW PENRICE: GLAM/148, back, dated 1245 x 1253
NLW PENRICE: GLAM/145, seal 1, back, dated 1246

SEAL 1232
Round, 35
Bulla of Innocent IV
NLW PENRICE: GLAM/141, dated 1244

SEAL 1233
Round, 28
Lion rampant facing right
Legend: + SIGILLVM RICARDI LAEL[. .]
NLW PENRICE: GLAM/142, dated 1244

SEAL 1234
Round, 27
Stylised lily with three pellets either side of the lower stem
Legend: + SIGILL'. THOME GRAMVS
NLW PENRICE: GLAM/1991, dated 1225 x 1274
NLW PENRICE: GLAM/2014, dated 1225 x 1274
NLW PENRICE: GLAM/144, dated 1245
NLW PENRICE: GLAM/1990, dated 1225 x 1274
NLW PENRICE: GLAM/168, dated 1258
NLW PENRICE: GLAM/167, dated 1261
NLW PENRICE: GLAM/166, dated 1254
NLW PENRICE: GLAM/165, dated 1254
NLW PENRICE: GLAM/2055, dated 1238
NLW PENRICE: GLAM/172, dated 1261

SEAL 1235
Pointed oval, 26x19
stylised lily
Legend: ⁊ S'.LESSANTABMORGAN
NLW PENRICE: GLAM/145, seal 3, dated 1246

SEAL 1236
Round, 23
Stylised lily
Legend: +S'OWEINF'ELAITho
NLW PENRICE: GLAM/145, seal 5, dated 1246

SEAL 1237
Round, 27
Eleven-petalled flower
Legend: SIGILL:RESI:FILII[.]ANTHVRI
NLW PENRICE: GLAM/145, seal 6, dated 1246
NLW PENRICE: GLAM/2056, dated 1200 x 1250

SEAL 1238
Round, 25
Eight-petalled flower
Legend: +S'CRADOC[. .]AB.A[. . .]ThO
NLW PENRICE: GLAM/145, seal 7, dated 1246

SEAL 1239
Pointed oval, c.26x20
Stylised lily, inverted
Legend: [.] SIGILL' : GRIFINI : VOI[. .]
NLW PENRICE: GLAM/146, dated 1225 x 1250

SEAL 1240
Pointed oval, c.28x18
Arrow, point down
Legend: + SIGILL'. [. . . . . .]B I[?V]AN
NLW PENRICE: GLAM/146, seal 2, dated 1225 x 1250

SEAL 1241
Round, 20
Stylised eight-petalled flower
Legend: +S'GRIFINIF'CRAD'
NLW PENRICE: GLAM/150, dated 1200 x 1299

SEAL 1242
Pointed oval, nm
Man vested for Mass standing full-face holding book in left hand
Legend: [section lost] IS:CLAR[section lost]
NLW PENRICE: GLAM/151, seal 1, dated 1249

SEAL 1243
Pointed oval, nm
Man standing full-face ?vested for Mass
Legend: [section lost][.]B.[. . . .]D[.][section lost]
NLW PENRICE: GLAM/151, seal 2, dated 1249

SEAL 1244
Pointed oval, nm
Man vested for Mass standing full-face
Legend: [section lost]ATI[. . .][section lost]
NLW PENRICE: GLAM/151, seal 3, dated 1249

SEAL 1245
Pointed oval, nm
?Tonsured man standing facing half left holding pastoral staff in his right hand, a book in his left hand
Legend: +[.]IGILL[. . . . .]
NLW PENRICE: GLAM/151, seal 4, dated 1249

SEAL 1246
Pointed oval, 29x20
Stylised lily
Legend: + S' PhILIP[.]I . LE PAVM'
NLW PENRICE: GLAM/153, dated 1200 x 1299

SEAL 1247
Round, 25
Stylised twelve-petalled flower
Legend: + S' IOhIS : PORCh :
NLW PENRICE: GLAM/155, dated 1200 x 1299

SEAL 1248
Pointed oval, 25x20
Gem: figure standing full-face holding ?spear upright in right hand, large oval shield held

close to body on left side
Legend: +SIGIL[.] T[.]OME DE [. . . .]
NLW PENRICE: GLAM/157, dated 1205

SEAL 1249
Pointed oval, *c*.65x*c*.40
Mitred man vested for Mass standing full-face holding pastoral staff in left hand, a stylised lily in the field to the right
Legend: [.] S GVIDO [rest lost]
NLW PENRICE: GLAM/159, front, dated 1251

SEAL 1250
Round, 29
Mitred suppliant man half length facing right, GVI in field to right
Legend: + S' SECRE[.]V. EP [rest lost]
NLW PENRICE: GLAM/159, back, dated 1251

SEAL 1251
Pointed oval, 29x16
A bird ?perched on a branch facing right
Legend: * S' SIMON LE WI[.]C
NLW PENRICE: GLAM/160, dated 1252

SEAL 1252
Round, 24
Stylised ?lily (very elaborate, with 'roots' at the base)
Legend: + SIGILL[. . . . .]LIPI : D' [. . . .]ELI
NLW PENRICE: GLAM/163, dated 1225 x 1274

SEAL 1253
Pointed oval, 35x24
Stylised lily
Legend: [.] S'IOHANNIS BARED CEL[. . .]I
NLW PENRICE: GLAM/164, dated 1225 x 1274

SEAL 1254
Round, 39
Armoured man holding a sword in his right hand and blowing a horn in his left hand, on a horse galloping to the right

Legend: + SIGI[. . . . . .] ¶ BERTI [section lost]
NLW PENRICE: GLAM/169, dated 1258

SEAL 1255
Round, nm
Stylised ?eight-petalled flower (alternate 'normal' petals and ?stylised stamens)
Legend: [section lost] AN . AB . G [section lost]
NLW PENRICE: GLAM/170, dated 1258

SEAL 1256
Unknown, nm
?Feet resting on a corbel
Legend: lost
NLW PENRICE: GLAM/170, seal 2, dated 1258

SEAL 1257
Round, 21
Bird facing right perched on a crescent with six-pointed star below
Legend: + S' WILLI' : SC[. . .]AG
NLW PENRICE: GLAM/170, seal 3, dated 1258

SEAL 1258
Round, 33
Bulla of Alexander VI
NLW PENRICE: GLAM/171, dated 1260
NLW PENRICE: GLAM/173, dated 1261

SEAL 1259
Pointed oval, 29x21
Stylised lily
Legend: [. . .]OME . CAPE[. . . .]I . DE . KENEFE[.]
NLW PENRICE: GLAM/175, dated 1264

SEAL 1260
Round, 23
Six-petalled flower with a shield of arms (three chevrons) in each petal
Legend: +SIGIL[. . . . . .]BERTIDECLARE
NLW PENRICE: GLAM/176, dated 1265
NLW PENRICE: GLAM/177, seal 2, dated 1265

SEAL 1261
Pointed oval, nm
Man standing full-face with a book in his right hand and a staff in his left, with a crescent facing up to the left and a star to the right and pellets in the field
Legend: N/A
NLW PENRICE: GLAM/177, dated 1265

SEAL 1262
Pointed oval, c.52x38
Mitred man vested for Mass ?standing full-face blessing with right hand, holding a book up to his chest in his left hand, to the right a pastoral staff
Legend: [. . . . . .] [section lost] ET VE[.] LETRE[.] EPI
NLW PENRICE: GLAM/179, front, dated 1265

SEAL 1263
Round, 14
Arm emerging from right, hand holding two keys pointing up
Legend: [.] AVE MARIA
NLW PENRICE: GLAM/179, back, dated 1265

SEAL 1264
Round, 21
Many-petalled flower
Legend: +S'.PhILIPPI . LE . PALMHRE
NLW PENRICE: GLAM/181, dated 1266

SEAL 1265
Pointed oval, 31x19
Stylised lily (ornate)
Legend: *S' WILELMI [.]RAVNKCIEYN
NLW PENRICE: GLAM/182, dated 1267

SEAL 1266
Round, 28
Seven-petalled flower
Legend: + SIGILL' : THOME : FILII : [ROB]'TI
NLW PENRICE: GLAM/183, dated 1267

SEAL 1267
Drop-shaped, 26x20
Stylised lily (inverted)
Legend: +S':WILEL[.]I:COGH:
NLW PENRICE: GLAM/184, dated 1225 x 1274

SEAL 1268
Round, 34
Bulla of Clement IV
NLW PENRICE: GLAM/185, dated 1268

SEAL 1269
Round, 24
Stylised lily
Legend: * S' DAVIT [.]PVDVR :
NLW PENRICE: GLAM/188, dated 1281
NLW PENRICE: GLAM/187, dated 1281
NLW PENRICE: GLAM/186, dated 1281

SEAL 1270
Round, 28
Stylised seven-petalled flower (Tudor-style rose)
Legend: + S hE[. . . . . . .] : ALEX
NLW PENRICE: GLAM/189, seal 1, dated 1283

SEAL 1271
Pointed oval, c.40x28
Shallow cup with long stem and knop (?chalice) with six-pointed star ?on faint circle (?host) above, eight-pointed star below
Legend: [.] AMABILLE . FILIE : ALEXA'[.]
NLW PENRICE: GLAM/189, seal 2, dated 1283

SEAL 1272
Pointed oval, 30x19
To left a lion facing right attacking wyvern facing left
Legend: +SIGILLVMTRAhARN AP RES
NLW PENRICE: GLAM/191, dated 1305

APPENDIX

SEAL 1273
Hexagonal, 16x18
Lamb of God facing right
Legend: + S' MAT[.]EI [.]E[. . . .]S
NLW PENRICE: GLAM/191, seal 4, dated 1305

SEAL 1274
Hexagonal, 21x19
Shield of arms (chequy, a fess ?ermine), foliate tendrils in the field
Legend: *S' PAGAnI DE : TVRBEVILE
NLW PENRICE: GLAM/193, dated 1312

SEAL 1275
Round, nm
Uncertain; ?stylised flower
Legend: [section lost] EVIL'
NLW PENRICE: GLAM/193, seal 2, dated 1312

SEAL 1276
Round, 20
Shield of arms (three estoils)
Legend: +S'hENRICI:SCURLAG
NLW PENRICE: GLAM/195, dated 1262 x 1290

SEAL 1277
Hexagonal, 21
Shield of arms (cross floretty)
Legend: *S'IOhA[. . . . .]N[. . . . .]S
NLW PENRICE: GLAM/196, dated 131E

SEAL 1278
Round, c.22
Stylised lily, star (?six pointed) in upper left, crescent in upper right
Legend: + [. .] [section lost] MORG'
NLW PENRICE: GLAM/197, dated 1316

SEAL 1279
Rounded oval, 32x24
Stylised lily
Legend: + S' ALICIE PERVAT .
NLW PENRICE: GLAM/198, dated 1320

SEAL 1280
Round, 34
Four conifer branches with four pellets in the angles (one between each branch)
Legend: + S' : COMVNE : DE : KENEF'
NLW PENRICE: GLAM/2059, seal 2, dated 1250 x 1299
NLW PENRICE: GLAM/200, seal 2, dated 1325
NLW PENRICE: GLAM/199, seal 2, dated 1320
NLW PENRICE: GLAM/198, seal 2, dated 1320

SEAL 1281
Round, 25
Eight-petalled stylised flower
Legend: +SALI[.]IE[.]VA
NLW PENRICE: GLAM/199, dated 1320

SEAL 1282
Rounded oval, 38x30
Stylised lily, ?star below left and right
Legend: +S'IOhIS:nICOLDEKE[?n']
NLW PENRICE: GLAM/200, dated 1325

SEAL 1283
Rounded oval, c.20xc.17
Stylised lily
Legend: + S [section lost] [?E?L]
NLW PENRICE: GLAM/201, dated 1325

SEAL 1284
Round, 28
Eight stylised branches arranged radially ('snowflake' design)
Legend: + S' ThOME DE SCO DONAT'
NLW PENRICE: GLAM/202, dated 1275 x 1324

SEAL 1285
Round, 17
Crossed hands, lily above
Legend: LELAMIAVET:
NLW PENRICE: GLAM/203, seal 13, dated 1329

SEAL 1286
Round, 17
Hare facing left
Legend: [. .]PRI[. . . . . .]
NLW PENRICE: GLAM/203, seal 14, dated 1329

SEAL 1287
Round, 18
Head face up in shallow bowl with low base (head of St John the Baptist), eagle displayed above
Legend: *O[. . . . . .]OhAN[. . .]
NLW PENRICE: GLAM/203, seal 15, dated 1329

SEAL 1288
Round, 19
Shield of arms (saltire lozengy)
Legend: *S'IOhANN[section lost]VOL
NLW PENRICE: GLAM/203, Seal 16, dated 1329

SEAL 1289
Rounded oval, 19x20
Barrel on its side, foliate stems in the field
Legend: [. .]OHANNIS:[. . . . .]
NLW PENRICE: GLAM/203, Seal 17, dated 1329

SEAL 1290
Round, 16
Two heads facing in, a bird facing left above
Legend: *LOVEMEANDEIIE.
NLW PENRICE: GLAM/203, Seal 18, dated 1329

SEAL 1291
Round, 19
Shield of arms (saltire between four escallops)
Legend: [section lost]RIGR[section lost]
NLW PENRICE: GLAM/203, Seal 19, dated 1329

SEAL 1292
Unknown, nm
Three shields of arms arranged in a radial pattern with bases touching (vairé; maunch; barry of six a bend)
Legend: N/A
NLW PENRICE: GLAM/203, Seal 20, dated 1329

SEAL 1293
Round, 19
Stylised four-petalled flower
Legend: illegible
NLW PENRICE: GLAM/203, dated 1329

SEAL 1294
Round, 19
Squirrel facing left in a tree
Legend: *[section lost] YO[. .]METE
NLW PENRICE: GLAM/203, seal 3, dated 1329

SEAL 1295
Rounded oval, nm
Gem: griffin facing left
Legend: [?+]S'RE[. . . .]D[section lost]
NLW PENRICE: GLAM/203, seal 4, dated 1329

SEAL 1296
Round, 17
Four-petalled flower (?four-leafed clover)
Legend: LELA[section illegible]
NLW PENRICE: GLAM/203, seal 6, dated 1329

SEAL 1297
Rounded oval, nm
Four-petalled flower
Legend: N/A
NLW PENRICE: GLAM/203, seal 9, dated 1329

SEAL 1298
Round, 74
Obverse: Armoured man with armorial surcoat (bezantee) and shield (ten bezants) on a horse with armorial caparisons (bezanty) and head-crest galloping to the right, on a diaper ground

APPENDIX

Reverse: within a cusped octofoil, a woman in veil and long dress standing full-face on a corble holding two shields of arms (dexter; three lions passant guardant: sinister; three chevrons), on a diaper ground
Legend: Obverse: ¶ S' ¶ WILLI : LA ¶ ZOVChE : DOMINI ¶ DE ¶ GLAMORGAN
Legend: Rev: + SIG[. . .] WILLELMI : LA ZOVChE : DOMINI : DE GLAMORGAN
NLW PENRICE: GLAM/205, front and back, dated 1329
NLW PENRICE: GLAM/204, front and back, dated 1329

SEAL 1299
Round, 30
Within an ornate trefoil, a shield of arms (ten bezants) an armorial lozenge (three chevrons) above, armorial lozenges (three chevrons) to left and right
Legend: [. . . .]L[. . . . .]ILLE[. . . . .] ZOVChE
NLW PENRICE: GLAM/206, dated 1329
NLW PENRICE: GLAM/208, dated 1331

SEAL 1300
Round, 24
Within ornate architectural-style interlacing with a central circle a shield of arms (per pale: dexter three chevrons; sinister ?five bezants), in a circle above an armorial lozenge (three lions passant guardant), in a circle to the lower right a lozenge (quarterly ?blank and a fret, over all a bend)
Legend: SIGIL [rest lost]
NLW PENRICE: GLAM/206, seal 2, dated 1329

SEAL 1301
Round, 20
Shield of arms (three chevrons), with the Lamb of God facing left with a trefoil to its left above, wyverns either side of the shield
Legend: + S' . IOHIS § DE.AVENE § §
NLW PENRICE: GLAM/217, seal 2, dated 1341
NLW PENRICE: GLAM/207, dated 1330
NLW PENRICE: GLAM/219, dated 1341
NLW PENRICE: GLAM/218, seal 2, dated 1341

SEAL 1302
Round, 21
Shield of arms (a bend cotised with three martlets in chief and three ?towers in base) couche, a helm above, on a field semé with trefoils
Legend: [section lost] ?EMO [section lost]
NLW PENRICE: GLAM/210, dated 1333

SEAL 1303
Round, nm
?Head of a crozier within an ornate architectural border
Legend: [section lost] TCO[.] [section lost] ABBA [section lost]
NLW PENRICE: GLAM/211, dated 1336

SEAL 1304
Round, 78
Obverse: Armoured man with armorial shield (quarterly, 1 and 4 diapered, 2 and 3 a fret, a bend over all) on a horse with armorial caparisons (quarterly, 1 and 4 diapered, 2 and 3 a fret, a bend over all) galloping to the right.
Reverse: within an ornate cusped octofoil, a shield of arms (quarterly, 1 and 4 diapered, 2 and 3 a fret, a bend over all) flanked by a tree to the left and a tree to the right, a lion passant guardant above, on a field semé with stars
Legend: Obverse:
S'hVG¶ONIS:LE:DE¶SPENSER:D-NI:GLAMO¶RGANCIE: ET:MORGANCII¶
Legend: Rev: +S'hVGONIS:LE:DESPENSER:DO[. . .]IS:GLAMORGANCIE ET MORGANCIE
NLW PENRICE: GLAM/212, front and back, dated 1338
NLW PENRICE: GLAM/2065, front and back, dated 1338
NLW PENRICE: GLAM/212/b, front and back, dated 1338
NLW PENRICE: GLAM/221, front and back, dated 1347

SEAL 1305
Rounded oval, 25x20
Within a cusped border, Virgin and Child standing facing right, to right a kneeling suppliant figure facing left with three ?flowers on stems in the field above
Legend: illegible
NLW PENRICE: GLAM/214, dated 1339

SEAL 1306
Pointed oval, 65x42
Beneath an ornamental canopy, a mitred man standing full-face on an ornate corbel blessing with right hand and holding a pastoral staff in his left hand, to the left a shield of arms (three lions passant) to the right a shield of arms (stork statant), on a diapered field
Legend: ¶.S'FRAT[section lost]IA EPISC [section lost]
NLW PENRICE: GLAM/215, dated 1339
NLW PENRICE: GLAM/216, dated 1339

SEAL 1307
Round, 20
Shield of arms (per pale, dexter a fess between six ?roses, sinister three chevrons) suspended from a strap, foliate tendrils in the field
Legend: *S' MARG[. .]ETE:DEAVENE
NLW PENRICE: GLAM/218, dated 1341
NLW PENRICE: GLAM/217, dated 1341

SEAL 1308
Round, 22
In an ornate ?trefoil, a shield of arms (includes three chevrons and a label)
Legend: [section lost]VE [section lost]
NLW PENRICE: GLAM/222, dated 1350

SEAL 1309
Round, c.45
Within an ornate border a shield of arms (a lion rampant) flanked by two wyverns facing in
Legend: [section lost] OVB[. . .] [section lost] [.]RBRE[.]RE E[. . . . . . .]
NLW PENRICE: GLAM/223, dated 1350 x 1351

SEAL 1310
Unknown, nm
Eight-petalled stylised flower
Legend: [section lost]A[section lost]
NLW PENRICE: GLAM/224, dated 1351

SEAL 1311
Round, 112
Sixth Great of Seal Edward III
NLW PENRICE: GLAM/225, dated 1353

SEAL 1312
Pointed oval, nm
Beneath a canopy, the Virgin and Child ?seated
Legend: + SE [section lost] RIE
NLW PENRICE: GLAM/226, dated 1354

SEAL 1313
Round, 19
Shield of arms (a saltire between four pheons) flanked by wyverns facing in
Legend: * S IOhANNIS L[. .]EL
NLW PENRICE: GLAM/227, seal 2, dated 1354

SEAL 1314
Round, 20
Within an ornate border, head of a man facing right, on the right an ornament (?speech scroll)
Legend: [section lost]LE
NLW PENRICE: GLAM/228, dated 1357

SEAL 1315
Round, 83
Obverse: Man in armour with crested helm (a ?griffin's head) and armorial shield (quarterly, 2 and 3 a fret, a bend over all) on a horse with armorial caparisons (quarterly, 1 and 4 ?diapered, 2 and 3 a fret, a bend over all) galloping to the right
Reverse: within a cusped border, a shield of arms (quarterly, 1 and 4 diapered, 2 and 3 a fret, a bend over all) hanging from a bush
Legend: Obverse: ¶ Sigillum:Edwardi ¶ le:despense[. . . . .]morg[. . . .]morg::

APPENDIX

Legend: Reverse: ⸿ Sigillum [. . . . .]
de [. . . . .]o [. . . . . . .]NLW PENRICE:
GLAM/230, front and back, dated 1338
NLW PENRICE: GLAM/229, front and back, dated 1358

SEAL 1316
Pointed oval, 32x19
Within a cusped border, a boar walking left over rocky ground, a tree behind
Legend: *S'.DE[. . .]N[. . .]DE.GRONYTh
NLW PENRICE: GLAM/232, dated 1365

SEAL 1317
Round, c.28
Within a cusped border, a shield of arms (paly of six, on a bend three ?quatrefoils), foliate tendrils in the field
Legend: [. . . . .] DE § STRATEL[. . .]
NLW PENRICE: GLAM/234, dated 1366

SEAL 1318
Round, 35
Bulla of Urban VI
NLW PENRICE: GLAM/236, dated 1383

SEAL 1319
Pointed oval, 79x45
Within an ornate canopied niche, a mitred man seated full-face blessing with his right hand and holding a pastoral staff in his left, on the left outside the niche the word: 'theleau', above, a shield (indistinct), below, within a niche formed by a rounded arch, a full-face three quarter length mitred supplicant man, on the left a shield of arms (quarterly France ancient and England), on the right a shield of arms (a pile, diapered)
Legend: S:th[remainder lost]
NLW PENRICE: GLAM/237, dated 1384

SEAL 1320
Round, 35
Bulla of Boniface IX
NLW PENRICE: GLAM/238, dated 1394

SEAL 1321
Rounded oval, 28x25
Within an ornately canopied niche, Virgin and Child seated full-face to the left, to the right a kneeling suppliant man facing left holding up a crozier before him
Legend: ⸿ SECRETVMThOME ABBIS[.]EV[.]ESBVR'
NLW PENRICE: GLAM/239, dated 1394
NLW PENRICE: GLAM/251, dated 1440

SEAL 1322
Pointed oval, 42x28
Mitred man vested for Mass seated full-face blessing with right hand, left hand holding a pastoral staff, two keys point up with a cross bottone beneath to the left, a sword point up with a cross bottone beneath to the right, below, beneath a pointed arch, a suppliant ?tonsured man half-length facing right
Legend: ⸿ SIG[.]L OFFICIALI⸿T[. . . . .]
NLW PENRICE: GLAM/242, dated 1397

SEAL 1323
Round, nm
Second Great Seal of Henry V
NLW PENRICE: GLAM/243, dated 1415

SEAL 1324
Round, 70
Man in armour with armorial sleeves and shield (quarterly England and France modern) and wearing a cap of maintenance on a horse with armorial caparisons (quarterly England and France modern) galloping to the right, foliate tendrils in the field
Legend: Obverse: [sectio lost] [. . . . .]pro Principatu Southwa[. .]
NLW PENRICE: GLAM/244, front, dated 1422
NLW PENRICE: GLAM/244, back, dated 1422

SEAL 1325
Round, 34
Bulla of Martin V
NLW PENRICE: GLAM/245, dated 1423

SEAL 1326
Pointed oval, nm
Within an ornate canopied architectural niche, nimbed and bearded man with long hair standing full-face wearing skin robes, holding the Lamb of God up in his left hand and pointing to it with his right hand (St John the Baptist) with below, beneath an ogee arch, a kneeling suppliant tonsured man facing left, a shield of arms (bendy of six) on either side
Legend: [section lost] doc'to[. . .] [section lost]
NLW PENRICE: GLAM/246, dated 1423
NLW PENRICE: GLAM/247, dated 1423
NLW PENRICE: GLAM/248, dated 1423

SEAL 1327
Pointed oval, nm
In a compartment beneath a ?pedestal a shield of arms (bendy of six, on chief a pierced cinquefoil)
Legend: lost
NLW PENRICE: GLAM/249, dated 1423

SEAL 1328
Round, 15x12
Scallop
Legend: none
NLW PENRICE: GLAM/250, dated 1440

SEAL 1329
Octagonal, 15x12
Eagle with spread wings walking left
Legend: torborvyill
NLW PENRICE: GLAM/250, seal 2, dated 1440

SEAL 1330
Rounded oval, 28x25
Within an ornately canopied niche, Virgin and Child seated full-face to the left, to the right a kneeling suppliant man facing right holding a crozier up before him
Legend: S'[.]ECRETV'W[. . . . .]S TEVKESBVR'
NLW PENRICE: GLAM/254, dated 1442
NLW PENRICE: GLAM/252, dated 1441

SEAL 1331
Round, 13
Crowned letter 'I' with foliage either side
Legend: none
NLW PENRICE: GLAM/255, dated 1443

SEAL 1332
Rounded oval, 29
Within an ornate canopied niche, on the left Virgin and Child seated full-face, on the right a kneeling suppliant man facing right holding up a crozier before him
Legend: ¶[section lost][. . . . .]BIS.TEVK [. . . .]R'
NLW PENRICE: GLAM/258, dated 1449
NLW PENRICE: GLAM/256, dated 1444
NLW PENRICE: GLAM/259, dated 1449 x 1450
NLW PENRICE: GLAM/257, dated 1447

SEAL 1333
Round, nm
Obverse: ?man holding sword on horse in armorial caparisons (three chevrons) ?galloping to (facing) right
Reverse: shield of arms (?per pale, dexter, lost; sinister, three chevrons), abstract decoration in the field
Legend: lost
NLW PENRICE: GLAM/261, front and back, dated 1450
NLW PENRICE: GLAM/260, front and back, dated 1450

SEAL 1334
Round, nm
Obverse: Armoured man with armorial shield (a saltire with a label of three points) on horse with armorial caparisons galloping to the right
Legend: Obverse: fragments which remain are chiefly indecipherable minims
NLW PENRICE: GLAM/263, front, dated 1452
NLW PENRICE: GLAM/262, front, dated 1452

APPENDIX

NLW PENRICE: GLAM/262, back, dated 1452
NLW PENRICE: GLAM/263, back, dated 1452

SEAL 1335
Round, nm
Obverse: armoured man, holding a sword in the right hand and a shield of arms (see reverse) in the left, mounted on a horse galloping to right, with foliage in the field
Reverse: shield of arms (per pale: [1] France (modern) and England, quarterly, with a label of three points; per fess: [2] a fess between six crosses crosselet; [4] chequy, chevron ermine) surrounded by foliage
Legend: lost
NLW PENRICE: GLAM/266, dated 1471

SEAL 1336
Pointed oval, nm
Within an ornate canopied architectural niche, a man ?vested for Mass standing full-face, ?blessing with right hand
Legend: lost
NLW PENRICE: GLAM/267, dated 1477

SEAL 1337
Pointed oval, 56x40
Within a canopied architectural niche, Virgin and Child standing full-face, shield of arms (three clarions) with a crescent and sun below to the left of the niche, a shield of arms (three chevrons) with a sun and crescent below to the right of the niche, with below, beneath a pointed arch, the head and shoulders of a suppliant man facing right with a crozier held up in their arms
Legend: ❡ SIGILL ❡ VM ABBATIS ET ❡ CONVENTVS DE ❡ MARGAN
NLW PENRICE: GLAM/2073, dated 1528
NLW PENRICE: GLAM/279, dated 1518
NLW PENRICE: GLAM/2071, dated 1519
NLW PENRICE: GLAM/268, dated 1484
NLW PENRICE: GLAM/273, dated 1509
NLW PENRICE: GLAM/277, dated 1516
NLW PENRICE: GLAM/280, dated 1518
NLW PENRICE: GLAM/281, dated 1521
NLW PENRICE: GLAM/274, dated 1509
NLW PENRICE: GLAM/276, dated 1514
NLW PENRICE: GLAM/285, dated 1532
NLW PENRICE: GLAM/2072, dated 1520
NLW PENRICE: GLAM/2068, dated 1509
NLW PENRICE: GLAM/2074, dated 1530

SEAL 1338
?Pointed oval, nm
Within an ornate canopied tripartite niche, full-length standing Virgin in supplicant pose (the Assumption) in a wavy oval with an angel above and below, to the left a tonsured and nimbed man holding two keys and book (St Peter), to the right a nimbed and bearded man holding sword and book (St Paul), Holy Trinity (Throne of Mercy) in a compartment above
Legend: lost
NLW PENRICE: GLAM/269, dated 1486

SEAL 1339
Round, 12
Bird (?eagle displayed)
Legend: N/A
NLW PENRICE: GLAM/271, seal 3, dated 1493

SEAL 1340
Unknown, nm
Shield of arms (two fleur-de-lys)
Legend: none
NLW PENRICE: GLAM/275, dated 1510

SEAL 1341
Round, nm
Shield (charge illegible)
Legend: none
NLW PENRICE: GLAM/282, dated 1521

SEAL 1342
Round, 11
Monogram ?dH
Legend: none
NLW PENRICE: GLAM/283, dated 1527

SEAL 1343
Round, nm
Boar's head facing left, ?foliate stem (?water) below, unidentified object in upper left
Legend: none
NLW PENRICE: GLAM/284, dated 1527

SEAL 1344
Round, 9
Two-headed eagle
Legend: none
NLW PENRICE: GLAM/286, dated 1536

SEAL 1345
Round, 17
Head lying face up in dish with shallow foot (head John the Baptist)
Legend: [.] CA[.]V D IO [section lost]
NLW PENRICE: GLAM/299, dated 1282

SEAL 1346
Round, 15
Stylised lily
Legend: SI [section lost] OM[. . .]
NLW PENRICE: GLAM/299, seal 2, dated 1282

SEAL 1347
Round, nm
Lion to the left facing right fighting a ?wyvern facing left
Legend: * PRI [section lost] POI CONV
NLW PENRICE: GLAM/304, dated 1315

SEAL 1348
Rounded oval, 24x22
Head of man with wavy hair facing left
Legend: *SIGIL [section lost] [?D]EGVIS[. .]
NLW PENRICE: GLAM/305, dated 1315

SEAL 1349
Unknown, nm
Eagle displayed
Legend: LEL [section lost]
NLW PENRICE: GLAM/307, seal 2, dated 1315

SEAL 1350
Rounded oval, nm
Within a canopied niche, to left a nimbed figure standing holding a rectangular object up in their left hand, to right a kneeling suppliant figure facing left
Legend: [section lost]DE PENE[. . . .]GE
NLW PENRICE: GLAM/311, dated 1320

SEAL 1351
Round, 18
Shield of arms (three bars)
Legend: + [. . . . . .]VS[.] [section lost] AN[. .]
NLW PENRICE: GLAM/312, seal 2, dated 1323

SEAL 1352
Round, 19
Shield of arms (party per pale dancetty) with a star above and foliate stems either side
Legend: *S' ROBERTIDEPENRES'
NLW PENRICE: GLAM/314, seal 3, dated 1323
NLW PENRICE: GLAM/313, dated 1323
NLW PENRICE: GLAM/318, dated 1320 x 1323
NLW PENRICE: GLAM/2804, seal 4, dated 1341
NLW PENRICE: GLAM/315, dated 1323
NLW PENRICE: GLAM/316, seal 3, dated 1323

SEAL 1353
Round, 19
Four leaves (four-leafed clover)
Legend: *[section lost] [. .]A[.]ET¶
NLW PENRICE: GLAM/314, dated 1323

SEAL 1354
Round, 19
Sacred monogram (IHC), stylised 'crown' above
Legend: +PRIVESV
NLW PENRICE: GLAM/314, seal 2, dated 1323

APPENDIX

SEAL 1355
Round, 15
Eagle displayed
Legend: *PRIVESV[.]
NLW PENRICE: GLAM/314, seal 4, dated 1323

SEAL 1356
Round, 18
Two lions passant facing left
Legend: [section lost] [. .] MAR
NLW PENRICE: GLAM/314, seal 5, dated 1323

SEAL 1357
Round, 24
Three ?flowers (?ears of grass) on stem
Legend: +S[. .]ENR'FIL'.WILL'I.
NLW PENRICE: GLAM/314, seal 6, dated 1323

SEAL 1358
Round, 17
Crossed hands, a flower above
Legend: *TE [.]FEIVAI
NLW PENRICE: GLAM/314, seal 7, dated 1323

SEAL 1359
Round, 19
Lion rampant facing left
Legend: +SIGILLUM ¶ IOE[. . . .]
NLW PENRICE: GLAM/316, seal 2, dated 1323

SEAL 1360
Round, 19
Grotesque (bird with man's head) walking to left
Legend: * IEO SVY [.]E NVTEL[.]
NLW PENRICE: GLAM/317, dated 1323

SEAL 1361
Pointed oval, 28x19
Stylised four-petalled flower with ?leaves between petals
Legend: *S'ISABELL'DEPENRES
NLW PENRICE: GLAM/322, dated 1325

SEAL 1362
Round, 18
A merchant mark on a shield (includes inverted Y, letters IO) a cross-tipped staff and banner emerging from top
Legend: +SIOhISDESTOTISBV[. .]
NLW PENRICE: GLAM/324, seal 2, dated 1336

SEAL 1363
Unknown, nm
Indistinct
Legend: lost, if any
NLW PENRICE: GLAM/325, dated 1340

SEAL 1364
Rounded oval, 16x10
Gem: head and shoulders (of ?woman) facing right
Legend: none
NLW PENRICE: GLAM/329, dated 1383

SEAL 1365
Round, 24
Within an eight pointed border, shield of arms (per pale, indented)
Legend: [. . .]ILLU.IOhIS.PE[. . .] Y [. . . . .] .OXENW[. . . .]
NLW PENRICE: GLAM/330, dated 1394

SEAL 1366
Round, 24
Man in long gown standing full-face holding up disk with Lamb of God in his left hand (St John the Baptist), within an ornate architectural niche with canopy extending into legend band
Legend: ¶ § S § iohanis § [?T]aseman
NLW PENRICE: GLAM/331, dated 1394

SEAL 1367
Round, 11
Head and neck of eagle facing left with foliage below, letters in the field
Legend: Ir [section lost] e[. . .]c
NLW PENRICE: GLAM/332, dated 1428

SEAL 1368
Round, 15
Crowned letter R
Legend: none
NLW PENRICE: GLAM/336, seal 11, dated 1461

SEAL 1369
Round, 13
Shield of arms (charge illegible)
Legend: illegible
NLW PENRICE: GLAM/337, seal 1, dated 1483

SEAL 1370
Round, 13
Shield (charge indistinct) with letters (indistinct) in the field
Legend: none
NLW PENRICE: GLAM/337, seal 2, dated 1483

SEAL 1371
Round, 15
Abstract lines forming A either side of a diagonal band (upper right to lower left)
Legend: none
NLW PENRICE: GLAM/340, dated 1493

SEAL 1372
Rectangular, 11x8
Letter W with ?knot above
Legend: none
NLW PENRICE: GLAM/342, seal 1, 11 and 12, dated 1487

SEAL 1373
Rectangular, 12x10
Merchant mark (includes letters I, ?M)
Legend: none
NLW PENRICE: GLAM/342, seal 3, 6, 7, 8, 10 dated 1487

SEAL 1374
Round, 12
Merchant mark (includes patriarchal cross with banner above)
Legend: none
NLW PENRICE: GLAM/342, seal 2, 4, 5 and 9, dated 1487

SEAL 1375
Rectangular, 11x9
Shield of arms (a chevron between three maunches)
Legend: none
NLW PENRICE: GLAM/343, dated 1511
NLW PENRICE: GLAM/345, dated 1511

SEAL 1376
Rounded oval, 11x8
Crowned letter I, ?branches either side
Legend: none
NLW PENRICE: GLAM/344, dated 1511

SEAL 1377
Round, 10
Five-petalled flower
Legend: none
NLW PENRICE: GLAM/348, seal 1, dated 1514

SEAL 1378
Round, 12
Merchant mark (includes letters b, ?h)
Legend: none
NLW PENRICE: GLAM/348, seal 2, dated 1514

SEAL 1379
Round, 13
Pelican in piety facing left
Legend: none
NLW PENRICE: GLAM/348, seal 3, dated 1514

SEAL 1380
Round, nm
Hand emerging from the right holding a dagger point up, object in upper left
Legend: none
NLW PENRICE: GLAM/350, dated 1516

APPENDIX

SEAL 1381
Square, nm
Letter S
Legend: none
NLW PENRICE: GLAM/351, dated 1517

SEAL 1382
Undetermined, 15x15
Within an ornate border, boar's head facing left
Legend: none
NLW PENRICE: GLAM/352, dated 1520

SEAL 1383
Rounded oval, 12x10
Shield of arms (a maunch)
Legend: none
NLW PENRICE: GLAM/2078, dated 1543
NLW PENRICE: GLAM/355, dated 1534

SEAL 1384
Undetermined, 15x15
Monogram: within a bead border, letters 'TO'
Legend: none
NLW PENRICE: GLAM/356, dated 1536

SEAL 1385
Round, 14
Letters 'I B', pattern above
Legend: none
NLW PENRICE: GLAM/357, dated 1537

SEAL 1386
Round, nm
Second Great Seal of Henry VIII
NLW PENRICE: GLAM/359, dated 1540

SEAL 1387
Round, 14
Letter ?G (damaged)
Legendnone
NLW PENRICE: GLAM/360, dated 1540

SEAL 1388
Unknown, nm
Shield (charge illegible)
Legend: none
NLW PENRICE: GLAM/361, dated 1541

SEAL 1389
Round, 126
Third Great Seal of Henry VIII
NLW PENRICE: GLAM/366, dated 1546
NLW PENRICE: GLAM/362, dated 1543
NLW PENRICE: GLAM/1188, dated 1543

SEAL 1390
Unknown, nm
A maunch (uncertain if on a shield; seal too worn)
Legend: none
NLW PENRICE: GLAM/364, dated 1544
NLW PENRICE: GLAM/363, dated 1543

SEAL 1391
Round, 15
Letters R M, stylised branch above and below
Legend: none
NLW PENRICE: GLAM/364, seal 2, dated 1544

SEAL 1392
Rounded oval, 14x19
Gem: galley (?with fish below)
Legend: illegible
NLW PENRICE: GLAM/379, back, dated 1150 x 1199

SEAL 1393
Round, nm
Armoured man on horse galloping to right
Legend: lost
NLW PENRICE: GLAM/379, front, dated 1150 x 1199

SEAL 1394
Round, 11
Cross with ?branches in the angles (uncertain motif)
Legend: none
NLW PENRICE: GLAM/382, dated 1275 x 1324

SEAL 1395
Round, 25
Stylised sixteen-petalled flower
Legend: *.S'WILL'[. . . . .]NER'
NLW PENRICE: GLAM/383, dated 1275 x 1324

SEAL 1396
Round, 23x24
Sun with eight rays that curve clockwise
Legend: *S' IOHIS D[. .]ARRY
NLW PENRICE: GLAM/384, dated 1275 x 1299

SEAL 1397
Round, 23
Sixteen-petalled flower (four large petals, four smaller ones, eight tiny petals in the angles of the larger ones)
Legend: + S' . SEMONIS WEBIR
NLW PENRICE: GLAM/385, dated 1275 x 1299

SEAL 1398
Pointed oval, 31x21
Tonsured head facing left with a star to the left, a hand, blessing, emerging from top right (Manus Dei)
Legend: [. . . .] I KEThEROCh : CAPILL'[.]
NLW PENRICE: GLAM/386, dated 1283

SEAL 1399
Round, nm
Stylised lily between four pellets
Legend: *S'NIC[. . . .]IL'IOh'ANE
NLW PENRICE: GLAM/387, dated 1250 x 1299

SEAL 1400
Unknown, nm
Motif lost
Legend: S':[remainder lost]
NLW PENRICE: GLAM/388, dated 1250 x 1299

SEAL 1401
Round, c.19
Shield of arms (five lozenges conjoined in a bend), foliate sprigs in the field
Legend: * S' SIMONIS [. . . . .]
NLW PENRICE: GLAM/389, seal 1, dated 1299

SEAL 1402
Round, 17
Stylised lily
Legend: S' E[. . . . .]
NLW PENRICE: GLAM/389, seal 13, dated 1299

SEAL 1403
Round, nm
Shield of arms (a bend)
Legend: *S [. . . . .][?A]LE[. .]
NLW PENRICE: GLAM/389, seal 2, dated 1299

SEAL 1404
Round, nm
Shield of arms (cross fleuretty between ?eight billets)
Legend: [section lost] LE . N [section lost]
NLW PENRICE: GLAM/389, seal 4, dated 1299

SEAL 1405
Round, nm
Motif indistinct
Legend: none
NLW PENRICE: GLAM/391, front, dated 1305 x 1306

SEAL 1406
Round, 23
Lozenge (charge lost)
Legend: S' [section lost]LE[section lost]I[.]E[. . . . .]S
NLW PENRICE: GLAM/391, back, dated 1305 x 1306

SEAL 1407
Round, 28
Elaborate four-petalled flower
Legend: S' AMICIE . LE NIVLESTAR'
NLW PENRICE: GLAM/392, dated 1310

APPENDIX

SEAL 1408
Round, 28
Stylised eight-petalled flower with eight small half-petals in the angles
Legend: S' C[. . .]TIANE.ALINC
NLW PENRICE: GLAM/393, dated 1321

SEAL 1409
Round, 17
Within a six-petalled flower, a ?leopard's head full-face
Legend: *E[?N][. .]E[.]OSEL[. . . . . .]
NLW PENRICE: GLAM/396, seal 1, dated 1332

SEAL 1410
Unknown, nm
Figure ?vested for Mass (fragment only)
Legend: N/A
NLW PENRICE: GLAM/396, seal 3, dated 1332

SEAL 1411
Round, 23
Within a cusped sexfoil, a shield of arms (three bars)
Legend: *SIGILL[.]MRICARDI . SCVRLAG
NLW PENRICE: GLAM/398, dated 1366

SEAL 1412
Rounded oval, 25x20
Man standing facing half right holding a roundel with the Lamb of God up in his left hand and pointing to it with his right hand (St John the Baptist)
Legend: ECCE AG[. .]S DEI
NLW PENRICE: GLAM/399, dated 1366

SEAL 1413
Pointed oval, nm
Within niches, to the left a figure in robes standing ?full-face, to the right a figure ?vested for Mass, in a niche below a mitred man standing facing half left holding up and object
Legend: none
NLW PENRICE: GLAM/400, seal 1, dated 1367

SEAL 1414
Pointed oval, nm
Building with rounded arched door and central circular window, a tower with conical spire above, to the right a tower with a conical spire (left side lost)
Legend: [. . . . . .]VM [remainder lost]
NLW PENRICE: GLAM/400, seal 2, dated 1367

SEAL 1415
Round, nm
Obverse: horse with caparisons facing right
Reverse: shield of arms (quarterly; 2 a fret, 4 a bend (1 & 3 lost)), a ?wing to the right
Legend: illegible
NLW PENRICE: GLAM/404, dated 1394

SEAL 1416
Rounded oval, nm
Flat-topped pear shape, voided (?possibly a strap-end rather than seal matrix)
Legend: none
NLW PENRICE: GLAM/406, dated 1417

SEAL 1417
Round, 12
Scallop-shell shaped outline with ?horseshoe inside
Legend: none
NLW PENRICE: GLAM/406, seal 2, dated 1417

SEAL 1418
Round, nm
Obverse: armoured man on horseback, riding right
Reverse: shield of arms (impaled: dexter, lion rampant; sinister, lion rampant; with supporters)
Legend: lost
NLW PENRICE: GLAM/407, dated 1417

SEAL 1419
Rounded oval, 14x10
Crowned letter E
Legend: none
NLW PENRICE: GLAM/408, seal 1, 4, 5, 6
dated 1419

SEAL 1420
Unknown, nm
?Letter
Legend: none
NLW PENRICE: GLAM/408, seal 3, dated 1419

SEAL 1421
Octagonal, 8x10
Large leaf (?vine leaf), with letters around the edge
Legend: [. . .]ane [. .]en[. . .]
NLW PENRICE: GLAM/409, seal 2, dated 1427

SEAL 1422
Octagonal, 12x10
Letter C with small letter n inside
Legend: none
NLW PENRICE: GLAM/409, seal 3, dated 1427

SEAL 1423
Rounded oval, 12x10
Within a chaplet with roses, crowned letter I and foliage on either side
Legend: none
NLW PENRICE: GLAM/409, seal 4, dated 1427

SEAL 1424
Octagonal, 10x8
Shield of arms (a bird (?eagle) rising) hanging from stems of two ivy leaves
Legend: in vous ma fye
NLW PENRICE: GLAM/409, seal 5, dated 1427

SEAL 1425
Round, 15
Griffin passant facing left
Legend: none
NLW PENRICE: GLAM/411, seal 1, dated 1456

SEAL 1426
Round, 42
Within an ornate double-canopied niche, Virgin standing full-face to left, man in short gown holding object up in right face (John the Baptist), foliate stem between them
Legend: ¶C[. . . .]VNE ABBIS ET [. . . . . .] S DE STANLEYA IN [. . .]
NLW PENRICE: GLAM/411, seal 2, front, dated 1456

SEAL 1427
Round, 18
Monogram: letters 'AC', with foliage above and below
Legend: none
NLW PENRICE: GLAM/411, seal 2, back, dated 1456

SEAL 1428
Round, 20
Shield of arms (three bars)
Legend: none
NLW PENRICE: GLAM/414, dated 1474

SEAL 1429
Round, 12
Crowned letter R
Legend: none
NLW PENRICE: GLAM/415, dated 1489

SEAL 1430
Round, 11
Stag's head full-face with a cross between the antlers and a pellet each side of the head
Legend: none
NLW PENRICE: GLAM/415, seal 2, dated 1489

SEAL 1431
Round, nm
?Conifer branch with pellet to right

APPENDIX

Legend: S[. . .] [section lost] II
NLW PENRICE: GLAM/415, seal 3, dated 1489

SEAL 1432
Round, 9
Bird with wings raised facing right
Legend: none
NLW PENRICE: GLAM/416, dated 1489

SEAL 1433
Rectangular, 13
Letter I flanked by flowers on stems, ?small flowers above and below
Legend: none
NLW PENRICE: GLAM/418, dated 1502

SEAL 1434
Round, 12
Stag seated facing left, letter I to left, ?letter ?w (?m) to right
Legend: none
NLW PENRICE: GLAM/418, seal 2, dated 1502

SEAL 1435
Unknown, 12
Includes letter 'P'
Legend: none
NLW PENRICE: GLAM/421, dated 1520

SEAL 1436
Undetermined, 14x18
Monogram: letters 'I ?h'
Legend: none
NLW PENRICE: GLAM/422, dated 1535

SEAL 1437
Round, 13
Letters T h, stylised branch above and below
Legend: none
NLW PENRICE: GLAM/423, dated 1538

SEAL 1438
Round, 11
Letters W b
Legend: NLW PENRICE: GLAM/2813, seal 1, 2 3 and 4, dated 1542
NLW PENRICE: GLAM/424, seal 1, 2, 3 and 4, dated 1542

SEAL 1439
Rounded oval, 8x9
Gem: winged horse rearing on hind legs, facing right
Legend: none
NLW PENRICE: GLAM/426, seal 1 and 2, dated 1546

SEAL 1440
Round, 12
Stag standing facing left
Legend: none
NLW PENRICE: GLAM/426, seal 3, dated 1546

SEAL 1441
Round, 23
Shield of arms (three chevrons)
Legend: [.] S' hE[. . .] [section lost]
NLW PENRICE: GLAM/439, dated 1250 x 1299

SEAL 1442
Octagonal, 12x11
A heart, sprouting from it three stems with four-petalled flowers
Legend: none
NLW PENRICE: GLAM/442, dated 1422

SEAL 1443
Round, 14
Letters hK interlaced at right angles, small letters ene above the K
Legend: none
NLW PENRICE: GLAM/443, seal 1, dated 1424

SEAL 1444
Round, 18
Two heads both facing in
Legend: * AMIE . DOVZ PE[.]SE [. . . .]RS
NLW PENRICE: GLAM/443, seal 2, dated 1424

SEAL 1445
Rounded oval, 21x17
Gem: figure (?man) standing facing right, gesturing to right with left hand, right arm on staff held behind them
Legend: +S[. . . . .]V. WILL'[. .]DE LON [. . .]IIS
NLW PENRICE: GLAM/522, dated 1205 x 1214

SEAL 1446
Pointed oval, nm
Within ornate architectural canopied niches the Annunciation, to the left a nimbed man standing full-face holding saltire cross (St Andrew), to the right a man standing full-face wearing a large hat, holding a pilgrim staff and carrying a bag (St James), with below, beneath a rounded arch, a half-length full-face mitred supplicant man with a pastoral staff, to the left a shield of arms (three clarions), to the right a shield of arms (lion rampant)
Legend: lost
NLW PENRICE: GLAM/526, front, dated 1484

SEAL 1447
Rounded oval, 28x23
Virgin and Child seated full-face, to the right a kneeling ?mitred supplicant man holding a pastoral staff facing left, all within a canopied niche
Legend: S' richu's . abbatis de . t[. . . .]burie III
NLW PENRICE: GLAM/526, back, dated 1484

SEAL 1448
Rounded oval, nm
Uncertain (?gem with ?bust)
Legend: none
NLW PENRICE: GLAM/528, dated 1516

SEAL 1449
Rectangular, 12x11
Letter T
Legend: none
NLW PENRICE: GLAM/530, dated 1516

SEAL 1450
Round, nm
Letter G to the right, stylised branch above and below
Legend: none
NLW PENRICE: GLAM/540, seal 1, dated 1546

SEAL 1451
Round, nm
Merchant mark on a shield (includes inverted Y)
Legend: none
NLW PENRICE: GLAM/540, seal 2, dated 1546

SEAL 1452
Octagonal, 14x14
Pelican in its piety facing right
Legend: none
NLW PENRICE: GLAM/554, dated 1515

SEAL 1453
Square, 9x10
Monogram: 'IS'
Legend: none
NLW PENRICE: GLAM/555, dated 1518

SEAL 1454
Unknown, nm
Letters ?B e
Legend: none
NLW PENRICE: GLAM/562, seal 1, dated 1539

SEAL 1455
Rounded oval, nm
A pellet (may be impression from a cameo bezel, not an intaglio matrix)
Legend: none
NLW PENRICE: GLAM/562, seal 2, dated 1539

APPENDIX

SEAL 1456
Rounded oval, 17x14
Shield of arms (lion passant guardant between three fleur-de-lys), a helm with a chaplet and mantling, letters ?E N above
Legend: none
NLW PENRICE: GLAM/564, dated 1543
NLW PENRICE: GLAM/1187, dated 1543

SEAL 1457
Rounded oval, 14x11
Gem: man holding sword up in right hand kneeling facing left wearing ancient-style helm with shield on his back
Legend: none
NLW PENRICE: GLAM/566, dated 1543
NLW PENRICE: GLAM/565, dated 1544 x 1545
NLW PENRICE: GLAM/2081, dated 1547

SEAL 1458
Unknown, nm
?Figure (very worn)
Legend: none
NLW PENRICE: GLAM/567, dated 1546

SEAL 1459
Unknown, 12x12
A maunch
Legend: none
NLW PENRICE: GLAM/568, dated 1546

SEAL 1460
Round, 15
Indistinct
Legend: none
NLW PENRICE: GLAM/569, dated 1547

SEAL 1461
Round, 16
Letter I with star above and ?foliage (?text) to left and right
Legend: none
NLW PENRICE: GLAM/569, seal 2, dated 1547

SEAL 1462
Round, 14
Letters M L with two stars in between, stylised branch above and below
Legend: none
NLW PENRICE: GLAM/570, dated 1548

SEAL 1463
Round, 12
Letter L
Legend: none
NLW PENRICE: GLAM/784, dated 1463

SEAL 1464
Round, 13
Stylised lily
Legend: none
NLW PENRICE: GLAM/787, dated 1533

SEAL 1465
Rounded oval, 14x11
Shield of arms (quarterly: 1 three fleur-de-lys; 2 and 3 cross saltire fleury; 4 ?bird)
Legend: none
NLW PENRICE: GLAM/788, seal 1, dated 1537

SEAL 1466
Rounded oval, 11x9
?Gem: man's bearded head facing left, wearing a ?helm (?wreath)
Legend: none
NLW PENRICE: GLAM/788, seal 2, dated 1537

SEAL 1467
Round, 13
Animal facing left
Legend: none
NLW PENRICE: GLAM/790, seal 1 and 2, dated 1550

SEAL 1468
Round, 13
Letter W
Legend: none
NLW PENRICE: GLAM/1177, dated 1534

SEAL 1469
Unknown, nm
?quadruped walking to right
Legend: none
NLW PENRICE: GLAM/1178, dated 1536

SEAL 1470
Rounded oval, 11x8
Undetermined
Legend: none
NLW PENRICE: GLAM/1179, dated 1536

SEAL 1471
Scutiform, 12x10
Shield of arms (three chevrons)
Legend: none
NLW PENRICE: GLAM/1179, seal 2, 3, and 4, dated 1536

SEAL 1472
Round, 13
Letter h to right, stylised branch above and below (letter to left obscured)
Legend: none
NLW PENRICE: GLAM/1181, dated 1538

SEAL 1473
Round, 15
Shield of arms (on a chief a dog passant) couchee, helm above
Legend: none
NLW PENRICE: GLAM/1183, dated 1538
NLW PENRICE: GLAM/1182, dated 1538

SEAL 1474
Round, 13
Letters in five rows: L, [.] ?T[.], LIB[.], RTA, S
Legend: none
NLW PENRICE: GLAM/1185, dated 1540

SEAL 1475
Second Seal of the Court of Augmentations of Henry VIII
NLW PENRICE: GLAM/1189, dated 1544

SEAL 1476
Rectangular, 10x18
Boar's head facing left, letter H in upper left
Legend: none
NLW PENRICE: GLAM/1565, dated 1546
NLW PENRICE: GLAM/1564, dated 1546

SEAL 1477
Square, nm
Letter W
Legend: none
NLW PENRICE: GLAM/2106, dated 1531
NLW PENRICE: GLAM/2107, seal 1 and 3, dated 1531
NLW PENRICE: GLAM/2109, seal 2, dated 1532
NLW PENRICE: GLAM/1792, dated 1531
NLW PENRICE: GLAM/2111, seal 3, dated 1532

SEAL 1478
Seal of the Court of Great Session, Glamorgan
NLW PENRICE: GLAM/1794, dated 1543
NLW PENRICE: GLAM/2816, dated 1548

SEAL 1479
Round, nm
Armoured man with armorial shield (two lions passant guardant) on horse galloping to the right
Legend: [section lost] SANGLIE:[. . . .]N[. .]
NLW PENRICE: GLAM/1947, front, dated 1193

SEAL 1480
Rounded oval, 23x19
Gem: head facing right
Legend: illegible
NLW PENRICE: GLAM/1947, back, dated 1193

SEAL 1481
Round, nm
Stylised eight-petalled flower (small petals at end of long stems in rosette pattern)

APPENDIX

Legend: [. .]GILL' R[. . . . . . .]E PENARD[.]
NLW PENRICE: GLAM/1949, dated 1230

SEAL 1482
Round, 41
Bow with arrow (point down) ready for shooting
Legend: + SIGILL' WILLELMI.GILLEM'
NLW PENRICE: GLAM/1952, dated 1175 x 1203

SEAL 1483
Round, 40
Stylised eight-petalled flower ('petals' on long stems)
Legend: +SIGILL' ALAIT[.] FILII [. . . .]ARdI
NLW PENRICE: GLAM/1954, dated 1175 x 1225
NLW PENRICE: GLAM/1959, dated 1200 x 1225

SEAL 1484
Round, 39
Stylised eight-petalled flower (Tudor-style rose)
Legend: + SIGIL' LVELIN MAPRIREd
NLW PENRICE: GLAM/1955, dated 1175 x 1225
NLW PENRICE: GLAM/1956, dated 1175 x 1225

SEAL 1485
Round, 33
Lion walking to right
Legend: + SIGILL' : MORGANI : FILII : KADRY
NLW PENRICE: GLAM/1957, dated 1217 x 1228

SEAL 1486
Pointed oval, 45x30
Two stylised seeded lilies, one facing up one facing down, points touching in centre of seal
Legend: + SIGILL.ALAITHVRFIL.ITHENARd
NLW PENRICE: GLAM/1958, dated 1175 x 1225

SEAL 1487
Round, 41
Stylised eight-petalled flower ('petals' on long stems)
Legend: + SIGIL' IORVERdIFILII [. . . . .]dI
NLW PENRICE: GLAM/1960, dated 1200

SEAL 1488
Round, 29
Stylised sixteen-petalled flower
Legend: +SIGILL':VALAVET.VAChAN
NLW PENRICE: GLAM/1961, dated 1225 x 1250

SEAL 1489
Round, 30
Bird walking left
Legend: +SIGILL'.GRIFIN:FILIIKNAI
NLW PENRICE: GLAM/1962, seal 1, dated 1231

SEAL 1490
Round, 36
Stylised six-petalled flower
Legend: +SIGILL':MADOCFIL'KNAITHVR
NLW PENRICE: GLAM/1962, seal 2, dated 1231

SEAL 1491
Round, 34
Bow and arrow pointing down ready to shoot
Legend: +SIGILL:ENEIRFILII:KNA[.] TAVR
NLW PENRICE: GLAM/1962, seal 3, dated 1231

SEAL 1492
Pointed oval, 43x27
Crescent with an eight armed sun above, letters RVP below
Legend: +SIGILL'.[.]NAIROD.FILKNAI
NLW PENRICE: GLAM/1962, seal 4, dated 1231

SEAL 1493
Round, 38
Bow and arrow pointing down ready to shoot
Legend: +SI [. . .] E[N?]
IAVN:FILII:RIERIDI
NLW PENRICE: GLAM/1963, dated 1175 x 1217

SEAL 1494
Round, 34
Stylised eight-petalled flower (petals formed by balls on end of long stems)
Legend: [section lost] A [section lost] ADAR[section lost]
NLW PENRICE: GLAM/1965, dated 1175 x 1225

SEAL 1495
Drop-shaped, 41x35
Lily-type plant facing down in relation to legend
Legend: +SIGILLVMIORVERFILII:GISTELAR
NLW PENRICE: GLAM/1967, dated 1225 x 1250

SEAL 1496
Drop-shaped, 32x29
Seeded stylised lily (upside-down in relation to legend), a pellet on upper right and left of field
Legend: +SIGILL'hOELLAB : WRVNV:
NLW PENRICE: GLAM/1968, dated 1225 x 1274

SEAL 1497
Round, 49
Ornate stylised lily
Legend: +SIGILL'KENWERC FIL' hERBERTI
NLW PENRICE: GLAM/1970, dated 1200
NLW PENRICE: GLAM/1971, dated 1200 x 1225

SEAL 1498
Pointed oval, 35x31
Seeded stylised lily
Legend: +SIGILL':MADOCI:KANAITI
NLW PENRICE: GLAM/1973, dated 1225 x 1250

SEAL 1499
Round, 29
Stylised eight-petalled flower with small pellets between the petals
Legend: +SIGILL' : kEDIC : FIL : kENERIC
NLW PENRICE: GLAM/1974, dated 1225 x 1250

SEAL 1500
Pointed oval, nm
Stylised lily
Legend: [section lost] AB OEIN [section lost]
NLW PENRICE: GLAM/1975, dated 1200 x 1225

SEAL 1501
Round, 33
Stylised lily
Legend: +SIGILL'.MEVRICFIL'LEWEL'
NLW PENRICE: GLAM/1977, seal 1, dated 1230 x 1240

SEAL 1502
Round, 33
Stylised eight-petalled flower
Legend: +SIGIL[. . . . . .]FI[.]:LEV[. . .]L
NLW PENRICE: GLAM/1977, seal 2, dated 1230 x 1240

SEAL 1503
Pointed oval, 43x28
Man facing right holding a spear, point over his shoulder, in his right hand and blowing a horn held up in his left hand
Legend: +SIGILL'ROG¶ERISTVRMIIV¶NIOR
NLW PENRICE: GLAM/1986, dated 1193 x 1218

SEAL 1504
Round, 25
Eight-petalled stylised flower with points in the angles

APPENDIX

Legend: +S':MARGERIE:FIL'E:ROGE'I
NLW PENRICE: GLAM/1993, dated 1233 x 1271

SEAL 1505
Drop-shaped, 27x23
Stylised leaf
Legend: +SIGILL'MEVRIC:AbTRA[..]N
NLW PENRICE: GLAM/1994, dated 1225 x 1250
NLW PENRICE: GLAM/1995, dated 1235

SEAL 1506
Round, 43
Eight branches in a radial pattern
Legend: +SIGILLVM RESI:GhOG:
NLW PENRICE: GLAM/1998, dated 1207
NLW PENRICE: GLAM/1997, dated 1200 x 1208

SEAL 1507
Round, 30
Bow and arrow pointing down ready to shoot, two stars below, two sets of three pellets above
Legend: +SIGILL'DIVERICI
NLW PENRICE: GLAM/1999, dated 1175 x 1225

SEAL 1508
Round, 27
Stylised lily
Legend: +SIGILL'PhILIP[section lost][.]I
NLW PENRICE: GLAM/2004, dated 1225 x 1274

SEAL 1509
Rounded oval, 22x20
Gem: animal with long horns (gazelle?), resting on haunches, facing left
Legend: +SIGILLVM:SECRETI:
NLW PENRICE: GLAM/2006, dated 1200 x 1225

SEAL 1510
Round, 38
Lion walking right
Legend: +SIGILLUMTHOME[...]LES
NLW PENRICE: GLAM/2009, dated 1175 x 1200
NLW PENRICE: GLAM/2008, dated 1175 x 1200

SEAL 1511
Round, 26
Stylised four-petalled flower
Legend: +S'ROBERT:MAGOR:
NLW PENRICE: GLAM/2011, dated 1250 x 1299

SEAL 1512
Round, 35
Stylised lily (very ornate)
Legend: + SIGILL' MAYOC : BOHAN
NLW PENRICE: GLAM/2012, dated 1230 x 1240

SEAL 1513
Round, 48
Grotesque (man's head on long neck, body of bird, foliate tale enclosing heart-shaped tendrils) walking to right
Legend: + SIGILLV[......] I : NORREIS :
NLW PENRICE: GLAM/2013, dated 1175 x 1231

SEAL 1514
Round, 43
Stylised eight-petalled flower (small petals at end of long stems radiating from central pellet)
Legend: + SIG[.......]IC : FILII : MEILERI
NLW PENRICE: GLAM/2028, dated 1200 x 1225

SEAL 1515
Round, 43
Armoured man on a horse galloping to the right
Legend: + SIGILL' OWENI FIL' M¶ ORGAN ¶ I
NLW PENRICE: GLAM/2033, dated 1208 x 1217
NLW PENRICE: GLAM/2032, dated 1208 x 1217

SEAL 1516
Round, 33
Stylised lily with crescent in upper left (reversed) and upper right
Legend: + SIGILLVM MORGANI . CA'
NLW PENRICE: GLAM/2035, dated 1217 x 1240

SEAL 1517
Round, 29
Stylised eight-petalled flower
Legend: +SIGILL' IORVART AB ESPVS
NLW PENRICE: GLAM/2040, dated 1200 x 1250

SEAL 1518
Round, 69
Armoured man on horse galloping to the left
Legend: lost
NLW PENRICE: GLAM/2045, back, dated 1217 x 1218
NLW PENRICE: GLAM/2046, back, dated 1218 x 1230
NLW PENRICE: GLAM/2047, back, dated 1200 x 1225
NLW PENRICE: GLAM/2044, back, dated 1217 x 1218

SEAL 1519
Round, 32
Armoured man on a horse galloping to the right
Legend: illegible, partially lost
NLW PENRICE: GLAM/2050, seal 1, dated 1200 x 1225

SEAL 1520
Round, 29
Stylised lily
Legend: +SIG[. . . .]ILL'I DE SVMERI
NLW PENRICE: GLAM/2050, seal 2, dated 1200 x 1225

SEAL 1521
Pointed oval, c.38x18
Stylised lily
Legend: [section lost] ?F?I[section lost] [.]O[.]
NLW PENRICE: GLAM/2050, seal 3, dated 1200 x 1225

SEAL 1522
Pointed oval, c.34x30
Man wearing short tunic standing facing right holding a cup in his left hand and a square object in his right hand
Legend: [. . .]ILLVM [. . . . . . .]CER[.]
NLW PENRICE: GLAM/2050, seal 4, dated 1200 x 1225

SEAL 1523
Round, 27
Stylised twelve-petalled flower
Legend: +SIGILL':OWENI:FILII:ALIThVRI
NLW PENRICE: GLAM/2056, seal 2, dated 1200 x 1250

SEAL 1524
Round, 31
Stylised eleven-petalled flower
Legend: +SIGILL'׃CRADOCIFILII:ALAITh
NLW PENRICE: GLAM/2056, seal 3, dated 1200 x 1250

SEAL 1525
Drop-shaped, 36x32
Stylised lily (upside-down in relation to legend), on the right and left five pellets, above, on either side, one pellet
Legend: +SIGILLVMWALTERILVVEL
NLW PENRICE: GLAM/2057, dated 1253

SEAL 1526
Round, 25
Stylised lily
Legend: +S'WALTERI:LOVEL:
NLW PENRICE: GLAM/2059, dated 1250 x 1299

SEAL 1527
Round, 28
Stylised eight-petalled flower
Legend: +SIGILLTATHERECDV
NLW PENRICE: GLAM/2061, dated 1197 x 1201

APPENDIX

SEAL 1528
Round, 21
Stylised lily
Legend: *S'DAVITSPVDVR:
NLW PENRICE: GLAM/2063, dated 1201
NLW PENRICE: GLAM/2062, dated 1201

SEAL 1529
Round, 22
Eight dots arranged in a circular pattern around a pellet
Legend: S'.IENANA'MADOC
NLW PENRICE: GLAM/2064, dated 1291

SEAL 1530
Rounded oval, 22x18
Pelican in its piety facing right
Legend: *SV[. . . .]ICANVS DEI
NLW PENRICE: GLAM/2066, seal 2, dated 1350

SEAL 1531
Round, 25
In an ornate border, shield of arms (chequey)
Legend: illegible, partially lost
NLW PENRICE: GLAM/2067, dated 1360

SEAL 1532
Scutiform, 17x14
Letters T S, stylised branch between, a sow walking to the left below
Legend: none
NLW PENRICE: GLAM/2073, dated 1528

SEAL 1533
Round, 16
Letter T with small letter S within flanked by stylised branches, stylised
foliage emerging from top of T
Legend: [. . . .] M [. . .] OdLEI
NLW PENRICE: GLAM/2073, dated 1528

SEAL 1534
Round, nm
Shield of arms (on a chevron three mullets of five points between three ?lion's heads erased)
Legend: [. . . . .] SNRA[.]YNGMETA[.]R
NLW PENRICE: GLAM/2076, dated 1537

SEAL 1535
Rounded oval, nm
Stylised lily
Legend: none
NLW PENRICE: GLAM/2096, dated 1495

SEAL 1536
Rectangular, nm
?Five diagonal lines (two top left to right, three left to right) intersecting in centre to form diaper pattern
Legend: none
NLW PENRICE: GLAM/2098, dated 1515

SEAL 1537
Rectangular, nm
Saltire cross (formed by four thin lines) with a small pellet either side
Legend: none
NLW PENRICE: GLAM/2098, seal 2, dated 1515

SEAL 1538
Unknown, nm
Two horizontal and two short vertical lines forming a 'ladder' design
Legend: none
NLW PENRICE: GLAM/2099, seal 1, dated 1515

SEAL 1539
Square, nm
Saltire cross with a pellet in each of the angles
Legend: none
NLW PENRICE: GLAM/2099, seal 2, dated 1515
NLW PENRICE: GLAM/2100, dated 1515

SEAL 1540
Round, 13
Merchant mark (includes letter YY interlinked)
Legend: none
NLW PENRICE: GLAM/2101, dated 1516

SEAL 1541
Square, 14x14
Letter R
Legend: none
NLW PENRICE: GLAM/2104, dated 1521

SEAL 1542
Rectangular, nm
?Letters s n (?stylised foliate tendrils)
Legend: none
NLW PENRICE: GLAM/2106, seal 2, dated 1531

SEAL 1543
Unknown, nm
Uncertain (?Stylised foliage)
Legend: none
NLW PENRICE: GLAM/2109, dated 1532

SEAL 1544
Square, 11x11
Uncertain design (?stylised leaves and ?flower /?ear of grass)
Legend: none
NLW PENRICE: GLAM/2110, seal 1 and 2, dated 1532
NLW PENRICE: GLAM/2111, seal 2, dated 1532

SEAL 1545
Round, 14
Letters I ?D, stylised branch above and stylised foliage below
Legend: none
NLW PENRICE: GLAM/2111, dated 1532

SEAL 1546
Rounded oval, 13x10
Gem: naked figure (?man) ?wearing a ?helm and holding a ?branch up in his right hand (?Hermes), leaning against a small pillar facing left
Legend: none
NLW PENRICE: GLAM/2112, dated 1537

SEAL 1547
Round, 12
Pelican in its piety facing left
Legend: none
NLW PENRICE: GLAM/2113, dated 1541

SEAL 1548
Rounded oval, 14x12
Letters T P with a looped cord between them
Legend: none
NLW PENRICE: GLAM/2115, dated 1540
NLW PENRICE: GLAM/2114, dated 1540

SEAL 1549
Round, 12
Letter W
Legend: none
NLW PENRICE: GLAM/2118, dated 1549
NLW PENRICE: GLAM/2116, dated 1549

SEAL 1550
Round, 24
Stylised eight-petalled flower (chevron design on petals)
Legend: S' AMABILIE : LE MILERO
NLW PENRICE: GLAM/2798, dated 1250 x 1299

SEAL 1551
Pointed oval, c.28x21
Bird walking to the left
Legend: + S' ELEN[. . . . . .] ROGERI
NLW PENRICE: GLAM/2799, dated 1200 x 1299

SEAL 1552
Round, c.23
Shield of arms (barry of six)
Legend: [. .]ALTERI DE S[. . . . . .]
NLW PENRICE: GLAM/2803, seal 1, dated 1225 x 1275

SEAL 1553
Round, 25
Shield of arms (?chequy, a saltire)

APPENDIX

Legend: [. . . . . . .]E[. . . . . .]D[.]
NLW PENRICE: GLAM/2803, seal 11, dated 1225 x 1275

SEAL 1554
Round, 22
Eagle displayed
Legend: lost
NLW PENRICE: GLAM/2803, seal 1, dated 1225 x 1275

SEAL 1555
Pointed oval, 20x29
Gem: an animal with ?horns / ?long ears (?antelope / ?hare) running to the left
Legend: [. . . . .]OMEDENER[. . .]ToT [Start point uncertain]
NLW PENRICE: GLAM/2803, seal 5, dated 1225 x 1275

SEAL 1556
Round, 18
Four ?clover leaves
Legend: lost
NLW PENRICE: GLAM/2804, seal 1, dated 1341

SEAL 1557
?Rounded oval, c.10xc.15
Animal (?horse) walking to right
Legend: none (or lost)
NLW PENRICE: GLAM/2804, seal 2, dated 1341

SEAL 1558
Round, 24
Shield of arms (?two beasts ?combatant) within an ornate border
Legend: lsot
NLW PENRICE: GLAM/2804, seal 5, dated 1341

SEAL 1559
Rounded oval, 24xc.16
Tonsured man sanding full-face holding a gridiron, a ?flame above (St Lawrence)
Legend: [Lost} [. .][A][. . .]

NLW PENRICE: GLAM/2804, seal 6, dated 1341

SEAL 1560
Rounded oval, 15x12
Letter ?T with ?crown above
Legend: none
NLW PENRICE: GLAM/2807, dated 1521

SEAL 1561
Rounded oval, 12x10
Monogram H d (or d H)
Legend: none
NLW PENRICE: GLAM/2808, dated 1527

SEAL 1562
Undetermined, 13x14
Letters W P
Legend: none
NLW PENRICE: GLAM/2809, dated 1520

SEAL 1563
First Seal of Court of Augmentations of Henry VIII, obverse and reverse
NLW PENRICE: GLAM/2812, front, dated 1539
NLW PITORD/1556, front, dated 1539 x 1540
NLW PENRICE: GLAM/2812, back, dated 1539
NLW PITORD/1556, back, dated 1539 x 1540

SEAL 1564
Rectangular, 15x18
Letters (uncertain)
Legend: none
NLW PENRICE: GLAM/2814, dated 1543

SEAL 1565
Seal of Henry VIII as Lord of Glamorgan and Morgan (Chancery of Cardiff)
NLW PENRICE: GLAM/2815, dated 1526

SEAL 1566
Rounded oval, 14
Shield of arms (per bend sinister; dexter, three horns; sinister, ?dragon rampant), letters ?c d above
Legend: none
NLW PENRICE: GLAM/2830, seal 1, dated 1549
NLW PENRICE: GLAM/2839, dated 1549

SEAL 1567
Round, 16
Bird facing left, on left letter T, on right letter B
Legend: none
NLW PENRICE: GLAM/2830, seal 2, dated 1549

SEAL 1568
Round, 16
Letters I . T
Legend: none
NLW PENRICE: GLAM/2830, seal 3, dated 1549

SEAL 1569
Round, 16
Letters N P, stylised branch above and below
Legend: none
NLW PENRICE: GLAM/2841, dated 1550

SEAL 1570
Round, 17
Letters R I, a looped cord between
Legend: none
NLW PENRICE: GLAM/2841, seal 2, dated 1550

SEAL 1571
Round, 10
Double-headed eagle displayed
Legend: none
NLW PENRICE: GLAM/5915, dated 1547

SEAL 1572
Round, 27
Stylized seven-petalled flower
Legend: S'REGINAL'BOLDI'
NLW PITORD/2, dated 1297 x 1298
NLW PITORD/359, dated 1297 x 1298
NLW PITORD/70, dated 1275 x 1299

SEAL 1573
Round, 26
Stylised ?eight-petalled flower.
Legend: S'[. . . . . . .]?N[. .]E[. . . .]
NLW PITORD/3, dated 1321 x 1322

SEAL 1574
Round, 19
Indistinct Legend: [. .]G[. . . . . . .]E?I[. . .]
NLW PITORD/4, dated 1348 x 1349

SEAL 1575
Round, 32
Stylised eight-petalled flower
Legend: S' GALFRIDI : DE CAN[.]RhN
NLW PITORD/6, dated 1275 x 1299

SEAL 1576
Round, 19
Within two interlaced squares, an animal (?Lamb of God) facing right
Legend: Lost
NLW PITORD/7, dated 1293 x 1294

SEAL 1577
Rounded oval, 20x17
?Man's head facing right above four leafy branches, a sleeping lion facing right below
Legend: *EXULTATEDEOFLO[.]C[....]A[...]ELEO
NLW PITORD/8, dated 1279 x 1280

SEAL 1578
Scutiform, 16x14
Stag's head full-face, a cross patty between the antlers, in band at top 'LEL(?)O'.
Legend: N/A
NLW PITORD/9, dated 1323 x 1324
NLW PITORD/219, dated 1325 x 1326

SEAL 1579
Round, 17

APPENDIX

Three hares running counter clockwise with three conjoined ears forming a triangle with a pellet at centre
Legend: VN . . . . ?R . . [...]
NLW PITORD/10, dated 1329 x 1330

SEAL 1580
Round, 19
Squirrel facing left
Legend: I CRA[.]E NOT[. .]
NLW PITORD/11, dated 1344 x 1345

SEAL 1581
Round, 18
Hawk taking a duck facing left
Legend: ALASIESUP[.]IS[.]
NLW PITORD/12, dated 1345

SEAL 1582
Round, 32
Four conifer branches with four pine cones in the angels
Legend: *S'SY[. . .]IS.hYLLOT (hY conjoined)
NLW PITORD/13, dated 1289 x 1290

SEAL 1583
Rounded oval, 22x19
Gem: head and shoulders facing right.
Legend: § [?W]ILL'[.]DI[?E?C?A][. . .]?HOTA
NLW PITORD/14, dated 1325 x 1326
NLW PITORD/53, dated 1326 x 1327

SEAL 1584
Round, 21
Within an ornate quatrefoil, a shield of arms (a bar between three ?roundels (?crescents))
Legend: S' RO[.]TI DE PIChFO[.]D
NLW PITORD/15, dated 1343 x 1344

SEAL 1585
Pointed oval, 39x25
Stylised seven-petalled flower.
Legend: S' P[. . . .]NILL' [. . . . .] (N reversed)
NLW PITORD/16, dated 1275 x 1299

SEAL 1586
Rounded oval, 25x23
Christ crucified flanked by Mary and John, sun and moon above.
Legend: [. . . .]?CI [. . . .]NV[. .]
NLW PITORD/17, dated 1356 x 1357

SEAL 1587
Pointed oval, 34x22
Cross with rays in the angles (?stylised four-petalled flower with four with small petals in between
Legend: + S'CECILIE RAISON
NLW PITORD/18, dated 1297 x 1298

SEAL 1588
Round, 19
Bird walking to left looking back with foliage in its beak
Legend: SIGILL'WI[. . . .]?CITOR?E
NLW PITORD/19, dated 1275 x 1299

SEAL 1589
Rounded oval, 23x20
Gem: ?Animal (?lion) facing left
Legend: illegible
NLW PITORD/20, dated 1344 x 1345

SEAL 1590
Rounded oval, 28x18
Virgin and Child seated
Legend: * AVE R[. . . .] [section lost] [. . . .]
NLW PITORD/22, dated 1308 x 1309
NLW PITORD/21, dated 1308 x 1309

SEAL 1591
Round, 18
Lion sleeping facing right
Legend: illegible
NLW PITORD/23, dated 1343 x 1344
NLW PITORD/24, dated 1343 x 1344

SEAL 1592
Round, 20
Squirrel facing left
Legend: * [. . . . . . .]
NLW PITORD/25, dated 1343 x 1344

SEAL 1593
Round, 18
Two human heads facing in, between them a stylised lily on a long stem
Legend: *LOVEMEANDEWE
NLW PITORD/57, dated 1340 x 1341
NLW PITORD/26, dated 1341 x 1342
NLW PITORD/404, dated 1340 x 1341
NLW PITORD/58, dated 1340 x 1341

SEAL 1594
Round, 20
Within a six-pointed star, a shield (charge unclear)
Legend: [. . . . .] ?IO [. . . . . .]
NLW PITORD/27, dated 1340 x 1341

SEAL 1595
Round, 32
Eight ?wheatears (conifer branches)
Legend: [Lost] [. . . . .]E[.]EWTER[.]
NLW PITORD/28, dated 1275 x 1299

SEAL 1596
Octagonal, 13x9
Crowned letter T, small S within looped descender
Legend: none
NLW PITORD/568, dated 1413
NLW PITORD/82, dated 1413 x 1414
NLW PITORD/29, dated 1413 x 1414

SEAL 1597
Round, 18
Bird walking to left with foliage in its beak
Legend: *?I[. . . . . .]?T[. .]
NLW PITORD/2449, dated 1339
NLW PITORD/31, sup1, dated 1338 x 1339

SEAL 1598
Round, 18
Animal with long tail (?lion) facing left
Legend: lost
NLW PITORD/31, seal 2, dated 1338 x 1339

SEAL 1599
Rounded oval, 16x19
Cockerel facing left
Legend: *[. .]I?V[. . . . .]
NLW PITORD/33, dated 1347 x 1348
NLW PITORD/32, dated 1347 x 1348

SEAL 1600
Round, 28
Four conifer branches with three petals in the angles
Legend: *S'WILL'IBOLDING:§
NLW PITORD/34, dated 1315 x 1316

SEAL 1601
Unknown [fragment], 19
Indistinct fragment wrapped in wool
Legend: N/A
NLW PITORD/36, dated 1305 x 1306

SEAL 1602
Round, 20
Within an octofoil a shield of arms (two ?heads full-face in chief, a wheatsheaf in base) hanging from a bush.
Legend: ¶ § S : ade : De : Smah[. . .] § ¶
NLW PITORD/37, dated 1389 x 1390

SEAL 1603
Rounded oval, 22x19
Woman wearing a long dress and a veiled headdress (?long side-plats) standing full-face holding a shield (fess) in her right hand, her left hand against her breast (?holding cord from cloak).
Legend: * S' A[. . . . .]V¶[. .]
NLW PITORD/1293, dated 1358 x 1359
NLW PITORD/38, dated 1356 x 1257
NLW PITORD/46, dated 1359 x 1360
NLW PITORD/537, seal 2, dated 1349

SEAL 1604
Round, 19
Indistinct
Legend: lost
NLW PITORD/39, dated 1347 x 1348

APPENDIX

SEAL 1605
Round, 22
Woman standing full-face holding a ?wheel up in her right hand (?St Katherine), five (?) stars in a radial pattern in the field.
Legend: illegible
NLW PITORD/47, dated 1350 x 1351

SEAL 1606
Round, 23
Within an octofoil, merchant mark on a shield (includes letter I), a long cross and banner extending from the top
Legend: * [. . . . .]?OVR
NLW PITORD/48, dated 1368 x 1369

SEAL 1607
Pointed oval, 32x19
Stylised lily
Legend: + VVILPANNIG
NLW PITORD/49, dated 1322 x 1323

SEAL 1608
Round, 19
Stag facing left
Legend: ALASB[?O]V[. . . .] (start point *c*.290º)
NLW PITORD/51, dated 1350 x 1351
NLW PITORD/439, dated 1350 x 1351
NLW PITORD/409, dated 1293 x 1294

SEAL 1609
Pointed oval, 26x38
A lion attacking a grotesque (bird's body with dragon head and long tail ending in a foliate motif) from behind, both facing right.
Legend: §[.]OST TENEBRA[.] SPEROLVCEM
NLW PITORD/52, dated 1294 x 1295

SEAL 1610
Round, 19
Within an ornate quatrefoil, a shield of arms (chequy)
Legend: N/A
NLW PITORD/54, seal 1, dated 1373 x 1374

SEAL 1611
Round, 17
Shield of arms (lion rampant), with a ring above linking shield to cross in legend, crescent to left and right.
Legend: + . . . hA . . . . AD . .
NLW PITORD/54, seal 2, dated 1373 x 1374

SEAL 1612
Rounded oval, 23x19
Woman standing full-face wearing a veil and long gown holding a flowering stem in her right hand, to the left a ?bush.
Legend: illegible
NLW PITORD/60, dated 1341 x 1342

SEAL 1613
Round, 22
Within a sexfoil, a merchant mark / pseudo-armial device on a shield (three roundles on a fess between W in chief and P in base, Latin cross extending from the top of the shield
Legend: SIG[. . .]WILL[. . . . .]
NLW PITORD/61, dated 1344 x 1345

SEAL 1614
Rounded oval, 19x16
Eagle displayed
Legend: [. . .]V . . . . OE . .
NLW PITORD/62, dated 1319 x 1320

SEAL 1615
Round, 17
Lamb of God facing left
Legend: [Illegible]
NLW PITORD/63, seal 1, dated 1342 x 1343

SEAL 1616
Round, 19
?Hare facing right
Legend: * [. . . .]ov[. . . .]v
NLW PITORD/63, seal 2, dated 1342 x 1343

SEAL 1617
Round, 18
Two hands crossed, a heart above
Legend: §[. . . . .]LE[.]
NLW PITORD/63, seal 3, dated 1342 x 1343

SEAL 1618
Rounded oval, 18x16
Uncertain; central elongated blob
Legend: [Lost]
NLW PITORD/67, dated 1322 x 1323

SEAL 1619
Rounded oval, 9x7
?Gem: (?head in profile)
Legend: None
NLW PITORD/71, dated 1471 x 1472

SEAL 1620
Round, 29
Stylised eight-petalled flower.
Legend: [section lost]OHANNISGAL[.]RIDI
NLW PITORD/72, dated 1291 x 1292

SEAL 1621
Round, 22
Within an octofoil, h with a ?star above and a trefoil leaf within the descenders of the letter
Legend: + S' hENRICI LE GOLDSMYTH §
NLW PITORD/75, dated 1351 x 1352
NLW PITORD/382, dated 1349 x 1350

SEAL 1622
Round, 17
An ?arm extending from right holding up two keys, to the left a ?star.
Legend: Illegible
NLW PITORD/76, dated 1329 x 1330

SEAL 1623
Round, 24
A stylised lily within a circle with a small stylised lily above flanked by stylised trees
Legend: +S'IEhANLESCVL . . [. . .]S . . LES . ?M . AI .
NLW PITORD/79, seal 1, dated 1396 x 1397
NLW PITORD/160, seal 3, dated 1391 x 1392

SEAL 1624
Undetermined, 13
Three circles
Legend: N/A
NLW PITORD/79, seal 3, dated 1396 x 1397

SEAL 1625
Rounded oval, 12x10
Sacred monogram (ihc) with crown above
Legend: none
NLW PITORD/79, seal 4, dated 1396 x 1397

SEAL 1626
Round, 18
Two hands crossed, a stylised lily above
Legend: *FEIMETE[.]T
NLW PITORD/80, dated 1310 x 1311

SEAL 1627
Unknown, 15x10
Uncertain
Legend: N/A
NLW PITORD/84, dated 1499 x 1500

SEAL 1628
Round, 22
Crowned woman standing full-face holding a wheel (st Katherine) within a canopied niche
Legend: ¶ S . V . KATERI DEO . . ¶
NLW PITORD/85, dated 1358 x 1359

SEAL 1629
Round, 20
Four clover leaves
Legend: S [. . . . . .]V?E[. . .]
NLW PITORD/87, dated 1339 x 1340

SEAL 1630
Round, 29
Stag's head full-face

Legend: * S' GWYDON'. D' GLAZELEYE
NLW PITORD/1144, dated 1301 x 1302
NLW PITORD/88, dated 1316 x 1317

SEAL 1631
Pointed oval, 38x26
Stylised eight-petalled flower
Legend: +S' [?E]MME PRIDE
NLW PITORD/90, dated 1275 x 1299

SEAL 1632
Rounded oval, 24x18
Virgin and Child ?seated (?three-quarter length)
Legend: SA[. . . . .]
NLW PITORD/94, dated 1350 x 1351

SEAL 1633
Round, 32
Four conifer branches with rays in the angels
Legend: +[.] hENRICI DE W'[. . . .]DE
NLW PITORD/95, dated 1225 x 1274

SEAL 1634
Round, 13
Letters I O, five small pellets to the left, stylised branch below
Legend: none
NLW PITORD/97, dated 1468 x 1469

SEAL 1635
Round, 21
Within a sexfoil, letter M
Legend: * SIGILLV . IOhIS DE LA hVLL
NLW PITORD/314, dated 1354 x 1355
NLW PITORD/533, dated 1352 x 1353
NLW PITORD/98, dated 1352 x 1353
NLW PITORD/580, dated 1353 x 1354

SEAL 1636
Round, 21
Virgin and Child seated full-face within an architectural niche with below, beneath a rounded arch, head and shoulders of a suppliant figure facing left
Legend: ¶ S [.]ILLI . DE [.]STO[. . . .]
NLW PITORD/99, dated 1354 x 1355

SEAL 1637
Round, 31
Stylised four-petalled flower with stylised branches in the angels
Legend: *S' I[.]HIS [. .] [section lost] [.] I[. . .]
NLW PITORD/100, dated 1322 x 1323

SEAL 1638
Rounded oval, 24x18
Lion sleeping facing left, with above two branches flanking a central ?flower (?head) on a broad stem
Legend: * S [.] [section lost] [. .]ROB'TI
NLW PITORD/101, dated 1301 x 1302

SEAL 1639
Round, 30
Stylised twelve-petalled flower
Legend: S'[.]IMO[.] 'FIL'TIR[.]L'WE'
NLW PITORD/102, dated 1298 x 1299

SEAL 1640
Round, 18
Squirrel facing right eating a nut
Legend: [?C]RE[.]E [. . . . .]
NLW PITORD/104, dated 1328 x 1329

SEAL 1641
Round, 17
Squirrel facing left
Legend: + ... AE . . M . .
NLW PITORD/105, dated 1348 x 1349

SEAL 1642
Round, 21
Seven-(?eight) petalled flower
Legend: S[. . . . .]
NLW PITORD/106, dated 1341

SEAL 1643
Unknown, 22x18
Uncertain (wax only)
Legend: N/A
NLW PITORD/109, dated 1327 x 1328

SEAL 1644
Rounded oval, 23x21
Within an ornate quatrafoil, a shield of arms (?fess)
Legend: illegible
NLW PITORD/110, dated 1361 x 1362

SEAL 1645
Pointed oval, 34x24
Stylised lily
Legend: [. .]' MATILDI[. .]IL' hEN[. . .]
NLW PITORD/112, seal 1, dated 1275 x 1324

SEAL 1646
Round, 30
Stylised lily
Legend: [. .] MATILDE : FIL' . hEN[?R] [. . .]
NLW PITORD/112, seal 2, dated 1275 x 1324

SEAL 1647
Round, 18
Hawk taking a duck, both facing left
Legend: * AL[?A][.]I[. . .]P[. . .]
NLW PITORD/113, dated 1334 x 1335

SEAL 1648
Unknown, 24
Trace of a round legend band but no trace of design
Legend: N/A
NLW PITORD/114, dated 1340

SEAL 1649
Round, 20
Crossed hands with a bird above
Legend: *DELA . . . VE+
NLW PITORD/115, dated 1342 x 1343
NLW PITORD/117, dated 1342
NLW PITORD/116, dated 1342 x 1343

SEAL 1650
Round, 22
In an ornate quatrafoil, shield of arms (on chief a lion passant, below letters 'IH' with an abbreviation mark)
Legend: +S:IOhANNIS:FIL':IOhANNIS:CROV[.]E
NLW PITORD/421, dated 1344 x 1345
NLW PITORD/495, dated 1347 x 1348
NLW PITORD/1297, dated 1338 x 1339
NLW PITORD/1298, dated 1338 x 1339
NLW PITORD/2468, dated 1332 x 1333
NLW PITORD/144, dated 1354 x 1355
NLW PITORD/120, dated 1344 x 1345

SEAL 1651
Round, 29
Four conifer branches with four ?cones in the angles
Legend: *[.] A [. . . .] D[. .]RE[?S]TV[?N]
NLW PITORD/121, dated 1297 x 1298

SEAL 1652
Round, 29
Shield of arms (paly, on a fess three crosses)
Legend: [...]OH'IS D [...]
NLW PITORD/122, dated 1300 x 1301

SEAL 1653
Rounded oval, 11x9
Merchant mark (includes tall cross, letters P and sR
Legend: none
NLW PITORD/124, dated 1451 x 1452
NLW PITORD/346, dated 1451 x 1452

SEAL 1654
Rectangular, 10x14
Letters W l (BL) with line above W, stylised branch to lower left
Legend: none
NLW PITORD/125, dated 1492 x 1493

SEAL 1655
Round, 16
Crowned letter 'M', ?foliage to the left
Legend: + [. . .]e[. .]lp'$[. . . . . . .]
NLW PITORD/126, dated 1410 x 1411

APPENDIX

SEAL 1656
Pointed oval, 30
Eagle displayed
Legend: [section lost]ILL'WA[. . . . .]ME[section lost]
NLW PITORD/128, seal 1, dated 1200 x 1299

SEAL 1657
Round, 25
Stylised lily (quite absract)
Legend: [section lost]ENEDEALPRAM
NLW PITORD/128, seal 2, dated 1200 x 1299

SEAL 1658
Unknown, 25x21
To right a figure standing full-face holding shield in right hand, to left a figure standing full-face holding an object in left hand
Legend: lost
NLW PITORD/129, dated 1350 x 1351

SEAL 1659
Round, 19
Within a cusped quatrafoil, a shield of arms (chief, a ?bordure)
Legend: * S'[.]EhAR[. . . . .]
NLW PITORD/407, seal 5, dated 1346 x 1347
NLW PITORD/131, seal 1, dated 1346 x 1347

SEAL 1660
Rounded oval, 26x22
Within a twelve-lobed border, a woman standing facing half right holding a spiked wheel up in her left hand (St Katherine), to the right a suppliant kneeling figure facing left with a flowering stem in the field above
Legend: *S[?V?D]E[.]ORIS . [. .]E[. . . .]ER [. . . .]VE
NLW PITORD/131, seal 2, dated 1346 x 1347
NLW PITORD/407, seal 2, dated 1346 x 1347

SEAL 1661
Round, 20
Lion rampant facing left
Legend: *SVM [.]EOFO[. . . .]
NLW PITORD/131, seal 3, dated 1346 x 1347
NLW PITORD/407, seal 4, dated 1346 x 1347

SEAL 1662
Rounded oval, 24x18
Virgin and Child seated full-face within a canopied nich with below, beneath a rounded arch, a half-length supplicant figure facing right
Legend: AVEM[.]RE ¶ IAGRAC[?A]
NLW PITORD/132, dated 1346 x 1347
NLW PITORD/131, seal 4, dated 1346 x 1347
NLW PITORD/407, dated 1346 x 1347

SEAL 1663
Round, 15
Stylised lily
Legend: [.]I[. .] ¶ [. . . .]
NLW PITORD/134, dated 1346 x 1347

SEAL 1664
Round, 14
Tudor-style rose (with ?letters in the centre)
Legend: none
NLW PITORD/133, dated 1492 x 1493

SEAL 1665
Round, 25
Shield of arms: includes two wheat sheaves (one in second quarter)
Legend: none
NLW PITORD/135, front, dated 1377 x 1378

SEAL 1666
Round, 19
Lamb of God facing left
Legend: + ECCE AGNVS DEI
NLW PITORD/136, dated 1346 x 1347

SEAL 1667
Pointed oval, 42x25
Woman standing full-face holding a pot up in her left hand, pointing to it with her right hand (Mary Magdelane), with below, beneath a pointed arch, head and shoulders of a suppliant tonsured man facing left
Legend: S': OFFICIALITATI : D❡ ECANE DE BRVG
NLW PITORD/236, dated 1355 x 1356
NLW PITORD/1233, dated 1316
NLW PITORD/587, dated 1341
NLW PITORD/1420, dated 1349
NLW PITORD/137, dated 1327
NLW PITORD/227, seal 3, dated 1338 x 1339
NLW PITORD/537, dated 1349
NLW PITORD/1322, seal 2, dated 1426 x 1427

SEAL 1668
Rounded oval, 9x13
Lion's head full-face, to the left 'I', to the right 'c'
Legend: none
NLW PITORD/138, dated 1451 x 1452
NLW PITORD/343, dated 1451 x 1452
NLW PITORD/202, dated 1451 x 1452

SEAL 1669
Octagonal, 13x10
Merchant mark (includes cross-tipped h, letter t, inverted Y
Legend: none
NLW PITORD/140, dated 1463 x 1464

SEAL 1670
Round, 20
Shield of arms (large covered cup between two small covered cups, a star (dexter) and crescent (sinister) in chief, a star in base)
Legend: S' hE❡NRICI ❡ [. . .]NE ❡
NLW PITORD/168, dated 1334 x 1335
NLW PITORD/143, dated 1322 x 1323

SEAL 1671
Round, 21
Within an octofoil, a shield of arms (crescent with a star above and a ?star below)
Legend: SIGILL:WILLELMI : DE : W[. . .] YE
NLW PITORD/145, dated 1376 x 1377
NLW PITORD/204, dated 1391 x 1392
NLW PITORD/160, dated 1391 x 1392

SEAL 1672
Round, 20
Bird walking to right with foliage in its beak
Legend: *PORTO SIGNV' CLEM[. . .]I DEI
NLW PITORD/146, dated 1275 x 1276

SEAL 1673
Scutiform, 19x18
Bird facing right perched on a bush with two branches
Legend: ?VAS?A
NLW PITORD/147, dated 1287 x 1288

SEAL 1674
Round, 17
Four clover leaves
Legend: *[. . .]VE?S[. .]
NLW PITORD/148, dated 1336 x 1337

SEAL 1675
Round, 18
Squirrel facing left
Legend: * [. . .] [section lost] OTTS
NLW PITORD/150, dated 1348 x 1349

SEAL 1676
Rounded oval, 25x20
Christ crucified, a figure to left and right facing in (?Mary and John), sun and moon above
Legend: *IESUS [...]
NLW PITORD/151, dated 1334 x 1335

SEAL 1677
Round, 28
Cresent with sun above
Legend: + S'ALANI : LETVRNOVR
NLW PITORD/153, dated 1278 x 1280

APPENDIX

SEAL 1678
Round, 19
Branch with three lobes
Legend: illegible
NLW PITORD/154, dated 1316 x 1317

SEAL 1679
Round, 17
Crossed hands
Legend: illegible
NLW PITORD/154, seal 2, dated 1316 x 1317

SEAL 1680
Round, 18x16
Woman full-face holding right hand up to body, flowers on stem in field to left (fragment only)
Legend: [section lost] [?D]RO[. .]
NLW PITORD/158, dated 1350 x 1351

SEAL 1681
Round, 26
Stylised ?eight-petalled flower
Legend: [section lost] [?I]S[?P][.] [section lost]
NLW PITORD/159, dated 1275 x 1299

SEAL 1682
Round, 19
?Winged creature facing ?left
Legend: lost
NLW PITORD/162, seal 1, dated 1343 x 1344

SEAL 1683
Round, 19
Lion sleeping facing right
Legend: illegible
NLW PITORD/162, seal 2, dated 1343 x 1344

SEAL 1684
Pointed oval, 16x24
Lion walking to right (?rampant facing right)
Legend: [.] S[. . . . . .]E[. . . . .]
NLW PITORD/163, dated 1302 x 1303

SEAL 1685
Round, 29
Stylised eight-petalled flower
Legend: *S'Ioh'FIL':AMARI
NLW PITORD/164, dated 1300 x 1301
NLW PITORD/165, dated 1299 x 1300

SEAL 1686
Round, 28
Stylised eight-petalled flower
Legend: *S'NICh'I:FIL'MATh'IAVRIFABR'
NLW PITORD/166, dated 1300
NLW PITORD/517, dated 1309 x 1310

SEAL 1687
Round, 18
Two hands crossed, above them a heart
Legend: § [. . .] [section lost] V[?A] . [. . . .]
NLW PITORD/167, dated 1357 x 1358

SEAL 1688
Round, 38
Crescent with a star above
Legend: [. .]IG[. . .] W[.]LL' BO[section lost]
NLW PITORD/169, dated 1200 x 1299

SEAL 1689
Round, 15
Letter R
Legend: . V. RLVE
NLW PITORD/170, dated 1348 x 1349

SEAL 1690
Octagonal, 11x11
Letter ?G
Legend: none
NLW PITORD/172, dated 1429 x 1430

SEAL 1691
Octagonal, 11x9
Lion rampant facing right, letter 'b' in lower right
Legend: none
NLW PITORD/173, dated 1439 x 1440

SEAL 1692
Round, 18
Crossed hands with a bird facing left above
Legend: +[.]E[. . . . . . .]
NLW PITORD/175, dated 1325 x 1326

SEAL 1693
Pointed oval, 29x21
Stylised lily
Legend: illegible
NLW PITORD/176, dated 1284 x 1285

SEAL 1694
Round, 30
Stylised eight-petalled flower
Legend: S' AD[. . .]E[. . . . .]
NLW PITORD/177, seal 1, dated 1294 x 1295

SEAL 1695
Pointed oval, 29x20
Pelican in its piety facing right
Legend: illegible
NLW PITORD/177, seal 2, dated 1294 x 1295

SEAL 1696
Pointed oval, 42x28
Building with large round-arched ?doorway, with tall central tower flanked by shorter towers with round-arched windows to left and right.
Legend: S'[. . . . . .] [. .]LE[. . .]ISDE[. . . .] E[?L]
NLW PITORD/179, dated 1337 x 1338

SEAL 1697
Round, 31
Stylised lily
Legend: +S'WILL'LEM[...]DONITV
NLW PITORD/180, dated 1275 x 1299

SEAL 1698
Round, 21
Within a quatrafoil, the head of Christ within a central circle surrounded by the symbols of the Evangelists
Legend: marc' ¶ math ¶ luc[.] ¶ ioh's ¶
NLW PITORD/542, dated 1436 x 1437
NLW PITORD/491, dated 1403 x 1404
NLW PITORD/182, seal 1, dated 1436 x 1437
NLW PITORD/504, dated 1436 x 1437
NLW PITORD/2465, seal 2, dated 1400 x 1499
NLW PITORD/1345, dated 1401 x 1402

SEAL 1699
Octagonal, 13
Crowned letter R, stylised branch to left, ?cable below and to right
Legend: none
NLW PITORD/182, seal 2, dated 1436 x 1437
NLW PITORD/504, seal 2, dated 1436 x 1437

SEAL 1700
Round, 11
Crowned letter I with foliage either side
Legend: none
NLW PITORD/184, dated 1420 x 1421

SEAL 1701
Rounded oval, 20x16
Eagle displayed
Legend: [...]T[...]
NLW PITORD/185, dated 1314 x 1315

SEAL 1702
Pointed oval, 30x21
Four conifer branches with long-stemmed stylised lilies in the angles
Legend: S' [.]WAIN' F[.]L' LEV[. . . . .]
NLW PITORD/186, dated 1200 x 1299

SEAL 1703
Round, 24
Man in long gown standing full-face holding disk with the Lamb of God in his left hand and pointing to it with his right hand (St John the Baptist), within an ornate canopied niche extending into the legend band
Legend: Sig: iohis ¶ de : gray ¶

APPENDIX

NLW PITORD/188, seal 1, dated 1375 x 1376
NLW PITORD/505, dated 1374 x 1375

SEAL 1704
Round, 29
Within a cusped quatrafoil, to left a tonsured man standing full-face holding a key up in his left hand gesturing to it with his right hand, to the right a bearded man standing full-face holding a sword up in his right hand (SS Peter and Paul), between them a column
Legend: *§ SIGILLVM § ROBERTI § DE § BREDONE §
NLW PITORD/188, seal 2, dated 1375 x 1376
NLW PITORD/310, seal 3, dated 1369 x 1370
NLW PITORD/505, seal 2, dated 1374 x 1375

SEAL 1705
Round, 30
Within a cusped trefoil with small stylised roses in interior cusps, a shield of arms (four lions rampant) hanging from a ?lion's head full-face
Legend: : Sigillum: ⸱ iohannes : de ⸱ :lutte[.]ye §
NLW PITORD/191, seal 1, dated 1415 x 1416

SEAL 1706
Round, 20
Within a quartafoil, a shield of arms (three ?roses (round objects), a chevron cotised).
Legend: [.]E[. . . .]
NLW PITORD/191, seal 2, dated 1415 x 1416

SEAL 1707
Round, 16
Boat with central mast and rigging fore and aft
Legend: [...]VE[...]
NLW PITORD/192, dated 1340

SEAL 1708
Square, 8x8
Bird with wings raised behind walking to left
Legend: none
NLW PITORD/193, dated 1410 x 1411

SEAL 1709
Round, 21
Shield (charge lost) surmounted by a cross
Legend: lost
NLW PITORD/194, dated 1340 x 1341

SEAL 1710
Round, 12
Merchant mark (includes inverted Y, letter V
Legend: none
NLW PITORD/196, dated 1471 x 1472

SEAL 1711
Round, 12
A star (asymmetrical pentagram)
Legend: none
NLW PITORD/197, seal 1, dated 1420 x 1421

SEAL 1712
Round, 14
Crowned T, stylised branch either side
Legend: none
NLW PITORD/197, seal 2, dated 1420 x 1421

SEAL 1713
Round, 24
Within a deeply angled quatrafoil, a shield of arms (an eagle displayed)
Legend: [. . .] ⸱ [. . .] ⸱ R[.]N ⸱ [. . .] ⸱
NLW PITORD/199, dated 1377 x 1378

SEAL 1714
Octagonal, 10x12
Heart within a shackle
Legend: S : Willi : locard
NLW PITORD/271 up.1, dated 1422 x 1423
NLW PITORD/1087, dated 1419 x 1420
NLW PITORD/200, dated 1420
NLW PITORD/1117, dated 1419 x 1420

SEAL 1715
Undetermined, 11x10
Interlaced pattern
Legend: none
NLW PITORD/201, dated 1524 x 1525

SEAL 1716
Round, 20
Lion facing left
Legend: lost
NLW PITORD/203, dated 1358 x 1359

SEAL 1717
Rounded oval, 11x10
Squirrel facing right holding a nut
Legend: none
NLW PITORD/204, seal 2, dated 1391 x 1392

SEAL 1718
Unknown, 19
Within a cusped quatrafoil, a shield of arms (?chevron; most of charge lost)
Legend: Sh[...]E[...]
NLW PITORD/205, dated 1375 x 1376

SEAL 1719
Round, 19
Squirrel facing left
Legend: [.] C[. . . .] NO[.] [section lost]
NLW PITORD/207, dated 1347 x 1348

SEAL 1720
Round, 16
Within an octofoil, a ?lion's head with a long cross above, I to the right
Legend: +S[. . .]IL[. . . . .]E
NLW PITORD/213, dated 1346 x 1347

SEAL 1721
Round, 23
Within an octofoil with flowers on stems in the cusps, a shield of arms (a bend cotised)
Legend: *S' § PETRI § DE § BRVG[. . .] ORTH
NLW PITORD/215, dated 1375 x 1376

SEAL 1722
Unknown, 17
Indistinct
Legend: [...]AE[...]
NLW PITORD/216, dated 1316 x 1317

SEAL 1723
Pointed oval, 34
Stylised eight-petalled flower
Legend: [...]WA[...]
NLW PITORD/221, dated 1339 x 1340

SEAL 1724
Pointed oval, 18x28
Bird with foliage in its beak walking to the right
Legend: S' IOH'IS . DE . B[.]LE
NLW PITORD/592, dated 1330 x 1331
NLW PITORD/223, dated 1331 x 1332

SEAL 1725
Unknown, 30
?circular pattern
Legend: none
NLW PITORD/225, dated 1507 x 1508

SEAL 1726
Round, 24
Within an ornate border, a shield of arms (a bird facing dexter on a crosshatched ground) hanging from a bush
Legend: ¶ Sigill : Willelmi : de : Worthyn ¶
NLW PITORD/328, dated 1383 x 1384
NLW PITORD/670, dated 1374 x 1375
NLW PITORD/226, seal 1, dated 1383 x 1384

SEAL 1727
Round, 19
Stag's head full-face with a cross between the antlers
Legend: [. . . . . . .]E[. . .]
NLW PITORD/226, seal 2, dated 1383 x 1384

SEAL 1728
Round, 17
Hawk facing left on a gloved hand and arm

APPENDIX

emerging from the left
Legend: * PRIVE SVEAME
NLW PITORD/227, seal 1, dated 1338 x 1339

SEAL 1729
Round, 21
Stag's head full-face with a cross between the antlers
Legend: * IESVS MERCI
NLW PITORD/227, seal 2, dated 1338 x 1339

SEAL 1730
Round, 19
Crossed hands with a bird above
Legend: *LE[...]
NLW PITORD/228, dated 1343 x 1344

SEAL 1731
Round, 26
?Shield (indistinct)
Legend: lost
NLW PITORD/229, dated 1351 x 1352

SEAL 1732
Round, 13
Uncertain
Legend: lost, if any
NLW PITORD/231, dated 1496 x 1497

SEAL 1733
Round, 20
Within an octofoil with flowers on stems in the cusps, a shield of arms (two lions rampant addorsed reguardant (?conjoined at the waist))
Legend: [section lost][......]s d'swenlegh
NLW PITORD/232, dated 1364 x 1365

SEAL 1734
Round, 23
Within an octofoil, a shield of arms (broad arrow head pointing up, in dexter chief letter ?R, in sinister chief letter ?P, a ?mullet in base dexter and sinister)
Legend: * [....]llu[section lost][......]
NLW PITORD/233, dated 1377 x 1378

SEAL 1735
Rounded oval, 11x9
An object within rays
Legend: none
NLW PITORD/234, dated 1458 x 1459

SEAL 1736
Round, 20
Two ?lions rampant both facing in, in the centre a vertical line
Legend: * S[...]LL[..........]
NLW PITORD/235, dated 1309 x 1310

SEAL 1737
Pointed oval, 34x20
Three-quarter length figure standing full-face wearing a gown with wide sleves with below, beneath trefoil arch, a wheatsheaf with a lion's head to the left and a spade-shaped object to right
Legend: [section lost]ES[section lost]
NLW PITORD/239, dated 1349

SEAL 1738
Round, 19
Animal (?lion) running to right
Legend: S[..]IL[........]
NLW PITORD/240, dated 1275 x 1299

SEAL 1739
Octagonal, 10x12
Tonsured head with two-pointed beard full-face
Legend: none
NLW PITORD/242, dated 1483 x 1484

SEAL 1740
Round, 15
Arm emerging from left holding an object with a diamond-shaped top, thin handle and square base (?candlestick / ?monstrance), to the right a small Latin cross, foliage in the ground
Legend: none
NLW PITORD/242, seal 2, dated 1483 x 1484

SEAL 1741
Round, 29
Stylised eight-petalled flower
Legend: +SRICARDI.FIL'.PETRI
NLW PITORD/244, dated 1275 x 1299

SEAL 1742
Round, 22
Within an ornate octofoil, a shield of arms (three bars with letters CO[. . .] between the top and middle bar) with a cross extending form the top
Legend: SIGI [. . . . .]
NLW PITORD/1102, dated 1383 x 1384
NLW PITORD/328, seal 2, dated 1383 x 1384
NLW PITORD/245, dated 1383 x 1384

SEAL 1743
Round, 19
Hare running to left, a hawk above, to right a dog running to left
Legend: *S[...]§[...]E[...]E[...]
NLW PITORD/246, dated 1351 x 1352

SEAL 1744
Rectangular, 14x11
Uncertain
Legend: none or lost
NLW PITORD/247, seal 1, dated 1448 x 1449

SEAL 1745
Round, 10
Eagle with wings outstretched walking to left
Legend: none
NLW PITORD/247, seal 2, dated 1448 x 1449
NLW PITORD/321, seal 2, dated 1448 x 1449

SEAL 1746
Round, 17
Lion sleeping facing right
Legend: [.]A[. .]MENO[.]A[?N]
NLW PITORD/248, dated 1323 x 1324

SEAL 1747
Pointed oval, 58x37
Man standing full-face vested for Mass holding a cross-tipped staff in his left hand and blessing with his right hand (?St Thomas Becket), within an ornately canopied architectural niche
Legend: S':COE:GA[. . .]IE:S[. . . .]OS[. . .]AR[.]DA[. . . ..]
NLW PITORD/249, dated 1456 x 1457

SEAL 1748
Round, 26
Stylised lily
Legend: illegible
NLW PITORD/250, dated 1359 x 1360

SEAL 1749
Rounded oval, 20x16
Two shields of arms (dexter, two bars; sinister, a fess charged with objects), half length woman holding up a spiked wheel (St Katherine) above, half length full-face woman with a veil below
Legend: [. . . . . .]OVST[. . . .]¶ [. . . .]VO [. . . . .]
NLW PITORD/1126, dated 1349 x 1350
NLW PITORD/566, dated 1349
NLW PITORD/251, dated 1349 x 1350

SEAL 1750
Round, 19
?Animal (?Lamb of God) facing left
Legend: illegible
NLW PITORD/252, dated 1388 x 1389

SEAL 1751
Round, 20
M with ?stylised flower emerging from top
Legend: none
NLW PITORD/253, dated 1386 x 1387

SEAL 1752
Round, 27
Shield of arms (eagle displayed, head to sinister) suspended from a bush in the legend band
Legend: ¶ Sigillu' M[. . . .] § : [?B]r[. . .] : §

APPENDIX

NLW PITORD/345, dated 1493
NLW PITORD/1056, dated 1530 x 1531
NLW PITORD/809, seal 1, dated 1530 x 1531
NLW PITORD/255, dated 1492
NLW PITORD/1276, dated 1491 x 1492

SEAL 1753
Round, 35
Four conifer branches with three-pointed stems in the angles
Legend: +S' ROB' : FIL' ADE
NLW PITORD/256, dated 1275 x 1299

SEAL 1754
Round, 21
Within an ornate cusped border, a shield of arms (between three crescents a fess charged with four crosses saltire) hanging from a stylised bush
Legend: §SIGILLV[. .] OHIS:DE:SCOLEHALL
NLW PITORD/258, dated 1370 x 1371

SEAL 1755
Round, 13
trefoil ?leaf
Legend: none
NLW PITORD/262, seal 1, dated 1469 x 1470

SEAL 1756
Unknown, 14x11
Legend: none or lost
NLW PITORD/262, seal 2, dated 1469 x 1470

SEAL 1757
Rounded oval, 19x11
Merchant mark
Legend: none
NLW PITORD/267, seal 1, dated 1478 x 1479

SEAL 1758
Round, 12
Letter R, stylised branch to left

Legend: none
NLW PITORD/315, dated 1478 x 1479
NLW PITORD/1323, dated 1478 x 1479
NLW PITORD/600, seal 2, dated 1478 x 1479
NLW PITORD/267, seal 2, dated 1478 x 1479

SEAL 1759
Octagonal, 14x10
Merchant mark on a shield, long cross-tipped staff with banner emerging from top
Legend: illegible
NLW PITORD/271, seal 2, dated 1422 x 1423

SEAL 1760
Round, 13
Letter W with star above
Legend: none
NLW PITORD/271, seal 3, dated 1422 x 1423

SEAL 1761
Rounded oval, 12x17
Shield of arms (chevron between three stags heads caboshed)
Legend: none
NLW PITORD/273, dated 1548 x 1549

SEAL 1762
Hexagonal, 14x12
Letter T with small cross above
Legend: none
NLW PITORD/274, dated 1536 x 1537

SEAL 1763
Round, 10
Letters (uncertain) with looped cords
Legend: none
NLW PITORD/282, dated 1539 x 1540

SEAL 1764
Round, 21
Shield of arms (eagle displayed, head to sinister)
Legend: lost
NLW PITORD/283, dated 1491 x 1492

SEAL 1765
Rounded oval, 13x14
Letters ?CC
Legend: none
NLW PITORD/286, dated 1530 x 1531

SEAL 1766
Unknown, 14x8
Lost (fragment of cusped border)
Legend: illegible
NLW PITORD/290, dated 1491 x 1492

SEAL 1767
Round, 13
Illegible fragment
Legend: none or lost
NLW PITORD/295, dated 1467 x 1468

SEAL 1768
Unknown, 28x24
Building with central tower and large ?doorway, with flanking towers (faint fragment)
Legend: lost or none
NLW PITORD/301, dated 1460 x 1461

SEAL 1769
Round, 23
Rabbit facing right with arrow shaft protruding from its back
Legend: * ALAS : [. . .][?C]RV
NLW PITORD/302, seal 1, dated 1364 x 1365

SEAL 1770
Round, 22
Creature with tufty tail (?rabbit) standing on top of a ?lion curled up, both facing right, with stylised foliage to right and left
Legend: none
NLW PITORD/302, seal 2, dated 1364 x 1365

SEAL 1771
Round, 27
Four conifer branches with three-pointed stems in the angles
Legend: +S'IOh':LE:MAYLER
NLW PITORD/303, dated 1275 x 1299

SEAL 1772
Rounded oval, 29x24
Man standing full-face holding large keys up in left hand (St Peter), three flowers on stems to the left
Legend: * S[. . . . .]VS
NLW PITORD/308, dated 1356 x 1357

SEAL 1773
Rounded oval, 11x9
Barrel on its side with ?lid open (?handle) at one end and ?spike protruding from base (?butter churn), flanked by stylised branches
Legend: none
NLW PITORD/309, seal 1, dated 1474 x 1475

SEAL 1774
Round, 12
Crowned letters R I, stylised leaves in field
Legend: none
NLW PITORD/309, seal 2, dated 1474 x 1475

SEAL 1775
Round, 18
Figure standing facing right holding a long object (?sword / ?keys) up in front of them (?St Peter), branch to the left
Legend: none
NLW PITORD/310, seal 1, dated 1369 x 1370

SEAL 1776
Round, 20
A shield of arms (a chevron)
Legend: lost
NLW PITORD/310, seal 2, dated 1369 x 1370

SEAL 1777
Round, 20
A large standing cup with star above, on either side a peacock addorsed with its head turned back to drink from cup

APPENDIX

Legend: *[. . . . . . .][?E] . [. . . . . . .]
NLW PITORD/310, seal 4, dated 1369 x 1370

SEAL 1778
Round, 21
Stag running to left
Legend: * PRIVE [. . . . . .]
NLW PITORD/311, dated 1354 x 1355

SEAL 1779
Round, 16
Uncertain (?Animal)
Legend: Lost
NLW PITORD/313, dated 1322 x 1323

SEAL 1780
Round, 33
Stylised eight-petalled flower
Legend: S' IOhANNIS FIL' ROGERI
NLW PITORD/316, dated 1295 x 1296

SEAL 1781
Round, 12
Bird flying downwards, ?foliage in its beak, ?flames above (?descent of the Holy Spirit)
Legend: [. .][?m]e[. . .]o
NLW PITORD/317, seal 1, dated 1403 x 1404

SEAL 1782
Round, 13
Letter S
Legend: none
NLW PITORD/317, seal 2, dated 1403 x 1404

SEAL 1783
Round, 20
Bird walking to the left looking back
Legend: lost
NLW PITORD/319, dated 1275 x 1299

SEAL 1784
Round, 37
Four conifer branches with wavy lines in the angles
Legend: SIGILL' SIMONIS DE SABRINA
NLW PITORD/320, dated 1275 x 1299

SEAL 1785
Unknown, 18x10
No evidence of seal matrix impression; looks as though flattened against a table-top
Legend: none
NLW PITORD/321, seal 1, dated 1448 x 1449

SEAL 1786
Pointed oval, nm
Wheatsheaf beneath a crenellated canopy (fragment only)
Legend: lost
NLW PITORD/1281, dated 1337
NLW PITORD/322, dated 1377
NLW PITORD/1394, dated 1377

SEAL 1787
Unknown, 23
Illegible fragment
Legend: lost or none
NLW PITORD/323, dated 1357 x 1358

SEAL 1788
Round, 24
Within an octofoil, a closed helm with crest (a crown), facing left
Legend: § SIG[. . .]T[. . . . .]ANI : DE [. . . .]DESI
NLW PITORD/324, dated 1351 x 1352

SEAL 1789
Round, 20
Stag's head full-face, cross patty between the antlers
Legend: [.] IR [.] VESV?M?C [. .]
NLW PITORD/325, dated 1342 x 1343

SEAL 1790
Round, 33
Shield of arms (eagle displayed with a label of three points) suspended from a bush in the legend band
Legend: [. . . . .]§IOhAN§bru[section lost]
NLW PITORD/326, dated 1462 x 1463

SEAL 1791
Round, 24
Hare, blowing a horn, riding a hound running to right
Legend: * S[.] h [. . . . .]
NLW PITORD/327, dated 1322 x 1323

SEAL 1792
Round, 17
Eagle displayed
Legend: *?PI[section lost]
NLW PITORD/1242, dated 1329 x 1330
NLW PITORD/329, dated 1329 x 1330

SEAL 1793
Pointed oval, 34x24
Stylised lily
Legend: [. .]WILL'IDE [. . . . .]RV[. .]
NLW PITORD/330, dated 1275 x 1299

SEAL 1794
Rounded oval, 23x19
Within a wavy border, a lion passant guardant
Legend: [.]'WILL'I[.]L[[section lost]
[. . . . . .]
NLW PITORD/331, dated 1349
NLW PITORD/488, dated 1331 x 1332

SEAL 1795
Rounded oval, 21x19
Within an ornate quatrefoil, a merchant mark on a shield (includes inverted Y, letters E P) cross emerging from top
Legend: §S'ED§M§VDI§§[. .
.]§[.]§FOR§D§
NLW PITORD/332, dated 1352 x 1353
NLW PITORD/333, dated 1343 x 1344
NLW PITORD/1311, seal 2, dated 1371 x 1372
NLW PITORD/1322, dated 1426 x 1427
NLW PITORD/1310, dated 1371 x 1372
NLW PITORD/375, dated 1346 x 1347

SEAL 1796
Round, 18
Uncertain
Legend: [. . . . .]E (start point uncertain)
NLW PITORD/334, dated 1357 x 1358

SEAL 1797
Round, 20
Lamb of God facing left
Legend: + [.]CC[. . . . .]SDEI
NLW PITORD/335, dated 1336 x 1337

SEAL 1798
Rounded oval, 18x16
Animal (?lion) facing left attacking a creature in the lower left
Legend: illegible
NLW PITORD/336, dated 1341 x 1342

SEAL 1799
Round, 36
Stylised eight-petalled flower
Legend: S'ROBERTIFIL'ROGER'S
NLW PITORD/337, dated 1298
NLW PITORD/1353, dated 1304 x 1305
NLW PITORD/338, dated 1275 x 1299

SEAL 1800
Round, 18
Shield of arms (?fess, in base cross-hatched) or merchant mark on shield
Legend: *S' RO[. . . . .]
NLW PITORD/339, dated 1357 x 1358

SEAL 1801
Round, 32
Stylised eight-petalled flower
Legend: S' RICA[section lost][. . . . .]
NLW PITORD/340, dated 1316 x 1317

SEAL 1802
Round, 16
Human leg wearing hose with laces loose at top facing right
Legend: [. . .]V[. . .]
NLW PITORD/341, dated 1321 x 1322

SEAL 1803
Round, 21
Stag facing left

APPENDIX

Legend: [. . .]E[. . .][lost]
NLW PITORD/342, dated 1353 x 1354

SEAL 1804
Round, 20
Shield of arms (?paly)
Legend: [section lost][. .]O[. . .]
NLW PITORD/345, seal 2, dated 1493

SEAL 1805
Round, 19
Within an octofoil, a shield of arms (checky), in place of legend band tendrils with flowers
Legend: none
NLW PITORD/348, dated 1325

SEAL 1806
Round, 18
Lamb of God facing right
Legend: +ECCEAGNVSDEI
NLW PITORD/349, dated 1356 x 1357
NLW PITORD/1341, dated 1356 x 1357
NLW PITORD/1328, dated 1356 x 1357
NLW PITORD/487, dated 1351 x 1352

SEAL 1807
Round, 24
Within a six-pointed star, three ?leaves (?flowers) on a stem
Legend: none
NLW PITORD/350, seal 1, dated 1368 x 1369

SEAL 1808
Round, 19
Shield of arms (a chevron)
Legend: *[. .][section lost][. . .][section lost][. . . . .]E
NLW PITORD/350, seal 2, dated 1368 x 1369

SEAL 1809
Rounded oval, 24x19
Within a cusped border, a ?woman standing full-face, to the left a kneeling suppliant figure facing right
Legend: illegible
NLW PITORD/351, dated 1352 x 1353

SEAL 1810
Round, 22x20
Shield of arms (lozengy) between three swords (one above, one either side) with three stars above and below the blades
Legend: *S' ThOME : DVn*F*O*Y*L
NLW PITORD/520, dated 1341 x 1342
NLW PITORD/352, dated 1341

SEAL 1811
Round, 25
Within an octofoil, a shield of arms (diapered, in chief ?uncertain)
Legend: [. . . . .]OBI.DE.AVDELE[. .]
NLW PITORD/354, dated 1352

SEAL 1812
Round, 17
Crowned letter I with ring around ascender
Legend: S' IOhIS DO[. . . .][?E][. . .]
NLW PITORD/355, dated 1401 x 1402
NLW PITORD/492, dated 1399 x 1400

SEAL 1813
Unknown, 14
Two human heads both facing in, an object between them
Legend: illegible, part lost
NLW PITORD/356, dated 1322 x 1323

SEAL 1814
Rounded oval, 25x18
Virgin and Child standing full-face, to the left a ?wheatsheaf
Legend: *AVEMA[. . . . . .]CI[.]
NLW PITORD/357, dated 1363 x 1364

SEAL 1815
Round, 17
In a cusped quatrafoil, Virgin and Child standing full-face, to left a kneeling suppliant figure facing right
Legend: [. . . . .]E[?N][.]
NLW PITORD/358, dated 1481 x 1482

SEAL 1816
Round, 20
Lion sleeping facing right
Legend: *WAKEME[.]O[. . .]
NLW PITORD/361, dated 1339 x 1340

SEAL 1817
Round, 24
Within an ornate quatrefoil, a merchant mark / pseudo-armorial device on shield (broad arrow pointing up, in dexter chief a crescent, in sinister chief a mullet, in sinister base letter R) cross above
Legend: *SIGILLVM.RICARDI.BRV[. .]
NLW PITORD/373, dated 1374 x 1375
NLW PITORD/1311, dated 1371 x 1372
NLW PITORD/565, dated 1363 x 1364
NLW PITORD/1310, dated 1371 x 1372
NLW PITORD/450, dated 1369 x 1370
NLW PITORD/362, dated 1374 x 1375

SEAL 1818
Round, 19
Within a ?sexfoil, a shield (charge illegible)
Legend: [. . . . . . .]O[. . .][section lost]
NLW PITORD/363, dated 1344 x 1345

SEAL 1819
Pointed oval, 39x25
Stylised lily
Legend: +S'WILMIF[. .]WIL'BOLDING
NLW PITORD/364, dated 1200 x 1224

SEAL 1820
Rounded oval, 13x11
Gem: naked woman seated on ground facing right holding left arm up to a swan with wings outstretched facing left (?Leda and Zeus)
Legend: none
NLW PITORD/366, dated 1541 x 1542

SEAL 1821
Round, 20
A figure facing right holding a ?wheel (?St Katherine) beneath an ornate canopy
Legend: illegible
NLW PITORD/368, dated 1356 x 1357

SEAL 1822
Round, 23
Pelican in piety facing left
Legend: [. . .]IVE[. . . .]D[. . . .]
NLW PITORD/369, dated 1358 x 1359

SEAL 1823
Pointed oval, 37x27
Four conifer branches with small ?cones in angles
Legend: +S'TI[.]RICI:FIL'hENRICI
NLW PITORD/370, dated 1275 x 1299

SEAL 1824
Pointed oval, 24
Stylised lily
Legend: [section lost] ICE [section lost]
NLW PITORD/371, dated 1305 x 1306

SEAL 1825
Round, 18
Within a six-lobed border, a ?bearded head facing right, to the right a small object
Legend: SV[?E]IT[. . .]E[. . . . .]
NLW PITORD/372, dated 1339
NLW PITORD/412, dated 1339

SEAL 1826
Rounded oval, 20
Lion sleeping facing right
Legend: lost, if any
NLW PITORD/377, dated 1306 x 1307

SEAL 1827
Round, 26
Cross moline voided
Legend: [section lost] I RICARDI D[.] [section lost]
NLW PITORD/378, dated 1275 x 1299

SEAL 1828
Round, 28
Stylised eight-petalled flower
Legend: +S'RICARD'FVHEAR
NLW PITORD/379, dated 1298 x 1299

APPENDIX

SEAL 1829
Round, 12
Crowned letter I flanked by stylised branches
Legend: none
NLW PITORD/536, dated 1406 x 1421
NLW PITORD/380, seal 1, dated 1420 x 1421

SEAL 1830
Round, 12
Six-spoked spiked wheel, within the gaps between spokes 'n l i n e i'
Legend: none
NLW PITORD/380, seal 2, dated 1420 x 1421

SEAL 1831
Round, 17
Bird facing right with foliage above
Legend: * PRI [. . . . . .]
NLW PITORD/381, seal 1, dated 1377 x 1378

SEAL 1832
Round, 20
Within a quatrafoil, a shield of arms (fess, in base ?letter ?T)
Legend: none
NLW PITORD/381, seal 2, dated 1377 x 1378

SEAL 1833
Rounded oval, 18x14
Uncertain (?gem)
Legend: none
NLW PITORD/381, seal 3, dated 1377 x 1378

SEAL 1834
Rounded oval, 22x19
In an octofoil, a pelican in its piety facing right
Legend: * SVM PEL[. . . . .]S DEI
NLW PITORD/382, seal 2, dated 1349 x 1350

SEAL 1835
Round, 26
Stylised ?sixteen-petalled flower
Legend: + S[. . . . .]
NLW PITORD/384, dated 1302 x 1303

SEAL 1836
Pointed oval, 33x23
Stylised lily
Legend: + S' EMME P[. .]N DENORTWO'
NLW PITORD/385, dated 1275 x 1299

SEAL 1837
Round, 32
Stylised eight-petalled flower
Legend: [.]S'RICAR[section lost]
NLW PITORD/386, dated 1316 x 1317

SEAL 1838
Round, 18
Hare sitting facing left
Legend: *[. . . . .]IV[. .]
NLW PITORD/387, dated 1324 x 1325
NLW PITORD/388, dated 1325 x 1326

SEAL 1839
Round, 25
?Two figures ?holding ?shields
Legend: lost
NLW PITORD/390, dated 1349 x 1350

SEAL 1840
Round, 19
Virgin and Child standing facing half right, to the right a kneeling suppliant figure facing left, between them a spray of ?flowers, all within an ornate niche
Legend: illegible, part lost
NLW PITORD/391, dated 1377 x 1377

SEAL 1841
Round, 19
Shield of arms (diapered, in chief letters RO)
Legend: *S'ROB[section lost]EREhAM
NLW PITORD/392, dated 1351 x 1352

SEAL 1842
Round, 19
Shield of arms (charge lost) couche, a hem (?with crest) above
Legend: illegible
NLW PITORD/393, dated 1352 x 1353

SEAL 1843
Round, 18
In a cusped quatrafoil, crossed hands
Legend: illegible
NLW PITORD/394, dated 1361 x 1362

SEAL 1844
Round, 47
Building with (?three) towers, a crenellated wall, and a round arched door.
Legend: lost
NLW PITORD/397, dated 1302 x 1303

SEAL 1845
Round, 32
Shield of arms (a bend with a label of three points) couche, a crested helm (a ?dolphin (large fish)) with mantling above, all on a diaper field
Legend: *[. . . .]LLVM IOhAN[. . . . .]
NLW PITORD/400, dated 1342 x 1343
NLW PITORD/585, dated 1344 x 1345

SEAL 1846
Round, 15
Four clover leaves
Legend: [. . .]VE S[. .]
NLW PITORD/402, dated 1338 x 1339

SEAL 1847
Round, 13
Hare facing right
Legend: illegible
NLW PITORD/405, seal 1, dated 1321 x 1322

SEAL 1848
Rounded oval, 19
Shield of arms (charge illegible), a ?wyvern above
Legend: *S'IO[. . .] : D[. . .]OVL[. .]I
NLW PITORD/405, seal 2, dated 1321 x 1322

SEAL 1849
Round, 23
Within a cusped border, a shield of arms (a ?chevron between three objects)
Legend: S'I[. . . . .]CO?N[. . . . .]
NLW PITORD/407, seal 3, dated 1346 x 1347

SEAL 1850
Round, 19
Sacred Monogram (ihc), crown above and branch below
Legend: none
NLW PITORD/413, seal 1, dated 1401 x 1402

SEAL 1851
Round, 20
Uncertain
Legend: illegible
NLW PITORD/413, seal 2, dated 1401 x 1402

SEAL 1852
Round, 23
Six-pointed star, voided in centre, with leaves on stems between the arms of the star; tendril with flowers in place of letters in legend band
Legend: none
NLW PITORD/456, dated 1417 x 1418
NLW PITORD/413, seal 3, dated 1401 x 1402

SEAL 1853
Round, 17
Within a quatrafoil, R, flanked by four-petalled flowers
Legend: none
NLW PITORD/413, seal 4, dated 1401 x 1402

SEAL 1854
Rounded oval, 25x23
Gem: figure ?seated facing left
Legend: *S'RIC [. .]FIL RIC' : CLERICI
NLW PITORD/414, dated 1300 x 1301

APPENDIX

SEAL 1855
Round, 23
Mitred man vested for Mass standing full-face blessing with right hand and holding a cross-tipped staff in his left hand, flanked by stylised branches
Legend: [. . . .]?OTV[.]¶ [. . . . . .]
NLW PITORD/415, dated 1341 x 1342

SEAL 1856
Octagonal, 15x13
Crowned letters RA (?RH)
Legend: none
NLW PITORD/416, dated 1492

SEAL 1857
Round, 29
Three shields of arms (each charged with three leaves) arranged radially pointing in with a stylised branch between each shield
Legend: S' [section lost] [.]AT'IN' D' GLASE[.]
NLW PITORD/418, dated 1317 x 1318

SEAL 1858
Round, 14
Looped cords above letters (illegible)
Legend: none
NLW PITORD/420, dated 1489 x 1490

SEAL 1859
Round, 19
Quadruped facing left
Legend: [. . .]VES[.][?M][. . . .]
NLW PITORD/422, seal 1, dated 1376 x 1377

SEAL 1860
Round, 21
Stag running to left
Legend: illegible
NLW PITORD/422, seal 2, dated 1376 x 1377

SEAL 1861
Rounded oval, 22x18
Mitred man standing full-face blessing with right hand and holding a crozier in his left hand, to the left a kneeling suppliant figure facing right
Legend: ¶ S' RO[.]ER[. . . .]ET[. . . . .]
NLW PITORD/426, dated 1339

SEAL 1862
Round, 18
Crowned letter ?R
Legend: none
NLW PITORD/427, dated 1403 x 1404

SEAL 1863
Round, 14
I flanked by stylised branches
Legend: none
NLW PITORD/428, dated 1403 x 1404

SEAL 1864
Round, 14
Crowned letter h, foliage left and right
Legend: none
NLW PITORD/429, dated 1402 x 1403

SEAL 1865
Round, 28
In a quatrafoil, a shield of arms (a fess between three martlets)
Legend: [section lost][. . . .]EW[?C]L[. . .]
NLW PITORD/430, dated 1402 x 1403

SEAL 1866
Round, 30
Hand emerging from right holding up a?bell (?cleaver) by the handle, to the left a small ?bell hanging from a chain
Legend: +S' RICARDI . DE . WAREWIC
NLW PITORD/431, dated 1200 x 1224
NLW PITORD/433, dated 1200 x 1224

SEAL 1867
Pointed oval, 26x16
Bird walking right with wings outstretched
Legend: [.]S:IOhANNIS:GRUND
NLW PITORD/432, dated 1200 x 1224

SEAL 1868
Round, 23
In a cusped trefoil, a shield of arms (bend with three lions passant, in sinister chief a mullet of six points pierced).
Legend: *[. . .]ILLROBER[. .]D [section lost] ILIOHE
NLW PITORD/436, dated 1352 x 1353

SEAL 1869
Round, 22
Shield of arms (two arrows pointing up saltire tied with a ribbon between two mullets of six points)
Legend: [section lost][. . .][section lost] DE ROGE[. . . .]
NLW PITORD/437, dated 1342 x 1343

SEAL 1870
Rounded oval, 24
Flower and two leaves on short stems emerging from ?pot
Legend: illegible
NLW PITORD/441, dated 1302 x 1303

SEAL 1871
Round, 19
Shield of arms (a ?fess)
Legend: *.S'ROBER(?I) COR(?B)ET§
NLW PITORD/442, dated 1301 x 1302

SEAL 1872
Round, 17
Hawk taking a rabbit, facing left
Legend: +S' IOh[. .]S[. .]OTE :
NLW PITORD/443, dated 1272 x 1273

SEAL 1873
Round, 20
Two birds addorsed, heads turned back with beaks touching ?flower on stem (?cross-tipped staff) between them
Legend: SIG[. . . .]A[. .]T[. . .]
NLW PITORD/444, dated 1300 x 1301

SEAL 1874
Round, 15
Long-legged bird facing left with foliage in the field
Legend: none
NLW PITORD/445, dated 1471 x 1472

SEAL 1875
Round, 20
In a cusped quatrafoil, a shield of arms (three mullets of six points between an object)
Legend: none
NLW PITORD/446, dated 1427 x 1428

SEAL 1876
Round, 20
Hare, blowing a horn, on a hound running left
Legend: [. . . .]VI[. . . .]
NLW PITORD/447, dated 1322 x 1323

SEAL 1877
Round, 35
Four conifer branches with rays in the angles
Legend: +S'ROBER[. .]FIL':R[section lost] RICh
NLW PITORD/448, dated 1200 x 1224

SEAL 1878
Round, 21
Virgin and Child seated full-face, to the right a kneeling suppliant figure facing left
Legend: illegible
NLW PITORD/449, seal 1, dated 1302 x 1303

SEAL 1879
Undetermined, 33x21
Stylised eight-petalled flower
Legend: + S' [?I]SABEL[.] B[.]VN
NLW PITORD/449, seal 2, dated 1302 x 1303

SEAL 1880
Round, 21
Shield of arms (charge illegible) hanging from a ?bush in legend band
Legend: illegible
NLW PITORD/453, dated 1338 x 1339

APPENDIX

SEAL 1881
Rounded oval, 20x16
Man in long gown holding a staff in his left hand
Legend: ¶IESULEI¶PAVM(?E)R
NLW PITORD/454, dated 1351 x 1352
NLW PITORD/464, dated 1342 x 1343

SEAL 1882
Hexagonal, 14x13
Shield of arms (broad arrowhead pointing down), above left ?i, below left t, below right ?h
Legend: none
NLW PITORD/456, seal 2, dated 1417 x 1418

SEAL 1883
Round, 31
Stylised lily
Legend: +SIGILL'RICARDIFILIIPhILIPPI
NLW PITORD/457, dated 1275 x 1299

SEAL 1884
Round, 18
Within a cusped octofoil, a lion's head with a cross-tipped staff emerging from the top between letters I and ?h
Legend: [. .]GILL [. .]O[.]E [. . . . . .]
NLW PITORD/462, dated 1380 x 1381

SEAL 1885
Round, 18
Stylised lily
Legend: [. . . . . . .]OV[.]E[. . . .]
NLW PITORD/463, dated 1351 x 1352

SEAL 1886
Round, 20
Stag's head full-face, a cross between the antlers
Legend: [. . . . .]IONIS DE A[. . . .]?E[. . .]
NLW PITORD/465, dated 1310 x 1311

SEAL 1887
Round, 17
Head and shoulders of man facing right
Legend: * CREDECAPITI
NLW PITORD/466, dated 1323 x 1324

SEAL 1888
Pointed oval, 29x18
?Crenellated tower
Legend: S'ALE[.]A[section lost]
NLW PITORD/468, dated 1284 x 1285

SEAL 1889
Round, 20
Stag's head full-face, an object in the field either side
Legend: lost
NLW PITORD/469, dated 1349 x 1350

SEAL 1890
Rounded oval, 24x20
Within an octofoil, Virgin and Child standing full-face, to the right a kneeling suppliant figure facing left
Legend: * S' R[.]G[. . . . .]E[?T][. .]
NLW PITORD/470, dated 1369 x 1370

SEAL 1891
Round, 12
Merchant mark on a shield, cross emerging from top
Legend: none
NLW PITORD/472, seal 2, dated 1435 x 1436

SEAL 1892
Round, 23
Within a cusped quatrafoil, Lamb of God facing right
Legend: [. . . .]LVM § [. . .]ELMI [.]E TERV[. .]
NLW PITORD/475, seal 1, dated 1402 x 1403

SEAL 1893
Round, 19
Crowned letter B flanked by stylised branches
Legend: none
NLW PITORD/475, seal 2, dated 1402 x 1403

SEAL 1894
Round, 22
Crowned and veiled head full-face within a spiked circle (head of St Katherine)
Legend: illegible
NLW PITORD/477, dated 1358 x 1359

SEAL 1895
Round, 17
Crossed hands bird facing left above
Legend: illegible
NLW PITORD/478, dated 1349 x 1350

SEAL 1896
Round, 18
Shield (charge lost)
Legend: lost
NLW PITORD/480, dated 1341 x 1342

SEAL 1897
Rounded oval, 19x25
Gem: winged animal with human head seated facing right (Sphinx).
Legend: [.]A[section lost]VMO[section lost]
NLW PITORD/483, dated 1364 x 1365

SEAL 1898
Round, 14
Merchant mark (includes long cross crosslet)
Legend: none
NLW PITORD/484, dated 1330

SEAL 1899
Round, 12
Merchant mark on a shield (inverted Y), patriarchal cross emerging from the top
Legend: none
NLW PITORD/485, dated 1468 x 1469

SEAL 1900
Unknown, 23
Indistinct
Legend: illegible, part lost
NLW PITORD/486, dated 1302 x 1303

SEAL 1901
Round, 18
Lion sleeping facing left
Legend: *W[. . .][section lost]
NLW PITORD/489, dated 1302 x 1303

SEAL 1902
Rounded oval, 22x18
Stag's head full-face, a cross ?potent between the antlers
Legend: illegible
NLW PITORD/490, dated 1318 x 1319

SEAL 1903
Round, 20
Within a cusped border, a woman in a long gown standing full-face holding a staff in her right hand, a dragon below (St Margaret)
Legend: illegible
NLW PITORD/493, dated 1393 x 1394

SEAL 1904
Rounded oval, 23x18
Lion sleeping facing left with head between two branches above
Legend: [.]S'RICHAR[section lost]F'IL'[.]OB[section lost]
NLW PITORD/496, dated 1313 x 1314

SEAL 1905
Round, 19
?bear with a collar and leash sitting up facing right
Legend: *[. . . . . .][section lost]
NLW PITORD/497, dated 1298 x 1299

SEAL 1906
Round, 18
Bird facing right
Legend: illegible
NLW PITORD/498, dated 1299 x 1300

SEAL 1907
Scutiform, 14x10
?Crossed hands with ?flower above
Legend: none
NLW PITORD/499, dated 1300 x 1301

APPENDIX

SEAL 1908
Rounded oval, 22x19
Within a cusped border, man standing full-face holding a roundel up in left hand (St John the Baptist), shields of arms (charge illegible) in field on either side with below, beneath a rounded arch, half length suppliant figure facing left
Legend: illegible
NLW PITORD/500, dated 1344 x 1345

SEAL 1909
Round, 21
In an ornate border, a shield: (Letter 'I' flanked by roundels)
Legend: +[...]A[.]R[section lost]?DOM[.]?EE[..]S
NLW PITORD/503, dated 1366 x 1367

SEAL 1910
Round, 25
Shield of arms (quarterly; 1 a martlet, 2 illegible, 3 ?ermine, 4 illegible) hanging from stylised branches
Legend: illegible
NLW PITORD/506, dated 1426 x 1427

SEAL 1911
Round, 18
Shield (charge illegible) surmounted by a cross
Legend: illegible, partially lost
NLW PITORD/508, dated 1300 x 1399

SEAL 1912
Pointed oval, nm
Virgin and Child standing on a small corabl facing half right with a tendril of lilies in the field on either side
Legend: illegible, partially lost
NLW PITORD/509, dated 1349

SEAL 1913
Hexagonal, 19x16
Within an ornate cusped trefoil, a shield of arms (two bends, in chief a ?talbot passant, a canton of two swords)
Legend: S' hVGOnIS DE [. .]ISPOR[.]
NLW PITORD/510, dated 1352 x 1353
NLW PITORD/1167, dated 1355 x 1356

SEAL 1914
Round, 19
Crossed hands with a bird facing left above
Legend: +[....]T[..]OTIS
NLW PITORD/511, dated 1326 x 1327

SEAL 1915
Round, 32
Four conifer branches with four ?cones in the angles
Legend: [.]S[.]MONIS : E[. .]OTE
NLW PITORD/513, dated 1289 x 1290

SEAL 1916
Round, 25
Stylised eight-petalled flower
Legend: +S[section lost][.]NA[. .]E[. .]
NLW PITORD/514, dated 1275 x 1299

SEAL 1917
Scutiform, 19x14
Shield of arms (lion rampant)
Legend: *SV[. . . . .]
NLW PITORD/515, dated 1387 x 1388

SEAL 1918
Round, 19
Letter M
Legend: X . [?I] . I . N . [?L] . I . V . A
NLW PITORD/518, dated 1410 x 1411

SEAL 1919
Pointed oval, 33x21
Bird facing left
Legend: + [. . . . .]INO[.] B[.]VGIE : [. . . .]
NLW PITORD/519, dated 1306

SEAL 1920
Round, 20
Lion walking to left
Legend: *[. .]IV[.] [. . .]SVI
NLW PITORD/521, dated 1345 x 1346

SEAL 1921
Round, 14
Indistinct
Legend: lost
NLW PITORD/522, dated 1316 x 1317

SEAL 1922
Unknown, nm
In a quatrafoil, a shield (charge lost)
Legend: lost
NLW PITORD/525, dated 1400 x 1401

SEAL 1923
Round, 20
Within a cusped quatrofoil, a shield (?M, with central descender forming base of a Latin cross)
Legend: S G[.]V[. . . . .]
NLW PITORD/527, dated 1363 x 1364

SEAL 1924
Round, 14
Merchant mark on a shield (includes letter R W), staff with banner emerging from top
Legend: none
NLW PITORD/529, dated 1467 x 1468

SEAL 1925
Round, 20
Hawk taking a rabbit, facing left
Legend: [. . . .] V S [section lost]
NLW PITORD/530, dated 1342 x 1343

SEAL 1926
Round, 19
Stag facing left
Legend: illegible
NLW PITORD/531, dated 1354 x 1355

SEAL 1927
Round, 19
Lion rampant facing right
Legend: [. . . . .]E[. . . . .]
NLW PITORD/532, dated 1200 x 1224

SEAL 1928
Pointed oval, nm
Stylised ?eight-petalled flower
Legend: illegible, partially lost
NLW PITORD/535, dated 1294 x 1295

SEAL 1929
Round, 9
Elephant facing left with a tower on its back
Legend: none
NLW PITORD/538, seal 1, dated 1474 x 1475

SEAL 1930
Square, 9x7
Shield of arms (three ?leaves)
Legend: N/A
NLW PITORD/538, seal 2, dated 1474 x 1475

SEAL 1931
Round, 14
Shield of arms (?vair en point), a cardinal's hat above
Legend: none
NLW PITORD/541, seal 1, dated 1477 x 1478

SEAL 1932
Rounded oval, 15x12
Bird (?pigeon) walking to left, surrounded by ears of corn
Legend: [?g]la[. .][?s]
NLW PITORD/541, seal 2, dated 1477 x 1478

SEAL 1933
Round, 10
Woman with long hair, half length, holding up a roundel (?mirror) in her right hand, an object in her left hand (?mermaid)
Legend: god [?be] g[. .]
NLW PITORD/541, seal 3, dated 1477 x 1478

SEAL 1934
Rounded oval, 15x10
Crowned letter W

Legend: none
NLW PITORD/543, seal 1, dated 1401 x 1402

SEAL 1935
Round, c.25
Squirrel facing left
Legend: none
NLW PITORD/543, seal 4, dated 1401 x 1402

SEAL 1936
Rounded oval, 23x18
In an ornate octofoil, a man's head full-face wearing a papal tiara, to left a key, to right a sword (St Peter)
Legend: *AS[. . . . .]V[. .]ISMEPETRE GY[. . . . .]
NLW PITORD/544, dated 1408 x 1409

SEAL 1937
Round, 22
Within a cusped border, a shield of arms (a fess, quarterly; 1,4 a mullet ?voied, 2 lost, 3 fretty)
Legend: [section lost][.]E[. . . . . . .]
NLW PITORD/548, dated 1364 x 1365

SEAL 1938
Rounded oval, 9x11
Crowned letter I flanked by branches
Legend: none
NLW PITORD/594, dated 1424 x 1425
NLW PITORD/551, dated 1424 x 1425

SEAL 1939
Round, 29
Within an ornate cusped border, a shield of arms (an eagle displayed) suspended from a bush in the legend band
Legend: §Sigillum:iohis § : bruyn :
NLW PITORD/553, dated 1399 x 1400
NLW PITORD/2482, seal 5, dated 1427

SEAL 1940
Round, 38
Stylised lily

Legend: +SIG[. . . . .]ANTREN
NLW PITORD/557, dated 1200 x 1224

SEAL 1941
Round, 14
Letter T
Legend: none
NLW PITORD/558, dated 1537
NLW PITORD/1063, dated 1530 x 1531

SEAL 1942
Round, 26
Indistinct
Legend: lost, if any
NLW PITORD/571, dated 1309

SEAL 1943
Round, 12
Letters N h, stylised foliage above
Legend: none
NLW PITORD/572, seal 1, dated 1549 x 1550

SEAL 1944
Rounded oval, 17x14
Bust of man facing right
Legend: none
NLW PITORD/572, seal 2, dated 1549 x 1550

SEAL 1945
Round, 18
Merchant mark cross, small cross above
Legend: illegible
NLW PITORD/574, dated 1319

SEAL 1946
Round, 18
Hare facing left
Legend: illegible, partially lost
NLW PITORD/586, dated 1324 x 1325

SEAL 1947
Round, 22
Within an octogram, a squirrel facing left
Legend: lost, if any
NLW PITORD/589, dated 1353 x 1354

SEAL 1948
Undetermined, 11x11
?Winged creature with ?human head and front leg raised facing right
Legend: none
NLW PITORD/596, dated 1442 x 1443

SEAL 1949
Round, 13
Shield (wheatsheaf, T to left h to right)
Legend: none
NLW PITORD/600, seal 1, dated 1478 x 1479

SEAL 1950
Pointed oval, 54x34
Within an ornate niche with three pointed arches and an architectural canopy, Virgin and Child standing full-face, to the left a woman standing facing half right holding an object in her right hand and a jar in her left hand (St Mary Magdalene), to the right a tonsured man vested for Mass standing full-face blessing with his right hand, holding a pastoral staff in his left hand, beneath the niche a shield of arms (England)
Legend: [.] COMV[. . . . .] [section lost] NO[. .]
NLW PITORD/605, seal 1, dated 1337

SEAL 1951
Pointed oval, 36x22
Noli me tangere, with below, beneath a rounded arch, a half length suppliant figure facing right
Legend: +S' GARdINO [?F][. . . . .] BRVGIENORTH'
NLW PITORD/605, seal 2, dated 1337

SEAL 1952
Pointed oval, nm
Within an architectural niche Virgin and Child standing full-face, to the left a crowned and veiled woman standing full-face holding a pastoral staff in her right hand and object in her left hand, to the right a ?woman standing holding a wheel (?St Katherine), below, within a rounded niche, a half-length suppliant mitred man facing half left holding a pastoral staff, to left a shield of arms (lion rampant, a bordure), to right a shield of arms (two keys addorsed in bend with a ?sword bend sinister)
Legend: [section lost]p[section lost]
NLW PITORD/606, dated 1486

SEAL 1953
Pointed oval, nm
Man seated full-face vested for Mass and wearing a papal tiara holding a patriarchal cross in his right hand and two keys in his left hand (St Peter)
Legend: [section lost] mune [section lost] ti § petri § Glouc[. . . . . .]
NLW PITORD/608, front, dated 1538 x 1539

SEAL 1954
Round, 20
Shield of arms (two keys saltire, over all a sword in pale hilt downwards)
Legend: illegible
NLW PITORD/608, back, dated 1538 x 1539

SEAL 1955
Round, 17
Horse's head facing half right
Legend: none
NLW PITORD/615, dated 1535 x 1536

SEAL 1956
Rounded oval, 15x12
Small figure facing left, large oval to left
Legend: none
NLW PITORD/632, dated 1523 x 1524

SEAL 1957
Round, 11
Bird facing left
Legend: none
NLW PITORD/634, dated 1529 x 1530

APPENDIX

SEAL 1958
Round, 14
Letters RP, stylised branch above
Legend: none
NLW PITORD/1455, dated 1545 x 1546
NLW PITORD/646, dated 1545 x 1546

SEAL 1959
Round, 11x8
Animal ?seated facing left
Legend: none
NLW PITORD/683, seal 1, dated 1486 x 1487

SEAL 1960
Round, 10
Barrel on its side
Legend: ioh'n [. . . . . .] :
NLW PITORD/683, seal 3, dated 1486 x 1487

SEAL 1961
Round, 14
Letters R B with foliage above and below
Legend: none
NLW PITORD/689, dated 1530 x 1531

SEAL 1962
Round, 14
R ?B, with a ?barrel on its side below
Legend: none
NLW PITORD/710, dated 1544 x 1545

SEAL 1963
Round, 11
Sacred Monogram (ihs), interlinked
Legend: none
NLW PITORD/712, dated 1403 x 1404

SEAL 1964
Round, nm
Shield of arms (?quarterly, 1 ?barry dancerty, 2 ?billette, 3 lost, 4 lion rampant, in escutcheon a lion rampant), sinister a supporter (a ?griffin)
Legend: [section lost] dni lovell : [section lost]
NLW PITORD/803, dated 1484 x 1485

SEAL 1965
Round, 16
Wyvern facing left
Legend: none
NLW PITORD/930, dated 1534 x 1535
NLW PITORD/809, seal 2, dated 1530 x 1531

SEAL 1966
Round, 23
Letter M with small D interlaced through central descender
Legend: * sigillum g[. . .]quevar holbache
NLW PITORD/848, dated 1429 x 1430

SEAL 1967
Rounded oval, 10x11
Animal (?dog) walking left
Legend: none
NLW PITORD/849, dated 1473 x 1474

SEAL 1968
Scutiform, 12x8
Letter T (?Tau cross), object above and crescent facing down below
Legend: none
NLW PITORD/918, seal 1, dated 1518 x 1519

SEAL 1969
Rectangular, 14x11
Uncertain (?purse / ?cup with rounded base)
Legend: none
NLW PITORD/918, seal 2, dated 1518 x 1519

SEAL 1970
Great Seal of Henry VII
NLW PITORD/924, dated 1485
NLW PITORD/1397, dated 1499 x 1500
NLW PITORD/1396, front, dated 1485 x 1486

SEAL 1971
Rounded oval, 25x13
Woman standing full-face holding up a spiked wheel (St Katherine), flanked by stylised foliage
Legend: * S[. . . . .]A[.]A[.]E[. .]
NLW PITORD/935, dated 1357 x 1358

SEAL 1972
Round, 22
Shield of arms (quarterly, 1 & 4 goutty, 2 & 3 paly of 3)
Legend: ioh Knyg[.]t[.]ley
NLW PITORD/1312, dated 1424 x 1425
NLW PITORD/937, dated 1424 x 1425

SEAL 1973
Round, 14
Crowned letter I flanked by foliage
Legend: none
NLW PITORD/938, dated 1389 x 1390

SEAL 1974
Rounded oval, 14x9
?Tree (?palm tree)
Legend: none
NLW PITORD/940, dated 1421 x 1422

SEAL 1975
Unknown, nm
Shield of arms (three ?wheatsheaves)
Legend: lost, if any
NLW PITORD/943, seal 1, dated 1543 x 1544

SEAL 1976
Undetermined, 11
Letter ?E (?M) within diamond
Legend: none
NLW PITORD/943, seal 2, dated 1543 x 1544

SEAL 1977
Round, 13
Bird displayed
Legend: none
NLW PITORD/963, dated 1539

SEAL 1978
Round, 34
Stylised lily
Legend: + [section lost] XORIC' FIL' TH'
NLW PITORD/967, dated 1275 x 1324

SEAL 1979
Unknown, 12
Six lines arranged in a radial pattern
Legend: none
NLW PITORD/968, dated 1538 x 1539

SEAL 1980
Rounded oval, 9x6
Letter ?W
Legend: none
NLW PITORD/993, seal 3, dated 1492 x 1493

SEAL 1981
Scutiform, 18x16
Hawk taking a hare facing left, ?text above
Legend: none
NLW PITORD/995, dated 1384 x 1385
NLW PITORD/994, dated 1384 x 1385

SEAL 1982
Pointed oval, nm
Within a roundel in an architectural setting, a ?tonsured head full-face (top fragment); a kneeling suppliant figure facing left (bottom fragment)
Legend: lost
NLW PITORD/1057, dated 1333

SEAL 1983
Pointed oval, nm
Christ carrying a flourishing cross, facing right
Legend: + S ¶ [. . . . .]C[.]S [section lost] NIE ¶
NLW PITORD/1057, seal 2, dated 1333

SEAL 1984
Round, 14
R, with a (?conifer) branch to the left
Legend: none

APPENDIX

NLW PITORD/1074, seal 1, dated 1397 x 1398

SEAL 1985
Scutiform, nm
Shield of arms (?barrel on its side, in chief a label of ?three points)
Legend: none
NLW PITORD/1074, seal 2, dated 1397 x 1398

SEAL 1986
Octagonal, 9x11
Letter b (?v) interlaced with letter ?v (?ll)
Legend: none
NLW PITORD/1082, seal 1, dated 1410 x 1411

SEAL 1987
Octagonal, 11x9
Wolf rampant erased
Legend: MEVIE
NLW PITORD/1082, seal 2, dated 1410 x 1411

SEAL 1988
Octagonal, 15x12
Monogram I P interlaced
Legend: none
NLW PITORD/1082, seal 3, dated 1410 x 1411

SEAL 1989
Octagonal, 11x9
Interlaced crowned monogram I I
Legend: none
NLW PITORD/1086, seal 2, dated 1449 x 1450

SEAL 1990
Round, 12
Eagle with ?foliage in its beak and wings raised walking to the left
Legend: none
NLW PITORD/1117, seal 2, dated 1419 x 1420
NLW PITORD/1087, seal 2, dated 1419 x 1420

SEAL 1991
Pointed oval, 27x19
Head and shoulders of suppliant man facing right, a star in the top right
Legend: * CAPVD SERVI [. .]I
NLW PITORD/1101, dated 1277

SEAL 1992
Unknown, nm
?Plant ?displayed
Legend: [section lost] EA [section lost]
NLW PITORD/1103, dated 1323 x 1324

SEAL 1993
Hexagonal, 19x18
Within a cusped trefoil, a shield of arms (a ?chevron)
Legend: [. . . . . . .]N [?S]PER[.]
NLW PITORD/1104, dated 1349 x 1350

SEAL 1994
Hexagonal, 12x11
Head and shoulders of man facing left, stylised lily on each side
Legend: none
NLW PITORD/1120, dated 1440 x 1441
NLW PITORD/1114, seal 1, dated 1440 x 1441

SEAL 1995
Hexagonal, 9x12
Monogram intertwined W ?L with flower on stem woven through ascenders of W
Legend: none
NLW PITORD/1114, seal 2, dated 1440 x 1441
NLW PITORD/1120, seal 2, dated 1440 x 1441

SEAL 1996
Unknown, nm
Letter I
Legend: none
NLW PITORD/1116, seal 1, dated 1440 x 1441

SEAL 1997
Unknown, nm
Crowned letter ?I
Legend: none
NLW PITORD/1116, seal 2, dated 1440 x 1441

SEAL 1998
Round, nm
Within an ornate border, a shield of arms (?three roundels and a chevron)
Legend: Foliate tendrils in legend band
NLW PITORD/1118, dated 1322 x 1323

SEAL 1999
Rounded oval, nm
Eagle displayed
Legend: *S[section lost]AMORI
NLW PITORD/1119, dated 1410 x 1411

SEAL 2000
Pointed oval, 29
Stylised lily
Legend: *S WIL[.]I DE CANTRE[..]
NLW PITORD/1123, dated 1290 x 1291

SEAL 2001
Round, 31
Six-petalled flower
Legend: S[. . . . .]VIL
NLW PITORD/1124, dated 1200 x 1224

SEAL 2002
Rounded oval, 20x18
Two heads facing in, between them a tree, below two hands clasped
Legend: [section lost] [. . .]E[.]
NLW PITORD/1141, dated 1342 x 1343

SEAL 2003
Pointed oval, 29x18
Bearded head in a long-stemmed cup (head John the Baptist, with hand emerging from upper right, blessing (manus Dei)
Legend: *CAPVTIOhANNIS[. .]IS[.]O
NLW PITORD/1143, dated 1299 x 1300

SEAL 2004
Rounded oval, 18x14
Lion sleeping facing left
Legend: Foliate tendrils in legend band
NLW PITORD/1145, dated 1304 x 1305

SEAL 2005
Pointed oval, 37x23
Eight-petalled stylised flower
Legend: [.]S'ALICI[. .]VN[.]T
NLW PITORD/1149, dated 1295 x 1296

SEAL 2006
Round, 21
Shield of arms (barry of eight, a label of three points, inescutcheon illegible) hanging from a bush in legend band, two wyverns in the field
Legend: ¶S'hUGONIS DE MORTV[. . . .]
NLW PITORD/1151, dated 1327 x 1328

SEAL 2007
Round, 14
Monogram interlaced WA (seal has to be turned upside down to read the two letters)
Legend: none
NLW PITORD/1153, dated 1541 x 1542
NLW PITORD/1593, dated 1540 x 1541

SEAL 2008
Round, 36
Shield of arms (England) between three trees
Legend: * SIGILLVM BAL[. .]VORV' SALOPIE
NLW PITORD/1155, dated 1547 x 1553

SEAL 2009
Rounded oval, 15x11
Letter B
Legend: none
NLW PITORD/1157, dated 1536

SEAL 2010
Round, 14
Head and shoulders of a woman full-face with long hair, wearing ornate necklace, to left a ?star, to right a ?leaf

APPENDIX

Legend: none
NLW PITORD/1158, dated 1515 x 1516

SEAL 2011
Hexagonal, 11x12
Crescent facing up surmounted by a triangle with a circle above (?balance / ?horn on strap)
Legend: none
NLW PITORD/1160, seal 1, dated 1518 x 1519

SEAL 2012
Round, 21
Two heads facing in, between them a tree
Legend: [.]AV[. . . .]ESA[. . . . . . .]
NLW PITORD/1162, seal 2, dated 1342 x 1343

SEAL 2013
Round, 20
A sickle facing left, three stalks of corn to the left
Legend: * S' RICA[.]DI DE [. . . .]EFORD'
NLW PITORD/1165, seal 1, dated 1354 x 1355

SEAL 2014
Rounded oval, 22x18
Annunciation with below, beneath a rounded arch, a half-length suppliant man in clerical dress facing right
Legend: * SIGIL[.] RIC ꝗ ARDI CA[.]E
NLW PITORD/1165, seal 2, dated 1354 x 1355

SEAL 2015
Round, 22
Bearded head facing up in a shallow dish with a low foot (head of John the Baptist)
Legend: *S'IOhIS L[.][section lost]PREBIT[.]
NLW PITORD/1166, dated 1361 x 1362

SEAL 2016
Round, 20
A shield of arms (quarterly, 1 and 4 a bend, 2 and 3 chief indented) suspended from a bush
Legend: § Sigillum : Ricardi de : [...]bto

NLW PITORD/1168, dated 1321 x 1322
SHA 322/2/208, dated 1386 x 1387

SEAL 2017
Rounded oval, 22x21
Gem: figure facing left holding a staff in their ?right hand seated on a chair with 'x' shaped support and tall back
Legend: illegible
NLW PITORD/1169, seal 1, dated 1391 x 1392

SEAL 2018
Round, 11
Lion walking to right
Legend: none
NLW PITORD/1169, seal 2, dated 1391 x 1392

SEAL 2019
Round, 11
Letters ?h (?n) c
Legend: none
NLW PITORD/1169, seal 3, dated 1391 x 1392

SEAL 2020
Square, 4x4
Letter ?M
Legend: none
NLW PITORD/1184, dated 1550

SEAL 2021
Round, 55
A shield of arms (quarterly, 1, barry nebulee of uncertain number, 2, ?goutty, a bar dancetty, 3, barry of uncertain number, a bend over all, 4, lion rampant, in escutcheon a lion rampant) couchee, a crest with a helm (a lovel gorged with a coronet, padlock to dexter), supporters (lions rampant guardant) and mantling
Legend: Sigillum : johannis dmi' ꝗ lowell burnell & de holand ꝗ
NLW PITORD/1210, front, dated 1462 x 1463
NLW PITORD/1188, dated 1463
NLW PITORD/1215, front, dated 1463 x 1464

SEAL 2022
Round, 13
On a shield surmounted by a cross crosslet, a merchant mark (includes inverted Y)
Legend: god bri[. . . . . . .]el
NLW PITORD/1189, seal 1, dated 1462 x 1463

SEAL 2023
Square, 12x8
Shield of arms (six objects)
Legend: none
NLW PITORD/1189, seal 2, dated 1462 x 1463

SEAL 2024
Round, 21
Within a cusped sexfoil, a shield of arms (six ?roses)
Legend: D¶AV¶ID ¶ RV¶S[. .]
NLW PITORD/1193, dated 1342 x 1343

SEAL 2025
Rounded oval, 16x11
Crowned letter W
Legend: none
NLW PITORD/1194, dated 1432 x 1433

SEAL 2026
Round, 14
A key facing up
Legend: S [?P]d[.]r[.] voll[. .]t
NLW PITORD/1195, dated 1435 x 1436

SEAL 2027
Rounded oval, 8x12
Gem: ?antelope (quadruped with thin straight horns) facing left
Legend: none
NLW PITORD/1196, dated 1426 x 1427

SEAL 2028
Octagonal, 10x12
Letters H I, small Greek cross to the right
Legend: none
NLW PITORD/1198, seal 1, dated 1523 x 1524

SEAL 2029
Round, 12
Shield of arms (chains saltire joined at the centre with a ring, a star on chief)
Legend: none
NLW PITORD/1198, seal 2, dated 1523 x 1524

SEAL 2030
Round, 13
Boar's head (?dog's head) facing left
Legend: none
NLW PITORD/1201, seal 3, dated 1531 x 1532

SEAL 2031
Round, 18
Hare blowing a horn on a dog running to left
Legend: * [. .]hOV [.]O[. . .]
NLW PITORD/1205, dated 1321 x 1322

SEAL 2032
Round, 22
Indistinct; damaged fragment
Legend: Includes I[?E?N]
NLW PITORD/1206, dated 1424 x 1425

SEAL 2033
Round, 17
Squirrel facing left
Legend: [.] I CRA[. . . .]TIS
NLW PITORD/1207, dated 1320 x 1321

SEAL 2034
Round, 14
A padlock (?fetterlock) with a key in it
Legend: none
NLW PITORD/1215, back, dated 1463 x 1464
NLW PITORD/1210, front, dated 1462 x 1463

SEAL 2035
Rectangular, 9x11
Letters RH (Rom caps)
Legend: none
NLW PITORD/1211, dated 1529 x 1530

APPENDIX

SEAL 2036
Round, 22
Merchant mark on a shield (includes inverted Y, with letter R), to the lower left a ?bird facing right, to lower right a stylised branch (?wing), patriarchal cross extending from top
Legend: + S' RICARDI HERN[. .]S'
NLW PITORD/1216, dated 1367 x 1368

SEAL 2037
Unknown, 15n
Uncertain; stylised ?wreath to one side
Legend: none
NLW PITORD/1220, seal 1, dated 1540 x 1541

SEAL 2038
Round, 12
Letter ?E, stylised foliage to left
Legend: none
NLW PITORD/1220, seal 2, dated 1540 x 1541

SEAL 2039
Round, nm
Letters I?L with horizontal stylised branch between them, curved branch above
Legend: none
NLW PITORD/1223, seal 1, dated 1475 x 1476

SEAL 2040
Round, 13
Crowned letter ?R, stylised branches to either side
Legend: none
NLW PITORD/1223, seal 2, dated 1475 x 1476

SEAL 2041
Rounded oval, nm
Figure standing facing half right holding a ?staff in left hand, to the left a ?tree
Legend: [section lost] ME [section lost]
NLW PITORD/1226, dated 1200 x 1224

SEAL 2042
Round, 32
Stylised four-petalled flower with four small petals in the angles
Legend: S' ?M [remainder lost]
NLW PITORD/1227, dated 1258 x 1259

SEAL 2043
Round, 27
Four stylised branches, four small roundels in the field
Legend: * S' WALTERI : [. . . . . .]D :
NLW PITORD/1230, dated 1314 x 1315

SEAL 2044
Round, 14
Merchant mark (includes 4 shape, letters r and ?c)
Legend: none
NLW PITORD/1231, dated 1544 x 1545

SEAL 2045
Rounded oval, 25x19
Within an architectural niche, Virgin and Child seated full-face, to right a kneeling suppliant figure facing left
Legend: ¶ MATER DEI MEME[. . .] MEI .
NLW PITORD/1234, dated 1394 x 1395

SEAL 2046
Round, 18
Stag's head full-face, item between antlers
Legend: *I[. . . . .]I
NLW PITORD/1235, dated 1350 x 1351

SEAL 2047
Round, 53
Shield of arms (chief indented with a label of three points) couche, closed helm with a crest (covered cup) and supporters (dexter, a falcon with wings extended, sinister, a male griffin), all on a diaper field
Legend: Sigillu [section lost] [. . .] § ¶ [. . . . . .] : orm[. . . . .]
NLW PITORD/1237, front, dated 1445 x 1446

SEAL 2048
Round, 16
Within a trefoil, a shield of arms (chief indented, a label of three points)
Legend: none
NLW PITORD/1237, back, dated 1445 x 1446

SEAL 2049
Unknown, 14x14
'cross' within a half circle; ?interlaced letters
Legend: none
NLW PITORD/1239, seal 1, dated 1417 x 1418

SEAL 2050
Unknown, 15x15
?Gem: figure standing full-face holding object up in right hand
Legend: none
NLW PITORD/1239, seal 2, dated 1417 x 1418

SEAL 2051
Round, 36
Lion facing right
Legend: [.] SIGILLVM M[.]RASCOTI
NLW PITORD/1241, dated 1150

SEAL 2052
Rounded oval, 28x23
Within an ?eight lobed border, a woman standing full-face holding up a spiked wheel (St Katherine), to left a kneeling supplicant figure facing right, ?flowers on stems in the field
Legend: illegible, partially lost
NLW PITORD/1244, dated 1344 x 1345

SEAL 2053
Rounded oval, 23x17
Woman standing full-face holding a spiked wheel up in her left hand (St Katherine), a bush to left and right
Legend: +SAVNCTA[.]ATE[. .]NA
NLW PITORD/1357, dated 1349 x 1350
NLW PITORD/1245, dated 1349 x 1350

SEAL 2054
Round, 24
Shield of arms (a pierced cinquefoil between six martlets), tendrils in the field
Legend: * S' RADVL[.]I DE PhICFORD
NLW PITORD/1247, dated 1293 x 1294

SEAL 2055
Round, 44
Armoured man on a horse galloping to right
Legend: §+SIGILL' hAM§ONIS FILII§ MARSCOT
NLW PITORD/1249, dated 1175 x 1199
NLW PITORD/1248, dated 1175 x 1199

SEAL 2056
Rounded oval, 20x18
Gem: animal (?horse) facing right
Legend: [. . . . .]ASTON
NLW PITORD/1250, dated 1344 x 1345

SEAL 2057
Round, 25
Within an ornately cusped border, Virgin and Child seated full-face on a bench with below, beneath a trefoil arch, half-length suppliant figure facing left
Legend: * SIGILL' [.]ILLEL¶[.] DE CEST[?R?I]A
NLW PITORD/1251, seal 1, dated 1368 x 1369
NLW PITORD/1375, dated 1368 x 1369

SEAL 2058
Rounded oval, 15x13
Gem: head with two faces (?head of Janus)
Legend: *S ALICI[. . . .]TEYN
NLW PITORD/1251, seal 2, dated 1368 x 1369
NLW PITORD/1375, seal 2, dated 1368 x 1369

SEAL 2059
Round, 27
Stylised eight-petalled flower
Legend: [.]S'IOh'LEkIN[.].
NLW PITORD/1254, dated 1298 x 1299

APPENDIX

SEAL 2060
Pointed oval, 28x20
Stylised eight-petalled flower
Legend: + S' WIL' DE FARNAL'
NLW PITORD/1256, dated 1250 x 1299

SEAL 2061
Rounded oval, 24x20
Within a cusped border, a ?crested helm (?standing figure), to left a ?shield with a ?stylised lily above, uncertain object to right
Legend: illegible
NLW PITORD/1257, dated 1344 x 1345

SEAL 2062
Round, 14
Short-legged quadruped (?elephant / ?hippo) walked to left on uneven ground, a palm tree behind
Legend: none
NLW PITORD/1260, dated 1470 x 1471

SEAL 2063
Pointed oval, 34x27
Stylised eight-petalled flower
Legend: [.]NICOL'[. .]L'[.]L[. . . . .]
NLW PITORD/1262, dated 1301 x 1302

SEAL 2064
Round, 21
Stylised four petalled flower with leaves in the angles
Legend: +S'ROB[. .]E[. . . .]
NLW PITORD/1263, dated 1278 x 1282

SEAL 2065
Rounded oval, nm
Letters ?A T
Legend: none
NLW PITORD/1265, seal 1, dated 1473 x 1474

SEAL 2066
Round, 11
Quadruped (?dog) facing right
Legend: none
NLW PITORD/1265, seal 2, dated 1473 x 1474

SEAL 2067
Round, 17
?animal
Legend: illegible
NLW PITORD/1267, dated 1473 x 1474

SEAL 2068
Round, 20
Hare blowing a horn riding a ?dog walking to left
Legend: SO[. . . . . . .]
NLW PITORD/1268, dated 1473 x 1474

SEAL 2069
Pointed oval, 30x19
Lamb of God facing right
Legend: + E[.]CEAG[.]VSDEI
NLW PITORD/1269, dated 1295 x 1296

SEAL 2070
Rounded oval, 10x8
Letter T with curved loop of descender terminating in stylised leaf, stylised branch above
Legend: N/A
NLW PITORD/1270, dated 1467 x 1468

SEAL 2071
Round, 20
Bird walking left with a branch in its beak
Legend: + [?R][. . . .] SDIV[.]
NLW PITORD/1273, dated 1353 x 1354

SEAL 2072
Round, nm
In a cusped quatrefoil, shield of arms (charge illegible)
Legend: N/A
NLW PITORD/1275, dated 1360

SEAL 2073
Round, nm
Shield (charge lost) hanging from a bush in the legend band
Legend: lost
NLW PITORD/1276, seal 2, dated 1491 x 1492

SEAL 2074
Rounded oval, 10x13
?Gem: bird with human head walking to right
Legend: none
NLW PITORD/1278, dated 1534 x 1535

SEAL 2075
Rounded oval, 16x12
Letter W, zigzag pattern above
Legend: none
NLW PITORD/1280, dated 1419

SEAL 2076
Rounded oval, 20x17
Lion rampant facing left (?gem)
Legend: *[.]V[.........]
NLW PITORD/1284, dated 1320 x 1321

SEAL 2077
Round, 22
Within an oval border, a shield of arms (paly of six, in chief sinister a ?rose, a sinister canton (a bend)) couche, a helm with a crest (?an animal's head) above
Legend: ¶ [...]ART ¶ [....]
NLW PITORD/1285, seal 1, dated 1545 x 1546

SEAL 2078
Round, 14
Merchant mark on a shield (includes inverted Y, letter ?L)
Legend: none
NLW PITORD/1285, seal 2, dated 1545 x 1546

SEAL 2079
Rounded oval, 20x15
Ship with central mast and rigging on waves
Legend: + [.........]OV
NLW PITORD/1287, dated 1325 x 1326

SEAL 2080
Pointed oval, 37x24
Stylised four-petalled flower with leaves in the angles
Legend: [.]SMARG[.]R[section illegible]
NLW PITORD/1289, dated 1306 x 1307

SEAL 2081
Rounded oval, 18x21
Bird walking to left with a branch in its beak
Legend: [.]ESV[......]
NLW PITORD/1295, dated 1347 x 1348

SEAL 2082
Round, 22
In a cusped quatrafoil, a shield of arms (a fess between three ?roses)
Legend: SIGILL'[.......] DE[......]
NLW PITORD/1296, seal 2, dated 1361 x 1362

SEAL 2083
Unknown, nm
Stylised plant (?ornate stylised lily with thin stems)
Legend: [section lost] DE M[section lost]
NLW PITORD/1300, dated 1200 x 1299

SEAL 2084
Pointed oval, 36x25
Stylised eight-petalled flower
Legend: + S' TOME FIL' HERBERTI
NLW PITORD/1303, dated 1200 x 1299

SEAL 2085
Round, 15
Hare blowing a horn on a dog running to left
Legend: *ALO[?N][.............]
NLW PITORD/1306, dated 1316 x 1317

SEAL 2086
Round, 17
Pelican in piety facing left
Legend: * SV[.........]SDEI
NLW PITORD/1309, dated 1392 x 1393

SEAL 2087
Round, 31
Bird with wings raised walking to left
Legend: * S' WILELI LAVN[...]IN
NLW PITORD/1313, dated 1225 x 1274

APPENDIX

SEAL 2088
Round, 21
Within an ornate cusped border, a shield of arms (charge illegible)
Legend: none
NLW PITORD/1314, dated 1353 x 1354

SEAL 2089
Pointed oval, 32x20
Four conifer branches with four cones in the angles
Legend: S' EDAYNE : F' : SIMONIS
NLW PITORD/1316, dated 1200 x 1224

SEAL 2090
Round, 12
Animal (?boar) facing left
Legend: S[. . . . . .]
NLW PITORD/1318, dated 1295 x 1296

SEAL 2091
Round, 25
Stylised eight-petalled flower
Legend: *S'WILLELMI:LECW
NLW PITORD/1319, dated 1200 x 1299

SEAL 2092
Rounded oval, 29x24
Head and shoulders of man facing left, blowing a horn held up in left hand
Legend: *S' [. .]ANI DE MONTEGOMERI
NLW PITORD/1320, dated 1275 x 1299

SEAL 2093
Round, nm
Within an ornate trefoil with four-petalled flowers in the cusps, a shield of arms (charge illegible)
Legend: S' hEN ¶ RI [section lost]
NLW PITORD/1324, dated 1391

SEAL 2094
Round, 29
Within a deeply cusped trefoil, a shield of arms (a chevron between three clarions)
Legend: Si[. .]llu' ¶ iohanni[.] ¶ arthur ¶
NLW PITORD/1325, dated 1426 x 1427

SEAL 2095
Round, 21
Lion (guardant) walking to left
Legend: [. .]A[. .]E[.][?E][. . . . . . .]
NLW PITORD/1332, dated 1292

SEAL 2096
Round, 18
Indistinct
Legend: illegible
NLW PITORD/1333, dated 1317 x 1318

SEAL 2097
Round, 37
Bird with wings raised running to the right
Legend: + SIGILL' NICOLAI : DE : SALLOWE
NLW PITORD/1335, dated 1200 x 1299
NLW PITORD/1334, dated 1200 x 1299

SEAL 2098
Pointed oval, 41x29
Two peacocks addorsed with heads turning back, between them a staff surmounted by a stylised lily
Legend: [.]ThOME DE [. . . .]IN[.]E[. .]
NLW PITORD/1340, dated 1275 x 1299

SEAL 2099
Round, 20
Lion walking right
Legend: illegible, partially lost
NLW PITORD/1346, dated 1250 x 1299

SEAL 2100
Round, 20
Within a cusped quatrafoil, a shield of arms (on a lozenge, a ?rose)
Legend: [.] ROBERTI [.]E COT[. .]
NLW PITORD/1348, dated 1314 x 1315

SEAL 2101
Round, 24
Figure standing to left ?holding up ?wheel (?roundel), to the right a ?suppliant figure ?facing left, between them ?trees
Legend: illegible, partially lost
NLW PITORD/1349, dated 1319 x 1320

SEAL 2102
Round, 17
Bird walking to left with foliage in its beak
Legend: SVP[. . . . .]
NLW PITORD/1350, dated 1329 x 1330

SEAL 2103
Round, 22
Four conifer branches
Legend: +S'Y[section lost].BLEThVN
NLW PITORD/1351, dated 1285 x 1286

SEAL 2104
Rounded oval, 26x20
St Andrew crucified
Legend: *S'A¶NDRE[. .]¶OLD[. .]¶[G D' BRVG ¶
NLW PITORD/1352, dated 1297 x 1298

SEAL 2105
Pointed oval, nm
Stylised ?eight-petalled flower
Legend: illegible, partially lost
NLW PITORD/1354, dated 1295 x 1296

SEAL 2106
Round, 20
Woman standing full-face with cross-tipped staff in her right hand, with base of staff in mouth of dragon upon which she is standing (St Margaret)
Legend: ¶ [. . .]IC[. . .]E[.]O[. . . . . .]E
NLW PITORD/1356, dated 1368 x 1369

SEAL 2107
Rounded oval, 12x14
Indistinct
Legend: none
NLW PITORD/1360, dated 1397 x 1398

SEAL 2108
Pointed oval, nm
Woman standing full-face on a corbel within ornate canopied architectural niche, holding a ?palm branch in her left hand and a ?jar up in her right hand (St Mary Magdalene)

Legend: ¶Sigi[section lost] [. . . . .] § [. .] § bruge
NLW PITORD/1361, seal 1, dated 1469

SEAL 2109
Round, 18
Virgin and Child standing full-face, stylised foliage to the left
Legend: *AVEMARIAGRAC
NLW PITORD/1361, seal 2, dated 1469

SEAL 2110
Unknown, nm
Letter ?R
Legend: none
NLW PITORD/1364, dated 1440 x 1441

SEAL 2111
Round, 14
?Letters
Legend: none
NLW PITORD/1365, dated 1325 x 1326

SEAL 2112
Round, 33
Stylised lily
Legend: +[. .]G[.]
LL'WILLELMIFIL:TEBALD
NLW PITORD/1367, dated 1100 x 1199

SEAL 2113
Round, 29
Stylised lily
Legend: SIGILL'PETRI:FIL'ROBERTI
NLW PITORD/1368, dated 1100 x 1199

SEAL 2114
Round, nm
Boar's head facing right
Legend: lost
NLW PITORD/1369, dated 1342 x 1343

SEAL 2115
Round, 21
Within a cusped border, a figure in a long gown standing full-face, ?holding an object up in their left hand

Legend: illegible
NLW PITORD/1370, dated 1390 x 1391

SEAL 2116
Round, 33
Bird walking to right
Legend: +SIGILL WILL'I D' LABEChE
NLW PITORD/1391, dated 1200 x 1250
NLW PITORD/1372, dated 1200 x 1299

SEAL 2117
Rounded oval, nm
Merchant mark on a shield (includes letter ?W), cross crosslet emerging from the top
Legend: [section lost] M[. . . . .]
NLW PITORD/1373, dated 1405 x 1406

SEAL 2118
Round, 20
Eight-rayed sun
Legend: +[?. .] ER [?.]L' [. .]BE?R
NLW PITORD/1377, dated 1292 x 1293

SEAL 2119
Round, 11
Plant (?teasel) with large oval flower and two leaves
Legend: lel[.]¶ [.]u[.]
NLW PITORD/1382, dated 1458 x 1459

SEAL 2120
Pointed oval, nm
Man (?vested for Mass) standing full-face within an ornate canopied architectural niche, holding a pastoral staff in his left hand and blessing with his right hand, to the right a figure standing full-face, to the left ?Virgin and Child ?seated
Legend: § SI:GILLV[. . . .]AR [sectio lost] [.]x EPI +
NLW PITORD/1389, dated 1520

SEAL 2121
Octagonal, 13
Letter ?I
Legend: none
NLW PITORD/1390, dated 1464 x 1465

SEAL 2122
Round, 18
Stag's head full-face
Legend: IESV[.]?M [. . . . .]
NLW PITORD/1392, dated 1350 x 1351

SEAL 2123
Rounded oval, nm
Within a niche with canopy above, a figure ?(woman) standing full-face, to the right a kneeling suppliant figure facing left
Legend: ¶ [section lost][?E]IO[. . . .]GRA[. . . . . . .]
NLW PITORD/1401, dated 1346 x 1347

SEAL 2124
Round, nm
?Four conifer branches
Legend: +SIG[section lost]CI
NLW PITORD/1409, dated 1200 x 1299

SEAL 2125
Round, 34
Four-petalled stylised flower with curved leaves in the angles
Legend: +[section lost]D[.]
NLW PITORD/1410, dated 1259 x 1260

SEAL 2126
Round, 57
Armoured man on a horse galloping to the right
Legend: + SIGILLVMHVG[.]NI[. . . . .] ORDIC ¶¶
NLW PITORD/1414, dated 1182 x 1194

SEAL 2127
Rounded oval, 27x30
Gem: Two figures both facing in standing holding ?swords up in ?right hand, between them a ?fountain (?tree on raised pedestal)
Legend: + SIGILLVM [. .]OLI . FIL'I AN [. . . . .]
NLW PITORD/1415, seal 1, dated 1275 x 1299

SEAL 2128
Pointed oval, 40x26
Stylised lily
Legend: + S' ROGERI FILII : OSBERTI :
NLW PITORD/1415, seal 2, dated 1275 x 1299

SEAL 2129
Pointed oval, 38x26
Stylised lily (atypical)
Legend: [.]SIGILL' : hEN RICI [.]ILII : M[.]L'
NLW PITORD/1415, seal 3, dated 1275 x 1299

SEAL 2130
Round, 43
Armoured man on a horse galloping to right
Legend: ¶SIGILL'TO[.]EDECOS TENTIN
NLW PITORD/1416, dated 1200 x 1224

SEAL 2131
Round, 34
Lion walking to right
Legend: +SIGILL'GILBERTID'LACI
NLW PITORD/1417, dated 1200 x 1299

SEAL 2132
Round, nm
Within an ornate cusped border, a shield of arms (quarterly, 1 & 4 a lion rampant, 2 & 3 ?lucies hauriant), shield held by half-length man full-face in plate armour
Legend: s' hen[. . . .] de p[. . . . .] [section lost]
NLW PITORD/2488, dated 1397 x 1398
NLW PITORD/1419, dated 1397 x 1398

SEAL 2133
Round, 44
Armoured man on a horse galloping to the right
Legend: + SIGILL' GALFRIDI D[. . .] V¶ERTVN¶
NLW PITORD/1421, dated 1200 x 1299

SEAL 2134
Pointed oval, 57x36
Within an ornate canopied architectural niche, a mitred man vested for Mass standing full-face ?blessing with his right hand, left hand holding a cross-tipped staff diagonally across his body
Legend: ¶[section lost][. .]E[.]CH[.] ARIES[.]I [.]§[. .]SI[. . . . . . .] DEBRVGG
NLW PITORD/1422, dated 1456 x 1457

SEAL 2135
Round, nm
Illegible; central ?cross-shape
Legend: illegible, partially lost
NLW PITORD/1424, dated 1200 x 1224

SEAL 2136
Round, 11
Crowned letter T
Legend: none
NLW PITORD/1450, seal 1, dated 1542 x 1543
NLW PITORD/1450, seal 2, dated 1542 x 1543

SEAL 2137
Rectangular, 10x11
Letter ?R (?B)
Legend: none
NLW PITORD/1454, seal 1, dated 1520

SEAL 2138
Square, 12x12
Letter ?R (?B)
Legend: none
NLW PITORD/1454, seal 2, dated 1520

SEAL 2139
Octagonal, nm
Merchant mark (includes inverted Y, letters I ?t)
Legend: none
NLW PITORD/1459, seal 2, dated 1424 x 1425

APPENDIX

SEAL 2140
Rounded oval, 13x10
?Bearded head with long hair full-face (?Vernicle head of Christ / ?head St John the Baptist)
Legend: lost, if any
NLW PITORD/1459, seal 3, dated 1424 x 1425

SEAL 2141
Round, 13
Illegible
Legend: none
NLW PITORD/1462, dated 1534 x 1535

SEAL 2142
Round, 17
Sacred Monogram (IhC), crown above
Legend: [section lost] ?R?E?V[section illegible]
NLW PITORD/1588, dated 1272 x 1273

SEAL 2143
Round, 24
Within a cusped border with ornate interlaced pattern, a roundel with ?the Sacred Monogram (?ihc)
Legend: [.]IGI[.]L[. .]IO[. . . . .]
NLW PITORD/2387, dated 1406 x 1407

SEAL 2144
Round, 32
Eight-petalled flower
Legend: * S' WIL' : FIL' WILE'L
NLW PITORD/2440, dated 1293

SEAL 2145
Pointed oval, nm
Within an architectural niche, a man
Legend: * S' WIL' : FIL' WILE'L
NLW PITORD/2441, dated 1419

SEAL 2146
Pointed oval, 34
Eight-petalled stylised flower
Legend: +S'GOhANNISDEhA
NLW PITORD/2443, dated 1293

SEAL 2147
Pointed oval, nm
Stylised eight-petalled flower
Legend: illegible, partially lost
NLW PITORD/2445, dated 1275 x 1299

SEAL 2148
Rectangular, 23
In a cusped quatrefoil, merchant mark on a shield (includes letter ?I I) cross emerging form top of shield
Legend: +S[section lost]hS' ChAV[. . .]Len
NLW PITORD/2447, dated 1354

SEAL 2149
Round, nm
Hindquarters of a ?lion (?horse) running to right
Legend: lost
NLW PITORD/2456, dated 1100 x 1199

SEAL 2150
Round, nm
Shield of arms (charge illegible)
Legend: illegible, partially lost
NLW PITORD/2461, seal 1, dated 1335

SEAL 2151
Round, 17
Eagle displayed
Legend: illegible, partially lost
NLW PITORD/2461, seal 2, dated 1335

SEAL 2152
Rounded oval, 25x22
Gem: man holding ?shield walking to left, small ?figure in lower left
Legend: illegible
NLW PITORD/2464, dated 1367 x 1368

SEAL 2153
Round, 19
Within a cusped border, a woman in a long gown standing full-face holding a ?palm up in her right hand and a ?staff in her left hand, an ?animal beneath her feet (?St Margaret)

Legend: [.....]VE I[.][?h]I[?S] [....]
NLW PITORD/2465, dated 1400 x 1499
NLW PITORD/2478, dated 1404

SEAL 2154
Rounded oval, 14x12
Hare facing right
Legend: illegible
NLW PITORD/2467, dated 1341 x 1342

SEAL 2155
Round, 15
Within an octofoil a ?bird ?flying left (?hands clasped) with five dashes (?letters) around edge of field
Legend: none
NLW PITORD/2470, dated 1390 x 1391

SEAL 2156
Unknown, 14
?Ermine spot (?flower)
Legend: none
NLW PITORD/2481, dated 1417 x 1418
NLW PITORD/2472, seal 1, dated 1417 x 1418

SEAL 2157
Unknown, 13
Legend: none
NLW PITORD/2472, seal 2, dated 1417 x 1418
NLW PITORD/2481, seal 2, dated 1417 x 1418

SEAL 2158
Unknown, nm
Shield of arms (charge illegible) couchant, a helm with a crest (illegible) above
Legend: lost, if any
NLW PITORD/2477, dated 1327 x 1377

SEAL 2159
Rounded oval, 22x16
Figure standing to left ?facing right, to right a kneeling suppliant figure facing left, between them a ?tree
Legend: illegible
NLW PITORD/2478, seal 2, dated 1404

SEAL 2160
Rounded oval, 10x12
Letters HC
Legend: none
NLW PITORD/2478, seal 3, dated 1404

SEAL 2161
Octagonal, 10x12
Crowned letter M flanked by four-petalled flowers on stems
Legend: none
NLW PITORD/2478, seal 4, dated 1404

SEAL 2162
Round, 10
Letters ?hC
Legend: none
NLW PITORD/2480, seal 1, dated 1404

SEAL 2163
Round, 13
Crowned 'I'
Legend: none
NLW PITORD/2480, seal 2, dated 1404

SEAL 2164
Pointed oval, nm
Nimbed man standing full-face holding in his right hand a stemmed cup with snake emerging and a palm branch in his left hand (St John the Evangelist), to the left a crowned and veiled woman standing full-face holding a pastoral staff in her right hand and a ?book in her left hand (St ?Winfried), to the right a nimbed woman with long hair standing full-face holing a jar up in her left hand, pointing to it with her right hand (St Mary Magdalene), all three within ornately canopied architectural niches
Legend: lost
NLW PITORD/2482, seal 1, dated 1427

SEAL 2165
Pointed oval, nm
?Nimbed and veiled woman standing full-face holding a pastoral staff in her right hand and a book in her left hand (?St Milburga /

APPENDIX

?St Winfried) within an ornate architectural niche, with below, beneath a rounded arch, head and shoulders of a suppliant figure facing left
Legend: lost
NLW PITORD/2492, seal 2, dated 1418
NLW PITORD/2482, seal 2, dated 1427

SEAL 2166
Round, 19
Within an ornate cusped quatrefoil, a shield of arms (lion rampant), with an ?eagle above
Legend: none
NLW PITORD/2482, seal 3, dated 1427

SEAL 2167
Round, 13
Hawk wearing jesses facing left
Legend: g ¶ stun
NLW PITORD/2482, seal 4, dated 1427

SEAL 2168
Rounded oval, 13
Crowned letter T loop of descender terminating in stylised leaf)
Legend: none
NLW PITORD/2482, seal 7, dated 1427

SEAL 2169
Round, 24
Within an ornate quatrefoil, seated Virgin and Child, left a crowned head, right mitred head, below a supplicant
Legend: lost, if any
NLW PITORD/2484, dated 1353
NLW PITORD/2485, dated 1356

SEAL 2170
Unknown, nm
Shield of arms (charge illegible)
Legend: [section illegible]T[. .][section lost]
NLW PITORD/2486, dated 1346 x 1347

SEAL 2171
Round, 13
Helm surmounted by a heron

Legend: S IOhISD[section illegible]
NLW PITORD/2487, dated 1383 x 1384

SEAL 2172
Pointed oval, nm
Figure standing full-face ?holding a ?staff in their right hand with shaft diagonally across the body, within an ornate canopied niche
Legend: lost
NLW PITORD/2492, seal 1, dated 1418

SEAL 2173
Hexagonal, 11x14
A barrel on its end, to the left letter l, to the right e, to far left a small flower
Legend: none
NLW PITORD/2492, seal 3, dated 1418

SEAL 2174
Octagonal, 9x10
Uncertain; central tapered ?column flanked by ?sacks with six small roundels, letters (illegible) above
Legend: none
NLW PITORD/2492, seal 4, dated 1418

SEAL 2175
Round, 35
In an ornate trefoil, shield of arms (strewn with fleur-de-lys)
Legend: none
NLW PITORD/2501, dated 1431

SEAL 2174
Round, nm
Shield of arms (?per pale; sinister, a lion rampant), helm with crest (a ram's head) above, sinister a supporter (a ?hert), mantling in the field
Legend: S . henri' gray [remainder lost]
NLW Strata Marchella, dated 1446 x 1447

SEAL 2177
Unknown (?round), c.40x c.34
Armoured man on horse ?galloping to right
Legend: lost
NLW Strata Marchella/5, dated 1183

SEAL 2178
Pointed oval, c.45xc.42
Man vested for Mass standing full-face holding a ?pastoral staff up in his left hand, ?blessing with his right hand
Legend: lost
NLW Strata Marchella/16, dated 1195 x 1196

SEAL 2179
Pointed oval, c.33x26
Man vested for Mass standing full-face on a corbel blessing with his right hand and holding a pastoral staff in his left hand
Legend: [. .]GILLVM ¶ [. . . . .] R [. . .]
NLW Strata Marchella/16, back, dated 1195 x 1196

SEAL 2180
Round, c.35
Armoured man on horse galloping to the right
Legend: lost
NLW Strata Marchella/18, dated 1198

SEAL 2181
Round, 48
Armoured man on horse galloping to the right
Legend: SIGILLV[. . . . .] I'[.]VI ¶ [section lost] [?C] ¶
NLW Strata Marchella/33, dated 1201
NLW Strata Marchella/51, dated 1197 x 1202

SEAL 2182
Round, 57
Armoured man on horse galloping to the right
Legend: §SIGILL'GVEN§VNWINDE§KE-VEILIAVC
NLW Strata Marchella/34, front, dated 1201
NLW Strata Marchella/53, front, dated 1207
NLW Strata Marchella/50, front, dated 1197 x 1216
NLW Strata Marchella/41, front, dated 1205

SEAL 2183
Round, c.59
Armoured on horse galloping to the right
Legend: ¶ SIGIL[. . . . .]
V[?C] ¶
NLW Strata Marchella/62, dated 1215
NLW Strata Marchella/35, dated 1197 x 1216

SEAL 2184
Round, 68
Armoured man on horse galloping to the right
Legend: SIG[section lost] [.]P[.] [section lost]
NLW Strata Marchella/58, dated 1209

SEAL 2185
Round, nm
Armoured man on a horse ?walking to right
Legend: SIG[section lost]IR§
NLW Strata Marchella/59, dated 1215

SEAL 2186
Round, 52
Armoured man on a horse galloping to the right
Legend: lost
NLW Strata Marchella/60, dated 1215

SEAL 2187
Round, c.53
Armoured man a horse galloping to the right
Legend: + [.] [section lost][.]IC
NLW Strata Marchella/65, dated 1216 x 1226
NLW Strata Marchella/64, dated 1216 x 1226

SEAL 2188
Round, nm
Three-quarter length ?tonsured man standing full-face, in his right hand a pastoral staff, in his left hand a book
Legend: +SIGI[section lost]SIS
NLW Strata Marchella/70, dated 1227

APPENDIX

SEAL 2189
Round, 46
Armoured man on a horse galloping to the right
Legend: + S' [. . . . .] AS ¶ [. . . .] AVN
NLW Strata Marchella/80, dated 1232

SEAL 2190
Round, c.60
Armoured man on a horse galloping to the right
Legend: lost
NLW Strata Marchella/88, dated 1367

SEAL 2191
Pointed oval, c.50xc.38
?Crowned figure ?seated within niche, to left a ?suppliant figure with large crozier above
Legend: illegible, partially lost
NLW Strata Marchella/91, dated 1490

SEAL 2192
Round, nm
Figure on horse facing right
Legend: lost
NLW Strata Marchella/101, dated 1207

SEAL 2193
Pointed oval, c.35x20
Two keys crossed, facing up
Legend: lost
NLW WIGFAIR/8, back, dated 1355

SEAL 2194
Round, c.48xc.37
Man vested for Mass standing full-face within a niche, to the right a nimbed angel standing facing left holding up a ?candle
Legend: lost
NLW WIGFAIR/8, front, dated 1355

SEAL 2195
Round, 20
Within a cusped border, a ?dragon walking left
Legend: [. . . . . .] ?R [. . . . .] SI [. . . . .]
NLW WIGFAIR/13, dated 1404

SEAL 2196
Round, 15
Lion sleeping facing left beneath a tree
Legend: none
NLW WIGFAIR/13, seal 2, dated 1404

SEAL 2197
Round, 22
Lamb of God facing left
Legend: [. . .]EAGNUSDEI
NLW WIGFAIR/13, seal 3, dated 1404

SEAL 2198
Round, c.35
Shield of arms (quarterly; 1, barry, in chief three torteaux; 2, ?3, quarterly, 1, 4 a maunch, 2, 3, barry of eight, an orle of ten martlets; fourth quarter lost)
Legend: [section lost] ?wa[. . . . .]
NLW WIGFAIR/15, dated 1437

SEAL 2199
Round, 19
Lamb of God facing left
Legend: ECC[. . . . .]
NLW WIGFAIR/256, dated 1346

SEAL 2200
Octagonal, 13x13
Shield of arms (chevron, two stars in chief)
Legend: none
NLW WIGFAIR/258, dated 1389

SEAL 2201
Unknown, nm
Shield of arms (griffin statant)
Legend: lost
NLW WIGFAIR/268, dated 1475

SEAL 2202
Round, 14
Lion facing left springing on a ?deer in lower left
Legend: none
NLW WIGFAIR/270, dated 1479

SEAL 2203
Round, 16
Three vertical and five horizontal lines forming interlaced pattern
Legend: none
NLW WIGFAIR/274, dated 1493

SEAL 2204
Square, 11x11
Letter ?H
Legend: none
NLW WIGFAIR/277, dated 1500

SEAL 2205
Round, c.49
Ornate naturalistic lily-plant, to right and left a ?peacock (?wyvern) addorsed with head turned back
Legend: [. . . .]LL [. . . . .]DSTOC[. .]
NLW WIGFAIR/627, front, dated 1275 x 1299

SEAL 2206
Round, 18
Stag's head full-face, a cross between the antlers
Legend: + TIMETEDEVM
NLW WIGFAIR/627, back, dated 1275 x 1299

SEAL 2207
Round, 26
Eight-petalled stylised flower
Legend: *S'ROBTIFILIIWILLMI
SHA 20/5/2, dated 1275 x 1324

SEAL 2208
Pointed oval, 26
Indistinct
Legend: lost, if any
SHA 20/5/4, dated 1275 x 1324

SEAL 2209
Unknown, nm
?eight petalled stylised flower
Legend: [. .]?BE[remainder lost]
SHA 20/5/5, dated 1273 x 1274

SEAL 2210
Round, 22
Stylised lily
Legend: *S'PETRI FIL' ROB'TI D'STOKS
SHA 20/5/7, dated 1311 x 1312

SEAL 2211
Rounded oval, 27x24
Within an eight-pointed star, a squirrel facing right
Legend: [. . . . .] EFIL'WILL'IDE [. . .]
[section lost]
SHA 20/5/9, dated 1334 x 1335

SEAL 2212
Round, 16
Hare (?rabbit) facing left, stylised foliage above
Legend: *SOHO [. . . .] E [. . .] ¶
SHA 20/5/10, dated 1334 x 1335
SHA 20/5/83, dated 1340 x 1341

SEAL 2213
Rounded oval, 26x21
Within a niche, woman standing facing half right holding up a spiked wheel (St Katherine), to right a kneeling suppliant figure facing left, stylised tree in field
Legend: [. . .]ATER [. . . . . .]S [.] RERE:D[. . .]
SHA 20/5/11, dated 1381 x 1382

SEAL 2214
Octagonal, 11x10
Eagle with wings raised facing left
Legend: [. . . . .]
SHA 20/5/16, dated 1453 x 1454
SHA 20/5/55, dated 1448 x 1449

SEAL 2215
Pointed oval, 37x22
Four conifer branches
Legend: [. .]LICIE . FIL' R [. . . . . .]
SHA 20/5/19, dated 1300 x 1301

APPENDIX

SEAL 2216
Round, 11
Woman kneeling full-face holding object in both hands
Legend: Wa[. . . . .]a
SHA 20/5/22, dated 1427 x 1428
SHA 20/5/21, dated 1427 x 1428

SEAL 2217
Round, 9
Merchant mark (includes letters ?, I)
Legend: none
SHA 20/5/22, seal 2, dated 1427 x 1428
SHA 20/5/21, seal 2, dated 1427 x 1428

SEAL 2218
Rectangular, 9x7
Woman standing full-face holding a spiked wheel up in right hand, sword point down in left hand (St Katherine)
Legend: none
SHA 20/5/22, seal 3, dated 1427 x 1428
SHA 20/5/21, seal 3, dated 1427 x 1428

SEAL 2219
Round, 10
Pair of wings
Legend: none
SHA 20/5/22, seal 4, dated 1427 x 1428
SHA 20/5/21, seal 4, dated 1427 x 1428

SEAL 2220
Round, 12
Head and shoulders of man facing left, letter R on chest, in field to left and right a stylised lily
Legend: none
SHA 20/5/24, seal 1, dated 1430 x 1431
SHA 20/5/23, dated 1430 x 1431

SEAL 2221
Rectangular, 12x15
Letter W, stylised foliage to right
Legend: none
SHA 20/5/24, seal 2, dated 1430 x 1431
SHA 20/5/23, seal 2, dated 1430 x 1431

SEAL 2222
Hexagonal, 11x10
Eagle displayed, letter (illegible) to left and right
Legend: none
SHA 20/5/24, seal 3, dated 1430 x 1431
SHA 20/5/23, seal 3, dated 1430 x 1431

SEAL 2223
Rectangular, 12x9
letter ?G
Legend: none
SHA 20/5/51, dated 1425 x 1426

SEAL 2224
Round, 13
Leaf (?Maple-type)
Legend: none
SHA 20/5/53, dated 1448 x 1449
SHA 20/7/34, dated 1436 x 1437
SHA 20/5/55, seal 2, dated 1448 x 1449
SHA 20/5/56, dated 1448 x 1449
SHA 20/6/62, dated 1435 x 1436
SHA 20/6/64, dated 1447 x 1448
SHA 20/7/52/A, dated 1447 x 1448
SHA 20/7/58, dated 1458 x 1459

SEAL 2225
Rounded oval, 13x11
Letter G
Legend: none
SHA 20/5/53, seal 2, dated 1448 x 1449

SEAL 2226
Rounded oval, 23x20
Shield (charge indistinct: merchant mark?), a cross-tipped staff and banner emerging from top
Legend: ⁋ S'ThOME.DE ⁋ [. .] LETVN
SHA 20/5/54, dated 1448 x 1449

SEAL 2227
Rounded oval, 12x8
Crowned letter I, stylised foliage to left and right
Legend: none
SHA 20/5/54, seal 2, dated 1448 x 1449

SEAL 2228
Round, 27
Four conifer branches with four cones in the angles
Legend: S' ROG'I COTEREL
SHA 20/5/66, dated 1274 x 1275
SHA 20/5/65, dated 1309 x 1310

SEAL 2229
Rounded oval, 40x32
?Gem: head and shoulders of bearded man wearing a hat with a brim facing right
Legend: * SCIGILLVM HENRICI MONETARII:
SHA 20/5/67, dated 1313 x 1314
SHA 20/5/68, dated 1313 x 1314
SHA 20/5/71, dated 1315 x 1316
SHA 20/5/70, dated 1315 x 1316

SEAL 2230
Round, 18
Hawk taking a bird facing left
Legend: * ALASI[.]S[. . .]PRIS
SHA 20/5/72, dated 1323 x 1324
SHA 20/5/75, dated 1338 x 1339

SEAL 2231
Round, 19
Hare facing right with foliage behind
Legend: * S'PETRIDE ST[. . .]TON
SHA 20/5/73, dated 1333 x 1334
SHA 20/5/76, dated 1347 x 1348
SHA 20/5/85, dated 1341 x 1342
SHA 20/5/74, dated 1333 x 1334

SEAL 2232
Octagonal, 11x10
Letters I G interlaced
Legend: none
SHA 20/7/50, dated 1425 x 1425
SHA 20/5/77, dated 1422 x 1423
SHA 20/7/48, dated 1407 x 1408
SHA 20/7/49, dated 1407 x 1408

SEAL 2233
Round, c.19
?Four ?conifer branches with pellets in the angles
Legend: [. .]V[.] [rest lost]
SHA 20/5/80, dated 1300 x 1349

SEAL 2234
Round, 13
Hare facing right
Legend: illegible
SHA 20/5/81, seal 1, dated 1324 x 1325

SEAL 2235
Round, 17
Letter T
Legend: none
SHA 20/5/81, seal 2, dated 1324 x 1325

SEAL 2236
Round, 17
Sacred Monogram (ihc)
Legend: [. . . .]ESV
SHA 20/5/82, dated 1327 x 1328

SEAL 2237
Round, 20
Shield of arms (charge illegible)
Legend: illegible
SHA 20/5/83, seal 2, dated 1340 x 1341

SEAL 2238
Round, 19
?Tonsured man standing full-face holding two large keys up in his left hand (St Peter), three ears of wheat in the field
Legend: [. .]A[. . . . . .]ETR[. .]
SHA 20/5/84, dated 1341 x 1342

SEAL 2239
Round, 19
Within a cusped border, a shield of arms (charge illegible)
Legend: N/A
SHA 20/5/85, dated 1341 x 1342

SEAL 2240
Round, 25
Dog (?lion) running to right

APPENDIX

Legend: S IACOB[. . . . .]
SHA 20/5/86, dated 1342 x 1343

SEAL 2241
Round, 17
Lamb of God facing right
Legend: +E[. . . . .]NV[. . . .]
SHA 20/5/87, dated 1347 x 1348

SEAL 2242
Round, 25
Within a cusped border, a merchant mark on a shield (includes inverted Y, ?letters), staff with banner emerging from the top
Legend: + SIGILV[.]: [.]ILLI : DE : SCHROVIS[.]ERI
SHA 20/5/88, dated 1356 x 1357

SEAL 2243
Round, 19
Shield of arms (on a bend ?cotised, three mullets], a cross-tipped staff emerging from the top
Legend: + [. .]OhA[. . . . . . .]hEYNE
SHA 20/5/89, seal 1 and 2, dated 1366 x 1367

SEAL 2244
Round, 12
Crowned letter W
Legend: none
SHA 20/5/90, seal 1, dated 1417 x 1418

SEAL 2245
Round, c.19
?Shield of arms (charge lost)
Legend: lost
SHA 20/5/90, seal 2, dated 1417 x 1418

SEAL 2246
Round, 16
Within a quatrefoil, a shield of arms (charge uncertain)
Legend: [. . . .] : Ioh[. .] : [. . . . .]
SHA 20/5/92, dated 1474

SEAL 2247
Round, 13
Uncertain (very worn and distorted)
Legend: lost
SHA 20/5/95, dated 1438 x 1439

SEAL 2248
Round, 10
Crowned letter I
Legend: none
SHA 20/5/97, dated 1482

SEAL 2249
Round, 19
To left, Virgin and Child seated facing right, to right ?kneeling suppliant figure facing left
Legend: +IES [. .] EL [.]A [.] V [.] LEL
SHA 20/5/141, dated 1200 x 1299

SEAL 2250
Round, 32
Cross fleury with eight pointed stars in the angles
Legend: +SIGILL' SYMONIS: GERNVN:
SHA 20/6/1, dated 1228 x 1243

SEAL 2251
Round, 66
Armoured man on horse galloping to the right
Legend: [section lost] LACI
SHA 20/6/2, dated 1200 x 1249

SEAL 2252
Rectangular, 11x7
Crowned letter I, stylised foliage to left and right
Legend: none
SHA 20/6/15, dated 1485 x 1486

SEAL 2253
Round, 21
Four ?clover leaves
Legend: [section lost] [.] DIVE [.] [section lost]
SHA 20/6/35, dated 1407 x 1408

SEAL 2254
Round, 16
Indistinct
Legend: [section illegible] S [section illegible]
SHA 20/6/35, seal 2, dated 1407 x 1408

SEAL 2255
Round, 29
Stylised eight-petalled flower
Legend: * S' WI[.....] COR[.]TONE
SHA 20/6/49, front, dated 1295 x 1296

SEAL 2256
Unknown, c.18
?Dog running to the left
Legend: none
SHA 20/6/49, back, dated 1295 x 1296

SEAL 2257
Round, 18
Suppliant figure ?kneeling (?half length) facing right holding ?flower up in their hands, stylised branch to the left
Legend: illegible
SHA 20/6/50, dated 1354 x 1355

SEAL 2258
Round, 20
Uncertain central device
Legend: N/A
SHA 20/6/52, dated 1353 x 1354

SEAL 2259
Rounded oval, 18x9
Uncertain
Legend: illegible
SHA 20/6/54, dated 1360 x 1361

SEAL 2260
Round, 19
Bird with foliage in its beak walking to left
Legend: [....]VESDI'
SHA 20/6/55, dated 1379 x 1380

SEAL 2261
Round, 18
Within an octofoil, a shield of arms (charge lost)
Legend: lost
SHA 20/6/56, dated 1403 x 1404

SEAL 2262
Round, 23
?Pelican in its piety
Legend: D[.........]
SHA 20/6/57, dated 1409 x 1410

SEAL 2263
Round, 13
Crowned letters IC
Legend: none
SHA 20/6/58, dated 1410 x 1411

SEAL 2264
Octagonal, 14x12
Monogram: AIh (?LIH) with crown above and below
Legend: none
SHA 20/6/60, dated 1430 x 1431

SEAL 2265
Round, c.15
Shield of arms (?dog's head erased)
Legend: none
SHA 20/6/61, dated 1434 x 1435

SEAL 2266
Round, 15
Crowned letter M
Legend: none
SHA 20/6/66, dated 1452 x 1453

SEAL 2267
Octagonal, 29x29
Letters I ?V
Legend: none
SHA 20/6/67, dated 1452 x 1453

SEAL 2268
Rectangular, 9x8
Crucifixion
Legend: none
SHA 20/6/68, dated 1466 x 1467

APPENDIX

SEAL 2269
Round, 29
Shield of arms (lion rampant) hanging from bushes
Legend: ⁌ S' iohis : [. . . . . .]d[. .]e[. . . .]
SHA 20/6/120, dated 1394 x 1395

SEAL 2270
Round, 24
Four-petalled flower
Legend: S' RICA[. . . . .]ENVTO[.]
SHA 20/6/121, dated 1319 x 1320

SEAL 2271
Round, 19
To hands crossed, above them a bird flying to the left
Legend: INVET[.]LELAM
SHA 20/6/122, dated 1357 x 1358

SEAL 2272
Round, 23
Within a quatrefoil, to left a man standing facing half right holding up a saltire cross (St Andrew), to right a man in short gown holding up a roundel with Lamb of God (St John the Baptist), in lower centre a half-length suppliant man facing right with crowned M above
Legend: [.]O[. . .]TIS[. . . . .] OH'I
SHA 20/6/123, dated 1374 x 1375

SEAL 2273
Round, 20
Within an ornate architectural niche with a double canopy, Virgin and Child standing full-face to left, to right a kneeling suppliant figure facing left
Legend: * LEYEDI . PREY . FOR ME:
SHA 20/6/124, dated 1385 x 1386

SEAL 2274
Round, c.18
Within a cusped border, a shield of arms (?ragged cross)
Legend: [section lost] de . horn[.]o[.]
SHA 20/6/125, seal 2, dated 1388 x 1389

SEAL 2275
Round, 19
Merchant mark on a shield, cross emerging from top with star to the left, crescent to the right
Legend: IE[.]V[.]EAL'
SHA 20/6/125, seal 3, dated 1388 x 1389

SEAL 2276
Round, 17
Hawk taking a large bird, facing left
Legend: * [. . . .]E[. .]E[.]O[. . .]E
SHA 20/6/125, seal 4, dated 1388 x 1389

SEAL 2277
Round, 28
Seven conifer branches arranged radially
Legend: [.]ROB' IV[. .][?M]ISBRV[?I]
SHA 20/7/1, dated 1200 x 1299

SEAL 2278
Round, 17
Two heads facing in, a bird above
Legend: [. .]VE[.]EA[. . . . .]
SHA 20/7/2, dated 1322 x 1323

SEAL 2279
Round, 16
Squirrel facing right
Legend: ICR[. . . .]ENOTIS
SHA 20/7/3, dated 1322 x 1323

SEAL 2280
Round, 19
Within a cusped quatrefoil, a shield of arms (a chevron between two objects in chief and a crescent in base)
Legend: *[. . . . .]E
SHA 20/7/4, dated 1323 x 1324

SEAL 2281
Round, c.13
Hare facing right blowing a horn
Legend: * SOH[.][lost]
SHA 20/7/7, dated 1341 x 1342

SEAL 2282
Round, 20
Virgin and Child standing full-face, to right a kneeling suppliant figure facing left with foliate stem above hands
Legend: AVE MA[. . .]GRACIA P[.]ENA ¶
SHA 20/7/8, dated 1341 x 1342

SEAL 2283
Round, 19
Cross recercely
Legend: * WA[. . .]E[. . .]AR[?S][?I I]
SHA 20/7/9, dated 1349 x 1350

SEAL 2284
Rounded oval, 24x c.20
Figure (?woman) standing full-face holding a circular object up in their left hand, an ear of wheat in the lower right
Legend: * EC[?CE] AN[?C][. . . .]O[. . .]
SHA 20/7/11, dated 1352 x 1353

SEAL 2285
Round, 21
Shield of arms (chequy) suspended on strap
Legend: * SIG[. .]L [. . . . . .]IS D[. . . . . . .] ON
SHA 20/7/14, dated 1367 x 1368

SEAL 2286
Scutiform, 18x15
Bearded head face up on a shallow dish, a sword pointing left above, in chief letters X S [.]
Legend: none
SHA 20/7/15, dated 1369 x 1370
SHA 20/7/46, dated 1379 x 1380

SEAL 2287
Round, 22
Within a six-pointed star, a lion's head full-face, a ?crescent below, decoration in the outer angles of the star
Legend: none
SHA 20/7/16, dated 1370 x 1371

SEAL 2288
Rounded oval, 26x20
Within an ornate architectural canopy, Virgin and Child standing facing half right, to right a kneeling suppliant man facing left with three trefoil flowers on stems above his hands
Legend: ¶ MATER DEI [. . .]ERERE MEI
SHA 20/7/17, dated 1380 x 1381

SEAL 2289
Round, 22
Within a cusped quatrefoil a crowned woman standing to the left facing half right holding up a spiked wheel in their left hand (St Katherine), to the right a kneeling suppliant figure facing left, foliate stems in the field
Legend: illegible
SHA 20/7/18, seal 1, dated 1380 x 1381

SEAL 2290
Round, 23
Within a cusped border, a shield of arms (a chief)
Legend: *SIGI[. .]V[. . . . .]
SHA 20/7/18, seal 2, dated 1380 x 1381

SEAL 2291
Round, 18
Stag running to the left
Legend: [. .][?D]IVES[. . . .]
SHA 20/7/19, seal 1, dated 1382 x 1383
SHA 20/7/20, seal 1, dated 1382 x 1383

SEAL 2292
Round, 21
Within a cusped rectangle, a shield of arms (a ?maunch)
Legend: lost, if any
SHA 20/7/19, seal 2, dated 1382 x 1383

SEAL 2293
Round, 23
Dragon walking to the left
Legend: *I[. .]VES[?N][. .]
SHA 20/7/21, dated 1382 x 1383

APPENDIX

SEAL 2294
Round, 24
Within an ornate architectural niche, a man standing full-face holding a ?book up in his right hand and a grid-iron in his left hand (St Lawrence), with below a shield of arms (diaper, two ?mullets on a chevron)
Legend: S' [?R][. . . . . . .] th[. . . . .]
SHA 20/7/22, dated 1384 x 1383

SEAL 2295
Rounded oval, 16x18
Gem: griffin walking to right
Legend: * [.]E[. . .]N[. . .]V[.]VER §
SHA 20/7/23, dated 1393 x 1394

SEAL 2296
Rounded oval, 14x11
Crowned letter I, stylised branches to left and right
Legend: none
SHA 20/7/23, seal 2, dated 1393 x 1394

SEAL 2297
Round, 26
Crowned letters TL
Legend: none
SHA 20/7/25, dated 1402 x 1403
SHA 20/7/26, dated 1402 x 1403

SEAL 2298
Round, 20
Within a cusped quatrefoil, a shield of arms (charge illegible)
Legend: *S[. . . . .]
SHA 20/7/27, dated 1402 x 1403

SEAL 2299
Round, 21
Four ?clover leaves
Legend: * PROLIVES.
SHA 20/7/28, dated 1404 x 1405

SEAL 2300
Rounded oval, 10x15
Letters TH
Legend: none
SHA 20/7/29, dated 1408 x 1409

SEAL 2301
Rounded oval, 11x10
Bearded head full-face
Legend: illegible
SHA 20/7/31, dated 1414 x 1415

SEAL 2302
Octagonal, 14x9
Crowned letter I, stylised branches to left and right
Legend: none
SHA 20/7/32, dated 1427 x 1428

SEAL 2303
Round, 14
Crowned letter ? D
Legend: none
SHA 20/7/33, dated 1409 x 1410

SEAL 2304
Octagonal, 13x12
Letter I, stylised foliage to left and right
Legend: none
SHA 20/7/36, dated 1400 x 1499

SEAL 2305
Round, 22
Stag running left, tree behind
Legend: S [. . . . . . .] E [. .]
SHA 20/7/37, dated 1404 x 1404

SEAL 2306
Pointed oval, 31x20
Four conifer branches with ?cones in the angles
Legend: [section lost] S' DIONISIIL' [. . . .]h?S
SHA 20/7/38, dated 1300 x 1301

SEAL 2307
Rounded oval, 18x17
Within an ornate border, a shield of arms (cross, in dexter chief a ?martlet / ?owl)
Legend: * [. . . .]E [. . . . .]
SHA 20/7/43, seal 2, dated 1398 x 1399
SHA 20/7/41, dated 1386 x 1387

SEAL 2308
Unknown, nm
Man standing full-face holding a gridiron (St Lawrence)
Legend: [section lost] AVRENT [section lost]
SHA 20/7/42, dated 1351 x 1352

SEAL 2309
Rounded oval, 24x21
Crowned man standing full-face fastened to a tree, to left and right archers facing in (martyrdom of St Edmund)
Legend: *[.]A[. . . . .] EADEM [section lost] [section illegible] D [.]
SHA 20/7/43, dated 1398 x 1399

SEAL 2310
Round, 15
Letter L, stylised branch to left
Legend: none
SHA 20/7/44, dated 1409 x 1410

SEAL 2311
Rectangular, 11x9
Crowned letter R, stylised branches to left and right
Legend: none
SHA 20/7/45, dated 1417 x 1418

SEAL 2312
Unknown (?Rounded oval, fragment), c.20xc.15
Head of man wearing a ?mitre facing left, to left a ?staff, foliate stem in the field (fragment only)
Legend: lost
SHA 20/7/50, seal 2, dated 1425 x 1425

SEAL 2313
Octagonal, 10x12
Monogram IS
Legend: none
SHA 20/7/51, seal 1, dated 1425 x 1426

SEAL 2314
Rectangular, 11x8
Crowned letter M
Legend: none
SHA 20/7/51, seal 2, dated 1425 x 1426

SEAL 2315
Octagonal, 11x13
Letter T
Legend: none
SHA 20/7/52/A, seal 2, dated 1447 x 1448

SEAL 2316
Round, 53
Armoured man on a horse galloping to the right
Legend: ¶ S[. . . . .]E ¶ [. . .]OR ¶ D
SHA 322/2/8, dated 1186 x 1190

SEAL 2317
Round, 30
Shield of arms (indistinct)
Legend: +SIGIL [section lost] CORBET
SHA 322/2/10, dated 1200 x 1299

SEAL 2318
Pointed oval, 44x26
Long foliate tendril in reversed-S shape
Legend: SIGILL'AMMEVXORISWILL'IBANAST'
SHA 322/2/14, dated 1250 x 1299

SEAL 2319
Round, c.54
Armoured man on a horse walking to the right
Legend: ¶ SIG[. . . . .]IVIANI FIL [.]¶ [. . . . .]
SHA 322/2/16, dated 1200 x 1299

SEAL 2320
Round, 30
Shield of arms (four crescents (?horseshoes))
Legend: +SIGILLVMOSBERT[. . . . . . .]
SHA 322/2/21, dated 1200 x 1299

SEAL 2321
Round, 30
Stylised lily
Legend: S'IOHANNIS P'WYEFORT
SHA 322/2/23, dated 1200 x 1299

APPENDIX

SEAL 2322
Hexagonal, 10
Four-petalled stylised flower (?quatrefoil)
Legend: none
SHA 322/2/25, dated 1252 x 1252

SEAL 2323
Round, 24
Shield of arms (two lions passant to sinister, a bordure of roundels)
Legend: S'hENRICIDEHEL[?IN]TI
SHA 322/2/29, dated 1200 x 1299

SEAL 2324
Round, 20
Shield of arms (a chevron between two estoils of many points)
Legend: S[. .]A[.]E[. . . . . .]
SHA 322/2/30, seal 1, dated 1275 x 1325

SEAL 2325
Round, 33x21
Dragon walking to the left
Legend: [?S]IV¶ E[.]MV[. . .]
SHA 322/2/30, seal 2, dated 1275 x 1325

SEAL 2326
Round, 32
Stylised lily, inverted in relationship to legend
Legend: +S'LVCERELICTEELIBOTE
SHA 322/2/31, dated 1200 x 1299

SEAL 2327
Round, 24
Shield of arms (two lions passant ?guardant, a border of roundels)
Legend: [. . . . . . .]DEERDI[. . . . .]
SHA 322/2/36, dated 1200 x 1299

SEAL 2328
Round, c.18
?Eight-petalled flower
Legend: + S [section lost] YE
SHA 322/2/38, dated 1200 x 1299

SEAL 2329
Pointed oval, 33x21
Stylised lily
Legend: [. . .]IL'.WILE[. . .]S[. . . . . .]
SHA 322/2/39, dated 1274 x 1275

SEAL 2330
Round, 22
Shield of arms (letter R between three fleur-des-lys)
Legend: + [. .]GILL' RO§ GERI P'VDE
SHA 322/2/42, dated 1285 x 1286

SEAL 2331
Round, 24
Shield of arms (three annulets)
Legend: +S'R [. . .]ERIDEACTVN:
SHA 322/2/45, dated 1287 x 1288

SEAL 2332
Round, 25
Shield of arms (two lions passant)
Legend: * S' HENRI[. .] DE ERDINTONE
SHA 322/2/49, dated 1275 x 1324

SEAL 2333
Round, 17
Within an ornate border, a shield of arms (cross saltire embattled between ?three objects)
Legend: [. . . . . .[DE[. . .]A[. . . .]
SHA 322/2/50, dated 1300 x 1399

SEAL 2334
Round, 21
Four (?clover) leaves
Legend: [start point uncertain] [. .]A [. . . . . . .]
SHA 322/2/56, dated 1300 x 1399

SEAL 2335
Unknown, nm
Indistinct
Legend: [section lost] PHILIPPID [section lost]
SHA 322/2/59, dated 1300 x 1399

SEAL 2336
Round, 20
Eight-petalled stylised flower
Legend: [. . .]ESDE[. .]A[. .]
SHA 322/2/61, dated 1275 x 1324

SEAL 2337
Round, 22
Within a pointed octofoil, a shield of arms (a chevron between ?three ?roundels)
Legend: ¶SI¶[..]¶[..]¶[..]¶[..]¶[..]¶E[.]¶[..]
SHA 322/2/63, dated 1275 x 1324
SHA 322/2/137, dated 1339 x 1340

SEAL 2338
Round, 17
Eagle displayed
Legend: + [.] hEDE [section lost]
SHA 322/2/66, dated 1286 x 1287

SEAL 2339
Round, 30
Eight-petalled stylised flower
Legend: S' [section lost] [.] I' ROB' D' N [. .] BAL
SHA 322/2/72, dated 1300 x 1349

SEAL 2340
Round, 19
Within an ornate border, a shield of arms (indistinct)
Legend: [.]SI [. .]LL [section lost] COR [. . .]
SHA 322/2/74, dated 1275 x 1324

SEAL 2341
Round, 36
Stylised lily
Legend: *S [section lost] [.] TE
SHA 322/2/76, dated 1320 x 1321

SEAL 2342
Round, 47
Leopard walking to right
Legend: +SIGILLVM [. . . .] ES [. . .] ?RV [. .] ALOPESBERIE
SHA 322/2/85, dated 1327 x 1328

SEAL 2343
Round, 19
Beast (?griffin) rampant
Legend: [section lost] E [section lost]
SHA 322/2/86, dated 1320 x 1321

SEAL 2344
Round, 22
Within an eight-pointed star, a shield of arms (barry of four)
Legend: * [.] ROGERI.CORBET
SHA 322/2/88, dated 1323 x 1324
SHA 322/2/87, dated 1323 x 1324

SEAL 2345
Round, nm
Shield of arms (charge illegible)
Legend: lost
SHA 322/2/89, dated 1323 x 1324

SEAL 2346
Round, 22
Within an ornate border, shield of arms (indistinct), a roundel above and to right and left
Legend: * [. . . . . . .] ROBERT [. .] CORBE [.]
SHA 322/2/101, dated 1300 x 1349

SEAL 2347
Round, 17
Squirrel facing left
Legend: *[. . . . .]
SHA 322/2/110, dated 1333 x 1334

SEAL 2348
Unknown, c.22
Hawk taking an animal (?rabbit)
Legend: lost, if any
SHA 322/2/111, dated 1333 x 1334

SEAL 2349
Round, 18
Shield of arms (a chevron with three charges (illegible))
Legend: illegible
SHA 322/2/112, dated 1333 x 1334

APPENDIX

SEAL 2350
Round, 18.
Hawk taking a bird facing right
Legend: * M[. . . .]O[. . .]VE
SHA 322/2/113, dated 1333 x 1334
SHA 322/2/113, seal 2, dated 1333 x 1334

SEAL 2351
Round, 17
Indistinct (?head)
Legend: illegible
SHA 322/2/113, seal 3, dated 1333 x 1334

SEAL 2352
Round, 24
Shield of arms (a fess chequy between six crosses paty) couche with a crested and mantled helm above
Legend: none (foliate stems in place of letters)
SHA 322/2/117, seal 1, dated 1336 x 1337

SEAL 2353
Round, 25
Three shields of arms (in chief, a fess chequy between six cross patys; dexter, a chevron, in chief (? charge illegible); sinister, a chevron between ?three objects), between them three ?wyverns lodged
Legend: * S' ELE LA BOTIL[. . . . . . .]
M[.]E
SHA 322/2/117, seal 2, dated 1336 x 1337

SEAL 2354
Round, 19
Pelican in its piety facing left
Legend: illegible
SHA 322/2/119, dated 1337 x 1338

SEAL 2355
Round, 19
Squirrel eating a nut facing right
Legend: I [.]RACNVTE[. .]
SHA 322/2/120, dated 1337 x 1338

SEAL 2356
Round, 21
Shield of arms (charge illegible) couche, a helm above, ?mantling in the field
Legend: [section lost] LE WEL [section lost]
SHA 322/2/123, dated 1338 x 1339
SHA 322/2/124, dated 1338 x 1339
SHA 322/2/125, dated 1338 x 1339

SEAL 2357
Round, 23
Circle quartered: (1, 2: indistinct; 3: letter 'W', 4: letter 'G') surmounted by a cross
Legend: +[. . . . . .] M [section lost]
SHA 322/2/128, dated 1338 x 1339

SEAL 2358
Round, 23
Within a sexfoil, a shield of arms (a martlet), an annulet above, to left and right
Legend: *SIG[. . . . . .]OB[. . .]I CORBET
SHA 322/2/143, dated 1340 x 1341
SHA 322/2/131, dated 1338 x 1339
SHA 322/2/151, dated 1345 x 1346

SEAL 2359
Round, *c*.19
Four (?clover) leaves
Legend: [.]I[. . . . . .]I
SHA 322/2/134, dated 1339 x 1340

SEAL 2360
Round, 20
Pelican in its piety facing left
Legend: * SVM [. . . . .]
SHA 322/2/135, seal 1, dated 1339 x 1340

SEAL 2361
Round, 18
Squirrel facing left
Legend: [.]AL[. . . . . .]
SHA 322/2/135, seal 2, dated 1339 x 1340

SEAL 2362
Round, *c*.19
?Cross (?merchant mark)
Legend: S M[rest lost]
SHA 322/2/136, dated 1339 x 1340

SEAL 2363
Round, c.26
Within a quatrefoil, a shield of arms (?vair, a fess), three lions passant in the top, right and left cusps of the quatrefoil
Legend: illegible
SHA 322/2/138, dated 1366 x 1367

SEAL 2364
Round, 21
Shield of arm (a ?fess) ?held by a ?figure (?hanging from a small bush)
Legend: S' IOHAN [rest lost]
SHA 322/2/139, dated 1340 x 1341

SEAL 2365
Pointed oval, 54x38
Virgin and Child seated full-face
Legend: [section lost]EA[?C][?M][section lost]
SHA 322/2/142, dated 1340 x 1341

SEAL 2366
Unknown, nm
Lost
Legend: [section lost] ?A [section lost]
SHA 322/2/145, dated 1341 x 1342

SEAL 2367
Round, nm
Indistinct
Legend: [section lost] [. . . .]
SHA 322/2/150, dated 1344 x 1345

SEAL 2368
Unknown, nm
Lamb of God facing left
Legend: +E[. . . . .]I
SHA 322/2/152, dated 1346 x 1347

SEAL 2369
Round, 18
Four ?clover leaves
Legend: lost
SHA 322/2/155, dated 1348 x 1349

SEAL 2370
Round, 17
Squirrel facing left
Legend: * IE [. . .] A [. . .]
SHA 322/2/158, dated 1350 x 1351

SEAL 2371
Round, 19
Shield of arms (a chevron between three lion's heads erased) hanging from a strap
Legend: * S' IOHANNIS DE WY[. . .]ORD
SHA 322/2/162, dated 1353 x 1354

SEAL 2372
Round, 19
Two figures standing facing in holding a foliate stem up between them
Legend: *[. .]S[. . . . . . .]
SHA 322/2/164, dated 1353 x 1354

SEAL 2373
Round, 18
Within a trefoil, three lion's heads caboshed
Legend: * S' WILLI : DE [?M]ORTON [. .' .]E[.]
SHA 322/2/165, dated 1353 x 1354
SHA 322/2/176, dated 1360 x 1361

SEAL 2374
Round, 19
Shield of arms (corbie) hanging from a bush
Legend: *SIGILL'ROBERTICORBET¶
SHA 322/2/173, dated 1359 x 1360
SHA 322/2/177, dated 1361 x 1362
SHA 322/2/168, dated 1347 x 1348
SHA 322/2/178, dated 1361 x 1362
SHA 322/2/179, dated 1362 x 1363
SHA 322/2/194, dated 1374 x 1375

SEAL 2375
Round, 23
Within an ornate border: shield of arms (two ?lions, a bendlet)
Legend: +SI'EGIDII DE ERDEN [. . .]
SHA 322/2/171, dated 1357 x 1358

APPENDIX

SEAL 2376
Round, nm
Shield of arms (charge indistinct)
Legend: illegible, partially lost
SHA 322/2/174, seal 1, dated 1359 x 1360

SEAL 2377
Round, 20
Within an ornate border, on the left, a man standing full-face holding a ?sceptre and a sheaf of arrows (St Edmund), to the right a ?kneeling supplicant facing left
Legend: * [.]' ED[.]V [.] D [.] DE MEVA [. .] E
SHA 322/2/174, seal 2, dated 1359 x 1360

SEAL 2378
Round, c.21
Shield of arms (?bend between ?objects)
Legend: lost
SHA 322/2/182, dated 1363 x 1364

SEAL 2379
Unknown, c.23xc.14
Shield of arms (chequey, a fess diapered) hanging from a bush
Legend: lost, if any
SHA 322/2/187, dated 1365 x 1366

SEAL 2380
Round, 20
Hare facing left
Legend: [. . .]O[?T]VED[. .]
SHA 322/2/191, dated 1370 x 1371

SEAL 2381
Round, 22
Shield of arms (a maunch charged with a mullet, a bordure engrailed)
Legend: * Sigillu : Thome : Banastre
SHA 322/2/191, seal 3, dated 1370 x 1371

SEAL 2382
Round, c.23
Within a quatrefoil, a shield (charge illegible)
Legend: illegible, partially lost
SHA 322/2/192, dated 1373 x 1374

SEAL 2383
Round, 20
Virgin and Child seated full-face
Legend: [. . .]g : roberti [. . . .]e[. . . . .]
SHA 322/2/195, seal 1, dated 1375 x 1376

SEAL 2384
Round, 15
Letter ?n, stylised branches to left and right
Legend: none
SHA 322/2/195, seal 2, dated 1375 x 1376

SEAL 2385
Round, 20
Building with three crenellated towers, a crescent to the left, a star to the right
Legend: [. . . . .] [?D?E][. .]VM[. . .]
SHA 322/2/197, dated 1377 x 1378

SEAL 2386
Round, 24
Shield of arms (barry of six, a bendlett over all)
Legend: * SIG RADVLPHI DE [L]ONGEYNE
SHA 322/2/198, dated 1379 x 1380

SEAL 2387
Round, 21
Within an ornate border, a shield of arms (two corbies)
Legend: * SIGILLVM ROGERICORBET
SHA 322/2/200, dated 1378 x 1379
SHA 322/2/199, dated 1378 x 1379

SEAL 2388
Round, 30
Within an ornate border, a shield of arms (a fess diapered, in chief two mullets pierced) surmounted by a crested helm, foliate tendrils in the field to left and right
Legend: ¶ SIG [section lost] : [. . . .]TON:
SHA 322/2/201, seal 1, dated 1378 x 1379

SEAL 2389
Round, 36
Within an ornate border, a shield of arms (diapered (?a fess diapered), in chief ?two mullets pierced, a label of three points) a crested helm above, foliate tendrils to left and right
Legend: [section lost] NTON: [section lost]
SHA 322/2/201, seal 2, dated 1378 x 1379

SEAL 2390
Round, 19
Within a trefoil border, shield of arms (vair, a bar)
Legend: [section lost] : ?R [section lost]
SHA 322/2/201, seal 3, dated 1378 x 1379

SEAL 2391
Round, 21
Figure standing full-face holding an object up in their left hand
Legend: illegible, partially lost
SHA 322/2/201, seal 4, dated 1378 x 1379

SEAL 2392
Round, nm
Crucifixion, with Mary and John
Legend: none
SHA 322/2/201, seal 5, dated 1378 x 1379

SEAL 2393
Round, 10
Letter B
Legend: none
SHA 322/2/201, seal 6, dated 1378 x 1379

SEAL 2394
Round, 19
Within a cusped border, an animal (?lion) seated facing right
Legend: illegible, partially lost
SHA 322/2/201, seal 7, dated 1378 x 1379

SEAL 2395
Round, 13
Letter A, stylised foliage to right
Legend: none
SHA 322/2/204, dated 1383 x 1384

SEAL 2396
Round, 21
Within an ornate border, a shield of arms (a fess between three lions passant)
Legend: *SIGILLUM : [. . . . .]
SHA 322/2/208, seal 2, dated 1386 x 1387

SEAL 2397
Unknown, nm
Shield of arms (corbie)
Legend: lost
SHA 322/2/209, dated 1388 x 1389
SHA 322/2/210, dated 1389 x 1390

SEAL 2398
Hexagonal, 11x14
Stag's head full-face, a cross formy to right and left and between the antlers
Legend: none
SHA 322/2/211, dated 1391 x 1392

SEAL 2399
Round, 20
Shield of arms (a chevron, a canton of five objects (?ermine))
Legend: *[. . . .]ll[. . . . .]
SHA 322/2/212, dated 1393 x 1394

SEAL 2400
Unknown, c.22xc.14
Shield of arms (?per pale; dexter, a chevron, a ?corbie in chief; sinister, a chevron between ?six roundels (three visible)) hanging from a bush
Legend: lost, if any
SHA 322/2/213, dated 1393 x 1394

SEAL 2401
Round, 9
Letters T A with a crown above
Legend: none
SHA 322/2/214, seal 1, dated 1393 x 1394

SEAL 2402
Round, 19
Within a cusped quatrefoil, a shield of arms (a chevron between three objects, on chief a label of three points)

APPENDIX

Legend: * S[. . . . .]
SHA 322/2/214, seal 2, dated 1393 x 1394

SEAL 2403
Round, 20
Crowned letter I, stylised branches to right and left
Legend: none
SHA 322/2/215, seal 1, dated 1394 x 1395

SEAL 2404
Round, 20
Within an ornate quatrefoil, an uncertain design
Legend: illegible
SHA 322/2/215, seal 2, dated 1394 x 1395

SEAL 2405
Round, 19
Shield of arms (?Pelican in its Piety)
Legend: S' § Robertus § de § Kendel §
SHA 322/2/216, dated 1469 x 1470

SEAL 2406
Round, 20
Scallop shell
Legend: [section lost] [. . . .]don[. . . . .]
SHA 322/2/218, dated 1396 x 1397

SEAL 2407
Round, 14
Letter I, stylised branches to right and left
Legend: none
SHA 322/2/219, dated 1396 x 1397
SHA 322/2/237, dated 1422 x 1423

SEAL 2408
Round, nm
Shield of arms (two bars, a canton diaper)
Legend: lost, if any
SHA 322/2/225, dated 1405 x 1406

SEAL 2409
Rounded oval, 20x19
Gem: Figure standing ?facing left
Legend: + [. . . .]NNISDE [. . . . . . .]
SHA 322/2/226, dated 1406 x 1407

SEAL 2410
Round, 20
Head of man with long hair and long beard facing left
Legend: IESU [. . . . . .] T?V [.] ?OISER [. . . . . .]
SHA 322/2/227, dated 1406 x 1407

SEAL 2411
Round, 15
Letter A, stylised foliage to right
Legend: none
SHA 322/2/228, seal 1, dated 1415 x 1416

SEAL 2412
Round, 16
Stylised lily
Legend: illegible, partially lost
SHA 322/2/228, seal 2, dated 1415 x 1416

SEAL 2413
Round, 14
Letter W, stylised foliage to left and right
Legend: none
SHA 322/2/241, dated 1427 x 1428

SEAL 2414
Round, 22
Pelican in its piety facing left
Legend: * SV[. . . . .]
SHA 322/2/243, dated 1431 x 1432

SEAL 2415
Rectangular, 11x9
Crowned letter M
Legend: none
SHA 322/2/244, dated 1435 x 1436

SEAL 2416
Round, 12
?Deer (?hare) facing left, flowers on stems to left and right, a wicker fence below (?deer in a park)
Legend: none
SHA 322/2/245, dated 1435 x 1436

SEAL 2417
Round, nm
Obverse: shield of arms (quarterly: 1 & 4, two bars, a canton; 2, ?3, three corbies) a ?crested helm above, supporters (wyverns)
Legend: lost
SHA 322/2/254, front, dated 1444 x 1445

SEAL 2418
Round, 10
Letter ?Bp
Legend: none
SHA 322/2/259, dated 1447 x 1448

SEAL 2419
Round, 11
Indistinct
Legend: none
SHA 322/2/263, dated 1455

SEAL 2420
Round, 12
?Pelican in piety
Legend: N/A
SHA 322/2/267, dated 1467 x 1468
SHA 322/2/266, dated 1467 x 1468

SEAL 2421
Round, 15
Hand from the right holding five flowers
Legend: N/A
SHA 322/2/267, seal 2, dated 1467 x 1468
SHA 322/2/266, seal 2, dated 1467 x 1468

SEAL 2422
Octagonal, 11x8
?Flower, on the left, letters 'to'
Legend: N/A
SHA 322/2/267, dated 1467 x 1468
SHA 322/2/266, seal 3, dated 1467 x 1468

SEAL 2423
Round, 13
Crowned letter I, foliage on either side
Legend: N/A
SHA 322/2/266, seal 4, dated 1467 x 1468
SHA 322/2/267, seal 5, dated 1467 x 1468

SEAL 2424
Unknown, 16
Indistinct
Legend: N/A
SHA 322/2/266, seal 5, dated 1467 x 1468
SHA 322/2/267, seal 6, dated 1467 x 1468

SEAL 2425
Round, 11
Bird facing left
Legend: N/A
SHA 322/2/267, seal 4, dated 1467 x 1468

SEAL 2426
Triangle pointing up, 17x13
Letters H I interlaced within a rectangle and diamond
Legend: none
SHA 322/2/272, dated 1471 x 1472

SEAL 2427
Round, c.10
Letter R, stylised branch to the left
Legend: none
SHA 322/2/276, dated 1473 x 1474
SHA 322/2/273, dated 1473 x 1474
SHA 322/2/274, seal 2, dated 1473 x 1474

SEAL 2428
Round, 8
Uncertain (?letters ?grotesque head facing left)
Legend: none
SHA 322/2/275, dated 1473

SEAL 2429
Rounded oval, 8x10
Letter I, stylised foliage to left and right
Legend: none
SHA 322/2/279, seal 3, dated 1480 x 1481

SEAL 2430
Rounded oval, 12x9
Virgin and Child seated full-face
Legend: none
SHA 322/2/280, seal 1, dated 1484 x 1485

APPENDIX

SEAL 2431
Round, 11
?Animal
Legend: none
SHA 322/2/280, seal 2, dated 1484 x 1485

SEAL 2432
Rounded oval, 13x9
Virgin and Child ?half-length full-face
Legend: none
SHA 322/2/280, seal 3, dated 1484 x 1485

SEAL 2433
Rounded oval, 12x10
Crowned letter R
Legend: none
SHA 322/2/280, seal 4, dated 1484 x 1485

SEAL 2434
Unknown, 12x12
Letter P, stylised foliage to left and right
Legend: none
SHA 322/2/280, seal 5, dated 1484 x 1485

SEAL 2435
Round, 41
Lion walking to the right
Legend: + SIGILL' WILELMI EX[. . .]NEI
SHA 972/1/1/427, dated 1175 x 1225

SEAL 2436
Pointed oval, 58x35
Eagle displayed
Legend: +SIGILL'ROG'ICAPLL'NIDE.S'CAMARIA
SHA 972/1/1/428, dated 1175 x 1224

SEAL 2437
Round, 32
Bird with wings raised walking left
Legend: SIGILL'ROBERTIHAGERWAS
SHA 972/1/1/429, dated 1210

SEAL 2438
Pointed oval, 42x26
Bird with wings outstretched walking to the left
Legend: + SIGILL' ISABELLE VXOR PAIN
SHA 972/1/1/432, dated 1230 x 1240

SEAL 2439
Round, 33
Stylised lily
Legend: +SIGILL'IOh'ISFIL'IOh[. .] CALVI
SHA 972/1/1/434, dated 1230 x 1250

SEAL 2440
Round, 25
Latin cross, ?sun in upper left, a crescent in upper right, letter 'alpha' in lower left, letter 'omega' in lower right
Legend: SIGILL'IOhANI[.] T [section lost] IS
SHA 972/1/1/436, dated 1245

SEAL 2441
Round, 34
Boar running to the right, three stylised trees behind, ?acorns in lower field
Legend: + [. . .]GINALDECHESB'
SHA 972/1/1/437, dated 1245

SEAL 2442
Pointed oval, 36x23
Four conifer branches with leaves in the angles
Legend: *S'SIBILLEVXO[.] IOh'IS
SHA 972/1/1/438, dated 1252 x 1265

SEAL 2443
Pointed oval, c.24x19
Pelican in its piety facing right
Legend: [. . . . .][?R]N[. .]E
SHA 972/1/1/439, dated 1260 x 1270

SEAL 2444
Round, 29
Sixteen-petalled stylised flower
Legend: *S'IOhANNIS: [. . . . .]L ¶
SHA 972/1/1/440, dated 1272

SEAL 2445
Round, 24
Gem: naked man wearing a hat walking to right, holding a ?cloth out in his left hand, right arm resting on ?spear behind him
Legend: *S'GALEFRIDI:RONDOLNF+
SHA 972/1/1/443, dated 1304 x 1305

SEAL 2446
Round, 27
Pair of open shears, points up, to the left a ?leaf, to the right a ?staff, small four-petalled flowers above and below
Legend: + S' ROERI SISSOR'
SHA 972/1/1/442, seal 1, dated 1275

SEAL 2447
Pointed oval, 29x18
Eight-petalled stylised flower
Legend: + S' ISOTEIVXIRROGER
SHA 972/1/1/442, seal 2, dated 1275

SEAL 2448
Pointed oval, 32x19
Stylised lily
Legend: +S'AL [section lost] OGERI
SHA 972/1/1/598, dated 1284 x 1285

SEAL 2449
Round, 24
Eight-petalled stylised flower
Legend: + S'ROGERID [section lost] DELIE
SHA 972/1/1/598, seal 2, dated 1284 x 1285

SEAL 2450
Pointed oval, 32x19
Fish facing up
Legend: +S' MATILDIS F' WILL'I RO[. .]I
SHA 972/1/1/599, seal 1, dated 1284 x 1285

SEAL 2451
Round, 24
Stylised plant ('weeping willow' style)
Legend: + S' ROBERTI LE SAY
SHA 972/1/1/599, seal 2, dated 1284 x 1285

SEAL 2452
Round, 24
Bird with wings raised walking to left
Legend: REGINA[section illegible]TW [section illegible]
SHA 972/1/1/600, dated 1294 x 1295

SEAL 2453
Pointed oval, 28x18
Eagle displayed
Legend: +S'IVLIANE F'WILL'
SHA 972/1/1/600, seal 2, dated 1294 x 1295

SEAL 2454
Round, 16
Sacred monogram: (IHC)
Legend: + [. .] [section lost] [. .]
SHA 972/1/1/605, seal 1, dated 1325 x 1326
SHA 972/1/1/607, dated 1342 x 1343

SEAL 2455
Round, 18
Shield of arms (chess rook), a crescent above, foliate motifs to left and right
Legend: [. . . . .] DE [. . .] E [. . . .]
SHA 972/1/1/605, seal 2, dated 1325 x 1326

SEAL 2456
Unknown, c.18xc.14
Foliate stems (?wheat)
Legend: lost
SHA 972/1/1/601, seal 1, dated 1300 x 1349

SEAL 2457
Pointed oval, c.30x 28
Man vested for Mass holding a staff in his right hand and a book in his left hand standing full-face beneath a canopy supported by thin columns
Legend: [section lost] LILLISHVL[. . . . . .]
SHA 972/1/1/603, seal 1, dated 1308 x 1330

SEAL 2458
Round, 19
Uncertain; impression very worn or poorly impressed

Legend: lost, if any
SHA 972/1/1/608, dated 1343 x 1344

SEAL 2459
Round, 19
?Hawk taking a bird (very worn)
Legend: lost, if any
SHA 972/1/1/609, dated 1344 x 1345

SEAL 2460
Round, 19
Lion sleeping facing left with two heads facing in above, a heart with an ?arrow emerging from the top between the heads
Legend: none
SHA 972/1/1/610, seal 1, dated 1344 x 1345
SHA 972/1/1/611, dated 1344 x 1345

SEAL 2461
Round, 19
Hare blowing a horn mounted on a hound running to the left
Legend: *SOhO ?V [.] O [. . . . .]
SHA 972/1/1/610, seal 2, dated 1344 x 1345

SEAL 2462
Rounded oval, 24x20
Within an ornate canopied niche, to the left a woman standing full-face holding a cross in her right hand (St Helen), to the right a kneeling supplicant figure facing left, a foliate motif above
Legend: VIRGOSANCT [.] ELENA ?P[.] OME [. . .]
SHA 972/1/1/612, seal 1, dated 1344 x 1345

SEAL 2463
Rectangular, 20
Merchant mark with cross-tipped staff emerging form top
Legend: [.] HENR[.]CI DIC[.]I [. . . . .]
SHA 972/1/1/615, dated 1351 x 1352

SEAL 2464
Round, 17
Grotesque: bipedal creature with a human face walking left

Legend: *V [. .] [section lost] ?VTI
SHA 972/1/1/612, seal 2, dated 1344 x 1345

SEAL 2465
Round, 21
Lion sleeping facing left beneath a tree
Legend: [. . . . . .]CI . DE : ERA[.]E[.]E[. . .]
SHA 972/1/1/615, seal 2, dated 1351 x 1352

SEAL 2466
Round, 25
Within a cusped quatrefoil, a shield of arms (a chevron between a crescent in sinister chief and an object in base; dexter chief illegible) hanging form a strap
Legend: illegible
SHA 972/1/1/618, dated 1385 x 1386

SEAL 2467
Round, 19
Sacred Monogram (Ihc), ?crown above, zigzag lines below and at each side
Legend: none
SHA 972/1/1/619, dated 1387 x 1388

SEAL 2468
Round, 17
Shield of arms (indistinct) hanging from a bush
Legend: illegible
SHA 972/1/1/621, dated 1390 x 1391

SEAL 2469
Round, 21
Within a cusped trefoil, Virgin and Child seated full-face
Legend: +S' GVILLILEVIGI [. . . .] DE [. .] R?ALEV
SHA 972/1/1/621, seal 2, dated 1390 x 1391

SEAL 2470
Rounded oval, 22xc.17
Within a cusped octofoil, to the right a woman standing facing half left holding a staff up in her right hand with the tip in the mouth of a dragon beneath her feet (St Margaret), to the left a kneeling supplicant

man facing right with three small ?flowers above him
Legend: [.]E [section lost] [. . .][?I]hIER[. . .]
SHA 972/1/1/620, dated 1389 x 1390

SEAL 2471
Round, 13
Letters ?th?i
Legend: none
SHA 972/1/1/622, dated 1394 x 1395

SEAL 2472
Round, 16
letter 'T', stylised foliage to left
Legend: none
SHA 972/1/1/623, dated 1396 x 1397

SEAL 2473
Rectangular, 11x9
Letter R
Legend: none
SHA 972/1/1/624, dated 1416 x 1417

SEAL 2474
Rectangular, 13x8
Crowned letter I
Legend: none
SHA 972/1/1/625, dated 1417 x 1418

SEAL 2475
Round, 19
Stag seated facing left
Legend: [. .]VITES
SHA 5981/B/2/256/2, seal 3, dated 1392 x 1393

SEAL 2476
Round, 20
Shield of arms (lion rampant)
Legend: * S' EDMV[.]DI DE MORTONE
SHA 5981/B/2/256/5, dated 1413 x 1414
SHA 5981/B/2/256/4, dated 1410 x 1411
SHA 5981/B/2/262/16, dated 1425 x 1426

SEAL 2477
Octagonal, 14x11
Crowned letter T, small ?star each side
Legend: none
SHA 5981/B/2/256/6, dated 1421 x 1422

SEAL 2478
Rounded oval, 10x12
Crowned letter I
Legend: none
SHA 5981/B/2/256/7, dated 1454 x 1455

SEAL 2479
Round, 9
?Animal (?squirrel) / ?person ?seated facing left, two ?tendrils in the field
Legend: none
SHA 5981/B/2/256/9, dated 1466 x 1467

SEAL 2480
Undetermined, 13x5
Long strip with slight indentations (not proper matrix?)
Legend: none
SHA 5981/B/2/256/11, dated 1496 x 1497

SEAL 2481
Round, 18
Shield of arms (indistinct)
Legend: +S' [remainder illegible]
SHA 5981/B/2/262/4, dated 1376 x 1377

SEAL 2482
Round, 23
?Spiked wheel
Legend: none
SHA 5981/B/2/262/5, dated 1376 x 1377

SEAL 2483
Round, 20
Within an ornate border, a shield of arms (uncertain, a mullet in base)
Legend: *S' ROBERTIATTE. [.] ERW [.] .
SHA 5981/B/2/262/6, dated 1388 x 1389

SEAL 2484
Round, 21
Within a cusped border, a shield of arms (eagle displayed, a bend over all)
Legend: * Sigillum Thome [. . . . .]

APPENDIX

SHA 5981/B/2/262/12, seal 2, dated 1420 x 1421
SHA 5981/B/2/262/7, dated 1406 x 1407

SEAL 2485
Rounded oval, 23x18
Within a scalloped border, a ?large plant with a ?small ?quadruped facing left jumping up to the right (indistinct)
Legend: none
SHA 5981/B/2/262/10, dated 1419 x 1420

SEAL 2486
Round, 14
Crowned letter W, stylised branches to left and right
Legend: none
SHA 5981/B/2/262/10, seal 2, dated 1419 x 1420
SHA 5981/B/2/262/14, dated 1424 x 1425

SEAL 2487
Octagonal, 12x12
Shield of arms (fleur-de-lys)
Legend: none
SHA 5981/B/2/262/11, dated 1420 x 1421
SHA 5981/B/2/262/15, dated 1424 x 1425

SEAL 2488
Hexagonal, 13xc.8
Letter ?h (?b)
Legend: none
SHA 5981/B/2/262/12, seal 1, dated 1420 x 1421

SEAL 2489
Octagonal, 15x10
Merchant mark on a shield (includes letters I h,)
Legend: none
SHA 5981/B/2/262/13, dated 1420 x 1421

SEAL 2490
Rounded oval, 15x12
Letters ?t i interlaced
Legend: none
SHA 5981/B/2/262/17, dated 1463 x 1464

SEAL 2491
Round, 13
Pelican in its piety facing left
Legend: none
SHA 5981/B/2/262/18, dated 1463 x 1464

SEAL 2492
Round, 8
?Nimbed head full-face (?Vernicle head of Christ)
Legend: none
SHA 5981/B/2/262/19, dated 1463 x 1464

SEAL 2493
Round, c.18
Letter P
Legend: none
SHA 5981/B/2/262/19, seal 2, dated 1463 x 1464

SEAL 2494
Round, 14
Crowned letters ?D W
Legend: none
SHA 5981/B/2/262/19, seal 3, dated 1463 x 1464

SEAL 2495
Unknown, nm
?Letter
Legend: none
SHA 5981/B/2/262/19, seal 4, dated 1463 x 1464

SEAL 2496
Round, 11
Letter n (?crown above)
Legend: none
SHA 5981/B/2/262/19, seal 5, dated 1463 x 1464

SEAL 2497
Round, c.20
Letter h
Legend: none
SHA 5981/B/2/262/19, seal 6, dated 1463 x 1464

BIBLIOGRAPHY

Unpublished primary sources

For a full list of collections consulted, see appendix

TNA, SC 2/216/10-2/220/9 (Dyffryn Clwyd court rolls; data available at *http://www.data-archive.ac.uk/* (last accessed 26 January 2016) arising from Economic and Social Research Council project, 'Dyffryn Clwyd Court Roll Database, 1294–1422', award numbers: R000232548; R000234070).

Printed primary sources

Henry de Bracton, *On the Laws and Customs of England*, ed. G. E. Woodbine and S. E. Thorne, 4 vols (Cambridge, 1968).
The Acts of the Welsh Rulers, 1120–1283, ed. H. Pryce (Cardiff, 2005).
Calendar of Inquisitions Miscellaneous (Chancery) Preserved in the Public Record Office, vol. 3 (London, 1937).
The Cartulary of Haughmond Abbey, ed. Una Rees (Cardiff, 1985).
The Chronicle of Battle Abbey, ed. E. Searle (Oxford, 1980).
Chronicles of the Mayors and Sheriffs of London, ed. Henry Thomas Riley (London, 1863).
Earldom of Gloucester Charters: The Charters and Scribes of the Earls and Countesses of Gloucester to AD 1217, ed. R. B. Patterson (Oxford, 1973).

English Episcopal Acta 7. Hereford, 1079–1234, ed. Julia Barrow (Oxford, 1993).
English Episcopal Acta X. Bath and Wells, 1061–1205, ed. M. F. Ramsey (Oxford, 1995).
English Episcopal Acta 31. Ely, 1109–1197, ed. N. Karn (Oxford, 2005).
English Episcopal Acta 35. Hereford, 1234–1275, ed. Julia Barrow (Oxford, 2009).
Llandaff Episcopal Acta 1140–1287, ed. D. Crouch (Cardiff, 1989).
Select Cases Concerning the Law Merchant. Vol. 1. Local Courts, 23, ed. C. Gross (Selden Society, 1908).
The Charters of the Abbey of Ystrad Marchell, ed. G. C. G. Thomas (Aberystwyth, 1997).
The Treatise on the Laws and Customs of England Commonly Called Glanville, ed. and trans. G. D. G. Hall (Oxford, 1993).
Wace, *The Roman de Rou*, trans. G. S. Burgess, with the text of A. J. Holden and notes by G. S. Burgess and E. van Houts (St Helier, 2002).

Secondary works

A London Antiquary, 'Curious notices of antiquities of London', *The Gentleman's Magazine and Historical Chronicle*, 54, 2 (1784), 733.
Adams, N., J. Cherry and J. Robinson (eds), *Good Impressions: Image and Authority in Medieval Seals* (London, 2007).
Ailes, A., 'Heraldry in twelfth-century England: the evidence', in D. Williams (ed.), *England in the Twelfth Century: Proceedings of the 1988 Harlaxton Symposium* (Woodbridge, 1990), pp. 1–16.
— 'The knight, heraldry and recognition and the origins of heraldry', in C. Harper Bill and R. Harvey (eds), *Medieval Knighthood IV: Papers from the Fifth Strawberry Hill Conference 1990* (Woodbridge, 1992), pp. 1–21.
— 'The knight's alter ego: from equestrian to armorial', in N. Adams, J. Cherry and J. Robinson (eds), *Good Impressions: Image and Authority in Medieval Seals* (London: 2007), pp. 8–11.
— 'Governmental seals of Richard I', in P. R. Schofield (ed.), *Seals and their Context in the Middle Ages* (Oxford, 2015), pp. 101–10.
Alexander, J., and P. Binski (eds), *Age of Chivalry: Art in Plantagenet England, 1200–1400* (London, 1985).
Angold, M. J., G. C. Baugh, M. M. Chibnall, D. C. Cox, D. T. W. Price, M. Tomlinson and B. S. Trinder, 'Friaries: Franciscan friars', in ed. A. T. Gaydon and R. B. Pugh, *A History of the County of Shropshire*, vol. 2 (1973), pp. 89–91, http://www.british-history.ac.uk/report.aspx?compid=39934 (last accessed 11 July 2014).
Archibald, M. M., 'The lion coinage of Robert earl of Gloucester and William earl of Gloucester', *British Numismatic Journal*, 71 (2001), 71–86.

Ayre, K., *Medieval English Figurative Roundels*, CVMA (GB) Summary Catalogue 6 (Oxford, 2002).
Bailey, M., *The Decline of Serfdom in Late Medieval England. From Bondage to Freedom* (Woodbridge, 2014).
Baker, A., *English Panel Paintings 1400–1558*, ed. and updated by A. Ballantyne and P. Plummer (London, 2011).
Baltrušaitis, J., *Le Moyen-Âge Fantastique*, new edn (Paris, 1981).
Barrell, A. D. M., R. R. Davies, O. J. Padel and Ll. B. Smith, 'The Dyffryn Clwyd Court Roll project, 1340–1352 and 1389–1399: a methodology and some preliminary findings', in Z. Razi and R. M. Smith (eds), *Medieval Society and the Manor Court* (Oxford, 1996), pp. 260–97.
Barron, C., 'Chivalry, pageantry and merchant culture in medieval London', in P. Coss and M. Keen (eds), *Heraldry, Pageantry and Social Display in Medieval England* (Woodbridge, 2002), pp. 219–41.
Bartlett, R., 'Heartland and border: the mental and physical geography of medieval Europe', in H. Pryce and J. Watts (eds), *Power and Identity in the Middle Ages. Essays in Memory of Rees Davies* (Oxford, 2007),pp. 23–36.
Bautier, R. H. (ed.), *Vocabulaire International De La Sigillographie* (Rome, 1990).
Bedos-Rezak, B. M., 'Women, seals and power in medieval France, 1150–1350', in M. Erler and M. Kowaleski (eds), *Women and Power in the Middle Ages* (Athens, GA, and London, 1988), pp. 61–82.
— 'Towns and seals: representation and signification in medieval France', *Bulletin of the John Rylands Library*, 72/3 (1990), 35–49.
— 'Medieval women in French sigillographic sources', in J. T. Rosenthal (ed.), *Medieval Women and the Sources of Medieval History* (Athens, GA, and London, 1990), pp. 1–36.
— 'Signe d'identité et principes d'altérité au XIIe siècle', in B. M. Bedos-Rezak and D. Iogna-Prat (eds), *L'Individu au Moyen Âge. Individuation et individualisation avant la modernité* (Paris, 2005), pp. 43–57.
— 'Replica: images of identity and the identity of images', in J. F. Hamburger and A-M. Bouché (eds), *The Mind's Eye: Art and Theological Argument in the Middle Ages* (Princeton, 2006), pp. 46–64.
— 'In search of a semiotic paradigm: the matter of sealing in medieval thought and praxis (1050–1400)', in N. Adams, J. Cherry and J. Robinson (eds), *Good Impressions: Image and Authority in Medieval Seals* (London, 2007), pp. 1–7.
— 'Outcast. Seals of the medieval West and their epistemological frameworks (XIIth–XXIst centuries)', in C. Hourihane (ed.), *From Minor to Major: the Minor Arts in Medieval Art History* (Princeton, 2012), pp. 122–40.
Bennett, M., 'Wace and warfare', in M. J. Strickland (ed.), *Anglo-Norman Warfare: Studies in Late Anglo-Saxon and Anglo-Norman Military Organization and Warfare* (Woodbridge, 1992), pp. 230–50.

— 'Poetry as history? The "Roman de Rou" of Wace as a source for the Norman Conquest', *Anglo-Norman Studies*, 5 (1982), 21–39.
Binski, P., Becket's Crown. *Art and Imagination in Gothic England 1170–1300* (New Haven and London, 2004).
Birch, W. de Grey, *A History of Margam Abbey* (London, 1897).
— *Catalogue of Seals in the Department of Manuscripts in the British Museum*, 6 vols (London, 1887–1900).
Brand, P., 'Aspects of the law of debt, 1189–1307', in P. R. Schofield and N. J. Mayhew (eds), *Credit and Debt in Medieval England c.1180–c.1350* (Oxford, 2002), pp. 19–41.
— 'Seals and the law in thirteenth century England', in P. R. Schofield (ed.), *Seals and their Context in the Middle Ages* (Oxford, 2015).
Briggs, C., *Credit and Village Society in Fourteenth-Century England* (Oxford, 2009).
— and P. R. Schofield, *Select Pleas in Manorial Courts* (Selden Society, forthcoming).
Britnell, R., (ed.), *Pragmatic Literacy, East and West* (Oxford, 1997).
Burke, J., *A Genealogical and Heraldic History of the Landed Gentry of Great Britain and Ireland*, 4 vols (London, 1838).
Bynum, C. W., *Jesus as Mother* (Berkeley and Los Angeles, 1982).
— 'Men's use of female symbols', in L. K. Little and B. K. Rosenwein (eds), *Debating the Middle Ages: Issues and Readings* (Oxford, 1998), pp. 277–89.
Camille, M., *Mirror in Parchment. The Luttrell Psalter and the Making of Medieval England* (London, 1998).
Carpenter, D., 'The English royal chancery in the thirteenth century', in A. Jobson (ed.), *English Government in the Thirteenth Century* (Woodbridge, 2004).
Carr, A. D., Medieval Anglesey (Llangefni, 1982).
— ' "This is my act and deed": the writing of private deeds in late medieval north Wales', in H. Pryce (ed.), *Literacy in Medieval Celtic Societies*, Cambridge Studies in Medieval Literature, 33 (Cambridge, 1998), pp. 223–37.
— 'Inside the tent looking out: the medieval Welsh world-view', in R. R. Davies and G. H. Jenkins (eds), *From Medieval to Modern Wales: Historical Essays in Honour of Kenneth O. Morgan and Ralph A. Griffiths* (Cardiff, 2004), pp. 30–44.
Carver, M., 'Sculpture in action: contexts for stone carving on the Tarbat peninsula, Easter Ross', in S. M. Foster and M. Cross (eds), *Able Minds and Practiced Hands: Scotland's Early Medieval Sculpture in the 21st Century* (Leeds, 2005), pp. 13–36.
Chaplais, P., *English Royal Documents: King John–Henry VI 1199–1461* (Oxford, 1971).
— *English Diplomatic Practice in the Middle Ages* (Hambledon and London, 2003).
Chassel, J-L., (ed.), *Sceaux et usages de sceaux. Images de la Champagne médiévale* (Paris, 2003).

Cherry, J., 'Seal matrices', in P. Saunders and E. Saunders (eds), *Salisbury Museum Medieval Catalogue*, part 1 (Salisbury, 1991), pp. 29–39.
— 'Medieval and post-medieval seals', in D. Collon (ed.), *7000 Years of Seals* (London, 1997), pp. 124–42.
— 'Personal and impersonal impressions: identity revealed through seals', in S. Worrell, G. Egan, J. Naylor, K. Leahy and M. Lewis (eds), *A Decade of Discovery: Proceedings of the Portable Antiquities Scheme Conference 2007*, BAR British Series, 520 (Oxford, 2010), pp. 225–34.
— 'Ie su sel nul tel: no seal like it?', in M. Gill and J-L. Chassel (eds), *Pourquoi Les Sceaux. La sigillographie nouvel enjeu de l'histoire de l'art* (Lille, 2011).
Chibnall, M. M., 'Houses of Augustinian canons: abbey of Lilleshall', in ed. A. T. Gaydon, *A History of the County of Shropshire*, vol. 2 (Oxford, 1973), pp. 70–80.
Clanchy, M. T., *From Memory to Written Record, England 1066–1307*, 2nd edn (Oxford, 1993).
Clarke, C., 'Women's names in post-conquest England: observations and speculations', *Speculum*, 80 (1978), 223–51.
— 'English personal names ca.650–1300: some prosopographical readings', *Medieval Prosopography*, 8 (1987), 31–60.
Clark-Maxwell, W. G., 'The College of St Mary Magdalene, Bridgnorth, with some account of its deans and prebends. Part 1. The college', *Archaeological Journal*, 84 (1927), 1–23.
Clinch, G., 'Seal of the vicar of Reculver', *Archaeologia Cantiana*, 23 (1918), 169–70.
Coss, P., *The Lady in Medieval England, 1000–1500* (Stroud, 1998).
— 'Knighthood, heraldry and social exclusion in Edwardian England', in P. Coss and M. Keen (eds), *Heraldry, Pageantry and Social Display in Medieval England* (Woodbridge, 2002), pp. 39–68.
— *The Origins of the English Gentry* (Cambridge, 2003).
— and M. Keen (eds), *Heraldry, Pageantry and Social Display in Medieval England* (Woodbridge, 2002).
Crouch, D., 'The earliest original charter of a Welsh king', *Bulletin of the Board of Celtic Studies*, 26 (1989), 125–31.
— *The Image of Aristocracy in Britain, 1000–1300* (London, 1992).
— *The Birth of Nobility: Constructing Aristocracy in England and France, 900–1300* (Harlow, 2005).
— *The English Aristocracy, 1070–1272: A Social Transformation* (New Haven and London, 2011).
Dalrymple, W., *From The Holy Mountain: A Journey in the Shadow of Byzantium*, rev. edn (London, 2011).
Dalton, J. P., *The Archiepiscopal and Deputed Seals of York, 1114–1500*, Borthwick Texts and Calendars 17 (York, 1992).

Danbury, E., 'Queens and powerful women: image and authority', in N. Adams, J. Cherry and J. Robinson (eds), *Good Impressions: Image and Authority in Medieval Seals* (London, 2007), pp. 17–24.
Davies, R. R., *Lordship and Society in the March of Wales 1282–1400* (Oxford, 1978).
— *Domination and Conquest: The Experience of Ireland, Scotland and Wales, 1100–1300* (Cambridge, 1990).
— *The Matter of Britain and the Matter of England* (Oxford, 1996).
— *The Age of Conquest: Wales 1063–1415* (Oxford, 2000).
Davis, J., *Medieval Market Morality. Life, Law and Ethics in the English Marketplace, 1200–1500* (Cambridge, 2012).
Diederich, T., 'Reflexions sur la typologie des sceaux', J*anus: revue archivistique*, 1 (1993), 48–68.
Ellis, R. H., *Catalogue of Seals in the Public Record Office: Personal Seals*, vols 1 and 2 (London, 1978–81).
— *Catalogue of Seals in the Public Record Office: Monastic Seals* (London, 1986).
Elmhurst, E., *Merchant Marks*, Harleian Society (London, 1959).
Eyton, R. W., *The Antiquities of Shropshire*, 12 vols (London, 1854–60).
Fabre, M., *Sceau Medieval: Analyse D'une Pratique Culturelle* (Paris, 2001).
French, K., *The People of the Parish. Community Life in a Late Medieval English Diocese* (Philadelphia, 2001).
Gillingham, J., 'The travels of Roger of Howden and his views of the Irish, Scots and Welsh', *Anglo-Norman Studies*, 20 (1998 for 1997), 151–69.
— *The English in the Twelfth Century: Imperialism, National Identity and Political Values* (Rochester, NY, 1999).
— 'Civilizing the English: the English histories of William of Malmesbury and David Hume', *Historical Research*, 74 (2001), 17–43.
Goody, J., *The Logic of Writing and the Organization of Society* (Cambridge, 1986).
Graham, R., 'The Order of St Antoine de Viennois and its English commandery in Threadneedle Street', *Archaeological Journal*, 84:1 (1927), 341–406.
Gray, M., *Images of Piety: The Iconography of Traditional Religion in Late Medieval Wales*, BAR British Series, 316 (Oxford, 2000).
Griffiths, R. A., and P. R. Schofield (eds), *Wales and the Welsh in the Middle Ages* (Cardiff, 2011).
Hamilton Thompson, A., 'The College of St Mary Magdalene, Bridgnorth, with some account of its deans and prebends. Part 1. The deans and canons of Bridgnorth', *Archaeological Journal*, 84 (1927), 24–87.
Harper-Bill, C. (ed.), *Blythburgh Priory Cartulary*, 2 parts, Suffolk Records Society, Suffolk Charters, Il–III (1980–1).
Harvey, P. D. A., 'Personal seals in thirteenth-century England', in G. A. Loud and I. N. Wood (eds), *Church and Chronicle in the Middle Ages: Essays Presented to John Taylor* (London, 1991),

— 'Computer catalogue of seals in the Public Record Office, London', *Janus*, 2 (1996), 29–36.
— 'Seals and the dating of documents', in M. Gervers (ed.), *Dating Undated Medieval Charters* (Woodbridge, 2000), pp. 207–12.
— and A. McGuiness, *A Guide to British Medieval Seals* (London, 1996).
Henig, M., 'The re-use and copying of ancient intaglios set in medieval personal seals, mainly found in England: an aspect of the Renaissance of the twelfth century', in N. Adams, J. Cherry and J. Robinson (eds), *Good Impressions: Image and Authority in Medieval Seals* (London, 2007), pp. 25–34.
Heslop, T. A., 'The Virgin Mary's regalia and 12th century English seals', in A. Borg and A. Martindale (eds), *Studies Presented to Christopher Hohler* (Oxford, 1981), pp. 53–62.
— 'Seals', in G. Zarnecki, J. Allen and T. Holland (eds), *English Romanesque Art 1066–1200* (London, 1984), pp. 298–319.
— 'Cistercian seals in England and Wales', in C. Norton and D. Park (eds), *Cistercian Art and Architecture in the British Isles* (Cambridge, 1986), pp. 266–83.
— 'Peasant seals', in E. King (ed.), *Medieval England, 1066–1485* (Oxford, 1988), pp. 214–15.
— 'Towards an iconology of Croziers', in D. Buckton and T. A. Heslop (ed.), *Studies in Medieval Art and Architecture Presented to Peter Laslo* (Stroud, 1994), pp. 36–45.
— 'Art, nature and St Hugh's choir at Lincoln', in J. Mitchell (ed.), *England and the Continent in the Middle Ages*, Harlaxton Medieval Studies, VIII (Stamford, 2000), pp. 60–74.
Hilton, R. H., 'Gloucester Abbey leases of the thirteen century', *University of Birmingham Historical Journal*, iv (1953–4), 1–17.
Holt, J. C., 'More battle forgeries', *Reading Medieval Studies*, 11 (1985), 75–86.
Hope, W. St John, 'The seals of English bishops', *Proceedings of the Society of Antiquaries*, 2nd ser., 11 (1885–1887), 271–306.
Hough, C., 'Women in the landscape: place-name evidence for women in north-west England', *Nomina*, 31 (2008), 45–61.
Hyams, P. R., Kings, *Lords and Peasants in Medieval England* (Oxford, 1980).
Insley, C., 'From rex Wallia to princeps Wallie: charters and state formation in thirteenth-century Wales', in J. R. Maddicott and D. M. Palliser (eds), *The Medieval State: Essays Presented to James Campbell* (London, 2000).
Jenkins, D., 'The medieval Welsh idea of law', *Tijdschrift voor Rechtsgeschiedenis/Legal History Review*, 49 (1981).
— and M. E. Owen (eds), *The Welsh Law of Women: Studies Presented to Professor Daniel A. Binchy on his Eightieth Birthday, 3 June 1980* (Cardiff, 1980).
Jenkinson, H., 'A money-lender's bonds of the twelfth century', in H. W. C. Davis (ed.), *Essays in History Presented to Reginald Lane Poole* (Oxford, 1927), pp. 190–210.

— *A Guide to Seals in the Public Record Office* (London, 1968).
— 'The study of English seals: illustrated chiefly from examples in the Public Record Office', *Journal of the British Archaeological Association*, 3rd ser., i (1937), 93–125, reprinted in *Selected writings of Sir Hilary Jenkinson* (Gloucester, 1980), pp. 147–85.
Jobson, A. (ed.), *English Government in the Thirteenth Century* (Woodbridge, 2004).
Johns, S. M., Noblewomen, *Aristocracy and Power in the Twelfth-Century Anglo-Norman Realm* (Manchester, 2003).
— *Gender, Nation and Conquest in the High Middle Ages: Nest of Deheubarth* (Manchester, 2013).
— 'Seals, gender, identity, and social status in the late twelfth and early thirteenth centuries in Wales', in S. Solway (ed.), *Medieval Coins and Seals: Constructing Identity, Signifying Power* (Turnhout, 2015), pp. 347–58.
Jones, D., *The Church in Chester 1300–1540*, Chetham Society, 3rd. ser., vol. 8 (1957).
Justice, S., *Writing and Rebellion. England in 1381* (Berkeley, 1994).
Kaye, J. M., *Medieval English Conveyances* (Cambridge, 2009).
Keen, M., *Origins of the English Gentleman: Heraldry, Chivalry and Gentility in Medieval England, c.1300–c.1500* (Stroud, 2002).
— 'Heraldry and the medieval gentlewoman', *History Today*, 53 (2003), 24.
Kemp, B., 'Family identity: the seals of the Longespées', in P. R. Schofield (ed.), *Seals and their Context in the Middle Ages* (Oxford, 2015), pp. 137–50.
Kingsford, H. S., 'The seals of the Franciscans', in A. G. Little (ed.), *Franciscan History and Legend in English Mediaeval Art* (Manchester, 1937).
— 'Some medieval seal-engravers', *Archaeological Journal*, 97 (1940), 155–80.
Klingender, F., *Animals in Art and Thought to the End of the Middle Ages* (London, 1971).
Lancaster, R. K., 'Artists, suppliers and clerks: the human factors in the art patronage of King Henry III', *Journal of the Warburg and Courtauld Institutes*, 35 (1972).
Lechler, G., 'The tree of life in Indo-European and Islamic cultures', *Ars Islamica*, 4 (1937), 369–419.
Lewis, C. P., and A. T. Thacker, *A History of the County of Chester*, vol. 5, 2, (Woodbridge, 2005).
Lewis, D., 'The Hospital of St Anthony [of Vienne]', in C. M. Barron and M. Davies (eds), *The Religious Houses of London and Middlesex* (London, 2007), pp. 228–31.
Lewis, K., *The Cult of St Katherine of Alexandria in Late Medieval England* (Woodbridge, 2002).
Little, A. G., (ed.), *Franciscan History and Legend in English Mediaeval Art* (Manchester, 1937), pp. 84–5.
— *Franciscan Papers, Lists and Documents* (Manchester, 1943).

Lloyd-Morgan, C., 'More written about than writing? Welsh women and the written word', in H. Pryce (ed.), *Literacy in Medieval Celtic Societies*, Cambridge Studies in Medieval Literature, 33 (Cambridge, 1998), pp. 149–65.

Lodge, R., 'Language attitudes and linguistic norms in France and England in the 13th Century', in P. R. Coss and S. Lloyd (eds), *Thirteenth-Century England IV* (Woodbridge, 1982), pp. 73–83.

McEwan, J., 'Occupation and identity in medieval London', in C. M. Barron and A. F. Sutton (eds), *The Medieval Merchant,* Harlaxton Medieval Studies, XXIV (Donnington, 2014), pp. 357–9.

— 'Making a mark in medieval London: the social and economic standing of seal-makers', in P. R. Schofield (ed.), *Seals and their Context in the Middle Ages* (Oxford, 2015), pp. 77–88.

— 'The challenge of the visual: making medieval seals accessible in the digital age', *Journal of Documentation*, 71 (2015), 999–1028.

— and E. A. New (eds), *Seliau yn eu Cyd-destun: Cymru o'r Mers yn yr Oesoedd Canol / Seals in Context: Medieval Wales and the Welsh Marches* (Aberystwyth, 2012).

McGuinness, A. F., 'Non-armigerous seals and seal-usage in thirteenth-century England', in P. R. Coss and S. D. Lloyd (eds), *Thirteenth-Century England V* (Woodbridge, 1995), pp. 165–77.

Maddison, J., *Ely Cathedral: Design and Meaning* (Ely, 2000).

Mate, M. E., *Women in Medieval English Society* (Cambridge, 1999).

Maxfield, D. K., 'St Anthony's Hospital, London: a pardoner-supported alien priory, 1219–1461', in J. L. Gillespie (ed.), *The Age of Richard II* (Stroud, 1997), pp. 225–47.

Menuge, N. J., (ed.), *Medieval Women and the Law* (Woodbridge, 2003).

Miller, E., and J. Hatcher, *Medieval England: Rural Economy and Society, 108–1348* (Abingdon, 1978).

Millett B., and J. W. Brown (eds), *Medieval English Prose for Women: Selections from the Katherine Group and Ancrene Wisse* (Oxford, 1990).

Morgan, F. C., and P. E. Morgan, *A Concise List of Seals Belonging to the Dean and Chapter of Hereford Cathedral* (Hereford, 1966).

Morgan, P., 'Making the English gentry', in P. R. Coss and S. D. Lloyd (eds), *Thirteenth-Century England V* (Woodbridge, 1995), pp. 21–35.

Morris, D., 'The rise of Christian names in the thirteenth century: a case study of the English nobility', *Nomina*, 28 (2005), 43–54.

Mundill, R. R., 'Jewish and Christian lending patterns and financial dealings during the twelfth and thirteenth centuries', in P. R. Schofield and N. J. Mayhew (eds), *Credit and Debt in Medieval England* (Oxford, 2002).

Murray, P., and L. Murray, T*he Oxford Companion to Christian Art and Architecture* (Oxford, 1996).

New, E. A., 'Christological personal seals and Christocentric devotion in later medieval England and Wales', *Antiquaries Journal*, 82 (2002), 47–68.
— 'Signs of community or marks of the exclusive? Parish and guild seals in later medieval England', in C. Burgess and E. Duffy (eds), *The Parish in Late Medieval England*, Harlaxton Medieval Studies, XIV (Stamford, 2006), pp. 113–28.
— 'Seals and status in medieval English towns: a case study of London, Newcastle and Durham', in N. Adams, J. Cherry and J. Robinson (eds), *Good Impressions: Image and Authority in Medieval Seals* (London, 2007).
— 'Representation and identity in medieval London: the evidence of personal seals', in M. Davies and A. Prescott (eds), *London and the Kingdom*, Harlaxton Medieval Studies, XVI (Stamford, 2008), pp. 246–58.
— *Seals and Sealing Practices*, British Records Association Archives and the User 11 (London, 2010).
— 'Biblical imagery on seals in medieval England and Wales', in M. Gill and J-L. Chassel (eds), *Pourquoi les sceaux? La sigillographie nouvel enjeu de l'histoire de l'art* (Lille, 2011), pp. 451–68.
— 'Lleision ap Morgan makes an impression: seals and the study of medieval Wales', *Welsh History Review*, 27:1 (2013), 327–50.
— '(Un)conventional images. A case-study of radial motifs on personal seals', in P. R. Schofield (ed.), *Seals and their Context in the Middle Ages* (Oxford, 2015), pp. 151–60.
— 'Text and image: the language of seals in medieval England and Wales', in M. Carruthers (ed.), *Multilingual Networks in Medieval Britain*, Harlaxton Medieval Studies, XXV (Donnington, 2015), pp. 59–73.
— 'The common seal and civic identity in medieval London', in S. Solway (ed.), *Medieval Coins and Seals: Constructing Identity, Signifying Power* (Turnhout, 2015), pp. 297–31.
Nicholl, L. D., *The Normans in Glamorgan, Gower and Kidweli* (Cardiff, 1936).
Ormerod, G., *The History of the County Palatine and City of Chester. Vol. II: Containing the Hundreds of Edisbury, Wirral and Broxton* (London, 1819).
Ortner, S., 'Is female to male as nature is to culture?', in M. Rosaldo and L. Lamphere (eds), *Women, Culture and Society* (Stanford, 1974), pp. 67–87.
Panofsky, E., *Studies in Iconology: Humanistic Themes in the Art of the Renaissance* (New York, 1939).
Patterson, R. B., *The Scriptorium of Margam Abbey and the Scribes of Early Angevin Glamorgan: Secretarial Administration in a Welsh Marcher Barony* (Woodbridge, 2002).
Pearce, C., 'The cult of St Margaret of Antioch', *Feminist Theology: The Journal of the Britain and Ireland School of Feminist Theology*, 16 (1997), 70–85.

Postan, M. M., 'Private financial instruments in medieval England', *Vierteljahrschrift für Sozial und Wirtschaftsgeschichte*, 22 (1930); reprinted in M. M. Postan, *Medieval Trade and Finance* (Cambridge, 1973), pp. 28–64.
Postles, D., 'The distinction of gender? Women's names in the thirteenth century', *Nomina*, 19 (1996), 78–89.
—— 'Identity and identification: some recent research into the English medieval "forename" ', in D. Postles and J. T. Rosenthal (eds), *Studies on the Personal Name in Later Medieval England and Wales* (Kalamazoo, MI, 2006), pp. 29–62.
—— *The North through its Names: A Phenomenology of Medieval and Early Modern Northern England*, English Surnames Survey, 8 (Oxford, 2007).
Pryce, H., (ed.), *Literacy in Medieval Celtic Societies* (Cambridge, 1998).
—— *Native law and the church in Medieval Wales* (Oxford, 1993).
—— 'Lawbooks and literacy in medieval Wales', *Speculum*, 75 (2000).
—— 'Culture, power and the charters of Welsh rulers', in M. T. Flanagan and J. Green (eds), *Charters and Charter Scholarship in Britain and Ireland* (Basingstoke and New York, 2005), pp. 184–202.
—— 'Anglo-Welsh agreements, 1201–77', in R. A. Griffiths and P. R. Schofield (eds), *Wales and the Welsh in the Middle Ages* (Cardiff, 2011), pp. 1–19.
Pugh, T. B., (ed.), *A History of Glamorgan. Vol. III: The Middle Ages* (Cardiff, 1971).
Radiker, L., 'Observations on cross-cultural names and naming patterns in medieval Wales and the March', *Proceedings of the Harvard Celtic Colloquium*, 26/27 (2006–7), 160–98.
Rees, W., *South Wales and the March, 1284–1415. A Social and Agrarian Study* (Oxford, 1924).
Richards, G., *Welsh Noblewomen in the Thirteenth Century: An Historical Study of Medieval Welsh Law and Gender Roles* (Lewiston, NY; Queenston, Ontario; and Lampeter, 2009).
Rigby, S. H., *English Society in the Later Middle Ages: Class, Status and Gender* (Basingstoke, 1995).
Robinson, D., (ed.), *The Cistercian Abbeys of Britain: Far from the Concourse of Men* (London, 1998).
Round, J. H., 'The introduction of knight service into England', in J. H. Round, *Feudal England: Historical Studies on the Eleventh and Twelfth Centuries* (London, 1895; repr. London, 1964), pp. 182–245.
Rubin, M., *Corpus Christi: The Eucharist in Late Medieval Culture* (Cambridge, 1991).
Saxl, A. F., 'The Ruthwell Cross', *Journal of the Warburg and Courtauld Institutes*, 6 (1943), 1–19.
Schofield, P. R., 'Intestat et testaments paysans en Angleterre et Pays de Galles au XIIIe siècle et au début du XIVe siècle', in N. Vivier (ed.), *Ruralité française et britannique, xiiie–xxe siècles. Approches comparées* (Rennes, 2005), pp. 207–18.

— 'The market in free land on the estates of Bury St Edmunds: sources and issues', in L. Feller and C. Wickham (eds), *Le marché de la terre au Moyen Âge* (Rome, 2005), pp. 273–95.
— 'Peasant debt in English manorial courts: form and nature', in J-M. Claustre (ed.), *Endettement privé et justice au Moyen Âge* (Paris, 2007), pp. 55–67.
— 'English law and Welsh marcher courts in the late-thirteenth and early-fourteenth centuries', in R. A. Griffiths and P. R. Schofield (eds), *Wales and the Welsh in the Middle Ages* (Cardiff, 2011).
— 'Seals and the peasant economy in England and marcher Wales, c.1300', in S. Solway (ed.), *Medieval Coins and Seals: Constructing Identity, Signifying Power* (Turnhout, 2015).
— (ed.), *Seals and their Context in the Middle Ages* (Oxford, 2015).
Sheehan, M. M., *The Will in Medieval England* (Toronto, 1963).
Short, I., 'Tam Angli quam Franci: self-definition in Anglo-Norman England', *Anglo-Norman Studies*, 18 (1996 for 1995), 153–75.
Siddons, M. P., 'Welsh seals in Paris', *Bulletin of the Board of Celtic Studies*, 29 (1981), 531–44.
— 'Welsh equestrian seals', *National Library of Wales Journal*, 23 (1983–4), 292–318.
— 'Welsh equestrian seals: additions', *National Library of Wales Journal*, 33 (2003), 217–18.
— *The Development of Welsh Heraldry*, 4 vols (Aberystwyth, 1991–2006).
— *Heraldic Badges of England and Wales. II.2: Non-Royal Badges* (Woodbridge, 2009).
Smith, J. B., 'Dynastic succession in medieval Wales', *Bulletin of the Board of Celtic Studies*, 33 (1986), 199–232.
— 'The succession to Welsh princely inheritance: the evidence reconsidered', in R. R Davies (ed.), *The British Isles, 1100–1500: Comparisons, Contrasts and Connections* (Edinburgh, 1988), pp. 64–81.
Smith, J. B., 'The kingdom of Morgannwg and the Norman conquest of Glamorgan', in T. B Pugh (ed.), *Glamorgan County History, Volume 3: The Middle Ages* (Cardiff, 1971), pp. 1–44.
Smith, Ll. B., 'The gage and the land market in late medieval Wales', *Economic History Review*, 29 (1976), 537–50.
— 'Tir prid: deeds of gage of land in late medieval Wales', *Bulletin of the Board of Celtic Studies*, 27 (1977).
— 'Inkhorn and spectacles: the impact of literacy in late medieval Wales', in H. Pryce (ed.), *Literacy in Medieval Celtic Societies* (Cambridge, 1998), pp. 202–22.
Späth, M., 'The body and its parts: iconographical metaphors of corporate identity in 13th century common seals', in J-L. Chassel and M. Gil (eds), *Pourquoi les sceaux? La sigillographie nouvel enjeu de l'histoire de l'art* (Lille, 2011), pp. 383–99.

— 'Memorialising the glorious past. Thirteenth-century seals from English cathedral priories and their artistic contexts', in P. R. Schofield (ed.), *Seals and their Context in the Middle Ages* (Oxford, 2015), pp. 161–72.

Steiner, E., *Documentary Culture and the Making of Medieval English Literature* (Cambridge, 2003).

Stenton, D. M., *The Englishwoman in History* (London, 1957).

Stenton, F. M., *First Century of English Feudalism* (Oxford, 1932).

Stephenson, D., 'The politics of Powys Wenwynwyn in the thirteenth century', *Cambrian Medieval Celtic Studies*, 7 (1984), 39–61.

Stevens, M. F., *Urban Assimilation in Post-Conquest Wales. Ethnicity, Gender and Economy in Ruthin, 1282–1348* (Cardiff, 2010).

Swanson, R. N., 'Peculiar practices: the jurisdictional jigsaw of the pre-Reformation Church', *Midland History*, 26 (2001), 69–95.

— *Indulgences in Medieval England: Passports to Paradise?* (Cambridge, 2007).

Taylor, A. J., 'Count Amadeus of Savoy's visit to England in 1292', *Archaeologia*, 106 (1979), 125–6.

Thacker, A. T., 'Churches and religious bodies: the collegiate church of St John', in ed. C. P. Lewis and A. T. Thacker, *A History of the County of Chester*, vol. 5, part 2, (Woodbridge, 2005), pp. 125–33.

Trueman, J. H., 'The privy seal and the English ordinances of 1311', *Speculum*, xxxi (1956).

Varty, K., *Reynard the Fox. A Study of the Fox in Medieval English Art* (Leicester, 1967).

Vincent, N. 'King Henry II and the monks of Battle: the Battle Chronicle unmasked', in R. Gameson and H. Leyser (eds), *Belief and Culture in the Middle Ages: Studies Presented to Henry Mayr-Harting* (Oxford, 2001), pp. 264–86.

— 'The seals of King Henry II and his court', in P. R. Schofield (ed.), *Seals and their Context in the Middle Ages* (Oxford, 2015), pp. 7–33.

Walker, S. S., 'Introduction', in S. S. Walker (ed.), *Wife and Widow in Medieval England* (Ann Arbor, MI, 1993), pp. 1–16.

Weinstein, D., and R. M. Bell, *Saints and Society: The Two Worlds of Western Christendom 1000–1700* (Chicago and London, 1982).

Whatley, L. J., 'Visual self-fashioning and the seals of the Knights Hospitaller in England', in N. Paul and S. Yeager (eds), *Remembering the Crusades. Myth, Image and Identity* (Baltimore, 2012), pp. 252–69.

Whitehead, D., 'St Ethelbert's Hospital, Hereford', in G. Aylmer and J. Tiller (eds), *Hereford Cathedral: A History* (London and Rio Grande, 2000), pp. 599–609.

Williams, D. H., *Welsh History through Seals* (Cardiff, 1982).

— 'Catalogue of Welsh ecclesiastical seals as known down to 1600 AD. Part I. Episcopal seals', *Archaeologia Cambrensis*, cxxxiii (1984).

— 'Catalogue of Welsh ecclesiastical seals as known down to 1600 AD. Part II. Seals of ecclesiastical jurisdiction', *Archaeologia Cambrensis*, cxxxiv (1985).
— 'Catalogue of Welsh ecclesiastical seals as known down to 1600 AD. Part IV. Seals of Cistercian Monasteries', *Archaeologia Cambrensis*, cxxxvi (1987), 133–55.
— *Atlas of Cistercian Lands in Wales* (Cardiff, 1990).
— *Catalogue of Seals in the National Museum of Wales. Vol. 1: Seal Dies, Welsh Seals, Papal Bullae* (Cardiff, 1993).
— *Catalogue of Seals in the National Museum of Wales. Vol 2: Ecclesiastical, Monastic and Collegiate Seals with a Supplement Concerning Wales* (Cardiff, 1998).
— 'Welsh seals at Canterbury', *Archaeologia Cambrensis*, 148 (2001 for 1999), 146–53.
— 'The seals of Strata Florida Abbey', *Ceredigion*, 14 (2003).
— 'Medieval Cistercian seals with special reference to "hand-and-staff" seals', *Archaeologia Cambrensis*, 154 (2007 for 2005), 153–78.
— *Images of Welsh History* (Aberystwyth, 2007).
— 'The judicial seals of the Welsh Courts of Great Sessions', in N. Adams, J. Cherry and J. Robinson (eds), *Good Impressions: Image and Authority in Medieval Seals* (London, 2007), pp. 60–5.
— 'Seal finds in Wales', in P. R. Schofield (ed.), *Seals and their Context in the Middle Ages* (Oxford, 2015), pp. 196–7.
Winstead, K. A., *Virgin Martyrs: Legends of Sainthood in Late Medieval England* (Ithaca, NY, and London, 1997).
Yates, M., 'The market in freehold land, 1300–1509: the evidence of feet of fines', *Economic History Review*, 66 (2013), 579–600.
Zarnecki, G., J. Holt and T. Holland, *English Romanesque Art 1066–1200* (London, 1984).

Unpublished

Andrew, S., 'Late medieval bosses in the churches of Devon' (unpublished PhD, University of Plymouth, 2011).
Julian-Jones, M.,'Land of the raven and the wolf: a comparative study of family power and strategy in the Welsh March, *c.*1199–1300' (unpublished Cardiff University PhD, 2014).
Sillence, M. J., 'The cardinal's seal of dignity and the representation of identities, 1378–1533' (unpublished PhD thesis, University of East Anglia, 2009).

INDEX

Aug.: Augustinian; Bened.: Benedictine; Cist.: Cistercian

Aaron, rod of 69
Aberchwiler (Denbighshire) 43
Aberystwyth (Ceredigion) 4
Abingdon, Edmund of, Archbishop of Canterbury (1234–40) 67, 74 n. 50
accounts 123
Acton Burnell (Shropshire) 53
advowson 62
Afan (lordship) 107
Aigueblanche, Peter of, bishop of Hereford (1240–68) viii, 63
Albus, William, of Hereford 66
Amadeus, count of Savoy (d. 1323) 13, 31 n. 1
amobwr (heriot) 52
Andrew, Susan 114
Anglesey 51
annulment 64
Anselm le Gros, bishop of St Davids (1230–47) 74, n. 49
Anselm, Preceptor General in England of the Hospital of St Anthony (London) viii, 62–3, 71 n. 12
Appeleye, Alice, wife of Roger of 66
Appeleye, Roger of 66
apprentice 53
arbitration 68
archdeaconry of Chester 64
archdeacons 41, 62
authentication 19–21, 24, 28, 36, 40, 42–3, 62, 65–7, 77, 79, 80, 81–3, 85, 87 n. 30, 98, 110

Bagod, Walter 65
bailiff 40, 98
Ballieul, Gilbert de 18–19
Bangor (Gwynedd) 1, 63, 111; bishop of *see* Cadwgan
banneret 82, 93, 106, 107
bards 108, 116 n.15
Basset, Henry vii, 53
Basset, Thomas 59 n. 20
Basset, William vii, 53
Bath Abbey (Bened., Somerset) 62, seal of 70 n. 8

Battle Abbey (Bened., Sussex) 18–19, 79
Bayville (Carmarthenshire) 56–7
Becket, Thomas, St Thomas of Canterbury 68, 115 n. 4, 196, 268
Bedos-Rezak, Brigitte 8, 84, 94, 105
Benedict XII, pope (1334–42) 68
Bewsey, Joan, daughter of William Troutbeck, wife/widow of William Butler of 63, 71–2 n. 20
Bingham, Robert, bishop of Salisbury (1228–46) 74 n. 49
Biþ Welle, Alice, daughter of Christine de 102 n. 29
Birch, Walter de Gray 2
Bleddyn, Margaret, wife/widow of Gruffydd ap 40
Bleddyn, Meurig ap 82
Bleddyn, Rhys ap 82
Bleddyn, Wrunu ap 82
Blythburgh Cartulary 74 n. 48
bonds 53, 57, 60 n. 50, 84, 122
bondsmen 52, 53, 59 n. 19, 84
Boneville, family of 50
Boniface IX, pope (1389–1404) 62, 233
Bonneville, William de x, 113
Bonnwyn, David ap Dyc (c.1476) 99
Bonveville, John de (c.1183–1218) ix, 83
Bonville, Sibyl de 108
Bonvilston (Glamorgan) 108
borrowing 24, 38, 65, 73 n. 34, 117 n. 40
Boxley Abbey (Cist., Kent) 68, seal of 74 n. 56
Bratton, Henry of, justice 24
Bremesberg, Nicholas of / Bremburgh (?Bramburgh) 66, 73 n. 45
Bridgend (Glamorgan) 6
Bridgnorth (Shropshire) 8, 56, 98, 114, 117
Bridgnorth collegiate church, royal free chapel of St Mary Magdalene 64, 69, 73 n. 35
Bridgnorth communal seal (burgesses) vii, 41–2, 46 n. 38, 66
Bridgnorth, Convent of Franciscan Friars viii; seal of guardian of viii

Bridgnorth, John (c.1358), son of Thomas, son of Robert of 98–9, his mother 98
Bridgnorth, Official and Dean of viii, 66
Bridgnorth, Robert of (c.1360) 98, 103 n. 37, 117
Bridgnorth, Hospital of St James 9
Bridgnorth, St Leonard's Church, 73 n. 35
Bridgnorth, St Mary Magdalene, church of 64–5, 73 n. 35
Bridgnorth, Thomas *cognomina Robard* of 65
Bristol 57, 109
Bromfield, court of 43
Brun, Reginald 66
Brun, Richard le, rector of All Saints Hereford 62
Brun, Richard, of Bridgnorth ix, 109
Bruyn, Alice, widow of Richard le (senior) 72 n. 24
Bruyn, Alice, wife of Richard le 117 (possibly identifiable with widow of Edmund de Pitchford)
Bruyn, Alice, wife/widow of Richard le 64
Bruyn, Richard le (senior) 64
Burdin, Agnes, wife of Gilbert 81
Burdin, Gilbert 23, 81
burgesses vii, 41, 42, 46 n. 38, 56, 68; *see also* towns/townspeople
Burghill, John, bishop of Llandaff (1396–8; d. 1414) 41
Burton, Sibilla, widow of William Waters of (1368 x 1369) ix, 100
Bury St Edmunds Abbey (Bened., Suffolk) 75 n. 70
Butler, William, of Bewsey 71 n. 20
bynames 96–7, 109

Cadwgan, bishop of Bangor (1215–38) 74 n. 49
Caerleon (Gwent) 81
Caernarfon (Gwynedd) 53, 56
Callow, Isabel, daughter of John 50
Callow, Isabella, widow of John 44
Callow, John 50

INDEX

Canne, John, clerk 99
Canne, William, of Bridgnorth 65
Canterbury, archbishops of 115; *see also* Edmund of Abingdon, Hubert Walter, Thomas Becket, Richard Wethershed
Caradoc *Uerbeis* 38
Caradoc, Morgan ap 81, second seal of 82
Caradoc, Morgan ap, *Margan ap Caradoc* (d. *c.*1208) of Glamorgan
Caradog, Lleision ap Morgan ap 82, 88 n. 47
Caradog, Owain ap Morgan ap 82, 88 n. 47
Cardiff (Glamorgan) 50; castle 39
Cardiff, Adam the porter/gatekeeper (*portarius*) of ix, 106
Carlisle, Statute of (1307) 41, 68
Carmarthen, seal of Principality of South Wales 208
Carmarthenshire 6
Carpenter, John the 109
Carpenter, John, Master of the House of St Anthony of Vienne 63
Carr, A. D. 36, 44, 78
carving 111
Cecilia (*c.*1365 x 65), daughter of Hugh, son of Hugh de Hauthryn 99
Ceredigion, county of 3, 6
chamberlain of North Wales 147, 148, 149; *see also* North Wales
charter production and diplomatic norms England and Wales 85
Cherry, John 94
Cheshire 111
Chester 14–15, 56, 63, 64, 109, 117, 155
Chester, St John's Church, 64, 72 n. 26
Chetwynd, John of (*c.*1330) 66
chirograph 24, 39, 46 n. 38, 66
chivalry 93
Christian agreements 24
Christina, widow of William Canne of Bridgnorth 65
Christogram *see* seals; motifs; Christ; imagery
churchwardens 74 n. 47
Cistercian 2–3, 41, 62, 67–8, 106, 122
Citharedi, William, the harper 108

Clairvaux Abbey (Cist.; Champagne, France), seal of 68, 75 n. 58
Clanchy, Michael 84
Clare family 107; *see also* Alianora (Eleanor); Gilbert
Clare, Gilbert de (d. 1230), fifth earl of Gloucester 40, 81
Clare, Gilbert de (d. 1295), seventh earl of Gloucester and sixth earl of Hertford 38, 87 n. 28
classification 3–5, 16–17, 32 n. 18, 33 n. 45, 93, 96
Clement IV, pope (1265–8) 62
Clerk, Margery, wife of Roger the 94
Coity lordship (Glamorgan) 106
Colington, Peter of 99
Colion commote, Dyffryn Clwyd 39–40, 42, 46 n. 30
Common seal 41, 42, 44, 66, 68, 69
concubine 56, 94
confraternity, letters of 71 n. 17
conjoint sealing 68, 82, 94; *see also* family group sealing
consanguinity 64
Conwy (Clwyd) 114
coptic art 63
corporate identity 16, 73 n. 44, 68
Corpus Christi 114
co-sealing, women and 96–7
countergifts 66
counterseal 38, 41, 91, 92, 114
courts, Marcher 42
Coventry and Lichfield, diocese of 63; bishop of *see* Stainsby, Alexander
creditors, Jewish 84
Crouch, David 80, 82–3, 85, 106–7
cultural diffusion 18–19, 77–80; *see also* seals, increase in use
Cwmhir Abbey (Cist; Powys) 3
Cymer Abbey (Cist.; Gwynedd) 3

d'Avene family 107
dating, problems of 14–15
Davies, Susan 2–3, 4

debt 19, 54, 65, 79, 84
Deheubarth 78, 80
Denbigh (Clwyd) 6
Denemede, Roger of 68, 75, n. 64
Despenser, *Alianora le Depenser*, Eleanor de Clare (1292–1337), wife/widow of Hugh Despenser the Younger (d. 1326), and wife/consort of William de la Zouche (d. 1352), first lord Zouche 40, 87 n. 28
Despenser, Hugh (d. 1349), lord of Glamorgan and Morgannwg 39, 87 n. 27
Dey, Gruffydd ap Dafydd 51
diocesan commissary court 73 n. 38
diocesan officers Archdeacons and seals, rural deans and seals 41
dispute 18, 19, 24, 36, 39–41, 44, 46, 48, 68, 122
Dod, Simon 65
Dogfeiling (Denbighshire) 54, 59 n. 23
dower 94
Dunham (Cheshire) 71 n. 20
Durham 118
Dyffryn Clwyd 39–40, 42–3, 54
dynastic rivalry 85

earls 16
East Anglia 113
ecclesiastical identity 68
ecclesiastical office and seals 41
economic exchange and seals 49–54
Edgebolton (Shropshire) 95
Edward I, king of England (1272–1307) 38; and conquest of Wales 78
Edward II, king of England (1307–27) 38
Edward III, king of England (1327–77) 194
Edward IV, king of England (1461–83) 149, seal of chamberlain 81
Edward, Prince of Wales, son of King Henry VI 154
effigy type 67–8
Eionion ap Bleddyn 43–4, 47 n. 48
Ela la Botiliere, 'Lady Wem of Shropshire' (*c*.1337) ix, 97, 103 n. 31

Ely Cathedral 67; bishops of *see* Hugh of Northwold, Nigel
Emma (*c*.1240), wife of (1) Simon de *Jagdon*; (2) William Banastre (3) Adam ix, 95
English law 93
Englishry 6, 7
estate administration 40
ethnicity 83
Eucharist 113, 114
Eugenius IV, pope (1431–47) 71 n. 17
Exchequer 140
exclusion 78–9
excommunication 62
executors 64, 65, 72 n. 24
Exeter, Statute of (1285) 84
Eyton, family of (Denbighshire) 55
Eyton, Robert 2

Facham, Robert of 65
family and seals 26, 38, 81–3, 85, 91–4, 97–101, 103 n. 33, 106–8, 111–13, 123–4
family group sealing 50, 54, 55, 57, 83
Fauconberg, Eustace of, bishop of London (1221–80) 74 n. 49 and n. 52
Filipp son of Wurkin 88 n. 38
finished goods 52
Flesshewer, William 55, Agnes his wife 55
Flintshire 6
forgery 19, 32 n. 23
Fostone, William de 116 n. 28
Fountains Abbey (Cist., Yorkshire) 68, 74 n. 56
Franciscan Order 68–9
free status 52
Frere, Thomas 56
Fromberg, Alice *de* 97
Fychan, Espus ap Iorwerth 82
Fychan, Ifor (Ivor Vaghan) ix, 82
Fychan, Iowerth sons of *see* William, Madog, Espus Fychan
Fychan, Lleision ap Morgan ap Morgan of Glamorgan 107
Fychan, Madog ap Iorwerth 82

INDEX

Fychan, Owain ab Llywelyn ab Owain 80
Fychan, William ap Iorwerth 82

Gate, Robert at 65
gender and seals 8, 93–101, 105
genealogy 92
gentlemen as social category 93
Glamorgan 14, 19, 20
Glamorgan lordship 107, 108, 111, 116;
 Court of the Great Session 246
Glanville 79, 84
glass 109, 113
Gloucester Abbey (St Peter's; Bened.,
 Gloucestershire) 18, 57
Gloucester, earls of 38
Gloucester, FitzRobert, William (d. 1183),
 second earl of 38, 91
Gloucester, Isabella, countess of (d. 1217)
 ix, 91
Gloucester, Robert, first earl of (d. 1147)
 19, 91
Gogerddan Estate Records 3
gonfanons 82
Gough, Ifor, father of Ieuan 'le Tayllour'
 ix, 110
Gough, Ieuan 'le Tayllour', son of Ifor
 ix, 110
Gournay, Hugh de 94
Gournay, Milicent de 94
Gower, chancellery, seal of 209
Gower, John 79
grant in free alms 66
Great seals 38–9; *see also individual English
 kings for references to great seals*
Grenehilles, William, of Preston 56
Grey, John de 39
Grey, Reginald de (Dyffryn Clwyd) 39
Gronw son of Philip 88 n. 38
Gruffith, William 63
Gruffudd a Bud rei hosan 80
Gruffudd ab Ivor (Ifor Meurig Ifor Bach,
 Griffin ab Ivor) 38
Gruffudd, Cadel ap (d. 1175) of
 Deheubarth 80

Gruffudd, Dafydd ap (d. 1283), prince of
 Wales 39
Gruffudd, Llywelyn ap 78
Gwenllian, daughter of Gwerfil ix
Gwenllian, daughter of Phillip ix
Gwenwynwyn ab Owain Cyfeiliog (d. 1216)
 of Powys Wenwynwyn (Gwenwynwyn son
 of Owain) 20, 79, 85
Gwerful *ferch*/daughter of Adda 43–4,
 47 n. 48
Gwilym ap Gruffydd ap Gwilym 111; *see also*
 Johanna, his wife
Gwilym, William ap Gruffith ap 52
Gwrgant, Nicholas ap (d. 1183), Bishop of
 Llandaff 20
Gwynedd 6, 36, 78, 85
Gwyneth, Maurice, of Shrewsbury ix, 108

Hafadheuolog Grange (?Glamorgan) 66,
 73 n. 41
Hampton, John, brother of William de 40
Hampton, William 40
Hampton, William de 40
Harley, John 53
Harvey, Paul 5, 4, 19, 21, 24, 28
Hastings, battle of and memory of 82
Haughmond Abbey (Aug., Shropshire) 80,
 85, 95
Haukeston, George, 110
Hauthryn, Margery (*c.*1365 x 65), daughter
 of Hugh son of Hugh de 99
heiress 94
Helisand, wife of Nicholas of *Bremesberg*
 (?Bramburgh), daughter of William Albus
 of Hereford 66
Henry II, king of England (1154–89) 79;
 Great seal 216
Henry III, king of England (1216–72) 62;
 Great seal 224
Henry of Blois, bishop of Winchester
 (d. 1171) 116
Henry V, king of England (1413–22) 147,
 148, as Chamberlain of Wales viii, 81;
 Great seal 233

Henry VI, king of England (1422–61, 1470–1) 148
Henry VII, king of England (1485–1509) 140, 285
Henry VIII, king of England (1509–47), First Great Seal 212; Second Great Seal 239, 246; Third Great Seal 239; Court of Augmentations, First seal of 253
heralds 110
Hereford 14–15, 66; bishop of *see* Peter of Aigueblanche
Hereford Cathedral Dean and Chapter, seal of 73 n. 45
Hereford, church of All Saints, 62
Hereford, Dean and Chapter of 66–7
Hereford, Elias of Bristol, canon of (*c*.1225) 73 n. 46
Hereford, Hugh of 20, 23
heriot *see amobwr*
Hermes 252
Hesketh, John de viii, 56
Heslop, T. A. 14, 75 n. 57
hierarchy 32 n. 18, 54, 77, 89, 92–3, 106–9
Holbache, Gwenhyfar (*c*.1430) 99
Holt, James 18–19
Hospital, St Anthony of Vienne (S.E. France), order of, (London) ix, 62–3, 71 n. 18 and n. 19
Hospital, St Anthony's, London 71 n. 18 and n. 19
Hospitallers 66
hospitals 62; *see also* St Anthony (London); St Ethelbert (Hereford); St James (Bridgnorth); St John of Jerusalem
Host 108, 116
Howel, Gwenhwyfar ferch Griffith ap Cynwrig ap (*c*.1415) 96
Howel, Gwenllian ferch Griffith ap Cynwrig ap (*c*.1415) 96
Hubert Walter, archbishop of Canterbury (d. 1205) 115
Hugh le Vilein 44, 50
Hugh, son of Robert of Lancarfon *Lantcarvan* 19

Hulle, John de, bailiff of Bridgnorth (*c*.1360) 98
Hulle, Richard de la, rector of Pitchford Church 104 n. 53
humour 26, 110–12
hunting, hunters ix, 17, 24, 25, 29, 30, 55, 56, 108, 110
Hwlkin Bach 52
Hywel (*Howl*) ap Jankyn 113

Idenard (*c*.1250) ap Kedic ix, 82
identity 74, 79, 83–5, 91–101, 105–15
Ieaun, Rhys ab (*c*.1225–50); *Resus ab Yewan ab Yustin* Iwan ab Iestyn 83
Iestyn, Gruffud Foil ab Iwan ab (*Griffin Voil, ab Yewan ab Yustin*) 83
illegitimacy 65
indented licence 68
indulgence 63, 67, 71 n. 17, 74 n. 49
Innocent III, pope (1198–1216) 62
Innocent IV, pope (1243–54) 225 bulla
International Council of Archives 16, 32 n. 15
Iollyn, Margaret verch Dafydd ap 64
Iorwerth, Llywelyn ap (d. 1240) of Gwynedd 81, 85
Isabella, wife of Roger ix, 95

Jagdon, Roger, son of Simon de, and Emma 95
Jenkyn, William ab Howl ap 113
Jews 24
John, king of England (1199–1216) 92; Great Seal of 220
John, son of Richard de Leigh of High Hall (Cheshire) 63, 71 n. 16
Julius II, pope (d. 1513) (Julian, later Giuliano Della Rovere, cardinal bishop of Sabina) viii, 63–4, 72 n. 21

Kedic, Madog ap (*c*.1250) ix, 82
Kedic, Philip (*c*.1250) ap viii, 82
Kenfig (Glamorgan) vii, 41, 42, 50–1, 56, 82–3, 91

INDEX

Kenwric, son of Robert 88 n. 38
Keynsham (Somerset) 62
kings of England 16, 37; *see also* Edward I; Edward II; Edward III; Edward II; Edward III; Edward V; Edward VI; Edward VII; Edward VIII; John; Richard II
kingship 93
Kinnersley (Herefordshire) viii, 66–7
Kinnersley (Herefordshire), Phillip, parson of 66

Lancarfan, Robert of, *Lantcarvan* (Glam) 19
land, conveyance of 37–8
language 24, 52, 83, 84–5, 93, 95, 100, 102 n. 20
law, seals and 6, 7, 35–9, 42–4, 51–5, 57, 78, 79, 81, 84; *see also* Welsh law
leases 42, 51, 55, 66, 85
legend (seal) 24–5, 33, 80, 91, 94–5
legitimacy 16
Leigh, Johanna, wife of John, son of Richard de 63
Leominster (Herefordshire) 67
letters closed 39
Lewes, Robert of, bishop of Bath (1136–66) 62
licence, sexual 111
Lichfield, diocese of *see* Coventry and Lichfield
life-cycle 93–4, 98, 100–1
Lilleshall Abbey (Aug., Shropshire) 50–1, 55, 73 n. 42
Lincolnshire 15
lineage 38, 50, 55, 83, 92, 97–9, 124
linguistic change 95
literacy 36, 45 n. 44, 78, 84, 101
Llandaff Cathedral (Glamorgan) 20, 41; bishop of *see* Burghill, John; Nicholas ap Gwrgant
Llanerch, court of 46 n. 25
Llanwys (?Monmouth) 56
Llywelyn, Lleucu ferch Ieuan ap 99
Llywelyn, William ap Ievan ap Gruffith ap Iorwerth ap 52

loans 24
location 4, 7, 14, 50, 55–7, 66, 110
Locksmith, John, son of Robert the x, 114
London 24, 109, 110; bishop of, *see* Fauconberg, Eustace of; seal of city of 74 n. 52
London, William de 82
Lucy, Richard de (d. 1179), justiciar 18, 79
Luvel, family of 50

Mansell, Rees; *Resio Mauncell* 53
manumission 52–3, 58 n. 15
manuscripts 111, 114
March *see* Wales and the March
Margam Abbey (Cist., Glamorgan) 2, 19–20, 38–9, 40, 50, 53, 55–6, 59 n. 34, 62, 66, 68, 81–3, 88 n. 49, 91, 103 n. 46, 107, 114; seal of 75 n. 60
Margery, daughter of Roger viii, 56
maritagium 94
marital status (and seals) 96–7
marriage 64, 98, 125
Marshal, William (I), fourth earl of Pembroke (*c*.1146–1219) 87 n. 30
Marston, Roger, provincial minister of the Franciscans in England (*c*.1292–8) 68
Martin V, pope (1417–31) 62; bulla 233
Matilda, daughter of William 99
McGuinness, A. F. 19, 24
mendicant houses viii, 62
mercantile bonds and trade 53, 57, 124
Meurig, Kedic ap (*c*.1250) 82
Meurig, Madog ap (*c*.1250) ix, 82, 89 n. 49
Meylys, Elisabeth 64
Meylys, William 64
Middelton, John de, of Lancaster 56
military ethos 93
Miller, Amabilia, daughter of Walter the (of Kenfig, Glamorgan) vii, 51
misuse of seals 43–4
Mitdehorguill, Milisant, daughter of William de 19
Mitdehorguill, William de 19
Monmouthshire 6

monogram 13, 15, 26, 56
monstrance 108, 116
Montfort, Eleanor de (d. 1282), princess of Wales 39
Montgomery, Treaty of (1272) 78, 80
moveable goods 52–3
murder 65
music 108, 118 n. 51
Mygnoth, John 114

names on seals 24, 96–7
National Archives, The 15
National Library of Wales, The 2, 4
Neath Abbey (Savignac / Cist., Glamorgan) 62, 68, 81
Newborough (Anglesey) 56
Newcastle (Glamorgan) 39, 62, 91
Newcastle (Tyne and Wear) 117 n. 32
Nigel, Bishop of Ely (d. 1169) 116
Nigg Stones 63
nobility and seals 20, 39, 54–5, 77, 93, 97, 106
Norfolk 94
Norries family of Penllyn 118
Norries, Ralph 111
Norries, Richard ix
North Wales, deputed great seal of 198; *see also* chamberlain of
Northwold, Hugh of, bishop of Ely (1229–54) 67, 74 n. 50
Nussa, Terrricus de, Prior and master of Hospital of St John of Jerusalem 66

oaths 36
oral agreements 78–9
oral evidence 42–3
oral proof under Welsh law 53
orchard 98
Orreby, Felicia, wife of Phillip of (*c.*1360) 98
Orreby, Phillip (*c.*1360) 98
Osemund, Gilbert, of Foxherd viii, 52–3; *see also* Peter, his son; Ida, his wife
Osemund, Peter, son of Gilbert 52–3

Osumend, Elen, daughter of Gilbert 52–3
Osemund, Ida, wife of Gilbert, of Foxherd 52–3
Oxford (Oxfordshire) 109

painter 65
Palmer, Philip, son of Robert vii, 51
Panofsky, Erwin 16
papacy 122, 147; *see also individual* Popes
papal officials, seals of 62
parish seals 67, 74 n. 47
Parvus, Roger 18
Passion 114
Pembroke, Chancery of, seal of 200
Pembrokeshire 6, 109
Pendar Abbey (Cist., Glamorgan) 38
Pennarth, Robert, commissary of the bishop of St Asaph 64
Penteulu 81
Peole, John 117
personal seals 42, 56; *see also* secret seal and privy seal
Pervath, Alice, wife of John vii, 51
Pervath, John, of Kenfig (Glamorgan) vii, 51; *see also* Alice his wife 51
Philip, Grunu ap ix
photography, digital 121–2
piety and seal motifs 28, 53
Pitchford manor 117
Pitchford, Agnes, illegitimate daughter of Edmund de 65
Pitchford, Alice de, wife/widow of Edmund de Pitchford ix, 65, 99, 109
Pitchford, Alice, wife of Edmund de 109–10, 117
Pitchford, Chantry of 69
Pitchford, Edmund de (Bridgnorth) ix, 65, 98, 73 n. 36, 109–10, 117; *see also* Alice de Pitchford
Pitchford, family of *see* Alice de Pitchford; Edmund de Pitchford; Joan de Pitchford; Nicholas de Pitchford
Pitchford, Joan de Pitchford, wife of Nicholas de 68–9

INDEX

Pitchford, Joanna, wife/widow of Nicholas de 99
Pitchford, Nicholas of (Shropshire), provost of Bridgnorth 68–9, 75 n. 62, 99
Pitchford, Prebendary of 65
Pitchford, Robert de 65, 117
Pitchford, William de 117
poetry 107
Pontefract (Yorkshire) 46 n. 38
Ponti, Nicholas 88 n. 43
popes *see* papacy: and individual Popes, Benedict: Boniface: Eugenius: Clement: Innocent: Julius: Martin: Urban
Portable Antiquities Scheme (PAS) 6, 9, 124
Postles, David 96
Powys 6, 36
priests 108
Principality of South Wales, Carmarthen, seal of 208
privy seals 35, 38, 43, 84
probate 65
propaganda 1
pseudo-armorial devices 32 n. 18, 109, 110, 257, 274
Pulley (Pihley), John 65
puns 98–9
pura Wallia 4, 6, 122, 124
purity 92
Pykemere (*Pylmere*), John 99, 103 n. 51, 111, 118
Pykemere, Johanna, wife of John of (formerly wife of Gwilym ap Gruffudd ap Gwilym) x, 103 n. 51, 111

quadruped 201, 208, 246, 277, 293, 325
quitclaim 20, 44, 82, 95, 99

Ranulf de Blondeville (d. 1232), earl of Chester 15
Raul, Robert, son of Robert (Glam) vii, 51
Reading Abbey (Cluniac; Berkshire) 67
Reculver (Kent), vicar of 74 n. 48
Redman family arms 72 n. 23

Redman, Richard, bishop of St Asaph (1471–95) 72 n. 23
reliefs 52
religion 8, 61–70, 112
religious institutions and seals 55, 155
Rhondda Cynon Taf 6
Richard II, king of England (1377–99) 209
Richard, John ap Thomas ap (?Glamorgan) 66
Richard, Richard ap Thomas ap (Glamorgan) 66
Robert Scissor ix, 109
Robert the locksmith 114
Roc, William, chaplain 66
Rome 62–3
Rondulph, John 98, 109–10
Rudge, William of 65
Rudwell Cross (Northumbria) 63
rural deans 62
Russell, Alexander 114
Ruthin 42, 58 n. 15
Ruthin, Great Court of, 40, 46 n. 23 and n. 26

sacred monogram *see* Christogram
saints 124
St Andrew 111, 195, 244, 296, 309
St Anthony 63, 159, 193
St Bonaventure 69
St Edmund x, 113, 197, 312, 317
St Ethelbert, Hospital of, Hereford 66–7, 73 n. 46
St Etheldreda 197
St Helen 100
St James 244
St James the Great 66
St John 262, 318
St John of Jerusalem, Hospital of 66
St John the Baptist 113, 114, 157, 185, 189, 213, 230, 234, 236, 237, 241, 242, 264, 281, 288, 289, 299, 309
St John the Evangelist 300
St Katherine 99–100, 104 n. 53, 109, 118, 186, 189, 257, 258, 261, 268, 274, 280, 284, 286, 292, 304, 310

St Lawrence 253, 311–12
St Leonard (Newcastle, Glamorgan) 39, 62
St Margaret 296, 299, 323,
St Margaret of Antioch 100
St Mary Magadalene 69, 262, 284, 300
St Michael 194
St Milburga 100, 300
St Oswald 157
St Paul 197, 212, 235, 265
St Paul the Hermit 63, 193
St Peter 193, 235, 265, 270, 283-84, 306
St Thomas of Canterbury *see* Becket, Thomas
St Vigeans stones 63
St Winifrid 100, 300–1
Says, Thomas ap Dafydd 64
Scheynton, Adam of 65
sculpture 113
Scurlage, David 40
Scurlage, family of 50
seals
  and amercements 40
  ancillary seals 35
  anonymous 24–8, 33 n. 45, 65, 103 n. 40, 108, 110, 111
  colour 5, 63, 84, 89, 91, 101 n. 1
  increased use of 4, 14, 15–28, 30, 35–40, 42, 44, 49, 50–1, 52, 56–7, 81; *see also* cultural diffusion
  motifs
    abstract design 238
    acorns 321
    altar 200
    angel 173, 235, 255, 259, 303
    animals 23, 99, 141, 155, 157, 158, 162, 175, 178, 198, 201, 207, 208, 214, 218, 245, 256, 267–8, 272, 285, 290, 292–3, 295, 314, 321, 324–5; *see also* antelope; ape; ass; bear; boar; bull; calf; deer; fox; goat; hare; horse; hound; lamb; lion; pig; rabbit; serpent; snake; squirrel; stag; wolf; *also those listed under* beasts, mythical
    annunciation 158, 164, 167, 225, 244, 289

antelope 214, 253, 290
ape 186
arabic script 134, 219
archangel 131
archers 312
arm 228, 258, 267; *see also* hand
arms/armour/armorial devices
  see heraldic devices
armoured man, dismounted 191, 209;
  see also equestrian figures
arms of England 69, 284
arrows 99, 136, 174, 182, 197, 218, 223, 226, 247, 248, 249, 267, 270, 274, 278, 279, 317, 323; *see also* bow
ass 186
assumption 235
banner *see* pennon
barrel 203, 230, 270, 285, 287, 301
bear 157
beasts 162, 214, 314; mythical *see* centaur; dragon; griffin; grotesques; hippocampus; mermaid; unicorn; wyvern; yale
bell 159, 277
bird ix *passim*, 15, 17, 21, 22, 23, 25, 26, 27, 29, 140, 142, 148, 153, 154, 155, 156, 157, 158, 159, 160, 164, 165, 166, 167, 171, 172, 173, 174, 175, 177, 179, 181, 184, 189, 191, 192, 195, 196, 206, 207, 213, 216, 221, 227, 230, 235, 242–3, 247, 252, 254, 255, 256, 260, 262, 265–7, 271, 275, 277, 278, 284, 286, 293–7, 300, 306, 308–9, 321; *see also* cock; eagle; goose; hawk; pigeon; raven; stork
boar 153, 154, 156, 160, 182, 236, 233, 236, 239, 246, 290, 295, 296, 321
boat 265
bow and arrow 82, 136, 218, 223, 247, 248, 249; *see also* arrows
building 132, 133, 134, 159, 188, 213, 215, 221, 241, 264, 270, 276
bull 166, 187, 218

350

INDEX

bust ix *passim*, 17, 18, 21, 27, 29–31, 37, 98, 130, 147, 168, 180, 244, 255, 283, 287–8, 290, 292, 299, 305, 306, 309, 310, 312, 319; *see also* head
butter churn 270
butterfly 203, 204, 208
calf 160
candle 108, 303
candlestick 267
caparisons *see* equestrian
canting images *see* rebus
centaur 165
chalice 39, 78, 114, 219, 228
Christ, imagery ix *passim*, 17, 25, 27, 28, 29–30, 68–9, 113, 132, 142, 143, 147, 148, 149, 158, 164, 156, 167, 182, 186, 191, 192, 193, 194, 196, 197, 198, 199, 228, 250, 255, 262, 264, 286, 277, 298, 299, 314–15
cleaver 82, 277
clover 148, 152, 159, 175, 206, 214, 230, 236, 253, 258, 262, 276, 307, 311, 313, 315, 316
cockerel 131, 149, 154, 158, 205, 210, 256
column 265, 301 322
conifer branches 142, 143, 144, 145, 146, 153, 179, 181, 184, 185, 186, 189, 195, 197, 229, 242, 255, 256, 259, 260, 264, 269, 270, 271, 274, 278, 281, 286, 295, 296, 297, 304, 306, 309, 311, 321
coronet *see* crown
cows 189
crafts 108
crescent 132, 141, 143, 165, 179, 182, 185, 187, 191, 193, 196, 211, 214, 225, 227, 228, 229, 235, 247, 250, 255, 257, 262, 263, 269, 274, 285, 289, 309, 310, 312, 317, 321, 322, 323
cross 14, 69, 75 n. 69, 99, 134, 141, 146, 149, 152, 156, 158, 161, 167, 172, 174, 175, 176, 180, 187, 190, 195, 196, 198, 199, 203, 205, 206, 208, 211, 212, 223, 233, 239, 251, 255, 268, 274, 280, 292, 307, 310, 313, 318, 321
crown 100, 140, 144, 145, 146, 147, 148, 149, 150, 151, 152, 155, 156, 157, 159, 160, 162, 163, 166, 168, 171, 173, 179, 183, 184, 186, 187, 188, 189, 194, 198, 199, 204, 206, 211, 212, 213, 214, 215, 234, 236, 238, 242, 253, 256, 258, 260, 264, 265, 270, 271, 273, 275, 276, 277, 279, 280, 282, 283, 284, 286, 290, 291, 298, 299, 300, 301, 303, 305, 307, 308, 309, 310, 311, 312, 318, 319, 320, 321, 323, 324, 325
crozier 132, 193, 195, 196, 197, 215, 231, 233, 234, 235, 277, 303
crucifixion 69, 296, 308, 318
cup 137, 195, 228, 250, 262, 270, 285, 288, 290, 300
dagger 82, 238
deer 30, 172, 303, 319
diamond 149, 176, 201, 267, 286, 320
distaff 217
dog 29, 165, 180, 198, 212, 246, 268, 285, 290, 293, 246, 294, 306, 308; *see also* hound
dolphin 276
dragon 81, 163, 169, 170, 177, 194, 198, 254, 257, 280, 296, 303, 310, 313, 323
duck 255, 260
eagle 91, 135, 141, 144, 150, 152, 153, 163, 171, 181, 186, 191, 193, 194, 201, 208, 212, 213, 216, 230, 234, 235, 236, 237, 242, 253, 254, 257, 261, 264, 265, 268, 269, 271, 272, 283, 287, 288, 299, 301, 304, 305, 314, 321, 322, 324
ecclesiastical imagery x, 20–1, 131, 132, 133, 147, 149, 155, 191, 192, 193, 195, 196, 197, 215, 216, 223–4, 228, 235, 302, 305, 311, 322

elephant 154, 282, 293
equestrian images ix *passim*, 2, 17, 21, 22, 23, 25, 28–30, 37, 55, 80–1, 85, 106, 107, 130, 135, 136, 137, 139, 147, 168, 170, 178, 190, 192, 193, 198, 215, 216, 217, 218, 222, 224, 225, 227, 230–5, 239, 241, 250, 292, 297–8, 301, 302, 303, 307, 312
ewer 161
figure on seal 275, 276, 284, 299, 303, 319
fish 99, 103 n. 51, 151, 219, 239, 276, 219, 322
flames 203, 271
fleur de lys 18, 99, 177, 235, 245, 301; *see also* lily flower
flowers 14, 53, 82, 89 n. 49, 114, 130, 131, 132, 133, 134, 135, 136, 137, 138, 139, 141, 142, 143, 144, 145, 146, 149, 150, 151, 154, 157, 162, 163, 165, 166, 167, 169, 170, 171, 172, 174, 176, 177, 180, 182, 184, 185, 186, 187, 188, 189, 190, 191, 195, 203, 206, 207, 208, 212, 213, 218, 219, 220, 226, 227, 228, 229, 232, 237, 238, 240, 241, 243, 246, 247, 248, 249, 250, 252, 254, 255, 257, 258, 259, 261, 263, 264, 266, 267, 268, 270, 271, 272, 273, 274, 275, 276, 278, 280, 281, 282, 287, 288, 291, 292, 293, 294, 295, 296, 297, 299, 300, 301, 304, 308, 309, 310, 313, 314, 319, 320, 321, 322, 324; *see also* lily flower; fleur de lys
flute 8, 111, 148
foliate motif 15, 83, 95, 162, 164, 169, 189, 212, 218, 222
fountain 297
fox 8, 99, 103 n. 51, 111, 118 n. 51, 148, 151
galley 239
garb *see* wheat / wheatsheaf
gazelle 249
gems 21, 38, 83, 91, 112, 118 n. 57, 130,
134, 137, 147, 153, 164, 167, 188, 190, 191, 192, 197, 199, 200, 209, 210, 213, 214, 216, 217, 218, 219, 221, 226–7, 230, 237, 239, 243, 244, 245, 246, 249, 252, 253, 255, 258, 274, 275, 276, 280, 289, 290, 292, 294, 297, 299, 306, 311, 319, 322
geometric design 215
goat 186, 197
goose 150
griffin 13, 14, 151, 160, 170, 198, 208, 214, 230, 232, 242, 285, 291, 303, 311, 314
grotesque 111, 237, 249, 257, 320, 323
hand imagery ix *passim*, 17, 23, 29, 67–8, 81–2, 88 n. 38 and n. 44, 106, 108, 132, 133, 135, 138, 139, 171, 180, 189, 193, 194, 202, 207, 216, 218, 220, 224, 229, 237, 238, 244, 258, 263–4, 266–7, 280–1, 309, 322
hare(s) ix *passim*, xi, 17, 25, 28, 29, 30, 32 n. 18, 56, 99, 110–11, 114, 146, 155, 165, 177, 180, 182, 208, 230, 253, 255, 257, 268, 272, 275, 276, 278, 283, 286, 290, 293, 294, 300, 304, 306, 309, 317, 319, 323; *see also* rabbit
harp 108, 116, 135
hat 134, 244, 282, 306, 322
hawk ix *passim*, 17, 25, 29, 30, 110, 131, 155, 160, 173, 180, 181, 192, 193, 207, 255–6, 260, 266, 268, 273, 278, 282, 284, 286, 286, 301, 306, 309, 314–15, 323
head imagery ix *passim*, 28, 230, 236, 240, 243, 264, 267, 274, 286, 294, 299, 301; *see also* bust
head of Christ 68, 150, 264, 299, 325
heart 14, 15, 140, 151, 162, 163, 166, 176, 180, 198, 203, 243, 258, 263, 265, 323
helm/helmet 92, 109, 128, 139, 147, 154, 163, 164, 168, 170, 182, 183, 198, 204, 208, 209, 219, 231, 232,

INDEX

245, 246, 252, 271, 276, 289, 290, 291, 293, 294, 300, 301, 315, 317, 318, 320
heraldic devices 2, 72, 97, 72 n. 23, 81, 81, 107, 108, 109, 110, 113, 123, 131, 132, 134, 136, 139, 140, 141, 142, 144, 145, 146, 147, 149, 150, 151, 153, 154, 155, 157, 158, 159, 160, 161, 162, 163, 164, 165, 168, 169, 170, 172, 177, 178, 179, 180, 181, 183, 185, 187, 188, 190, 194, 195, 196, 198, 199, 200, 201, 202, 203, 204, 207, 208, 209, 210, 211, 212, 214, 215, 222, 225, 227, 229, 230–3, 235, 236, 237, 238, 239–46, 251–7, 260–2, 265–70, 272–9, 280–95, 299, 301, 303, 305–7, 309–12, 314–18, 320, 322–4, 277, 282, 298, 300, 313, 319, 325
heron 185, 301
hippo 293
hippocampus 191
Holy Spirit 271
Holy Trinity 112, 114, 235
hop flowers 203
horn 17, 25, 29, 56, 99, 139, 155, 165, 182, 217, 227, 248, 253, 254, 272, 278, 289, 290, 293–4, 295, 309, 323
horse 44, 149, 156, 166, 177, 181, 192, 243, 253, 284, 292, 299; *see also* equestrian images
horseshoe 241, 312
hound ix *passim*, 17, 25, 29, 56, 99, 110–11, 155, 157, 165, 182, 198, 208, 212, 278, 290, 293, 294
human head 98, 149, 191, 256, 273, 280, 284, 294
intaglios *see* seals; motifs; gems
interlaced pattern 266
jar 284, 296, 300
key 72 n. 23, 82, 106, 138, 147, 166, 193, 228, 233, 235, 258, 265, 270, 283, 284, 290, 303, 306
kneeling figure *see* suppliant

lamb ix *passim*, 160
Lamb and Staff ix *passim*, 14, 17, 29–30, 99; *see also* Lamb of God
Lamb of God 99, 113, 132, 133, 134, 140, 145, 158, 164, 165, 172, 175, 179, 180, 181, 185, 189, 193, 200, 202, 207, 229, 231, 234, 237, 241, 254, 257, 261, 264, 268, 272, 273, 279, 293, 303, 307, 309, 316
lance *see* spear
leaf/leaves 218, 236, 242, 249, 269, 301, 305; *see also* clover
leg 272, 281
leopard 241, 314
lily flowers 17–18, 21, 22, 23, 25–8, 30, 31, 38, 53, 58 n. 16, 82–3, 91, 92, 98, 99, 103 n. 32, 106, 112, 114, 115 n. 9, 130–1, 132, 134, 136, 137, 138, 139, 142, 143, 144, 147, 153, 154, 156, 158, 159, 162, 165, 167, 170, 171, 172, 179, 182, 186, 187, 188, 189, 190, 191, 193, 194, 201, 202, 203, 205, 206, 207, 208, 209, 211, 215, 216, 217, 218, 219, 220, 221, 222, 223, 225, 226, 227, 228, 229, 236, 240, 245, 247, 248, 249, 250, 251, 256, 257, 258, 260, 261, 264, 268, 272, 274, 275, 279, 281, 283, 286, 287, 288, 293, 294, 295, 296, 298, 304, 305, 312, 313, 314, 319, 321, 322
lion ix *passim*, 14–18, 21–3, 27–8, 30, 32 n. 18, 36, 54, 56, 83, 126, 129, 131, 134, 137, 139, 141, 149, 151, 153, 154, 155, 159, 162, 164, 167, 170, 172, 173, 175, 180, 186, 187, 190, 191, 195, 197, 207, 212, 216–17, 219–20, 224, 228–9, 239, 262, 279; *see also* lion sleeping
lion sleeping x, 17, 25–6, 29, 30, 32, 149, 151, 153, 154, 255, 259, 263, 268, 274, 280, 288, 295, 303, 323
lords and lordship 8, 40, 77–85, 100
man seated 284

353

man standing 215–17, 221–8, 232–5, 37, 250, 253, 264–5, 265, 268, 270, 277, 279, 281, 297–8, 302, 303, 306, 312
Marian imagery *see* Mary, Blessed Virgin; *see also* Virgin and Child
Mary, Blessed Virgin 68, 112, 132, 142, 143, 147, 149, 164, 165, 167, 182, 186, 192, 193, 194, 196, 197, 199, 235, 242
maunch 198, 230, 239, 245, 303, 310, 317
merchant mark ix *passim*, 17, 27, 29, 30, 53, 56–7, 59 n. 20, 109, 110, 140, 147, 157, 165, 166, 169, 175, 176, 177, 180, 183, 188, 200, 203, 206, 207, 209, 237, 238, 244, 251, 257, 260, 262, 265, 269, 272, 274, 279, 280, 282, 283, 287, 288, 290, 291, 294, 297, 298, 299, 305, 307, 309, 315, 323, 325
mermaid 152, 282
moon 143, 149, 214, 255, 262
motto 25, 95, 98, 256, 284
naked figure 122, 197, 252, 274, 322
necklace 288
nimbus/nimbed figure 159, 189, 191, 194, 197, 234, 235, 236, 244, 300, 303, 325
ostrich 208
owl 186, 210
padlock 289, 290
pastoral staff 67, 81, 131, 132, 133, 135, 192, 195, 196, 197, 215, 217, 220, 221, 223, 224, 225, 226, 227, 228, 232, 233, 244, 284, 297, 300, 302
peacock x, 53, 58 n. 16, 114, 270, 295, 304
pelican in piety ix *passim*, 17, 25, 26, 27, 29, 30, 32 n. 18, 59 n. 20, 99, 103 n. 49, 113, 118 n. 63, 140, 142, 148, 149, 151, 153, 167, 172, 176, 180, 184, 199, 200, 211, 212, 238,

244, 251, 252, 264, 274, 275, 294, 308, 315, 319, 320, 321, 325
pellets *see* heraldic device
pennon 29, 82, 88 n. 38, 96, 106–7, 116 n. 15, 130, 138, 169, 185, 188, 208, 212, 215, 216, 220, 223, 282
pig 63, 71 n. 15 and n. 16, 159, 203
pigeon 282
pilgrim staff 244
pipe (musical instrument) 197
portcullis 159, 213
pot 262
rabbit 99, 114, 270, 278, 282, 304, 314; *see also* hare
radial device ix *passim*, 17–18, 21, 22, 25–30, 50, 54, 55, 56, 57, 99, 136, 137, 138, 143, 145, 161, 182, 229, 230, 249, 257, 277, 286, 309
raven 63
rebus 105, 110, 111
rose(s) 242, 261
saddle-tree 200
saint *see under individual saints' names*
scallop *see* shell
sceptre 188, 197, 317
scroll 216
serpent *see* snake
shell 66, 138, 172, 173, 195, 198, 210, 222, 234, 241, 319
shears 109, 110, 185, 322
shield vii, 16–18, 22–3, 25–7, 29, 31, 87 n. 27, 98, 231, 233, 235, 237, 245, 256, 261, 265, 267, 274–5, 280–82, 284, 290–1, 293, 299, 305; *see also* Heraldic device
ship 294
sickle 289
snake 107, 151, 169, 195, 300
spear 55, 81–2, 88 n. 38, 106–7, 116, 137, 138, 139, 190, 194, 216, 220, 221, 223, 226, 248, 322
spire 67, 133, 197, 241
squirrel ix *passim*, 8, 17, 25, 26, 30, 31, 99, 103 n. 52, 111, 118, 141, 148,

INDEX

titles 85, 92, 97, 105
tombs 109
Totnes Priory (Bened., Devon) 80
towns/townspeople 4, 35, 41–2, 49, 51–2, 66, 109, 113; *see also* burgesses
trade 49, 122, 124
trespass 43
Trinity, Holy 112
Trotinale, Alice, wife of Hugh de 98
Trotinale, Hugh de 98
Tudor, Jasper, earl of Pembroke and duke of Bedford (*c.*1431-95) 81
Turberville, Payne (III) de (d. *c.*1208) 106
Turberville, Payne (III) de *see* Turberville
Twemlow (Cheshire) 66
typology 16; *see also* classification

Uchaf (Caernarvonshire) 52
urban sealing 51
Urban VI, pope (1378–89) 62, bulla 233
use of another's seal 20, 66; *see also* borrowing
uxor formula and seals 95–6

Vale of Glamorgan 6
validation *see* authentication
Vaughan, Sir Roger, of Tretower (Powys) 107
Vaughan, Thomas 107
Vawr, Gwalter ap Gourwared of Bayville (Carmarthenshire) viii, 57
villeins 52
virginity 92

Wace 82
Wales and the March, sealing practice in 2–6, 16, 35–9, 43–4, 84, 106, 110
Walter, son of Richard of Stokes 53, 114
Warden Abbey (Cist., Bedfordshire) 68; seal of 74 n. 56
Warwick, Richard de (*c.*1200) 88 n. 45
Waters, Sibilla, widow of William Waters of Burton *see* Sibilla

Welere, Iseuda la (*c.*1339) ix, 100
Wells, Jocelin of Wells, bishop of (1206–42) 74 n. 49
Welsh elite, use of seals by 37, 79–80
Welsh law 22, 36–7, 42–3, 51, 53–4, 78, 93
Welshpool (Powys) 51, 55–6, 66
Welshry 7
Westhall (Suffolk), 71 n. 15
Westminster 98
Wethershed, Richard, archbishop of Canterbury (1229–31) 74 n. 51
Whitbourne (Herefordshire), bishop's palace of 63
White, Amy (*c.*1530) 103 n. 52
Whitford (Flint) 110
widows, and seals 92, 95, 95, 99–100
will 64, 65, 72 n. 24, 73 n. 34, 98, 103 n. 37
William the chaplain ix, 116 n. 28
William the clerk (Glamorgan) 20
William the harper 89 n. 55
William the tailor 109
William, son of Susanne 103 n. 29
Williams, David H. 2–3, 40, 41, 67
witness/witnessing 20, 36, 42–3, 47 n. 45, 54, 57, 69, 99, 111, 114
wives 94
women 9, 88–9 n. 47, 81, 87 n. 27, 91, 97–100, 104 n. 53, 106
wool 53
Worcester Cathedral Chapter House 69,
Worcester Franciscans viii, 68–9
Wrexham 6, 9
written culture 79

Yeruard Du (*c.*1225–50) *Yewan ab Yustin Iwan ab Iestyn* 83
Ynge, John, of Acton Burnell (Shropshire) 53
Ystrad Marchell Abbey (Cist., Powys) 50

Zouche, William de la, lord of Glamorgan and Morgan 40, 81